AF889455

All in One

English Communicative
CBSE Class 10

Reading, Writing, Grammar & Literature | Review Exercises | Sample Papers & Board Papers

Recommended by Teachers
Trusted by Toppers

All in One®

English Communicative
CBSE Class 10

Reading, Writing, Grammar & Literature | Review Exercises | Sample Papers & Board Papers

Author
Parneet Kaur

arihant
SUCCESS AND NOTHING LESS

SUCCESS AND NOTHING LESS

ARIHANT PRAKASHAN

(School Division Series)

卐 ADMINISTRATIVE & PRODUCTION OFFICES

Regd. Office

'Ramchhaya' 4577/15, Agarwal Road, Darya Ganj, New Delhi -110002
Tele: 011- 47630600, 43518550; Fax: 011- 23280316

卐 *Head Office*

Kalindi, TP Nagar, Meerut (UP) - 250002, Tel: 0121-7156203, 7156204

卐 SALES & SUPPORT OFFICES

Agra, Ahmedabad, Bengaluru, Bareilly, Chennai, Delhi, Guwahati, Hyderabad, Jaipur, Jhansi, Kolkata, Lucknow, Nagpur & Pune.

PO No : TXT-XX-XXXXXXX-X-XX

Published By Arihant Publications (India) Ltd.

For further information about the books published by Arihant, log on to www.arihantbooks.com or e-mail at info@arihantbooks.com

Follow us on

卐 PRICE ₹ 450.00

PRODUCTION TEAM

Publishing Managers
Mahendra Singh Rawat & Keshav Mohan

Cover Designer
Rakesh Rawat

Inner Designer
Ankit Tyagi

Project Head
Manju

Page Layouting
Lalit Chaprana

Proof Readers
Harsh Agarwal, Naina Rajya

Index *cum* Study Planner

SECTION D : LITERATURE

One Book- Endless Features

to Help you Succeed

Chapter Summary

In each chapter of the Prose, Poetry & Drama, Summary of the chapter & Explanation is given in simple and easy to understand language. It will help the students to understand theme of the chapter easily.

CHAPTER 1

Two Gentlemen of Verona

by A.J. Cronin

CHAPTER SUMMARY The story is set in Verona, Italy, after the Second World War. The story begins with the narrator driving down the foothills of the Alps where he encounters the two brothers, Nicola and Jacopo. The story recounts the hard life chosen by two young boys so that they could pay for the treatment of their sister afflicted with tuberculosis. The boys' sacrifice, their sincerity and devotion to the cause, and the maturity they display in their actions gives a new hope for humanity.

Word Meaning

In each chapter of the Prose, Poetry and Drama, difficult words are given along with their meaning. This will help students to understand difficult words easily.

Word Meaning

Word	Meaning	Word	Meaning
outskirts	the parts of a city or town that are farthest from the centre	far beyond their years	of someone much older
		ran errands	made short trips for particular purposes
Verona	a city in Northern Italy	deserted	uninhabited
shabby	untidy, disordered	emigrate	leave one's own country in order to settle permanently in another
worn	old and damaged as a result of much use		
earnest	serious, sincere	vexation	annoyed
slackened	decreased in speed or intensity	put out	annoyed or offended
Juliet's tomb	the place where Juliet, the heroine of Shakespeare's play 'Romeo and Juliet' was buried	vestibule	a hall or lobby
		cubicle	a small partitioned area of a room, for example a desk in an office
demeanour	appearence and behaviour	intrude upon	disturb
artless	simple, innocent	scarce	insufficient, not enough
engaging	charming and attractive	dear	expensive

Format of Formal Letters

You are Gunjan, a resident of Delhi. You are a subscriber of a weekly magazine named Outlook. Lately, you have not been receiving the copies of the magazine on a regular basis. Write a letter to the Circulation Manager, Education Tunes regarding the non-receipt of copies. (120 Words)

Sender's address	WZ-1263, XYZ New Delhi-110088
Date	20th May, 20XX
Receiver's name/rank and his/her address	The Circulation Manager Education Times New Delhi-110024
Subject	**Subject** Non-Receipt of Copies of Education Times Magazine
Salutation	Sir/Ma'am
Body of the letter	This is to inform you that I am a subscriber of Education Times with subscription no. 120124. Unfortunately, I have not been receiving copies of the magazine on a regular basis since the past few weeks. At times, the copies do not arrive on time or are not delivered at all. I have also called your helpline number but the issue has not been fixed. I would appreciate if you could look into the issue and make sure that I get the copies on time. Looking forward to your speedy action.
Subscription/ Complimentary close and Signature	Thanking you Yours sincerely Gunjan (A subscriber)

Formats in Writing Section

In Writing section standard format has been given. This will help students to learn proper format of each writing task.

One Book- Endless Features

to Help you Succeed

Textbook Folder

Here, we have covered questions of CBSE Textbook (Intext & Exercise) with their detailed answer in simple and easy language.

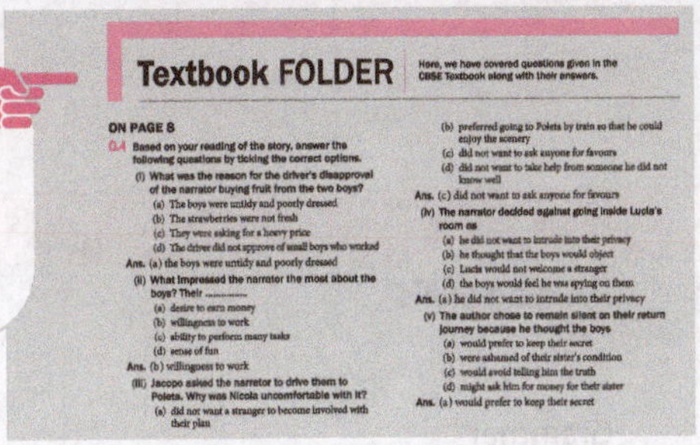

Textbook FOLDER Here, we have covered questions given in the CBSE Textbook along with their answers.

ON PAGE 8

Q.1 Based on your reading of the story, answer the following questions by ticking the correct options.

(i) **What was the reason for the driver's disapproval of the narrator buying fruit from the two boys?**
(a) The boys were untidy and poorly dressed
(b) The strawberries were not fresh
(c) They were asking for a heavy price
(d) The driver did not approve of small boys who worked

Ans. (a) the boys were untidy and poorly dressed

(ii) **What impressed the narrator the most about the boys? Their ....**
(a) desire to earn money
(b) willingness to work
(c) ability to perform many tasks
(d) sense of fun

Ans. (b) willingness to work

(iii) **Jacopo asked the narrator to drive them to Poleta. Why was Nicola uncomfortable with it?**
(a) did not want a stranger to become involved with their plan
(b) preferred going to Poleta by train so that he could enjoy the scenery
(c) did not want to ask anyone for favours
(d) did not want to take help from someone he did not know well

Ans. (c) did not want to ask anyone for favours

(iv) **The narrator decided against going inside Lucia's room as**
(a) he did not want to intrude into their privacy
(b) he thought that the boys would object
(c) Lucia would not welcome a stranger
(d) the boys would feel he was spying on them

Ans. (a) he did not want to intrude into their privacy

(v) **The author chose to remain silent on their return journey because he thought the boys**
(a) would prefer to keep their secret
(b) were ashamed of their sister's condition
(c) would avoid telling him the truth
(d) might ask him for money for their sister

Ans. (a) would prefer to keep their secret

Assessment Exercise

At the end of the chapter, there are unsolved questions for practice and assessment of students. By practising these questions, students can assess their preparation level for the chapter.

Review Exercise

Each chapter cover all types of questions like Extract Based Questions, Short Answer & Long Answer Type Questions.

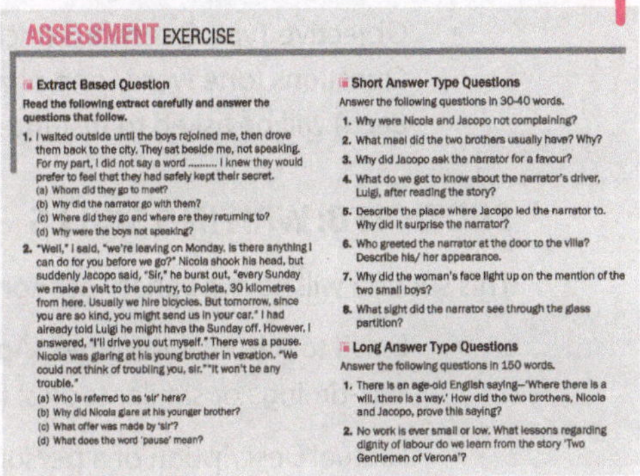

ASSESSMENT EXERCISE

Extract Based Question

Read the following extract carefully and answer the questions that follow.

1. I waited outside until the boys rejoined me, then drove them back to the city. They sat beside me, not speaking. For my part, I did not say a word .... I knew they would prefer to feel that they had safely kept their secret.
(a) Whom did they go to meet?
(b) Why did the narrator go with them?
(c) Where did they go and where are they returning to?
(d) Why were the boys not speaking?

2. "Well," I said, "we're leaving on Monday. Is there anything I can do for you before we go?" Nicola shook his head, but suddenly Jacopo said, "Sir," he burst out, "every Sunday we make a visit to the country, to Poleta, 30 kilometres from here. Usually we hire bicycles. But tomorrow, since you are so kind, you might send us in your car." I had already told Luigi he might have the Sunday off. However, I answered, "I'll drive you out myself." There was a pause. Nicola was glaring at his young brother in vexation. "We could not think of troubling you, sir." "It won't be any trouble."
(a) Who is referred to as 'sir' here?
(b) Why did Nicola glare at his younger brother?
(c) What offer was made by 'sir'?
(d) What does the word 'pause' mean?

Short Answer Type Questions

Answer the following questions in 30-40 words.

1. Why were Nicola and Jacopo not complaining?
2. What meal did the two brothers usually have? Why?
3. Why did Jacopo ask the narrator for a favour?
4. What do we get to know about the narrator's driver, Luigi, after reading the story?
5. Describe the place where Jacopo led the narrator to. Why did it surprise the narrator?
6. Who greeted the narrator at the door to the villa? Describe his/ her appearance.
7. Why did the woman's face light up on the mention of the two small boys?
8. What sight did the narrator see through the glass partition?

Long Answer Type Questions

Answer the following questions in 150 words.

1. There is an age-old English saying–'Where there is a will, there is a way.' How did the two brothers, Nicola and Jacopo, prove this saying?
2. No work is ever small or low. What lessons regarding dignity of labour do we learn from the story 'Two Gentlemen of Verona'?

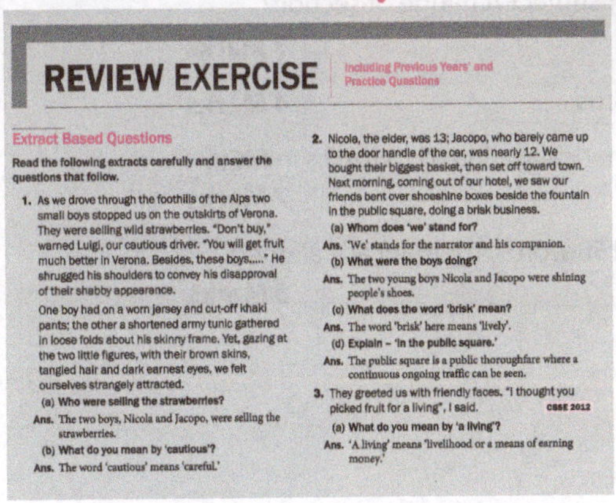

REVIEW EXERCISE Including Previous Years' and Practice Questions

Extract Based Questions

Read the following extracts carefully and answer the questions that follow.

1. As we drove through the foothills of the Alps two small boys stopped us on the outskirts of Verona. They were selling wild strawberries. "Don't buy," warned Luigi, our cautious driver. "You will get fruit much better in Verona. Besides, these boys....." He shrugged his shoulders to convey his disapproval of their shabby appearance.

One boy had on a worn jersey and cut-off khaki pants; the other a shortened army tunic gathered in loose folds about his skinny frame. Yet, gazing at the two little figures, with their brown skins, tangled hair and dark earnest eyes, we felt ourselves strangely attracted.

(a) **Who were selling the strawberries?**

Ans. The two boys, Nicola and Jacopo, were selling the strawberries.

(b) **What do you mean by 'cautious'?**

Ans. The word 'cautious' means 'careful.'

2. Nicola, the elder, was 13; Jacopo, who barely came up to the door handle of the car, was nearly 12. We bought their biggest basket, then set off toward town. Next morning, coming out of our hotel, we saw our friends bent over shoeshine boxes beside the fountain in the public square, doing a brisk business.

(a) **Whom does 'we' stand for?**

Ans. 'We' stands for the narrator and his companion.

(b) **What were the boys doing?**

Ans. The two young boys Nicola and Jacopo were shining people's shoes.

(c) **What does the word 'brisk' mean?**

Ans. The word 'brisk' here means 'lively'.

(d) **Explain – 'In the public square.'**

Ans. The public square is a public thoroughfare where a continuous ongoing traffic can be seen.

3. They greeted us with friendly faces. "I thought you picked fruit for a living", I said. **CBSE 2012**

(a) **What do you mean by 'a living'?**

Ans. 'A living' means 'livelihood or a means of earning money.'

Latest Course *Structure*

Section		Total Weightage
A	Reading Skills	22
B	Writing Skills	22
C	Grammar	10
D	Literature Textbook	26
	TOTAL	80

SECTION A: READING SKILLS **(12+10=22 Marks)** **50 Periods**

- The section will have two unseen passages with the maximum word limit of 750 words. The passages can have continuous and non-continuous text inspired from the themes in prescribed books. Please refer to the Main Course Book (MCB) for types of non-continuous texts. (For example –Unit 1 has lists, tables, cues, message, telephone conversation, etc.).
- Objective Type Questions (including Multiple Choice Questions), Very Short Answer Type Questions (one word/ one phrase / one sentence) and Short Answer Type Questions (30-40 words each) will be asked to test interpretation, analysis, inference, evaluation and vocabulary in context.

SECTION B: WRITING SKILLS **22 Marks** **50 Periods**

This section will have a variety of short and long writing tasks.

- Email to school authorities (Application for leave/ change of subject /change of section/ bus-timings or similar topics) in maximum 50 words **3 Marks**
- Factual Description of a person/object in maximum 100 words **4 Marks**
- One out of two formal letters, in maximum 120 words, thematically aligned to topics in MCB. **7 Marks**
- One out of two articles based on verbal cues, in maximum 150 words, thematically aligned to MCB topics. **8 Marks**

SECTION C: GRAMMAR 10 Marks 20 Periods

Grammar items will be taught and assessed over a period of time.

1. Tenses
2. Modals
3. Subject–verb concord
4. Reported speech
   - Commands and Requests
   - Statements
   - Questions
5. Clauses
   - Noun clauses
   - Adverb clauses
   - Relative clauses
6. Determiners
   - The above items may be tested through test types as given below
   - Gap filling 3 marks
   - Editing or Omission 4 marks
   - Sentences Reordering or Sentence Transformation in context. 3 marks

SECTION D: LITERATURE TEXTBOOK 26 Marks 50 Periods

- Two out of three extracts from prose/poetry for reference to the context. Very Short Answer Questions will be asked to assess global comprehension, interpretation, inference and evaluation. 8 marks (4+4)
- Five Short Answer Type Questions out of six from the Literature Reader to test local and global comprehension of theme and ideas, analysis, evaluation and appreciation (30-40 words each) 5 x2 = 10 Marks

- One out of two Long Answer Type Questions to assess how the values inherent in the text have been brought out. Creativity, evaluation and extrapolation beyond the text and across the texts will be assessed. This can also be a passage-based question taken from a situation/plot from the texts. (150 words). 8 marks

Prescribed Books: Interact in English Series by CBSE (available on www.cbseacademic.nic.in)

- Main Course Book (Revised Edition)
- Literature Reader (Revised Edition)
- Workbook (Revised Edition)

NOTE: Teachers are advised to

(i) encourage classroom interaction among peers, students and teachers through activities such as role play, group work, etc.,

(ii) reduce teacher-talk time and keep it to the minimum,

(iii) take up questions for discussion to encourage pupils to participate and to marshal their ideas and express and defend their views.

Assessment of Listening and Speaking Skills: 50 Periods Guidelines for the Assessment of Listening and Speaking Skills are given at Annexure I.

CHAPTER 1

Reading Comprehension

Let's REVISE Reading Comprehension is a language activity that involves a thorough understanding of a given passage consisting of one or more paragraphs. It tests the understanding powers and analytical skills of a student with questions that evaluates the reader's ability to—

- find the main idea or a suitable title for the text.
- find information directly specified in the passage.
- draw conclusions from the given passage.
- determine the meaning of words used in the passage.
- determine the author's style, mood or point of view.

The CBSE Class X Communicative exam, Reading Comprehension comprises 22 marks

Types of Passages

In CBSE Class X Communicative exam, question from two types of passages are asked.

- Continuous passage includes paragraphs taken from stories, articles, reports, etc.
- Non continuous passage includes lists, tables, cues, message, telephone conversation, etc.

Types of Questions

In the examination, the students are tested on a variety of questions that assess their interpretation, analysis, inference, evaluation and vocabulary in context.

The questions can be

- Objective type questions (including multiple choice questions)
- Very short answer type questions (one word/phrase/sentence)
- Short answer type questions (30-40 words)

Steps to Attempt Reading Comprehension

- Read each and every line of the passage carefully. Reading the passage twice is always helpful, as it makes it easier for the student to find answers.
- Underline the difficult words while reading the passage, as you might be tested on them.
- While answering, be sure that you've clearly understood the question. Answer must be relevant to the question.
- Ensure that you answer the question according to the marks it carries.
- Try to use your own language and frame the answer in clear and simple language.
- In the answers, make sure that you use the same tense in which the question has been asked.
- In MCQs, analyse the questions and options carefully before selecting the correct option as the options can be closely related.

SOLVED EXAMPLES

Continuous Passages

PASSAGE 1

1. Drishti was a young woman who had always been fascinated by the supernatural. She had read countless books and watched numerous documentaries about ghosts and otherworldly beings. So, when she heard about an abandoned hotel on the outskirts of town that was said to be haunted, she knew she had to investigate.
2. One night, Drishti decided to sneak into the dilapidated hotel with a few of her friends. As they made their way through the dark, eerie corridors, they heard strange noises and felt cold spots. They were convinced that they were not alone.
3. Suddenly, they came across a room that was different from the rest. It was filled with old cooking equipment and strange symbols etched into the walls. Drishti felt a chill run down her spine as she entered the room. She knew that this was where the most paranormal activity occurred. As they were examining the room, they heard a loud bang coming from the hallway. They froze in fear, not knowing what was coming their way. They could hear footsteps approaching and they knew they had to hide.
4. They quickly ducked behind some old shelves as the footsteps grew louder. The sound of breathing was getting closer and closer until, finally, they saw a figure appear in the doorway. It was a man wearing a chef's hat, with a face that was twisted in a sinister smile. Drishti and her friends felt their blood run cold as the man approached them. They could feel his cold breath on their faces as he leaned in, whispering in a deep voice, 'You shouldn't be here.'
5. Drishti and her friends were frozen with fear as they stared into the chef's eyes. But, suddenly, the lights flickered on and the figure disappeared. They looked around the room and everything seemed normal. They had been so scared that they hadn't realised they were in a room with faulty wiring.
6. Disappointed, they realised that their ghost hunt had been a bust. They left the hotel feeling deflated and let down. They had hoped for an exciting, spine-tingling adventure but all they got was a scary moment caused by faulty wiring.

   As they drove home, they couldn't help but feel foolish for getting so worked up over nothing. They had been so convinced that they would find evidence of the paranormal that they had overlooked the simple explanation for the noises they had heard.
7. Drishti learned an important lesson that night. Sometimes, the scariest things are the ones that we create in our own minds. She realised that she didn't need to chase after the supernatural to experience thrills and excitement. The world around her was full of mystery and wonder and she was content to experience it without the need for ghosts and ghouls.

CBSE SQP 2023

Answer the following questions based on the passage given above.

1. How does the setting contribute to the overall mood and atmosphere of the story?
   (a) It creates a sense of nostalgia.
   (b) It provides a sense of false security.
   (c) It adds to the suspense in the story.
   (d) It presents a contrast with the real world.

2. What is the main flaw in Drishti's approach to investigating the haunted hotel?
   (a) She was too focused on finding evidence of the paranormal.
   (b) She was too skeptical and refused to believe in the possibility of ghosts.
   (c) She relied too heavily on other people's accounts of the supernatural.
   (d) She didn't take enough precautions to ensure her safety.

3. Complete the sentence appropriately.
Based on the use of the word 'dilapidated' to describe the hotel, in Paragraph 2, we can infer that its condition was ....

4. Rectify the given false statement.
The reason Drishti and her friends visited the abandoned hotel was to prove the existence of ghosts.

5. What is the most significant lesson that Drishti learns from her experience in the haunted hotel?

6. After which paragraph of the story, would the following paragraph most likely be placed?
They commenced walking through the hotel, Drishti's torchlight barely illuminating the darkness around her. Suddenly, they heard a loud creaking noise behind them. Drishti whipped around, pointing her flashlight in the direction of the noise. Nothing. Shaken, they all quickened their pace.

7. Why would the title, The Hotel Haunting be an inappropriate title, as compared to The Unsettling Encounter at the Abandoned Hotel for the passage?

8. Briefly explain (in 30-40 words) any two elements that classify the story as scary.

9. List two ways how the disappointment that Drishti and her friends felt after their ghost hunt is analogous to the feeling of waking up from a dream. Answer in 30-40 words.

Answers

1. (c) It adds to the suspense in the story.
2. (a) She was too focused on finding evidence of the paranormal.
3. in a state of decay, disrepair and neglect. It was old, damaged, and possibly unsafe.
4. Drishti and her friends visited the abandoned hotel to investigate the rumours of ghosts.
5. A significant lesson that Drishti learns from her experience in the haunted hotel is the need to be more sceptical of the supernatural.
6. It would be placed after Paragraph 2, because Drishti and her friends had just begun exploring. This paragraph segues into Paragraph 3 as it begins with 'Suddenly...' , indicating that something happens after 'they all quickened their pace'. The other likely paragraphs could have been 3,4 and 5 but they aren't suitable as the apparent encounter has already taken place.
7. If the title, 'The Hotel haunting' is given to the passage, it would be inappropriate in comparison to 'The Unsettling Encounter at the Abandoned Hotel' because it makes assumptions about the presence of ghosts unlike the appropriate title which accurately reflects a spooky and unsettling experience at an abandoned hotel.
8. Elements that classify the story as scary are—
   (i) **Suspense** The story creates a sense of suspense, unease and tension through its use of foreshadowing, eerie descriptions, and unexplained phenomena.
   (ii) **Eerie Atmosphere** The hotel setting contributes to the overall sense of fear and dread, with its dilapidated and abandoned state.
   (iii) **Supernatural Element** The unexplained noises, movements, and apparitions suggest the presence of supernatural forces or entities. *(Any two)*
9. The disappointment that Drishti and her friends felt after their ghost hunt is analogous to the feeling of waking up from a dream was
   - Both involve a sense of disappointment that reality didn't live up to their expectations.
   - In both cases, they may have had high hopes for what they would experience, only to find that it was not as exciting or satisfying as they had hoped.
   - Just as waking up from a dream can leave us feeling let down, Drishti's realisation that the haunted hotel was not as spooky as she had imagined was a letdown for her and her friends. *(Any two)*

PASSAGE 2

1. With eager anticipation we awaited the next stage. A tailor was called in to measure us, five boys and one girl, Mary Lila Rao, for the sports kits. I was filled with happiness, just like a child who had been given a bag full of candy. After all, I would be fulfilling my dream to wear a blazer with INDIA written on it!
2. A week later, we left for Australia. The night before we left I could not sleep. My small suitcase had been packed with my kit and bedding and I waited for the Sun to rise. Excited by the prospect of what lay ahead, we boarded the train to Bombay, the first lap of our long journey across the seas to far-off Australia. When we reached Bombay's Churchgate station, we were taken by bus to the Astoria Hotel. It was the first time that I had seen such a grand place and I could barely believe my eyes. What was I, a simple village boy doing in such a different world? While we were at the Astoria, Commander Rekhi, our manager, showed us how to knot a tie and gave us lessons on table manners.
3. When we reached Santa Cruz, the entire atmosphere at the terminal seemed unreal—its bright lights, the strange sounds, the rush of people. Except for Mary Lila Rao, none of us had flown before. I was scared and confused. I had no bedding and no food.
   Where would I sleep? What would I eat? How would the plane take off with so many people, their luggage and other cargo? Would it crash under so much weight? I followed my companions towards the huge monster that awaited us, and blindly climbed up the ramp into the cabin. I was asked to fasten my seatbelt, but naturally I did not know what to do and was fumbling with the straps when the air-hostess kindly helped me.
4. When the plane started to taxi along the runway, I closed my eyes and prayed to my God. I had butterflies in my stomach as the plane ascended. And then we were airborne. When I looked out of the window I saw smoke pouring out of the engines and raised an alarm, thinking that the plane was on fire. The air-hostess calmed me down, patiently explaining that it was only the fuel burning. I felt very foolish and laughed with relief.

(Adapted from the Autobiography of Milkha Singh)

Answer the following questions based on the passage given above.

1. Why was Milkha Singh excited to get measured by a tailor?

(a) His dream of wearing a blazer came true
(b) He had met an expert tailor
(c) He was going to sit on a plane
(d) He was going to a foreign nation

2. Why does Milkha call his stay at Astoria Hotel to be 'a different world'?
   (a) As a village boy, he had not visited such a grand hotel
   (b) It was very different from the hotels he had been to
   (c) It was too luxurious for his taste
   (d) Both (a) and (b)
3. Complete the sentence appropriately.
   He prayed to his God because ....
4. Rectify the given false sentence.
   Milkha Singh was bored to see such a grand hotel.
5. Why did the air-hostess need to help him?
6. Substitute the underlined word in the sentence with the word from the passage which means the same.
   The kite slowly arose in the sky.
7. Give any two reasons responsible for Milkha's worry or confusion?
8. What made the atmosphere of Santa Cruz seem unreal?
9. Why couldn't Milkha Singh sleep the night before they left?

Answers

1. (a) His dream of wearing a blazer came true
2. (d) Both (a) and (b)
3. he was scared of the plane
4. Milkha Singh was fascinated to see such a grand hotel.
5. The air-hostess was needed to him because he did not know how to fasten his seatbelt and was fumbling with it.
6. ascended
7. Milka was worried and confused because he had never ever travelled by or flown in a plane before. Further, he was worried how he would sleep without any bedding and what they would eat.
8. The atmosphere of Santa Cruz was unreal because of its bright lights, strange sounds and the huge rush of people there.
9. Milkha Singh could not sleep the night before they left because he was excited to go to Australia.

Non-Continuous Passages

PASSAGE 1

Study the State-Wise Literacy Rate in India According to 2021 Census.

S.No.	State/Union Territory	Literacy rate in % (Person)	Literacy rate in % (Male)	Literacy rate in % (Female)
1.	Kerala	94.0	96.1	92.1
2.	Lakshadweep	91.8	95.6	87.9
3.	Mizoram	91.3	93.3	89.3
4.	Goa	88.7	92.6	84.7
5.	Tripura	87.2	91.5	82.7
6.	Daman and Diu	87.1	91.5	79.5
7.	Andaman & Nicobar Island	86.6	90.3	82.4
8.	NCT of Delhi	86.2	90.9	80.8
9.	Chandigarh	86.0	90.0	81.2
10.	Puducherry	85.8	91.3	80.7
11.	Himachal Pradesh	82.8	89.5	75.9
12.	Maharashtra	82.3	88.4	75.9
13.	Sikkim	81.4	86.6	75.6
14.	Tamil Nadu	80.1	86.8	73.4
15.	Nagaland	79.6	82.8	76.1
16.	Manipur	79.2	86.1	72.4
17.	Uttarakhand	78.8	87.4	70.0
18.	Gujarat	78.0	85.8	69.7
19.	West Bengal	76.3	81.7	70.5

20.	Dadra and Nagar Haveli	76.2	85.2	64.3
21.	Punjab	75.8	80.4	70.7
22.	Haryana	75.6	84.1	65.9
23.	Karnataka	75.4	82.5	68.1
24.	Meghalaya	74.4	76.0	72.9
25.	Odisha	72.9	81.6	64.0
26.	Assam	72.2	77.8	66.3
27.	Chhattisgarh	70.3	80.3	60.2
28.	Madhya Pradesh	69.3	78.7	59.2
29.	Uttar Pradesh	67.7	77.3	57.2
30.	Jammu and Kashmir	67.2	76.3	56.4
31.	Andhra Pradesh	67.0	74.9	59.1
32.	Jharkhand	66.4	76.8	55.4
33.	Rajasthan	66.1	79.2	52.1
34.	Arunachal Pradesh	65.4	72.6	57.2
35.	Bihar	61.8	71.2	51.5

Answer the following questions based on the table given above.

1. Complete the sentence appropriately.
   The overall literacy rate is 91.3% for ....
2. Complete the sentence appropriately.
   67.2% : Literacy rate :: ....: Male literacy rate
3. In which state is the difference between the male literacy rate and female literacy rate highest?
   (a) West Bengal (b) Bihar
   (c) Rajasthan (d) Tamil Nadu
4. Which of the following can be said for all states?
   (a) The female literacy rate is decreasing.
   (b) The female literacy rate is improving.
   (c) The female literacy rate is stagnant.
   (d) The female literacy rate is inconsequential.
5. Name the States/UTs with female literacy lower than 60%.
6. Name the State/UTs with the highest female literacy.
7. What does the lower gap between male literacy rate and female literacy rate show?
8. Discuss reasons why male literacy is higher than female literacy in India.

Answers

1. Mizoram
2. 76.3%
3. (b) Bihar

MCB Theme : Education

4. (b) The female literacy rate is improving.
5. The States or UTs with female literacy lower than 60% are—Madhya Pradesh, Uttar Pradesh, Jammu and Kashmir, Andhra Pradesh, Jharkhand, Rajasthan, Arunachal Pradesh and Bihar.
6. The State or UT with the highest female literacy rate is Kerala.
7. The low gap between male literacy rate and the female literacy rate shows that the regressive attitude that places males as superior to females is reducing. More and more parents are sending their girls to schools and getting them educated. Further, it also means that education facilities are improving, especially for girls.
8. The low literacy rate is usually higher than the female literacy rate because of the regressive mindset of the society wherein boys are to be educated and girls are supposed to take care of the household. Further, the lack of proper school and facilities also leads the parents to not send the girls to schools.

PASSAGE 2

Our history makes it evident that the Indian Plastics Industry made a vigorous beginning in 1957 but it took more than 30 years for it to pervade Indian lifestyles. In 1979, 'the market for plastics' was just being seeded by the state-owned Indian Petro-Chemicals and it was only in 1994 that plastic soft drink bottles became a visible source of annoyance.

In the same year, people in other cities were concerned about the state of public sanitation and also urged regulatory bodies to ban the production, distribution and use of plastic bags. However, the challenge was greater than it appeared at first.

The massive generation of plastic waste in India is due to rapid urbanisation, spread of retail chains, plastic packaging from grocery to food and vegetable products, to consumer items and cosmetics.

The projected high growth rates of GDP and continuing rapid urbanisation suggest that India's trajectory of plastic consumption and plastic waste is likely to increase.

Global plastics production 1950 to 2020 Annual global polymer resin and fiber production (plastic production), measured in metric tonnes per year.

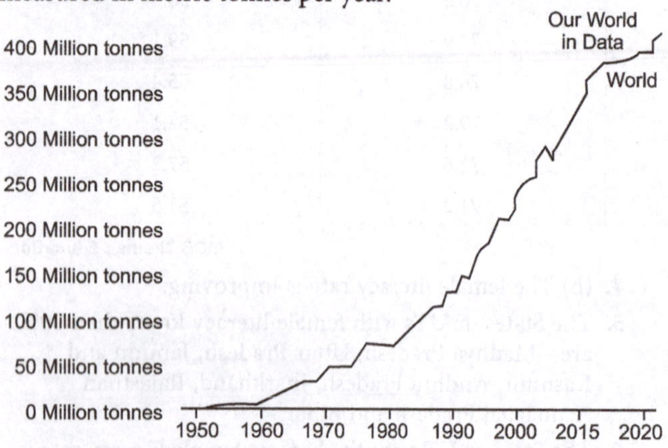

Source : Geyeretal (2017)

According to the United Nations Environment Programme (UNEP) report of 2018, India stands among few other countries like France, Mongolia and several African countries that have initiated total or partial national level bans on plastics in their jurisdictions. A world of greater possibilities has now opened up to initiate appropriate and concrete actions to build up the necessary institutions and systems before oceans turn, irreversibly into a thin soup of plastic. In this context, thereafter ten states (Andhra Pradesh, Chhattisgarh, Himachal Pradesh, Karnataka, Madhya Pradesh, Meghalaya, Odisha, Rajasthan and Tamil Nadu) are currently sending their collected waste to cement plants four co-processing, twelve other states/UTs are using platic waste for polymer bitumen road construction and still four other states are using the plastic waste for waste-to-energy plants and oil production. A world of greater possibilities has now opened up to initiate approparaite and concrete actions to build up the necessary institutions and systems before oceans turn, irreversibly into a thin soup of plastic.

However, there is no one single masterstroke to counter the challenges witnessed by the staggering plastic waste management in the country. The time is now to formulate robust and inclusive National Action Plans and while doing so, the country will establish greater transparency to combat the plastic jeopardy in a more sustainable and holistic way.

Answer the following questions based on the passage given above.

1. Complete the sentence appropriately.

   The market for plastic was introduced by ....

2. Complete the sentence appropriately.

   The last paragraph of the passage ....

3. Select the option that displays how the challenge had increased.

   (a) Increase in plastic waste

   (b) Increased environmental concerns

   (c) Increase in burning of plastic

   (d) Increased plastic production

4. How can plastics be reused?

   1. Road construction   2. Energy production

   3. Oil production   4. Toys

   5. Bags

   Options

   (a) 1 and 2   (b) 3 and 4

   (c) 1, 2 and 3   (d) All of these

5. What does the upward trend of the graph indicate?
6. Which country had not initiated partial national level bans on plastics?
7. What created a demand for plastics in India?
8. What steps are taken to combat the challenges of plastic waste management in India? What will be its impact?

Answers

1. Indian Petro-Chemicals
2. states the need for effective plastic waste management
3. (a) Increase in plastic waste
4. (c) 1, 2 and 3
5. India's trajectory of plastic consumption and waste would increase.
6. Italy
7. Rapid urbanisation, the spread of retail chains, plastic packaging from grocery, food and vegetable products to consumer items and cosmetics created a demand for plastics in India.
8. Ten states of India are sending their plastic collected waste to cement plants for co-processing, 12 other states are using plastic waste for polymer bitumen road construction and others use it for waste to energy plants and oil production.

   Its impact would be seen on oceans with less plastic waste and would help combat plastic jeopardy in a sustainable and holistic way.

REVIEW EXERCISE

Including Continuous and Non-Continuous Passages

Continuous Passages

PASSAGE 1

1. India, often celebrated as a land of diversity, is a unique blend of various cultures, languages, religions, and traditions. Known for its rich historical heritage, India stands as a testament to the coexistence of a multitude of identities harmoniously under one nation.
2. The Indian subcontinent is home to a multitude of languages. The Constitution of India recognises 22 official languages, with Hindi being the most widely spoken. Besides, there are over a thousand dialects spoken across the country. This linguistic diversity is reflective of India's cultural richness and its people's adaptability and acceptance of varied means of expression.
3. Religion plays a central role in the lives of many Indians, contributing significantly to the country's cultural diversity. India is the birthplace of major religions such as Hinduism, Buddhism, Jainism, and Sikhism, and also harbours significant populations of Muslims, Christians, Sikhs, Buddhists, and other communities. Religious festivals like Diwali, Eid, Christmas, and Vesak are celebrated with great enthusiasm, showcasing this unity in diversity.
4. The Indian cuisine is another example of regional diversity turning into a national treasure. From the fiery dishes of the South to the rich curries of the North, and from the sweets of Gujarat to the street food of Mumbai, each region contributes to the subcontinent's eclectic palate This culinary variety not only highlights India's diverse geography but also brings people together through a shared love for food.
5. Cultural practices vary widely across regions. Traditional dance forms like Bharatanatyam from Tamil Nadu, Kathak from North India, and Odissi from Odisha, along with classical music forms like Carnatic and Hindustani, illustrate the rich tapestry of regional art forms that together represent India's cultural unity.
6. The principle of unity in diversity is perhaps best reflected in the Indian democratic system, where people from diverse backgrounds come together to participate in the world's largest democracy. The Indian Constitution guarantees Fundamental Rights and freedoms to all its citizens, ensuring equality and justice by transcending regional and cultural barriers.
7. Challenges to this unity arise, such as regional conflicts and cultural misunderstandings, but the overarching narrative of mutual coexistence persists. India's ability to embrace diversity as a strength rather than a hindrance sets it apart globally as a symbol of unity.

CBSE 2025

Answer the following questions based on the passage given above.

1. The celebration of various festivals in India demonstrates given
   (a) Expertise (b) Skills
   (c) Regionalism (d) Diversity
2. What role does language play in Indian diversity?
   (a) It is a unique blend of various religions.
   (b) It stands as a testament to South-East Asia.
   (c) It reflects India's cultural richness.
   (d) It ensures justice for all.
3. Complete the following suitably.
   India stands as a testament to the coexistence of a multitude of identities harmoniously because ....
4. Rectify the given false statement.
   The linguistic diversity is reflective of the people's intolerance of varied means of expression.
5. List any one classical music form mentioned in the passage.
6. What does the Indian Constitution guarantee to all its citizens?
7. How is Indian cuisine an example of regional diversity?
8. Explain in about 30-40 words, how the various Indian art forms represent cultural unity.
9. What is the overarching narrative of India's existence as per the passage?

PASSAGE 2

1. It was a bleak, rainy day, and I had no desire to drive up the winding mountain road to my daughter Garolyn's house. But she had insisted that I come and see something at the top of the mountain.
2. So, here I was, reluctantly making the two-hour journey through fog that hung like veils. By the time I saw how thick it was near the summit, I'd gone too far to turns back. Nothing could be worth this, I thought , as I inched along the perilous highway.
3. "I' ll stay for lunch, but I'm heading back down as soon as the fog lifts," I announced when I arrived. "But I need you to drive me to the garage to pick up my car," Carolyn said. "Could we at least do that ?"
4. "How far is it ?" I asked. "About three minutes," she said. "I' II drive I'm used to it".
5. After ten minutes on the mountain road, I looked at her anxiously. "I thought you said three minutes." She grinned, "This is a detour."
6. Turning down a narrow track, we parked the car and got out. We walked along a path that was thick with old pine needles. Huge black-green evergreens towered over us. Gradually, the peace and silence of the place began to fill my mind.
7. Then we turned a corner and stopped-and I gasped in amazement. From the top of the mountain, sloping for several acres across folds and valleys, were rivers of daffodils in radiant bloom, A profusion of colour - from the palest ivory to the deepest lemon to the most vivid salmon-blazed like a carpet before us. It looked as though the sun had tipped over and spilled gold down the mountainside.
8. At the centre, cascaded a waterfall of purple hyacinths. Here and there were coral-coloured tulips. And as if this bonanza were not enough, western bluebirds frolicked over the heads of the daffodils, their tawny breasts and sapphire wings like a flutter of jewels .
9. A riot of questions filled my mind. Who created such beauty ? Why ? How ? As we approached the home that stood in the centre of the property, we saw a sign that read : "Answers to the Questions I Know You are Asking".
10. The first answer was : "One woman-Two Hands, Two Feet," The second was : "One at a Time". The third : "Started in 1958".
11. As we drove home, I was so moved by what we had seen, I could scarcely speak. "She changed the world," I finally said, "One bulb" at a time. She started almost 40 years ago, probably just the beginning of an idea, but she kept at it.
12. The wonder of it would not let me go. ' Imagine', I said, "If I'd had a vision and worked at it, just a little bit every day, what might I have accomplished ?" Carolyn looked at me sideways, smiling. 'Start tomorrow,' said she "Better yet, start today".

CBSE 2024

Answer the following questions based on the passage given above.

1. State why the author was reluctant to make a two-hour journey.

2. "This is a detour." On what occasion did Carolyn say this to the author? (30 - 40 words only)

3. The author started liking the place because
(a) of its forest and sandy sea beach.
(b) of the black-green evergreens towering over them.
(c) of the bleak and rainy day.
(d) of reaching the place in just three minutes.

4. The place, where the author went with her daughter, had a beautiful panoramic view. Justify this statement with reference to the passage, in about 40 words.

5. Why was the narrator's mind filled with questions?

6. Complete the following sentence appropriately
"The wonder of it would not let me go."
From this sentence, we can infer that the author was deeply ....

7. State whether the given assertion is True or False.
A field of flowers opens one woman's eyes to the world of the possibilities.

8. What is the lesson the author learns form her experience?
(a) To drive to such places more often
(b) To start working for nature
(c) To change the world with a new vision
(d) That there is a huge world of possibilities

9. Find a word from Paragraph 1, Which means the same as 'cheerless and gloomy'.

10. Substitute the word 'perilous' with a word which is its synonym.
(a) dangerous (b) cunning
(c) devastating (d) secured

PASSAGE 3

1. For most of us, a strong immune system implies fewer sick leaves and being able to avoid seasonal colds, stomach bugs or just about any infection. But research shows that a ramped up immune system goes much further: it helps us age better and live longer.
2. Lifestyle plays a crucial role in proper functioning of your immune system. Chronic stress, such as prolonged job insecurity or a difficult marriage, takes a toll on many aspects of your health, including

immunity. There's compelling evidence that this kind of stress, causes a measurable decline in the immune system's ability to fight infections. Try activities that relax you - yoga, meditation, trekking, volunteering or learning a new skill.

3. The more physically fit and active you are, the less likely you are to fall ill. Exercise helps flush out toxins, and increases the circulation of the body's immune system cells. You need to exercise at least 30 minutes each day. Practice yoga and pranayama that focuses on deep breathing.
4. A nutritionally balanced diet is a key for a strong immunity. Fill your plate with fruits and vegetables, especially purple, blue, green, red, orange and yellow veggies that are rich in antioxidants.
5. Excessive exposure to pollution can cause inflammation. Besides putting you at a higher risk for asthma and other respiratory diseases, breathing polluted air over a long time can damage your immune system. To avoid pollution, plan outdoor activities early in the morning or late evening as air pollution is highest during rush hours. Use the recycled air option on your air conditioner to cut down fumes while driving and cover your nose and mouth while outdoors.
6. You may eat healthy, sleep eight hours, and exercise daily, but researchers have discovered a much simpler way to boost immunity, and it's as easy as watching a sunrise. Positive emotions like awe, the feelings you get on seeing the wonders of nature, help boost immunity. Explore the great outdoors. Look for reasons to feel lucky every day. Make time for a favourite activity, or simply help another person - it will bring a smile to your face. **CBSE 2024 C**

Answer the following questions based on the passage given above.

1. Four friends Aman, Ayesha, Alok and Drishti ate from a roadside food outlet while coming back from school. Alok started having a stomach ache and developed fever in the evening.
   Why do you think it happened with Alok and not with the other three friends?
2. List two ways discovered by the researchers to boost your immunity. Answer in 30 - 40 words.
3. According to the majority of us, a strong immune system implies
   (a) sleeping peacefully (b) falling less ill
   (c) ageing better (d) living longer
4. Briefly explain in 30 - 40 words how stress affects our immunity.
5. In order to avoid pollution, which is the most suitable time to go for outdoor activities ?
6. Substitute the underlined word in the following sentence with a word from paragraph 2 that means the same.
   Yoga and meditation help cure <u>persistent</u> diseases.
7. What is the most appropriate way to flush out toxins from the body?
   (a) Sleeping (b) Eating antioxidants
   (c) Exercising (d) Dieting
8. Complete the following appropriately. Based on the use of the word 'ramped up' to describe the immune system, in Paragraph 1, we can infer that the immune system is ....
9. Complete the sentence appropriately.
   If the title, 'Build Up Your Immunity' is given to this passage, it would be an appropriate title, as compared to 'Health and Yoga' because ....
10. State whether the given assertion is True or False.
    A balanced diet is the most important way to build a strong immunity.

PASSAGE 4

In a world dominated by digital technology, the way we capture, store, and share memories has evolved significantly. Traditional photo albums and digital photo galleries are two primary methods for preserving personal and family memories, each with its own unique characteristics. Though both share the common goal of keeping memories alive, they offer different experiences, advantages, and disadvantages.

Photo albums represent a tangible and tactile way to capture memories. A physical album filled with printed photographs provides a sense of reminiscence and can be passed down through generations, becoming a family heirloom. The process of selecting photos, printing them, and placing them in an album can be a personal and intimate experience, allowing one to reflect on the moments captured.

One of the primary advantages of photo albums is their permanence. Unlike digital files, which can be lost or corrupted, physical photographs in a well-maintained album can last for decades, if not centuries. Albums also provide a sensory experience; flipping through the pages, feeling the texture of the paper, and smelling the aging prints can evoke strong emotional responses.

Additionally, photo albums require little to no technology to enjoy. This makes them accessible to a wider range of people, including those who may not be tech-savvy. Albums can be taken to family gatherings or passed around during holidays, creating a shared experience among family and friends.

However, photo albums come with certain disadvantages. They take up physical space and are vulnerable to damage from environmental factors like water, fire, or sunlight. Albums are also limited in capacity; once they are filled, creating additional albums can become cumbersome. Furthermore, the process of creating a photo album can be time-consuming and costly. Printing photographs, purchasing albums, and maintaining them can add up.

Digital photo galleries have transformed the way we capture and share memories. With the rise of smartphones and digital cameras, taking and storing photos has become more convenient than ever.

The main advantage of digital photo galleries is their convenience and capacity. With a single device, you can store thousands of photos and access them from anywhere. Digital galleries also offer powerful organisation tools, allowing users to sort and categorise their photos with metadata, tags, and dates. Sharing digital photos is effortless; you can send them via email, social media, or cloud-based platforms, enabling friends and family to enjoy memories instantly. Digital galleries also allow for easy editing and enhancement of photos, helping to correct imperfections and improve quality.

Despite their convenience, digital photo galleries have their drawbacks. The reliance on technology means that photos can be lost due to hardware failure, software corruption, or accidental deletion. Additionally, the ephemeral nature of digital files makes them less tangible and more prone to being overlooked or forgotten among the vast array of digital content. Security and privacy are also concerns with digital galleries. Sharing photos online opens up the risk of unauthorised access or data breaches, leading to potential misuse of personal images.

Ultimately, the choice between traditional photo albums and digital photo galleries depends on personal preferences and priorities. Photo albums offer a tactile, enduring connection to memories, while digital galleries provide convenience, flexibility, and ease of sharing. A combination of both methods can offer the best of both worlds, ensuring that cherished memories are preserved and enjoyed for years to come. **CBSE SQP 2024**

Answer the following questions, based on the passage given above.

1. What do traditional photo albums and digital photo galleries share in common?
   (a) Both use digital technology to store photos.
   (b) Both are methods of preserving personal and family memories.
   (c) Both are tangible and can be passed down through generations.
   (d) Both rely on external power sources to function.
2. What aspect of traditional photo albums makes them a cherished item for families?
   (a) The convenience of digital technology.
   (b) The ability to store thousands of photos.
   (c) The sense of nostalgia they provide.
   (d) The option to access them from anywhere.
3. Complete the following suitably.
   The personal experience associated with photo albums is important because ....
4. Rectify the given false statement.
   The main benefit that photo albums have over digital files is the sensory experience.
5. List any one way the photo albums can contribute to an enjoyable family time.
6. Why has it become cumbersome to create additional photo albums, according to Paragraph 5?
7. Why does the writer say that digital cameras, have made taking and storing photos 'more convenient than ever'?
8. How can we say that digital photographs may not always represent reality?
9. Explain why we can say that the writer did not choose sides?

PASSAGE 5

1. His heavy bat was a major talking point whenever Sachin Tendulkar battled injuries in his over-two-decade-long career but the iconic cricketer said he was never convinced about giving it up for a lighter one as his timing got affected every time he tried the change. In his autobiography 'Playing It My Way', Tendulkar wrote that he was asked several times to try a lighter bat but it never worked for him.
2. "I used a pretty heavy bat and I was sometimes encouraged to move to a lighter one. Again, I did try but I never felt comfortable, as my whole bat swing depended on that weight. When I was hitting a drive, I needed the weight to generate the power. It was all to do with the timing", he explains. The all-time leading scorer in the game also offered an interesting take on how to hold the bat. "To me the bat should be an extension of your arm, and if you've reached the stage where it's become an extension of your arm, why do you need to change? What mattered to me most when I was batting was feeling comfortable. As long as I felt comfortable, it didn't matter where I was playing or who I was playing against. If you make technical adjustments, such as moving to a lighter bat, to cope

with different conditions, there's a risk of making yourself feel uncomfortable and of thinking too much about your technique", he says.

3. Tendulkar has advised budding batsmen against too much experimentation, saying, "the bat should be an extension of your arm" and there is no need for a change in technique if "you have reached that stage". "People have often commented on my own grip, which is very low down on the handle. It all goes back to when I started playing cricket when I was eleven, with my brother Ajit, who is ten years older. As I didn't have a bat of my own, I had to use Ajit's full-size bat and the only way I could cope with the weight at that age was to hold the bat right at the bottom of the handle", Tendulkar writes. "Some coaches suggested changing my grip, and I did experiment, but it never felt right. I had got used to feeling the end of the handle pressing against the inside of my forearm and if I gripped the bat further up I didn't have that and batting just didn't feel natural. That's not to say that my technique didn't change at all, though. Throughout my career, I was always looking to improve and constantly tried new things to cope with different situations."

4. Tendulkar said one must try to read the bowler's mind rather than thinking too much about 'your own batting'. "I've always felt that I've batted best when my mind has been at the bowler's end of the pitch, not at my end. In fact, for both batsmen and bowlers, I've always believed that cricket is played best when your mind is at the opposite end and that problems occur when your mind is stuck at your own end. "For example, if a bowler is thinking too much about bowling no-balls, he's not going to be able to bowl what he wants to bowl. Instead, his mind should be at the batsman's end, focusing on where he's going to pitch the ball, which way he's going to swing it and so on. As a batsman, if I'm not consciously worrying about my footwork or my backlift or my wrist-work, then I know that I'm in the right space, because my mind needs to be at the opposite end, figuring out what the bowler is trying to do. There's no time to think about both ends at the same time", he says.

Answer the following questions based on the passage given above.

1. According to Tendulkar, when did the players need to make technical adjustments?
(a) When playing against different teams
(b) In different conditions
(c) To suit the weather in which they were playing
(d) To get a better grip

2. The given passage seems to be ....
(a) instructional (b) factual
(c) emotional (d) observation

3. Complete the sentence appropriately.
To Tendulkar, the bat was an ....

4. Rectify the given false statement.
Tendulkar was not very compassionate to the budding batsmen.

5. List a problem faced by a cricketer in making technical adjustments?

6. Why was Tendulkar's bat was a major talking point?

7. What advice did Tendulkar give to budding batsmen?

8. Why did the advice given by coaches not work for him?

9. Why is it important to read a bowler's mind?

PASSAGE 6

1. The time Uncle Ken and I went for a walk and he insisted on going the zigzag way, I did the same. It was fun. But like all things to do with Uncle Ken, it landed us in a situation where we had to make a hasty exit. While we were being chased away by an irate man from his fields and were dashing away, Uncle Ken's hat flew off. Later, when we had stopped panting, I remembered what Granny had said about looking at the funny side of situations and had a good laugh. Unfortunately, I don't think Uncle Ken saw the lighter side at that moment.

2. It helps to have such an outlook on finding oneself in the oddest of circumstances. Like the time I was in Mumbai and my belt decided to have some fun by getting entangled with a fellow passenger's luggage. After that, I sat quietly at the book festival I had been taken to attend, to keep my belt out of trouble. And it's not just belts that get me into trouble. There was the time I was sharing a taxi to Delhi with a gentleman with a fierce moustache. He was carrying a book written by me with him. When I told him it was my book, he looked offended that I was trying to lay a claim to his property. I gave up on the conversation quickly and filed it away for future use in a story.

3. I have even been accused by some of my younger audience for being too funny. Once a girl asked me disapprovingly why my ghost stories are not scary enough. "Your ghosts are too funny," she grumbled. So, I tried to write a few scary ghost stories. But I find benign, friendly ghosts just as delightful. So, I also wrote about my friend Jimmy, who discovered he was a jinn.

That meant he could elongate his arms at will. This ensured that he had a starring role to play in the school basketball team. Mostly, I feel I have been able to live this life enjoying its small moments of happiness and been able to laugh when needed. **CBSE 2020 Modified**

Answer the following questions based on the passage given above.

1. While on a walk, what did Uncle Ken insist on?

(a) On going towards the lake

(b) On going in a zig-zag manner

(c) To run

(d) To make an exit

2. What happened when Uncle Ken was chased away from the field by an irate man?

(a) He fell down (b) He started laughing

(c) He was angry (d) His hat flew off

3. Complete the sentence appropriately.
Uncle Ken .... to his hat flying off.

4. Rectify the given false statement.
The narrator was a frustrated man.

5. Complete the sentence appropriately.
The narrator had an .... life.

6. Substitute the underlined word in the sentence with the word from the passage which means the same.
He was as <u>amiable</u> as your father.

7. What was the oddest situation that the narrator had faced in Mumbai?

8. "I was trying to lay claim to his property." What is the 'property' referred to in this sentence?

9. What did the girl accuse the narrator of?

PASSAGE 7

1. Choice of profession and career is of great importance. Success depends on the right and timely choice of a career. There are a great variety of careers and professions. The lack of proper counselling worsens the situation. It also results in unemployment and frustration which means a lot of waste of money, time and energy. The students should take the help of elders, teachers and professionals in deciding their careers. They should choose their career according to their aptitude and resources.

2. Young people are ambitious, impatient and eager to achieve good positions. They want to become high officials, executives and have top positions without considering their qualifications, skills, etc. This is a wrong attitude. One should be realistic. One may dream of becoming a super film star and end up as a mere casual artist. Such high ambitions lead to disillusionment and unhappiness.

3. It is better to choose a career at the high school level than go for higher studies aimlessly. One should go for a vocational course at this stage. There are many careers, professions and vocations to choose from. There are teaching, engineering, medicine, law, technology, business, trade, computer application career, government employment, positions in the police and army etc. But each of these requires special aptitude, training, and resources. One may have proper qualifications and aptitude for a career of a doctor or engineer. But if there are no financial resources to train for it, one cannot choose it as one's career.

4. Choice of a career is not simply a matter of likes and dislikes. Financial resources play a very important role in deciding to choose a profession. For lack of funds, one will have to choose a far humbler career. One can take to politics if one has an aptitude for public life. It is a profession of hard labour and perseverance. If you have strong optimism, ambition for fame and are prepared to face the worst, you are best suited for politics. If you have enough money and resources and want to grow very rich, you can choose business as your career. Therefore, be practical, logical and reasonable in choosing your profession. This is a crucial choice. **CBSE 2020**

Answer the following questions based on the passage given above.

1. What leads to disillusionment and unhappiness among young people?

(a) Lack of success

(b) Unrealistic ambitions

(c) Monotonous lifestyle

(d) Gap between qualifications and achievements

2. What are the qualities needed to become a politician?

(a) Oratory skills (b) Fame

(c) Aptitude for public life (d) Funds

3. Complete the sentence appropriately.

Lack of proper counselling leads to ....

4. Rectify the given false statement.

The author negates the importance of the role of counsellors.

5. What are the qualities associated with the young people?

6. Substitute the underlined word in the sentence with the word from the passage which means the same.
We need the <u>guidance</u> of the elders to solve this riddle.

7. State the factors that can help young people decide their career.

8. What is the right time to make a career choice? Why?

9. Why are financial resources important while choosing a career?

PASSAGE 8

1. Sleep is crucial to maintaining one's health. Without it, we increase our susceptibility to an astonishing array of health problems, including heart disease, stroke, diabetes, obesity and depression.
2. Not sleeping enough can compromise your immune system, says Stanley Coren, noted professor of psychology and author of the very popular book 'Sleep Thieves'. You eat well and exercise in order to keep your immune system up, Coren goes on to explain, but if you aren't sleeping, you undo all that good work. "The immune system works best when you are sleeping," he says. "That's when your natural killer cells are generated."
3. Natural killer cells are produced in the bone marrow and found in the blood and lymph fluid. They are part of the body's defence mechanism against viruses, bacteria, even cancer and they do not work properly in the persons who are sleepdeprived.
4. It's not just our immune system that gets adversely affected when we cut down on sleep. According to Dr. Michael Sole, a Canadian cardiologist, there is a higher rate of heart failure among people with sleep disorders and sleep disturbances. He goes on to emphasise that there is increased evidence of C-reactive protein, an indicator of heart disease risk, in people suffering from sleep loss.
5. Sleep disturbances increase the likelihood of prediabetic state of glucose intolerance and insulin resistance. Both these are also markers for heart ailments. Dietician Ramona Josephson notes that insufficient sleep may affect three hormones that can contribute to obesity.
6. There's a decrease in leptin, the appetite-suppressing hormone found in our fat tissue, she says. Ghrelin, the hormone controlling hunger pangs increases with lack of sleep causing greater feelings of hunger. "The less you sleep, the more your chances of obesity," Josephson concludes.
7. Sleep is important in keeping not only our waistline trim, but also ensuring a balanced brain activity. During sleep, brain neurotransmitters-the chemicals that deliver messages between nerve cells in the brain-are replenished. When we do not sleep well, our brain chemicals deplete which leads to emotional disturbances like depression, anxiety and general feelings of sadness, anger and irritation.

MCB Theme : Health and Medicine

Answer the following questions based on the passage given above.

1. What does lack of sleep do?
(a) Decreases laziness.
(b) Weakens the body's capacity to combat diseases.
(c) Helps youngsters do well in their examinations.
(d) Prevents a person from gaining weight.

2. What does natural killer cells do?
(a) Make a person look old pretty quickly.
(b) Are produced in large numbers when we stay awake.
(c) Help us fight viruses and bacteria.
(d) Work well even for sleep-deprived people.

3. Complete the sentence appropriately.
If we sleep well, ...

4. Complete the sentence appropriately.
Lack of sleep increases the chances of ....

5. How does C-reactive protein affect our body?

6. Substitute the underlined word in the sentence with the word from the passage which means the same.
They have <u>discovered</u> the pathway that leads to the river.

7. How does sleep promote immunity?

8. How does sleep deprivation affect one's immunity?

9. Sleep deprivation can lead to long term effects. Elaborate.

PASSAGE 9

1. The plant world is an immense store of active chemical compounds. Nearly half the medicines we use today are herbal in origin, and a quarter contains plant extracts or active chemicals taken directly from plants. Across the globe, the hunt will always be on to find species that could form the bases of new medicines.
2. Thousands of years ago, the ancient Egyptians discovered simple ways to extract and use the active ingredients within plants. Egyptian papyrus manuscripts from 2000 B.C. record the use of perfumes and fine oils, aromatic oils and gums in the embalming process.

3. In ancient Greece in the 5th and the 4th centuries B.C., Hippocrates, the father of medicine, was already recommending asparagus and garlic for their diuretic qualities, poppy as a way of inducing sleep and willow leaves to relieve pain and fever.

4. As a result of trade with Africa and Asia, the Western world's store of herbal medicines was enriched by the inclusion of camphor, cinnamon, ginger, ginseng, nutmeg, sandalwood, turmeric and henna. For a long time, however, the use of both local plants and those with more distant origins was based on more or less fanciful beliefs. From the Renaissance onwards, scientists and their scientific studies, discoveries and inventions came to the fore, rejecting alchemists' elixirs and other magical remedies. Local plants were carefully collected and widely used to make infusions, decoctions and ointments. These plants make up the major part of the traditional cures that we have inherited.

5. One tree that generated considerable interest among scientists was the willow. In the early 1800s, chemists from Germany, Italy and France began the search for the compounds responsible for the acclaimed pain-relieving effects of its bark. In 1828, the German pharmacist, Johann Buchner, was the first to obtain salicin, the major compound in a pure form. In 1838, the Italian chemist, Raffaele Piria also obtained salicylic acid from the bark by various chemical processes.
But these early compounds caused blisters in the mouth, and stomach upsets when ingested. In 1853, a French chemist, Charles Frederic Gerhardt, synthesised a modified form of salicylic acid-acetylsalicylic acid. But still it wasn't further developed for more than 40 years until a German chemist, Felix Hoffman, working for Bayer, rediscovered Gerhardt's compound. Hoffman gave it to his father who suffered from arthritis and reported the beneficial effects.

6. From the 1930s onwards, advances in chemistry have made it much easier to reproduce the active ingredients in plants. But plants will continue to have a medicinal importance in their own right. Their active constituents may be slightly modified to improve their efficiency or to reduce their undesirable effects, but they are still vital for the treatment of disorders such as cancers and heart diseases or as a means of combating malaria. And they remain the essence of herbal medicine-an area that has still not been fully understood and explored. **MCB Theme : Health and Medicine**

Answer the following questions based on the passage given above.

1. Why is there a hunt to find new species of plants?
(a) To make bases for the medicine
(b) To discover new species for human use
(c) For scientific discovery
(d) For study of ayurveda

2. What were found in the Egyptian papyrus manuscripts from 2000 B.C.?
(a) Inclusion of camphor, cinnamon, ginger, ginseng, nutmeg, sandalwood, turmeric and henna.
(b) Record of the use of perfumes and fine oils, aromatic oils and gums in the embalming process.
(c) How to obtain tartaric acid from grapes, citric acid from lemons and malic acid from apples?
(d) Our ancestors discovered which plants were medicinally beneficial and which were highly toxic.

3. Complete the following sentence appropriately.
Hoffman gave .... to his father who suffered from arthritis and reported the beneficial effects.

4. State whether the assertion is True or False.
Hippocrates recommended poppy as a way of inducing sleep and willow leaves to relieve pain and fever.

5. Complete the following sentence appropriately.
Africa and Asia are called ....

6. Substitute the underlined word in the following sentence with a word/phrase from passage, that means the same.
In the late 1700s, Carl Wilheim Scheele, a gifted Swedish chemist, <u>obtained</u> tartaric acid from grapes, citric acid from lemons and malic acid from apples.

7. The plant world is an immense store of active chemical compounds. List any two points to justify it.

8. In which paragraph would the following lines most likely be placed.
First came the isolation of morphine from the opium poppy in 1803, then caffeine from coffee beans in 1819, quinine from cinchona bark and colchicines from meadow saffron both in 1820 and atropine from deadly nightshade in 1835.

9. Even though advances in chemistry have made it much easier to reproduce the active ingredients, plants would never lose their significance in medicine. Justify in 40 words.

PASSAGE 10

When on 1st April, 2010, the Right of Children to Free and Compulsory Education Act became a reality, this historic step became the first Fundamental Right that has been added to the Constitution since India attained independence. The act makes it obligatory on the State to guarantee Right to Education and "ensure compulsory admission, attendance and completion of elementary education by every child of 6 to 14 years." According to the act, financial constraints should not prevent a child from completing elementary education, which means, even if a child lives in a remote area, providing free transportation will be part of the child's entitlement to education. Some of the salient features of the act include-providing for school teachers at 1: 30 teacher - pupil ratio at the primary school and 1: 35 ratio at the upper primary level within six months, with these schools having only trained school teachers in five years. The norms for the schools in the Act, include one room for every teacher, subject-wise teachers, toilets and drinking water, a library and a playground within three years. The Right to Education (RTE) Act has three basic goals—(a) bringing children of marginalised sections into the ambit of school education; (b) ensuring that all schools and their teachers meet some specified norms; and (c) ensuring that all children receive quality schooling free from any kind of discrimination.

The RTE Act says that private schools should reserve a fourth of their seats for the poor and other categories of children. The RTE Act says that all schools should now be 'recognised'. Given the shortage of trained teachers in the country, there is a need to do some rethinking on this stipulation and explore the possibility of hiring para- teachers to run these schools until sufficient number of trained teachers are available. Studies in Uttar Pradesh and Bihar by Kingdon and Banerji show that children taught by parateachers are as good if not better than those taught by regular trained teachers. If the RTE Act is implemented successfully, India can emerge as a global leader in achieving the Millennium Development Goal of ensuring that all children complete their elementary education by 2015.

MCB Theme : Education

Answer the following questions based on the passage given above.

1. What is special about the RTE 2010?
   (a) First addition to the Constitution after Indian Independence
   (b) First Fundamental Right
   (c) Made education obligatory
   (d) Made education an important criterion for growth
2. What are the challenges of RTE?
   (a) Shortage of trained teachers
   (b) Lack of school infrastructure
   (c) Financial constraints
   (d) All of the above
3. Complete the sentence appropriately.
   To handle the problem of lack of trained teachers, ... can act as substitutes.
4. Rectify the given false statement.
   RTE can promote SDG's.
5. Complete the sentence appropriately.
   According to the RTE, ... in private schools.
6. What should be the students and teacher ratio according to RTE
   (a) 1 : 30 (b) 30 : 1 (c) 35 : 1 (d) 40 : 1
7. What action will be taken if some parents don't send children to schools?
8. What is the implication of 'free education' in the act?
9. What is the Right to Education?

PASSAGE 11

Vocational Education prepares learners for jobs that are based on manual or practical activities. It has traditionally been considered non-academic and totally related to a specific trade, occupation or vocation. Hence, it is sometimes referred to as technical education. It is generally given at the secondary or post-secondary level.

It focuses on development of skills that are needed for specific trades and hence, practical work is given greater importance than bookish learning.

There is an urgent need to respond to the growing skill requirement so that the momentum of the economy can be sustained. By focusing on employability, our education system can fulfill the requirements of skilled manpower. Further, vocational education also creates more employment opportunities by equipping learners with entrepreneurial skills. It also addresses the changing face of technology through diversified courses.

However, there are many concerns, foremost among them being low motivation amongst students to pursue vocational education. It is compounded by the rigid mindset of parents and educators in accepting vocational courses. It is also a painful fact that many vocational courses that are being offered have become obsolete. Since there is poor linkage between institutions offering vocational courses and the private sector, students often find it difficult to secure proper employment immediately after completing their courses.

As a result of globalisation, new sectors in both manufacturing and service industries have opened up. Hospitality, fashion technology, film and television, information technology, retail, health care etc. are some of the emerging areas that require skilled man power.

MCB Theme : Education

Answer the following questions based on the passage given above.

1. Which of the following qualities would you apply to vocational education?
   (a) Knowledge based (b) Practical
   (c) Experience based (d) Both (b) and (c)
2. What does vocational education focus on?
   (a) Application (b) Skills
   (c) Theoretical knowledge (d) All of these
3. Complete the following sentence appropriately.
   ...., new sectors in both manufacturing and service industries have opened up.
4. Rectify the given false statement.
   Students often find it easy to secure proper employment immediately after completing their courses.
5. Complete the following sentence appropriately.
   There is .... institutions offering vocational courses and the private sector.
6. Substitute the underlined word in the following sentence with a word/phrase from passage, that means the same.
   It focuses on development of skills that are needed for specific trades and hence, practical work is given greater importance than theoretical learning.
7. Why is vocational education called technical education?
8. On the basis of the paragraph how would you define vocational education?
9. How is vocational education important to our society? Answer in about 40 words.

PASSAGE 12

Solar Power

With energy consumption being the buzzword in developing economies around the world, fears of an energy crisis looming ahead are not totally unfounded.

The non-renewable nature of fossil fuels makes complete dependence on these for future energy needs, a very dicey affair. Renewable energy sources are the best bet in the scenario. And what can be a better renewable energy resource than the Sun?

In a country like India, if the abundant amount of sunlight available is harnessed properly it could mean an end to the energy crisis. It is the most abundant source of energy. The average global solar radiation is around 5 Kilowatt Hours (KWH) per square meter per day with the sunshine hours ranging between 2300-4300 per year. The country receives solar energy equivalent to more than 5000 trillion KWH per year, which is far more than its total annual energy consumption.

Besides, it is a renewable and clean energy source. Taking both environmental and economic cost, solar energy works cheaper than fossil fuel resources. Once we master techniques to harness solar energy, it can be a vital source of power on all planets.

Electric Motors

Imagining a future where clean air is no longer a dream and our cities are not smog filled concrete jungles, this could well become a reality in the coming years if the world begins to increasingly adopt the use of cleaner options like alternate-fuel vehicles.

The rise in economic activity and the burgeoning population have led to a tremendous demand in the transport sector, especially in urban India. With India's ever growing population, pollution is also increasing manifold. Thus, a very critical issue of keeping air and noise pollution in urban areas under control has emerged.

The need to reduce air pollution along with the availability of new advanced batteries have allowed EVs to reappear as a clean alternative to internal combustion vehicles. Electric drive systems are virtually non-polluting and extremely energy efficient. While internal combustion vehicles can convert about 20% of the chemical energy in gasoline into useful work, 75% or more of the energy from a battery has productive power in an electric vehicle.

Apart from being environment and user-friendly, there are several other reasons for alternative fuel cars to flourish in India. Firstly, electricity for EVs can be produced from various sources for which India has natural resources and does not need to depend on the import of oil. Although EVs will not replace LPG, CNG or petrol and diesel for intercity use, the infrastructure required for EVs in the form of electricity distribution infrastructure, is already available in all the major cities and minimum costs are required to install additional capacity.

In order to do that, a holistic approach involving the government, public and auto majors is needed to promote EVs in India. Appropriate government policies and adequate support from business houses and institutions, for instance, purchasing a fixed percentage of vehicles for their fleets and offering subsidies and tax exemptions, will go a long way in promoting the industry in India.

Finally, people have to become more informed about these technologies. The media must play its role in educating the public about alternative fuel vehicles and their advantages.

MCB Theme : Science

Answer the following questions based on the passage given above.

1. What can bring about a change in the energy crisis in India?
   (a) Solar energy (b) Technological development
   (c) Wind energy (d) Renewable energy
2. India receives 5000 trillion KWH/year which means ....
   (a) India needs to develop the technology to utilise it
   (b) India has an abundance of solar energy
   (c) India is a powerhouse of renewable sources of energy
   (d) India can change the face of energy crisis
3. Complete the sentence appropriately.
   The media can help by ....
4. Rectify the given false statement.
   Establishing solar power generating units is too expensive.
5. Complete the sentence appropriately.
   Tax exemptions and subsidies are required to ....
6. Substitute the underlined word in the sentence with the word from the passage which means the same.
   The modified version of this car will be available next month.
7. Why is dependence on non-renewable sources of energy said to be a very dicey affair?
8. What had led to a tremendous increase in the transport sector in India?
9. How does an electric vehicle work?

PASSAGE 13

D.1 Koko Village, Nigeria

Mr. Sunday Nana, his wife and four small children live in Koko Village, Nigeria. The village is like any other African village-picturesque, colourful and noisy. The Nana family's house, too, is the same as all the other houses in the village with mud walls and a rusting corrugated iron roof and with children and chickens sharing the compound.

There is one difference, however. Outside Mr. Nana's front are three large empty metal drums, the bright red paint now flaking away, but the skull and crossbones symbol clearly visible on each. And in a clearing 200m away from the village, next to a stream that the villagers get their drinking water from, is an enormous pyramid of identical drums, reaching to the sky. Some of them are badly corroded, their slimy contents of various colours - grey, dark green, bright orange, etc.-leaking out, down, on to the baked African Earth and into the stream. Some have fallen down and rolled-or been rolled by playful children - into the bush. Some are smoking in the midday heat. Some are swelling, as if their contents are bursting to get out. Some have already burst.

"They came on a Wednesday", said Sunday, "Many, many big lorries". They took all day unloading them. Noone told us what was in them. They gave the Chief a brown paper bag-I saw him smiling as the lorries drove away. This was five years ago. Then three months ago, one of the brightest boys in the village-Thomas Agonyo - started university in Lagos. He came home one weekend with a new Chemistry book and spent all day looking at the drums and writing things down and talking to himself and shaking his head. We all thought he had gone mad. Then he called a meeting of the village and told us that the drums contained poisonous chemicals. He said they had come from Italy. But I don't know where that is. Is it in Europe?

Mr. Sunday Nana stopped, frowning, a troubled look on his face, "In the last five years, 13 people have died in this village, my own elder brother being one of them. They have been in pain, terrible pain. We have never seen deaths like that before. Lots of our children are sick. We have asked the government to take the drums away, but they do nothing. We have written to Italy, but they do nothing. The Chief says we should move our houses to another place. But we have no money to buy land. We have no choice. We have to stay here. And they ......" pointing to the mountain of death in the clearing - "are our neighbours".

D.2 Ponnimanthuri Village, India

"I can remember the time", she said wistfully, "when all the fields around this village were green and the harvests good. Her outstretched arm described a complete circle as she stood in the morning Sun. Then they built those monsters, those…". Her voice spluttered in anger as she shook her fist at a collection of ominous-looking black buildings on the horizon, covered in a low-lying shroud of thick smoke. "They said that factories need leather to make shoes, handbags and clothes. They said our menfolk would get jobs. They said we would all become rich."

We stood silent, each thinking our own thoughts. Yes, they told you all that. But there is so much they didn't tell you. They didn't tell you that to change animal skins into leather - which they call tanning - uses as many as 250 different chemicals, including heavy metals such as cadmium, arsenic and chromium. They didn't tell you that these chemicals are discharged into the environment from those chimney stacks and fall to Earth for miles around, polluting the earth below. They didn't tell you that this would poison your fields, so that nothing will grow.

"They didn't tell us that the chemicals would be dumped in open fields and into our rivers", sighed Vijayasama. We had been thinking the same thoughts. "They didn't tell us that our women would have to walk ten kilometers every day.

They didn't tell us that we would get ulcer and sores on our bodies. They didn't tell us..." Her voice trailed off. There is so much they didn't tell you, I thought.

"We don't buy leather shoes or leather handbags or leather clothes", she said.

MCB Theme : Environment

Answer the following questions based on the passage given above.

1. How is Mr. Nana's village described?
   (a) Vibrant (b) Poor
   (c) Picturesque (d) Both (a) and (c)
2. What were in the drums?
   (a) Water (b) Poisonous chemicals
   (c) Slimy liquid (d) Some common chemicals
3. Complete the sentence appropriately.
   It was .... who told everyone in the village that the drums contained poisonous chemical.
4. State whether the given assertion is True or False.
   Mr. Nana had asked the government to take the drums away.
5. How does Vijayasama feel when she says "I can remember the time"?
6. Substitute the underlined word in the sentence with the word from the passage which means the same.
   They had <u>poured</u> the drink in the cup.
7. Why do you think there are 'three large, empty metal drums' outside Mr. Nana's front door?
8. What are the monsters? Why are they called so by Vijayasama?
9. Where were the chemicals used in the leather factories dumped?

PASSAGE 14

India is the current tourism hot spot. The other epithets used while referring to the nation include 'Destination of the Millennium' and 'Land of All Seasons'. Spanning an area of 3,287,263 square kilometers, India is a vast country and includes dry desert areas, evergreen forests, snowy Himalayas, a long coast, and fertile plains. The natural beauty and cultural diversity of the place echo a rich tradition. India flaunts of equal grandeur bays and beaches, deserts and mountains, enigmatic green valleys and backwaters. There exists in India a comfortable juxtaposition of contrasts- the existence of bustling haats and swanky malls, emergence of nuclear families but a reluctance to let go on the joint family system, a rush to embrace modernity yet a firm resolve to preserve traditions; destination for both ayurveda and modern medical tourism; bustling communities and indigenous tribes.

India has a rich heritage and culture of warm hospitality. In India, it is believed that honouring guests equals to honouring God. A guest is welcomed into our home and hearth with cheerful gratitude. The Sanskrit adage 'Atithi Devo Bhavah' dictates the respect granted to guests in India. This wonderful tradition of our country has become the unique selling point of the modern tourism industry. Ministry of Tourism, Government of India has pioneered an initiative that will help tap into the full potential of tourism in India. Ministry of Tourism, Government of India has introduced "Atithi Devo Bhavah Programme"- a nation wide campaign that aims at sensitising key stakeholders towards tourists, through a process of training and orientation. The endeavour is to boost tourism in India, which in turn would act as a catalyst for India's economic growth. The 'Incredible India' Campaign has been launched to create awareness about the effects of tourism and sensitising people about preservation of our rich heritage and culture, cleanliness and warm hospitality. It also re-instills a sense of responsibility towards tourists and reinforces the confidence of foreign tourists towards India as a preferred holiday destination.

MCB Theme : Travel and Tourism

Answer the following questions based on the passage given above.

1. India is said to be a land of contrasts because of the presence of ....
   (a) haats and malls
   (b) nuclear and joint families
   (c) ayurveda and advanced medicine
   (d) All of the above
2. The adage 'Atithi Devo Bhavah' is taken from ....
   (a) Sanskrit (b) Hindi
   (c) Tamil (d) Kannada
3. Complete the sentence appropriately.
   In India, guests are given the same treatments as ....
4. Complete the sentence appropriately.
   The adage was pioneered by ....
5. What does the adage 'Atithi Devo Bhavah' mean?
6. Why is the adage 'Atithi Devo Bhavah' important?
7. What are the epithets used for India? Why?
8. What is the 'Atithi Devo Bhavah Programme'?
9. What kind of land does India have?

PASSAGE 15

Mile Sur Mera Tumhara

Ek sur (meaning One Tune) or 'Mile Sur Mera Tumhara' as it is better known, is an Indian song and accompanying video feature promoting national integration and unity in diversity. The concept for Mile Sur was developed in 1988 by Lok Seva Sanchar Parishad, and promoted by Doordarshan and India's Ministry of Information. The song was composed by Ashok Patki, co-composed and arranged by Louis Banks, written by Piyush Pandey (then an Accounts Manager and presently the Executive Chairman and Creative Head of Ogilvy and Mather, India). The project was conceived and directed by Suresh Mullick (then All India Creative Director, Ogilvy and Mather) and recorded by a group of people from all walks of life, including a super group of popular Indians - musicians, sports persons, movie stars, etc.

The national integration video was intended to instill a sense of pride and promote unity amongst Indians, highlighting the different linguistic communities and societies that live in India - India's unity in diversity, so to speak.

Mile Sur was telecast for the first time on Independence Day 1988, after the telecast of the Prime Minister's speech from the ramparts of the Red Fort. It quickly captivated India, gaining and maintaining near-anthem status ever since.

The song's lyrics are unique; One phrase, repeated in fourteen Indian languages: 'Mile sur mera tumhara, to sur bane hamara', meaning "When my musical note and your musical note merge, it becomes our musical note".

The song itself ends by fading into the final notes of the Indian National Anthem.

Languages used were Hindi, Kashmiri, Urdu, Punjabi, Sindhi, Tamil, Kannada, Telugu, Malayalam, Bangla, Assamese, Oriya, Gujarati and Marathi. 'Phir Mile Sur Mera Tumhara': Twenty years after the original debut, the song has been re-recorded with an updated cast for telecast on 26th January, 2010 by Zoom TV. This version titled Phir Mile Sur Mera Tumhara features Indian musicians, singers, sportspersons and film personalities from the current generation. The current version (16 min 17 sec) runs longer than the older version (6 min 9 sec) and has been directed by Kailash Surendranath who had produced the original version of Mile Sur Mera Tumhara as well. The new version also retains music composer/arranger Louis Banks who had co-composed/arranged the original Mile Sur Mera Tumhara as well.

MCB Theme : National Integration

Answer the following questions based on the passage given above.

1. What is the motto of Mile Sure Mera Tumhara?
   (a) Patriotism
   (b) Unity
   (c) Pleasure
   (d) Both (a) and (b)
2. Mile Sure Mera Tumhara was sung by......... .
   (a) Suresh Mullick
   (b) athletes
   (c) popular Indians
   (d) common man
3. Complete the sentence appropriately.
   The national integration video highlights ....
4. State whether the given assertion is True or False.
   Languages used were Hindi, Kashmiri, Urdu, Punjabi, Sindhi, Tamil, Kannada, Telugu, Malayalam, Bangla, Assamese, Oriya, Gujarati and Rajasthani.
5. Complete the sentence appropriately.
   The song has been re-recorded with an updated cast for telecast ....
6. Substitute the underlined word in the following sentence with a word/phrase that means the opposite.
   The new version also <u>retains</u> music composer/arranger Louis Banks who had co-composed/arranged the original Mile Sur Mera Tumhara as well.
7. Who is Piyush Pandey?
8. Who came up with the project of composing the song Mile Sur Mera Tumhara?
9. Briefly explain why the song is unique? Answer in 40 words.

PASSAGE 16

As the population of India comprises many different races, religions, cultures and language groups, the importance of national integration comes to the forefront. In order to establish peace and stability and ensure progress, all different societies must be brought into one single nation with a national consciousness. National integration should aim at improving socio-cultural relations, reducing economic inequalities and strengthening unity and solidarity. If we ask what the forces that challenge national integration are, the answers are not difficult to find. Regionalism, communalism, religious fanaticism, lingualism and now terrorism are the main forces among others.

The patriotic doctrine that for a citizen, the country comes first and all other issues come second, doesn't always work to motivate the people for national causes.

Regional aspirations of the people, if not controlled, may be dangerous for the country as it may break it up or create more and more new states. Communalism may encourage clashes between communities. No community should be placed above the nation. Lingual preferences should be peacefully dealt with so that no excessive bias or favour for any one language brings about agitation in the country. Religious fanaticism is another dangerous force that often leads to violence, not only in India, but all over the world. India is a secular country, but that hasn't solved all problems. Let us recollect what our secularist founding fathers thought about religions.

In order to achieve national integration, we must first identify the force that may blissfully bind the people of the country, create an emotional bond and help them share common ideas and values. Constitution, territorial continuity, art, literature, music, national festivals, national flag, national anthem, sports and, let us not forget, Bollywood- these are the vital aspects that may be exploited to promote national integration. Economic development of the unprivileged and underprivileged regions should get primary importance. More facilities should be extended to distant regions and tribal groups. The education system in general should be revised with the aim of fostering national integration. Some special means should be adopted within the education system to instill a sense of belonging and unity in the mind from childhood.

Last but not the least, I would like to mention a very special point, often ignored, that may be considered extremely vital for national integration. Exercise of power and authority may be successful temporarily, but fails in the long run. It's essential to attain internal freedom for the people first, by which I mean a mind free of selfish ego and aware of basic values and humanity in general, a conscience always awakened and strong, and love and true spirit in the core of heart. Such a free mind remains open to other cultures, religions and languages and will easily accept different people of the country.

MCB Theme : National Integration

Answer the following questions based on the passage given above.

1. Why is national integration important for a country like India?
(a) Because of diversity
(b) For growth
(c) For peace and stability
(d) All of the above

2. The passage mentions a patriotic doctrine. What is it?
(a) That for a citizen, the country comes first
(b) That safety of the country is important
(c) That progress at any cost is important
(d) None of the above

3. Complete the sentence appropriately.

A person with a free mind remains open to ....

4. State whether the given assertion is True or False.

Regional aspirations of the people, if not controlled, may be dangerous for the country as it may break it up or create more and more new states.

5. What is essential for freedom?

6. Substitute the underlined word in the following sentence with a word/phrase that means the same.

It's essential to attain internal freedom for the people first, by which I mean a mind free of selfish ego and aware of basic values and humanity in general, a <u>conscience</u> always awakened and strong.

7. What are the aims of national integration?

8. What are the forces that challenge national integration?

9. What are the steps that we should take to strengthen the nation and its unity?

Non-Continuous Passages

PASSAGE 1

Why do people travel?

1. There are many reasons for travel. Most tourist trips can be placed under the following categories.
2. Leisure tourism trips make up 42% of travel. The main purpose is relaxation, rest and enjoyment. Most holidays are taken in family groups, couples or with groups of friends. Sometimes, people may choose to go on holiday by themselves to be on their own, or perhaps to meet new friends. Short breaks of less than one week are also becoming increasingly popular as second holidays. People choose to spend 2 or 3 nights away from home on a short break over a weekend or mid-week to relax and destress. These holiday choices are driven by what memorable experiences we hope to create and what we class as our definition of spending quality time together.
3. Health and fitness tourism, such as a cycling tour, trekking, or a walking holiday (5%), is growing in popularity amongst the youth today. Also, sports tourism (3%) wherein sports tours are taken as a spectator, such as a visit to a major sporting event like the Olympics or a World Cup in another city or country.
4. Health tourism (10%) implies going to a different country to have an operation or medical treatment not available or too expensive in the country where the person usually lives. This is making India a popular destination because of the excellent medical facilities it has to offer.
5. Educational tourism (3%) covers school and college visits and foreign language exchanges linked directly to study experiences and are short visits made by high school students as they prepare for further studies.
6. Spiritual tourism (2%) is where people travel both inbound and outbound to places of worship according to their beliefs.
7. Business tourism (35%) many people have to travel in the course of their business life apart from making a regular journey to and from where they normally work. It may involve driving to a meeting or flying to another country for conferences or corporate events business tourism is very important to the travel and tourism industry as it takes place all through the year and some travel and tourism businesses, such as budget hotel chains, rely heavily on income from business travellers. **CBSE 2025**

Answer the following questions based on the passage given above.

1. Complete with a suitable reason.

   People go on holidays together to ....
2. Fill in the blank with an appropriate word/phrase.

   The phrase 'driven by' in paragraph 2 suggests that the choice of holiday destination .... people's experiences.
3. Short holidays of 2-3 days are becoming popular.

   (a) because people have limited holidays.
   (b) because people have increased their holiday budgets.
   (c) to take a break from the stress of daily life.
   (d) to visit historical places.
4. Why do tourists travel abroad for sports tourism?

   I. It is more economical.
   II. To watch family members play.
   III. To be spectators at world events.
   IV. It doubles up for both sports and leisure.
   V. To train for sporting events.

   Select the correct option.

   (a) Only I (b) II and V
   (c) II, III and IV (d) Only III
5. Why is India a popular destination for health tourism?
6. Which is the most popular form of tourism and why?
7. Explain why business tourism is important for the travel industry.
8. According to the above statistics, which form of tourism is the least popular at the present moment?

PASSAGE 2

Read the following table displaying the performance and interest of four students of different calibre in academics and co-curricular activities.

Name	Mathematics	Science	English	Overall Average (100)	Interest in Co-curricular Activities	Performance in the Inter - School Competition
Ravi	75	80	70	75	Sports (Cricket , Football)	Won 1st place in Inter - School Football Tournament
Mohit	95	90	85	90	Debate, Quiz, Elocution	Awarde Best Speaker in Inter-School Debate Competition
Raghu	55	60	50	55	Painting, Drama, Photography	Displayed artwork in Inter-School Art Exhibition
Lata	100	96	95	97	Robotics, Coding, Chess	Secured 2nd place in Inter-School Robotics Challenge

CBSE 2024

Answer the following questions based on the above table.

1. Identify the student from the above table who has <u>artistic ideas</u>.

2. Lata has interest in Robotics and Coding. Choose the best career option for her from the given options.
   (a) Event Organiser
   (b) App Developer
   (c) Choreographer

3. Which interest(s) of Raghu can help him to relax whenever he is stressed?

4. Give one justification each to prove that
   (a) Lata's actions are based on accurate calculations, and
   (b) Lata is capable of cracking any competitive examination.

5. Select the correct option to fill in the blank and complete the analogy.
   Guitar : Music : : .... : Photograph

6. Complete the given sentence with the appropriate reason, with reference to the information in the given table.
   From the table given above, we can infer that even though Raghu is an average student yet he is .... than Lata.

7. Explain why situation (C) showcases the sportsmanship quality of Ravi.
   (a) In an Inter-School cricket tournament, Ravi played well and helped the team to win the match.
   (b) In an Inter-School cricket match, it was Ravi who cheered his team as a captain and took important decisions to win the match.
   (c) After an Inter-School cricket match, Ravi Congratulate the opposite team for winning the match.

8. Choose the correct option which proves that Mohit is a good Debater.
   (a) Mohit shouts at the beginning of any discussion and does not let others speak.
   (b) Mohit argues without any facts while presenting his ideas.
   (c) Mohit can convince others with valid points and facts.

PASSAGE 3

Student Council Unveils School's First Student-Made Drone Programme

by Tanveer Siddiqui, Secretary, Student Council

Bengaluru, 10th November The Student Council at ABC School has initiated a ground-breaking project involving the construction and operation of drones made by students. The programme was introduced at the school's monthly public presentation on 7th November, attracting significant interest from students, faculty, and parents alike.

Mr. J. Rao, the school's vice-principal, and the head of the Student Council, Priya Desai, kicked off the event by explaining the motivation behind the project. They noted that the programme aims to provide students with hands-on experience in technology and engineering while promoting teamwork and creativity. The Student Council collaborated with local engineers and technology experts to ensure safety and compliance with regulations.

During the event, the council members demonstrated a live drone flight, showcasing the capabilities of the drones built by the students. They performed a variety of manoeuvres, including aerial photography and obstacle course navigation.

The Student Council has planned several future activities to keep the momentum going. These include a drone-building workshop, a photography contest using the drones, and an inter-school drone race in the spring. The programme is designed to engage students in innovative ways and foster a deeper interest in technology and engineering. **CBSE SQP 2024**

Answer the following questions based on the report above.

1. Complete with a suitable reason.

   The most likely reason why the student council secretary was chosen to draft the report was because ....

2. Fill in the blank with an appropriate word/ phrase.

   The term 'ground-breaking' project suggests that the project is .... and reflects a level of creativity.

3. What was the primary goal of the Student Council's drone programme at National Public School?

   (a) To encourage teamwork and creativity among students
   (b) To demonstrate the latest drone technology to the public
   (c) To generate interest in aerial photography
   (d) To promote engineering skills and provide hands-on experience

4. Who did the Student Council turn to, to ensure safety and regulatory compliance?

   1. Faculty and parents
   2. Vice-Principal
   3. Local Engineers
   4. Head of Student Council
   5. Technology experts

   Options

   (a) Only 1 (b) Only 5
   (c) 2 and 4 (d) 3 and 5

5. What was the most likely purpose of showcasing the capabilities of the drones during the event?

6. What in the passage suggests that the live drone demonstration aimed to engage and excite the audience?

7. What skills are the students expected to develop through the photography contest using drones?

8. Explain how the Student Council's Drone Programme at National Public School align with the school's goals of promoting holistic education.

PASSAGE 4

Name	Motto	Participation in activities	Achievements	Awards	Personal Qualities	Drawbacks	Other notable things
Rohit	"Together we can achieve greatness"	Debate club, Quiz club	1st prize in Science Olympiad	Best Student	Diligent, confident, empathetic	Sometimes tends to be overly competitive	Volunteer at a local NGO
Sanya	"Service before self"	Social service club, Drama club	1st prize in Debate competition	Best Orator	Compassionate, organised, responsible	Can be overly critical times	Participated in a Model United Nations conference
Rajat	"Never give up, always rise up"	Sports club, Music club	2nd position in Chess competition	Best Sportsperson	Perseverant, team player, adaptable	Can sometimes be indecisive	Plays in a local band
Aryan	"Success through hard work"	Photography club, Science club	1st prize in Photography competition	Budding Innovator	Creative, curious, detail-oriented	Can sometimes procrastinate	Built a working model of a wind turbine for a science fair
Ananya	"Strive excellence"	Dance club, Art club	1st prize in Art competition	Creative Mind	Confident, hardworking, imaginative	Tends to overthink things	Published her own poetry collection

CBSE SQP 2023-24

Answer the following questions based on the above table.

1. Complete the given sentence with the appropriate reason, with reference to the information in the table.

   We can infer that Aryan's overall performance may be negatively impacted by his weakness in time management because ....

2. Select the correct option to fill the blank and complete the analogy.

   .... : Paint brush :: Rajat : Tabla

3. Which house captain is most likely to struggle the most with handling stress during the school's annual inter-house sports tournament?

   (a) Rohit
   (b) Sanya
   (c) Rajat
   (d) Ananya

4. Select the option that correctly matches the House Captains (A) - (C), to the trophies (i) - (v).

   HOUSE CAPTAINS–(a) Rajat (b) Ananya (c) Aryan

(i)

(ii)

(iii)

(iv)

(v)

(a) (A)-(ii), (B)-(ii), (C)-(iii) (b) (A)-(i), (B)-(v), (C)-(iv)
(c) (A)-(v), (B)-(iii), (C)-(ii) (d) (A)-(iii), (B)-(iv), (C)-(i)

5. Based on the personal qualities of the House Captains, why is Rajat the most likely to be a collaborative worker?

6. Explain briefly why situation (b), from the three situations given below, showcases Ananya's motto, 'Lead by example'?

   (a) During a group project, Ananya assigns each team member specific tasks and sets a high standard for the project's quality. She tells them to actively participate in the project and take it to fruition.

   (b) During a house debate competition, Ananya notices that a few of her house members are struggling to articulate their arguments effectively. Ananya takes the time to listen to their concerns and provides constructive feedback and support.

   (c) During a fundraising event, Ananya volunteers to be in charge of organising and coordinating the event but she frequently delegates tasks to others and attends to her school assignment while her team completes the task successfully.

7. Identify the person who is likely to ask many 'why' questions, and support your choice with one reason.

8. Give two justifications for Sanya being the best fit to lead a school-wide initiative to promote mental health and well-being among students.

PASSAGE 5

The following data is based on a survey to assess percentage of activities done by different age groups during their free time

Age Group	Reading	Outdoor Sports	Gym	Vacation	Meeting Friends	Social Media	Watching
10-15 yrs	5	25		20	25	10	15
16-25 yrs			30		10	50	10
26-40 yrs	30		30	20	20		
1-55 yrs	10			25		35	30
56-70 yrs	10	20			10	20	40

CBSE 2024 C

Answer the following questions based on the above table.

1. Identify the age group from the above table that spends the least time reading.

   (b) 10-15 yrs (b) 26-40 yrs
   (c) 41-55 yrs (d) 56-70 yrs

2. The age group of 16-25 yrs prefers going to the gym rather than .... for physical fitness.

   (a) play carrom (b) go for a walk
   (c) watch a movie (d) cook a meal

3. Which activities can help the 56-70 yrs group make more friends?

   (a) Watching TV, gym, and reading
   (b) Social media, reading, and meeting friends
   (c) Vacation, social media, and watching TV
   (d) Outdoor sports, social media, and vacation

4. Give one justification each to prove that
(a) The 26-40 yrs old age group is more outgoing.
(b) Reading is the least popular activity among most age groups.

5. Select the correct option to complete the analogy:
Noise : Sound :: .... : Silence

6. Complete the given sentence with the appropriate reason with reference to the information in the given table.
The 16-25 yrs age group prefers more indoor activities to outdoor ones because......... .

7. Validate why, based on the above information, the 10-15 yrs age group prefers to spend more time outside the home.

8. Which one is the correct option based on the above data?
(a) The 41-55 yrs group spends most of its free time going on vacation and playing outdoor sports.
(b) The 56-70 yrs group spends some free time reading and on social media with no time for physical activity.
(c) The 26-40 yrs group prefers meeting friends more than any other group.
(d) The 16-25 yrs group prefers virtual interaction more than any other group.

PASSAGE 6

Processing Common Steps	Activities Involved	Effects on the Millets and their nutrients
Removing the Husk	Removing the husk from the grains because it is composed of cellulosic matter that the human body cannot digest.	As per a study, when this is done to pearl millets, their phytic acid and polyphenol contents drop. As per a paper published in 2021, millet husk can be briquetted and used as household fuel, and potentially alleviate energy poverty in North Nigeria.
Decorticating the grain	Decorticating the grain, that is, to remove any other outer covering and expose the seed.	Mechanical and hand-worked decortication do not have significance effects on the grain. Both remove crude and dietary fibre. They make the grain more edible and visually attractive, which are favourable factors when marketing them to urban centres.
Milling and Grinding	Milling to grind the grains into flour. Sieving to remove large 'impurities' including bran.	Whole-flour has a high content of 'total polyphenols and flavonoids.' Sieving makes the flour more digestible and its nutrients more accessible to the body. But it also reduces the nutrient content due to the loss of bran.
Germination and Fermentation	Grains are soaked in water for an extended duration.	A positive improvement in the overall nutritional characteristics of millets.
Polishing	Polishing is the process whereby brown rice, for example, is changed to white rice by rubbing off the bran and the germ.	As per a 2012 study, barnyard millet can be polished with a rice polisher for up to three minutes without significant nutrient loss. Polished millets are preferred by (i) Customers for the resulting taste and texture, shorter cooking time (ii) Retailers longer shelf life that is achieved by removing the bran

Answer the following questions based on the passage given above.

1. Complete the sentence given below appropriately.
It is necessary to remove the husk from the grains because ....

2. Select the correct option to fill the blank and complete the analogy.
.... : Positive effect on millet nutrition ::
Decorticate : Remove dietary fibre

3. Identify the main purpose of sieving the millets.
(a) Removing the outer covering of the millets
(b) Exposing the seeds of the millets
(c) Removing the impurities from the millets
(d) Rubbing off the bran

4. Where is this table likely to be found?
(a) A farm brochure
(b) A book on agricultural practices
(c) A nutritionist
(d) In a fact file

5. Which processing step can be linked to the fulfillment of energy requirements of households? Give reason in support of your answer.

6. Why are polished millets popular among the people? Mention any two reasons.

7. When grains are decorticated, their marketing to the urban centres becomes easy. What does it suggest about the urban population?

8. What does the 2012 study show?

PASSAGE 7

Moitra (HR Manager) Hello! Is this Vayu?

Vayu (Candidate) Yes, Vayu this side. May I know who this is?

Moitra Hi Vayu, Moitra this side from the HR department of ABC Ltd. Is this the right time to talk to you?

Vayu Yes Ma'am!

Moitra I have viewed your profile on Naukri.com. Let me know if you are available in the job market?

Vayu Yes, Ma'am. I am looking forward to a new job opportunity.

Moitra I called you for the position of Tech Support for our Noida office. Would you be comfortable with the profile and the location?

Vayu Yes, Ma'am. I am currently working as a Tech Support and I would be very much comfortable with the location.

Moitra What is your educational background?

Vayu I have completed my Bachelor of Technology degree in IT from ZYA, Jaipur with an aggregate of 87%.

Moitra That's great. Let me know about your working experience.

Vayu I started my career 4 years back as Tech Support.

Moitra Okay. With which company are you currently working?

Vayu I am working in the Tech Support department of Unique Solutions Ltd. for their Noida office.

Moitra Tell me something about your roles and responsibilities in your current company.

Vayu My job responsiblities include identifying hardware and software solutions, troubleshooting technical issues, diagnosing and repairing faults, resolving network issues, installing and configuring hardware and software, etc.

Moitra Excellent! Let me know what is your reason for the job change?

Vayu Actually, I have been working here for the past three years but the kind of work I am getting recently in the support profile is not exactly to my liking. Plus, to be honest, I am also looking for a good pay hike as well as new opportunities to upskill myself. I am looking for a new environment to grow.

Moitra Okay. Can you tell me what is your current salary expectation?

Vayu My current salary is 5 LPA. As per industry norms, I am expecting a miminum of 30-40% hike on my current CTC.

Moitra We will surely offer you a decent hike on your current CTC based on your interview.

Vayu Okay.

Moitra I am fixing your appointment for Monday at 2 pm. Is it fine with you?

Vayu Yes, I will be there for the interview.

Moitra Okay. See you Monday then. Goodbye!

Answer the following questions based on the passage given above.

1. Complete the sentence appropriately.
   It can be concluded from the last dialogue that Moitra would further Vayu's resume because ....

2. Complete the sentence appropriately.
   Vayu's responsibilities include troubleshooting technical issues. Here, 'troubleshooting' refers to ....

3. What is the main attraction for Vayu in ABC Ltd.?
   (a) Cooperative staff
   (b) Supportive managers
   (c) Endless learning opportunities
   (d) Non-challenging nature of jobs

4. Which of the following assertions can be sustained from the conversation?
   (a) Vayu was selected for the job by HR.
   (b) Vayu was convinced that HR has a good exposure and skillset.
   (c) Vayu was convinced that he was selected for the job.
   (d) HR was convinced that Vayu has a good exposure and skillset.

5. Vayu informed HR that he would be very much comfortable with their office location. Why was he comfortable?

6. Select the option to fill the blank and complete the analogy.
   Vayu : .... :: Moitra : Interviewer

7. Explain briefly two reasons why Vayu was looking for a new job?

8. After learning about Vayu's role and responsibilities in his current job, Moita remarks 'excellent'. Give any two probable reasons for her response.

PASSAGE 8

Sunday Times of India, New Delhi, 2nd January, 2011 (Article by B. Pradeep Nair)

Yesterday's gizmo is today's junk

More things have changed in the last few decades than in any other period of time. Many common-place utility gadgets have been dying off faster than one would have imagined. In fact, in the past few decades, a number of technologies have become so obsolete that it is difficult to even imagine we were, once upon a time, so contented with them.

Here are five of those which have vanished without a trace.

Floppy disks Computer CPUs had a slot where this could be inserted. Text and pictures could be copied on it and carried. It was notorious for its susceptibility to get infected by viruses that got passed on to PCs when it was inserted. The most common 3-1/2 disk had a storage capacity of 1.44MB. Now, these have been replaced by CDs, DVDs and pen drives that have higher capacity to carry. Of course, with cloud computing catching on at a fast pace, even these face extinction.

Pager The user had a number to which someone could send a short message *via* the paging company. It became very popular in the 1990s because it was the first portable communication device for the ordinary consumer. Typically the message sent on pagers were like. 'call me on (some landline number)' or 'reached home' etc. Pagers soon lost out to mobile phones once they became affordable.

Valve radio One 'got stations' by turning the tuning knobs. The concept of fine tuning never existed. Like a refrigerator, a radio had its place in a house; it was too big to be portable. Often the radio used to be switched on right in the morning and switched off only when it was realised that no one was paying any attention to it. The radio also functioned as a clock - people timed their schedules with the beginning or end of popular programmes.

Gramophone plate There was a stick-like lever that one kept over the disc so that the tiny needle at the end of that lever made contact with the invisible grooves on the disc. It then produced the favourite Mohd. Rafi and Kishore Kumar numbers. There were different discs depending upon the speed of revolution (RPM for revolution per minute). The plates had their amusing offerings as well. One often heard singers mysteriously repeating the same line of a song many times, until someone realised that the needle had got stuck on the same track. So much for getting lost in a tune!

TV antennas They were also status symbols so much so that it didn't matter if you had a cheap black and white TV or an expensive colour one. You had graduated into the next rung of the social ladder if you had one of those antennae sticking out of your roof. It was important to get its position right. And there were no sophisticated ways to do that—there was one guy on the rooftop and another monitoring the reception in the living room; and through a sequence of 'yes-no', the final position was arrived at.

MCB Theme : Science

Answer the following questions based on the passage given above.

1. Radio was placed in the house because ....
2. Complete the sentence appropriately.
   .... was used to play music.
3. Why have some technologies become obsolete?
   (a) New advancements (b) Lack of need
   (c) Lack of popularity (d) Both (a) and (b)
4. What has replaced Floppy disks?
   1. CDs 2. DVDs
   3. Pen drives 4. Hard disks
   5. Mobile phones

   Options
   (a) 1 and 2 (b) 2 and 3 (c) 1, 2 and 3 (d) Only 5
5. Why was floppy disk considered notorious?
6. Substitute the underlined word in the sentence with the word from the passage which means the same.
   Hena bought a dress that was <u>reasonable</u>.
7. Why do CDs, DVDs and pen drives face extinction?
8. What is a pager? Why had it become popular?

PASSAGE 9

Sunita Williams

Age 43

Astronaut since 1998

Space time Six months on the space station in 2006-2007, including more than 29 hours of space walks

With her 195 days in space, Sunita Williams broke Shannon Lucid's previous endurance record-until Peggy Whitson broke both the women's records in 2008.

Williams, a naval aviator and test pilot who grew up in the Boston area, also 'ran' the Boston Marathon from the station treadmill, with an unofficial time of 4 hours and 24 minutes (during which the International Space Station orbited the Earth about three times).

On being a rookie "Yes, it's unusual to stay in space for six months on a first flight. And yes, it's a little shift that you're going to be locked in a can with a couple of guys. But I embraced the idea. I mean, I prepared for almost eight years! All the training was definitely beneficial for living up there. And with my Navy background, I'd gone on deployments before, so I wasn't worried about leaving home for six months. The cosmonauts were very professional, and we all had mutual respect and understanding."

Flying versus walking "I learned after about a week how to fly gracefully without going too fast or jerking around. I had a hard time remembering how to walk. I prefer flying!"

Daily exercise "The treadmill harness is a little uncomfortable and takes some getting used to. I really like running outside and having the wind blow on you, even if it's hot and humid like in Houston. But I got into a routine. If you're healthy, your body can adapt to anything."

Her haircut "Long hair can be troublesome in space. It sticks to everything, and I didn't want to have my hair floating all around the space station. So, I decided to cut it as we were preparing to dock.

"I've had some friends who've had cancer and had to go through chemo. I know how traumatic that is, so I thought the least I could do was donate my hair. A friend's 12-year-old daughter had given her own hair to Locks of Love. So I put my hair in a plastic bag, sent it home on the space shuttle, and asked that someone give it to her. She donated it for me."

Tranquil view "When you have that perspective of being far away and looking back at the planet, you don't see the hustle and bustle or the borders. You see a very peaceful place. Gandhi tried to instil the feeling of oneness in all of us. Seeing our planet from space, you understand that."

MCB Theme : Science

Answer the following questions based on the passage given above.

1. Complete the sentence appropriately.
Sunita cut her long hair because ....

2. Complete the sentence appropriately.
Williams, 'ran' the Boston Marathon from the station treadmill ....

3. For how many days did Sunita Williams stay in space to break previous record?
(a) 200 days (b) 195 days
(c) 182 days (d) 180 days

4. What do you think is the purpose of the given extract?
(a) Inspire (b) Inform
(c) Present facts (d) Remember

5. Which record did Sunita Williams break? Who broke her record?

6. Why was Sunita not worried for leaving home for six months?

7. What makes Sunita Williams say that the Earth is a peaceful place?

8. What did Sunita decide to do with her hair? Why?

PASSAGE 10

1. It is generally accepted that leadership development should be a part of the education system's responsibility for preparing individuals to participate in a democratic and progressive society. Many schools, colleges and universities, across nations, provide their students with leadership courses, curricular programmes and co-curricular programmes that are designed to develop students' formal knowledge about leadership as well as opportunities and experiences to develop students as leaders and actually practise leadership. Yet, only a handful of studies have sought to understand leader development from the students' point of view, with students describing their own experiences and what they learned from them in their own words.

2. A recent descriptive study sought to understand student leadership with research through key events via the following research questions.

Research Question 1 What key events do student leaders in college report as significantly impacting their development as a leader?

Research Question 2 What lessons do student leaders in college report learning as a result of the key events they have experienced?

Research Question 3 Are certain key events more likely to be linked to particular lessons?

Approximately 130 students were contacted and the 72 interested, were interviewed. Two members of the research team were present for each 15–45 minute interview. One member served as the primary interviewer while the second ran the audio equipment. The results for lessons learned (Table 1), were varied but there were a few that were frequently quoted.

Lessons Learned	Responses
Identity	
Self Identity	58
Leadership Identity	54
Professionalism	30
Balancing Roles	19
Individual Competencies	
Delegation	17
Decision Making	15

Adaptability/Flexibility	38
Resilience/Persistence/Hard Work	18
Taking Initiative	36
Accountability/Responsibility	29
Big Picture	27
Learning to Teach/Learn	18
Support Systems	
Developing and Using Support Systems	36
Being a Support System	28
Working with Others	
Communication	59
Temwork	26
Conflict	21
Diversity	32
Inspiring and Motivating Others	17
Other Working with Others	30
Getting the Job Done	
Task Skills	55
Environment	54

3. This study described the rich array of leadership lessons that students are learning through their experiences. It revealed that student leaders are learning foundational leadership skills and competencies that have positively impacted how to accomplish work, how to work with others and how to be both supported by and support others.

Answer the following questions based on the passage given above.

1. Complete the sentence appropriately.
More than 50% of the identified student respondents were keen to participate in the 2014 study. We can say this because ....

2. Fill in the blank by choosing the correct word from the bracket.
The concluding sentence of the text makes a clear case for .... (collaboration/observation) by listing it as a core competency for student leadership.

3. Select the option that displays the most likely reason for including Research Question 3 in the 2014 study.
In order to find out if...
(a) learning opportunities shape students' overall personality
(b) leadership lessons are the result of the designed learning opportunities
(c) all learning opportunities cater to a specific lesson
(d) certain lessons are common in more than one learning opportunity

4. Complete the given sentence by selecting the most appropriate option.
The 2014 study attempts to understand student leadership by focussing on ....
(a) experiences that shaped students' overall personality
(b) lessons gained by students as they grew up
(c) relationship of key events with particular lessons
(d) students in leadership roles

5. Do you think the researchers of the study aimed to change the students' outlook towards the development of leadership skills, directly or indirectly? Support your answer with reference to the text.

6. The lessons for 'Individual competencies' had a range of responses. Give one reason why having the least number of responses for 'Decision Making' is a matter that needs attention.

7. Based on the reading of the text, state a point to challenge the given statement.
When theoretical knowledge about leadership suffices, it is a waste of funds by educational organisations to organise leadership camps and programmes.

8. Does the following statement agree with the information given in Paragraph 1?
The researcher believes that educational institutions have ideal resources to study impact of leadership skills on young adults.

PASSAGE 11

1. India is a country of many languages.
The Constitution recognises 22 languages officially, but over 121 unique languages have been identified in the country.
2. To preserve and encourage the literary function of language, the government introduced 'classical languages' in 2004. According to the Ministry of Culture, a classical language is one that is at least 1,500 years old and has ancient, valuable literature recorded in it. Further, such a language is original and not derived from another language. Based on these guidelines, six languages have been classified as classical languages: Tamil, Sanskrit, Kannada, Telugu, Malayalam and Odia.
3. The following graph shows the percentage of Indian people whose mother tongue is a classical language.

This is as per data collected by the census of 2011. The census was not conducted in 2021 due to the pandemic.

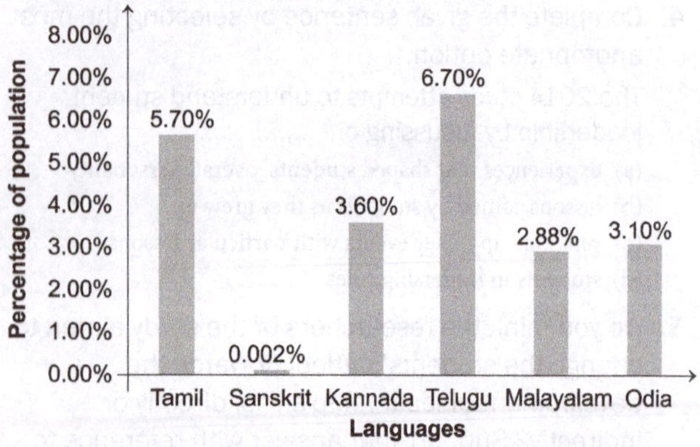

4. According to the graph, around 6.7% of the Indian population are native speakers of Telugu, whereas Sanskrit has been identified as a mother tongue by only 0.002% of the population, which is around 24,821 people. Malayalam has the second lowest number of native speakers, making up about 2.9% of Indians.
5. The 2011 census data also noted that a majority of the native speakers reside in the area that their mother tongue originated from. For example, 93% of Kannada speakers live in Karnataka. Similarly, 93% of Malayalam speakers live in Kerala.
6. Balancing preservation of culture and inclusivity is a delicate equation for a heterogeneous country like India. With growing awareness, concepts like 'classical languages' may help us achieve harmony.

Answer the following questions based on the passage given above.

1. Complete the sentence based on information from the passage.

If Tamil originated from Tamil Nadu, we can infer that .... of the native Tamil speakers would be living in Tamil Nadu.

2. Fill in the blanks with the appropriate option from those given in brackets.
Based on the passage, the .... (functional/historical) value of a language is of utmost importance while .... (preserving/categorising) it as a classical language.

3. Which of these sentences uses 'delicate' in the same way as Paragraph 6 does?
(a) She looked beautiful in the dress with the delicate floral pattern.
(b) He was frequently admitted to the hospital due to his delicate health.
(c) This discussion will require careful consideration as it is a delicate matter.
(d) Please handle these delicate items carefully during transportation as they break easily.

4. Which of these pieces of information can be confirmed by reading the passage?
(A) The number of people in India who speak Tamil
(B) Where the majority of native Sanskrit speakers live
(C) The reason Malayalam is considered a classical language
(D) When the idea of classical languages was introduced in India

(a) Only A (b) Only D (c) A and B (d) C and D

5. State an example from the passage that shows that India is a 'heterogeneous country'. Answer in one sentence.

6. Why has the writer stated the following line in the passage? Give a reason.

The census was not conducted in 2021 due to the pandemic.

7. Which of these hypothetical situations would help India achieve harmony? Justify your answer in about 40 words.
(a) If the majority of Indians who speak a classical language are settled abroad
(b) If more languages from remote and tribal areas of India are identified as classical languages
(c) If the percentage of Indians who are native Telugu speakers increases to more than 10 percent

8. Imagine that a committee was formed to ensure that classical languages have more native speakers by the time the next census is conducted. In 40 words, answer the following questions to help the committee achieve its objective.
(i) Which classical language needs its attention most urgently and why?
(ii) Which classical language would be third on its priority?

PASSAGE 12

1. Reduction in green areas has caused various environmental problems. People squeezed between concrete structures are looking for various ways to meet their longing for green. One of the ways to do so, is vertical gardens and green walls. Vertical gardening is a unique method of gardening where plants are grown in a vertical position or upward, rather than in the traditional method of planting them on the ground.

2. The purpose of vertical gardens and green walls, which arises from the studies of different disciplines (landscape architects, architects, engineers, etc.), is to close the cold image of concrete and increase the visual value. In these systems, nature and structures are integrated and thus, urban areas and the desired environment have become intertwined.
3. Vertical garden case studies often show that though functionality should be in the foreground, when vertical gardens are planned, they are generally made as aesthetic elements in the city's underpasses and city squares and decorative elements in residences, without seeking functionality.
4. Experts support that the visual quality and evaluation of landscape architecture is determined based on the satisfaction of the users. Hence, a survey questionnaire was prepared for residents of varied age groups from of a metropolitan city. The given Table 1, displays these responses.

Table 1 : Total number of participants : 400

No.	Survey statements	Strongly agree	Agree	Neutral	Disagree	Strongly disagree
Vertical gardens						
1.	Improve quality of life of people in urban areas	191	138	43	9	19
2.	Reduce noise pollution	128	164	77	25	6
3.	Increase air quality-indoors and outdoors	172	147	51	28	2
4.	Reduce energy and water consumption	58	47	125	68	2
5.	Positively impact global warming	114	144	106	30	6
6.	Have a relaxing and calming effect	161	177	44	7	11
7.	Cost too much	86	107	152	42	13
8.	Make plants look beautiful	195	139	44	6	16
9.	Add naturalness to the environs	135	173	55	25	12
10.	Are among the determining factor to visiting a place	59	133	141	54	13
11.	Are inconvenient indoors	9	84	123	126	48
12.	Can be applied in every place	71	132	97	77	23
13.	Have a functional feature	81	207	100	10	2
14.	Distract drivers	34	101	106	131	28
15.	Funds are best used for social issues	57	72	100	130	41

5. The study acknowledged that vertical gardening has the potential to transform urban spaces into green, sustainable areas and further research should explore the impact of vertical gardening on the environment and human well-being.

Adapted for academic usage - 2019 case-study -Investigating the vertical garden applications in Turkey

Answer the following questions based on the passage given above.

1. Complete the following analogy appropriately, based on your understanding of Paragraphs 1 and 2.
We can say thmat the situation of people living in concrete structures is comparable with a fish living in a fishbowl and the need for vertical gardens to the need for decorations in the fishbowl because ....

2. Fill the blanks with the appropriate option from those given in brackets, based on your understanding of Paragraph 2.
The statement that urban spaces have become more closely connected with the desired natural surroundings through the incorporation of nature and structures in vertical gardens and green walls, is a/an .... (fact/opinion) because it is a/an .... (subjective judgement/objective detail).

3. Which of the following is the main takeaway from the study mentioned in the passage?
(a) Vertical gardening has minimal impact on the environment or human well-being.
(b) Vertical gardening is a sustainable practice that can transform urban spaces into green areas.

(c) The impact of vertical gardening on the environment and human well-being has already been thoroughly explored.

(d) The study needs to include experts from horticultural firms to offer any recommendations for further research.

4. Select the option that correctly displays what 'intertwined' signifies. (Reference-Paragraph 2)

(i) (ii) (iii) (iv) (v)

(a) (i), (iv) and (v) (b) Only (ii)

(c) Only (iii) (d) (ii) and (v)

5. Based on the survey results, which two concerns should a city government, looking to install vertical gardens, address?

6. In Table 1, the Statement 3, "Vertical gardens increase air quality - indoors and outdoors," received the most neutral responses from participants, with 51 respondents indicating a neutral stance. State any one inference that can be drawn from this.

7. Infer one benefit and one drawback of vertical gardening, in comparison to other solutions, such as community gardens or parks. (Answer in about 40 words)

8. Justify the following, in about 40 words.

While the survey results suggest that vertical gardens may be effective in improving the quality of life in urban areas, further research and evaluation may be necessary to fully understand their effectiveness and potential drawbacks.

PASSAGE 13

'Devastating': 91% of reefs surveyed on Great Barrier Reef affected by coral bleaching in 2022

Mass Bleaching Event Coral bleaching impacted 91% of surveyed reefs on the Great Barrier Reef, marking the sixth recorded mass bleaching event. The report, titled "The Reef Snapshot: Summer 2021-22," confirmed the occurrence.

Survey Details Government scientists from the Great Barrier Reef Marine Park Authority and the Australian Institute of Marine Science conducted surveys on 719 reefs using helicopters. Results indicated bleaching on 654 reefs, with the central region between Cape Tribulation and the Whitsundays being the worst affected.

Extent of Bleaching Severe and extreme bleaching was most prevalent in areas highly visited by tourists, affecting both inshore and offshore reefs.

La Niña Year Surprisingly, this mass bleaching event occurred during a cooler La Niña year, contrary to expectations. The climate's ongoing changes were emphasised, with temperatures now 1.5°C warmer than 150 years ago.

Reactions and Concerns

I. The report was described as 'devastating news' for reef lovers, emphasising the need to prioritise cutting fossil fuel emissions.

II. Despite being a La Niña year with more cloud cover and rain, bleaching occurred in over 90% of surveyed reefs.

III. Calls for political commitment to emissions cuts aligned with global needs to save the reef, as current targets fall short.

Climate Change Impact The Intergovernmental Panel on climate change highlighted the critical difference between limiting global heating to 1.5°C or 2°C for tropical reef survival. Current emission reduction targets were deemed insufficient.

Scientists' Recommendations Dr Simon Bradshaw of the Climate Council emphasised the urgent need for substantial emission reduction in the 2020s to save coral reefs worldwide.

Bleaching Effects Coral bleaching occurs when corals are stressed by above-average water temperatures, leading to the expulsion of algae. While corals can survive, they may suffer sublethal effects, making them more susceptible to disease and limiting growth and reproduction.

UNESCO and World Heritage Status A United Nations mission visited the Great Barrier Reef in March, and their report, due before a world heritage meeting in June, is expected to provide insights into the reef's health and management.

Controversy and Call for Transparency The release of the report and maps was delayed, prompting calls for transparency. Concerns were raised about political interference, with suggestions that releasing survey results during the election campaign could breach caretaker conventions.

Answer the following questions based on the passage given above.

1. Complete the following sentence.

With the year 2022 being classified as La Nina year, the reefs had .... cloud cover and rain than normal.

2. How many reefs have indicated bleaching during the Great Barrier Reef survey?

(a) 91%

(b) 654

(c) 719

(d) Both (a) and (b)

3. How were the coral reefs examined for the purpose of this survey?

(a) By deep sea dives
(b) By using submarines
(c) By helicopters
(d) By reportings from local fishermen

4. What is the proposed temperature range by scientific communities beyond which the harm to the reefs would be 'catastrophic'?

(a) 1°C or 1.5°C (b) 1.5°C or 2°C
(c) 2°C or 3.5°C (d) 2.5°C or 4°C

5. According to the report, how has tourism affected this coral bleaching event?

6. What is the name of the report that published the findings on the coral bleaching event?

7. How are elevated temperature and coral bleaching related?

8. Why is the mass coral bleaching that occurred during 2022 considered 'surprising'?

PASSAGE 14

Sun Tourism in Mountainous Regions

Introduction to Sun Tourism

- Sun tourism is an emerging trend in the travel industry.
- Offers a distinctive experience of exploring mountainous regions in warm and sunny conditions.

Appeal of Sun Tourism

- Caters to mountain enthusiasts seeking a blend of scenic landscapes and warm weather.
- Provides an opportunity to enjoy outdoor activities while basking in the Sun.

Departure from Traditional Mountain Tourism

- Differs from conventional mountain tourism associated with winter activities like skiing and snowboarding.

Benefits of Sun Tourism

1. **Economic Growth** Extends the tourism season, generating income for local businesses and service providers.
   Supports growth and development, contributing to the sustainability of local communities.
2. **Sustainable Development** Encourages conservation efforts, eco-friendly infrastructure, and responsible tourism practices.
   Ensures the long-term preservation of natural resources.
3. **Regional Infrastructure** Drives development in mountainous areas, improving transportation, accessibility, and amenities.
   Creates employment opportunities and stimulates the local economy.
4. **Variety of Activities** Expands the range of activities available beyond winter sports, attracting diverse travellers.
   Enables a broader range of experiences for visitors with varying interests.
5. **Emotional Health** Promotes a profound connection with nature, offering sunrise and sunset views from mountain summits.
   Recognised as vital for mental well-being.

Conclusion Sun tourism in mountainous regions presents a shift from the traditional winter-centric approach, offering economic, environmental, and emotional benefits for both tourists and local communities.

Answer the following questions based on the passage given above.

1. Complete the following sentence.

Sun tourism is .... for mental health.

2. Which of the following does not benefit from sun tourism?

(a) Local business owners (b) Mental well being of tourists
(c) Camel tourism (d) Local employment sectors

3. What are the conventional mountain tourism activities?

(a) Skiing and snowboarding (b) Diving and reef-watching
(c) Canoeing and cliff-jumping (d) Restaurant hopping

4. Which of the following are the highlights of sun tourism?

(a) Scenic sunrise views (b) Scenic sunset views
(c) Scenic coral reef views (d) Both (a) and (b)

5. Which geographical area is exclusively connected to sun tourism?

6. How does a departure from the traditional winter-centric approach to mountain tourism affect tourists who do not like the winter season?

7. How does sun tourism affect the economy of the mountainous regions?

8. How does sun tourism extend the tourist season in mountain regions?

PASSAGE 15

When Brains Do More, Who Owns Us?

Elon Musk's company Neuralink has put its first wireless device in a human brain. This technological advancement can be pivotal in brain-computer interface tech.

What exactly is new?

Like all scientific advancements, this one is very much built on its predecessors. Neuralink's first human trial is preceded by the 2021 case of the Australian ALS patient Philip O'Keefe who used a neural interface to put out a social media update:

"hello, world! Short tweet. Monumental progress." In comparison, Neuralink doesn't use heavy equipment.

Who benefits today?

According to Musk, the initial users will be those who have lost the use of their limbs. For this category of patients, taking control of their phone or computer, and thereby almost any device, just by thinking, would be transformative.

Who could benefit tomorrow?

Another category of potential candidates is patients suffering from brain diseases. Theoretically, processes like deep-brain stimulation could help fight Alzheimer's and Parkinson's, even depression and addiction. Another potential benefit could be the usage of neural interfaces for memory and concentration enhancement.

Ethical concerns

This unprecedented access to the human mind raises the major concern for privacy. Will Neuralink enable authorities to monitor every detail of human lives? In such a scenario, who will own the data collected by such invasion of privacy? The access to this technology could also become a privilege and thus worsen the existing social inequalities.

Conclusion

Although Neuralink is nowhere near becoming accessible like cardiac pacemakers, it is very possible that the project will get plenty of funds to continue the research. But the innovation is surrounded by ethical questions such as privacy and social inequalities.

Answer the following questions based on the passage given above.

1. Complete the following sentence with a word from the passage which means 'something that has never happened before'.
   The way that snow fell on the national capital was entirely ....
2. Who is the owner of the company 'Neuralink'?
3. Which of the following are planned to be the initial users of the Neuralink?
   (a) People with brain ailments
   (b) People with addiction
   (c) People with memory issues
   (d) People who have lost their limbs
4. Which of the following is not counted in the list of potential candidates?
   (a) People with brain ailments
   (b) People with stuttering issues
   (c) People with memory issues
   (d) People who have lost their limbs
5. What was the message posted by the Australian ALS patient Philip O'Keefe using the neural interface in 2021?
6. How could Neuralink help patients suffering from brain diseases?
7. What are the ethical concerns connected to Neuralink?
8. How will the neuralink help patients who have lost their limbs?

PASSAGE 16

National Integration: Building Unity in Diversity

Understanding National Integration

- National Integration is the awareness of a common identity among citizens.
- It transcends differences in caste, religion, and language, emphasising a shared national identity.
- Arises through citizens' behaviour and determination.
- Dr S Radhakrishnan emphasises that national integration grows in people's minds through education.

Importance of National Integration

- Stabilises democracy, improves economic growth, and develops the nation.
- Challenges in achieving national integration in diverse countries like India.

Historical Background

- Ancient India saw a natural merging of cultures as people from different places integrated seamlessly.
- Tasks like promoting travel among Indians enhanced unity.

Two Forms of National Integration

1. Uniformity-Based Integration: Emphasises language, living, customs, and rituals.
2. Internal Unity: Focuses on a common attitude and thinking regarding national interests despite differences.

Need for National Integration

- Enables individuals to work together for the prosperity of the nation.
- Obstacles include religious or political divisions and communication barriers.

Supporting Elements in National Integration

- Democratic principles, fundamental rights and duties, unified justice system, secularism, national symbols, and festivals.
- India's diverse society requires these elements for unity.

Advantages of National Integration

- Increases brotherhood and unity.
- Reduces differences in religion, region, race, and culture.
- Supports the development of the nation.

Disadvantages of National Integration

- Social tension, corruption, and illiteracy.
- Lack of urbanisation in some states.
- Diversity-related issues.

Conclusion of National Integration

- India's vast diversity requires active participation in national integration.
- Following the ideals of great nationalists is crucial for fostering unity in a country with various cultures and traditions.

Answer the following questions based on the passage given above.

1. Complete the following sentence with a word from the passage that is the opposite of 'division'.
   The success of any nation depends on the seamless .... of its diverse population, fostering unity and shared values.
2. Which of the following are not the positive results of national integration?
   (a) Reduced communal tensions
   (b) Increase of illiteracy
   (c) Increased feeling of brotherhood
   (d) Development of the nation
3. What is not productive for enhancing national integration?
   (a) Being critical of other people's religions
   (b) Being aware of a common identity among citizens
   (c) Celebrating the diversity of Indian communities
   (d) Being appreciative of the feeling of brotherhood
4. Which of the following markers are superseded by national identity?
   (a) Caste (b) Religion (c) Language (d) All of these
5. What did Dr S Radhakrishnan say about national integration?
6. What is the importance of national integration?
7. What is the meaning of national integration? How is it related to diverse identities in a nations' population?
8. What are the two forms of national integration?

ANSWERS (REVIEW EXERCISE)

Continuous Passages

Passage 1

1. (d) Diversity
2. (c) It reflects India's cultural richness
3. Indian citizens embrace diversity as a strength rather than an hindrance.
4. The linguistic diversity is reflective of the people's adaptability and acceptance of varied means of expressions.
5. Carnatic Music form
6. Indian Constitution guarantees fundamental rights and freedoms to all its citizens.
7. Indian cuisine is an example of regional diversity as the palate of the whole country is flavourful and eclectic. We usually see fiery dishes in South, rich curries in the North, sweets in Gujarat and street food of Mumbai. The culinary variety brings together people through a shared love for food.
8. India has a wide cultural variety with multiple art forms across various regions. From traditional dance forms like Bharatanatyam, Kathak, Odissi, etc to music forms like Carnatic and Hindustani. These diverse forms represent the feeling of unity in India's cultural tapestry.
9. The overarching narrative of India's existence is Unity in Diversity. India does not count diversity as a hindrance, it is a strength for the country. Despite various challenges and diverse cultural background across states, there is a feeling of unity that fosters in the heart of people. India also safeguards its citizens by giving Constitutional rights and duties.

Passage 2

1. The author was reluctant to make a two-hour drive because it was a rainy day and the author did not want to drive up the winding road.
2. Carolyn, the author's daughter says this when she, in the pretext of taking the author to the garage to pick up her car which is a journey of three minutes, takes her father on a journey which crosses over 10 minutes.
3. (b) of the black green evergreens towering over them
4. It is true to say that the place, where the author's daughter took him, had a beautiful panoramic view. The landscape was magnificent with mountains covered in beautiful daffodils of different colours. The pale white and lemon yellow colours of the daffodils look as if the

sun had coloured them as it. In addition, there were purple hyacinths and coral-colored tulips all of which were surrounded by western bluebirds.

5. The narrator's mind was filled with questions because the landscape and its beauty mesmerised him so much that he wanted to know who created it, for what reason and how.
6. impacted and mesmerised by the beautiful landscape
7. False
8. (d) That there is huge world of possibilities
9. bleak
10. (a) dangerous

Passage 3

1. Alok had a stomach ache and developed fever after eating from a roadside food outlet because he had a weak immune system.
2. The two ways discovered by the researchers to boost your immunity are
   (i) Positive emotions like awe, the feelings you get on seeing the wonders of nature, help boost immunity.
   (ii) Explore the great outdoors. Look for reasons to feel lucky every day. Make time for a favourite activity or simply help another person - it will bring a smile to your face
3. falling less ill
4. According to the passage, stress affects our immunity because it takes a toll on many aspects of your health, including immunity. Chronic stress, such as prolonged job insecurity or a difficult marriage results in a measurable decline in the immune system's ability to fight infections.
5. In order to avoid pollution, plan outdoor activities early in the morning or late evening as air pollution is highest during rush hours.
6. prolonged
7. (c) Exercising
8. essential for a long and healthy life
9. the passage focuses on how a weak immune system impacts us and suggest ways in which we can boost it
10. True

Passage 4

1. (b) Both are methods of preserving personal and family memories.
2. (c) The sense of nostalgia they provide.
3. it allows us to reflect on the moments captured
4. Main advantage is permanence because digital files may get corrupted.
5. It can create the shared experience of passing it around at family gatherings.
6. Due to the time-consuming and expensive process of printing and creating a photo album, it has become cumbersome.
7. The digital cameras allow us to capture and store a large number of photos digitally, on our devices. This process does not require any physical film or complex processing. Therefore, the digital format also enables easy access, organisation, and sharing through various digital platforms like email or social media. This advancement has changed how we capture memories, making it more convenient than ever.
8. With the new advancements in technology, it has become very easy to edit the pictures available in digital formats. The editing softwares and applications allow the users to significantly change their appearances and manipulate or enhance the images. This is why digital photographs may not always represent reality.
9. The writer has avoided taking sides by choosing to share both, pros and cons of each method. This has allowed the readers to make their choice based on their preferences and without any influence from the writer.

Passage 5

1. (b) In different conditions
2. (a) instructional
3. extension of the arm
4. Tendulkar was very compassionate to the budding batsmen.
5. A problem faced by a cricketer in making technical adjustments is that one can become uncomfortable.
6. Tendulkar's bat was a major talking point because he used a heavy bat which is said to be the source of his injuries.
7. Tendulkar advised budding batsmen that the bat is like an extension of the arm. Once the bat feels so, there will be no need to change your technique.
8. The advice given by the coaches did not work for Tendulkar as then batting did not feel natural to him.
9. According to Tendulkar, it is important to read the bowler's mind because it makes your performance efficient. If one is stuck on one's own self, one cannot perform efficiently.

Passage 6

1. (b) On going in a zig-zag manner
2. (d) His hat flew off
3. didn't react well
4. The narrtor was a happy man.
5. enjoyable
6. friendly
7. The oddest situation faced by the author in Mumbai was that his belt got entangled with a fellow passenger's luggage.
8. The 'property' referred to in the sentence was a book written by the author.
9. The girl accused that the author's ghost story was not scary enough. According to her, his ghosts were funny and friendly.

Passage 7

1. (b) Unrealistic ambitions
2. (c) Aptitude for public life
3. worsening of the situation of unemployment and frustration among many young people
4. The author states the importance of the role of counsellors
5. The qualities associated with the young people are-educated, impatient and ambitions.
6. help
7. Help from counsellors, elders, teachers and professionals helps an individual to decide the right career on the basis of their aptitudes and the resources available to them.
8. The right time to make a career choice is when an individual is in high school. This is so because this will allow them to develop the special aptitude required for a career.
9. Financial resources are important to consider when choosing a career because lack of funds does not allow an individual to choose a career option that requires great education funding. Hence, with lack of funds, one will have to choose a humble career.

Passage 8

1. (b) Weakens the body's capacity to combat diseases
2. (c) Help us fight viruses and bacteria.
3. production of brain chemicals increases
4. heart failures, obesity and many more diseases
5. When C-reactive protein is produced more in the body it causes heart failure.
6. found
7. Sleep promotes immunity by building the immune system's natural killer cells.
8. Sleep deprivation has a negative impact on one's immunity. According to a study in Turkey, 24 hours of sleep deprivation leads to a decline of 37% natural killer cells in the body.
9. It is true that sleep deprivation can lead to long term effects because the loss of natural killer cells due to sleep deprivation could have left the body undefended and susceptible to infection.

Passage 9

1. (a) To make bases for the medicine
2. (b) Record of the use of perfumes and fine oils, aromatic oils and gums in the embalming process.
3. the rediscovered Gerhardt's compound
4. True
5. the Western world's store of herbal medicines
6. extracted
7. The plant world is an immense store of active chemical compounds. We can say this because half the medicines we use today are herbal in origin. Further, a quarter contains plant extracts or active chemicals taken directly from plants. In addition, many more are yet to be discovered, recorded and researched; only a few thousand have been studied.
8. The given lines would most likely be placed in paragraph 5 to state how different compounds were isolated during the 19th century.
9. Even though advances in chemistry have made it much easier to reproduce the active ingredients, plants will continue to have a medicinal importance in their own right. Their active constituents may be slightly modified to improve their efficiency or to reduce their undesirable effects. However, they are still vital for the treatment of disorders such as cancers and heart diseases or as a means of combating malaria.

Passage 10

1. (a) First addition to the Constitution after Indian Independence
2. (a) Shortage of trained teachers
3. para-teachers
4. False
5. 1/4th of the seats should be reserved for poor and other categories of children
6. (b) 30:1
7. According to the act, parents can be legally punished if they don't send their children to schools.
8. The 'free education' part of the act implies that financial constraint should not prevent a child from gaining elementary education. Even if a child lives in a remote area, a child is entitled to reach the school to get his/her education.
9. The Right to Education or the Right of Children to Free and Compulsory Education Act is the fundamental right which ensures compulsory admission, attendance and completion of elementary education by every child of 6 to 14 years.

Passage 11

1. (d) Both (b) and (c)
2. (b) Skills
3. As a result of globalisation
4. Students do not find it easy secure proper employment immediately after completing their course.
5. poor linkage between
6. bookish
7. Vocational education is called technical education as it has traditionally been considered non-academic and totally related to a specific trade, occupation or vocation.
8. Vocational education can be defined as the training given at the secondary or post-secondary level. It focuses on development of skills that are needed for

specific trades and hence, practical work is given greater importance than bookish learning.

9. Vocational education is important to our society to respond to the growing skill requirement so that the momentum of the economy can be sustained. By focusing on employability, our education system can fulfill the requirements of skilled manpower. Further, vocational education also creates more employment opportunities by equipping learners with entrepreneurial skills.

Passage 12

1. (a) Solar energy
2. (b) India has an abundance of solar energy
3. educating the people about alternative fuel vehicles and their advantages
4. Establishing solar power generating units is not too expensive.
5. promote EV in India
6. advanced
7. Dependence on non-renewable sources of energy is called a dicey affair because such sources of energy are present in limited quantities and may get finished up soon.
8. The rise in economic activity and the growing population have led to the tremendous increase in the transport sector in India.
9. Driving an electric vehicle is easier and more relaxing than any other vehicle. The EV uses electrical energy which is stored in batteries that feed the electric motor. The driver has to just turn the key and press the acceleration pedal. There is no speed gear and functioning noise.

Passage 13

1. (d) Both (a) and (c)
2. (b) Poisonous chemicals
3. Thomas Agonyo
4. True
5. Vijayasama felt nostalgic at the time.
6. discharged
7. The 'three large, empty metal drums' outside Mr. Nana's front door were brought by some people and left there. Neither Mr. Nana nor anyone else in the village knew what to do with it and hence, kept them where they were.
8. The monsters are large ominous looking buildings on the horizon giving out black smoke. These are factories that need leather to make shoes, handbags and clothes. They are called monsters because they have destroyed the landscape.
9. The chemicals used in the leather factories were dumped in the open fields and rivers.

Passage 14

1. (d) All of the above
2. (a) Sanskrit
3. God
4. Ministry of Tourism, Government of India
5. The adage 'Atithi Devo Bhavah' means that honouring a guest is next to honouring God.
6. The adage 'Atithi Devo Bhavah' is important as it has become the unique selling point of modern tourism industry of India.
7. The epithets used for India are 'Destination of the Millennium' and 'Land of all Seasons'. The reason for calling India these is that India is a vast country which includes dry deserts, evergreen forests, snowy Himalayas, long coast and fertile plains along with a beautiful cultural diversity which caters to every tourist.
8. The 'Atithi Devo Bhavah Programme' is an initiative launched by the Ministry of Tourism, Government of India. It aims at sensitising key stakeholders towards tourists, through a process of training and orientation.
9. The land in India is just as diverse as the nation itself. India includes dry desert areas, evergreen forests, snowy Himalayas, a long coast and fertile plains.

Passage 15

1. (d) Both (a) and (b)
2. (c) popular Indians
3. India's unity in diversity
4. False
5. on 26th January, 2010 by Zoom TV
6. Changes
7. Piyush Pandey is the writer of the song Mile Sur Mera Tumhara. He was an Accounts Manager at that time and presently is the Executive Chairman and Creative Head of Ogilvy and Mather, India.
8. The project of composing the song Mile Sur Mera Tumhara was conceived and directed by Suresh Mullick who was the then All India Creative Director of Ogilvy and Mather.
9. The song Mile Sur Mera Tumhara is unique as the song's lyrics are special. In the song, one phrase is repeated in fourteen Indian languages—'Mile Sur Mera Tumhara, to sur bane hamara', meaning "When my musical note and your musical note merge, it becomes our musical note". The song itself ends by fading into the final notes of the Indian National Anthem.

Passage 16

1. (d) All of the above
2. (a) That for a citizen the country comes first.
3. other cultures, religions and languages and will easily accept different people of the country
4. True
5. Internal freedom
6. Morality and thought
7. National integration should aim at improving socio-cultural relations, reducing economic inequalities and strengthening unity and solidarity.

8. Regionalism, communalism, religious fanaticism, lingualism and now terrorism are the main forces that challenge national integration.
9. In order to achieve national integration, we must pay attention to the economic development of the unprivileged and underprivileged regions. More facilities should be extended to distant regions and tribal groups. The education system should be revised with the aim of fostering national integration. Some special means should be adopted to instill a sense of belonging and unity in the mind from childhood.

Non-Continuous Passages

Passage 1

1. relax, rest and enjoy
2. influenced
3. (c) to take a break from the stress of daily life.
4. (c) II, III and IV
5. India is a popular destination for health tourism because it has excellent medical facilities available at a reasonable cost.
6. The most popular form of tourism is leisure tourism. This makes up for around 42% of travel. It is the most popular form because people love taking holidays for relaxation and recreation.
7. Business tourism is important for travel industry because it takes places throughout the year. Some travel businesses such as budget hotel chains rely heavily on income from business travellers.
8. According to the given statistics, spiritual tourism is the least popular form at the present moment.

Passage 2

1. Raghu is the student with artistic ideas.
2. (b) App Developer
3. Painting and photography can help Raghu to relax whenever he is stressed.
4. (a) Lata is great at mathematics and has even scored a complete score in the subject. Thus, it means that she makes accurate calculations.

   (b) Lata, besides doing accurate calculations, seems to be a good scorer in all the three subjects. This indicates that she prepares well and thus, can easily be successful in cracking any competitive examination.
5. Camera
6. more creative
7. Ravi's act of congratulating the opposite team for winning the match shows that Ravi knew that winning and losing are a part of all sports. He, thus, has to improve to be successful as them. Further, it also shows that he harbors no ill-will for the other team. This shows Ravi's sportsmanship.
8. (c) Mohit can convince others with valid points and facts.

Passage 3

1. the student council secretary is typically responsible for making reports about school programmes and maintaining a record of important events. This responsibility is given to him/her as they have direct access to all the necessary information to create a detailed report
2. innovative
3. (d) To promote engineering skills and provide hands-on experience
4. (d) 3 and 5
5. The showcasing of the capabilities of the drones and during the event highlights the technical skills and the creativity of the students that were part of the project.
6. The aerial photography and the obstacle course navigation suggest that the live demonstration aimed to engage and excite the audience.
7. The students are expected to develop the following skills
   - Operating the drones and controlling them to adjust to different angles for precise photography.
   - Developing a sense for selecting appropriate locations and advancing their problem-solving skills.
8. The Student Council's Drone Programme at National Public School aligns with the school's goals of promoting holistic education by offering students a multidimensional learning experience through such a technologically advanced programme. The programme lets the students gain technical skills in drone construction and operation, which helps develop their critical thinking and problem-solving abilities.

Passage 4

1. his drawback is procrastination which means that he may struggle with completing tasks on time
2. (d) Ananya
3. (a) Rohit
4. (d) (A)-(iii), (B)-(iv), (C)-(i)
5. Rajat is most likely to be a collaborative worker because of his personal qualities of being a team player and an adaptable person.
6. The second situation (b) aligns with Ananya's motto because she actively listens to her team members and provides support, ultimately helping them to succeed by leading through her actions and setting a positive example.

7. Aryan is likely to ask many 'why' questions because his personal qualities include curiosity, creativity, and a love of learning. These qualities suggest that he is likely to ask many 'why' questions in order to better understand the world around him. Further, Aryan's academic achievements and co-curricular activities demonstrate his strong critical thinking skills, which would likely lead him to ask thoughtful and insightful questions.
8. Sanya is the best fit to lead a school-wide initiative to promote mental health and well-being among students because her motto 'Service before self' and the activities she participates in shows a commitment to work with others and help others, which is essential for promoting mental health and well-being. Further, her personal qualities of compassion, organisation, and responsibility would be valuable in leading such an initiative.

Passage 5

1. (a) 10-15 yrs
2. (b) go for a walk
3. (b) Social media, reading, and meeting friends
4. (a) The 26-40 yrs old age group is more outgoing because they spend more time doing outdoor activities. They enjoy going on vacations and meeting friends.

   (b) Reading is the least popular activity among most age groups because people in all age group spend the least amount of time in reading.
5. Quiet
6. they spend most of their time scrolling on social media apps after spending much of their day in studies or building their careers.
7. The 10-15 yrs age group prefers to spend more time outside the home because at this age they had surplus energy which they must utilise in playing games with friends. At this age, they spend most of their time enjoying outdoor games instead of reading, watching TV or other indoor activities.
8. (d) The 16-25 yrs group prefers virtual interaction more than any other group.

Passage 6

1. it is composed of cellulosic matter that the human body cannot digest
2. Germinate and ferment
3. (c) Removing the impurities from the millets
4. (b) A book on agricultural practices
5. Removing the husk can be linked to the fulfillment of energy requirements of households as millet husk can be used as a household fuel.
6. Polished millets are popular among people because

   (i) It has a shorter cooking time and gives better texture as well as taste

   (ii) It has a longer shelf life
7. Decortication makes the millet/grain visually pleasing which makes marketing easy. This shows that the urban center or the urban population make decisions based on appearance and show.
8. As per a 2012 study, barnyard millet can be polished with a rice polisher for up to three minutes without significant nutrient loss.

Passage 7

1. she called him for the interview
2. solving problems
3. (c) Endless learning opportunities
4. (d) HR was convinced that Vayu has a good exposure and skillset.
5. Vayu informed HR that he would be very much comfortable with their office location. He must have been comfortable as he may have been working at the office location – Noida already.
6. Interviewee
7. Vayu was looking for a job change because he was not satisfied with the kind of work he was getting in the support profile. Further, he was also looking for a good pay hike as well as new opportunities to upskill himself while also looking for a new environment to grow.
8. Two probable reasons for Moitra's response are

   (i) She must have been impressed with Vayu's skills and experience that he has acquired while fulfilling his responsibilities in his current job.

   (ii) Her company must have been looking for an experienced and qualified person like Vayu to fulfill the same roles and responsibilities that he has been carrying out in his current job.

Passage 8

1. it was too big to be made portable
2. Gramophone plate
3. (a) New advancements
4. (c) 1, 2 and 3
5. The floppy disk was considered notorious because it was susceptible to get infected by viruses that passed into PCs when inserted.
6. affordable
7. CDs, DVDs and pen drives face extinction because of newer technology of cloud computing becoming popular.
8. A pager is a device used to send a short message to another user via a paging company. It had become popular because it was the first portable communication device for the ordinary masses.

Passage 9

1. she didn't want to have her hair floating all around the space station
2. with an unofficial time of 4 hours and 24 minutes
3. (b) 195 days
4. (a) Inspire
5. Sunita Williams broke Shannon Lucid's previous endurance record-until Peggy Whitson broke both the women's records in 2008.
6. Sunita was not worried for leaving home for six months because due to her Navy background, she had gone on deployments before.
7. The vision of the Earth from the space and looking from a perspective of being far away made Sunita Williams realise that Earth is a very peaceful place. From the space, she could see only the planet and not the chaos that is generally found on land.
8. Sunita decided to donate her long hair to a cancer patient through Locks of Love. She does this because some of her friends had cancer and had to go through chemo. So, she knew how traumatic that is and thought the least she could do was donate her hair.

Passage 10

1. 72 of 130 students consented and were interviewed
2. collaboration
3. (d) certain lessons are common in more than one learning opportunity
4. (c) relationship of key events with particular lessons
5. No, I do not think the researchers of the study aimed to change students' outlook towards the development of leadership skills, directly or indirectly. The aim of seeking students' perspectives was to enable a better designing and creation of the leadership programmes in educational institutions.
6. The least number of responses for 'Decision Making' is a matter that needs attention because it clearly indicates that the lessons created do not allow sufficient opportunity for development of this crucial skill.
7. I disagree with the belief posed by the statement that "When theoretical knowledge about leadership suffices, it is a waste of funds by educational organisations to organise leadership camps and programmes" because no amount of theoretical knowledge can aid students to actually apply their learning about leadership. Practical application of skills will promote effective application of skill and thus, will further the development of other skills.
8. No, the given statement does not agree with the information given in Para 1. The researcher indicates that educational institutions have opportunities and programmes to inculcate leadership skills. The passage indicates that educational institutions do not pay attention to study the impact of leadership skills on young adults.

Passage 11

1. majority
2. historical, categorising
3. (d) Please handle these delicate items carefully during transportation as they break easily.
4. (d) C and D
5. The fact that over 121 unique languages have been identified in the country highlights the fact that India is a 'heterogeneous country'.
6. By stating that the census was not conducted in 2021 due to the pandemic, the author of the given passage wants to state that the data is old and the numbers might have changed.
7. (b) India can move on the path of achieving harmony if more languages from remote and tribal areas of India are identified as classical languages.
   Most of the divides in the country are a result of lack of acknowledgment of the languages and cultures present in the nation. Thus, if we start recognising them, we can ensure harmony.
8. (i) As a committee that would ensure that classical languages have more native speakers by the time the next census is conducted, my first focus would be Sanskrit as it has only only 0.002% of the population, which is around 24,821 people. If this number reduces, Sanskrit would become a dead language.
   (ii) The third language on the priority list would be Odia with only 3.10% spakers.

Passage 12

1. a fish needs decorations such as plants or rocks, to simulate a natural environment and improve its quality of life. People living in urban areas need green spaces such as vertical gardens to improve their physical and mental wellbeing
2. opinion, subjective judgement
3. (b) Vertical gardening is a sustainable practice that can transform urban spaces into green areas.
4. (b) Only (ii)
5. A city government looking to install vertical gardens should consider addressing these two concerns: cost of installation and maintenance (should be reasonable), areas of installation should be where driver distraction is less of an issue.
6. It can be inferred that the participants did not have a strong opinion or preference regarding the effect of vertical gardens on air quality, which resulted in a neutral response.
7. A benefit of vertical gardening is that vertical gardens can be installed in small spaces, making them ideal for urban cities with limited space. A drawback of vertical gardening is that the cost of installation and maintenance of a vertical garden may be higher than for other types of green spaces.

8. The given sentence is true because the majority of participants agreed that vertical gardens can improve the quality of life, increase air quality and have a relaxing and calming effect. However, the survey does not provide information on the long-term effectiveness of vertical gardens or their potential impact on other aspects of urban life, such as traffic or community engagement.

Passage 13

1. increased
2. (d) Both (a) and (b)
3. (c) By helicopters
4. (b) 1.5°C or 2°C
5. According to the report, tourism has negatively impacted the coral bleaching event. Severe and extreme bleaching was most prevalent in areas highly visited by tourists, affecting both inshore and offshore reefs.
6. The name of the report that published the findings on the coral bleaching event is 'The Reef Snapshot: Summer 2021-22.'
7. Coral bleaching occurs when corals are stressed by above-average water temperatures, leading to the expulsion of algae. While corals can survive, they may suffer sublethal effects, making them more susceptible to disease and limiting growth and reproduction.
8. The mass coral bleaching that occurred during 2022 is considered 'surprising' because this mass bleaching event occurred during a cooler La Niña year, contrary to expectations. Since, coral bleaching occurs when corals are stressed by above-average water temperatures, this event is surprising.

Passage 14

1. essential
2. (c) Camel tourism
3. (a) Skiing and snowboarding
4. (d) Both (a) and (b)
5. Sun tourism is exclusively connected to mountainous regions.
6. The departure from the traditional winter-centric approach to mountain tourism affect the tourists who do not like the winter season positively since it allows them to enjoy the scenic landscapes in warm weather.
7. Sun tourism affects the economy of mountainous regions positively. It extends the tourism season, hence generating income for local businesses and service providers.It also supports growth and development, contributing to the sustainability of local communities.
8. Sun tourism extends the tourist season in mountain regions because it is not dependent on seasonal snowfalls which used to be the primary attraction of mountain tourism.

Since snowfall happens only for a limited period of time, every year it adversely affects the local employment by reducing earning opportunities.

Passage 15

1. unprecedented
2. Elon Musk
3. (d) People who have lost their limbs
4. (b) People with stuttering issues
5. The message posted by the Australian ALS patient Philip O'Keefe using the neural interface in 2021 was: "hello, world! Short tweet. Monumental progress."
6. Theoretically, processes like deep-brain stimulation could help fight Alzheimer's and Parkinson's, even depression and addiction. Thus, Neuralink could help patients suffering from brain diseases.
7. The access to the human mind provided by the Neuralink raises the major concern for privacy. Neuralink could enable authorities to monitor every detail of human lives. Such a scenario raises the question of ownership of the data collected by such invasion of privacy. The access to this technology could also become a privilege and thus worsen the existing social inequalities.
8. According to Musk, the people who have lost their limbs will be able to take control of their phone or computer, and thereby almost any device, just by thinking, which would be transformative.

Passage 16

1. integration
2. (b) Increase of illiteracy
3. (a) Being critical of other people's religions
4. (d) All of these
5. Dr S. Radhakrishnan emphasises that national integration grows in people's minds through education.
6. National integration is important because it could help stabilise the democracy, improve economic growth, and also result in further development of the nation.
7. National integration is the awareness of a common identity among citizens. It transcends differences caused by diverse identities such as caste, religion, and language while emphasising a shared national identity.
8. The two forms of national integration are uniformity and internal unity. Uniformity-Based Integration emphasises language, living, customs, and rituals. Internal Unity focuses on a common attitude and thinking regarding national interests despite differences.

ASSESSMENT EXERCISE

Continuous Passages

Read the given passages carefully and answer the questions that follow each passage.

Passage 1

Everybody wants to succeed in life. For some, success means achieving whatever they desire or dream. For many it is the name, fame and social position. Whatever be the meaning of success, it is success which makes a man popular.

All great men have been successful. They are remembered for their great achievements. But it is certain that success comes to those who are sincere, hardworking, loyal and committed to their goals.

Success has been man's greatest motivation. It is very important for all. Success has a great effect on life. It brings pleasure and pride. It gives a sense of fulfilment. It means all-around development. Everybody hopes to be successful in life. But success smiles on those who have a proper approach, planning, vision and stamina.

A proper and timely application of all these things is bound to bear fruit. One cannot be successful without cultivating these certain basic things in life. It is very difficult to set out on a journey without knowing one's goals and purposes. Clarity of the objective is a must to succeed in life. A focused approach with proper planning is certain to bring success. Indecision and insincerity are big obstacles on the path to success.

One should have the capability, capacity and resources to turn one's dreams into reality. Mere desire cannot bring you success. The desire should be weighed against factors like capability and resources. This is the basic requirement of success. The next important thing is the eagerness, seriousness and the urge to be successful. It is the driving force which decides the success. It is the first step on the ladder of success.

One needs to pursue one's goals with sincerity and passion. One should always be in high spirit. Lack of such spirit leads to an inferiority complex which is a big obstruction on the path to success. Time is also a deciding factor. Only the punctual and committed have succeeded in life. Lives of great men are examples of this. They had all these qualities in plenty which helped them rise to the peak of success.

Hard labour is one of the basic requirements of success. There is no substitute for hard labour. It alone can take one to the peak of success. Every success has a ratio of five percent inspiration and ninety-five percent perspiration. It is the patience, persistence and perseverance which play a decisive role in achieving success. Failures are the pillars of success as they are our stepping-stones and we must get up and start again and be motivated.

Answer the following questions based on the passage given above.

1. What does success bring to those successful?
(a) Luxuries
(b) Pride
(c) Sense of fulfilment
(d) Experience

2. Which of the following is a basic requirement of success?
(a) Hard labour and inspiration
(b) Desire should be proportional to capabilities and resources
(c) Eagerness, urge and seriousness
(d) 5% inspiration and 95% perspiration

3. Complete the sentence appropriately.
.... plays a decisive role in achieving success.

4. Rectify the given false statement.
Indecision and insincerity does not hamper success.

5. To whom does success come certainly?

6. What is certain to bring success?

7. What is the one basic requirement of success?

8. Explain "Failures are pillars of success."

9. How should goals be pursued?

Passage 2

I was born in the small but beautiful mountain village of Nakuri near Uttarkashi in Garhwal, with the gurgling, playful Bhagirathi River flowing nearby. My parents were a hard-working and extremely self-contained couple. Even though our family was poor, barely managing the essentials, my father taught us how to live and maintain dignity and self-respect – the most treasured family value till today. At the same time, my parents also practised the creed, 'kindness is the essence of all religion'. They were large-hearted, inviting village folk passing by to have tea at our home and gave grain to the sadhus and pandits who came to the house.

This characteristic has been ingrained in me so deeply that I am able to reach out to others and make a difference in their lives – whether it is in my home, in society or at the workplace.

I was the third child in the family – girl, boy, girl, girl and boy in that order – and quite a rebel. I developed a tendency to ask questions and was not satisfied with the customary way of life for a girl-child. When I found my elder brother, Bachchan, encouraging our youngest brother, Raju, to take up mountaineering, I thought why not me? I found that my brothers were always getting preferential treatment and all opportunities and options were open to them. This made me even more determined to not only do what the boys were doing, but to do it better.

The general thinking of mountain people was that mountaineering as a sport was not for girls. They considered themselves to be born mountaineers as they had to go up and down mountain slopes for their daily livelihood and even for routine work. On the other hand, as a student, I would look curiously at foreign backpackers passing by my village and wonder where they were going. I would even invite them to my house and talk to them to learn more about their travels. The full significance of this came to me later when I started working. The foreigners took the trouble to come all the way to the Himalayas in order to educate themselves on social, cultural and scientific aspects of mountaineering, as well as to seek peace in nature's gigantic scheme of things.

Answer the following questions based on the passage given above.

1. From the passage, we can gather that the narrator was
(a) a young girl (b) a mountaineer
(c) a young boy (d) a host

2. The society in which the narrator lived can be described as ....
(a) discriminatory (b) practical
(c) egotists (d) nomadic

3. Complete the sentence appropriately.
The mountain people consider themselves to be born mountaineers bacause ....

4. Rectify the given false statement.
The narrator grandparents loved calling foreign tourists to her home.

5. List the qualities that can be associated with the narrator.

6. Why were foreigners drawn to the Himalayas?

7. Give an example to show that the author's parents were very hospitable.

8. Why did the author invite foreign mountaineers to her house?

9. What does the author tell us about the financial condition of her parents? What is the most treasured value of the author's family?

Passage 3

1. The Canadian Rocky Mountains or the Canadian Rockies are breathtakingly beautiful mountains and a precious ecosystem with a wealth of wildlife, lush forests including a large variety of flora, ice-capped peaks and among the most picturesque landscapes you will see in the world. Glaciers, waterfalls, lakes, limestone caves, canyons and fossils of marine animals are part of this splendid landscape.

2. The Canadian Rocky Mountain Parks are a UNESCO World Heritage Site. According to UNESCO, this province has outstanding physical features—"Classic illustrations of glacial geological processes including ice fields, remnant valley glaciers, canyons and exceptional examples of erosion and deposition are found throughout the area. The Burgess Shale Cambrian and nearby Precambrian sites contain important information about the Earth's evolution." For all these reasons, these mountains are also great for activities like hiking, fishing, trekking, mountaineering, skiing, camping and sightseeing.
This presents a challenge to the authorities because these beautiful mountains and valuable ecosystem could be a likely target for commercial and economic exploitation.

3. So, how is this challenge being met? The Rockies are divided into many national parks. This means that these are protected areas with many controls in place regarding what can be done within the area, whether by commercial organisations, other groups or the private visitor. This World Heritage label also implies many responsibilities for protection and special care.
For example, there is the Canadian Rocky Mountain Parks World Heritage Site where four national parks are part of this site—Banff, which is the most popular and visited, Jasper, Kootenay and Yoho. Besides, there are three British Columbia Provincial Parks— Hamber Provincial Park, the Mount Assiniboine Provincial Park and Mount Robson Provincial Park. These parks are known for their scenic splendour and together receive millions of visitors annually.

4. The idea is to encourage tourism and allow visitors to enjoy the spectacular Rockies, but to ensure that it is done in harmony with the environment. Many hotels exhort their guests to help them in being environmentally friendly by asking them not to waste water or electricity. Some of them provide guestroom amenity containers which are biodegradable. There is a strong civic consciousness ingrained within the citizens so that the environment is preserved.

Answer the following questions based on the passage given above.

1. For what reason did the UNESCO deem the Canadian Rocky Mountain Parks as World Heritage Site?
(a) Biodiversity
(b) Outstanding landscape
(c) Adventure sports
(d) All of the above

2. Why are adventure sports a challenge for the authorities of Canadian Rocky Mountain Parks?
(a) Threat of commercial and economic exploitation
(b) Threat of extinction of endangered biodiversity
(c) Ecological disturbances
(d) Lack of civic consciousness among tourists

3. Complete the sentence appropriately.
The Canadian Rocky Mountain Parks are a .... World Heritage Site.

4. Rectify the given false statement. Glaciers, waterfalls, lakes, limestone caves and canyons are a part of the landscape of the Australian Rocky Mountain Parks.

5. What are known for their scenic splendour?

6. What helps in preserving the environment in the biodiversity parks?
7. For what activities are the Canadian Rocky Mountains good?
8. Name the four national parks which are a part of this site.
9. What is the idea behind Canadian Rocky Mountain tourism?

Passage 4

Fundamentals of Laughter Yoga

1. The most important principle behind Laughter Yoga or the most significant driving force behind the several Laughter Clubs is the theory that Motion Creates Emotion. Quite a few people wonder how a person can laugh when he is in no mood to laugh or when one doesn't have any reason to laugh. However, the answer is very simple. For, there is a well established link between the body and the mind. Whatever happens to the mind happens to the body as well. This is easily understood and observed too. If a person is sad or depressed, his body also appears quite lifeless and sluggish. Such a person doesn't walk or talk enthusiastically. But, what most people fail to understand is that the opposite is also true. Whatever happens to the body also happens to the mind. I remember my father once telling me, "Son, if you are sad or feeling a bit low, don't sit idle. Keep doing some physical work or go for a walk or do some jogging or go out to play some cricket or football. You'll feel better." And most of the times dad was proved correct. I would start feeling better quite soon. In an unhappy state of mind, if we bring ourselves to behaving or acting happy, soon enough we will start feeling light-hearted and chirpy indeed!
2. Laughter is all about playfulness. Have you ever wondered why children laugh 300 to 400 times a day whereas adults would consider themselves very fortunate if they manage laughter 10 to 15 times in a day? This is because of that seriously wicked and interfering tool called the brain! Adults use their brains or minds first to comprehend humour and then decide if they have to laugh. Very often, they suffer from what is called in Hindi the LKK Syndrome, that is "Log Kya Kahenge" or "What will people say?" This is called the "Mind-to-Body Model of Humour". On the other hand, children, who do not allow themselves to be too affected by the LKK Syndrome and don't use their brain too seriously do the comprehension first, laugh the most while playing. Their laughter comes straight from the body and happily they don't make use of intellectual capacity of the brain for it.
3. Laughter Yoga makes a clear distinction between Happiness and Joy. Happiness is a conditional response of the mind which is totally dependent on the fulfilment of certain desires of the mind. By its very nature, it is related to how one's life had been in the past or how it will be in the future. It is not there at all in the present moment. The ironical and sad fact is that even if some dreams, goals or aspirations are fulfilled, happiness disappears quite quickly as the mind starts chasing new goalposts-a new job, a new house, a bigger car etc.
On the other hand, joyfulness is the unconditional commitment to be happy each moment, to have fun for the moment, despite the problems and challenges of life, no matter how insurmountable they seem to the mind. It is the promise that the body makes to the mind to indulge in playfulness moment by moment and thereby give relaxation to it.

MCB Theme : Health and Medicine

Answer the following questions based on the passage given above.

1. What does the theory 'Motion Creates Emotion' suggest?
(a) Laughter is good
(b) There is connection between body and mind
(c) We need to laugh at all times
(d) Both (a) and (b)
2. Which of the following is true for Laughter Yoga?
(a) It is strenuous
(b) It is done with friends and family
(c) It is a voluntary physical movement
(d) It treats many heart disorders
3. Complete the sentence appropriately. According to the writer, joy is ....
4. Rectify the given false statement.
Laughter Yoga involves jumping exercises.
5. Why do children laugh heartily?
6. What is the difference between happiness and joy?
7. How can you justify that there is a connection between mind and the body?
8. What did the writer's father teach him/her?
9. Why do people don't laugh that often?

Passage 5

Fox was very happy that there were more than 50 admissions in his new school. He was determined to make it the best school in the jungle. He introduced everything in his curriculum: reading, writing, arithmetic, swimming, dancing, running, climbing trees, etc. and insisted that teachers should take classes regularly and test the students regularly. The teachers however were very unsatisfied with the results.
However much they tried, they couldn't teach the Lion to swim, the Tiger always failed in climbing trees and the Crow refused to sing. The teachers tried all the methods and regularly conducted classes. The students had to attend special classes. The peacock would help the teacher conduct dancing classes but the Pig could not get a single step correct. Likewise, the Owl did not want to learn to read and the Monkey could not swim. All the students failed in the exams and Fox was very worried. Then, the wise Bat told him to let the students take up the courses they wanted to and then conduct the exams.

The Monkey did not have to learn swimming anymore but the Crocodile could practise swimming and diving, the Crow could fly and learn to do somersaults in the air and the Squirrel could continue learning arithmetic. When the exams were conducted, all the animals passed with flying colours and the Fox was very proud of his school.

MCB Theme : Education

Answer the following questions based on the passage given above.

1. Why was Fox happy?
   (a) His school was popular
   (b) He had 50 new admissions to his school
   (c) He had made education reachable to all
   (d) All of the above
2. What characteristic could be attached to the teachers of Fox's school?
   (a) Regular (b) Determined
   (c) Punctual (d) Lazy
3. Complete the sentence appropriately.
   .... could not be taught how to swim.
4. Rectify the given false statement.
   Fox's school became popular after Bat's advice.
5. Who would conduct the dance lessons?
6. When did the school show good results?
7. What was Fox's goal?
8. What was wrong with Fox's school initially?
9. What were the reasons for improvement in the results?

Passage 6

1. Walter Hudson, who has died at Hempstead, New York, age 46, was once listed in The Guinness Book of World Records as the heaviest man on Earth.
2. About 183 cm tall and 274 around, with cherubic features set off by pigtails braided in the Cherokee style, he long devoted himself to the pleasures of the table. Four years ago, Hudson-then tipping the industrial scales at his top weight of 540 kg - gained worldwide notoriety (as 'Whopping Walter') when he became stuck in his bedroom door. He was wedged there for some four hours. It took eight firemen to free him.
3. Walter Hudson was born at Brooklyn in 1945 and, as he recalled, "began gorging at the age of six ." At 15, he was so obese his legs collapsed underneath him and he was confined to bed.
4. Indeed, except for the time when his family moved to Hempstead in 1970 and he was transported by motor-car (his then 266kg broke the seat), he remained inside. "I'm just a foodaholic," he once confessed, "I have no excuse."
5. Hudson's eating habits were fuelled by food brought in by members of his family. He would generally start his day with a breakfast of two pounds of bacon, 32 sausages, a dozen eggs, a loaf of bread, jam and coffee.
6. For lunch, Hudson favoured four enormous bowls of rice, four double cheeseburgers, eight boxes of fried potatoes, six pies, and six large bottles of coca-cola. For dinner he would eat six roasted corns, half-a-dozen yams and another six or seven baked potatoes, ending with a whole apple pie. Between these main meals, he would eat a chicken or two, followed by noodles, string beans, six large bottles of soda, not to mention colossal sandwiches, and copious amounts of ice-cream.
   "All I cared about," he recalled, "was food, FOOD!"
7. Hudson, though, was advised against sitting up for longer than five minutes because of the risk of being smothered by flab. The only exercise he engaged in was when he attended to his ablutions; it took him an hour to negotiate the six yards to the bathroom from his bedroom. Then in 1987, he found himself wedged in the door-way. "The day I got stuck in that door," he recalled, "that when the Lord got me the help I needed." The help to which he referred was offered by Dick Gregory, a comedian who masterminded the Slim Safe Diet Scheme.
8. Gregory placed Hudson on a 1,200 calorie-a-day diet of raw fruit and orange juice. For exercise, he was advised to lie in bed waving his arms about like a conductor. Hudson soon lost some four inches off his knees, and within three months had shed 178 kg. It began to look as if he might fulfill such ambitions as visiting his mother's grave, riding on the New York subway, driving into the country-and even flying to a clinic in the Bahamas, from which he envisaged emerging as a sylph of 13 stones.
9. But it was not to be. At the time of his death, of an apparent heart attack, Hudson reportedly weighed 508 kg. Rescue workers had to cut a large hole in the wall of his bedroom to remove the body. He was unmarried.

MCB Theme Health And Medicine

Answer the following questions based on the passage given above.

1. Why was Walter Hudson in the Guinness Book Record?
   (a) For eating habits
   (b) For being the heaviest man
   (c) For his height
   (d) For his food challenges
2. What characteristics would you apply to Walter Hudson?
   (a) Greedy (b) Lazy
   (c) Foodie (d) Both (b) and (c)
3. Complete the sentence appropriately.
   Rescue workers had to .... to remove the body.
4. Rectify the given false statement.
   Walter Hudson was married.
5. What did Walter weigh at the time of his death?
6. Substitute the underlined word in the following sentence with a word/phrase from the passage that means the same.
   Then in 1987, he found himself <u>wedged</u> in the door-way.

7. After which paragraph would you place the following paragraph?

When not eating and sleeping, he would watch television, listen to tapes and read the Bible-he had a particular penchant for the psalms and was apt to recite Psalm 121. "I will lift up mine eyes unto the hills..."

8. Why do you think he did not go on a serious diet when he was much younger, so that he could have lived a fuller life?

9. What advice would you have given Walter on his diet?

PASSAGE 7

Vorobyov Village, Ukraine (formerly USSR) "It happened on April the 26th 1986. I remember the date because it was my mother's birthday. We heard the explosion early in the morning. We didn't worry, because there had been explosions before from Chernobyl. But this one was bigger. Everyone stopped what they were doing and listened. Then we ran out into the garden. We could see a cloud of white smoke coming from the nuclear reactor." Natasha Revenko wiped her hands nervously on her apron. Tears came to the corners of her eyes, and slid slowly down her pinched, pale cheeks.

"It was a Saturday," she went on, still wiping her hands on her apron. "It was a lovely warm day, and the children played outside all weekend. Even when the dust began to fall, they still played outside. They picked up handfuls of it and threw it at each other, laughing. It was Wednesday before the loudspeaker van came to the village, telling us to keep our children indoors and not to touch the radioactive dust. They also told us to wash down our houses and roads with water. A week later the children began to vomit. Their hair fell out. They couldn't eat. They grew so thin, and sores appeared all over their little bodies. Two weeks after that, all three died-all three on the same day." She broke down now and cried quietly, as she had done so many times before. "They're buried over there." She pointed to the church graveyard. "Lots of village children are. And adults." I touched her gently on the shoulder, leaving her to her bitter-sweet memories, and walked on through the silence. It was a ghost town. No one lived there any more. They had either died or been forcibly evacuated. The fields were barren.

Nothing grew. Nothing ever would again. There was no bird-song. No rabbit peered at me. No cow endlessly chewed. No horse neighed. Natasha caught me up as we boarded the bus marked MOSCOW. "Thank you for coming with me." She said. "I wanted to see the graves and the house again, before I die."

MCB Theme : Environment

Answer the following questions based on the passage given above.

1. What does the author's calmness in the beginning show?
   (a) That she did not want the day to be spoilt.
   (b) That the explosions were common.
   (c) That it was her mother's birthday.
   (d) Both (a) and (c)

2. What does the speaker feel when he/she states the events of the disaster?
   (a) Arrogant (b) Despair
   (c) Dejection (d) Both (b) and (c)

3. Complete the sentence appropriately.
   The nuclear explosion left Natasha's hometown ....

4. Rectify the given false statement.
   Natasha now moved back to her hometown.

5. Natasha and other families were warned to stay away from the dust. Justify?

6. Why does Natasha point to the graveyard?

7. How did the children react to the dust?

8. What can be the appropriate title of the passage?

9. How did the dust impact the children?

PASSAGE 8

Ecotourism means responsible travel to natural areas conserving the environment and improving the well-being of local people. The Ecotourism Society of India is dedicated to the promotion of sustainable development in tourism and to develop responsible practices in and among the tourism fraternity. It works towards continuous identification of new ecotourism destinations, strengthening ecotourism and making India a preferred ecotourism destination. Its objectives are

- Make strategy for ensuring perpetual sustenance of the environment.
- Work with empowered bodies to establish carrying capacity and sustainable tourism practices which include conservation of nature and wildlife, and allow local communities to benefit from tourism.
- To balance tourists and visitors' numbers and ensure good tourism practices that would allow nature to regenerate itself.
- To work with government bodies to develop policies and code of conduct for promotion of sustainable tourism, and help implement the same.
- To work towards certification of tourism service providers.
- To act as watchdog for excessive consumption of natural resources and any negative impact in the tourism sector.
- To support research in tourism environment related areas.
- Work with service providers to enhance quality of their product and eco-friendly services.
- Encourage use of appropriate local practices, materials, art, craft, architecture, food.
- Encourage minimal conspicuous consumption and prevent excessive consumption of energy.
- Encourage energy saving practices, water harvesting, use of solar and other natural energy sources.
- Encourage good waste management practices, especially non-biodegradable materials.
- Encourage low pollution-generating practices to minimise carbon footprint.

- Organise training and other activities to create awareness on ecotourism, sustainable and responsible tourism.
- To collaborate with like-minded bodies and implement ecotourism objectives all over the world.

Answer the following questions based on the passage given above.

1. Eco tourism promotes
   (a) preservation
   (b) conservation
   (c) mindfulness
   (d) All of the above
2. Which of the following does not ascertain to ecotourism?
   (a) Identification (b) Strengthening
   (c) Modifying (d) Developing
3. Complete the sentence appropriately.
   We need to organise training and other activities to ....
4. Rectify the given false statement.
   Local communities can not really benefit from tourism.
5. Ecotourism society worked with government bodies. Why?
6. Which characteristics can be associated with ecotourism?
7. What is the purpose of The Ecotourism Society of India?
8. What is the purpose of the passage?
9. What does The Ecotourism Society of India encourage us to do?

Non-Continuous Passages

Passage 1

With the enormous amount of information potentially available to travellers, the Internet constitutes an important platform for information exchange between the consumer and industry suppliers (e.g. hotels, transportation sectors, attractions), intermediaries (e.g. travel agents), controllers (e.g. governments and administrative bodies), as well as many non-profit organisations such as destination marketing organisations.

Different technological interfaces, such as search engines, online travel booking sites and websites of destination marketing organisations facilitate the information exchange between online travellers and the so-called 'online tourism domain'.

Particularly, it has been argued that understanding the nature of the online tourism domain, i.e. the composition of online tourism related information potentially available to travellers, provides an important stepping-stone for the development of successful marketing programmes and better information systems in tourism.

The importance of social media is identified by Xiang and Gretzel (2010). Their analysis showed that social media constitutes a substantial part of the search results, indicating that search engines linked the travellers directly to social media sites. Since more and more travellers seem to tap into this 'collective intelligence' available on the Web, this will challenge the established marketing practices of many tourism businesses and destinations.

One of the popular travel social media site Expedia Media Solutions partnered with ComScore, shed some insightful details of how travellers consume and share content prior to, during and after a trip.

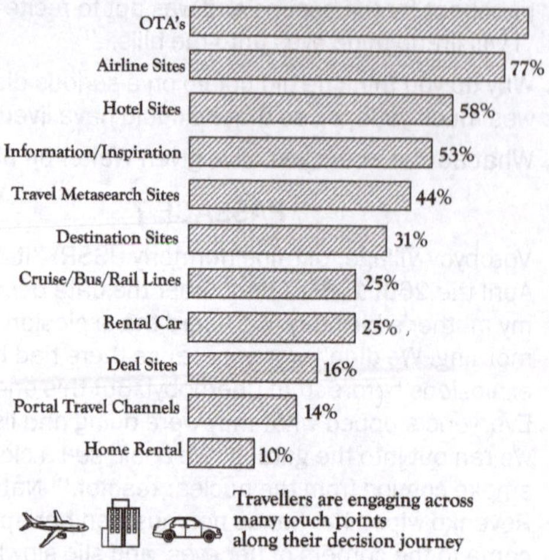

Travel Buyer Reach

It is no wonder that destinations, airlines, hotels and most travel marketers are embracing social networks such as pinterest, photo/video applications such as Instagram and Vine, as part of their storytelling toolkit, reaching out to growing crowds of travellers.

Answer the following questions based on the passage given above.

1. Complete the given sentence by selecting the most appropriate option.
   According to the passage, the internet ....
2. Complete the sentence appropriately.
   Online tourism domain can be understood as ....
3. What does the given passage focus on?
   (a) The increasing role of social media in tourism.
   (b) The increasing demand of tourism.
   (c) The need to boost tourism in India.
   (d) The Indian Tourism marketing needs.
4. Based on the given graphical representation of data in the passage, choose the option that lists the statements that are True with respect to the usage of social media networks.
   1. Online travel agencies are an important source across all platforms and throughout all stages of the booking process.
   2. Through media visibility, companies are able to complicate their market standing.
   3. Different technological interfaces facilitate the information exchange between online travellers.
   4. Travellers seem to move away from the 'collective intelligence' available on the Web.

   (a) 1 and 3 (b) 2 and 4
   (c) 1 and 4 (d) 2 and 3

5. Who are the controllers in the field of tourism?
6. What is called the collective intelligence?
7. According to the given data graph, which marketing field shows the greatest influence of tourists?
8. What facilitates the exchange of information between online travellers and online tourism domain?

Passage 2

Chronobiology might sound a little futuristic – like something from a science fiction novel, perhaps – but it's actually a field of study that concerns one of the oldest processes life on this planet has ever known: short-term rhythms of time and their effect on flora and fauna.

When it comes to humans, chronobiologists are interested in what is known as the circadian rhythm. This is the complete cycle our bodies are naturally geared to undergo within the passage of a twenty-four hour day. Aside from sleeping at night and waking during the day, each cycle involves many other factors such as changes in blood pressure and body temperature.

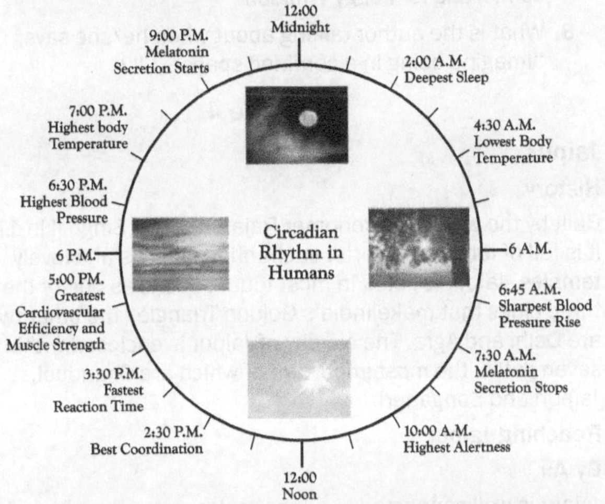

Knowledge of chronobiological patterns can have many pragmatic implications in our day-to-day lives. While contemporary living can sometimes appear to subjugate biology – after all, who needs circadian rhythms when we have caffeine pills, energy drinks and shift work and cities that never sleep? – keeping in sync with our body clock is important.

The average urban resident, for example, rouses at the eye-blearing time of 6:04 a.m., which researchers believe to be far too early. One study found that even rising at 7:00 a.m. has deleterious effects on health unless exercise is performed for 30 minutes afterward. The optimum moment has been whittled down to 7:22 a.m.; muscle aches, headaches and moodiness were reported to be lowest by participants in the study who awoke then.

Once you're up and ready to go, what then? If you're trying to shed some extra pounds, dieticians are adamant: never skip breakfast. This disorients your circadian rhythm and puts your body in starvation mode.

The recommended course of action is to follow an intense workout with a carbohydrate-rich breakfast.

Morning is also great for breaking out the vitamins. For improved supplement absorption, naturopath pain stone, suggests pairing supplements with a food in which they are soluble and steering clear of caffeinated beverages. Finally, Stone warns to take care with storage; high potency is best for absorption and warmth and humidity are known to deplete the potency of a supplement.

After-dinner espressos are becoming more of a tradition, but to prepare for a good night's sleep we are better off putting the brakes on caffeine consumption as early as 3 p.m. With a seven hour half-life, a cup of coffee containing 90 mg of caffeine taken at this hour could still leave 45 mg of caffeine in your nervous system at 10 o'clock that evening. It is essential that, by the time you are ready to sleep, your body is rid of all traces.

Answer the following questions based on the passage given above.

1. Complete the sentence appropriately.
   In the given image, a relation is shown between ....
2. "We are better off putting the brakes on caffeine consumption as early as 3 p.m."
   The idea of putting off the caffeine is to ....
3. Which time has been identified as the best time to wake up as per the researchers?
   (a) 6:04 a.m. (b) 7:00 a.m.
   (c) 7:04 a.m. (d) 7:22 a.m.
4. Pick the option that lists statements that are not true according to the passage.
   1. Chronobiology is the study of how living things have evolved over time.
   2. Circadian rhythms identify how we do different things at different times.
   3. A 'night person' can still have a healthy circadian rhythm.
   4. New therapies can permanently change circadian rhythms without causing harm.

   (a) 1 and 2 (b) 2 and 3
   (c) 3 and 4 (d) 1 and 4
5. What is chronobiology?
6. How should supplements be taken for maximum benefit?
7. Why is the knowledge of the chronobiological pattern central to our day-to-day activities?
8. With reference to the figure, write one conclusion about the chronological pattern followed by the human body.

Passage 3

4 Women Astronauts Talk About Space Exploration

By Julie Bain

Peggy Whitson

Age 48

Astronaut since 1996

Space time Two six-month tours on the International Space Station, in 2002 and 2007-2008

Imagine being in a confined space for six months with no easy means of escape and only a cosmonaut or two to keep you company. Peggy Whitson did it-twice, the second time as the first woman commander. The former Iowa farm girl racked up 377 days in space on two of her missions, more than any other US astronaut. Her space walks totaled to nearly 40 hours, more than any other woman astronaut. She's now a walking laboratory for the long-term effects of zero gravity (zero-g) on the human body. And hers, by the way, is ripped like an Olympic athlete's.

Getting used to zero-g "Fitness is a lot more important than strength. So is your ability to think in 3-D and intuit how to move objects in a different way than on Earth. The second time I went to the station, it felt like coming home. I adapted and got comfortable much quicker."

The best zero-g side effect "It's a nice plus that without the effects of gravity, everything is lifted while you're up there, so you look younger!"

Staying in shape "With no gravity for resistance, muscles and bones deteriorate quickly up there, so every day we do an hour of cardio on a specially designed cycle or treadmill and an hour of resistance training. You need strength for space walks, as every motion works against the pressure of the space suits we wear, and it's very fatiguing. Exercising always made me feel more positive and upbeat afterward too."

Poetic moment "As we orbited every 90 minutes, the view of the Earth's curvature was incredible. You could see the layers of atmosphere extend beyond the surface to meet with the blackness of space beyond. It seemed impossibly thin, yet it carried all the shades of blue closest to the planet a glowing blue, like sunlit water over white sand, extending to the deepest blue-purple mixture that holds the blackness at bay."

Returning to gravity "At first, being back on earth is not pleasant. My agility and quick motions, like playing basketball and the timing to dribble and do a layup, were severely hindered. But I had my physical fitness assessment about a month after my return and I'm back to preflight norm, which I'm really happy about."

Inspiration "Exploration is a very important part of who we are, and if we want to literally expand our horizons, we have to keep doing it. Construction of the International Space Station shows we can expand those horizons culturally as well."

MCB Theme : Science

Answer the following questions based on the passage given above.

1. Complete the sentence appropriately.

   .... had made Peggy more upbeat and positive.
2. Complete the sentence appropriately.

   Returning to Earth is not very positive for a few days because ....
3. What is more important for Peggy Whitson?

   (a) Fitness (b) Mindfulness
   (c) Strength (d) Training
4. How many days had Peggy Whitson spent in the International Space Station?

   (a) 365 days (b) 366 days
   (c) 345 days (d) 377 days
5. What inspires Peggy Whitson to go to the International Space Station?
6. What is the effect of lack of gravity on the human body?
7. Why was the second journey to the space station more comforting for Peggy Whitson?
8. What is the author talking about when he/she says, "Imagine being in a confined space......"?

Passage 4

Jaipur

History

Built by the warrior-astronomer Raja Sawai Jai Singh II in 1727, it is full of formidable forts, enchanting palaces and lovely temples. Jaipur is listed in most tourist books as one of the three cities that make India's Golden Triangle - the other two are Delhi and Agra. The old city of Jaipur is enclosed within seven gates, the most important of which are Chandpol, Jaipuri and Sanganeri.

Reaching Jaipur

By Air

Jaipur is well connected to all the major cities which include Delhi, Mumbai, Kolkata, Jodhpur and Udaipur. Recently, flights to Dubai have also started from Jaipur by Indian Airlines.

By Bus

Rajasthan Roadways run very comfortable deluxe and air conditioned buses from Delhi (Bikaner House, Nr. India Gate) to Jaipur. The roads are very good and it takes around 5-6 hrs from Delhi. You can also come by taxi.

By Train

Jaipur is on the Broad Gauge and hence connected to all the metro cities of India. There are daily trains from Delhi in morning (Shatabdhi Exp) and evening (Intercity Exp).

Getting Around

In the city you can travel by un-metered auto-rickshaws, buses, cycle-rickshaws or you can also use car cabs and car-taxi. The Rajasthan Tourism Development Corporation operates regular bus service for local city tour.

General Information

Weather

In summer 45° C (Max) – 25° C (Min)

In winter 22° C (Max) – 8° C (Min)

Rainy season July to mid Sept; very humid (upto 90%)

Our suggestion Best time to come – Oct to March

Accommodation Accommodation for tourists in Jaipur ranges from five star deluxe hotels to budget hotels. Heritage hotels also offer immaculate hospitality to guests.

Hot Attractions

Kite Festival A festival with a difference - as kites take to the sky all over Jaipur. In the evening, kites with lights in them and fireworks brighten the skies above. If you like kite flying, you should be here.

Elephant Festival A festival to celebrate Holi, this is a great occasion for the visitor to watch several elephant sports and also play this festival of colors.

Gangaur Fair A festival devoted to Goddess Parvati. It is time for young girls to dress up in their finery and pray for grooms of their choice while the married women pray for the well-being of their husbands.

Teej Festival A festival to mark the advent of monsoon. Essentially a women's festival, it is interesting to watch them enjoying in groups and at various bazaars where they turn up to shop in all their finery.

Local Sightseeing

Hawa Mahal Built in 1799, the Hawa Mahal (the Palace of winds) is one of Jaipur's major landmarks.

Amber Fort The magnificent Amber Fort, seeped in history, mesmerises the visitor with its grand architecture and grandiose history.

Galtaji A popular site with pilgrims, Galtaji's hilly location is full of surprising spires and peaks. Some of the temples here are quite old.

Cuisine Dal Batti Churma

Recognised as a Rajasthan speciality, Dal batti churma, is a wholesome Rajasthani meal. Dal, or lentil curry, is served with Batti, a roundel of stuffed flour that's baked in a charcoal fire or oven. Choorma is a sweet dish made with flour, jaggery or sugar and ghee.

Shopping

Johari Bazar This is where you can buy jewellery and tie and dye sarees.

Bapu Bazar and Nehru Bazar Here you can purchase textiles, local perfumes and shoes made of camel skin.

Visiting Jaipur is the most satisfying experience as the city is a fine balance of modern conveniences and great traditions. No wonder the pink city is a tourist's heaven.

MCB Theme : Travel and Tourism

Answer the following questions based on the passage given above.

1. Complete with one word/phrase .... marks the beginning of monsoons.
2. Complete the sentence appropriately.
   Visit the .... for tie and dye sarees.
3. How long does it take for bus to travel from Delhi to Jaipur?
   (a) 2-3 hrs (b) 5-6 hrs
   (c) 4-5 hrs (d) 6-7 hrs
4. What can you buy in the Bapu Bazar?
   (a) Local perfumes (b) Shoes made from camel skin
   (c) Textiles (d) All of these
5. What is Dal Batti Churma?
6. What is the best time to visit Jaipur?
7. What makes Jaipur a great tourist destination?
8. What reaction does the Amber Fort garner in the visitor?

PASSAGE 5

I. Cities	Ahmedabad, Gujarat	Miami-dade County, Florida	Vienna, Austria	Paris, France	Stuttgrat, Germany
II. Plans	Implemented its heat action plan after a deadly heatwave in 2010.	One of the first to have Chief Heat Officer.	Launched a 'cool streets' initiative as well as a state-of-the-art cooling park.	Has created a network of 100 'cooling islands'.	The city which sees very little wind, has created special spaces throughout the city.
III. Facilities Provided to Public	They have set up water supplies for the public, a cool roof initiative, early warning systems for vulnerable populations and training for healthcare professionals.	Initiatives planned include installing cool pavements and roofs, and creating tree canopies over pavements to increase shade cover. CHO Jane Gilbert told Bloomberg that officials moved to create a state-wide agreement with the local utility not to shut off power for a failure to pay bills when the temperature is above 35°C.	The streets will be permanently redesigned to be cooler, using tree planting and replacing asphalt with surfaces that reflect less heat. Plus, they have mobile shade dispensers and stations offering drinking water and spray cooling.	These cooling islands have spaces such as parks and pools which are linked by walkways. Residents can locate them using a smartphone app.	In these special spaces, there are tree-laden roads that help clean the air flow throughout the city.

Answer the following questions based on the passage given above.

1. Complete the given sentence with the appropriate reason, with reference to the information given in the table.

   We can infer that the network of cooling islands and pools have been linked by walkways because ....

2. Select the correct option to fill the blank and complete the analogy.

   Ahmedabad : Cool roof initiative :: Vienna : ....

3. In which of the following cities, the administration is confident about the digital proficiency of its citizens?

   (a) Ahmedabad (b) Miami-Dade
   (c) Stuttgart (d) Paris

4. Which of the following can be a title for the given passage?

   (a) Actions to tackle heat wave
   (b) Heat waves
   (c) Interesting places
   (d) Both (a) and (b)

5. Identify the city which is likely to face the risk of receiving late payment of electricity bills, and support your choice with one reason.

6. Based on the information given, why is Stuttgart the most likely to have an initiative named 'Ventilation Corridors'?

7. Give two significant arguments to prove that Ahmedabad, Gujarat is more concerned about the health of its people.

8. List the facilities provided to public by Vienna to tackle heat waves.

ANSWERS

Continuous Passages

PASSAGE 1

1. (c) Sense of fulfillment
2. (b) Desire should be proportional to capabilities and resources

PASSAGE 2

1. (a) a young girl
2. (a) discriminatory

PASSAGE 3

1. (b) Outstanding landscape
2. (a) Threat of commercial and economic exploitation

PASSAGE 4

1. (d) Both (a) and (b)
2. (c) It is a voluntary physical movement

PASSAGE 5

1. (b) He had 50 new admissions to his school
2. (b) Determined

PASSAGE 6

1. (b) For being the heaviest man
2. (d) Both (b) and (c)

PASSAGE 7

1. (b) That the explosions were common.
2. (d) Both (b) and (c)

PASSAGE 8

1. (d) All of the above
2. (c) Modifying

Non-Continuous Passages

PASSAGE 1

3. (a) The increasing role of social media in tourism.
4. (a) 1 and 3

PASSAGE 2

3. (d) 7:22 a.m.
4. (b) 2 and 3

PASSAGE 3

3. (a) Fitness
4. (d) 377 days

PASSAGE 4

3. (b) 5-6 hrs
4. (d) All of these

PASSAGE 5

3. (d) Paris
4. (d) Both (a) and (b)

CHAPTER 1

E-Mail Writing

E-mail or electronic mail is a message distributed through electronic means from one computer user to one or more recipients *via.* a network. With the advent of the digital age, e-mail plays an important part in everybody's life. It is the most popular and fastest way of sending messages anywhere in the world and is generally used in formal situations. So, a student should be well-versed with the e-mail technology. He/She should be familiar with the various features of an e-mail.

In the CBSE English Communicative Class X Exams, questions regarding e-mail to school authorities are asked. The question of email writing carries 3 marks.

Parts of an E-mail

1. **Recipient's Address** The first thing you need to enter when composing an e-mail is the recipient's address. An example of e-mail address is: sakshiwrites@gmail.com. When sending a message to multiple recipients, be sure to separate all addresses with a comma.
2. **Cc and Bcc** Another option when sending a message to multiple recipients is to use the Cc or **carbon copy**, and Bcc or **blind carbon copy** fields. When using the Cc feature, all recipients can see the e-mail addresses of everyone the message was sent to. If you want your communication to be more private, choose the Bcc option and the identities of the other recipients will not be shown.
3. **Subject Line** The subject line is the first part of your e-mail that the recipient will see. When entering the subject line, write what the e-mail is about.
4. **Salutation** Before writing the email, we need to address the recipient. We use either the name of the recipient or the formal modes of addressing someone.

   e.g. Mr. Kapoor

   Ms. Agarwal

   Sir/Ma'am

   Respected Sir/Ma'am
4. **Body** The body is where you actually write the message that you want to send.
5. **Attachments** Attachments are similar to enclosures in traditional mail. If you have files that you want to share with your recipient(s), you can include them as attachments in the e-mail.
6. **Complimentary Close** After writing the email, you need to end it properly. For the same, we express gratitude and close the mail with our name and designation.
7. **Signature** Some e-mail systems allow you to enter a signature that will appear automatically at the bottom of every mail you send. This feature is optional and can be turned off and on as needed.

E-mail Etiquettes

There are certain dos and don'ts of the things to do while writing e-mails. These are

1. **Do not leave the Subject line blank** The subject of the e-mail states what your e-mail is about. So, it should be brief and accurate, and must not be left blank.
   A few examples of a good subject line are
   (i) Assignment for Class X-English (ii) Time Table for Class X-B
2. **Include Proper Salutation as per the e-mail type** One must include proper salutation before starting to write an e-mail.
   e.g. Respected Sir/Ma'am
   Sir/Ma'am
3. **Avoid using Capital Letters** Words written in capital letters are interpreted as if the sender is angry or shouting at the recipient(s).
4. **Use of Abbreviations and Acronyms** One should avoid using abbreviations and acronyms in formal e-mails.
5. **Add Appropriate Closing** One should use proper closing of the e-mail before hitting the send button. The closing of the e-mail should be appropriate.
   e.g. Yours obediently
   Yours sincerely
   Yours faithfully

Format of an E-mail

Write an e-mail to the Principal of your school requesting him to make arrangement for new furniture for your classroom. Also give reason for your demand.

	New Message
Sender's address	**From** studentsgroup@gmail.com
Receiver's address	**To** principalxyz@gmail.com
Carbon copy	**Cc** abc@gmail.com
Date	**Date** 10th July, 20XX
Subject of e-mail	**Subject** Arrangement for new furniture
Salutation	Respected Sir
Body of the e-mail	This is to inform you that, we, the students of Class X-B are writing this mail to request you to arrange more furniture for our class. There are sixty students in Class X-B but the number of seats available can only seat 40 students. Further, even those seats are in bad shape. They seem to break easily and have injured 3 students in the past week. As a result, many of us have to keep standing for a larger part of the day. Such a situation does not allow us to focus on our studies.
	Therefore, we request you to make an arrangement for new furniture. We shall be highly obliged to you.
Complimentary close	Thanking you Yours sincerely
Name of the Sender	Students of Class X-B XYZ
	Sans Serif · B I U · Send

SOLVED EXAMPLES

1. You are Rishabh/Rishita, Class Prefect of Class IX A. Write an e-mail, in 50 words, to the Principal of your school, requesting him/her to provide an interactive board in your classroom. **CBSE 2025 (3)**

Include valid reasons for your request.

You may copy the given template to write your e-mail.

From	
To	
Cc	abc@xyzschool.com
Date	16th April, 20XX, 03:45 p.m.
Subject	

Ans. From rishitamishra66@gmail.com

To principal@xyzschoolsnoida

Cc abc@xyzschool.com

Date 16th April, 20XX, 03:45 p.m.

Subject Request for an Interactive Board in Class IX A

Respected Principal

I request you to kindly provide an interactive board in our classroom. It will enhance learning through visual explanations, make lessons more engaging, and improve understanding. Digital tools will also help teachers explain complex topics effectively. We believe this will greatly benefit our studies.

Thanking you

Yours sincerely

Rishita Mishra

Class Prefect, IX-A

2. As the school Head Girl, write an e-mail, in about 50 words, to the Teacher Coordinator, Student Enrichment Activities of your school, informing her/him of the need to schedule transport for the participants of the inter-school dance competition, at the mandated venue. Include a reason why you would need a smaller vehicle instead of the school bus. **CBSE SQP 2023**

You may copy the given template to write your e-mail.

From	
To	
Cc	transportoffice@gkschool.com
Date	10th September, 20XX, 07:30 p.m.
Subject	

Ans. From headgirlgkschool@gmail.com

To coordinatorcocurricularsgkschool@gmail.com

Cc transportoffice@gkschool.com

Date 10th September, 20XX, 07:30 p.m.

Subject Transport arrangements for Inter-School Dance competition

Respected Sir/Ma'am

This is regarding to the upcoming inter-school dance competition to be held on 12th September, 20XX, Friday, at the mandated venue. I would like to request a scheduled transportation for our team from the school premises at 8:30 a.m. Our school's participation is only in the senior category with 6 students. Hence, a mini-van would suffice for the journey. Hoping for the earliest reply of confirmation.

Thanking you

Yours sincerely

XYZ

(Head Girl)

3. Write an e-mail to the Principal of your school requesting her to introduce classes for some foreign languages.

You may copy the given template to write your e-mail.

From	
To	
Cc	
Date	
Subject	

Ans. From students@gmail.com

To principal.dps.2013@yahoo.com

Cc abc@gmail.com

Date 10th April, 20XX

Subject Request for introducing Foreign Language Classes

Sir/Ma'am

This is to request you to introduce classes/courses on foreign languages namely—Spanish, German and French for the students of Classes IX to XII.

The students feel that it is a great opportunity for them to get acquainted with foreign languages. They can be really helpful for the students in the future as being multilingual can be a great advantage for their careers.

They can also be helpful to them if they choose to study abroad or work in a foreign country. Also, having the understanding of multiple cultures enhances their overall worldview.

If the classes are organised then, each student can pick

one language to learn from the three given languages.
Kindly understand and oblige.

Thanking you
Yours faithfully
Anita Kumar
(Head Girl)

4. Write an e-mail to the Principal of your school requesting him/her to send a team of children from Class IX and X to participate in the open interactive session which will follow the play on 'World Water Day' celebration. **Competency Based**

Ans. From students@gmail.com
To principal.abc@xyzschool.com
Cc abc@gmail.com
Date 10th April, 20XX
Subject Interactive Session on World Water Day
Dear Sir/Ma'am

This is to inform you that, we, students of Class X have come to know that Delhi Public School, Delhi is going to organise a one-act play on World Water Day, i.e. 22nd March, 20XX in their School Auditorium to mark the occasion and create awareness. The play will be followed by an interactive session on the same.

Taking keen interest in the program, we request you to allow a team of children from Class IX and X to participate in the interactive session. It will be a great opportunity for us to interact with other students and improve our knowledge.

Kindly understand and oblige.

Thanking you
Regards
PQR
Student of Class X

5. As the Eco Club In-charge/President of your school, write an email, in about 50 words to the Principal of your school seeking permission to initiate a plantation drive in the nearby vicinity. You are Ridhi/Rohan.

You may copy the given template to write your e-mail.

From	
To	
Cc	ssc@abcschool.com
Date	10th April, 2024, 07:05 p.m.
Subject	

CBSE 2024 C

Ans. From students@gmail.com
To principal@abcschool.com
Cc ssc@abcschool.com
Date 10th April, 2024, 07:05 p.m.
Subject Permission to initiate a Plantation Drive in the nearby Vicinity
Respected Sir/Ma'am

We, the students of Class X, have written this mail to request you to allow us to initiate a plantation drive in the nearby vicinity. As we all are aware that our city has a very low Air Quality Index which is deteriorating every day. In this light, one of the ways, in which we can ensure that the quality of air that we breathe is maintained, is to plant more and more trees.

Hence, we all have planned to initiate a plantation drive in the nearby vicinity on 23rd October, 2024, at 11:00 a.m. Kindly grant us permission to do the same and reside in the drive as a chief guest.

Hoping for a positive reply.

Thanking you
Yours sincerely

Students of Class X

6. Write an e-mail to the Principal of your school requesting him/her to allow a team of three members to participate in the Quiz Competition held by STAR.

Ans. From students@gmail.com
To principal@bhairavschool.com
Cc abc@gmail.com
Date 10th April, 20XX
Subject Request to send a team for Inter-School Quiz competition
Sir/Ma'am

This is to inform you that STAR Organisation is organising an Inter-School Quiz Competition in the month of May. The quiz competition is an interesting programme that not only tests the knowledge of students but also organises many interactive knowledge sessions before the actual quiz. Thus, we, the students of Class X are extremely interested in participating in it.

Therefore, we request you to allow us to form a team and participate in the competition. We assure you that we will bring laurels to our school.

Thanking you
With regards
Ravi Saroha
(Head Boy)

7. You are Preeti Saraswat from Uttarakhand. Write an e-mail, in about 50 words, to your Principal, requesting early commencement of winter uniform usage for all. Include a valid reason.

You may copy the given template to write your e-mail.

From	
To	
Cc	principal.vjschool@gmail.com
Date	20th February, 2024, 05:10 p.m.
Subject	

CBSE SQP 2024

Ans. From preeti.xyz@gmail.com

To principal.vjschool@gmail.com

Cc coordinator.vjschool@gmail.com

Date 20th February, 2024, 05:10 p.m.

Subject Request for early commencement of winter uniform

Dear Madam

This is to request an early commencement of winter uniform for all the students due to the sudden drop in temperature in our area. This shall ensure students' comfort and well-being during the colder weather and facilitate their focus and productivity in classes too.

Thanking you for your consideration.

Warm regards
Yours sincerely
Preeti Saraswat
Class X-B

8. Write an e-mail to the Principal of your school requesting them for a change in subject. Invent necessary details and mention the reason.

Ans. From students@gmail.com

To principalruchi@thomas.org

Cc abc@gmail.com

Date 10th April, 20XX

Subject Application for change of subject

Respected Sir/Ma'am

This is to inform you that I, Vijay Kumar, am a student of Class 10th of your school. I have written this mail to request to change a subject for my board examinations. I took Computer Science as my optional subject and I hoped that I would obtain high marks in it. However, now my interest in the subject has wavered and I am not sure to achieve good marks in the board examinations.

I think that Hindi will be better for me and my future success.

Therefore, I request you to change my optional subject from Computer Science to Hindi so that I can go on with my studies without any problem.

Thanking you in anticipation.

Yours sincerely
Vijay Kumar

Class X
Roll No. 41

9. As Aarushi, a student of Class IX, write an email, in 50 words, to the Principal of your school, from IX-A to IX-B. Include a reason why you desire the change. **CBSE 2024**

You may copy the given template to write your e-mail.

From	
To	
Cc	ssc@xyzschool.com
Date	10th April, 2024, 07:05 p.m.
Subject	

Ans. From aarushi@gmail.com

To dubey.kumar@vidyarthi.org

Cc ssc@xyzschool.com

Date 10th April, 2024, 07:05AM

Subject Application for change of section

Respected Sir/Ma'am

This is to inform you that I, Aarushi Sinha, am a student of Class IX-A of your school.

I have written this mail to request you to change my section from section 'A' to 'B'. The reason for this request is that all of my old friends are in another section and I am facing adjustment problems with my new classmates.

Also, I am not feeling comfortable as the students constantly disturb me.

I hope you will consider my request as soon as possible.

Yours obediently
Aarushi Sinha
Class IX-A
Roll No. 23

10. Write an e-mail to the Principal of your school requesting them for a change in the timing of the school bus. Invent necessary details and mention the reason. **Competency Based**

Ans. From students@gmail.com

To principal@vps.org

Cc abc@gmail.com

Date 10th April, 20XX

Subject Application for change of bus timing

Respected Sir

This is to inform you that due to the installing of gas pipelines on the Jaha Street, the condition of the road is very pitiful. This is causing the students living in the nearby area, including me, to arrive late on the Main Road where the school bus arrives to pick us up. Consequently, most of the students miss the bus, especially due to it being rush hour, no matter how early we leave from our homes. I myself have missed it 5 times in the past two weeks. Therefore, I request you to change the timing of the bus from 7:20 a.m. for the span of the renovation of the road so that everyone can arrive on time

I hope you will accept my request as soon as possible.

Yours obediently

Garima Sethi
Class X-C
Roll No. 18

11. Write an e-mail to the Principal of a neighbouring school requesting him/her to send a team of teachers to judge the inter-class talent search.

Ans. From students@gmail.com

To principal@stflorence.org

Cc abc@gmail.com

Date 10th April, 20XX

Subject Request to appoint judges for a talent search event.

Sir/Ma'am

This is to inform you that I am Maya Gilani, the Cultural Secretary of the Student Council, St. Agnes' School. I have written this mail to inform you that our school is conducting a talent search contest for the students of Classes VIII, IX and X. This is to be held on the 24th of July, 2018, from 9 a.m. to 4 p.m. in music, art, dance, magic, acrobatics and stand-up comedy.

We request you to send a team of three teachers from your school to judge the talent search 'Everybody's Got Talent'.

Anticipating a positive response.

Yours faithfully

Maya Gilani
Cultural Secretary, Student Council
St. Agnes' School

12. You are the President of the Nature Club of your school. You wish to subscribe to the 'Nature for All' magazine for the school library. Write an e-mail to the Subscription Department of the magazine requesting them to send the details of the subscription plans. **Competency Based**

Ans. From : students@gmail.com

To theweek@subscriptionenquiring.com

Cc abc@gmail.com

Date 10th April, 20XX

Subject Subscription enquiry for 'Nature for All'

Sir/Ma'am

This is to inform you that I am the President of the Nature Club of Springdales School, Dhaula Kuan, New Delhi. I happened to go through a copy of your magazine at your stall in the recently concluded Book Fair at Pragati Maidan.

I found your magazine very interesting and wanted to subscribe to it for our school library so that students can benefit from it. Kindly send me the details of the cost of its subscription and the various plans available for the same. I would appreciate if you could give us some discount over and above the regular subscription rates as we would be using it for educational purposes.

Looking forward to your correspondence.

Yours faithfully

Naveen Paul
(President, Nature Club)
Springdales School

13. Write an e-mail to your School Counsellor requesting him/her to take a session on the topic 'How to choose the right stream in Class XI'. Invent necessary details.

You may copy the given template to write your e-mail.

From	
To	
Cc	
Date	
Subject	

Ans. From students@gmail.com

To pqr@gmail.com

Cc abc@gmail.com

Date 10th April, 20XX

Subject Session on choosing the right stream in Class XI

Sir/Ma'am

This is to inform you that I, Camilla Roy, am a student of Class X-D of your school. I have written this mail to request you to organise a career counselling session for students of Class X. As you know that after a few months, we would be promoted to Class XI and face the dilemma of choosing the right stream that is suitable to our aptitude. Making a wise decision at that stage is very important for students and their future career prospects.

Therefore, I request you to conduct a session on 'How to choose the right stream in Class XI' for us in our free period. This would help us in getting prepared in advance for the process and thus, avoid making a last minute blunder in the crucial decision-making process.

Thanking you
Yours obediently

Camilla Roy
Class X-D

14. You are Saurabh/Saumya of Class X of Happy School, Daryaganj, New Delhi. You wish to participate in a Robotics Contest being organised by an Infocom Private Company. Write an e-mail to your Principal requesting him to nominate your name for the Class IX-X level, giving him the detail of the Robot that you want to display in the contest. **Competency Based**

Ans. From saurabh@gmail.com

To principalhappyschool@gmail.com

Cc abc@gmail.com

Date 10th April, 20XX

Subject Nomination for entry in Robotics Contest

Respected Sir/Ma'am

This is to inform you that I, Saurabh Grover, am a student of Class X-B of your school. I have written this mail to request you to nominate my name in the Class IX-X category of the upcoming Robotics Contest being organised by Infocom Pvt. Ltd.

The Robot that I have made for the contest can mimic a human's voice. It is also capable of reciting a few nursery rhymes. I am quite confident that my entry would bag the first prize in the contest.

So, kindly nominate my name on behalf of our school.

Thanking you
Yours obediently

Saurabh Grover
Class X-B

15. Write an e-mail to the Principal of your school requesting him/her to send an invite to other school teams to participate. You have made the invite mail already as per his/her instruction.

Ans. From students@gmail.com

To principal.dps.2013@yahoo.co.in

Cc abc@gmail.com

Date 10th April, 20XX

Subject Request to send an invite to other school teams for participation in the Inter-school Music Competition

Dear Sir/Ma'am

This is with reference to the Inter-school Music Competition. As discussed, I request you to send the invites to other schools so that they can send their teams for participation. The invite mail written according to your instructions has been given below.

With great pleasure DPS school informs you that we are going to organise an Inter-school Music Competition on the 20th of September, 20XX. Five schools from the city have been selected to participate in the competition and you are one of them. The winning team will be honoured with Gold Medals and prize money.

Kindly send a team from your school to participate in the event. Please send a timely reply to confirm your attendance.

Thanking you
Yours faithfully

Anita Kumar
(Head Girl)

16. Write an e-mail to the Principal of your school requesting him/her to grant you permission to conduct the event and inviting her/him to judge the competition.

Ans. From students@gmail.com

To principalxyz@gmail.com

Cc abc@gmail.com

Date 10th April, 20XX

Subject Invitation to judge the dance competition of our school

Respected Sir/Ma'am

This is to inform you that we, the students of Classes IX to XII, have organised a dance competition with the help of our teacher as a part of inter-house activity. The event will take place on 15th May, 20XX from 12:00 pm onwards in the school auditorium. We would be honoured to have you as our chief guest and judge and look forward to seeing you in the event.

We hope for a positive reply.
Thanking you
Yours sincerely
XYZ
Class X

17. Write an e-mail to the Principal of your school, requesting her or him to ask students to participate in the charity drive.

Ans. From students@gmail.com
To principalxyz@gmail.com
Cc abc@gmail.com
Date 10th April, 20XX
Subject Charity drive on 22nd January, 20XX

Respected Sir/Ma'am

As you are already aware, we, the members of the Nature Club, are organising a 'Charity Drive' in our school on 22nd January, 20XX. It would be great help if you could make an announcement during the school assembly regarding the same.

The details of the charity drive are reiterated as such. Students are allowed to donate books, clothing, shoes, basic necessities which should be well within the expiration date, etc. All the items donated will be sent to non-profit organisations like Anish Charitable Trust, Happy Welfare Society, Bloom Charity and they will further distribute it to the poor and needy.

We would be grateful if you could convince more students to participate in this drive for it to be a success.

Thanking you
Yours sincerely
XYZ
Class X

18. Write an e-mail to your games in-charge requesting him to nominate you as the captain of your college football team.

Ans. From students@gmail.com
To principalxyz@gmail.com
Cc abc@gmail.com
Date 10th April, 20XX
Subject Request for nomination as captain of the college football team

Respected Sir/Ma'am

This is to inform you that I am PQR of Class X of your school. As you know, I am an active member of the sports team of the college and take part in the games actively.

I am a good footballer and that's why I request you to nominate me as the captain of the college football team.

I have good coordination with almost all the teammates and this will help me in leading them better. I hope you will consider me as the captain of the football team.
Anticipating your response.

Thanking you
Yours obediently
XYZ
Class X

19. Write an e-mail to the Principal of your school complaining against insufficient supply of water in your school.

Ans. From students@gmail.com
To principalxyz@gmail.com
Cc abc@gmail.com
Date 10th April, 20XX
Subject Insufficient water supply

Sir/Ma'am

This is to inform you that I am PQR of Class X of your school. I am writing this mail on behalf of all of the students to bring into your kind consideration the problem of insufficient water supply in our school.

Most humbly I want to inform you that these days we are not getting sufficient water to drink.

As you know, summer has started and temperature is soaring up. In such high temperatures, all of us require water. However, whenever we go to the water coolers, either the cooler is not working or the pressure of tap is so low that it takes almost 15 minutes to fill our water bottles. The result is that we all mostly remain thirsty for the fear of missing out important details in our classes.

We, therefore, request you to kindly order a booster pump installation to end the inconvenience to all of us.

Thanking you
Yours obediently
PQR

20. Write an e-mail to the Principal of your school requesting him for concession in fee.

Ans. From students@gmail.com
To principalxyz@gmail.com
Cc abc@gmail.com
Date 10th April, 20XX
Subject Request for fee-concession

Respected Sir/Ma'am

This is to inform you that I am PQR of Class X of your school. I have written this mail to request you to give me a fee concession. The financial condition of my family is not good. My father is the only earning member in the family and he is admitted in the hospital due to his illness. So, I am unable to pay my school fees.

So, kindly grant me full concession in the school fees. I will be highly obliged to you.

Thanking you
Yours obediently

PQR

20. Write an e-mail to the Principal of your school requesting him to grant you five-days leave to attend your sister's marriage.

Ans. From students@gmail.com

To principalxyz@gmail.com

Cc abc@gmail.com

Date 10th April, 20XX

Subject Leave for five-days to attend sister's marriage

Respected Sir/Ma'am

This is to inform you that I am PQR of Class X of your school. Most respectfully, I beg to say that I have to attend the marriage of my sister. It will take place on the 13th of this month. Being the only son of my parents, I have to help my father in making the arrangements.

Therefore, I request you to kindly grant me leave from 10th February to 15th February, 20XX. I would be highly obliged to you.

Thanking you
Yours obediently

PQR

ASSESSMENT EXERCISE

1. Write an e-mail to the Principal requesting him to send his team for the Inter-School Cricket Tournament to be held in Ramjas School on 28th November, 20XX.
2. You are Vikas/Vaishnavi Saha of Class X-C of Sanskriti School, Chanakyapuri, New Delhi. Write an e-mail to the Director, School of Foreign Languages, New Delhi asking him/her to send the e-catalogue of the books published by the school.
3. You are the Secretary of your school's Dramatics Club. Compose an e-mail to Akshara Theatre, New Delhi enquiring about the availability of the theatre in the last week of December so that you can stage your play there.
4. You are Chetan/Drishti Dhanraj, a student of a reputed school. Write an e-mail to the Tutorial Head of the secondary wing of your school requesting him/her to arrange a workshop on 'School Safety' for the students of your school.
5. Write an e-mail informing the office-bearers of a school's Science Society about their meeting with the Principal to chalk out details about the forthcoming Science Fair.
6. Write an e-mail, addressed to the principals of different schools located in the district/zone to inform the students about a three-day inter-school campaign for tree plantation, organised by the district administration. Assuming that you're the head of the campaign, request them to participate in the campaign and refer to some award to be given to the schools with most active participants.
7. Write an e-mail to the Principal of your school requesting him to issue your Transfer Certificate and Character Certificate as your father has been transferred to another city and you have to go along and join another institution.
8. Write an e-mail to the Principal of your school requesting him to grant you leave of four days as you have to visit your father who is getting treatment in a hospital.
9. Write an e-mail to the Principal of your school requesting him to grant you leave for a week to attend your sister's marriage.
10. Write an e-mail to the Principal of your school requesting him to make regular arrangement for evening games.

Descriptive Paragraph (Factual)

CHAPTER 2

A description is a detailed account of certain or salient aspects, characteristics or features of a person, place, thing, process, etc. A descriptive paragraph is a short composition which is objective and factual. It consists of some precise and factual information that helps us form the image of thing/person described. The information is placed in a manner that shows unity of thought and creates a clear understanding in the minds of the reader.

In CBSE English Communicative Class X, questions related to descriptions of person or object are asked. It carries 4 marks.

Description of a Person

Description of a person is a biosketch of the person. It begins with the date, place and time of birth if given or known. It includes the person's achievements, his/her physical appearance, habits, profession, intellectual and emotional qualities, special traits, social status or role in the society and his/her influence on the society (if he/she is a famous personality).

Description of Objects

Describing an object encourages students to expand their observation skills and thought process as they start thinking about an object as a whole.

Describing an object can include

- What category is the object in?
- What does it look like?
- What size is it?
- What sound does it make?
- What parts does it have?
- Where can you find it?
- What does the object do?
- What colour is it?
- What does it smell/taste like?
- What is it made of?
- What shape is it?
- Anything else you know about it.

Points to be Kept in Mind

- It should give complete details about the person or thing being described in it.
- One should use simple language and short sentences in writing the paragraph.
- The word limit of 100 words should be strictly adhered to.
- The visual and verbal clues given in the question can be used in constructing the descriptive paragraph.
- It should not include the opinion of the writer, personal comments or recommendations about the person, place or event being described in the paragraph.

SOLVED EXAMPLES

1. Write a factual description, in not more than 100 words, of a working model of 'Save Your Earth' that you have prepared for your school's Earth Day Exhibition. **CBSE 2025**

Ans. Our working model, 'Save Your Earth', is designed to spread awareness about simple yet effective ways to protect the environment. At the centre, a rotating globe represents our planet, surrounded by displays on afforestation, waste management, and renewable energy. A small solar panel powers an eco-friendly house, showing the benefits of clean energy. There's also a water filtration system and a composting unit to highlight conservation and recycling. Interactive buttons provide useful tips on reducing pollution and saving resources. Through this model, we hope to inspire others to take small but meaningful steps towards a greener future.

2. Write a factual description, in not more than 100 words, of an English Notebook that you have to submit to your teacher. **CBSE 2024**

Ans. I have an English Notebook for my school notes which is very important. It is an A4 sized hardbound notebook which has single lined pages. I bought it from a local market. I covered the notebook with a light orange paper cover and also put a pink name slip on it. The name slip has details of my name, class and roll number. The notebook is half filled with some of my class notes on the chapters that were completed in class. These notes have been checked by my English teacher for notes correction. It also includes homework that was given to us. I bring it to school daily.

3. Write a factual description, in not more than 100 words, of a mobile phone that you wish to gift your mother from the pocket money that you have saved. **CBSE 2024 C**

Ans. In the age of technology, mobile phones have become an integral part of our daily lives. They serve as tools for connectivity, sources of information and platforms for entertainment. As I look for the perfect gift to express my appreciation for my mother, I have decided to use the pocket money to purchase a mobile phone for her. In selecting the ideal mobile phone for my mother, I have carefully considered her preferences and needs. First and foremost, I want to choose a device that is user-friendly. I have also opted for a model with a large screen to make reading texts, viewing photographs and watching videos more enjoyable. Another essential feature is a good camera. My mother has a passion for photography, particularly capturing family moments. A mobile phone with a high-quality camera will allow her to take beautiful pictures of us and her adventures, preserving memories that we can cherish for a lifetime. By choosing a device that caters to her specific needs and enhances her daily life, I hope to empower her with technology while strengthening our bond.

4. With the help of the given clues, write a bio sketch of Subhash Chandra Bose in not more than 80-100 words. **Competency Based**

Name Subash Chandra Bose ; Netaji
Contribution Immense, Freedom Fighter
Born 23rd January, 1897 in Cuttack, Odisha.
Career Civil Services
Achievements Joined struggle; established Indian National Army
Motto Gain independence for India "Give me blood and I will give you freedom"
Setback Retreat after the defeat of Japan and Germany.
Death Air crash over Taipei, Taiwan on 18th August 1945.

Ans. Subhash Chandra Bose, affectionately called Netaji, was born on 23rd January, 1897 in Cuttack, Odisha. He was one of the most prominent leaders of Indian freedom struggle and is remembered today for his role in it. Deeply moved by the Jallianwala Bagh massacre, he gave up a promising career in the Civil Service to join the Freedom Movement. He founded the Indian National Army to overthrow British Empire from India. His famous line was "Give me blood and I will give you freedom". However, defeat of Japan and Germany in the Second World War forced INA to retreat and it could not achieve its objective. Subhash Chandra Bose was reportedly killed in an air crash over Taipei, Taiwan on 18th August, 1945.

5. Write a descriptive paragraph on a wrist watch.

Ans. A wrist watch is a small instrument to show time. It is so designed that it can be fastened around the wrist. There are markings or numbers from 1 to 12 to give us a sense of time. On its dials it has two hands or pointed needles to show the hours and the minutes. Sometimes watches also have a hand to show seconds. This dial is covered with a glass. There is a small knob attached on the exterior of the dial to bind the watch and set the time in mechanical watches. However, in electronic watches the knob is multi-functional. In such watches, a battery cell provides the energy and a quartz crystal functions as the timing device. Electronic watches are available in both analog and digital displays. These days there are innumerable brands of watches available according to choice and budget. You can wear any type of wrist watch you want and always be on time.

6. Describe the young Indian Chess Grandmaster, Gukesh Dommaraju. You can use the following hints to form your answer.

Early Life

- Mention his birthplace and birth date (Gukesh Dommaraju, born in 2006 in Chennai, India).
- Include his early interest in chess and when he started playing the game.

Chess Career

- Highlight his rise in the chess world, particularly his rapid ascent in international tournaments.
- Mention his achievement of becoming the youngest Indian to achieve the title of Grandmaster in 2019 at the age of 12 years and 7 months.

Significant Achievements

- Include key milestones in his career, such as notable tournament wins and his performance in international competitions.
- Talk about his achievements in Chess Olympiads, rapid, and blitz formats.

Style and Strengths

- Discuss his playing style and strategies, known for his aggressive and tactical approach.
- Mention any notable games or victories that have made him stand out.

Ans. Gukesh Dommaraju, born on 29th November, 2006 in Chennai, India, is one of the brightest young talents in the world of chess. He developed an early interest in the game and quickly demonstrated remarkable skill. Gukesh's determination and strategic thinking led him to rise through the ranks at a rapid pace. At the age of 12 years and 7 months, Gukesh achieved the title of Grandmaster in 2019, making him the youngest Indian to do so at that time. This achievement marked a significant milestone in his chess career and catapulted him into the international chess spotlight. His rise in the chess world was fueled by his victories in various tournaments, including strong performances in international events. Known for his aggressive and tactical playing style, Gukesh has earned a reputation for his sharp and precise moves. His games often display a deep understanding of the game. Gukesh's future in chess looks promising, as he continues to compete at the highest levels. His dedication, talent, and ability to thrive under pressure suggest that he is destined for even greater accomplishments in the world of chess.

7. Describe a calculator in your own words.

Ans. Doing mathematical calculations has become easy with the help of a device known as a Calculator. A calculator is, essentially, an electronic device used for doing calculations. These days we have all kinds of calculators in the market. The ordinary calculators perform simple arithmetical operations. Human minds can make error but not calculators. Speed and accuracy are the watchwords of a calculator. This small device looks like a small plastic box. The board contains numbers from 0 to 9 and +, —, x, ÷ marks. The push buttons carrying these numbers and signs are pressed to do the required calculations. Besides simple calculators, there are also sophisticated calculators to perform more complex operations. Moreover, there are scientific calculators too that can perform various scientific functions. So, if you have difficulty in doing math calculations, you know that you need to get a calculator.

8. Write a descriptive paragraph based on the visual clue given below.

Ans. Dr. APJ Abdul Kalam is a famous name in the whole world in several fields. He is among the greatest scientists of the 21st century. Moreover, he was the 11th President of India and served his country to bring about great changes in it. His contributions as a scientist and as a President are beyond comparison. Dr. Kalam's contribution to the ISRO (Indian Space Research Organisation) is so remarkable that it will always be remembered by the nation. He was the one who helped in the development of Agni and Prithvi missiles. For his involvement in the Nuclear Power in India, he was known as 'Missile Man of India'. And due to his contribution to the country, the government awarded him with the highest civilian award.

9. Write a factual description, in not more than 100 words, of a puzzle tht you purchased for yourself recently. **CBSE SQP 2024**

Ans. The puzzle that I recently purchased is a 1000-piece jigsaw puzzle featuring a picturesque beach landscape. The puzzle measures 26 by 20 inches when finished and comes in a sturdy cardboard box with a fully coloured reference image. The pieces are made of high-quality, durable cardboard, ensuring a satisfying puzzle-solving experience. The design showcases a beautiful sunset, palm trees and a mighty blue sea. Each puzzle piece has intricate details and vibrant colours having varying shapes and patterns.

10. Write a descriptive paragraph on the teacher of your favourite subject in school using the clues given below in 80-100 words.

Name of the teacher - Name of the subject - Their innovative teaching methods - Their qualities that appeal to you the most etc.

Ans. My favourite subject in school is History and Mrs. Patil, the History teacher, is awesome. She makes history exciting by telling stories with so much energy and passion that the boring history becomes very interesting. When she talks about events from the past, it feels like we're actually there. Her class is like a fun adventure through time. Being in her class is like going on a cool journey to the past that you never want to end. One of the coolest things is when she taught us about the Maratha empire. Mrs. Patil explained the different aspects so well, describing the battles and leaders in a way that made it all easy to understand. She even added interesting details that we would never find in the textbooks. She always teaches us that it is important to be aware of our past so that we won't make the same mistakes in the future.

11. Describe something that you have but you no longer use.

Ans. If life has taught us anything, it is that we should all be comfortable with the fact that everything in life is pretty much expendable at some point whether we like it or not. One such 'expendable' item which I held so dear to my heart once but sadly don't use anymore is my camera. I bought my popular branded and expensive camera about 10 years ago with the money which my late grandfather gave me as some 'gift'. The black colored small pocket fit Nikon camera has all the important features that a camera prevalent at that time had. It had a small SD card slot, a button and a charging point beside the huge lens. My camera was my best buddy and I carried it everywhere. However, now it has been replaced by my phone.

12. Write a descriptive paragraph about your favourite cartoon character based on the hints given below.

Name of the character - description - qualities - what you like the most about it.

Ans. I like to watch cartoons and there are many cartoon characters I like. Some of them are Tom, Doraemon, Mickey Mouse, etc. However, the cartoon character that I like the most is Jerry. Jerry is a mouse that appears in my favourite cartoon show, Tom and Jerry. Jerry is portrayed in the cartoon series as a small mouse which is brown in colour. Tom is much bigger than Jerry and is always after it. This is so because Jerry has a habit of teasing Tom. Jerry plays a lot of pranks on Tom and is not fearful of the big-sized cat at all. It is a lot of fun watching both of them running after each other. It seems obvious to viewers that Tom would be able to get a hold of Jerry but that doesn't happen. It is the prankster Jerry that wins in the end and steals the show. I enjoy this show so much and am always in awe of Jerry.

13. Describe an object/category of objects whose invention that you think is useful to people.

Ans. The invention of the automobile was one of the greatest inventions in the world. This invention has helped change society and enhanced people's lifestyle to a great extent. In fact, without the support of the automobile, it is impossible to travel. An automobile is essentially a transportation device that takes people or things from one place to another with the help of machines. Since the invention, the automobile has been playing an important role for all classes of people. Distance is no longer a barrier for people now. They can move from one place to another within a short time. Before the invention of the automobile, people had to travel on feet and it took a long time to reach their destinations. However now, they can reach their intended places smoothly and accomplish their respective tasks safely. At present, automobiles have become cheaper and they are manufactured in various countries of the world.

14. Write a descriptive paragraph based on the information given below.

- **Bama** Born 1958, creative Tamil, woman writer, committed teacher, social activist-popularly known as Karukku Bama.
- **Penname** Faustina Mary Fatima Rani.
- **Novels** Karukku, Sangati and Vanman-translated into other Indian languages, English and French.
- Wrote twenty short stories not published in book form.
- Honorary Doctorate Degree, Crossword Award for her semi-fictional autobiography Karukku.
- Invited by universities in India and abroad, lectures at various conferences.
- Multi-faceted personality woman with extraordinary courage, conviction, resistance to any form of oppression.
- Keen eye for beauty in nature, profound insight into issues pertaining to caste, religion, women.
- Clear thoughts and expression
- Dedicated to the upliftment of the downtrodden, passion-teaching, mission, building a casteless society.

Ans. Bama, popularly known as Karukku Bama, was born in 1958. She is a Tamilian woman writer, a committed teacher and a social activist. She goes by the penname Faustina Mary Fatima Rani. She is a prolific writer whose works include *Karukku*, *Sangati* and *Vanman*. These works have been translated into other Indian languages, English and French. She had also written twenty short stories which have not been published in the book form. She holds an honorary doctorate degree and has won the Crossword Award for her semi-fictional autobiography Karukku. She is regularly invited by Indian and foreign universities to lecture at various conferences. Bama is a multi-faceted personality and is a woman with extraordinary courage, conviction and resistance to any form of oppression. She has a keen eye for beauty in nature and shows profound insight into issues pertaining to caste, religion and women. She has a clarity in thoughts and expression. She is dedicated to the upliftment of the downtrodden, is passionate about teaching and her mission is to build a casteless society.

15. Describe a jewellery, fashion or cosmetic item you often use.

Ans. I am not like many girls who like to wear jewellery item almost always. In fact, I have only 2-3 jewellery items that I own and I do not always use all of them. The fashion bracelet made of gold and diamond is the only jewellery item that I often use. I use it almost every day except the days when I stay home or go out for swimming. I love the gold and diamond made bracelet because of its beautiful design. I find it fashionable, handy and easy to wear. This piece of jewellery is also very precious to me as it was a gift from my mother on my 15th birthday. At that time, I noticed that it was the most expensive gift I had ever gotten and the design and my mum's affection were both important to me. This was the first time I got somehow inspired and motivated to wear a jewellery item.

16. Write a descriptive paragraph on your role model based on the clues given below.

Name of the role model - why do you admire him/her- his/ her qualities that appeal to you the most - his/ her, traits, achievements, etc.

Ans. My father is my role model. He is the person I admire the most in my life. It is because he is a very hardworking and down-to-earth person. Although he was born in a very poor family, he defied all odds and became an engineer through his sheer hard work and will power. It is due-to-his efforts that I am able to live a comfortable life. He never boasts of his success and keeps working hard. The other quality that I like about him is that he treats everyone with respect, be it his superiors or subordinates, young or old, rich or poor. He is also calm and composed in times of difficulties and never gets bobbed down due to them. He is not only a father but also a friend to me. It is he who I consult first whenever I need any help or suggestion in my life. I believe in living life to his ideal which is 'Simple living and high thinking'.

17. Write a factual description, in not more than 100 words, of a potted plant that you and your sibling recently chose, to gift your parent. CBSE SQP 2023

Ans. We recently chose a potted plant called the Hibiscus as a gift for our mother for Mother's Day. The small plant in the elephant shaped mud pot looked very cute and enchanting. The plant itself was a small shrub with a height of about 1.5 feet. The leaves looked dark green and shiny, and had a slightly serrated edge. The plant had several buds and appeared to be healthy with one large, fully blossomed deep-red flower which had five petals and a prominent central stamen. The plant came in a small clay pot with a diameter of about 10 inches. It had a simple yellow and red abstract design that complemented the plant well. The soil in the pot looked moist and well-draining along with being enriched with organic matter.

18. Write a description of the most interesting person you have ever met. Competency Based

Ans. Every day we have a chance to meet and be with people. There are some that leave an impact on our hearts. It may be the way they carry themselves, the way they talk, their smile, the stories they share, how we see them with others or the kindness they have shown us that make them stay in our minds and hearts even long after we've seen them. There is one person who I feel is the most interesting person I have ever met. This person takes everyday as it comes and looks forward to each day with positivity and a lot of joy. The enthusiasm of this person is effortless and his sense of humor is amazing. He also possesses the ability to take decisions fast and efficiently. Apart from being so smart and interesting, this person is humble. Sure the person I am talking about is not completely perfect and does have some flaws but overall it is a lot of fun to talk and interact with him. I always appreciate the way this person looks at most situations and also has an opinion that I value.

19. Describe a photograph you have taken yourself.

Ans. To tell the truth, I have taken many pictures in my life, both randomly as well as on special occasions. However, none of those pictures really stands out as great as the one which I took 4 years ago. This picture portrays the serene nature of the rural life and ingenuine smile of a mother who was looking at her 2-year-old daughter. I submitted this photo in a competition organised by a magazine and won the second prize. The photograph I am talking about shows green paddy fields and a clear blue sky in the background. The main subject of the photograph was a young mother who was looking at her daughter and was smiling. Among other things, a flying eagle, two other women and a large green tree were visible in the photograph. I took the photograph when I went to one of my friends' hometown. It was actually a semester break and we wanted to enjoy our vacation in a remote and beautiful location. We stayed there for about 5 days and had a great experience in this beautiful place. I had my camera with me and whenever I found something worth capturing, I took the photo. When I took the photo, I knew that it was going to be a great scene and moment to capture in a frame.

20. Write a descriptive paragraph on Droupadi Murmu based on the information given below

- Former Cabinet Minister of Odisha and Governor of Jharkhand.
- Born into a humble family based in the remote village of Mayurbhanj, Odisha.
- Assistant teacher and a junior assistant in the Odisha State Irrigation Department.
- Started her political journey with the BJP in 1997.
- Worked as a councillor in Rairangpur.
- Worked as the President of the scheduled Tribe Morcha of the BJP Odisha unit.
- Elected twice to Odisha State Legislative Assembly.
- Felicitated with the best legislative member award.
- Personal life full of struggle and tragedy.
- Lost her husband and two grown-up sons.
- Created history as she became the first women Governor of Jharkhand, the first Tribal Governor of a tribal state, and the first Odisha-born woman to be a Governor.

Ans. Droupadi Murmu is the 15th and current President of India. She is also the former Cabinet Minister of Odisha and Governor of Jharkhand. She was born into a humble family based in the remote village of Mayurbhanj, a tribal district of Odisha. She had worked as an assistant teacher and a junior assistant in the Odisha State Irrigation Department. Murmu started her political journey with the BJP in 1997 and worked as a councillor in Rairangpur. She has also worked as the President of the Scheduled Tribe Morcha of the BJP Odisha unit before being elected twice to Odisha state legislative assembly on the BJP ticket where she was felicitated with the best legislative member award. Though her personal life remained full of struggle and tragedy, Murmu touched the pinnacle of public life and achieved monumental records in politics and social services. She lost her husband and two grown-up sons, but she stood strong on all occasions. Murmu created history as she became the First Women Governor of Jharkhand, the first Tribal Governor of a tribal state, and the first Odisha-born woman to be a Governor.

21. Describe a handcrafted item which you made yourself.

Ans. Kite flying is a popular activity in India and I have made different types of kites on various occasions all by myself. During the kite flying festival, many people, especially children play around with a variety of kites. On such an occasion, I made a kite which was more than 4 feet in length and looked like a red dragon. This sort of kite is usually called 'dragon kite' and it is quite tough to make and fly. It took me more than 4 days to complete this kite and I was required to purchase some special papers, colour, plastic, glue, ribbon and sticks for it. I was quite happy to see the final outcome and was convinced that it would fly without any obstacle. The wings of the dragon were more than 1 feet each and I had to be very careful while making it. Any wrong shape of the wing would actually ruin the whole project. I had to make it strong while keeping it light. That was a tough challenge but luckily I was quite successful in making the final kite.

22. Write a description of the great table master Zakhir Husaain. You can look at his image and other hints given below to form your answer.

Ans. Zakir Hussain, born on 9th March, 1951, in Mumbai, India, is one of the world's most renowned tabla Masters the world had ever seen. He hails from a family with a deep musical legacy, as his father was a legendary tabla maestro. Growing up in this environment, Zakir developed a passion for music at an early age and began his formal training. Zakir's unique playing style, which blends traditional Indian classical rhythms with innovative techniques, soon gained him recognition in India and abroad. His collaborations with some of the greatest musicians helped him gain international fame. His fusion of Indian classical music with jazz, world music, and other genres set him apart as a versatile and innovative artist. Throughout his illustrious career, Zakir has received numerous accolades, including the Padma Shri (1988), Padma Bhushan (2002), and Grammy Awards, underscoring his global recognition and impact on the world of music. In addition to his performance career, Zakir Hussain is a dedicated educator and philanthropist. He established the Zakir Hussain Foundation, which supports various musical and cultural initiatives, and works to preserve and promote Indian classical music for future generations. Zakir's ability to bridge the gap between traditional Indian music and global sounds has made him a cultural ambassador for India.

ASSESSMENT EXERCISE

1. Write a descriptive paragraph on a social figure you admire the most based on the clues given below.
   Name of personality - physical features - birth place/ date - reason for being famous - his/ her struggles - major achievements - qualities that you admire most about him/her.
2. Write a descriptive paragraph based on the visual clue given below (100 words).

3. Write a descriptive paragraph on Mother Teresa based on the clues given below.
   Founder of Missionaries of Charity - Albanian - Indian Roman Catholic Nun - received several awards including Nobel Peace Prize - admired for her charitable work.
4. Write a brief description of your grandfather.
5. Your school has a new Principal. Write a brief description of your new Principal.
6. Write a description of one of your classmates.
7. Write a description of an object found in your school bag.
8. Describe the most useful appliance in your household.
9. Describe an indoor board game that you enjoyed as a child.
10. Describe an item you would buy if you receive a large amount of money.

Formal Letters

CHAPTER 3

Letter writing is an essential skill. In spite of the prevalence of e-mail and text messages, letters are still one of the most important and popular means of communication. Commerce, trade, official correspondence, public representation, complaints and other dealings, transactions and communication with people are still conducted through letters.

Types of Formal Letters

In CBSE English Communicative Class X exams, questions from only formal letters are asked. They can be of 7 marks.

Formal letters can be broadly classified into many types. Some of are types from which questions are generally asked

1. **Complaint Letters** As the name suggests, these letters are written to lodge a complaint. They can be addressed to a public/private company or organisation.
2. **Enquiry Letters** These letters are written when a person wants to get more information about a product or service or to obtain a quotation for purchasing a product or service. These letters are the most common form of formal letters.
3. **Letters to the Editor** These letters are usually written on a topic of general concern and to influence public opinion. They may include suggestions on an issue concerning public interests, complaints or requests.
4. **Application Writing** These letters are usually written to school authorities like the Principal, Coach, Librarian to request for something.

Steps to Write a Letter

To write an effective Formal Letter, one must follow the correct format and the steps given below

1. **Sender's Address** Make sure that the sender's address is clear and precise. It is written at the top on the left hand corner of the page.

   e.g. 2334/31, Mangal Pandey Nagar
   Ekta Park
   Meerut-250002

   While writing the address, one must **NOT** put a comma at the end of each line.
2. **Date and Receiver's Address** While writing date, always remember the day is written in figures, month in words and year in full figures. The date on which the letter is written, followed by the receiver's address which comprises the receiver's name/designation and the complete address.

   e.g. 12th December, 20XX
   The Editor
   The Times of India
   Daryaganj
   Delhi-110002
3. **Subject** One of the most important parts of a formal letter is the subject. One must ensure that the subject expresses the main theme or crux of the letter clearly. It must be as brief as possible.

   e.g. Non-receipt of magazines

4. **Salutation** The salutation is a greeting to whom the letter is addressed. It depends on the relation and degree of intimacy between the writer and the addressee in personal letters. However, in official letters, we may use Sir/Madam or Respected Sir/Ma'am, keeping in mind the gender if specified in the question.
5. **Body of the Letter** The body of the letter is the part which contains all the information the writer (you) wants to convey. For this, start with introducing the purpose of writing. Then build up the topic.

   The body includes three main parts. It should be
   (i) **Introductory Paragraph/Sentence** States the purpose of writing.
   (ii) **Informative Paragraph** Gives details of the problem, cause, effect, possible solution, etc.
   (iii) **Concluding Paragraph/Sentence** States your hope, comment, request, suggestion, etc.
6. **Complimentary Close** This is a courteous way of ending a letter.

   For this, we write – Yours sincerely/Yours faithfully/Yours truly.

   The first letter of the second word (here 's', 'f,' 't') is never written in capital letter.
7. **Sender/Signature** Just below the complimentary close, sender's name is written as a mark of signing off. If applicable, the sender's designation may be added in brackets.

Note It Always leave one line space after writing the sender's address, date, receiver's address, subject and salutation.

Points to be Kept in Mind

- Answer the following questions while drafting the letter
  — Who are you writing to?
  — What is the reason for writing the letter?
  — What do you expect as the result of writing this letter?
- The subject line should match what is asked in the question.
- Get right to the purpose of the letter in polite and formal language. It should focus on the desired topic.
- Be clear, concise and to the point. Stick to the word limit of 120 words.
- Use simple language so that the letter is easy to understand.

Format of Formal Letters

You are Gunjan, a resident of Delhi. You are a subscriber of a weekly magazine named Outlook. Lately, you have not been receiving the copies of the magazine on a regular basis. Write a letter to the Circulation Manager, Education Tunes regarding the non-receipt of copies. (120 Words)

Sender's address	WZ-1263, XYZ New Delhi-110088
Date	20th May, 20XX
Receiver's name/rank and his/her address	The Circulation Manager Education Times New Delhi-110024
Subject	**Subject** Non-Receipt of Copies of Education Times Magazine
Salutation	Sir/Ma'am
Body of the letter	This is to inform you that I am a subscriber of Education Times with subscription no. 120124. Unfortunately, I have not been receiving copies of the magazine on a regular basis since the past few weeks. At times, the copies do not arrive on time or are not delivered at all. I have also called your helpline number but the issue has not been fixed. I would appreciate if you could look into the issue and make sure that I get the copies on time. Looking forward to your speedy action.
Subscription/ Complimentary close and Signature	Thanking you Yours sincerely Gunjan (A subscriber)

SOLVED EXAMPLES

Letters of Complaint

These letters are written to complaint against a defective product or poor service. Such a letter is addressed to the relevant person of the company/organisation/dealer/service provider. These letters include

- Details of the product / service
- Nature of the complaint
- Payment information like bill/cash memo number
- Date and place of purchase/service
- Model number (if applicable)
- Names of associated persons from supplier side (if applicable)
- Compensation or corrective action required, and
- Any other details necessary for resolving the complaint.

1. You had bought a mobile phone from a reputed showroom in Mumbai but after a month it developed a serious fault. Write a complaint letter to the Manager of the showroom asking for immediate replacement of the same. You are Sadiq/Razia, 123, South TT Nagar, Bhopal. (120 words).

Ans. 123, South TT Nagar
Bhopal - 462003

17th November, 20XX

The Manager
Multimedia Stores
345/ 7, Dr Bhadkamkar Marg
Mumbai - 400004

Subject Apple iPhone defective within warranty period

Sir/Ma'am

This is to inform you that, I had bought an Apple iPhone7 Sr No. 7778906 from your showroom on 16th October, 20XX. The Cash Memo number is MS/456/ 17-18. Unfortunately, the phone stopped working yesterday, which is very surprising for such a high quality product. It has not been damaged in any way and seems to be faulty.

Therefore, I request you to inform me the action to be taken for free replacement of this phone. You are welcome to contact me on mobile no. 98765XXXXX for any clarification.

Thanking you
Yours faithfully

Sadiq

2. Write a letter to the Director of the Archaeological Survey of India complaining about the damage caused to a historical monument in your city due to negligence in 120 words. **Competency Based**

Ans. 36, JL Nehru Road
Kolkata-700017

13th July, 20XX

The Director
Archaeological Survey of India
Kolkata - 700001

Subject Damage caused to monument

Sir/Ma'am

Through the medium of this letter I wish to bring to your notice the deplorable condition of the Victoria Memorial Monument and the grounds surrounding it.

Being old, the monument is in constant need of repairs, which are not being carried out periodically or when required. This should be arranged by your office as the Government of India has authorised you for this purpose.

Further, the grounds are littered with plastic bottles, paper scraps and polythene bags thrown by visitors, much to the disgust of foreign tourists. This monument is of prime importance to the history of our country and it is about time the civic authorities should realise this fact.

Hence, it is time that you step up and make sure that the monument is well maintained and repaired. Necessary repairs should be carried out to the interiors as well as exteriors of the monument. Security personnel should be increased to prevent littering of the grounds. If these measures are carried out, I am sure the Victoria Memorial will regain its lost glory.

Thanking you
Yours faithfully

Sonali Basu

3. You are Vinay Khosla, the Purchase Executive at Haven Book Store in Secunderabad, Andhra Pradesh. You had a telephonic discussion with a sales executive from Prakashan Book House, the wholesalers. The conversation pertained to the delivery of books, stationery, and art materials for your store. Despite the conversation, there has been no response from the Prakashan Book House, and attempts to contact them through the provided phone number have been unsuccessful. Write a complaint letter, in about 120 words, to the proprietor of Prakashan Book House, 60, Haveli Market Street, Hyderabad, A.P. **CBSE 2024 C**

Ans. The Haven Book Store
231, Gulmarg Bazaar
Secunderabad, A.P.

16th November, 20XX

The Proprietor M/s Prakashan Book House
(Wholesalers)
60, Haveli Market Street
Hyderabad, A.P.

Subject Unresolved issue with follow-up of delivery details

Sir/Ma'am

This is with reference to our previous conversation *via* telephone on 14th November, 20XX regarding to an order to be placed with your store for books, stationery, and art materials. I had a telephonic conversation with one of your sales executives, Khushi Sodhi, regarding the delivery schedule where we were told that we would be informed about the delivery soon. However, we have not received any updates or communication from your end. Attempts to contact your office using the listed telephone number have been unsuccessful, as the calls are not going through. This lack of communication and the absence of follow-up from your end have caused significant disruptions in our planned operations' schedule.

Therefore, I kindly request your prompt attention to this matter. Given the importance of our business relationship, we hope to resolve this issue amicably. Please feel free to reach out to me. Hoping for an early response.

Thanking you
Yours sincerely

Vinay Khosla
(Purchase Executive, Haven Book Store)

Letters of Enquiry

A letter of enquiry is written to ask for more information concerning a product, service or other information about a product or service. These letters are often written in response to an advertisement that we have seen in the paper, a magazine or on TV. In these letters, we include

- Place from where you found about the product or service
- The facility/product/service required
- Nature of the information required – this may be a quotation, a brochure or fare details, etc.
- Payment terms like credit
- Any other details required.

1. You are Samrat, a student of Class X and a resident of Mumbai. You are interested in learning French in your summer vacations. Write a letter to the Director of Language Learning Institute, Colaba, Mumbai, asking him about the various courses offered by the institute during the summers. (120 words)

Ans. A-46, Marine Drive
Mumbai - 400020

10th April, 20XX

The Director
Language Learning Institute
Colaba, Mumbai - 400005

Subject Query regarding French Classes in summer vacations

Sir/Ma'am

This is to inform you that I am a student of Class X residing in South Mumbai. I am interested in learning French during my summer vacations starting from 25th April. I would like to start with a beginner's course offered by you during the months of April-June.

Kindly send me the detailed information, fees applicable and any other relevant information. I would also like to have the brochure of your institute. You can send the information and brochure by post or at my email address samrat97@gmail.com. Also, kindly inform me the addresses and phone numbers of your branches in the Western and Eastern suburbs of Mumbai as many of my friends residing in those areas of the city want to learn French.

I look forward to your early response.

Thanking you
Yours sincerely

Samrat

2. You are Rajat Kumar, a resident of 79, Sector 4, RK Puram, New Delhi. You are interested in joining the course in Communication Skills advertised by the Elite School of Language, South Extension - II. Write a letter of enquiry for the same. (120 words)

Ans. 79, Sector 4, RK Puram
New Delhi - 110045

12th August, 20XX

The Director
Elite School of Language
South Extension - II
New Delhi - 110048

Subject Enquiry regarding Course on Communication Skills

Sir/Ma'am

This is with reference to an advertisement in 'The Times of India' dated 10th August, 20XX announcing the new course in communication skills that you have introduced. I have passed Class XII and plan to take up a part-time job as a Customer Care Executive in a reputed call centre. For this, I shall need to improve my communication skills and would appreciate it if you could forward me the details of the course.

Please let me know the duration of the course for beginners and the advanced course as well as the fees charged for both courses. I would like to know if they are diploma or certificate courses. Kindly furnish the details at the address mentioned above as early as possible, so that I can decide about enrolling myself in one of them.

Thanking you

Yours truly

Rajat Kumar

3. You are Sudhir/Sita, the Head Boy/Girl of ABC Public School, Jayanagar, Bengaluru. Your school has planned an overnight excursion of students and teachers to Mysuru and nearby areas. Write a letter to the Secretary, Ace Youth Hostel, Mysuru requesting him to send you a quotation for the costs of providing accommodation for 15 girls, 20 boys and two teachers for two days next month. Specify the dates when you want the accommodation and any other terms and conditions. (120 words)

Ans. ABC Public School
Jayanagar, Bengaluru - 560070

23rd October, 20XX

The Secretary
Ace Youth Hostel
Mysuru - 570001

Subject Accommodation required for Student Group on 10th and 11th November, 20XX

Sir/Ma'am

This is with reference to a poster advertisement placed outside XYZ regarding your hostel facilites. Our school is sponsoring an overnight excursion of senior students to visit Mysuru and nearby areas on 10th and 11th November, 20X

X. The group consists of 15 girls and 20 boys accompanied by two teachers. They will require overnight accommodation on the night of 10th November in Mysuru. The group will stay for two days, departing by 5 PM on the 11th November. Two dormitories (bedroom) will be required for the students, one for girls and one for boys. The teachers will require separate single rooms.

Hence, I request you to book the required accomodations for 10th and 11th November. If you require any further information, you may contact the undersigned on phone no. 97456XXXXX.

I hope I would get an early response.

Thanking you

Yours sincerely

Sudhir (Head Boy)

Letters to the Editor

These letters are written to the editor of a leading magazine or newspapers so that he/she may publish it. The purpose of these letters is to grab the reader's attention towards a social issue. These letters should

- Explain what the letter is about at the start.
- Explain why the issue is important.
- Give evidence of any praise or criticism.
- State the writer's opinion about what should be done.
- Any other details required for supporting the stand taken by the writer of the letter.

1. You are Arif/Amina. You recently visited Hyderabad and were captivated with the various heritage sites like the Golconda Fort, Tortoise Rock, etc. You may use ideas from Unit 4 - Environment, along with your ideas to write a letter to the Editor, in not more than 120 words, highlighting the threatening factors and suggesting ways of preserving the geological heritage. CBSE 2024 C

Ans. XYZ Apartments
New Delhi-110081

23rd October, 20XX

The Editor
The Times of India
New Delhi

Subject Preserving the geological heritage of Hyderabad

Sir/Ma'am

Through the columns of your esteemed newspaper, I wish to draw the attention of the concerned authorities towards the factors threatening the geological heritage of Hyderabad and ways of preserving them.

Hyderabad, the capital of the Indian state of Telangana, is a city that beautifully combines a rich historical narrative with a rapidly burgeoning cosmopolitan landscape. While Hyderabad is recognized for its cultural heritage, food, and technological advancements, it is also home to an invaluable geological heritage that includes unique rock formations, ancient mineral sites, and diverse soil types. Unfortunately, this geological wealth is threatened by a variety of factors, including urbanisation, industrialisation and climate change. Another significant threat to Hyderabad's geological heritage is the general negligence and lack of awareness among the public and policymakers alike.

Preserving this geological heritage is crucial not only for scientific research and education but also for maintaining the city's identity and ecological balance. Addressing the threats to Hyderabad's geological heritage requires a multifaceted approach that combines legislative action, community engagement, and education.

It is essential for the government to establish protective measures for key geological sites. Implementing guidelines that identify and protect geological heritage within urban development proposals can strike a balance between progress and conservation. Local communities should be actively involved in conservation efforts. We need to remember that a concerted effort today will ensure that the geological heritage of Hyderabad remains an enduring legacy, enriching the lives of its residents and the broader scientific community.

Thanking you
Yours truly

ABC

2. Many students from different parts of the country come to Delhi to study. Finding affordable accommodation is the main problem faced by them. Landlords charge exorbitant rents and in some cases refuse to rent rooms to them because of their different food habits and culture. The hostel facility provided by educational institutions is too inadequate to meet the demand. Write a letter in 120 words to the editor of a local daily drawing attention of the authorities and requesting them to take appropriate action. You are Raman/Raveena, 12, Station Road, Delhi.

Ans. 12, Station Road
New Delhi - 110054

25th July, 20XX

The Editor
The Times of India
New Delhi

Subject Inadequate hostel facility for students

Sir/Ma'am

Through the columns of your esteemed newspaper, I want to draw the attention of the concerned authorities towards the problem of inadequate hostel accommodation for college and university students who come from all over India to study in the various educational institutions and universities in Delhi. The hostel facility provided by educational institutions in Delhi is too inadequate to meet the rising demands. Consequently, many students have to hire private accommodation near to their place of study. As a result, landlords charge exorbitant rents and sometimes, even refuse to rent to students because of their different food habits and culture. Thus, these students face a serious accommodation problem, which interferes with their studies.

It is suggested that the educational authorities should provide more hostel accommodations in or near colleges and universities. Wherever possible, independent student hostels must be constructed near educational institutions to solve this problem. I hope that the concerned authorities will take speedy action on these suggestions.

Thanking you
Yours truly

Raveena

3. You are Sahil/Sahira, resident of 12, Mall Road, Kanpur. You recently visited an orphanage and saw many children living in poor conditions. You feel sympathy for them. They should get good food, healthy living conditions and proper education. Write a letter to the editor of a national daily requesting the authorities to take proper care of these helpless children. **CBSE 2020**

Ans. 12, Mall Road
Kanpur
14th November, 20XX

The Editor
The Times of India
New Delhi

Subject The Miserable Conditions of Children living in the Orphanages

Sir/Ma'am

Through the columns of your esteemed newspaper, I would like to draw the attention of the concerned authorities towards the disheartening condition of many orphanages today.

Recently, I went to ABC orphanage and the condition of the children was very miserable. They lack even the basic of necessities for healthy living like clean, hygienic and nutritious food, decent clothing and good education. I felt very sympathetic towards these innocent children who are already lacking parental love and affection. That cannot be compensated but they have every right to the necessities.
From what I understand, the orphanage gets good donations but it is not reaching the children due to inefficient management. Through your newspaper, I request the concerned authorities to take care of the children. They deserve better!

Thanking you
Yours sincerely

Sahira
Concerned citizen

Application Writing

We write letter to authority figures in school for various purposes. These include

- fee concession
- change of subject
- leave application
- addition of some facility, etc.

1. Write an application to the Principal of your school requesting him to make your library, which is dead, active in 120 words.

Ans. The Principal
XYZ School
Bahraich, UP

18th October, 20XX

Subject Providing Facility of Library

Sir/Ma'am

This is to inform you that we, the students of class X, have written this letter to request you to construct a library in our school premises. All of us want to read some other books apart from those we have in our curriculum. This will enhance our knowledge and will help in developing a good habit of reading. If we have this facility in our school, we can get books issued and read them at home in our leisure time. We will be very much grateful to you if you kindly consider our request.

Thanking you
Yours obediently

Students
Class X

2. Write an application to the Principal of your school requesting a fee concession. (120 words)

Ans. The Principal
PQR School
Delhi

22nd March, 20XX

Subject Application for Fee Concession

Sir/Ma'am

This is to inform you that I, Pankaj Soni, am a student of your prestigious school. I have written this letter to request you for a full fee concession so that I can continue my studies further.

I would like to inform you that I belong to a weaker section of the society. Thus, it becomes quite difficult for me to afford the tuition fees along with the study material. I had joined the institution earlier on a

2-year complete scholarship offered by the XYZ NGO. Now that I still have a year for graduation, I would be forever grateful if I get the concession. I would like to mention here that I am a good student and have always scored high percentage of marks in all subjects. I am a very hardworking and dedicated student. All the teachers appreciate me.

Therefore, I request you to kindly waive the fees and grant me the scholarship. I am sure you will find me the most deserving. I am confident you would certainly be kind enough to grant me the scholarship. I will be thankful to you. Hoping for a positive response.

Yours obediently

Pankaj Soni
(Student)

3. Write an application to the librarian of your college informing him that you have lost the book issued to you last week. (120 words)

Ans. The Librarian
ABC School
Kanpur, UP

12th December, 20XX

Subject Information about Loss of the Issued Book

Respected Sir/Ma'am

This is to inform you that I, XYZ, am a student of Class X D of your school. I have written this letter to tell you that I got a book issued from the library last week and it was to be returned tomorrow on 13th December. However, unfortunately I had lost the book. Hence, I apologise for the inconvenience.

I also request you to kindly let me know the price of the book so that I may make the payment to compensate it.

Thanking you

Yours obediently

XYZ

Letters Based on MCB Themes

MCB Theme 1 Health and Medicine

School students should study topics relating to health and medicine for several reasons. This area provides diverse career opportunities for them in future, enables them to work with people and help to make people happier. Health and medicine is a globally recognised field because there is a great need for good doctors and surgeons. Important factors that contribute to the health and wellness of individuals include, besides others, the following.

- Adequate and regular hours of sleep
- Humour and laughter
- A healthy diet to avoid obesity
- Adequate exercise, sports and games
- Use of natural and herbal medicines.

Solved Examples

1. You are a Sports Scout. Write a letter to the Governor of your region, drawing attention to the need for creating and upgrading sport facilities and practices to enable the local/indigenous sporting talent from your city to hone their skills. Include specific recommendations. Write the letter in not more than 120 words. **CBSE SQP 2023**

Ans. 12-A/F, Vaikunth Towers
Wagheilly, J.P.

17th August, 20XX

The Governor
Bharat Ghar
Ludnaam, J.P.

Subject Requirement of Sports Facilities to promote Local Talent

Sir/Ma'am

This is to draw your attention to the pressing need for creating and upgrading sports facilities in our region to support the development of local and indigenous sporting talent. Areas like Wagheilly have a vast pool of untapped sports talent and there is a pressing need to provide them with the necessary infrastructure to help them hone their skills.

As an experienced sports scout, I can vouch for the fact that facilities like multi-purpose indoor sports complexes, outdoor sports fields and running tracks with proper maintenance and lighting facilities are needed. Access to training and fitness centres and physiotherapy clinics, scholarships, mentorship programmes and tournaments can also promote talent and offer opportunities to local athletes to showcase their skills and earn recognition.

By investing in sports and promoting local talent, we can create a culture of excellence and inspire the youth to take up sports as a carrer. I hope that my suggestions would be taken into consideration and would add towards helping create a city that promotes sports and the growth of local and indigenous sporting talent.

Thanking you
Yours sincerely

XYZ
Sports Scout

2. You have observed that modern lifestyles in cities have made people follow the principle 'late to sleep and late to rise' instead of the other way round. As you understand the harm to a person's health due to this, write a letter to the Editor of a national daily making people aware of the problems that arise. Use ideas from the MCB unit on 'Health and Medicine' and your own ideas. You are Fazal/ Farzana of 106, Station Road, Kandivli West, Mumbai. *(120 Words)*

Ans. 106, Station Road, Kandivli West
Mumbai - 400067

13th January, 20XX

The Editor

The Indian Express
Mumbai - 400020

Subject Adequate Sleep Necessary for Good health

Sir/Ma'am

Through the columns of your esteemed newspaper, I wish to make everyone aware of the harm that lack of sleep can cause to our health. Adequate sleep on a regular basis is key to maintaining good health. Without it, we become susceptible to a variety of health problems including heart disease, obesity, diabetes, stroke, depression, etc.

Most adults require 7 to 8 hours of sleep every day. It is well known that even if we eat well and take adequate exercise, our immune system can get compromised if we do not sleep enough. Health watchers in many countries have reported that there is a higher rate of heart failure among people with sleep disorders and sleep disturbances.

However, even with the knowledge of the importance of sleep, we do not sleep properly. In our modern lives, our motto has changed to 'late to sleep and late to rise'. Hence, people today suffer from many lifestyle diseases.

Thus, it is suggested that people ensure that they get adequate sleep regularly to enjoy continued good health.

Thanking you
Yours sincerely

Farzana

3. Outdoor gyms installed by the D.D.A. in its parks have become very popular among the people. You are Sohan, a resident of Gopal Nagar. You want that an outdoor gym should also be installed in your area. However, repeated written requests to the authorities have not yielded a positive response. Write a letter in 100-120 words to the Editor, The Daily Times, drawing attention of the authorities to your request. **CBSE 2019**

Ans. Gopal Nagar
City PQR

7th June, 20XX

The Editor
The Daily Times
Gopal Nagar Office
City PQR

Subject Need of an Outdoor Gym at Gopal Nagar

Sir/Ma'am

Through the columns of your esteemed newspaper, I would like to draw the attention of the concerned authorities to the lack of an outdoor gym in Gopal Nagar.

In the recent years with increasing cases of lifestyle diseases as well as focus on physical exercises, the D.D.A. came with an innovative solution and named it Outdoor gyms. These outdoor gyms installed by the D.D.A. in its parks have become very popular among the people. It has been observed that people love to go to the parks where outdoor gyms have been installed. With much needed exercise in these parks, it has been noticed that the health of people has improved. Children have been benefitted the most. Now they go out, leaving TV and mobile aside. This is extremely beneficial for them.

Keeping the success of these gyms in mind, I also wished for this gym to be installed at Gopal Nagar Park. I have written many letters to the concerned authorities but no action has been taken yet. Through the medium of your esteemed daily I appeal to the authorities to do the same at the earliest.

Thanking you

Yours truly

Sohan

Resident of Gopal Nagar

MCB Theme 2 Education

In the present day world, education is vital because it gives people the knowledge and skills they require. Children require education to learn how to speak and to write. Students in higher education require knowledge in order to gain valuable information regarding what they are studying. Managers in companies require education to improve their decision making and adaptation skills to the changing environment. People cannot say that they do not need any further education no matter how smart they are, because there is always something new to learn.

Solved Examples

1. Vocational Education prepares learners for jobs that are based on manual or practical activities. Taking ideas from the unit 'Education', along with your own ideas, write a letter to the editor of a newspaper in about 120 words, providing information to the students about the growing need of Vocational Education in the present day world. **CBSE 2024**

Ans. R-4, RK Puram

New Delhi, 110052

10th May, 20XX

The Editor

The Times of India

New Delhi

Subject Importance of Vocational Education

Sir/Ma'am

Through the columns of your esteemed newspaper, I would like to draw the attention of today's youth towards a growing need and demand for vocational education.

Vocational Education involves a blend of practical skills and knowledge necessary to perform specific jobs or trades. It often focuses on hands-on training and real-world experiences, which are essential for many professions. Vocational education enhances employability by equipping individuals with job-specific skills that are in demand in the workforce. It helps individuals explore and pursue careers in fields such as healthcare, construction, automotive technology, information technology, culinary arts, and many others. Employers often prefer candidates who have received vocational training because they are ready to contribute to the workplace from day one. Therefore, choosing to learn some skills and vocations will help a person be ready for a job and be an asset for the country.

Hence, I would like to encourage today's youth to explore vocational education and learn some skills which would prove helpful for their career.

Thanking you

Yours truly

XYZ

2. Write a letter to the librarian, City Library, in not more than 120 words, for purchase and addition of popular fiction and non-fiction titles in Braille and also the intake of audio books to promote inclusion. You are an NGO employee, from the same city. You may use ideas from Unit 2 : Education, along with your own ideas to write this letter. **CBSE SQP 2023**

Ans. 53, Sithla Nagar

Villapuram

23rd July, 20XX

The Librarian

The City Library

30, Grande Avenue

Villapuram

Subject Request for Addition of Braille and Audio Books

Sir/Ma'am

This is to inform you that I am XYZ, an employee of NGO Chakshu and an avid reader. I have written this letter to request the inclusion of popular fiction and non-fiction titles in Braille and audio books in the City Library. I truly believe that the library should strive to promote inclusion and accessibility for all readers, including those with visual and other impairments. Many readers with visual impairment are often unable to access the same titles as others. By adding Braille and audio books to the library's collection, we can ensure that these readers have the same access to a wide range of books and can engage with the world of literature as fully as anyone else.

I urge you to take this matter into consideration and add Braille and audio books to the library's collection. I believe this move will help promote inclusion and accessibility in our community and help everyone to enjoy the benefits of reading.

Thanking you

Yours sincerely

XYZ

Co-ordinator, NGO Chakshu

3. In spite of the government's initiatives and provisions made for the girl child, the statistics given out by the government for the enrolment position of girls in primary and upper primary schools are poor and not improving significantly. Write a letter to the editor of a national daily, expressing your concern about the issue and the need to work on a war footing to counter the problem. Use ideas from the MCB unit on 'Education' and your own ideas. You are Ashok/ Ameeta of 23/7, New Hyderabad, Lucknow.

Or **The Government of India has consistently worked to ensure an alleviation in the status of the girl child. Write a letter to the editor of a national daily, expressing your appreciation towards the government initiatives and provisions made for girl child education and the importance of the same.**

Ans. 23/7, New Hyderabad
Lucknow - 226007

27th February, 20XX

The Editor
The Indian Express
Delhi - 110002

Subject Suggestions for Improving Enrolment of Girls in Schools

Sir/Ma'am

Through the columns of your esteemed newspaper, I wish to highlight the problem of poor enrolment of girls in schools inspite of various governmental initiatives and provisions. Government statistics inform us that less than half of the girls eligible for enrolment in schools are actually enrolled.

The reasons are not far to seek. In rural areas, girls are relegated to domestic duties and thus, not sent to school. Some parents are afraid that safety and security of the girls is inadequate in schools. Other reasons include lack of separate toilets for girls and regressive attitudes.

All these problems need to be tackled on a war footing. Parents should be explained the necessity of education for girls by qualified counsellors authorised by the government. Suitable measures for the improvement of the safety and security of girls at schools should be put in place. In addition, separate toilets for girls should be constructed and properly maintained in all schools which do not have them.

Thanking you

Yours sincerely

Ameeta

4. You want to go for vocational education in a technical trade after completing your Class X examination because you are from a poor family and want to take up a job as soon as possible to support your family. You have seen an advertisement in the classified section of a newspaper by a private ITI offering technical trades course. Write a letter of enquiry to the Principal of the ITI asking for their brochure and other details of courses. Use ideas from the MCB unit on 'Education' and your own ideas. You are Basavraj/ Beena of 462, Devraj Chowk, Hubli. (100–120 words) Competency Based

Ans. 462, Devraj Chowk
Hubli - 580020

3rd June, 20XX

Shastri Nagar ITI
Shastri Nagar
Dharwad - 580010

Subject Enquiry for Technical Courses

Sir/Ma'am

With reference to the advertisement in XYZ on 2nd June, 20XX, I wish to enquire regarding admission to technical courses of 2 years' duration leading to the award of an ITI trade certification. I am particularly interested in courses in the electronics and electrical trades.

I have recently passed the Class X Board exams with first division, At this juncture, I need to make a career choice. For the same, I feel that an ITI trade certification will help me secure a job either in government organisations or in the private sector.

Hence, to make a decision I need the following information.

- Syllabus
- Accomodation
- Scholarships
- Courses offered, etc.

Please send me your brochure and other details at the address given above.

Thanking you

Yours sincerely

Basavraj

5. You intend to join coaching classes at International Coaching Center situated in Raipur. The institute specialises in teaching science to Classes XI-XII. Write a letter of enquiry in 100-120 words addressed to the Administrator In-charge of the institute seeking clarification about the timings, duration, staff, transport and other necessary details for joining the institute. You are Rajesh/Rajni 2, Library Road, Jabalpur.

Ans. 2, Library Road

Jabalpur

18th March, 20XX

The Administrator In-charge

International Coaching Center

Raipur

Subject Information about Coaching for Science

Sir/Ma'am

With reference to your advertisement in 'The Hindu' dated 16th March, I would like to enquire about a science coaching offered by the institue. I have just appeared for my Class X CBSE Examination after which I have taken science stream to pursue my dream of becoming a doctor. For the same, I would like to join the coaching classes offered by your academy. I would be grateful if you could provide me with the following information for admission

- Procedure for admission and eligibility criteria
- Timings and duration of coaching classes offered by your academy
- Transport facility
- Course fee
- Any other relevant information

I am extremely keen to get good grades in my examinations and would appreciate if you could forward me all the necessary information related to the courses for it in your academy as soon as possible.

Thanking you

Yours sincerely

Rajesh

6. You wish to join hobby classes during summer break at Culture and Art Centre, Ambattur Road, Chennai.
You wish to learn instrumental music or an Indian dance. Write a letter of inquiry to the Director asking about details like charges and timings and describing your taste, experience, etc. You are Sahil/Sahira, resident of 12, Fort Road, Chennai.

Ans. 12, Fort Road

Chennai

18th March, 20XX

The Director

Culture and Art Centre

Ambattur Road, Chennai

Subject Information about Courses on Instrumental music and Indian Dance Forms

Sir/Ma'am

With reference to your advertisement in 'The Hindu' dated 16th March, I would like to enquire about a course. I have just appeared for my Class X CBSE Examination and have been looking for a hobby course. I was attracted by the variety of music and dance courses that your institution offers and would be delighted to join one of these. I wish to learn instrumental music or an Indian dance. Hence, kindly provide me the following details so that I can make the correct choice.

- Courses offered
- Procedure for admission and eligibility criteria
- Timings and duration of classes
- Course fee

I am extremely keen to learn either an instrument or a dance form and would appreciate if you could forward me all the necessary information related to the courses for it in your academy as soon as possible.

Thanking you

Yours sincerely

Sahira

MCB Theme 3 Science

Science is important in our lives because it teaches an understanding of natural phenomenon. It aims to stimulate our natural curiosity in finding out why things happen in the way they do. It also teaches methods of enquiry and investigation to stimulate creative thought. We learn to ask scientific questions and begin to appreciate the way science will affect our future on a personal, national and global level.

Some aspects of science which are relevant in modern times may be covered in writing letters. These are

- Alternative and renewable sources of energy
- Using the latest devices and gadgets as well as properly disposing of old gadgets
- Space travel – its usefulness and other aspects
- Aliens and life on other planets

Solved Examples

1. Write a letter to the Mayor of your city, addressing the issue of carelessness in transportation habits and advocating for initiatives to promote car-lessness in the community. Deliberate on the environmental, health, and social benefits of reducing reliance on cars and propose specific measures to encourage alternative modes of transportation. Also, emphasise the importance of community engagement and collaboration in achieving a more sustainable and liveable city. Use ideas from Unit 3: Science, along with your own to write this letter in not more than 120 words. CBSE SQP 2024

Ans. 123, Sundar Nagar
Chandigarh

5th September, 20XX

The Mayor
XYZ, Municipal Corporation Office
Chandigarh

Subject Movement from Carelessness to Car-lessness

Sir/Ma'am

I am writing to express my deep concern about the increasing reliance on cars in our city and to advocate for initiatives to promote car-lessness. Your efforts in combating these issues and promoting sustainability, while improving transportation infrastructure are remarkable and are already being implemented. However, as we have learned in our science class, excessive car use contributes significantly to air pollution, climate change, and public health issues. We could further improve our air quality by reducing our reliance on cars, reducing greenhouse gas emissions, and creating healthier communities. Additionally, car-less neighbourhoods can foster a stronger sense of community and promote physical activity, leading to improved health and well-being.

To encourage car-lessness in our city, I propose the following measures- expansion of public transportation, creating safe cycling and walking paths, and building dedicated infrastructure to promote cycling and walking as modes of transportation. Furthermore, implementation of carpooling programmes may also reduce the number of cars on the road.

I believe that by working together as a community, we can create a more sustainable and liveable city for everyone. Thank you for your attention to this important issue.

Yours sincerely
Vaibhav

2. You have read newspaper reports about the harm to the environment due to e-waste, meaning the electronic waste generated by people throwing away their obsolete, unwanted and non-functional electronic and electrical equipment and appliances like TV sets, radios, old refrigerators, etc. Write a letter to the Editor of a national daily making people aware of the problems that arise due to e-waste. Use ideas from the MCB unit on 'Science'. You are Anil/Neela of 221, Station Road, Ahmedabad. (120 words)

You are Nirmal Pillai, a concerned citizen from Aluva, Kochi. Compose a letter in about 120 words, to the Project Hend of the e-waste Management cell at Electronics Vatika, New Delhi, highlighting the adverse effects of e-waste pollution. Suggest measures for addressing its management through community engagement and government initiative.

Discarded electronic devices such as smarthphones, computers and televisions, which are no longer in use or have reached the end of their life cycle.

Ans. 221, Station Road
Ahmedabad - 380001
4th June, 20XX

The Editor
The Times of India
Ahmedabad - 380001

Subject Increasing Problems of Electronic Waste

Sir/Ma'am

Through the columns of your esteemed newspaper, I wish to make the people of our nation aware of the problems that arise due to waste. Electronic waste or e-waste is a waste that is formed when people throw away their unwanted and non-functional electronic equipment and appliances like TV sets, radios, old refrigerators, etc. when they buy either new or more advanced models.

The quantity of e-waste generated and recycled domestically is unknown but very little recycling is carried out by small operators to recover valuable metals like gold and silver. The remaining large waste is illegally disposed of in water bodies like rivers, ponds or in sewerage, which ultimately pollutes the water and land. This, not only worsens the problem of pollution but also creates many other problems like radioactive pollution which results in various ill effects on life.

All these matters should be investigated by the government so that India does not turn into a toxic scrap heap of land.

Thanking you

Yours sincerely

Neela

3. You had recently visited the Gujarat Solar Park at Charanka in district Patan. You realised the importance of solar energy as a permanent source of energy in the future. Write a letter to the Editor of a national daily newspaper highlighting the importance of solar energy. Use ideas from the MCB unit on 'Science' and your own ideas. You are Lalit/ Lalita of 243/2, Charkha Road, Vadodara. (120 words)

Ans. 243/2, Charkha Road
Vadodara - 390001
27th September, 20XX

The Editor

The Indian Express
Mumbai - 400020

Subject Importance of Solar Energy

Sir/Ma'am

Through the columns of your esteemed newspaper, I wish to highlight the importance of solar energy in the present world.

I recently visited the Gujarat Solar Park at Charanka in Patan district of that state where 1100 MW of power is being generated by the solar panels installed. There is absolutely no pollution whatsoever caused to the atmosphere or to the ecology by the solar panels. This made me realise that clean, renewable energy must become a priority for India to ensure that our economy grows, our health improves and we protect our environment. India should harness the power of the Sun to become a leader in solar energy development. Besides, it is a renewable and clean energy source.

Taking both environmental and economic cost into consideration, solar energy works out cheaper than fossil fuel resources like coal and petroleum. Once we master the techniques to harness solar energy efficiently, it can be a vital source of power making power shortage a thing of the past.

Thus, I believe that the government should find other areas of the country where adequate sunlight is available and harness this inexhaustible and non-polluting energy source for everyone's benefit.

Thanking you

Yours sincerely

Lalita

MCB Theme 4 Environment

Environment is an important component of the planet Earth which makes life possible. However, due to urbanisation and industrialisation, we have destroyed our environment. Activities like deforestation, pollution, poaching and overexploitation of resources have led to us to the present wherein we are facing effects of climate change. Hence, it is imperative for students to be aware of the concerns related to the environment and think about strategies to preserve it.

Solved Examples

1. Write a letter to the Director of the Geological Survey advocating for concerted efforts to preserve and protect geological heritage sites. Discuss the importance of these sites and highlight the threats they face. Propose specific measures to conserve these valuable natural assets and request her for proactive action to safeguard them for future generations. Use ideas from Unit 4: Environment, along with your own to write this letter in not more than 120 words. **CBSE SQP 2024**

Ans. 123, Sundar Nagar
New Delhi

5th September, 20XX

Director of Geological Survey
XYZ Office
Delhi

Subject Need to Work Towards Saving Our Geological Heritage

Sir/Ma'am

I am writing to express my deep concern for the preservation and protection of geological heritage sites. These sites are invaluable natural assets that offer a glimpse into our planet's history and provide vital information for scientific research and education. The steps that you have taken for environmental conservation are truly remarkable and appreciated.

The geological heritage sites are facing numerous threats, including urbanisation, industrialisation, and climate change. These activities can lead to erosion, pollution, and the destruction of unique geological formations. Therefore, it is imperative that we take immediate action to conserve these valuable resources for future generations.

I urge you to advocate for the establishment of protected areas around geological heritage sites and request you to implement stricter regulations to prevent their exploitation and protect them from vandalism. Additionally, it is essential to raise public awareness about the importance of these sites and to promote sustainable tourism practices that minimise their impact.

I believe that by taking concerted efforts to preserve and protect our geological heritage, we can ensure that these invaluable natural assets continue to inspire and educate us for centuries to come.

Thank you for your attention to this urgent matter.
Yours sincerely

Vani

2. With the help of the inputs given below, write a letter to the Editor of a newspaper on the colossal wastage of food in the lavish Indian weddings.

- Indians spend life's saving on weddings.
- Wedding market in India is approximately ₹ 1,50,000 crores per year.
- India also hosts one of the biggest armies of starving people in the world.
- No wastage more condemnable than wastage of food
- Responsibility of the guests to limit the size of the servings according to their appetite.
- Take spoonfuls of each to taste and decide, instead of filling the plate with every dish.

Ans. E-114, Nandanvan Colony
Nagpur

31st January, 20XX

The Editor
The Harbinger
9, Bund Marg
Hyderabad

Subject Colossal Wastage of Food in the Lavish Indian Weddings

Sir/Ma'am

Through the columns of your esteemed newspaper, I would like the attention of the public of our nation towards the wastage of food in the lavish Indian weddings.

Wedding is a special occasion for Indians. Money is spent lavishly on clothes, decorations, gifts and above all food. If we focus on only food, we will find that Indians spend a lot to get a variety of food in weddings. However, as one can see from the statistics of food wastage, one would find that these weddings are one of the largest food wasters in India. With so much variety, it has been noticed that.

Guests eat less and waste more in the marriages. Keeping this information in mind, lets face another fact that India hosts one of the biggest armies of starving people in the world. Millions of people hardly get a meal per day in India. The situation is dismal, calling for immediate action.

It is high time that we think about wastage of food and its social consequences. It is the responsibility of the guests to limit the size of the servings according to their appetite. Instead of filling the plate with every dish, the guests may take spoonfuls of each food item to taste first and decide how much to take.

I urge you to issue a special section on this issue to awaken the masses. This will bring a change in their thinking and attitude towards wastage of food as well as money in marriages.

Thanking you
Yours sincerely
PQR

3. **The National Bravery Awards are given to honour those children who have demonstrated selfless courage in the face of all odds. These awards serve as inspiration to other children and motivate them to follow in their footsteps. Similarly, the government should institute National Environment Crusader Awards for children who dedicate themselves to spreading awareness about saving the environment. Write a letter to the editor of a national daily, in 120 words, expressing your views on the above. Use you own ideas along with ideas from the unit Environment, to write the letter.** CBSE 2025

Ans. A4, 1202
Supertech Ecovillage 1
Noida- 201306

18th February, 20XX

The Editor
Times of India
Noida - 201301

Subject Request to Institute National Environment Crusader Awards for Children

Respected Sir/Ma'am

Through the columns of your esteemed newspaper I want to express my concern regarding environmental degradation and to propose an initiative that can inspire young mind to take action. The National Bravery Awards honour children who show extraordinary courage, inspiring others to do the same. Similarly, I strongly believe that the government should introduce National Environment Crusader Awards to recognise young environmentalists who actively promote eco-friendly practices.

Many children today are taking significant steps to protect nature-organising cleanliness drives, spreading awareness about pollution, and encouraging tree plantation. Recognising their efforts will not only reward their dedication but also inspire more young minds to take responsibility for our planet. At a time when environmental issues are a global concern, such an initiative will encourage future generations to work towards a sustainable future.

I hope my suggestion is considered.

Thanking you
Yours sincerely
Neha Vats

4. **In order to increase the green cover in their area, residents of Pioneer Housing Society, Vinod Vihar, New Delhi, planted saplings around their residential complex and also along the road. As Secretary of the Society, write a letter to the editor of a local newspaper requesting him to highlight the initiative taken by the society and urge other residential complexes to launch similar campaigns in their areas. You are Sugam/Sugandha.** CBSE 2019

Ans. Pioneer Housing Society
Vinod Vihar
New Delhi

7th June, 20XX

The Editor
The Daily Times
New Delhi

Subject Need of a Green Cover Initiative in all Residential Areas

Sir/Ma'am

Through the columns of your esteemed newspaper, I would like to draw the attention of the authorities of all residential complexes towards the need of organising a green cover initiative.

Recently, my locality- the Pioneer Housing Society- started a green cover initiative wherein the members of the society planted saplings in the region surrounding the society. Given that in the current scenario, planting more and more trees is essential to save our planet, the initiative can become a good start. We all are aware of the various benefits of trees and how it ensure life on the plant.

Hence, I would like to encourage all the members of residential complexes to organise such green cover initiatives so that our planet remains green and healthy.

Thanking you
Yours truly

Sugam
Secretary of Pioneer Housing Society

MCB Theme 5 Travel and Tourism

In today's world, nearly everyone enjoys a holiday and this has resulted in a positive impact on the travel and tourism sector and consequently, the global economy. This sector contributes almost 10% to the global economy and is growing rapidly, providing jobs to over 10% of the population.

Hence, it is essential for students to understand the various aspect of this sector, including

- Ecotourism
- Medical tourism
- Other Social issues

Solved Examples

1. Ecotourism means responsible travel to natural areas conserving the environment.
Imagine yourself as a member of the Ecotourism Society of India. Taking ideas from the units 'Environment' and 'Travel and Tourism', write a letter to the Ministry of Tourism, mentioning the ways to propagate Ecotourism by sensitising people. CBSE 2024

Ans. 104, Daryaganj
New Delhi
112233

10th March, 20XX

The Director
Ministry of Tourism

Subject Raising Awareness and Promoting Ecotourism to the Masses

Sir/Ma'am

Through the medium of this letter I would like to raise awareness and sensitise people about the importance of ecotourism, i.e. sustainable tourism practices that minimise negative impacts on the environment while benefiting local communities.

Ecotourism can be a boon for Earth and its ecological balance. Being mindful during travel can help us conserve natural resources and not harm the environment. Encouraging travellers to adopt responsible travel practices such as reducing waste, conserving water and energy, respecting wildlife, and supporting local economies by purchasing local products and services are some way to contribute. We can also involve local communities in ecotourism initiatives by providing training and employment opportunities, allocating funds and resources to support conservation projects, and promoting sustainable transportation options such as biking, hiking, public transit and carpooling to reduce carbon emissions.

I hope that the Ministry will consider these steps and raise awareness about Ecotourism by sensitising people and making them realise its positive effects on the environment.

Thanking you
Yours sincerely

Karan
Member, Ecotourism Society of India

2. You are Ravi/Riddhima, Proprietor of the travel operator M/S Creative Destinations. You have received an enquiry from a man enquiring about holidays for his wife and himself to the Lakshadweep Islands. Reply asking for the information you need before you can recommend a suitable hotel or package holiday. Use ideas from the MCB unit on 'Travel and Tourism' and your own ideas. (120 words)

Ans. M/S Creative Destinations
106/47, Siddharth Enclave
New Delhi - 110014

27th February, 20XX

Mr. Sanjeev Bajaj
47, Sahdev Chowk
Ambala Cantt - 133001

Subject Information on Trip to Lakshadweep Islands

Sir

Thank you for your letter dated February 20th enquiring about holidays in the Lakshadweep Islands.

We have a few excellent hotels in Lakshadweep, both in our all-inclusive package and in our independent traveller selection. However, I want to recommend the best holiday for you so I would appreciate it if you could give me some more information by answering the questions given below.

- What grade of holiday or resort are you looking for?
- When would you like to travel and from which airport?
- How long do you wish to stay?
- What type and standard of accommodation are you looking for? Do you have a preference for being close to the town or to the sea-front?
- Do you require any special facilities such as leisure activities, guided tours, boat rides, etc?

We look forward to receiving your reply so that we can process your request and suggest a suitable resort or hotel.

Thanking you
Yours sincerely
Ravi/Riddhima (Proprietor)

3. 'Atithi Devo Bhava' has been India's stand since times immemorial. However, you feel, to attract tourists, only tourism promotional drives do not suffice. It is important to sensitise those in the tourism industry to conduct themselves with propriety as hosts, and they must treat the tourists with respect, ensure their safety and support them during their visit. As Herbu R., write a letter to the Tourism Department expressing your concerns. Use your own ideas along with the ideas from the unit: Travel and Tourism, to write the letter in not more than 120 words. CBSE 2025

Ans. 1911, Maharani Bagh
New Delhi -110034

18th February, 20XX

The Director
Tourism Department
Delhi

Subject Promoting Responsible Conduct in the Tourism Industry

Respected Sir/Ma'am

I am writing this letter to express my concern regarding the need for greater senitisation among those working in tourism industry.

India has always believed in Atithi Devo Bhava, but to truly make tourists feel welcome, promotional campaigns alone are not enough. It is equally important to ensure that those in the tourism industry-guides, drivers, and hospitality staff-treat visitors with respect, offer help when needed, and prioritise their safety.

Unfortunately, incidents of overcharging, misguidance, and security concerns can leave tourists with a negative impression. Proper training and awareness programmes on responsible and ethical hospitality would make a huge difference. A positive experience encourages more travellers to visit, benefiting both tourism and the country's reputation. I sincerely hope the department takes steps to address this concern.

Thanking you
Yours sincerely

Herbu R.

4. It gives you a good feeling when you read in the newspapers how patients from abroad come to hospitals in India and get themselves treated at a fraction of expenses they will have incurred elsewhere. Write a letter to the editor of a national daily describing the importance of medical tourism for India. You are Karan/Karuna M 114, Mall Road, Kanpur.

Ans. M 114, Mall Road
Kanpur

7th February, 20XX

The Editor
The Times of India
Delhi

Subject Importance of Medical Tourism

Sir/Ma'am

Through the columns of your esteemed newspaper, I wish to highlight the importance of medical tourism in our country India. We feel good when we read about people from developed countries like the USA visit India for critical medical procedures to be performed on them. Heart bypass operations are only one instance of such cost effective and efficient medical procedures performed by expert Indian doctors.

This form of tourism, called 'Medical Tourism', earns valuable foreign exchange for the country, thus helping us to improve the balance of payments position and strengthening the value of the rupee vis-a-vis foreign currencies. It also publicises the competence and skill of Indian surgeons and nursing practitioners who are among the best in the world along with the world class medical facilities and infrastructure. No doubt, the government is promoting India as a healthcare destination in its incredible India campaign.

Today a 'modern' image of the country is becoming popular as compared to the earlier traditional image of India being a land of mystics and snake-charmers. The comprehensive solution for all medical needs and the alternative treatments as well as therapies provided by the country not only improves foreign relations but also enhances the image of modern India.

Thanking you
Yours sincerely

Karuna

MCB Theme 6 National Integration

Travellers to India appreciate the idea that India is one country embracing many lands and that the Indian nation has a multitude of castes, creeds, colours, convictions, cultures, cuisines, costumes and customs. Everywhere we can see festivals dedicated to seasons and harvests being celebrated. The Indians always seem to be displaying their pride in celebrating their diversity. It is interesting for people to see that inspite of this diversity, India is a united country.

Formal letters on national integration are usually written to editors of newspapers for making the general public aware about issues relating to this topic or reminding the relevant authorities about taking necessary action to maintain the integrity of the nation. These may include the following topics

- Unity in diversity
- Challenges to national integration
- The spirit of unity
- Promotion of national integration

Solved Examples

1. You are aware that there are many disruptive elements in the country trying to divide the people on the basis of religion, caste, etc. You feel that you must give suggestions to the government for methods to be adopted to promote national integration. Write a letter to the Editor of a national daily by using ideas given in the MCB unit on 'National Integration' and your own ideas. You are Mohit/Madhavi of 3/113, Shakti Nagar, Indore. (120 words). Competency Based

Ans. 3/113, Shakti Nagar
Indore - 452013
27th February, 20XX

The Editor
The Statesman
New Delhi-110001

Subject Ways to Promote National Integration

Sir/Ma'am

Through the columns of your esteemed newspaper, I wish to suggest some ways to promote national integration so that the relevant authorities can take suitable action.

The government can organise state festivals to make the public aware of the culture and tradition of different states.

At the school level, festivals of all states and communities should be celebrated. For instance, children will learn to celebrate Diwali, Eid, Christmas and Guruparb equally, irrespective of their own faith or religion. Advertisements on television and on hoardings can also contribute to national integration. Debates and discussions organised at a national level, along with other competitions based on the topic of 'Unity in Diversity' must be held. Highlighting the fact that our film industry and cricket team are the best examples of national integration will also help.

I hope that the public and concerned authorities will realise the importance of adopting these measures to promote national integration and will take appropriate action at the earliest.

Thanking you
Yours sincerely
Madhavi

ASSESSMENT EXERCISE

Letters of Complaint

1. Recently you travelled in a State Transport luxury bus from Chennai to Thiruvalluvar. To your shock, the air-conditioning in the bus was not working properly. The quality of the maintenance of the bus was also not up to the required standard of a luxury bus. Throughout the journey you spent the time in unbearable heat. Write a letter to the General Manager (Maintenance) of the State Transport for taking action in this matter in 120 words. You are Hema/ Ganesh, 25, Officers Quarters, Avadi, Chennai.

2. You are Rajeshwari/ Rajesh, President, RWA, Govindpuri, Bengaluru. The main park in your locality, which was once a model park, lies in a state of utter neglect. It has become a favourite spot for anti-social elements and also a permanent resting place for stray animals. Write a letter to the Municipal Commissioner requesting him to instruct the horticulture department to take prompt action and restore the park to its original condition. (120 words).

3. You are Ravi/ Renu of Ravidas Chowk, Sadar Bazar, Moradabad. You had bought a copy of the Social Science textbook of Class X, UP Board, from a nearby bookshop. After reading the book, you find that there is overlapping of print on a few pages. Also, some pages are missing due to defective binding. Write a letter of complaint to the publishers, M/S Sarojini Publishers, Bareilly, asking for a free replacement in 120 words.

4. You are Ashwini/ Aradhana of 1/169, Civil Lines, Agra. You have recently purchased a new washing machine from the showroom of M/S Vikki Sales Corporation. However, the performance of the machine leaves much to be desired. Write a letter complaining about the poor performance to the Customer Service In-charge of the company mentioning clearly the problems observed. Also state the action you want to be taken from their side. (120 words).

5. Write a letter to the Superintendent of Police of the district complaining about the unauthorised construction of a block of three shops adjacent to the public park in your area. You are Suresh/ Sarojini, President of the Residents' Welfare Association of your area. (120 words).

Letters of Enquiry

1. You are awaiting your class 10th results. Meanwhile, you would like to do a short-term course on personality development. Write a letter to the Director, Professional Careers Institute, Hyderabad, enquiring about the course details. You are Kailash/ Kusum of 148, Model Town, Delhi. (120 words)
2. As a health conscious person, you noticed an advertisement in the newspaper on yoga classes in your neighbourhood. Write a letter in 120 words to the organisers enquiring about the duration of the course and other relevant details. You are Rajesh/ Rajeshwari of 4/5, Saraswatipuram, Mysuru.
3. You are Salim/ Sarika, Administrative Officer of M/S Sanjeev Security Agencies, Saharanpur. You are opening your new vocational studies centre in the city for which you require suitable furniture. Draft an enquiry letter to M/S Office Suppliers, Saharanpur, asking for a quotation for the items required. Specify the number required of each item and ask for credit in payment. (120 words)
4. You are Chandan/ Chandni, Manager of Smart School, Patna. You require some cabinets for keeping books in your library. Specify the size / capacity of the items for the cabinets. (120 words)
5. Write an enquiry letter to the Manager of Saryu Banquet Hall, Udham Singh Nagar, for catering of the annual day ceremony of your school. (120 words)

Letters to the Editor

1. Influence of friends can have both positive and negative impacts on the students. Write a letter to the Editor of a national daily in 120 words discussing how we can make it positive and productive. You are Arun/Aruna, 24, Mall Road, Chennai.
2. The tourism industry can bring valuable income to the country. Using your ideas along with ideas from the MCB unit, Travel and Tourism, write a letter to the Editor of a popular daily on how the government and the public can boost the development of this industry. Write the letter in 120 words. You are Rama/ Ram 4, Rani Road, Ranchi.
3. There is a flood of advertisements on television channels these days. Useless commodities and superstitious beliefs are promoted through glamorous and exaggerated presentations. Write a letter to the Editor, 'New Indian Express', about the negative influence such advertisements have on the minds of the people. You are Radha/ Ramesh of Mayur Vihar, Lucknow.
4. Your grandfather is very upset about the rising prices and keeps thinking of his olden times when things were very cheap. You are very convinced that inflation has made life difficult for the common man. Write a letter in about 120 words to the Editor of a national daily describing the difficulties faced by poor families.
5. Write a letter to the Editor of a national newspaper regarding conducting awareness towards health and hygiene among rural people. You are Madhav/ Madhavi of Mahaveer Nagar, Jaipur.

Application Writing

1. Write an application to the Principal requesting him to take your class to a picnic spot. (120 words)
2. Write an application to your class teacher requesting him to put a zero period for your class. (120 words)
3. Write an application to your games teacher requesting him to issue new sports kit for the students. (120 words)
4. Write an application to the Principal requesting him to start the classes of foreign language in your school. (120 words)
5. Write an application to your Principal asking him to start skill development programmes in the school. (120 words)

CHAPTER 4

Article Writing

An article is a highly structured and directional piece of writing, written for a specific purpose, i.e. to inform, to persuade, to entertain or to convince the reader. It essentially has several paragraphs containing a distinct beginning, a middle and an end.

Writing an article is a very challenging task for anyone. It requires a high degree of creativity, a wide range of vocabulary and a thorough knowledge of the subject.

In CBSE Communicative English Class X, article writing carries 8 marks.

Elements of an Article

1. **Title/Heading** There are no predetermined rules as such on how to write the title of the article but it may comprise a single word, a phrase or a sentence of 4-6 words. The title should be thought-provoking, catchy and should highlight the theme.
2. **Name of the Writer** Sign off your article with your name in the form of a byline.
3. **Introduction** Keep the topic in perspective; specify it keeping the reader's interest intact by providing some surprising information or interesting facts related to the context.
4. **Description of the Topic** Highlight various facets of the topic like the causes and effects, advantages and disadvantages, etc.
5. **Ending** Wind up your article with your own views – criticism, suggestions, etc.
6. **Conclusion** End the article with a desire, an appeal or a warning.

Points to be Kept in Mind

- Understand the hints/information given in the verbal input.
- Arrange all the hints/ information in an order in which you want them to develop.
- Divide your article into several paragraphs when necessary. All the sentences in the paragraphs should logically lead to the objective for which the article is being written.
- The whole composition should not be disjointed or fragmented. There should be a continuity of thought according to the theme of the article.
- Language used should always be simple and grammatically correct. It should be straightforward and to-the-point.
- Articles are usually written in third person.
- Always remember to write your article within the word limit of 150 words.

Format of an Article

Hard work and punctuality are essential for a happy and successful life. They help in meeting the desired targets of our lives. You are Kavya/Kanha. Write an article highlighting the importance of hard work and punctuality in a student's life.

Use the following clues : foundations for future life of students - important characteristic - importance of time - source of discipline and confidence - meeting deadlines - wards off the stress - Life is full of challenges - no shortcuts. It trains a student's mind and body for future.

Title/Heading — **Importance of Hard Work and Punctuality in a Student's Life**

Byline (Name of the Writer) — *by Kavya*

Content —

Two of the basic foundations for future life of students are hard work and punctuality. A hardworking person can not only reach the sky but also beyond. Similarly, punctuality is a habit of a person to do any task on time. Thus, it is important to inculcate the qualities of– hard work and punctuality. Why, you may ask? Here is the answer. Punctuality is the most important characteristic that a student must display. Being punctual means to be on time as well as managing the task at hand in order to complete the task on time. A punctual person thus knows the importance of time and respects it. For a student, it is a source of discipline and confidence. It not only saves an individual from embarrassment but also helps in meeting deadlines set for students thus building a positive image. Not to forget, it wards off the stress that students face daily.

Hard work is another such necessary skill without which nothing can be achieved. Without hard work there is no success. Life is full of challenges that students must overcome with hard work as there are no shortcuts. It trains a student's mind and body for future.

We must remember that all great men achieved their glory because of their hard work.

Thus, both hard work and punctuality are very much important in a student's life.

SOLVED EXAMPLES

1. Recently you read about an incident in a newspaper in which a child tried to imitate the stunts shown on television and sustained serious injuries. Write an article in 150 words on the hazards of unsupervised television viewing by kids and how parents should guide them in this matter.

Clues

- TV for overall well-being of children
- Entices mind-effect greater than ever
- Ruin eyesight-lack of concentration
- Bad habits-copy actors-hero worship

Ans.

Hazards of Unsupervised Television Viewing by Kids

by XYZ

In the present times, television has begun playing a significant role in contributing to the overall well-being of children. Since the advent of television, its technology and capability to entice the mind of a child has grown exponentially through numerous shows directly targeted at children. With the average time of television consumption growing, the effect of television on a child is greater than ever.

While most people realise that television can ruin children's eyesight and cause lack of concentration, what they do not realise is that there are many other problems that one can associate with television. Just recently, there was a news about a child who tried to perform the stunts performed by an actor in PQR film and got serious injuries.

Such stunts performed by celebrities make children want to copy their favourite actors. The vulnerable young minds find the stunts thrilling, exciting and adventurous which leads them to dangers and fatal accidents.

Even though warning regarding these stunts are displayed, the font size is so small that no one seems to notice them. Hence, not just limited TV time but a guided and supervised TV time is needed. Parents and teachers can sensitise the students regarding the same so that the children know the pros and cons. Only then, we can reap the benefits of television.

2. Our rivers are drying up at a rapid pace. You have seen a Power Point presentation on how to revive the dried rivers. Write an article on 150 words on the topic 'How can We Revive our Dried Rivers?'. You can use the following cues

- Destruction of rivers due to pollution
- Threat
- Stop throwing garbage in rivers
- Waste management in industries
- Rainwater harvesting
- Reuse water

Ans. **How can We Revive our Dried Rivers?**

by PQR

In the modern world, only a few of us may have seen the mighty rivers of India full of clear water. Such an image is distant memory as these rivers are now reduced to a pool full of garbage. We know and understand that the reason Indian rivers are being destroyed is due to pollution and climate change. Most of these rivers hold a very sacred value to us and yet all the sewage, all the agricultural and industrial waste is just thrown in them. Dam construction, sand mining, deforestation, excessive groundwater used and improper management of current dams are some of the biggest threats faced by the Indian rivers. Keeping in mind that these rivers are the lifeline of the nation, it is high time we take action to revive them to their original glory.

For starters, we must stop throwing all sorts of things in the river for religious activities. It's not doing any good to the rivers. People should reduce their own waste and the way that they manage their waste. Second, people and the government need to pressure the industries to stop throwing their waste in the rivers with better strategies regarding the same. Third, we must practice rainwater harvesting. Reuse the water during the summer, untreated pollutants from mining should be stopped immediately and shouldn't be in the water at all!

This is important because by 2040 more than 40% of the Indian population won't have sufficient water and many cities are running out of water real quick.

3. The construction sector is believed to be quite hazardous and has the maximum number of fatal work injuries because apart from other causes, stakeholders in this sector tend to ignore safety regulations.

As a columnist for an e-zine, draft an article on the theme of the importance of worker safety in construction zones. Explore possible reasons for the prevailing situation and include suggestions for addressing it. Support your ideas with clues given below

Competency Based

Clues

- Construction workers' risk of accident due to fatigue
- Construction workforce health challenges in extreme weather conditions
- Construction worker fatality buried under soil heap
- Are construction managers from Mars and workers from Venus?
- Will training programmes revamp the safety standards?

Ans. **Importance of Safety in Construction Zones**

by XYZ

The present day's highly developed world is expanding at an exponential rate and so is its infrastructure. Everyday we come across new developments and new constructions being undertaken with the purpose of growth and development of our society. However, as the number of construction sites increase, so does the number of construction sites' accidents. It is not uncommon for us to hear a headline presenting a massive construction accident. It does not come as a surprise to any one of us as we are all aware of the lack of safety measures taken at the construction sites.

While we all know that this lack of occupation safety at sites is illegal, we do not seek to find why this lack exists. The reasons for this lack are many. First and foremost, the key stakeholders or the construction companies ignore safety regulations to save money. They exploit poor people to work in dingy and unsafe conditions without much pay. These people work without any consideration of the extreme weather conditions or even the health risks that the job poses. Further, they even ignore the fatigue and injuries of workers all the while overworking them to get the job done as early as possible.

This is high time that these organisations ensure that safety standards are maintained at their construction sites. To do so, the first step is to spread awareness about safety and the laws associated with it to not only construction companies but also the workers so that they are able to fight for their rights. Further, we need to enforce stricter laws and penalties that ensure that workers receive frequent training programmes to work efficiently and safely. We must also make policies that bridge the gap between the worker and the manager.

Only when these requirements are met, we can think of a safe workplace for construction workers- a workplace which is a reality for all.

4. Write an article titled 'Development of Cottage Industries in India'. You can use the following clues

- Great supply of labour
- Lack of access to low cost
- Offer subsidiaries
- Assistance to small businesses
- Department of Industries and Commerce's role

Ans. **Development of the Cottage Industries in India**

by PQR

With the introduction of industrialisation, the small scale manufacturing industry or cottage industry has taken a severe hit. In a country like India, where the enormous number of ancient cottage enterprises are well known, the cottage industry is frequently defined by its huge potential for job creation. While the industry is of critical importance to the economy and heritage of the nation, it is not wrong to say that the cottage industry faces severe problems. Starting from the scarcity of capital and great supply of labour, lack of access to low-cost, easy-to-get financing to marketing problems, the industry needs great support to survive. As a result, there is a pressing need to employ strategies that address their issues.

Efforts should be put toward the advancement of technology so that workers can live comfortably. The government could also offer subsidiaries to help cottage industries flourish, particularly in their early stages.

A variety of agencies needs to be established to assist small businesses and villages. Financial funding and raising the capital investment ceiling for small businesses should be a chief concern. The Department of Industries and Commerce should administer and effectively implement a number of programmes to aid existing and new industries with financial assistance, technical support and direction.

India's cottage industries are culturally and economically significant. They preserve ancient traditions while simultaneously employing a large number of people. Because these industries confront intense competition from other economies, society should provide support to prevent exploitation and further develop them.

5. Write an article titled 'Renovation of Heritage Sites'.

Ans. **Renovation of Heritage Sites**

by PQR

As we advance into the future, landmarks are sometimes unceremoniously destroyed by tourists or residents for their own selfish motives. Many people do not realise that what we lose is far more important than mere brick and mortar. As our heritage sites deteriorate, chunks of our history and identity will forever be wiped from the surface of the Earth.

Fortunately, conserving our built heritage is an integral part of our urban planning and development in India. We are a country where we can find old heritage buildings at every nook and corner , but that does not stop us from retaining the beauty, nostalgia and culture that lies within the walls of our heritage buildings. This vital component of our government's urban revitalisation efforts is most apparent in historic areas.

Conservation is not a mere preservation of a façade or freezing a building in time. By favouring restoration over replacement, we preserve the ambience, character and a living piece of our history. Most importantly, they also add variety and spark visual interest within the city. Heritage preservation is a long-term investment that benefits us today and leaves behind an invaluable resource for generations to come.

6. Write an article titled 'Free and Fair Print and Electronic Media- The Need of the Hour'.

Ans. **Free and Fair Print and Electronic Media- The Need of the Hour**

by PQR

Today, we are living in a society where information is everything and different forms of media have become the strapping tool of communication and connectivity. In the present world, with the advancement of digital technology and internet facilities, print and electronic media has become an even more powerful phenomenon as the most influential source of news, views, ideas and opinion.

In this world of globalisation, the impact and influence of free and fair media is all pervasive. The social setup of our civilisation relies heavily on media for not only information but also judgements and opinions. It is media which acts as an important pillar of democracy. It brings all these things to notice, creates public awareness and catalyses people to act, react and interact. The government utilises the power of mass media to explain, inform and support its policies and programmes. Further, it is the media which keeps people updated and informed so that everyone draws something from it.

The ability of the media to reach a wide audience with a strong and influential message has the potential to have a strong social, cultural and political impact upon society. Media has the supreme potential to educate, inform and condition people's minds. Hence, we must always promote free and fair print and electronic media.

7. Social media and excessive dependency on gadgets have impacted human interaction. Though life has become more comfortable, human relationships have taken a back seat. Write an article in about 150 words on "Our Dependency on Technology".

- Opening of new horizons
- Connecting with the world
- Emotional imbalance

CBSE 2024 C

Ans. **Our Dependency on Technology**

by XYZ

In the 21st century, technology has become an integral part of our daily lives, drastically altering the way we communicate, learn, work and even think. From smartphones and laptops to artificial intelligence and the Internet of Things (IoT), technology has woven itself into the very fabric of society, creating a dependency that is both profound and multifaceted. While this dependency offers numerous benefits, it also raises important concerns about our cognitive capabilities, the erosion of interpersonal skills, and the implications for future generations.

At the heart of our technological dependency is the access to information. The Internet has transformed how we seek knowledge; a query can be answered in seconds through a simple search engine inquiry. Moreover, the rise of social media and communication technologies has revolutionised interpersonal interactions. We can now connect with friends, family, and colleagues across the globe in real time, transcending geographical barriers. However, this reliance on digital tools has lead to many concerns. It raises questions about critical thinking and the ability to analyse and synthesise knowledge without digital assistance. Further, as we become more accustomed to conversing through screens, we risk losing the nuances of non-verbal communication, which play a crucial role in human interactions. This shift can lead to feelings of isolation and loneliness, despite being more 'connected' than ever. In addition, as automation and artificial intelligence continue to advance, there are growing concerns about job displacement and the future of work. Another significant aspect of our technological dependency is the effect it has on our privacy and security. As we integrate technology into nearly every aspect of our lives, we often sacrifice our personal information and privacy for convenience.

In conclusion, our dependency on technology is a double-edged sword; it offers countless benefits while posing significant challenges. As we continue to integrate technology into our lives, we must remain vigilant about its implications.

8. India has the world's largest cattle herd (buffaloes), largest area planted to grow wheat, rice, and cotton, and is the largest producer of milk, pulses, and spices in the world. It is the second-largest producer of fruit, vegetables, tea, farmed fish, cotton, sugarcane, wheat, rice and sugar.

Using the given information, write an article on the topic 'India- An Agricultural Country'.

Ans. **India–An Agricultural Country**

by PQR

Holding the second place in the world's agricultural productivity and land, it cannot be doubted that India is one of the major players in the agriculture sector. It is essentially the primary source of livelihood for about 58% of India's population historically.

India has the world's largest cattle herd (buffaloes), the largest area planted to grow wheat, rice and cotton, and is the largest producer of milk, pulses and spices in the world. It is the second-largest producer of fruit, vegetables, tea, farmed fish, cotton, sugarcane, wheat, rice and sugar. It is a sector that generates employment for about half of the country's population.

One can easily say that agriculture is crucial to the Indian economy. It has been the major contributor to the country's GDP which supports many other industries by providing them with raw material. It caters to the food requirement of the country's large population while also aiding the government to generate income in the form of exports.

Thus, in a country like India, the agricultural sector plays a critical role, and the Indian economy's prosperity is still heavily reliant on it. To conclude, India is an agro-economy.

9. Write an article on the topic 'Role of Women in Modern India'.

Ans. **Role of Women in Modern India**

by PQR

'Thy name is integrity and strength', these are very powerful words that give a woman her due position in the society. However, if we go back 10 years ago, women were discriminated and suppressed. They were limited due to the gender barriers created by the male dominated society. However, in the modern world, a woman stands equal to man in all fields.

While it cannot be said that women have been empowered completely, we cannot ignore the fact that we are in a time where women are trying to shatter the gender barriers created by the society and are proving themselves to be strong and independent individuals. They are taking leading roles in various MNCs, building their own enterprises, joining politics in large numbers, excelling in sports and academics and so on.

With the developments made by women, their future in India looks positive. Women have better access to education, health and opportunities than before even though it's still not equal. The government has played an important role in hastening the process of women's empowerment through various acts, schemes and provisions such as reservation in local panchayats. However it still needs to continue aggressive efforts to give an equal position to women. The cultural attitude towards women in India is changing with changing times, as women are getting educated, proving their mettle and showing that they can be positioned equal to men if they are given the same opportunities.

10. Write an article on the topic 'Steps for Making Cities Clean'.

Ans. **Steps for Making Cities Clean**

by PQR

We have all heard our elders tell us that 'Cleanliness is next to Godliness.' Therefore, all of us know that the importance of cleanliness is indisputable. However, the picture of the land before us stands contrary to belief. Our cities are littered with waste everywhere. People tend to pollute the environment either intentionally or unintentionally. With a greater need to focus on cleanliness of our cities, millions of people keep wondering how exactly they can make the city clean.

People can take certain measures to keep their cities clean. The first and foremost measure would be to replace single use plastic from everywhere. Instead of plastic cutlery, polythene bags and so on, we can use reusable cutlery and fabric bags which are long-lasting and less destructive to our environment. Bio waste can be effectively turned into bio-energy with careful disposal. Restaurant owners and communities can create compost pits where they can convert waste food into valuable manure. A good knowledge of waste management and use of dustbins must be promoted everywhere. People must encourage each other to take up the responsibility of keeping the city clean. The city government must administer policies that protect the city from contamination.

It is definite that no one likes walking in a litter-consumed city. It is annoying and frustrating. However, we know that keeping our city clean is easy. If we all follow the guidelines presented above then we can earn the right to have a better city to live in.

Articles Based on MCB Themes

MCB Theme 1 Health and Medicine

1. As sports captain of your school, write an article for your school magazine emphasising the need of adventure sports in youngsters' lives. You can use the following lines as clues.

Clues

- Craze for adventure sports
- Excitement and enjoyment
- Positive impact on mind and body
- Increases confidence
- Emotional and physical benefits

Ans. **Need of Adventure Sports in Youngsters' Lives**

by Rohit

The craze of adventurous and exciting sports among youngsters is skyrocketing like never before. Experiencing life outdoors and exploring unchartered terrains, those young at heart are taking to trekking, water rafting, canoeing, scuba diving, rock climbing and more to get an adrenaline rush. All these activities are classified adventure sport, which is a term given to sports that involve speed, height and a high level of physical exertion along with a highly specialised gear as they are performed under high risk or danger. These sports are great not only to get the real feel of excitement and enjoyment but also because it has a positive impact on the mind and the body.

Adventure sports have been instrumental in increasing confidence and physical abilities while preparing an individual to face any challenge of life. Consequently, it is not surprising that many parents encourage their children to take part in these sports to keep them healthy and fit.

India offers immense opportunity for adventure lovers throughout its length and breadth with its geographical diversity of mountains, hills, rivers and beaches. Today, adventure sports are known to teach self-reliance, teamwork and result in improved self-esteem. The emotional and physical benefits of adventure sports are impressive and numerous.

2. 'Laugh out loud and feel happy and fit inside out' for laughter is the best medicine. With stress mushrooming all around and among all ages, Laughter Yoga seems a great alternative way to physical and mental health. Use cues given below along with your own ideas and those you may have gathered from the unit: Health and Medicine, to write an article for your school magazine in about 150 words describing benefits of Laughter Yoga. **(8)**

- Improves Cardiovascular health
- Boosts Immune System → production of antibodies → activation of immune cells
- Reduces stress
- No special equipment required
- Cost effective

Ans. **Benefits of Laughter Yoga**

by XYZ

They say laughter is the best medicine and Laughter Yoga proves it! In today's stressful world, where people of all ages struggle with pressure, this simple and enjoyable practice offers many health benefits.

Laughter Yoga combines deep breathing with playful laughter exercises, improving heart health by boosting oxygen flow and blood circulation. It also strengthens the immune system, helping the body fight diseases. Most importantly, it reduces stress, lifts mood, and promotes a positive mindset. The best part is that it requires no special equipment and is completely free, making it easy for anyone to practise.

Whether young or old, anyone can enjoy Laughter Yoga and feel its benefits. It not only improves physical and mental health but also strengthens social bonds, making people feel happier and more connected. A few minutes of laughter everyday can make a big difference in our lives. So let's laugh more, stay healthy and live stress free!

3. You are Ram/Rajani, a nutritionist. Write an article on 'Healthy Food' pointing out how healthy food contributes to physical and mental well-being.

Ans. **Healthy Food**

by Rajani

Ann Wigmore, a holistic health practitioner, once said, "The food you eat can either be the safest and most powerful form of medicine or the slowest form of poison." Good health keeps our body and mind healthy and peaceful. It brings the feeling of well being physically, mentally, spiritually and socially. The criteria of health and fitness all over the world is expanding day-by-day. Men want to have a heavy muscle bound body whereas women want a slim and trim looking body.

It is a tough task, though not impossible for anybody. Being healthy and fit requires some diet tips to be followed daily with full dedication.

A good and nutritious diet not only maintains a good physical fitness level but also boosts mental abilities. Hence, healthy food is the key to physical and mental well-being. Following the given steps will ensure the health that you desire.

First, a heavy breakfast should be eaten on time. Next, dinner should be light and should be taken two to three hours before sleeping. Always eat fresh salad items with your meals. Don't keep yourself starved for long and then overeat subsequently. Avoid fast foods and canned foods. Eat heart-friendly foods like yellow, orange and green vegetables and fruits. Also, reduce the intake of food and exercise more as the age increases. Remember, our food contains chemicals that can boost memory, concentration, endurance and so on.

Thus, eating healthy food at the proper time will contribute to your physical and mental well-being.

4. You are Raghav/Mohini. You are concerned about the growing problem of obesity in children which leads to type II diabetes. Write an article titled 'Health- The Best Wealth,' throwing light on what problems arise if we eat junk food or overeat and neglect our health and how we can maintain good health through right food and good habits.

Ans. **Health-The Best Wealth**

by Mohini

'Health is Wealth' is an old saying which aptly sums up the importance of maintaining good health. If we are healthy, we are physically and mentally contented as we are away from medical conditions like hypertension, diabetes, heart ailments, etc.

It brings the ability to enjoy life and be a productive asset to our family, friends and the society. It brings happiness and contentment to our lives.

Unfortunately, most of us in a race to earn materialistic wealth, ignore it. As a result, in the past decade there has been an unprecedented rise in the growing problem of obesity in children. Children especially in the cities, binge on junk food or overeat, have sugar-sweetened beverages and include very few fruits and vegetables in their normal diet.

Consequently, they become overweight and vulnerable to lifestyle diseases like high blood pressure and type II diabetes.

It is imperative to ensure that children maintain a healthy lifestyle through right food and good eating habits. They should be encouraged to eat foods that provide adequate nutrition and an appropriate number of calories. An active lifestyle where they engage in physical activity daily should be encouraged. To effectively address the complex problem of childhood obesity, a sustained effort to promote a healthy lifestyle needs to be followed by parents and these strategies need to be initiated in children at a very early stage.

MCB Theme 2 Education

5. To meet the employment needs, the youth today are venturing into startups. As Veena/Veer of Class X-A, write an article in about 150 words, for your school magazine discussing the merits of startups as a boon to self-reliance. Use the cues given below along with your ideas and those you may have gathered from the unit: Education, to write the article.

- From job seeker to job creator
- Economic growth
- Self-reliance
- Decision-making freedom
- Flexible working conditions

Ans. **Startup as a Boon to Self-Reliance**

by XYZ

In today's world, where employment opportunities are limited, many young people are choosing to become job creators instead of job seekers. Startups have become a powerful way to achieve self-reliance, allowing individuals to turn their ideas into successful businesses.

One major benefit of startups is their role in economic growth. By creating jobs, they reduce unemployment and contribute to the nation's progress. Entrepreneurs also enjoy decision-making freedom, where they can shape their businesses according to their vision and creativity. Unlike traditional jobs, startups offer flexible working conditions, giving individuals the freedom to manage their time and work on their own terms.

Most importantly, startups empower young minds to think innovatively and take charge of their own success. Instead of depending on others for employment, they build opportunities for themselves and others. With passion, hard work, and the right mindset, startups are truly paving the way for a self-reliant future.

6. Choice of course after clearing Senior School Examination produces a great deal of stress on the minds of our students. Counselling can be of great help to them. Write an article on the topic, 'Role of Counselling in Choice of Course'. Use the following clues

- Deciding a career goal is important
- Discover their potential and interests, strengths and weaknesses
- Decide your career based on your aptitude, skills, interests, performance and personality
- Identifies that unique quality and guides informed choice

Ans. **Role of Counselling in Choice of Course**

by Ram

Choosing a definite career and deciding a career goal is very important especially once you have completed your senior secondary schooling. Unfortunately, not many students are able to discover their potential and interests and that is when the pressure starts building up.

There is no denying the truth that once we finish our school, we are faced with – what next? A student at the threshold of a new start has parents, teachers and friends as guides and each one speaks from his/her own perspective. It is at this juncture that a counsellor can help students in choosing a course that suits them. He/ She is the best person to guide you and help you decide your career based on your aptitude, skills, interests, performance and personality.

Human talent and potential is tremendous and can't be measured as such. Each individual has his/her strengths and weaknesses. A career counsellor identifies that unique quality and guides one to know the different career paths. With all this information, students can make an informed choice. Even in the future, counselling helps in setting goals and gives directions to life.

Thus, I would say that with the help of career counsellors students end up choosing the best profession well suited to their needs. They perform well and ultimately succeed in life. So, let us make an intelligent and professional move and step ahead in the right direction with the help of those who are more aware and informed.

7. Write an article on the topic– 'Inclusive Education is not an Alternative but an Inevitability', for publication in your school magazine. You may keep the following factors affecting Inclusive Education in mind

- Attitude of parents, teachers, classmates and the society
- Physical support
- Curriculum support
- Policy support
- Teacher support
- Infrastructure

Or **"Everyone is a genius. But if you judge a fish by its ability to climb a tree, it will live its whole life believing that it is stupid." Based on the above quote and using ideas from Unit-2 : Education, along with your ideas, write an article in about 150 words.** **CBSE 2024 C**

"The Transformative Power of Inclusive Education on Modern Education system."

Attitude of Parents, Teachers and Classmates

Physical Support

Curriculum Support

Or **Write an article, in about 150 words, as Gaurav Taneja, X-B, advocating for the implementation of inclusive education practices in schools, focusing on the benefits for students with diverse learning needs. Share advantages and discuss the importance of fostering an inclusive school environment. Additionally, propose any one recommendation for policymakers and educators to promote inclusivity in the education system. Use the given cues, along with your own ideas and those you may have gathered from Unit 2 : Education, to create this article.**

- Benefits of inclusive education for students with diverse learning needs
- Importance of fostering an inclusive school environment. **CBSE SQP 2024**

Ans. **Inclusive Education is not an Alternative but an Inevitability**

by XYZ

God Almighty has created each individual differently with peculiarities. Each child has unique mental and physical traits. Keeping these differences in mind, the same curriculum cannot be imposed on these differently talented children. It has to be tailormade(changed) for each different child.

For example, some children are prodigies while the others are very bright; similarly others are moderately brilliant and some are just average achievers; some are special children with special needs.

In such a situation, a new system of education needs to be implemented to cater to all students. With the advancement in teaching-learning methodology and the experience gained over the years, educationists have been coming up with better and more efficient methods of teaching and learning.

Inclusive education is one such new method of providing a conducive learning environment to students according to their abilities in the same classroom. Inclusive education ensures different curriculum for different children in the same environment. That is, each child has the option to pursue his curriculum according to his own talent, potential and interest. This not only makes education and learning more fruitful and productive but also much more entertaining. So, inclusive education should be adopted by all schools unanimously.

8. Based on the information provided in this section along with the input given below, write an article on "The Growing Need for Vocational Education"/ "Education Curriculum requires Fresh Perspective"

"In India every year 6,50,000 engineering graduates and approximately two million graduates pass out of colleges. Nearly two-thirds of the 6,50,000 engineering graduates need to be re-skilled, so that they can get jobs in the industry. The developed world requires knowledged workers and skilled professionals. By 2020, the developed world will have a shortage of 40 million working people, says a report. According to a survey, 72 per cent of our population is under the age of 35 and it is estimated that 300 million people between the ages of 18 and 50 seek employment of some form. While 57 per cent are unemployable, 46 per cent are registered with employment exchanges with little hope of finding work because there is a mismatch between the skilled manpower required and skilled man power available. A majority of the youth passing out of colleges do not have the specific skills required by various sectors in the market."

- Para 1- Introduction (The present education system- Vocational education how different)
- Para 2- The short comings of the system, its effect on the development of the country
- Para 3- Reasons of this mismatch in the market
- Para 4- Suggestions to bridge the gap

Ans. The Growing Need for Vocational Education

by XYZ

Education is a process which empowers a student to think for himself/herself and make his/her decisions in life. However, the present day education system puts emphasis on rote-learning and unhealthy competition. As a result, there exists a disparity between market demands and the skills of India's educated youth.

Various data revealed by surveys indicate that there is a gap in the education we receive and the skills we ought to have. For example, every year 6,50,000 engineering graduates pass out of whom nearly two-thirds need to be re-skilled so that they can get jobs in the industry. These figures reveal the shortage of skilled manpower in India in comparison to the jobs existing in the market. This mismatch occurs due to many reasons.

A few of them are low motivation amongst students to pursue vocational education, the rigid mindset of parents and educators in accepting vocational courses and thinking of them as obsolete courses. Further, there is poor linkage between institutions offering vocational courses and the private sector.

In order to keep up with the market demands of India, students should be encouraged to take up vocational education. They should be allowed to study the subjects they like. Teachers and parents must become more open minded about students' career and life choices. There should be enough infrastructure to support vocational education. Educational institutes could link up with Companies and Corporations so that students can be employed soon after they complete their studies. These are a few ways in which the gap between vocational education and market demand for skilled manpower can be bridged.

MCB Theme 3 Science

9. Space tourism, though in its early stages, is a reality. As Jagmeet Singh of Class X-D, write an article for your school magazine in about 150 words, discussing the opportunities and challenges of space tourism, the ethical considerations surrounding it and how it might impact society.

Use the given cues, along with your own ideas and those you may have gathered from Unit 3 : Science, to create this article.

- Safety concerns and potential accidents in space tourism
- Space debris and the need for responsible space traffic management
- Turning space in a commodity : the ethics of commercialising space

- Ensuring equality and access to space tourism opportunities
- Promoting responsible and sustainable practices in space tourism
- Balancing economic opportunities with environmental and social responsiblity.

CBSE SQP 2023

Ans. **Space Tourism: Balancing Opportunity and Responsibility**

By Jagmeet Singh, X-D

Space tourism, the idea of sending tourists into space for a few minutes or days, is becoming a reality. However, the opportunities and challenges of space tourism are complex and ethical considerations need to be taken into account.

One opportunity of space tourism is that it could inspire the next generation of scientists and engineers, providing a new way to get people interested in space exploration. However, space tourism also presents many challenges, including the potential impact on the environment. Space debris is already a major problem and increased space traffic from tourism could exacerbate this issue. What also causes concern is that it could contribute to the commodification of space, turning it into a playground for the rich rather than a shared resource for all humanity. There is also the question of putting paying tourists at risk for the sake of leisure activities.

As we move ahead with this exciting new industry, we must remain mindful of the impact on our planet, our society and the future of space exploration.

10. You are Rahul/Rekha. There are frequent power cuts in your locality. You strongly feel that it is time to shift to solar power. Write an article on the topic 'Solar Power: An Apt Global Solution for Energy Crisis'. Support your ideas with the clues given below.

- Renewable energy
- Reduce energy bill
- Completely clean, no water pollution, no greenhouse gas effects
- Carbon free, no emissions
- Low maintenance cost

Ans. **Solar Power: An Apt Global Solution for Energy Crisis**

by Rahul/Rekha

In the modern world wherein population and requirements are always increasing, the demand for energy has been on a constant rise. In this light, it is not unknown to us that our conventional sources of energy are depleting at an alarming rate. Consequently, the need of the hour to switch to renewable energy sources has time and again been taken up. Finally, we have a solution- solar power.

Solar power or solar energy is the most abundant and readily available source of energy on Earth. As a renewable source of energy, solar power offers various benefits to its users. First, it helps to reduce energy bills significantly. Once the initial installation cost is covered, solar energy is virtually free. Second, solar energy is completely clean and creates no pollution. It is carbon-free and emits no harmful gases. Hence, it is environmentally friendly and sustainable. Furthermore, solar energy requires low maintenance. It only needs to be cleaned periodically to remove dust and dirt. It is a one-time investment that has long-term benefits. Solar panels have a lifespan of 20-30 years and they can be used to generate electricity for a long period.

To conclude, solar power is an apt global solution for the energy crisis. It is renewable, environmentally friendly and cost-effective. Governments and individuals must take necessary steps towards shifting to solar power to ensure a sustainable and greener future. It is high time we realise the importance of renewable energy sources and take action towards creating a brighter and cleaner future.

11. Write an article on the topic 'Does Technology Limit Creativity'.

Ans. **Does Technology Limit Creativity**

by XYZ

Creativity and technology are two facets that have gained utmost importance in the modern contemporary world. However, with the emergence of technology which is improving day-by-day, a new topic of debate regarding these two facets has risen. People have taken sides when it comes to the effect of technology on creativity.

There are a category of people who believe that technology fosters creativity. It was a creative mind that gave birth to the internet and also other technologies. Similarly, the new devices, gadgets and technologies are the outcome of different creative minds. Creativity helps us to develop new things. When we need something, we think and try to fulfill our needs and, in this sequence, we develop something new. At the same time, people believe that technology has made us inactive which never encourages us to do something new. Laziness is something that never allows you to progress .We have become used to some technologies like our phones, social media, etc. All these distract us and when we have to submit our projects or assignments, rather than generating our own ideas we search it on the internet and complete our task quickly. This hinders us to think and develop new ideas.

It is important for us to note that it is our need which provokes us to invent something new. Thus, to judge whether technology has a negative impact on creativity would be wrong.

MCB Theme 4 Environment

12. EVs or Electric vehicles have now become a necessity. Keeping in mind how the rise in economic activity and burgeoning population has led to a tremendous demand of electric vehicles in the transport sector, especially in urban India, write an article on 'A World with Smog-free and Clean Air'. Use the given cues along with your own ideas from the Unit- 'Science'. (150 words) CBSE 2024

India's ever-growing population EV-Lower running costs	Critical issues of air and noise pollution
Zero tailpipe emissions	Electric vehicles-low maintenance costs

Ans. **A World with Smog-free and Clean Air**

by ABC

With the ever growing population of India and the growing concern for air pollution, the people of India have quickly welcomed EVs or Electric Vehicles. The reason behind this change is that Electric Vehicles have lower running costs compared to gasoline-powered vehicles. EVs have fewer moving parts which results in reduced maintenance requirements and lower long-term maintenance costs. Moreover, electricity is generally cheaper than gasoline on a per-mile basis, leading to lower fueling costs for EV owners.

One of the primary advantages of electric vehicles is their reduced environmental impact. EVs produce zero tailpipe emissions which help improve air quality and reduce pollution, both air and noise, in urban areas. Additionally, when powered by renewable energy sources such as solar or wind power, EVs can significantly lower greenhouse gas emissions compared to gasoline-powered vehicles. Electric vehicles reduce dependency on fossil fuels, which are finite resources and contribute to climate change.

Overall, electric vehicles play a crucial role in reducing greenhouse gas emissions, improving air quality, and transitioning to a more sustainable transportation system. As technology continues to evolve and adoption rates increase, electric vehicles will become increasingly integral to efforts to combat climate change and create a cleaner, greener future.

13. "The return of the cheetahs will help in the restoration of open forests and grassland ecosystems in India." Write an article in expressing your views on how this will help conserve biodiversity, wildlife and soil conservation. You Bela/Bhanu. Use the following cues along with your own ideas to compose your article.

- Ecological balance of nature
- Helps keep the food chain in place
- Maintains ecological stability
- Diversity ensures healthier ecosystems
- Cultural significance
- Good for mental health

Ans. **Return of the Cheetahs**

by Bela/Bhanu

In the time where the world is all focused on preservation and conservation, ideas regarding the flora and fauna, environment and ecological balance of the world, the return of the Cheetahs is a great milestone. The return of the Cheetahs will help in the restoration of open forests and grassland ecosystems in India which will further help maintain the ecological balance of nature.

Cheetahs are also needed to maintain the food chain. The big cat typically hunts the weak and slowest of several species of animals. If cheetahs no longer existed, there would be too many herbivores resulting in loss of vegetation, greater soil erosion, less available water and a negative impact on the health of the ecosystem.

To conclude, when a healthy environment is maintained, the world becomes a better and a happy place for all.

14. Scarcity of water is felt by people everywhere in villages, in towns and in big cities. Global warming has affected our rainfall and snowfall. Our population is increasing and demand for water is on the rise. Rainwater harvesting, conservation of water, along with control on its wastage shall help us meet our water needs in future. Write an article on the topic, 'Water Problem' using the clues given above.

Ans. **Water Problem**

by Ankita

The Earth is called the Blue Planet, and for reasons known well to all of us. About 97% of the earth is made of water and yet the scarcity of water available for use to man is nerve-chilling. India suffers from water shortage for cultivation and drinking despite the fact that many big rivers flow through some parts of India.

The cause of this scarcity is global warming which has led to irregularities in rainfall and snowfall, and depletion of underground water resources. Further, rapid urbanisation, industrialisation and the ever increasing population has led to an increase in demand of everything. As a result, all of the underground water is lost due to overexploitation. It is now estimated that by 2020, several Indian cities like Delhi and Bengaluru will have lost their groundwater recharge completely. India is blessed with rainfall in several regions which can be harvested to meet our needs. Schemes that promote proper town planning and water harvesting need to be launched on a big scale.

Eco clubs should be established in all the schools of the country to spread awareness among the students about the need to stop the reckless use of water and water conservation. Only then we can ensure a safe future for our coming generations, otherwise the day is not far when we may witness another world-war not for land, but for water.

15. Air pollution in our cities is increasing alarmingly. According to environmentalists, vehicles are one of the major contributors to air pollution. They recommend use of public transport by private vehicle owners. People in general are willing to switch over from private to public transport if there is a good system in place. Write an article on the topic, 'Importance of an Efficient Public Transport System'. You are Raghu/Ragini.

Ans. **Importance of an Efficient Public Transport System**

by Ragini Nair

A major factor contributing to the alarming air pollution of our country is private transportation. While private transportation is an important factor to urban sustainability, it also creates nuisance by giving rise to air and noise pollution. The increase in the number of cars and bikes has added to the various pollution problems. The smoke emitted from vehicles has turned the cities into living gas chambers. They affect our eyes and lungs, giving rise to all kinds of cardiovascular and respiratory diseases.

We, as the responsible citizens of India, must take steps to reduce these man-made problems and start using public transport as much as possible. We are well-aware that it can transport many more people in much less space than individual vehicles, which helps to lower traffic congestion, which in turn reduces air pollution; thus contributing towards a healthier environment. Not only that, it also offers a more economical, safe and energy efficient mode of transportation. It doesn't just improve the air quality and reduce the fuel consumption but also increases mobility and connectivity.

Public transportation is also linked with healthier lifestyles, as people who use public transportation are supposed to get more physical activity per day than those who don't, just from walking to and from their transit stops and their final destination. Thus, there is a need for an efficient public transport system.

MCB Theme 5 Travel and Tourism

16. Some people prefer solo travel while others enjoy travelling in a group. As Hema Joseph of Class X-C, write an article for your school magazine, in about 150 words, discussing the advantages and disadvantages of each preference and examining the factors that influence these choices.
Use the given cues, along with your own ideas and those you may gathered from Unit 5 : Travel and Tourism, to create this article. **CBSE SQP 2023**

- How can lonelines and safety concerns impact solo travel?
- What are some factors that can make solo travel more-expensive?
- How does travelling alone allow for personal growth and discovery?
- What are some advantage of being able to choose your itinerary and pace?
- How can conflicts and disagreements arise when travelling with others?
- What are some factors that can limit independence and freedom when travelling with a group?
- How does travelling with others provide opportunities to make friends?
- What are some ways that group travel can be more cost-effective?
- How can personality type influence travel preferences?
- How does budget impact travel choices?
- What role does the destination play in determining travel preferences?

Ans. Choosing Your Travel Style : The Benefits and Drawbacks of Solo and Group Travel

by Hema Joseph, X-C

Travelling is one of life's greatest pleasures and today many people have converted it into their professions. With many people taking to travelling, many different styles of travelling have come up. The way we prefer to travel varies from person to person. Factors that influence travel preferences include personality type, budget, destination and the purpose of travel. Some prefer solo travel while others enjoy travelling in a group. Each preference has its advantages and disadvantages.

Solo travel allows for complete independence and the freedom to choose the itinerary and pace. It also provides an opportunity for self-discovery and personal growth. However, solo travel can be lonely, expecially during meal times and at night. Besides this, it can be more expensive, as no costs are shared among the group. However, group travel requires more planning and coordination and sometimes compromises must be made. Additionally, some people may feel restricted by the group's itinerary and activities.

Extroverts may prefer group travel while introverts may opt for solo travel. Budget constraints may make group travel more feasible while adventure destinations may be better suited for solo travel. Ultimately, the decision to travel solo or in a group is a personal one. Both options have their pros and cons and travellers should weigh them carefully before embarking on their journey.

17. Tourism in India has been on the rise. Write an article in about 150 words, as Gaurav Taneja, X-B, discussing the surge in tourism in India since 2021, highlighting the key factors contributing to its growth. Propose additional recommendations to further boost tourism and predict the trajectory of the industry for the upcoming decade.

Use the given cues, along with your own ideas and those you may have gathered from Unit 5: Travel and Tourism, to create this article. **CBSE SQP 2024**

- Factors contributing to the tourism boom.
- Additional recommendations to sustain and enhance tourism
- Prediction for the future of Indian tourism; Plus and Minus

Ans. India's Tourism Boom : A Post-Pandemic Phenomenon

by Gaurav Taneja, X-B

India's tourism industry has witnessed a remarkable surge since the pandemic-induced slump in 2021. Several factors have contributed to this growth, including government initiatives, where the government's focus on infrastructure development, visa liberalisation, and promotional campaigns like 'Incredible India', has played a pivotal role in attracting international tourists. Also, digital advancements, such as the increasing penetration of the internet and social media has made it easier for travellers to research, plan, and book their trips. Furthermore, the unique cultural experiences where India's rich cultural heritage, diverse landscapes, and spiritual offerings continue to be major draws for tourists. Apart from these, India offers a unique blend of luxury and affordability, making it an attractive destination for travellers on a budget.

To further boost tourism, India can consider sustainable tourism by promoting eco-friendly practices and preserving natural heritage can attract environmentally conscious travellers. Also, encouraging tourism in rural areas can help revive local economies and promote cultural preservation. Leveraging India's world-class medical facilities to attract international patients seeking affordable healthcare would also help.

Looking ahead, the Indian tourism industry is poised for continued growth. With its diverse offerings, rich cultural heritage, and growing infrastructure, India has the potential to become a global tourism powerhouse. However, challenges such as infrastructure bottlenecks, safety concerns, and seasonality need to be addressed to ensure sustainable and inclusive growth.

18. You are Ram/Rajani. You feel that India, with its rich and varied heritage, linguistic and cultural diversity is an excellent destination for tourism. Promoting tourism will surely promote our economy. Write an article titled, 'Promoting Tourism is Promoting Ourselves' specifying the advantages of promoting tourism and how it can be accomplished.

Ans. Promoting Tourism is Promoting Ourselves

by Rajani

India has fascinated people from all over the world with its secularism and culture. There are historical monuments, places of religious interest, beaches and hill resorts that attract tourists. Every region is identified by its handicrafts, folk dances, music, fairs, people, etc. Bounded by the Himalayan mountain ranges in the North, by the Arabian Sea, Indian Ocean and the Bay of Bengal on the other three sides, India can give a delightful experience to the tourists. The enchanting backwaters, hill stations and landscapes make India a beautiful country to visit.

No doubt, Indian landscape has been one of the most preferred tourist destinations. Tourism plays a vital role in the economic development of a country. It is the second largest foreign exchange earner for India. The tourism industry employs a large number of skilled as well as unskilled persons. It also promotes national integration and international brotherhood. Thus, we should promote it for our own benefit.

The government's Department of Tourism promotes international and domestic tourism in the country. The Tourism Advisory Board recommends measures for promotion of tourist traffic to India. However, international tourism has been adversely affected by terrorism as well as pollution. Sincere efforts to combat such problems are required to further develop this industry. Thus, tourism, one of the fastest growing industries today, plays a vital role in the economic development of our country. By promoting tourism, we will be promoting ourselves.

19. Write an article on 'The Two Sides of Tourism Industry'.

Ans. **The Two Sides of Tourism Industry**

by XYZ

Tourism and the Hospitality Industry are the most promising and fast flourishing industries of the world. Thus, it is not surprising that many leaders feel that tourism in India has the potential to promote faster, sustainable and more inclusive growth.

Tourism brings with itself many advantages to the nation. It stimulates the economy by generating income from visitor expenditures, including accommodation, food, transportation and attractions. This infusion of money can boost local businesses, create job opportunities, improve the standard of living and contribute to poverty reduction. Further, it allows people to experience different traditions, customs and ways of life. This cultural interaction fosters mutual understanding, tolerance and appreciation for diversity. In addition, tourism can contribute to the preservation and conservation of historical sites, natural landscapes and cultural heritage.

While tourism brings economic growth, employment opportunities and cultural exchange, it can also lead to overcrowding, environmental degradation and cultural commodification. Popular tourist destinations can become overcrowded which can strain local infrastructure, public services and natural resources. Tourism leads to increased construction of hotels, resorts and infrastructure which leads to deforestation, habitat destruction and pollution. Additionally, the carbon emissions from transportation and waste generated by tourists can contribute to climate change and damage fragile ecosystems.

Thus , the tourism industry has a dual nature, offering both benefits and challenges. It has the potential to drive economic growth, provide employment, foster cultural exchange and preserve heritage. However, it also poses risks such as overcrowding, environmental degradation, cultural commodification and unequal wealth distribution. To maximise the positive impacts and mitigate the negative ones, sustainable tourism practices and responsible travel are crucial.

MCB Theme 6 National Integration

20. India represents a harmonious oneness in spite of distinctions. Taking ideas from the unit 'National Integration', and using the given cues along with your own ideas, write an article in 150 words for your school magazine on 'The Importance of Diversified Culture'. CBSE 2024

India–a land embracing many cultures	India–festivals dedicated to seasons and harvests
India–multitude of castes, creed, colour, convictions, culture, cuisines, costumes and customs	India national festivals-pride, sense of patriotism-promote national integration

Ans. **The Importance of Diversified Culture**

by XYZ

The importance of diversified culture is multifaceted and deeply ingrained in human society. India is one such nation that embraces many cultures. It celebrates a myriad of festivals throughout the year, reflecting its cultural and religious diversity. Diwali, Holi, Eid, Christmas, Navratri and Durga Puja are examples of just a festivals celebrated with great fervour and enthusiasm across the country. Many of these festivals are dedicated to seasons like Basant Panchmi, Baisakhi and Lohri while those dedicated to harvest include Makar Sankranti, Bihu, Pongal and Onam, to name a few.

India also has a multitude of castes, creed, colour and convictions. Indian cuisine is also incredibly diverse, with each region offering its own unique flavours, ingredients and cooking techniques which are widely popular. Naturally, traditional Indian clothing varies widely from region to region, with sarees, salwar kameez, dhotis and kurta-pyjamas being some of the most common attires, which are also loved by foreigners visiting the country.

India celebrates several national festivals that hold significant cultural, historical and religious importance some of which are, Republic Day (January 26), Independence Day (August 15) and Gandhi Jayanti (October 2). Such festivals bring the nation together and fill the citizens with a sense of pride, patriotism and eventually promote national integration.

21. Write an article on 'Degeneration of Democratic Values in India'.

Ans. **Degeneration of Democratic Values in India**

by PQR

The Republic of India, with its varied topography, extraordinary ethnic mix, 22 official and 780 spoken languages and diverse religions and cultures, has moved decisively on the path of progress overcoming existential threats and garnering attention as one of the world's most powerful democracies. However, with this title came degeneration of many values that were essential to maintaining an effective democracy.

The democratic values of accountability, transparency, social equity, justice, etc. have degenerated extensively. Today, no authority takes responsibility for the lack the country faces. Problems of illiteracy, discrimination, unemployment, poverty, etc. have gripped society more tightly and instead of looking for solutions we are playing a blame game. Drug abuse in some states has reached alarming proportions. The education system has let the country down, producing millions of unemployable people, all of which have been severely exacerbated due to the pandemic. Ironically, there is no dearth of policies, programmes and funds to deal with these issues.

Therefore, it is important that we stop and reflect upon the various deficiencies and drawbacks of our current state of democracy. We must forcefully reassert our democratic conscience.

22. Write an article on 'Journalism and Its Work in a Democratic Set-up'.

Ans. **Journalism and Its Work in a Democratic Set-up**

by PQR

Democracy is described as the government by the people, for the people or the rule of the people through their elected representatives. However, for the democratic system to operate effectively, the participation on the part of the public is also imperative. This needs a continuous circulation of reliable information to the masses. This is where Journalism comes in.

Journalism, since time immemorial, has been used to make the public aware about various social, political and economic activities. A news media, be it in print form or TV/radio, informs people about unbiased news without any censorship or tampering. As a result, people have come to always trust actual and honest news. Thus, it is not surprising that media plays an indispensable role in the proper functioning of a democracy. It has become a connecting link between government and people that provides citizens with knowledge about government acts, policies and inefficiencies. Media's functions within electoral contexts often focuses on their 'watchdog' role: by scrutiny and discussion of the successes and failures of candidates, governments, and electoral management bodies, the media can inform the public of how effectively they have performed and helped to hold them to account. It is also a forum where public can communicate, debate or discuss their concerns, opinions and needs. Further, media is a public educator. It educates and makes people aware of all topics of paramount importance to society.

Considering the increasing significance of media in the world, it was termed as the fourth pillar of democracy.

23. Write an article on 'Destabilising Forces Within a Country: Challenges to a Nation'.

Ans. **Destabilising Forces Within a Country: Challenges to a Nation**

by PQR

The culture, civilisation and tradition of India is approximately 12,000 years old. The spirit of tolerance has made it possible for our civilisation to survive the test of time. But with the passage of time, the growing attachment to one's own ethnic, religious, racial or cultural group rather than being a part of a wider circle of the entire social milieu, has posed one of the gravest problems of modern times. Fear, suspicion and a sense of insecurity towards the other communities has given rise to hatred which acts as a fuel, feeding the flame of many problems that challenge the integrity of the nation.

The forces that challenge national integration can simply be termed as regionalism, communalism, religious fanaticism, lingualism and terrorism. The growing attachment with one's own community, religion and language has lead to a thinking that they are superior. The result is national unrest and riots. Besides these internal conflicts, terrorism has also rooted itself deep in the country.

Thus, time and again our leader has talked about the need to destroy these disruptive forces. To achieve national integration and to crush divisive and disruptive forces, we must create an emotional bond of common ideas and values that can bind all the people of India. We, as responsible citizens, should continuously and ferociously guard our great secular heritage. Communal differences should be nipped in the bud itself and not be allowed to rise and flourish. Children should be taught to appreciate the diversity of the country. They should be taught to learn divergent cultures and ways of living.

Remember that it is us who have to make our nation strong and united.

24. Write an article in 150 words on 'Importance of Festivals in Our Social Life'. You are Anu/Anupam.

Ans. **Festivals of India**

by Anu

India is a secular country having diverse religions, languages, customs and traditions. Thus, it is not surprising why Indians celebrate many festivals throughout the year. Festival celebration brings happiness and joy to all. This is the occasion which creates a gathering where all the family members, relatives, friends and loved ones can meet and share their happiness.

Festivals play an important role in our lives. As we are living in the fast-paced world leading a stressful life, festivals are the ideal occasions to take a break from stress and create memorable times. It is also during the festivals that people belonging to different religions can celebrate different festivals thus uniting the country.

The beauty of the festivals is that each one of them is celebrated differently as per certain rituals and beliefs. While some festivals are celebrated by the whole nation, other festivals are confined to specific regions. But all the festivals are celebrated with great enthusiasm. Based on rituals and religions, festivals have been categorised. There are Hindu festivals, the dates of which are fixed on the basis of the Hindu calendar. These include Diwali, Dussehra, Holi, Lohri, Janamasthmi, Raksha Bandhan, etc. Then there are festivals celebrated by Muslims including Ramzan, Id-Ul-Milad, Bakra-Id, Muharram, etc. Sikhs celebrate the birthdays of their ten Gurus. The Christians celebrate Good Friday, Easter and Christmas.

The uniqueness of our country lies in the fact that in spite of the cultural differences, we celebrate and enjoy the numerous festivals with a sense of oneness. India is a land of diversity therefore, it is suffice to say that the number of festivals we enjoy is one of the ways in which it makes us feel proud of our national heritage.

ASSESSMENT EXERCISE

1. You are Dikshit, a sportsman. You are worried about the decreasing interest of students in sports and games. Write an article to be published in a magazine on the need for sports and games. Use the hints given below.

- Lack of physical activity
- Builds confidence, interpersonal skills
- Makes one disciplined
- More importance to examination results

2. Every teenager has a dream to achieve something in life. What they are going to become tomorrow depends on what our youth dreams today. Write an article on 'What I Want to be in Life'. You are Simranjit/Smita.

3. For admission to colleges, there is a lot of competition today. For one available seat, there are hundreds of candidates. Such a situation leads to stress on the minds of students in the schools. However, the practice of Yoga can help them to feel calm and stress-free. Write an article on the topic, 'Importance of Yoga to Students'. You are Karan/Karuna.

4. Mid-day meal scheme in the schools introduced by the government serves several purposes. Millions of children from the deprived sections of society get nutritious food leading to good health, are attracted to the schools, kept from going astray and developed into good citizens. The scheme may have some drawbacks too. Write an article on all aspects of the scheme. You are Navtej/Navita.

5. Morning assembly in the schools gives a cool and calm start to the otherwise hectic schedule of the day. It can be a means of passing important information to the students. What are your views on this significant event of the day? Write an article on 'Importance of Morning Assembly'. You are Navtej/Navita.

6. You are Rohini/Rahul. In today's competitive age, the students' main focus is on academics and coaching classes for entrance examinations so they tend to neglect participation in outdoor games. Lack of open spaces is another reason for avoiding athletics and sports. Write an article on 'Poor Physical Fitness of School Students'.

7. When children watch TV the adults generally scold them, without realising that some programmes on TV can be educative too. Write an article in 150 words on 'TV as a Tool of Instruction'. You are Navtej/ Navita.

8. You saw a stray dog beaten to death by a group of boys. Their act infuriated you and you scolded them for their cruel act. Write an article in about 150 words on the topic 'Cruelty to Animals'. You are Nikhil/ Naina.

9. The Delhi administration has launched a campaign against the use of polythene bags. Write an article in 150 words on 'Hazards of Polythene Bags' for your school magazine. You can use the following clues.
   - Polythene bags–hazardous
   - Light, handy, attractive and strong
   - Big threat to our environment
   - Adverse effects-choke the drains
   - Ways to reduce its use

10. You believe that a positive attitude is needed to ensure happiness, health and success. You are Krish/Kavya. Write an article in 150 words on 'Advantages of a Positive Attitude.'

    Clues
   - Brings more happiness to your life
   - Helps you achieve goals and attain success
   - Increases your faith in your abilities
   - Enables you to show self-esteem and confidence

11. You see that the modern life is full of stress and strain. Write an article on the 'Importance of Hobbies' in 150 words using the following clues.
   - Stress, anxiety and depression
   - Hobbies to destress
   - Gives pleasure
   - Upskills
   - Mental relaxation and peace
   - Mind is rejuvenated

12. Using the notes given below write an article in 150 words on 'Obesity Among children'.

    Clues
   - Sedentary life
   - Health risks
   - Remedies
   - Prevention

13. It is a pity that we cannot meet the natural calamities in a proper way. Write an article in 150 words on the 'Need of Disaster Management' using the notes given below.

    Clues
   - Effects of calamities
   - Causes of calamities
   - Disaster management
   - Condition of India

14. Write an article in 150 words on the 'Need of Democracy'.

15. It is said that if you educate a boy, you educate a person and if you educate a girl you educate a family. Write an article on the importance of educating women. You are Suresh/Shobha.

16. You are Ram/Rajani. You feel that in India, with its rich and varied heritage, linguistic and cultural diversity, it is essential to live in harmony which alone will lead to prosperity and peace. Write an article on the topic 'Unity in Diversity', specifying the advantages of unity and how we can promote it in spite of our diversity in religion, culture and language. You may quote relevant examples.

Section C : Grammar

CHAPTER 1

Tenses

1.1 Definition of Tense

Tense is defined as the form of verb that gives the relation between time and action. It tells us when the action is done.

There are three phases of time

(i) **Present** (time that is now)

(ii) **Past** (time that has passed)

(iii) **Future** (time that is yet to come)

Let's consider the sentences given below

(i) He is an artist. (Present)

(ii) He was an artist. (Past)

(iii) He will be an artist. (Future)

We can observe that each sentence given above has a different meaning. The reason for this difference in meaning is that each sentence has a different form of verb. These different forms of verbs are called tenses.

1.2 Classification of Tenses

According to the phases of time, there are three tenses

(i) Present Tense

(ii) Past Tense

(iii) Future Tense

Each tense is further divided into four forms. Study the chart given below to understand more about all tenses and their forms.

TENSE

- **Present**
  - Indefinite
  - Continuous
  - Perfect
  - Perfect Continuous
- **Past**
  - Indefinite
  - Continuous
  - Perfect
  - Perfect Continuous
- **Future**
  - Indefinite
  - Continuous
  - Perfect
  - Perfect Continuous

Present Tense

Present Indefinite Tense (Simple Present Tense)

This tense is used in the following ways

(i) To express habit or custom.

e.g. • She goes for a walk every morning at 6 o'clock. (habit)

• She studies every morning. (custom)

(ii) To talk about a universal truth.

e.g. The Moon affects the ocean's tides on earth. (universal truth)

(iii) To indicate a future event which is part of a plan or arrangement.

e.g. • The institute reopens next month.

• The examination commences tomorrow.

(iv) To introduce quotes with the verb 'says'.

e.g. • J.R.R. Tolkein says, "not all those who wander are lost."

• Neil Armstrong says, "That's one small step for a man, a giant leap for mankind."

(v) Vivid narration, as a substitute for the simple past.

e.g. Robinhood fights to provide for the poor.

(vi) Exclamatory sentences that begin with here or there.

e.g. • Here he is!

• There she comes!

(vii) Time clauses and conditional clauses in place of simple future.

e.g. • If you do not run fast, you will miss the bus.

• If you do not eat properly, you will become weak.

Rules for Affirmative Sentences

- Singular subject + first form of verb + s/es + ...
- I/You/Plural subject + first form of verb + ...

e.g. • She runs fast.
• An atom consists of an electron, proton and neutron.

Rules for Negative Sentences

- Singular subject + does not + first form of verb + ...
- I/You/Plural subject + do not + first form of verb + ...

e.g. • I do not like playing outdoor games.
• They are not going to the theatre today.

Rules for Interrogative Sentences

- Do/does + subject + first form of verb + ...?
- Question word + do/does + subject + first form of verb + ...?

e.g. • Does your head still hurt from the fall?
• Why do you need to go now?

Present Continuous Tense

This tense is used in the following ways

(i) To describe an action in progress.

e.g. • I am going for a walk.
• The children are playing with the dogs at the park.

(ii) An action that is not happening at the time of speaking but is in progress.

e.g. • He is pursuing his Masters degree from M University.
• They are working as professional coaches.

(iii) An action that has been pre-arranged to take place in the near future.

e.g. • I am holding my birthday party next week.
• My uncle and aunt are celebrating their 25th wedding anniversary tomorrow.

(iv) Persistent and undesirable habit, especially with adverbs like always, continually, constantly, etc.

e.g. • Hera is continually snickering at the humans in Olympus.
• Mother is constantly reminding us to not skip breakfast.

Rules for Affirmative Sentences

- Singular subject + is/am + first form of verb + ing +.......
- You/Plural subject + are + first form of verb + ing +.......

e.g. • She is building a website.
• They are going for a trip to Maldives.

Rules for Negative Sentences

- Singular subject + is/am + not + first form of verb + ing +.......
- Plural subject + are + not + first form of verb + ing +.......

e.g. • Rama is not coming to school today.
• I am not feeling well.

Rules for Interrogative Sentences

- Is/are/am + subject + first form of verb + ing + ...?
- Question word + is/are/am + subject + first form of verb + ing + ...?

e.g. • Is Akshay reading a novel?
• When are you leaving for work?

Exceptions for Continuous Tense

The following verbs are not normally used in present continuous tense on account of their meaning

- Verbs of perception or senses, e.g. see, hear, smell, notice, recognise, etc .
- Verbs of appearance, e.g. appear, look, seem, etc.
- Verbs of thinking, e.g. think, suppose, believe, agree, consider, forget, know, imagine, mean, etc.
- Verbs of emotion, e.g. want, wish, desire, feel, love, prefer, etc.
- have, own, possess, be (except when used in the passive).

Present Perfect Tense

This tense is used in the following ways

(i) To express an action that has recently been completed.

e.g. • I have just taken bath.
• She has to reach the station by 6 o'clock.

(ii) To describe an action whose time is not given.

e.g. • Priya has completed her 12th class.
• I have read all the poems by Rumi.

(iii) To show how a past situation relates to the present.

e.g. • I have caught the last train so I am reaching home in an hour.
• I have finished my work so I can look after yours.

Rules for Affirmative Sentences

- Singular subject + has + third form of verb + ...
- I/You/Plural subject + have + third form of verb + ...

e.g. • He has seen the latest Marvel movie.
• We have been to Kerala.

Rules for Negative Sentences

- Singular subject + has + not + third form of verb + ...
- I/You/Plural subject + have + not + third form of verb + ...

e.g. • The bus hasn't arrived yet.
• They haven't got the chance to meet their favourite author.

Rules for Interrogative Sentences

- Has/have + subject + third form of verb +.....?
- Question word + has/have + subject + third form of verb + ... ?

e.g. • Have they left for the airport?
• Why hasn't she woken up yet?

Present Perfect Continuous Tense

This tense is used in the following ways to describe an action that began in the past and is still continuing.

e.g. • We have been living in this apartment since I was five years old.
• She has been singing for two hours now.

Rules for Affirmative Sentences

- Singular subject + has + been + first form of verb + ing + ... + for/since +......
- I/You/Plural subject + have + been + first form of verb + ing + ... + for/since +......

e.g. • The toddler has been playing since he woke up.
• We have been playing the guitar for half an hour.

Rules for Negative Sentences

- Singular subject + has + not + been + first form of verb + ing + ... + for/since +......
- I/You/Plural subject + have + not + been + first form of verb + ing + ... + for/since +......

e.g. • He has not been visiting his parents for a year.
• The students have not been studying for the upcoming exam.

Rules for Interrogative Sentences

- Has/Have + subject + been + first form of verb + ing + ... + since/for +.....?
- Question word + has/have + subject + been + first form of verb + ing + ...+ since/for + ...?

e.g. • Has he been staying here for a long time?
• What have you been doing since morning?

Past Tense

Past Indefinite Tense (Simple Past Tense)

This tense is used in the following ways

(i) To indicate an action that happened in the past and to report completed actions. It is used often in recounts.

e.g. • I saw her a few years ago. (*past action*)
• She completed her assignment. (*completed action*)
• They went to Manali last week. (*recount*)

(ii) To indicate past habits or repeated events that are now over.

e.g. • I went to bath in the river every day in my younger days. (*repeated event*)
• She always drank tea in the morning. (*past habit*)

Note The habitual past can also be expressed by using 'used to'.

e.g. • My brother used to play video games all night.
• I used to like coffee more than tea.

(iii) To indicate another action which happened in the middle of a longer action.

e.g. • The patient had passed away before the ambulance arrived.
• The children went out to play while the teacher was arranging the files.

Rule for Affirmative Sentences

- Subject/plural + second form of verb +......

e.g. • Tina shared the apple with her friend.
• They were afraid of the dark.

Rule for Negative Sentences

- Subject/plural + did not + first form of verb +......

e.g. • She didn't go to school yesterday.
• We couldn't attend the seminar.

Rules for Interrogative Sentences

- Did + subject/plural + first form of verb + ...?
- Question word + did + subject/plural + first form of verb +.......?

e.g. • Were you late at the function?
• Where was that sound coming from?

Past Continuous Tense

This tense is used in the following ways

(i) To indicate an action that was happening at some time in the past. The time of action may or may not be indicated.

e.g. • She was playing the piano the whole day.
• They were going on a trip to Goa.

(ii) Used with always, continually, etc. for persistent habits in the past.

e.g. • Rami was always working hard.
• The mother was continually feeding her child.

(iii) The past continuous is also used for an action that was going on during a given period or at a period of time in the past.

e.g. • While I was studying for my exams, my brother was watching Netflix.
• The technician arrived when I was having my lunch.

Rules for Affirmative Sentences

- Singular subject + was + first form of verb + ing +.....
- You/Plural subject + were + first form of verb + ing +.....

e.g. • He was shivering because of the cold.
• We were carrying the flowers to the main hall.

Rules for Negative Sentences

- Singular subject + was + not + first form of verb + ing +.....
- You/Plural subject + were + not + first form of verb + ing +.....

e.g. • I was not thinking clearly at that time.
• They were not forming a society of the intellectuals.

Rules for Interrogative Sentences

- Was/were + subject + first form of verb + ing +......?
- Question word + was/were + subject + first form of verb + ing +.....?

e.g. • Were you learning how to swim?
• How was she recuperating after the accident?

Past Perfect Tense

This tense is used in the following ways

(i) To indicate an action that was completed before a definite time or before another action that took place in the past.

e.g. • He had already gone back home when I reached the park.
• The thunder came after the lightning had struck the place.

(ii) It indicates desires in the past that have not been fulfilled.

e.g. • I wish I had gone to meet my grandparents more.
• I wish I had I studied harder when I still had time!

(iii) It expresses those conditions of the past that were impossible to fulfil.

e.g. • If I had been more careful, I would not have gotten into trouble.
• If only I had questioned his intentions, things would not have turned out like this.

Rule for Affirmative Sentences

- Subject/plural + had + third form of verb + ...

e.g. • I had dinner already.
• We had completed our assignments.

Rule for Negative Sentences

- Subject/plural + had + not + third form of verb + ...

e.g. • Rose had not asked for anything since then.
• My parents had not attended my convocation ceremony.

Rule for Interrogative Sentences

- Had + subject + third form of verb + ...?
- Question word + had + subject + third form of verb +.........?

e.g. • Had he already finished the painting?
• Why had you not studied?

Past Perfect Continuous Tense

It indicates an action which began in the past and continued up to a certain point of time in the past.

e.g. • When I saw him last year, he had been working as a research assistant for two years.
• I had been researching the impact of laser beams since the past ten years.

Rule for Affirmative Sentences

- Subject/plural + had been + first form of verb +ing + ... + since/for +.....

e.g. • She had been sleeping since evening.
• I had been laughing at this comic strip for some time now.

Rule for Negative Sentences

- Subject/plural + had + not + been + first form of verb + ing + ... + since/for +......

e.g. • I had not been accompanying him since my resignation.
• They had not been doing enough for the safety of the employees.

Rules for Interrogative Sentences

- Had + subject + been + first form of verb + ing + ... + since/for + ...?
- Question word + had + subject + been + first form of verb + ing + ...since/for+.....?

e.g. • Had you been going to the doctor lately?
• Why had you been coming late to work since two weeks?

Future Tense

Future Indefinite Tense (Simple Future Tense)

This tense is used in the following ways

(i) To indicate an action that will happen in the future.

e.g. • I shall go for an interview next Friday.
• They will organise a marathon in the coming months.

(ii) Things which we cannot control and are factual.

e.g. • A newborn baby will have around 300 bones.
• Water will boil at 100 degree Celsius.

(iii) To indicate an instant decision.

e.g. • I just decided that I shall go on a trip to Hanoi.
• They remembered that today is her birthday so they will buy a cake for her.

Rules for Affirmative Sentences

- You/He/She/It/They (Second and Third Person Pronouns) + will + first form of verb + ...
- I/We (First Person Pronouns) + shall + first form of verb + ...

e.g. • I shall always remember you.
• She will pursue her Bachelors degree next year.

Rules for Negative Sentences

- You/He/She/It/They (Second and Third Person Pronouns) + will + not + first form of verb + ...
- I/We (First Person Pronouns) + shall + not + first form of verb + ...

e.g. • He will not participate in the debate competition.
• We shall not offend the manager.

Rules for Interrogative Sentences

- Will/Shall+ subject + first form of verb +......?
- Question word + will/shall + subject + first form of verb + ...?

e.g. • Will you please move aside?
• What shall we do in this situation?

Future Continuous Tense

This tense is used in the following ways

(i) To indicate an action that will occur in the normal course in the future.

e.g. • I shall be attending school tomorrow.
• They will be going to work at 9 o'clock.

(ii) To indicate an action that will be in progress at a given point of time in the future.

e.g. • At this time next month, I shall be moving abroad for higher studies.
• We shall be cooking at the usual time tomorrow.

Rules for Affirmative Sentences

- You/He/She/It/They (Second and Third Person Pronouns) + will + be + first form of verb + ing + ...
- I/We (First Person Pronouns) + shall + be + first form of verb + ing + ...

e.g. • Reema will be visiting the Taj Mahal.
• We shall be writing a report on global hunger index.

Rules for Negative Sentences

- You/He/She/It/They (Second and Third Person Pronouns) + will + not + be + first form of verb + ing + ...
- I/We (First Person Pronouns) + shall + not + be + first form of verb + ing + ...

e.g. • I shall not be attending the swimming class.
• Ranjan and Ravi will not be arriving on time.

Rules for Interrogative Sentences

- Will/shall + subject + be + first form of verb + ing + ...?
- Question word + will/shall + subject + be + first form of verb + ing +.....?

e.g. • Shall I be making the cake now?
• How will they be correcting this huge mistake?

Future Perfect Tense

This tense is used to describe an action which will be completed at some point of time in the future.

e.g. • We shall have completed the task by tomorrow evening.
• Harison will have arrived at the station around this time tomorrow.

Rules for Affirmative Sentences

- You/He/She/It/They (Second and Third Person Pronouns) + will + have + third form of verb + ...
- I/We (First Person Pronouns) + shall + have + third form of verb + ...

e.g. • I shall have gone to meet him.
• They will have asked him for help.

Rules for Negative Sentences

- You/He/She/It/They (Second and Third Person Pronouns) + will + not + have + third form of verb + ...
- I/We (First Person Pronouns) + shall + not + have + third form of verb + ...

e.g. • He will not have done this on his own accord.
• We shall not have been so strict.

Rules for Interrogative Sentences

- Will/shall + subject + have + third form of verb +......?
- Question word + will/shall + subject + have + third form of verb ......?
  e.g. • Will he have finished reading the novel?
  • What shall we have done to avoid this tragedy?

Future Perfect Continuous Tense

It describes an action that will be in progress over a period of time but will end in the future.

e.g. • Mike will have been working on his art for three days now.
• At 3 o'clock, we shall have been playing with the kids for an hour.

Rules for Affirmative Sentences

- You/He/She/It/They (Second and Third Person Pronouns) + will + have + been + first form of verb + ing + ... + since/for + ...
- I/We (First Person Pronouns) + shall + have + been + first form of verb + ing + ... + since/for + ...
  e.g. • I shall have been looking for my cat for two hours now.
  • They will have been repairing the house for two days.

Rules for Negative Sentences

- You/He/She/It/They (Second and Third Person Pronouns) + will + not + have + been + first form of verb + ing + ... + since/for + ...
- I/We (First Person Pronouns) + shall + not + have + been + first form of verb + ing + ... + since/for + ...
  e.g. • Yena will not have been dancing for more than thirty minutes.
  • I shall not have been studying for much time.

Rules for Interrogative Sentences

- Will/shall + subject + have + been + first form of verb + ing + ... + since/for + ...?
- Question word + will/ shall + subject + have + been + first form of verb + ing + ... + since/for + ...?
  e.g. • Will he have been working at the MNC for a year in a month?
  • Where will you have been staying when you move away from the city?

REVIEW EXERCISE | Including Practice Questions

1. Read the following notes carefully and complete the paragraph by selecting the correct options from the given alternatives.

RK NARAYAN

Birth	10th October, 1906, Chennai
Occupation	Novelist, short story writer
Father	Headmaster
Brother	Famous cartoonist RK Laxman

The famous novelist and short story writer, RK Narayan *(i)* .... His father *(ii)* ...... and his brother, RK Laxman *(iii)* ....

(i) (a) was born at Chennai on 10th October, 1906 (b) was born in Chennai on 10th October, 1906
(c) born on Chennai on 10th October, 1906 (d) were born in Chennai on 10th October, 1906

(ii) (a) was a Headmaster (b) was the Headmaster
(c) was Headmaster (d) is the Headmaster

(iii) (a) was a famous cartoonist (b) were a famous cartoonist
(c) is this famous cartoonist (d) is famous cartoonist

2. Read the following passage. Fill in the blanks by choosing the most appropriate options from the ones given below.

Once Swami Vivekananda had *(i)* .... to Banaras. He was returning from a visit to the temple. The lane he took *(ii)* .... narrow. There was a wall on one side, and on the *(iii)* .... side was a large tank.

(i) (a) go (b) going (c) gone (d) went
(ii) (a) was (b) is (c) are (d) were
(iii) (a) another (b) other (c) either (d) neither

3. Fill in the blanks (i) - (iii) with the appropriate option from those in the brackets.

Prerna and Sushil *(a)* .... (has/have/had) spent years together. On growing up they *(b)* .... (had got/have got/got) separated and went their own ways. Sushil *(c)* .... (becomes/became/had become) a well-known sports personality while Prerna pursued her artistic passion. **CBSE 2025**

4. Fill in the blanks with the correct form of verb given in the brackets.

Malaria *(a)* .... (be) caused by female Anopheles mosquito. They *(b)* .... (be) also called carriers. When a mosquito *(c)* .... (bite) a person, the microbes enter into the bloodstream. That's why we should always *(d)* ...... (keep) the surrounding clean to avoid the breeding of mosquitoes. Disease causing microbes *(e)* ...... (be) called pathogens.

5. Complete the following dialogue using correct tenses.

Mother Rahul, where *(a)* .... ?
Rahul I *(b)* ....
Mother *(c)* .... ?
Rahul Yes, mom, I have finished my homework.
Mother When will you be back from your friend's house?
Rahul *(d)* ....

6. Fill in the blanks using the correct form of tenses.

Medileaks, a website that *(a)* .... (allow) stakeholders to register complaints and point out irregularities in healthcare, *(b)* .... (launch) in the capital yesterday. The website, *(c)* .... (inspire) by Wikileaks, *(d)* .... (allow) whistleblowers to *(e)* .... (post) information anonymously. This *(f)* .... (check) by a team of volunteers before *(g)* .... (share) on the portal. However, concerns are already *(h)* .... (raise) about how it *(i)* .... (address) the issue of medical negligence.

7. Fill in the blanks using the correct form of tenses.

British scientists *(a)* .... (develop) what they claim *(b)* .... (be) a super broccoli, which *(c)* .... (protect) people against heart diseases and cancers, a statement of the Institute of Food Research and John Innes Centre in Norwich *(d)* .... (say). The new strain, Beneforte, *(e)* .... (look) like normal broccoli, but it *(f)* .... (contain) three times as much of a health boosting nutrient *(g)* .... (call) glucoraphanin. Research *(h)* .... (show) that glucoraphanin can help protect against heart diseases and cancers.

8. Fill in the blanks with the correct form of verb given in the brackets.

I *(a)* .... (bath) three times yesterday. It was quite hot in the room, so I *(b)* .... (open) the window. It *(c)* .... (be) a Sunday evening so I *(d)* .... (watch) a movie till 7 pm. Suddenly, my mind *(e)* .... (wander) off to Anna's grandfather who was 90 years old. He *(f)* .... (die) last Sunday afternoon.

9. Read the following passage and fill in the blanks with the correct form of verb given in the brackets.

Just as Jai *(a)* .... (get) into the apartment, all the lights *(b)* .... (go) off. He *(c)* .... (feel) dejected as he *(d)* .... (hope) to come after a week. When his coordinator suddenly *(e)* .... (call) him to Delhi, he *(f)* .... (spend) a lot of his time frolicking about. It *(g)* .... (give) him a feeling of liberty as it *(h)* .... (tired) to be in the same place for a very long time.

10. Samaira wrote a short story but forgot to edit it. There is an error in each line. Write the incorrect word/ phrase and the correction.

	Incorrect	Correct
(a) There was living a farmer named Mohan	....	....
(b) who is very hardworking and honest. He	....	....
(c) has known across the village as a man	....	....
(d) of principles and thus loving by all. His	....	....
(e) fields been always green and he never	....	....
(f) sleeping on an empty stomach.	....	....
(g) After a drought, all the farmers was leaving,	....	....
(h) but Mohan was not ready to left his	....	....
(i) fields. The news was reaching the press and	....	....
(j) a reporter come to the village to	....	....
(k) got his side of the story.	....	....

11. **In the passage given below, there is an error in each line. Write the error and the correction in your answer sheet. The first one has been done for you.**

		Error	Correction
You recently ask me to submit a short report		ask	asked
in the progress made so far in the	(a)	....	....
Literacy Project. Initially the adults were reluctance	(b)	....	....
to learn. However, gradually they overcome their inhibitions.	(c)	....	....

12. **In the passage given below, one word has been omitted in each line. Write the missing word along with the word that comes before and the word that comes after it.**

	Before	Missing	After
(a) Experiments at the world's biggest particle smasher confirmed the existence of two subatomic particles.	....	....	....
(b) The discoveries part of the baryon	....	....	....
(c) family of particles. Baryons composite particles composed of three quarks. The	....	....	....
(d) work carried out in 2011 and 2012. A	....	....	....
(e) paper reporting the finding been submitted.	....	....	....
(f) The facility going through an upgrade	....	....	....
(g) now. A related baryonic particle found by an experiment in 2012.	....	....	....

ANSWERS

1. (i) (b) was born in Chennai on 10th October, 1906
   (ii) (a) was a Headmaster
   (iii) (a) was a famous cartoonist
2. (i) (c) gone (ii) (a) was (iii) (b) other
3. (a) have (b) got (c) became
4. (a) is (b) are (c) bites (d) keep (e) are
5. (a) are you going
   (b) am going to my friend's house
   (c) Have you finished your homework
   (d) I will be back by 6 o' clock
6. (a) allows (b) was launched
   (c) inspired (d) will allow
   (e) post (f) will be checked
   (g) sharing (h) being raised
   (i) would address
7. (a) have developed (b) to be
   (c) can protect (d) says
   (e) looks (f) contains
   (g) called (h) has shown
8. (a) bathed (b) opened
   (c) was (d) watched
   (e) wandered (f) died
9. (a) was getting (b) went
   (c) felt (d) was hoping
   (e) called (f) was spending
   (g) gave (h) was tiring
10.

	Incorrect	Correct
(a)	was living	lived
(b)	is	was
(c)	has	was
(d)	loving	was loved
(e)	been	were
(f)	sleeping	slept
(g)	was leaving	left
(h)	left	leave
(i)	was reaching	reached
(j)	come	came
(k)	got	get

11.

	Error	Correction
(a)	in	on
(b)	reluctance	reluctant
(c)	overcome	overcame

12.

	Before	Missing	After
(a)	smasher	have	confirmed
(b)	discoveries	are	part
(c)	Baryons	are	composite
(d)	work	was	carried
(e)	finding	has	been
(f)	facility	is	going
(g)	particle	was	found

CHAPTER 2

Modals

Modal Auxiliary Verbs or Modals are verbs that are used to express the mood or attitude of the speaker. They do not appear alone in the sentence and always have a main verb with them. Further, they are non-finite verbs meaning they do not change forms in any case.

For example

- You **should** regularly go for a morning walk.
- They **must** attend tomorrow's meeting.
- **May** I use your pen please?
- You **can** park the car in front of our house.

There are primarily 9 Modals : **Can, Could, Shall, Should, Will, Would, May, Might** and **Must.**

All these Modals suggest any of the following

- Permission
- Possibility
- Promise
- Request
- Wish or Prayer
- Ability
- Suggestion, Advice
- Intention
- Necessity
- Duty, Obligation

2.1 Functions of Modals

Will

(i) To show promise, intention, willingness, determination with the first person (I, we)

e.g.
- I **will** buy you a smart watch. (*promise*)
- I **will** be going outside since the weather is pleasant. (*intention*)
- We **will** join you on the trip. (*willingness*)
- I **will** win the scholarship this time. (*determination*)

(ii) To express request, invitation, assumption, characteristic or habit

e.g.
- **Will** you please remove the chair from the front? (*request*)
- She **will** be working in the office during these hours. (*assumption*)
- He **will** always come late to every meeting. (*characteristic, habit*)
- **Will** you come to my graduation party? (*invitation*)

- **Negative Form of will** : Will not/ Won't

e.g.
- I **will** not ask for help.
- They **won't** be studying today.

Would (Past Form of 'Will')

(i) To express past habit

e.g.
- Manish **would** read the newspaper in the morning.
- I **would** take the kids for a walk at the park.

(ii) For request

e.g.
- **Would** you pass the car keys from the table?
- **Would** you like to have some coffee?

(iii) To express wish

e.g.
- I wish my mother **would** always be happy and healthy.
- I **would** like to travel the world one day.

(iv) To express an imaginary condition

e.g.
- She **would** have been saved if she was careful while driving.
- I **would** have been able to buy a mansion if I lived in the 19th century.

- **Negative Form of Would** : Would not / Wouldn't

e.g.
- He **would** not eat breakfast properly.
- He **wouldn't** come to the get- together.

Shall

(i) To ask for suggestion and request, with the first person (I, We) in the interrogative

e.g.
- **Shall** we have some more cupcakes from the table? (*request*)
- **Shall** we build a new Ed-tech company? (*suggestion*)

(ii) In the second and third person to indicate threat, warning, command and promise.

e.g.
- If you don't wear your uniform properly, you **shall** be punished. (*threat/warning*)
- You **shall** come back right away. (*command*)
- I **shall** come to visit you next year. (*promise*)

- **Negative Form of Shall** : Shall not/ Shan't

  e.g. • Meera **shall** not come to school tomorrow.
  - We **shan't** be punished for things we didn't do.

Should (Past Form of 'Shall')

(i) To express duty or obligation

e.g. • I **should** take care of your parents. (*duty*)
- You **should** abide by the rules made by the Constitution. (*obligation*)

(ii) To express opinion

e.g. • They **should** have been careful while conducting the experiment.
- They **should** have reached the station by now.

(iii) To give or take advice

e.g. You **should** sleep on time. (*advice*)

(iv) After 'lest' when someone expresses fear

e.g. • Walk carefully **lest** you should fall down.
- They started early **lest** they should miss the train.

- **Negative Form of Should** : Should not /Shouldn't

  e.g. • You **should not** go out at night.
  - We **shouldn't** be lazy all the time.

Can

(i) To express an ability, capability, capacity or power

e.g. • I **can** study for six hours without any break. (*ability*)
- Rohan **can** jump over this wall easily. (*capability*)
- I **can** speak four languages. (*capacity*)
- Only our principal **can** grant us leave of absence. (*power*)

(ii) To show possibility

e.g. • She **can** come over to my house today.
- You **can** slip since the floor is yet to dry.

(iii) To take or give permission

e.g. • **Can** I borrow your backpack?
- You **can** start eating now.

- **Negative Form of Can** : Cannot /Can't

  e.g. • I **cannot** read Sanskrit.
  - **Can't** you study harder?

Could (Past Form of 'Can')

(i) To express ability/talent in the past

e.g. • He **could** speak three languages when he was young. (*ability*)
- She **could** paint masterpieces. (*talent*)

(ii) To express polite request

e.g. • **Could** you pass the salt?
- **Could** you please move ahead?

- **Negative Form of Could** : Could not/ Couldn't

  e.g. • I **couldn't** be there for her when she needed me.
  - **Could** you **not** ask such difficult questions?

May

(i) To show possibility or probability

e.g. • The army **may** conduct a combat operation today.
- We **may** win the game.

(ii) To give or take permission

e.g. • **May** I take this pen?
- Yes, you **may** take that pen.

(iii) To wish or pray

e.g. • **May** you achieve great success! (wish)
- **May** God be always with you! (prayer)

(iv) To show a purpose

e.g. • The farmer is ploughing the field so that he **may** sow the seeds during rainy season.
- They are training hard so that they **may** qualify for the nationals.

- **Negative Form of May** : May not

  e.g. • He **may not** arrive today.
  - I **may not** reach on time.

Might (Past Form of 'May')

(i) To express less possibility

e.g. • The coach **might** teach us other techniques.
- You **might** secure the first position this time.

(ii) For permission

e.g. • **Might** we begin the session on self-care?
- **Might** I ask you to speak louder?

(iii) To express a guess

e.g. • The cat crying in the garden **might** be yours.
- That knock **might** be on our door.

- **Negative Form of Might** : Might not/ Mightn't

  e.g. • I **might not** attend the meeting today.
  - They **mightn't** ask for a refund for the damaged goods.

Must

(i) To express necessity or obligation

e.g. • You **must** contact the ambulance at once. (*necessity*)
- We **must** serve our people and our motherland. (*obligation*)

(ii) To indicate assumption or conclusion

e.g. • She **must** be here in the morning. (*assumption*)
- The meeting **must** have ended on a good note. (*conclusion*)

(iii) In case of prohibition

e.g. • You **must not** smoke here.
- You **must not** speak loudly in the hospital.

- **Negative Form of Must** : Must not/ Mustn't

e.g. • You **must not** loiter around here.
• She **mustn't** write like that in exams.

2.2 Semi Modals

Need, need to, dare, used to and ought to are considered semi-modals because they can be act as both modals auxiliaries and main verbs.

Need/Need to

As a modal auxiliary verb, it is used in negative or interrogative sentences it indicates absence of obligation. It expresses the speaker's authority or advice and is used for the present and the future.

e.g. • **Need** she come back today? (*interrogative in the past*)
• She **needn't** have come back today. (*negative in the past*)

Dare

As a modal auxiliary, dare refers to being bold and courageous. It is used to challenge someone.

e.g. • I **dare** not come home late as my mother is strict.
• **Dare** you talk to me in that manner?

Used to

(i) A discontinued habit or a past situation which is not applicable in the present.

e.g. • My father **used to** write short stories.
• I **used to** exercise every morning.

(ii) Something existing in the past.

e.g. • This place **used to** be lively just a few years back.
• There **used to** be an orphanage here.

Ought to

(i) To express moral obligation or duty

e.g. • We **ought to** be loyal to our friends. (obligation)
• You **ought to** follow the rules and regulations of the school. (duty)

(ii) To give advice

e.g. • You **ought to** work hard in order to pass the exam with flying colours.
• You **ought to** eat healthy and nutritious food.

- **Negative Form of Ought to** : Ought not to

e.g. • She **ought not to** disrespect her teachers.
• You **ought not to** walk down the disastrous road.

REVIEW EXERCISE

Including Practice Questions

1. Fill in the blanks using appropriate modals.

People who *(a)* .... remain outdoor for film shootings *(b)* .... be given a chance to go abroad. But they *(c)* .... have their passports ready. They *(d)* .... get a free ticket for one of their family members, if only their passport *(e)* .... be arranged. The company would provide them spare money. So, the members *(f)* .... take more foreign exchange with them. If they do so they will *(g)* .... declare them at the checking counter. They *(h)* .... get into unnecessary trouble this way.

2. Fill in the blanks using appropriate modals from must, ought to, dare and used to.

How *(a)* .... you say such a thing! You *(b)* .... be ashamed of yourself. You never *(c)* .... be so bold before. You *(d)* .... behave from now on.

3. Fill in the blanks with suitable modals.

If we sit in an incorrect posture, we *(a)* .... strain our back. As far as possible, this *(b)* .... be avoided. If the posture becomes a part of habit, a low back pain invariably develops. It *(c)* .... be cured if we become conscious of our posture. We can also take time out to perform a few exercises. If the exercises are done regularly, the backache *(d)* .... certainly be cured. It *(e)* .... also improve the blood circulation within the spine.

4. Complete the passage using suitable modals.

Times have changed. Nowadays, you *(a)* .... rush off to a travel agent to book tickets for a journey. You *(b)* .... sit at home and book them over the Internet. However, the experience of one British couple *(c)* .... be a warning to everyone. You *(d)* .... assume that if you book on the net, mistakes won't happen. That's why you *(e)* .... always check bookings carefully. If you don't, you *(f)* .... find yourselves in the wrong part of the world. That's exactly what happened to Emma Dunn and Raoul Sebastian. They set off from London in a large plane, thinking they were on their way to Sydney, Australia. They *(g)* .... understand what was happening when they landed at an airport and were asked to transfer to a much smaller plane. It *(h)* .... been quite a shock when they finally discovered they were in Canada. They *(i)* .... read their tickets more carefully because they were booked for Sydney, Nova Scotia, Canada.

5. Complete the passage using suitable modals.

You *(a)* .... help the teacher to maintain a neat and organised classroom. You *(b)* .... regularly inspect classrooms and *(c)* .... assign duties to class monitors to participate. You *(d)* .... ensure drinking water is provided to all. You *(e)* .... impose a fine on students who are found littering.

6. Read the passage and fill in the blanks with suitable modals.

Seeing a crow eating a piece of bread, a fox thought how it *(a)* .... trick that fellow. It said, " *(b)* .... I talk to you, Sir?". The crow did not even look at the fox. The fox again said, " *(c)* .... you please pay a little attention to me ? What a nice bird you are! Your voice *(d)* .... be very sweet. I am sure you *(e)* .... sing very well." The crow who *(f)* .... not be persuaded till then now looked at the fox. It *(g)* .... have felt flattered. The crow said to itself, "I'll show this fox how well I *(h)* .... sing." It opened its beak. The piece of bread fell down and was eaten away quickly by the fox.

7. Fill in the blanks using appropriate modals.

The hotels *(a)* .... be full as it has been raining non-stop since we have arrived. It's not like we *(b)* .... change the weather. In this situation, *(c)* .... it be a good idea to stop by a restaurant to have breakfast? We *(d)* .... to have our stomachs full in order to think properly as to what *(e)* .... be done next.

8. Fill in the blanks using appropriate modals.

On the Annual Day celebration, the chief guest delivered a lecture, "Good Morning students, you all *(a)* .... be the future pillars of the nations, hence you *(b)* .... obey your teachers. You *(c)* .... always try to win over any hurdles with confidence. You must not leave any stone unturned and you *(d)* .... not worry about the result as long as you do your best. Take a pledge that you *(e)* .... obey and respect your elders. You *(f)* .... take whatever stream you like but excel in the path that you have chosen.

9. In the following paragraph, one word has been omitted in each line. In your answer sheet, remember to write the missing word along with the word that comes before and after it as shown below. The first one has been done as an example. **CBSE 2025**

No.	Text	Word before	Omission	Word after
e.g.	A particular mineral that will formed from a certain combination of elements.	will	be	formed
(i)	This depends the physical	....	....	....
(ii)	and chemical conditions under the material forms.	....	....	....
(iii)	This results a wide range of colours,	....	....	....
(iv)	hardness, crystal forms, lustre density that a particular mineral possesses.	....	....	....

10. Meera has written a dialogue between two friends. But she has used the wrong modals. Find the incorrect modals and replace them with the correct ones in each line.

	Incorrect	Correct
(a) Vrehaan Where's Anshul? He can have been here half an hour ago.	....	....
(b) Vicky He should have got lost. He is still new to this town.	....	....
(c) Vrehaan He can have forgotten all about the plan, I suppose.	....	....
(d) Vicky He may not have forgotten. We were talking about it this morning.	....	....
(e) Vrehaan Well, something can have delayed him.	....	....

ANSWERS

1. (a) would (b) must (c) should (d) can (e) can (f) may (g) need to (h) won't (g) must (h) can

2. (a) dare (b) ought to (c) used to (d) must

3. (a) might (b) should (c) can (d) will (e) will

4. (a) needn't (b) can (c) ought to (d) shouldn't (e) must (f) could (g) couldn't (h) must have (i) should have

5. (a) must (b) should (c) no modal (d) must (e) may

6. (a) could (b) may (c) would (d) must (e) can (f) could

7. (a) might (b) can (c) will (d) need (e) should

8. (a) will (b) ought to (c) should (d) need (e) shall (f) may

9.

	Word Before	Omission	Word After
(i)	depends	on	the
(ii)	and	the	chemical
(iii)	results	in	a
(iv)	forms	and	lustre

10.

Incorrect	Correct
(a) can	should
(b) should	may
(c) can	could
(d) may not	can't
(e) can	must

CHAPTER 3

Subject-Verb Agreement

While writing any sentence in English we are required to follow certain rules. One of the most important of rules is the Subject-Verb Agreement. It is a grammatical rule that states that the verb or verbs in a sentence must match the number, person and gender of the subject.

3.1 Rules Involved in Subject-Verb Agreement

(i) The basic rule is Singular Subject → Singular Verb
Plural Subject → Plural Verb

In other words, if the subject is singular, the verb should also be singular. If the subject is plural, the verb should also be plural.

- Singular Subject → Singular Verb

e.g. She **is** having her lunch.

- Plural Subject → Plural Verb

e.g. We **are** holding a photo exhibition this week.

(ii) When two or more singular subjects are joined together using 'and' plural verb is used.

e.g. Anand and Priya **attended** the seminar on sustainable development.

(iii) When two subjects together express one idea, singular verb is used.

e.g. The horse and carriage **has** arrived at the front gate. (Horse and carriage expresses one idea of a means of transportation).

(iv) Some nouns look like plurals but are, in fact, singular nouns. Hence, we use a singular verb with then.

e.g. Politics **is** an area of my interest.

(v) The collective nouns such as audience, congregation, crowd, group and family take singular verb if they act as a group.

e.g. The team **is** practising at the main stadium.

However, if the group is divided in ideas or judgement, that is if the members are considered individually, then plural verb is used.

e.g. The Board of Directors **were** having disagreements regarding the construction issue.

(vi) Everybody, somebody, nobody, anybody and anyone take a singular verb.

e.g. Somebody is trying to enter the house.

(vii) If subjects are joined by 'or', 'nor', 'either', 'neither', the verb agrees with the subject nearest to it.

e.g. • The members or the captain **is** asked to give a short interview before the game.

• Neither Riko nor her cousins **are** attending the marriage ceremony.

(viii) The title of a book, play, story or a musical composition, even though plural, takes a singular verb.

e.g. 'Angels in America' **is** a 1991 two-part play by American playwright, Tony Kushner.

(ix) If plural nouns are joined to a singular subject by 'with', a singular verb is used.

e.g. My brother, with his friends, **is** collecting funds to help the under-privileged children.

(x) If subjects are joined by 'as well as', the verb must agree with the first subject, irrespective of whether it is singular or plural.

e.g. • The assistants, as well as the mentor **were** seen leaving the laboratory early in the morning.

• Maya, as well as her parents **is** moving away to a far-off village.

(xi) Two nouns qualified by each or every, even though connected by 'and', require a singular verb.

e.g. Every child and each parent **was** told to run the marathon together.

(xii) None is singular but takes a plural/singular verb according to the sense involved in the sentence.

e.g. • None of the projects **were** given approval to carry forward.

• I wanted to buy a black shirt but none **was** available at the store.

(xiii) When the plural noun is a proper name for some single object or some collective unit, it must be followed by a singular verb.

e.g. • The United Nations for Children's Emergency Fund **is** going to send aid to the victims of war.

(xiv) Nouns like glasses (spectacles), pants, trousers, shoes, people, police, scissors always take a plural verb. Also, descriptive nouns like the rich, the blind, the guilty are always plural.

e.g. Those scissors **are** quite sharp.

But when used with 'a pair of', they are singular.

e.g. I need a pair of scissors which **is** sharp.

(xv) Uncountable nouns like advice, news, media, stationery, weather, progress, etc., are singular and take a singular verb.

e.g. The news from mainstream media **is** biased towards the powerful section.

(xvi) A singular verb is used when a plural noun denotes some specific quantity or amount.

e.g. • Five - hundred rupees **is** not enough to buy a bag nowadays.

• I have to travel 17 kilometres everyday which **is** a long distance.

REVIEW EXERCISE

Including Practice Questions

1. Fill in the blanks keeping subject-verb agreement in mind.

(a) Everyone .... finished reading the fairy tale.
(b) Some of the students .... left the classroom for lunch.
(c) Nobody .... come for the party yet. We're still waiting.
(d) Somebody .... spilt tea on the tablecloth.
(e) Each of the teachers .... willing to attend the meeting during the weekend.
(f) Neither of the two students .... in the library now.
(g) A pair of jeans .... in the bathroom.
(h) My glasses .... on the table this morning.
(i) Diabetes .... very common among people who consume too much fast food.
(j) Five and seven .... twelve.
(k) Forty per cent of the milk .... been sold since morning.
(l) Everyone at the supermarket .... looking for the missing girl.
(m) Either my uncle or my grandparents .... going to buy me a laptop.

2. Fill in the blanks with the correct form of verb for subject-verb agreement.

An anti-viral drug that *(a)*................. widely used to treat Hepatitis B *(b)*................. become a major curse for some people infected with HIV who have become resistant to the drug. A new study *(c)*................. suggested that this could *(d)*................. major implications for over four million people. This finding *(e)*................. important for people who *(f)*................. jointly infected with Hepatitis B and HIV. Scientists *(g)*................. hopeful of finding some more such drugs to cure Hepatitis B. Till now no cure *(h)*................. available for HIV.

3. Fill in the blanks with the correct form of verb for subject-verb agreement.

Headbands *(a)*................. (be) great for keeping the irritating locks out of your face and will stop you from touching your hair, which *(b)*................. (lead) to greasy strands. Bad hair days *(c)*................. (be) a thing of the past now. Headbands *(d)*................. (be) the perfect accessory for disguising greasy roots and taming flyaways. Donning a headband *(e)*................. (require) smooth hair to start with. Frizzy, unkempt hair *(f)*................. (be not) work with a headband. This *(g)*................. (be not) mean you have to *(h)*................. (be) straight hair.

4. Fill in the blanks with the correct form of verb given in brackets and subject-verb agreement.

Be sure your hair *(a)*................. (be) sleek and shiny. If your hair *(b)*................. (be) curly or wavy, running a smoothing cream through it and then letting your curls *(c)*................. (shine) can work wonders. Another option *(d)*................. (be) to pile hair up into a high ponytail. Straight hair *(e)*................. (look) great worn with a headband or braided. Make sure your hair *(f)*.......... (be) strong enough to prevent breakage due to headbands. Humidity *(g)*........... (make) hair dry and brittle, leading to hair fall.

Colouring the hair *(h)*........ (damage) the hair strands, leading to breakage.

5. Fill in the blanks with the correct form of verb and subject-verb agreement.

Dangers *(a)* .... (be) growing in cyberspace. Not only *(b)* .... (be) the thieves learning to illegally draw millions of credit card numbers but elaborate pieces of malware *(c)* .... (be) capable of spying on whole organisations. The new spyware *(d)* .... (be not) resemble the evasive bits of code that scoop up credit card data. Although the US military *(e)* .... (be) standing up to major cyber effort, private-sector networks in the nation *(f)* .... (be) overly exposed.

6. Fill in the blanks using appropriate form of the verb given in brackets for correct subject-verb agreement.

(a) Each of these options .... its own benefit. (be)

(b) The level of drunkenness .... from person to person for the same amount of wine. (vary)

(c) Mr Sanyal's family members .... going to USA next week. (be)

(d) Many of my friends .... working in the private sector. (be)

(e) A large number of people .... in the earthquake in Mexico. (die)

(f) The decoration of Mayank's home .... it look impressive. (make)

7. Read the information given below and fill in the blank spaces appropriately. Do not add any new information. Write the answers in your answer sheet against the correct blank number.

House – symbol–safe and secure – construct – lot of time and effort – bought best quality materials – ability to identify and purchase good materials – lay strong foundation.

A house *(a)* .... for a family. When a house *(b)*...... . The best quality materials *(c)*......... . You should be *(d)* .... For the house to last long *(e)* ....

8. In the following passage, one word has been omitted in each line. Write the missing word with the word that comes before and the word that comes after it.

	Before	Missing	After
(a) Winston Castle damaged in the fire	....	....	....
(b) last night. Although no one hurt,	....	....	....
(c) two people rescued from upstairs.	....	....	....
(d) It not that there was no damage.	....	....	....
(e) A number of priceless paintings destroyed.	....	....	....
(f) It not known how the fire started.	....	....	....
(g) Some wires which hanging loose	....	....	....
(h) might caused the fire.	....	....	....

ANSWERS

1. (a) has (b) have (c) has (d) has (e) is (f) is (g) is (h) were (i) is (j) is (k) has (l) was (m) are

2. (a) is (b) has (c) has (d) have (e) is (f) are (g) are (h) is

3. (a) are (b) leads (c) are (d) are (e) requires (f) doesn't (g) doesn't (h) have

4. (a) is (b) is (c) shine (d) is (e) looks (f) is (g) makes (h) damages

5. (a) are (b) are (c) are (d) does not (e) is (f) are

6. (a) has (b) varies (c) are (d) are (e) died (f) makes

7. (a) is a symbol of safety and security

(b) is constructed, a lot of time and effort is put in.

(c) are bought for the house.

(d) able to identify good materials while purchasing them.

(e) a strong foundation needs to be laid.

8.

	Before	Missing	After
(a)	Castle	was	damaged
(b)	one	was	hurt
(c)	people	were	rescued
(d)	It	was	not
(e)	paintings	were	destroyed
(f)	It	is	not
(g)	which	were	hanging
(h)	might	have	caused

CHAPTER 4

Determiners

Determiners are words which are used before a noun or noun phrase to show how the noun/noun phrase is being used. A determiner modifies the meaning of the noun in the sentence.

e.g.
- **This** is my cat. It is a Persian cat.
- **Some** people don't like to eat Chinese food.

4.1 Classification of Determiners

Determiners can be classified into

1. Articles
2. Demonstrative
3. Quantifiers
   (i) Definite (ii) Indefinite
   (iii) Distributive (iv) Difference
   (v) Comparative
4. Possessives

Articles – A, An, The

An article is used before a noun to point out the noun that is referred to in a sentence. It also tells us whether we are referring to a noun in general or to a specific noun.

e.g.
- My mother is **a** strong woman.
- Can I have **an** orange?
- **The** Prime Minster is about to start his speech.

Types of Articles

There are only three articles- A, An and The. These three articles can be categorised into two types- Definite and Indefinite articles.

Indefinite Articles

The words 'A' and 'An' are indefinite articles. They do not refer to any specific or unique noun. They make the noun general and are used only with singular nouns.

e.g,
- I saw **a** horse in the morning.
- Give **an** example.

Use of Article 'A'

The article 'A' is used before singular countable noun that starts with a consonant sound.

e.g.
- I would need to carry **a** bottle of water.
- She needs **a** new bag.

Note it In some cases, the article 'A' is used before words that start with a vowel letter. This is so because the words begin with a consonant sound.

e.g.
- He is **a European** man. (European starts with the sound of 'y')
- It is only **a one-time** password. (One- time starts with the sound of 'w')
- She doesn't have **a uniform**. (Uniform starts with the sound of 'y')
- The farmers have decided to form **a union**. (Union starts with the sound of 'y')

Use of Article 'An'

The article 'An' is used before singular countable noun that starts with a vowel sound.

e.g.
- Mona was searching for **an** ear-plug.
- I would need **an** egg and some sugar to make the dough.

Note it However, in some cases, the article 'An' is used before words that start with a consonant letter. This is so because the consonant letter is silent and the word starts with a vowel sound.

e.g.
- She is **an heiress** of a food packaging company. (Heiress starts with the sound of 'e')
- Mr Kumar is **an honest** man. (Honest starts with the sound of 'o')
- He has **an MA** degree in History. (MA starts with the sound of 'a')

In these sentences, the sound of 'h' and 'm' are silent. The words start with the sound of 'o' and 'a'.

Definite Article 'The'

The word 'The' is the only definite article. It is used to refer to particular nouns and is used with both countable and uncountable nouns.

Uncountable nouns do not have plural forms, for example we cannot say 'sugars', we will say 'the sugar'.

e.g. • **The** river near my place has dried up.
• Can you return **the** book that you borrowed last time?

Use of Definite Article 'The'

'The' is used

I. While talking about a particular person or thing or one already referred to (that is, when it is clear from the context which one do we mean).

e.g. This is **the** song you were searching for.

II. When a singular noun represents the whole class.

e.g. **The** horse can run very fast.

III. Before some proper names that denote physical features.

(i) Oceans and seas e.g. **The** Arctic Ocean, **The** Mediterranean Sea

(ii) Rivers e.g. **The** Ganges, **The** Mekong

(iii) Canals e.g. **The** Great Canal

(iv) Deserts e.g. **The** Arabian Desert

(v) Group of islands e.g. **The** Bahamas, **The** Philippines

(vi) Mountain ranges e.g. **The** Alps, **The** Aravalli Ranges

(vii) A few names of countries which include words like States, Republic or Kingdom e.g. **The** People's Republic of China, **The** United Kingdom, **The** USA, **The** Republic of Korea, **The** Hague, etc.

IV. Before the names of religious or mythological books.

e.g. **The** Vedas, **The** Upanishads, **The** Gita (but we say Homer's Iliad, Valmiki's Ramayana).

V. Before the names of things which are unique or one of their kind.

e.g. **The** Milky Way, **The** Universe.

VI. Before a proper noun, when it is qualified by an adjective or a defining adjectival clause.

e.g. • **The** Tsar of Russia, Akbar the Great.
• **The** Miss Nancy whom you had seen on the stage is my cousin.

VII. With superlative degrees.

e.g. Today is probably **the** coldest day of the year.

VIII. With ordinals (first, second, ... etc)

e.g. I am **the** second place holder in the class as per the last exam.

IX. Before musical instruments.

e.g. She wants to learn how to play **the** sitar.

X. Before an adjective when the noun is understood.

e.g. **The** white always have a superiority complex over **the** people of colour. (Here the word 'people' is understood.)

XI. As an adverb with comparatives.

e.g. **The** more we learn, **the** more we realise we don't know much about the world.

Omission of Article 'The'

'The' is omitted

I. Before material, abstract and proper nouns used in a general sense.

e.g. • This cake is made with flour, sugar, eggs and baking powder.
• He spent his entire childhood in poverty.
• Rajouri Garden is in West Delhi.

II. Before plural countable nouns used in a general sense.

e.g. Parents must look after their children.

III. Before names of people.

e.g. Zencho/Zomov

IV. Before names of continents, countries, cities, etc.

e.g. Russia, Australia, Noida

V. Before names of individual mountains.

e.g. Mount Abu

VI. Before names of meals used in a general sense.

e.g. Have lunch before you go.

VII. Before languages and words like school, college, university, church and hospital.

e.g. • I'm going to learn french.
• He is attending college regularly.

VIII. Before names of relations like father, mother, etc.

e.g. Has sister arrived yet?

IX. In certain phrases consisting of preposition followed by its object.

e.g. At home, in hand, by night, in case, on foot, by train, on demand, etc.

Demonstrative Adjectives (This, That, These, Those)

I. **This** (in case of plural, **these**)

It refers to person(s) or thing(s) near the speaker.

e.g. • Can you buy me **this** pouch?
• **These** games seem intriguing.

II. **That** (in case of plural, **those**)

It refers to person(s) or thing(s) far from the speaker.

e.g. • **This** blue pen is mine and **those** black ones are yours.
• **That** poster looks more interesting than **these** posters.

Quantifiers

A quantifier is a word or phrase which is used before a noun to indicate the amount or quantity. Quantifiers can be used in affirmative sentences, questions, requests or commands with both countable and uncountable nouns.

e.g. • Would you buy **some** milk on your way back home?
• I have got **a few** coins with me.

Some quantifiers can go only with countable nouns (e.g. friends, people, cups), some can go only with uncountable nouns (e.g. sugar, tea, money, advice), while some can be used with both countable and uncountable nouns.

Examples of quantifiers are given below

Only with Uncountable Nouns	With both Countable and Uncountable Nouns	Only with Countable Nouns
a little	no, none, not any	a few
a bit of	some, all	a number of
—	any	several
a great deal of	a lot of, lots of	a great number of
a large amount of	plenty of	a large number of

Uses of Quantifiers

Usage of quantifiers are as follows

I. Use of few/a few and little/a little

(a) **Few, a few, The few**

Few emphasises the lack of something.

e.g. I have brought **few** clothes with me.

A few emphasises that something still remains.

e.g. She has **a few** questions that she wants to ask her parents.

'The few' emphasises that it is not much but all that there is.

e.g. **The few** toffees I had were spoilt it.

(b) **Little, a little and the little**

There is not much difference between the use of few, a few, the few and little, a little and the little. The only difference is that little is used with countable nouns while few is used with uncountable nouns.

Little emphasises the lack of something.

e.g. There is **little** sugar left in the container.

A little emphasises that something still remains.

e.g. I see **a little** hope in the new generation.

'The little' emphasises that it is not much but all that there is present/available.

e.g. I had to spend **the little** money that I had on my school fees.

II. Use of much and many

(a) We use **much** with singular uncountable nouns and **many** with plural nouns.

e.g. • I don't have **much** patience for nonsensical things.
• I wish I had **many** talents to survive in this competitive world.

(b) We usually use much and many with interrogative sentences and negative sentences.

e.g. • I am going back since there isn't **much** to do here.
• Are there **many** files on your laptop?

III. Use of more, less and fewer (Comparative Determiners)

(a) We use more or less before singular uncountable nouns by adding them after it, or for an additional or lesser quantity of something.

e.g. • She has **less** work today.
• I want **more** ice-cream than my brother.

(b) We use **fewer** before plural countable nouns to refer to a group of things smaller than another.

e.g. • I have **fewer** clothes than last year.
• **Fewer** candidates have come for the interview than expected.

IV. Use of each and every (Distributive Determiners)

We use each when the number in the group is limited or definite, but every is used when the number is indefinite or unknown. Both of these are followed by singular countable nouns and singular verbs.

e.g. • **Each** student is given a certificate as a token of appreciation.
• I want **every** student to attend the lecture tomorrow.

V. Use of most, several and all

(a) We usually use **most** with plural uncountable nouns.

e.g. • **Most** people don't go for a walk these days.
• I have completed **most** of the work.

(b) We usually use several with plural nouns but it refers to a number which is not very large. (i.e. less than most)

e.g. • I have seen **several** people dressing up for the festival.
• **Several** blankets have been arranged for the internally displaced people.

(c) All requires a plural verb when used with a countable noun while, it requires a singular verb with an uncountable noun.

e.g. • **All** of us are leaving tonight for the trip.
• **All** that shines is not a star.

VI. Use of **another** and **other**

We use another only with singular countable nouns, whereas other can be used with singular countable, plural countable or uncountable nouns.

e.g. • Can I get book **another** table as more people are coming over?
• She likes the **other** cat that was sitting on the table.

VII. Use of **either** and **neither**

(a) We use either to refer to two things, people, situations, etc. It may mean one or the other of two or each of the two.

e.g. **Either** you or your brother has to go and pick up the flowers.

(b) We use **neither** with only singular countable nouns and a singular verb. **Neither** is the negative of either.

e.g. I can see **neither** Anil nor Rami there.

Possessives (My, Your, His, Her, Its, Our, Their, etc.)

Possessive determiners or possessive adjectives tell us who owns something. We use a possessive determiner before a noun to show who owns the noun we are talking about. They come in front of any other adjectives.

e.g. • Is this **your** car?
• That girl who is holding the play-card is **my** sister.

We use different possessive determiners depending on who owns the thing we are talking about.

Subject	Possessive Determiner	Used with Type of Noun
I	my	first person singular
We	our	first person plural
You	your	second person singular/plural
They	their	third person plural
He	his	third person singular masculine
She	her	third person singular feminine
It	its	third person singular neuter

REVIEW EXERCISE

Including Practice Questions

1. Fill in the blanks using correct determiners.

(a) Why am I living in .... country?

(b) Get me .... box from the table.

(c) Come .... way, please.

(d) The person .... car is not properly parked should be fined.

(e) Look at .... earrings. Jamie gave them to me.

2. Choose the correct answer from the options given below.

Unfortunately, *(a)* .... (a lot/few) of the companies where we sent offers showed interest in our products. Last month was a good month for the company.

We found *(b)* .... (many/either) new customers and also increased our profit.

We have to speed up, there is very *(c)* .... (few/little) time to finish the project.

There were *(d)* .... (fewer/all) people than usual in the supermarket to buy our product.

It will take me *(e)* .... (a little/neither) time, but I'm sure everyone will learn how to use the new software eventually.

I have *(f)* .... (many/little) money but more time than I did ten years ago.

3. **Fill in the blanks using correct determiners.**

(a) .... the children went to their respective classes.

(b) .... children like playing.

(c) Would you like to have .... fruits?

(d) Last year I went to Paris and Rome. I liked .... cities very much.

(e) Did you buy .... food?

(f) I don't know where Girish lives these days. I haven't seen him for .... years.

4. **Fill in the blanks with a, an or the in the newspaper report.**

There was *(a)* .... book launch and *(b)* .... interactive session with India's Mission Mars Dream Team at *(c)* .... Indian National Science Academy in *(d)* .... Capital in November. Through *(e)* .... book 'Reaching for The Stars: India's Journey to Mars and Beyond,' the authors relate *(f)* .... untold story of India's marathon to Mars. The writers chronicled *(g)* .... Martian adventure of *(h)* .... Indian Space Research Organisation (ISRO) as an insider's narrative of India's journey from *(i)* .... Red Fort in Delhi when *(j)* .... mission was announced in 2012.

The Chairman claimed that Mars Orbiter Mission is only *(k)* .... beginning. They are looking at *(l)* .... bigger scientific mission to Mars.

5. **Read the passage given below and fill in the blanks with the help of determiners.**

Medicine remains a dream career for *(a)* .... and *(b)* .... of the aspirants go abroad to train as doctors. While *(c)*........... majority look up to countries like *(d)* .... US for postgraduate training, *(e)* .... go to places such as China. Here are two experiences, one in *(f)* .... East and *(g)* .... in the West.

One relates that the education system in *(h)* .... People's Republic of China gives you *(i)* .... time to study by yourself.

Practical training is *(j)* .... better than classroom teaching.

6. **Fill in the blanks using correct determiners.**

(a) There were three pictures on the wall. I didn't like .... of them.

(b) Is your friend the English or American? '...................... . She's Australian'.

(c) We went away for two days but the weather wasn't good. It rained on .... the days.

(d) I invited Ram and Sheila to the party but .... of them came.

(e) Helena has got two sisters and a brother, ... the sisters are married.

7. **Fill in the blanks using correct determiners.**

(a) Julia gets up at 6:30 .... morning.

(b) The weather was nice yesterday, so we sat outside .... afternoon.

(c) My sister loves new cars. She buys one .... year.

(d) There aren't .... pictures in the gallery.

(e) I'm going to the post office. I need .... stamps.

8. **Two friends meet in their school canteen. They are going to have their lunch. Complete the conversation by filling in the blanks with suitable determiners.**

Namit You can share my lunch and I'll share *(a)*

Vipul Oh, that'll be nice. I'll have *(b)* .... good things to eat.

Namit I'm afraid. I don't have *(c)* .... to eat. There are only two sandwiches and *(d)* .... apple. Here's your sandwich. And you can take half of *(e)* .... apple.

Vipul Thanks. They look delicious. I have four toasts and some pickle. We can have two toasts each. And we will order *(f)* .... drinks. What would you like, tea or coffee?

Namit I'll have tea.

Vipul So shall I.

9. **Fill in the blanks with the appropriate determiners or articles from the options given.**

(i) I always keep .... cash in my purse for emergencies.

(a) any

(b) every

(c) some

(d) No determiner required

(ii) My family doctor advised me to eat .... apple every morning.

(a) the

(b) a

(c) an

(d) No determiner required

(iii) I've got to solve .... Science problems before I go to sleep.

(a) any (b) some (c) all (d) No determiner required

(iv) I haven't got .... pictures in my bedroom.

(a) some (b) any (c) many (d) No determiner required

(v) There aren't .... students in the class today.

(a) much (b) many (c) a lot (d) No determiner required

(vi) Could you bring me .... books I left in the garden?

(a) these (b) that (c) those (d) No determiner required

(vii) My grandmother doesn't drink .... tea.

(a) many (b) much (c) a lot (d) No determiner required

(viii) She gave a chocolate bar to .... child.

(a) any (b) all (c) each (d) No determiner required

10. The following passage has not been edited. There is an error relating to determiners in each line. Write the incorrect word and the correction in your answer sheet as given below. Remember to underline the word that you have supplied. The first one has been done for you.

	Incorrect	**Correct**
See here, Mr Allison, give me the break,	**the**	**<u>a</u>**
(a) won't you. I've got to get a story or an editor will	....	....
(b) fire me. Please do tell me anything about yourself.	....	....
(c) How did you happen to get into that work?	....	....
(d) Do you have some family? Please	....	....
(e) do give me a answer. Well, if you won't	....	....
(f) talk, I'll write mine own story, but you	....	....
(g) may not like the all story you'll read.	....	....
(h) You have few minutes to consider my offer.	....	....
I'll return after visiting the warden.		

11. The following passage has not been edited. There is an error in each line. Write the incorrect word and the correction in the space provided.

	Incorrect	**Correct**
Scientists who tracked five		
(a) leopards fitted with GPS collars gathered any	....	....
(b) new insights. Much of these leopards ventured as close as 25 metres to individual houses	....	....
(c) at night. Dogs appeared to be their both preferred	....	....
(d) prey. Other of the leopards, Jai and Lakshai, were	....	....
(e) captured from a densely populated area. Many leopard Ajoba was captured after he fell into a well.	....	....
(f) For the study, scientists collected data other	....	....
(g) three hours. Either that the study implied was that they were resident in their ranges. It appeared that	....	....
(h) relocation may some have only short term local	....	....
(i) effects or simply move the conflict to each area	....	....
or increase the level of conflict.		

12. **The following passage has not been edited. There is an error in each line. Write the incorrect word and the correction in your answer sheet against the correct blank number.**

	Incorrect	Correct
(a) Once there was the man called Hasan.	....	....
(b) He was one of the much great	....	....
(c) lords in the court of a Persian king.	....	....
(d) Hasan had the great wish to	....	....
(e) find any way of making himself	....	....
(f) invisible. To their good luck, he met	....	....
(g) the magician who agreed to sell him	....	....
(h) a magic wand for many gold.	....	....

ANSWERS

1. (a) this (b) that (c) this (d) whose (e) these

2. (a) few (b) many (c) little (d) fewer (e) a little (f) little

3. (a) All (b) All (c) some/ these (d) both (e) any (f) many

4. (a) a (b) an (c) the (d) the (e) the (f) the (g) the (h) the (i) the (j) the (k) a (*l*) a

5. (a) many (b) some (c) a (d) the (e) others (f) the (g) the other (h) the (i) more (j) much

6. (a) any (b) Neither (c) both (d) neither (e) both

7. (a) every (b) all (c) every (d) many (e) some

8. (a) yours (b) some (c) much (d) an (e) the (f) some

9. (i) (c) some (ii) (c) an (iii) (b) some (iv) (b) any (v) (b) many (vi) (c) those (vii) (b) much (viii) (c) each

10.

Incorrect	Correct
(a) an	the
(b) anything	something
(c) that	this
(d) some	any
(e) a	an
(f) mine	my
(g) all	whole
(h) few	a few

11.

Incorrect	Correct
(a) any	some
(b) Much	Most/ Many
(c) both	most
(d) Other	Two
(e) Many	Another
(f) other	every
(g) Either	All
(h) some	either
(i) each	another

12.

Incorrect	Correct
(a) the	a
(b) much	many
(c) a	the
(d) the	a
(e) any	some
(f) their	his
(g) the	a
(h) many	some

CHAPTER 5

Clauses

A clause is a group of related words containing a subject and a verb. A clause is a larger word group than a phrase and includes a little more information.

5.1 Types of Clauses

There are two types of clauses. These are

1. Independent Clause (Main/Principal Clause)

A main/independent clause is a group of words which contain a subject and a verb. It can be considered as a sentence and thus can function on its own.

The main properties of an independent clause are

- It contains a subject.
- It contains an action.
- It expresses a complete thought.

e.g.
- Let's start the play.
  (Here 'play' is the subject and 'Let's start' is the action.)
- The mobile is defective.
  (Here 'mobile' is the subject and 'is defective' is the action.)
- I will tell her about the paper pattern.
  (Here 'I' is the subject and 'will tell her about the paper pattern' is the action.)

2. Dependent Clause (Subordinate Clause)

Subordinate clause is a clause which is not complete in itself and doesn't express a clear meaning. Therefore, it cannot stand alone as a sentence.

It starts with a subordinating conjunction such as "when, who, that or if" and requires a main clause to make complete sense.

Dependent clauses are further divided into three kinds

Kinds of Dependent Clause

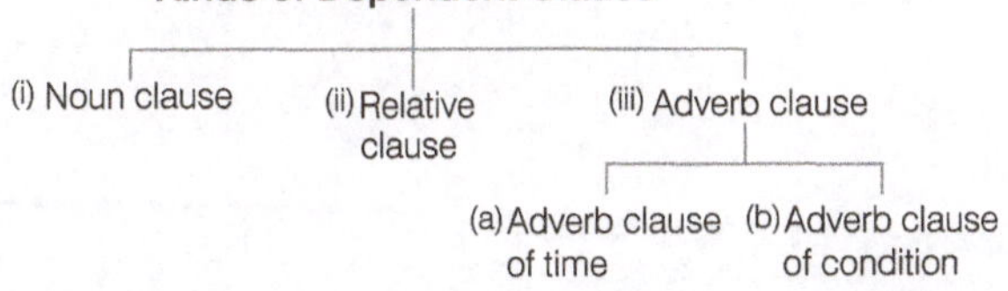

(i) Noun Clause

A noun clause is a dependent clause that acts as a noun. Noun clauses begin with words such as how, that, what, whatever, when, where, whether, which, whichever, who, whoever, whom, whomever and why.

These words generally come before the subject and the verb of the noun clause.

e.g.
- Choose a gift for **whomever you want.**
  ('*whomever you want*' is a noun clause and it contains the subject '*you*' and the verb '*want*')
- On weekends, we can do **whatever we want.**
  ('*whatever we want*' is a noun clause and it contains the subject '*we*' and the verb '*want*')

(ii) Relative Clause

Relative clauses are dependent clauses introduced by a relative pronoun (that, which, whichever, who, whoever, whom, whomever, whose and of which).

Relative clauses add extra information to a sentence by defining a noun. Relative clauses are also called adjective clauses. The introductory words used for various categories are

For people	who, whose or what
For things	which or that
For places	where
For times	when
For possession	whose

e.g.
- Rohan visited the office **where his mother works.**
  ('*where his mother works*' is a relative clause. It contains the relative adverb *where*, the subject *mother* and the verb *works*. The clause modifies the noun *office*)
- We're going to see a band **whose lead singer is a friend of ours.**
  ('*whose lead singer is a friend of ours*' *is a relative clause. It contains the relative pronoun whose*, the subject *singer* and the verb *is*. The clause modifies the noun *band*)

(iii) Adverb Clause

An adverb clause (also called adverbial clause) is a group of words or expressions in a sentence that functions as an adverb. It adds extra information about the time, place, manner, etc. to a sentence and modifies the verb.

e.g.
- I am sad **although you did a good job of trying to cheer me up.**
  (tells us under what conditions I am sad)
- You must go to bed **after we watch the fireworks tonight.**
  (tells us when you must go to bed)
- I will give you a chocolate **if you clean your plate**
  (tells us under what conditions the chocolate will be given)

Note it An adverbial clause is always an independent clause. It may come before or after the main clause. When it comes before the main clause, a comma is used to separate the two clauses. When it comes after the main clause, no comma is necessary.

Types of Adverb Clause

There are many types of adverb clauses. The two most commonly used are

(a) **Adverb Clause of Time** We use adverb clause of time to modify a verb in the main clause and to tell the time when an action takes place.

Subordinating Conjunctions used are when, whenever, anytime, before, after, till, until, while, since, just as, as soon as, as often as, now that, as long as, etc.

e.g.
- Will you wait here until **I am ready?**
- I was not at home **when he came to see me.**
- I always take a bath **before I go to bed.**
- **As soon as Teena finished that project,** she started working on the next.

(b) **Adverb Clause of Condition** We use adverb clause of condition to modify a verb in the main clause and to tell the condition under which an action takes place.

Subordinating Conjunctions used are if, even if, whether, if.....not, unless, supposing that, provided that, in the condition that, as long as that, etc.

e.g.
- **If it rains,** we shall stay at home.
- She will take this medicine **whether she likes it or not.**
- You won't pass **unless you work hard.**
- **As long as you have the time,** why don't you come for dinner?

Clauses at a Glance

Clauses	Definition	Begins with	Examples
Noun Clause	• Any clause that functions as a noun. • Ask the question 'what' to the main verb and the answer is always the noun clause.	**Connectives** like who, whose, whom, when, where, which, what, why, how, that, if and whether	• Nisha told me **that she was feeling unwell.** • Your success depends on **how you prepare yourself.**
Relative Clause/ Adjective Clause	• It describes a noun or pronoun. • It adds extra information to a sentence by defining a noun.	**Relative Pronouns** like who, whose, whom, that, which, whichever, whoever, of which	• They work in a factory **whose owner is cruel.** • This is the scarf **which I liked.**
Adverb Clause	• It functions as an adverb. It tells you something about how the action in the verb is done. **Adverb Clause of Time** It modifies a verb in the main clause to tell the time when the action takes place.	**Subordinating Conjunctions** like when, whenever, anytime, before, after, till, until, while, since, just as, as soon as, as often as, now that, as long as	• **As soon as he saw his mother,** he began to weep. • The world will always be the same **as long as men are men**
	Adverb Clause of Condition It modifies a verb in the main clause to tell the condition under which the action takes place.	**Subordinating Conjunctions** like if, whether, as long as, unless, provided, supposing, under the condition	• **If it rains,** we shall stay at home. • I won't pay for it **unless he sends me the bill again.**

REVIEW EXERCISE

Including Practice Questions

1. Choose the appropriate options to complete the sentences.

(i) The man .... house was robbed has still not been paid by the insurance company.

(a) which (b) that

(c) whose (d) No clause required

(ii) She failed the exam, ... came as a great surprise to us all.

(a) who (b) which

(c) that (d) No clause required

(iii) The bat is the only mammal .... can fly.

(a) who (b) that

(c) which (d) No clause required

(iv) Jasmine is a flower .... is white and very fragrant.

(a) which (b) who

(c) whom (d) No clause required

(v) The moment .... I learned the results of the art competition was one of the worst moments of my life.

(a) which (b) when

(c) where (d) No clause required

(vi) My sister Ankita had always wanted to go to a place .... she could speak her native tongue.

(a) which (b) whom

(c) where (d) No clause required

(vii) The 19th century artist, ... name I could not remember, was one of the best I had ever seen.

(a) which

(b) whose

(c) that

(d) No clause required

2. Fill in the blanks using correct introductory words for clauses.

(a) .... I'm late this evening, don't wait for me.

(b) I am going to do some shopping now. .... I come back, we can have lunch.

(c) Is it ok .... I close the window?

(d) I met a woman .... can speak six languages.

(e) Where is the picture ...... was hanging on the wall?

3. Fill in the blanks by choosing the correct option.

(i) .... you want my advice, I will be in my room.

(a) Even if (b) Only if

(c) In case (d) No clause required

(ii) You have to apologise to your friend Radhika .... you want to do it or not.

(a) whether (b) provided that

(c) unless (d) No clause required

(iii) .... your room is cleaned, you will be taken to a movie.

(a) Unless (b) Provided that

(c) Whether (d) No clause required

(iv) You can use your father's car .... you drive carefully.

(a) unless (b) as long as

(c) even if (d) No clause required

(v) You will never understand this topic .... Rehman helps you.

(a) unless (b) only if

(c) whether (d) No clause required

(vi) .... they have enough money, they are happy.

(a) Even if (b) Unless

(c) As long as (d) No clause required

(vii) .... he earns a lot, he won't buy this house.

(a) Even if (b) Whether

(c) Only if (d) No clause required

(viii) .... your wife leaves you, what will you do?

(a) Supposing that (b) As long as

(c) Even if (d) No clause required

4. In the following exercise, fill in the blanks to make correct adverbial clauses.

(a) Capital punishment should remain for assault or murder, ... justice for the victim and their family should take priority.

(b) It is important that the company financially assists theatre artists .... they can continue to provide entertainment to the people.

(c) I used to live .... you can now see that hotel. They demolished my house to build it.

(d) I will continue to use my scooter .... petrol prices remain low.

(e) Much of the seafood we eat would not actually last that long .... it were not for the chemicals it contains.

(f) Jack Smith, ... book 'English Made Simple' sold a million copies, died today.

5. Fill in the blanks in the following dialogue using appropriate connectors.

Aman (a) .... are the DVDs?

Disha (b) .... DVDs?

Aman The DVDs (c) ...... were lying on this table.

Disha Your friend has taken them.

Aman But I don't remember lending them to anybody.

Disha Your friend (d) .... visited us yesterday borrowed them from you.

Aman (e) .... forgetful of me!

6. Rearrange the following jumbled words/phrases to make meaningful sentences.

(a) Do you know where the shopkeeper keeps his money?
No, I don't. Where does he keep it?
is the / all the / in which / the shopkeeper / this / keeps / wooden box / cash

(b) Have you heard about the commotion that happened yesterday?
Is it about the robbery case? What happened to the thief?
man / police has / committed the / the / theft last / who / night / caught the

(c) Are you not feeling well?
No, I am not sick. I am just upset.
you tell / are / the reason / can / me / looking upset / why you

(d) The landlord was a proud man and he took pride in his strength.
was proud / his strength / despised the / who / tenants / the landlord / weakness of his / of

(e) Why didn't you attend my birthday party?
We were called by him urgently so we couldn't attend it.
he is / party / explain why / to / didn't / going / go to / they / the

(f) Do you have any idea whether she will be there by 5 o'clock?
I am not sure.
permission / come / or / will / depends on / whether she / her mother's / not / there

(g) She doesn't seem happy nowadays.
Why? Didn't she want to marry him?
not / really / if she / I sometimes / to marry / wonder / wanted / him or

(h) What is Ranvir doing now?
He's currently weeding the garden.
What is he doing afterwards?
he will / Ranvir finishes / the garden / the lawn / when / in / weeding / grass / cut the

(i) I have been listening to this podcast documenting the rise and fall of ancient civilisations.
What are podcasts?
want to / the internet / their favourite / radio programmes / allow people / podcasts on / to / whenever they / to / listen

(j) Where did Arvind go last month?
He went to Kuala Lumpur.
Has he gone abroad prior to that?
Kuala Lumpur / never been / month / until Arvind / outside India / he had / last / went to

ANSWERS

1. (i) (c) whose (ii) (b) which (iii) (b) that
(iv) (a) which (v) (b) when (vi) (c) where
(vii) (b) whose

2. (a) If (b) When (c) if
(d) who (e) which/that

3. (i) (c) In case (ii) (a) whether
(iii) (b) Provided that (iv) (b) as long as
(v) (a) unless (vi) (c) As long as
(vii) (a) Even if (viii) (a) Supposing that

4. (a) as (b) so that
(c) where (d) as long as
(e) if (f) whose

5. (a) Where (b) Which
(c) that (d) who
(e) How

6. (a) This is the wooden box in which the shopkeeper keeps all the cash.

(b) The police has caught the man who committed the theft last night.

(c) Can you tell me the reason why you are looking upset?

(d) The landlord, who was proud of his strength, despised the weakness of his tenants.

(e) He is going to explain why they didn't go to the party.

(f) Whether she will come there or not depends on her mother's permission.

(g) I sometimes wonder if she really wanted to marry him or not.

(h) When Ranvir finishes weeding the garden, he will cut the grass in the lawn.

(i) Podcasts on the internet allow people to listen to their favourite radio programmes whenever they want to.

(j) Until Arvind went to Kuala Lumpur last month, he had never been outside India.

CHAPTER 6

Reported Speech

6.1 Definition of Reported Speech

The act of reporting the words of a speaker is called Narration. There are basically two ways in which the words of the speaker can be conveyed in writing

(i) **Direct Speech** (Direct Narration) The reporting of the words of the speaker without making any changes to it is known as Direct Speech.
In a sentence in Direct Speech
- the exact words of the speaker are stated in double quotation marks ("").
- the direct speech of the speaker is separated from the introductory phrase using a comma (,).
- the exact words of the speaker start with a capital letter.
- the punctuation mark of the exact words of a speaker like question mark (?), full stop (.) and exclamation mark (!) come before the closing quotation mark.

(ii) **Indirect Speech** (Indirect Narration) The act of reporting the words of the speaker by making necessary changes to it is called Indirect Speech.
In a sentence in Indirect Speech
- the comma (,) and the double quotation (" ") marks are removed.
- the conjunction 'that' is generally used to join the introductory
phrase and the speech.
- the punctuation marks like the question mark (?) and exclamation mark (!) are replaced by a full stop (.).
- the tenses, pronouns and possessive adjectives along with words indicating nearness of time and position are also changed.

e.g. Irina said, "I have to reach the station in ten minutes." (Direct speech)
Irina said that she had to reach the station in ten minutes. (Indirect speech)
In sentence (i) we can notice that this is the speaker's direct narration as it is shown inside double quotation marks, but in sentence (ii) tense and pronouns are changed and quotation marks are removed.

Now, observe the following changes carefully.
- I said, "I am not feeling well." (Direct speech)
I said that I was not feeling well. (Indirect speech)
- They said, "We plan to work on the project as a group." (Direct speech)
They said that they planned to work on the project as a group. (Indirect speech)

General Rules for Changing Simple Direct Speech into Indirect Speech

Rules	Direct Speech	Indirect Speech
• The commas and the quotation marks are removed in indirect speech.	• She said, "I am staying at my friend's place."	• She said that she was staying at her friend's place.
• The conjunction 'that' is generally used to join the two parts of the introductory part and the exact words of the speaker.	• Antul said, "You have to study harder."	• Antul said that I had to study harder.
The reporting verb 'said' becomes 'told' when it is followed by an object.	• He said to me, "You are a good friend."	• He told me that I was a good friend.
	• Rahul said to me, "I have tried my best."	• Rahul told me that he had tried his best.

Beside these changes, we change the tense, pronouns, modals and time and place expressions. These are discussed below

Rules for Changes in Pronouns

Rules for Conversion	Direct Speech	Indirect Speech
• The pronoun in the indirect speech remains unchanged, if the speaker is in first person.	• I said, "I study at a college."	• I said that I studied at a college.
• The pronoun in the indirect speech is changed to second person, if the speaker is in second person.	• You said, "I have work tomorrow."	• You said that you had work the following day.
• The pronoun in the indirect speech is changed to third person in accordance with the gender of the speaker, if the speaker is in third person.	• She said, "I am learning how to swim."	• She said that she was learning how to swim.

Changes into Reported Speech with Respect to the Tense

When we convert a sentence from direct to indirect speech, the tense of the speech may or may not change depending on the reporting verb.

Note It The reporting verb of the sentence is the verb that is placed before the statement given in the inverted commas. e.g. She says, "I am leaving for work." (Herein 'says' is the reporting verb)

- If the reporting verb is in present tense, the tense of the verbs in the introductory phrase and exact words of the speaker does not change.

e.g. • My father says, "I am proud of you." (Direct speech)
• My father says that he is proud of me. (Indirect speech)

- If the reporting verb is in past tense, the tense of the speech in double quotation marks undergoes a change as given in the table

Present Tense

Rules of Conversion	Direct Speech	Indirect Speech
Simple Present changes into Simple Past	• I said, "I don't like apples." • They said,"We meet up on weekends."	• I said that I didn't like apples. • They said that they met up on weekends.
Present Continuous changes into Past Continuous	• He said, "I am going for a walk." • We said, "We are leaving tonight."	• He said that he was going for a walk. • We said that we were leaving that night.
Present Perfect changes into Past Perfect	• Ankita said, "I have eaten my lunch." • They said, "We have a project coming up regarding the nuances of art."	• Ankita said that she had eaten her lunch. • They said that they had a project coming up regarding the nuances of art.
Present Perfect Continuous changes into Past Perfect Continuous	• He said, "You have been studying since morning." • Mina said, "I have been learning about the Inuit."	• He said that I had been studying since morning. • Mina said that she had been learning about the Inuit.

Past Tense

Rules of Conversion	Direct Speech	Indirect Speech
Simple Past changes into Past Perfect	• She said, "I didn't like this movie." • My brother said to me, "You broke the vase."	• She told me that she had not like that movie. • My brother told me that I had broken the vase.
Past Continuous changes into Past Perfect Continuous	• He said, "I was not enjoying the concert." • She said to me, "You were looking rather pale in the morning."	• He said that he had not been enjoying the concert. • She told me that I had been looking rather pale in the morning.
Past Perfect remains Past Perfect (tense does not change)	• Mohan said, "I had learned how to code." • They said, "We had gone to Jaipur."	• Mohan said that he had learned how to code. • They said that they had gone to Jaipur.

Future Tense

Rules of Conversion	Direct Speech	Indirect Speech
Simple Future : **will/shall** changes into **would/should**	• Lomov said, "I will have to marry her." • They said, "We shall come over to help you."	• Lomov said that he would have to marry her. • They said that they should come over to help me.
Future Continuous: **will/shall be** changes into **would/should be**	• She said, "I shall be waiting for you." • Lencho said, "The post office employees will be stealing my money again."	• She said that she should be waiting for me. • Lencho said that the post office employees would be stealing his money again.
Future Perfect **will/shall have** changes into **would/should have**	• He said to me, "I shall have asked you for help." • You said, "You will have reached by now."	• He told me that he should have asked me for help. • You said that I would have reached by then.

Exception

1. Tense of speech does not change in cases of universal truth.
   e.g. • The teacher said, "The boiling point of water is 100°C." (Direct)
   • The teacher said that the boiling pont of water is 100°C. (Indirect)
2. As per the rules we have learnt so far, the Past Continuous Tense changes to the Past Perfect Continuous, but in practice it usually remains unchanged except when it refers to a completed action.
   e.g. • She said, "When I met her, she was reading a book." (Direct)
   • She said that when she met her, she was reading a book. (Indirect)
   Here, the action is not complete, so there is no change in the tense.
3. If the Past Tense describes a situation which still exists (unchanged) when the speech is reported, the tense of the reported speech remains unchanged.
   e.g. • Jackson said, "I left the job as the office got shifted near the border." (Direct)
   • Jackson said that he left the job as the office got shifted near the border. (Indirect)
4. Unreal or imagined past tenses after would, would rather/sooner and it is time do not change.
   e.g. • She said, "I would rather we left for the station early." (Direct)
   • She said that she would rather we left for the station early. (Indirect)

Rules for Changing Interrogative Sentences into Indirect Speech

(The reporting verb 'said' becomes 'asked' and 'to' is removed)

Rules	Direct Speech	Indirect Speech
Use 'if' or 'whether' in place of 'that' as a connector.	• He said to me, "Do you want a pen or pencil?	• He asked me whether I wanted a pen or pencil.
Remove the question mark while forming an assertive sentence.	• I said to her, "Do you have to go now?	• I asked her if she had to go then.
The questions starting with question words like **when, why, where,** do not use 'if' or 'whether'. The question words are retained to introduce the reported question.	• Rona said, "Where are you going?" • She said to me, "When do you leave for work?"	• Rona asked where I was going. • She asked me when I left for work.

Rules for Changing Imperative Sentences into Indirect Speech

(Commands, Requests and Suggestions)

Rules	Direct Speech	Indirect Speech
Use conjunction 'to' instead of 'that'.	• The teacher said to the students, "Don't run around in the corridor." • He said to me, "Close the door when you leave."	• The teacher ordered the students not to run around in the corridor. • He ordered me to close the door when I left.
In sentences beginning with 'Let', the reporting verb is changed to 'proposed' or 'suggested'.	• They said, "Let us go together."	• They suggested that we should go together.

Rules for Changing Exclamatory Sentences into Indirect Speech

Rules	Direct Speech	Indirect Speech
Words such as Alas, Bravo, Oh, Wow, Wah should be left out in indirect speech.	• Anil said, "Bravo! You secured the first place."	• Anil exclaimed with excitement that I had secured the first place.
Forms of the verb 'wish' is used if the sentence conveys a wish.	• The old man said, "Only If I were rich!"	• The old man wished to be rich/The old man wished that he were rich.

Time, Place, Expression and Other Changes

now	—	then
ago	—	before
today	—	that day
last night	—	the previous night or the night before
next week	—	the following week
here	—	there
hither	—	thither
this	—	that
thus	—	so

REVIEW EXERCISE

Including Practice Questions

1. Read the following conversation and complete the passage that follows.

Shylock I am unwell.

Duke What can I do for you, Sir?

Shylock Will you take me to the doctor?

Duke Yes, Sir.

Shylock told the Duke *(a)* .... The Duke asked respectfully *(b)* .... Shylock asked the Duke *(c)* .... The Duke replied in the affirmative.

2. Read the following conversation and complete the passage that follows.

Kanak Have you seen 'Three Idiots'?

Kartik I saw them yesterday in my class.

Kanak I was talking about the movie.

Kartik I thought that you were talking about the three idiots in the class.

Kanak asked Kartik *(a)* .... 'Three Idiots'. Kartik replied that *(b)* .... class. Kanak further said that *(c)* .... Kartik replied that *(d)* .... in the class.

3. Read the comic strip and fill in the blanks in the passage given below.

While making the list of what he wanted from Santa Claus, Charlie asked Patty how Santa *(a)* .... all those toys. Patty replied that it was possible, as everything *(b)* .... She could bet that *(c)* ...., he would find that Santa *(d)* .... big Eastern chain.

4. Read the following conversation and complete the passage that follows.

Utkarsh I have lost my wallet.

Inspector How did you lose it?

Utkarsh My pocket was picked.

Inspector Where did it happen?

Utkarsh In the local market, Sir.

Utkarsh reported to the inspector *(a)* .... lost his wallet. The inspector asked him *(b)* .... Utkarsh replied *(c)* .... The inspector further *(d)* .... Utkarsh respectfully replied that it had happened in the local market.

5. Read the dialogue and complete the following passage based on it. CBSE 2013

Susan Why have you not brought my party dress?

Jenny I haven't brought it because I had gone to my uncle's house with my parents, so I forgot to keep it.

Susan Don't give me silly excuses. I want to know the truth.

Jenny I am sorry Susan. I was chatting with my friends till late. I forgot that you needed it urgently today.

Susan asked Jenny *(a)* .... Jenny said that she *(b)* .... Susan *(c)* .... Jenny said that she was sorry and further added that she was chatting with her friends till late and she had forgotten that Jenny needed it urgently that day.

6. Read the following conversation and complete the passage that follows.

Dilip I've been watching the sea and there hasn't been any trace of a ship.

Ralph I told you yesterday too that we'll be rescued, so have patience.

Dilip Why do you ask me to keep quiet whenever I say something?

Ralph Have you ever said anything sensible?

Dilip said *(a)* .... Ralph replied *(b)* .... and so asked him to have patience. Dilip angrily asked Ralph *(c)* .... to which Ralph wanted to know *(d)* ....

7. Read the following conversation and complete the passage that follows.

Sanjay I am surprised to see you here in Delhi. When did you come?

Madan I came here yesterday. I have been offered a job here.

Sanjay told Madan *(a)* .... and asked *(b)* .... Madan replied that he had come there the previous day and added that *(c)* ....

8. **Change the following exclamatory sentences into Indirect Speech.**
(a) I said, "How happy he looks!"
(b) He said, "Alas! My friend is no more."
(c) The boys said, "Hurrah! We have overcome all our obstacles."
(d) Sheela said, "May God grant my wishes!"
(e) Arjun said, "Pooh! I can do better than him."

9. **Change the following sentences from direct to indirect speech.**
(a) "We'll have to decide", declared Rohan.
(b) "I'm looking for my car keys", announced Dad.
(c) "You can get the bus", said Mom.
(d) "It's your turn to make the dinner tonight, Rohan", said Richa.
(e) She said, "Do you like basmati rice?"

10. **You met Seema. Here are some of the things she said in direct speech.**
(a) "My parents are very well."
(b) "I'm going to learn to drive."
(c) "I want to buy a car."
(d) "Sumit has a new car."
(e) "I can't come to the party on Friday."
(f) "I don't have much free time."
(g) "I am going away for a few days, I'll phone you when I get back."
(h) "I shall keep you informed."

Later you tell somebody what Seema said. Use your words in indirect speech.

11. **Change the following sentences from direct speech into indirect speech.**
(a) He said, "I am tired."
(b) Mr. Bhatia said, "My son is a good player."
(c) You said, "He was a teacher."
(d) Mr. Mehta said, "I have written a book on grammar."
(e) He said, "They were quite healthy."

ANSWERS

1. (a) that he was unwell
(b) what he could do for him
(c) if he would take him to the doctor

2. (a) if he had seen
(b) he had seen them the day before in his
(c) she had been talking about the movie
(d) he had thought that she had been talking about the three idiots.

3. (a) could afford to give away
(b) those days was promotion
(c) if the truth was brought out
(d) was being financed by some

4. (a) that he had
(b) how he had lost it
(c) that his pocket had been picked
(d) asked him where it had happened

5. (a) why she had not brought her party dress
(b) hadn't brought it as she had gone to her uncle's house with her parents, so she had forgotten to keep it
(c) told her not to give silly excuses and further said that she wanted to know the truth

6. (a) that he had been watching the sea and that there had not been any trace of a ship
(b) that he had told him the day before that they would be rescued
(c) why he asked him to keep quiet whenever he said something
(d) if he had ever said anything sensible

7. (a) that he was surprised to see him there in Delhi
(b) when he had come
(c) he had been offered a job there

8. (a) I exclaimed that he looked very happy.
(b) He exclaimed with sorrow that his friend was no more.
(c) The boys exclaimed with joy that they had overcome all their obstacles.
(d) Sheela prayed to God to grant her wishes.
(e) Arjun exclaimed with contempt that he could do better than him.

9. (a) Rohan declared that they would have to decide.
(b) Dad announced that he was looking for his car keys.
(c) Mom said that I could get the bus.
(d) Richa told Rohan that it was his turn to make the dinner that night.
(e) She asked if I liked basmati rice.

10. (a) Seema said that her parents were very well.
(b) She said that she was going to learn to drive.
(c) She said that she wanted to buy a car.
(d) She said that Sumit had a new car.
(e) She said that she couldn't come to the party on Friday.
(f) She said that she didn't have much free time.
(g) She said that she was going away for a few days and would phone me when she got back.
(h) She said that she would keep me informed.

11. (a) He said that he was tired.
(b) Mr. Bhatia said that his son was a good player.
(c) You said that he had been a teacher.
(d) Mr. Mehta said that he had written a book on grammar.
(e) He said that they had been quite healthy.

Integrated Exercise

Type I : Gap Filling

1. Fill the blanks (a)-(c) with the appropriate option from those given in the brackets.

A house on my way to work **(a)** .... an American pit bull terrier. On the surface, it **(b)** .... to be a friendly dog. All it does **(c)** .... stand and grin through the fence.

(a) (i) had acquired (ii) has acquired (iii) acquired
(b) (i) seems (ii) seemed (iii) has seemed
(c) (i) was (ii) are (iii) is

2. Fill the blanks (a)-(c) with the appropriate option from those given in the brackets.

Solar energy **(a)** .... become a viable source of power generation in our near future. **(b)** .... both environmental and economic cost, it works cheaper **(c)** .... fossil fuels.

(a) (i) must (ii) should (iii) could
(b) (i) Take (ii) Taking (iii) Taken
(c) (i) then (ii) than (iii) those

3. Complete the following paragraph by filling in the blanks with the help of the given options.

During **(a)** .... hottest part of the year, many of our city streets seem to be on fire **(b)** .... masses of Gulmohar flowers. This **(c)** .... one of the most beautiful trees to view **(d)** .... summer.

(a) (i) a (ii) the (iii) an (iv) some
(b) (i) from (ii) by (iii) with (iv) over
(c) (i) is (ii) was (iii) are (iv) be
(d) (i) of (ii) at (iii) on (iv) during

4. Fill the blanks (a)-(c) with the appropriate option from those in the brackets. **CBSE SQP 2024**

In order to maintain a balanced lifestyle, we **(a)** .... prioritise self-care practices, such as regular exercise and healthy eating habits, to promote overall well-being. Individuals should also **(b)** .... in mindfulness activities, such as meditation or yoga, to improve mental health. Additionally, seeking support from friends, family, or mental health professionals **(c)** .... time one feels overwhelmed can contribute to a balanced and fulfilling lifestyle.

(a) (i) can (ii) should (iii) must
(b) (i) have engaged (ii) engage (iii) being engaged
(c) (i) every (ii) some (iii) any

5. Complete the following paragraph by filling in the blanks with the help of the given options.

He screamed so loudly that the pigeons pecking **(a)** .... the scattered grains in **(b)** .... courtyard **(c)** .... off in a flurry and **(d)** .... not return till evening.

(a) (i) on (ii) at (iii) over (iv) in
(b) (i) the (ii) a (iii) an (iv) some
(c) (i) take (ii) takes (iii) took (iv) taking
(d) (i) can (ii) should (iii) will (iv) did

6. **Fill in the blanks with the correct option from the two options given in brackets.**
(a) The quality of the mangoes .... (was/were) not good.
(b) Organic farming .... (is/are) one solution for reducing environmental pollution levels.
(c) Time and tide .... (wait/waits) for none.
(d) The news .... (was/were) too good to be true.
(e) Either the cat or the dog .... (has/have) been here.
(f) The shop with its contents .... (was/were) burnt down.
(g) Police .... (has/have) chased away the robbers.
(h) In the company, the Chairman and the Director always .... (help/helps) the employees.

7. **Complete the following paragraph by filling in the blanks with the help of the given options.**
Gauri was only eight years old, but (a) .... mountain of family responsibilities had already (b) .... (c) .... her head, as both her parents (d) .... *dead.*

(a)	(i) a	(ii) the	(iii) an	(iv) some
(b)	(i) descend	(ii) descending	(iii) descended	(iv) descends
(c)	(i) over	(ii) on	(iii) above	(iv) in
(d)	(i) are	(ii) is	(iii) became	(iv) were

8. **Fill in the blanks (a)-(c) with the appropriate option from those in the brackets.** **CBSE SQP 2023**
Time travel (a) .... (ought to/should/could) become a reality in the near future, (b) .... (allows/allowed/allowing) human beings to experience the thrill of travelling back in time. However, (c) .... (most/many/much) challenges must be overcome, such as ensuring safety and affordability for all potential time-travellers.

9. **Fill in the blanks in the following passage with one word only in each blank.**
The people in the restaurant seemed (a) .... lonely as the place itself. Two men in untidy work shirts (b) .... at the counter, (c) .... wearily at the cups of coffee. I thought that they (d) .... shift workers (e) ...., for some reason, didn't want to go home. A little away from them sat (f) .... couple. The man was staring into space, idly tapping his spoon on the table (g) .... the woman drew aimless parallel lines on her paper napkin with (h) .... fork.

10. **Fill in the blanks in the following passage with one word only in each blank.**
The ancient Egyptians believed that a person's soul lived after (a) .... body died. To make (b) .... soul live, they developed ways to prevent the body from (c) .... At first, they used to bury their bodies under (d) .... hot desert sand.

11. **Read the passage given below. Fill in the blanks by choosing the most appropriate words from the given options.**
Jesus Christ (a) .... of misleading the masses despite (b) .... fact (c) .... he was leading them from darkness towards light.

(a)	(i) accuse	(ii) was accused	(iii) will be accused	(iv) accuse
(b)	(i) a	(ii) the	(iii) an	(iv) that
(c)	(i) this	(ii) these	(iii) those	(iv) that

12. **Read the paragraph given below. Fill in the blanks by choosing the most appropriate words/phrases from the given options.**
(a) .... often the cause of accidents is the failure of the brake system, which means the owner of the vehicle does not bother to keep (b) .... machine in good condition. By attending to (c) .... vehicle regularly a lot of miseries (d) .... be avoided.

(a)	(i) Many	(ii) Much	(iii) Extremely	(iv) Very
(b)	(i) a	(ii) the	(iii) that	(iv) this
(c)	(i) a	(ii) an	(iii) the	(iv) that
(d)	(i) need to	(ii) could	(iii) must	(iv) should

13. Read the paragraph given below. Fill in the blanks by choosing the most appropriate words/phrases from the given options.

Children may quarrel all the time, drawing the elders into the fray. The neighbour's son may pick a flower or a fruit from your garden and **(a)** .... argument **(b)** .... erupt. Again, he may throw his ball to **(c)** .... window pane, damaging it. These are not unnatural so far as the younger one is concerned, but it is for the elders to **(d)** .... them with equanimity.

(a) (i) a	(ii) the	(iii) an	(iv) one
(b) (i) must	(ii) ought to	(iii) may	(iv) should
(c) (i) our	(ii) your	(iii) my	(iv) his
(d) (i) see	(ii) watch	(iii) view	(iv) look

14. Read the paragraph given below. Fill in the blanks by choosing the most appropriate words/phrases from the given options.

(a) .... think of road safety at all? It is because of the gruesome accidents that occur almost every day on the roads, in **(b)** .... all sorts of vehicles, human beings and even animals are endangered. These accidents **(c)** .... loss of life and property and, **(d)** .... importantly, obstruction to traffic.

(a) (i) Who	(ii) What	(iii) Where	(iv) Why
(b) (i) them	(ii) which	(iii) some	(iv) that
(c) (i) brings	(ii) give	(iii) mean	(iv) take
(d) (i) most	(ii) much	(iii) very	(iv) a lot

15. Complete the following passage by filling up the blanks with suitable prepositions. Write only the missing word in your answer sheet against the correct blank number.

The ultimate objective of demonetisation **(a)** .... to make India a cashless society. Though the people faced **(b)** .... lot of inconvenience owing **(c)** .... shortage of funds due to demonetisation, they did not criticise the government for **(d)** .... move.

16. Complete the following passage by filling up the blanks with the correct forms of the verbs given in brackets. Write only the missing words/phrases in your answer sheet.

Most man-made emissions of carbon dioxide **(a)** .... (be) through the **(b)** .... (burn) of fossil fuels, as well as through **(c)** .... (cut) down of carbon-absorbing forests. This **(d)** .... (cause) the greenhouse effect.

17. Read the following passage. Fill in the blanks by choosing the most appropriate options from the ones given below. Write the answers in your answer sheet against the correct blank numbers. Do not copy the whole passage.

Later, **(a)** .... asked about his decision, he said, " **(b)** .... first rule of sailing is, when you see **(c)**... ...... in trouble, you help **(d)** ...."

(a) (i) as	(ii) when	(iii) if	(iv) on
(b) (i) a	(ii) very	(iii) the	(iv) foremost
(c) (i) anyone	(ii) none	(iii) someone	(iv) one
(d) (i) one	(ii) them	(iii) her	(iv) him

18. Look at the notes given below and complete the following paragraph.

Florence Chadwick – goal – cross English Channel – first attempt unsuccessful – unable to see land – fog – second time determined – succeeded – broke men's record.

Florence Chadwick's goal was **(a)** .... She was not **(b)** .... because she could not **(c)** .... Her **(d)** .... helped her to win the second time. She not only swam across the channel but even succeeded in breaking the mens' record.

19. Fill in any four of the blanks in the sentences given below choosing the most appropriate options from the ones that follow. Write the answers in your answer sheet against the correct blank numbers.

(A) Concentration is **(a)**...... by alertness.

(B) Effective speaking **(b)**...... on effective listening.

(C) Economic growth **(c)**...... attitudes and lifestyle.

(D) The environment has always **(d)**...... in control of our destiny.

(E) They believe that logic **(e)**...... no place in faith.

(a) (i) help	(ii) will help	(iii) helps	(iv) helped
(b) (i) depends	(ii) depend	(iii) depended	(iv) depending
(c) (i) change	(ii) will change	(iii) changes	(iv) changed

(d) (i) is | (ii) be | (iii) been | (iv) was
(e) (i) has | (ii) have | (iii) had | (iv) having

20. Fill in the blanks in the paragraph given below by choosing the most appropriate options from the ones that follow. Attempt any four. Write the answers in your answer sheet against the correct blank numbers.

The sky was dark **(a)**...... monsoon clouds. It **(b)** ...... rained all night and **(c)**...... rain again. The monsoon rains **(d)**...... come early at **(e)**...... end of June.

(a) (i) from | (ii) with | (iii) over | (iv) in
(b) (i) has | (ii) was | (iii) have | (iv) had
(c) (i) will | (ii) would | (iii) shall | (iv) should
(d) (i) have | (ii) had | (iii) would | (iv) will
(e) (i) the | (ii) an | (iii) a | (iv) some

21. Fill in the blanks in the paragraph given below by choosing the most appropriate options from the ones that follow. Attempt any four. Write the answers in your answer sheet against the correct blank numbers.

As we got closer **(a)**...... the hills, the vegetation **(b)**...... more abundant and the fields smaller and **(c)**...... . By **(d)**...... time we branched**(e)**...... the jungle, it was quite dark.

(a) (i) in | (ii) from | (iii) to | (iv) over
(b) (i) grew | (ii) growing | (iii) grows | (iv) grown
(c) (i) few | (ii) fewest | (iii) fewer | (iv) a few
(d) (i) a | (ii) an | (iii) some | (iv) the
(e) (i) in | (ii) into | (iii) to | (iv) on

22. Fill in the blanks in the paragraph given below by choosing the most appropriate options from the ones that follow. Attempt any four. Write the answers in your answer sheet against the correct blank numbers.

In our school, the ground realities **(a)**...... different. We have not **(b)**...... our salaries for the last three months. The shortage of funds **(c)**...... hit the purchase of new books. But happy days are coming according **(d)**...... our Principal. An approval of funds **(e)**...... received from the Head Office.

(a) (i) is | (ii) were | (iii) are | (iv) be
(b) (i) received | (ii) been received | (iii) receiving | (iv) receives
(c) (i) have | (ii) had | (iii) has | (iv) having
(d) (i) for | (ii) on | (iii) to | (iv) of
(e) (i) is | (ii) are | (iii) were | (iv) has been

23. Fill in the blanks in the following sentences by choosing the most appropriate options from the ones given below. (Any four)

It was an old tree. A seed had been carried **(a)**...... the island by **(b)**...... strong wind some fifty years back. It **(c)**...... found shelter **(d)**...... two rocks and had **(e)**...... up to give shelter to a small family.

(a) (i) over | (ii) on | (iii) at | (iv) to
(b) (i) the | (ii) a | (iii) an | (iv) some
(c) (i) have | (ii) has | (iii) had | (iv) having
(d) (i) between | (ii) in | (iii) on | (iv) over
(e) (i) spring | (ii) sprang | (iii) sprung | (iv) springing

24. Fill in the blanks in the following by choosing the most appropriate options from the ones given below.

When I emerged **(a)**...... the anteroom, the waiting patients **(b)**...... relieved. Outside **(c)**...... street I hesitated **(d)** ...... a moment and **(e)**...... my feet homeward.

(a) (i) through | (ii) over | (iii) from | (iv) in
(b) (i) look | (ii) looked | (iii) looking | (iv) looks
(c) (i) the | (ii) a | (iii) an | (iv) some
(d) (i) over | (ii) for | (iii) in | (iv) from
(e) (i) turn | (ii) turns | (iii) turning | (iv) turned

25. Fill in any four of the following blanks choosing the most appropriate options from the ones given below.

(a) Politeness is said to (a)...... one of the important characteristics of a civilised person.
(b) The (b)...... enemy of politeness is ego.
(c) To be a polite person, you (c)...... to sacrifice your ego.
(d) It is difficult (d)...... an egoist to be polite.
(e) Polite actions (e)...... fine results.

(a) (i) is	(ii) be	(iii) are	(iv) being
(b) (i) less great	(ii) more great	(iii) greatest	(iv) greater
(c) (i) have	(ii) had	(iii) has	(iv) must
(d) (i) by	(ii) of	(iii) since	(iv) for
(e) (i) give	(ii) gave	(iii) gives	(iv) giving

26. Fill in the blanks (a) - (c) with the appropriate option from those given in the brackets.

A house on my way to work (a)...... (had acquired/has acquired/acquired) an American pit bull terrier. On the surface, it (b)...... (seems/seemed/has seemed) to be a friendly dog. All it does (c)...... (was/are/is) stand and grin through the fence.

Type II : Editing

Directions (Q. Nos. 1 to 29) The following passages have not been edited. There is one error in each line. Identify the wrong word and write it with the correction in the spaces given. The first one has been done for you in some questions as examples.

1. Neil Armstrong was the commander for Apollo 11.

		Incorrect	Correct
Neil Armstrong was the commander for Apollo 11.	e.g.	for	of
(a) He was the first to walk over		....	....
(b) the Moon. What many people do not knew		....	....
(c) is that, unlike most of their fellow		....	....
(d) astronauts, he was the civilian and not a soldier		....	....

2. The Gir National Park, also known by Gir Wildlife

	Incorrect	Correct
The Gir National Park, also known by Gir Wildlife	by	as
(a) Sanctuary, is situated in the state of Gujarat. It was	....	....
(b) one among the major wildlife sanctuaries to North India.	....	....
(c) It was establishment on 18th September, 1965	....	....
(d) as a forest reserve primary to conserve the Asiatic Lion.	....	....

3. According to tradition, Gautama Buddha sit

		Incorrect	Correct
According to tradition, Gautama Buddha sit	e.g.	sit	sat
(a) to meditate in the Bodhi tree at		....	....
(b) Bodh Gaya. Unfortunately, an original tree		....	....
(c) has disappeared and is replace		....	....
(d) through a successor — the Peepal tree.		....	....

		Incorrect	Correct
4.	(a) A priest is walking down the street one day	....	....
	(b) when he noticed the small boy	....	....
	(c) trying to press the doorbell of the house	....	....
	(d) across the street. And the boy was really	....	....
	(e) small and the doorbell was place at	....	....
	(f) normal adult height, which the little	....	....
	(g) fellow just can't reach. After watching	....	....
	(h) the boy's sorry efforts in some time, the priest stepped across the street and gave the doorbell a solid ring.	....	....

		Incorrect	Correct
5.	(a) To accomplish anything you need the driving	....	....
	(b) force. Motivation is this force. A wish	....	....
	(c) was not strong enough to make you take	....	....
	(d) action. A wish is the weak desire. Only	....	....
	(e) a desire could push you forward to act	....	....
	(f) and accomplish our goals. To get motivated,	....	....
	(g) you need for identify what you want,	....	....
	(h) possesses a strong desire and be willing to do whatever it takes to make things happen.	....	....

		Incorrect	Correct
6.	(a) A little girl was talking to his teacher	....	....
	(b) for whales. The teacher said it was	....	....
	(c) impossible to a whale to swallow	....	....
	(d) the human because, even though it	....	....
	(e) was the very large mammal, its	....	....
	(f) throat was very small. The little girl says,	....	....
	(g) "Jonah was swallow by a whale." The	....	....
	(h) teacher reiterated, "A whale couldn't swallow a human; it's impossible."	....	....

		Incorrect	Correct
7.	Walt Disney was our hero. He	e.g. was	is
	(a) left me a legacy that can	....	....
	(b) be enjoy time and again. He	....	....
	(c) knew who to entertain us so well.	....	....
	(d) He developed a process in creating animated films.	....	....

		Incorrect	Correct
8.	(a) It was necessary to understand that	....	....
	(b) we use ego at our everyday behaviour	....	....
	(c) and then we actually functions with	....	....
	(d) a healthy sense to self-esteem. It is said,	....	....
	(e) "Ego often had a voracious appetite; the	....	....
	(f) much you feed it, the hungrier it gets.	....	....
	(g) Hence, it was necessary to understand	....	....
	(h) where we are wrong. There was no harm in admitting our faults."	....	....

	Incorrect	Correct
9. (a) Thousands of bats emerge	....	....
(b) from under the bridge. It were	....	....
(c) a amazing sight. I learned	....	....
(d) a lot of fact about these creatures.	....	....

	Incorrect	Correct
10. (a) An one-eyed man was travelling	....	....
(b) through a bus one day. He was	....	....
(c) carrying a huge bag on him	....	....
(d) shoulder. Anyone sitting next to him asked, "May I help you?"	....	....

	Incorrect	Correct
11. (a) Often these days we hear and spoke of the conquest	....	....
(b) in nature, 'the taming of a river', 'the war against insects'	....	....
(c) and so on. Often these phrases being used without consciously	....	....
(d) attaching any value to them, but those have an	....	....
(e) underlying attitude of hostile towards nature and nature's	....	....
(f) creatures, a viewpoint which seeming to assume	....	....
(g) nature as an enemy that needs to being vanquished.	....	....
(h) Alternatively, nature is seen merely as the 'resource' to be 'exploited.'	....	....

	Incorrect	Correct
12. On reaching his room he entire broke	entire	entirely
(a) down, and became a prey for the most	....	....
(b) violent agitation. The vulgarity of those twins and	....	....
(c) the gross materialism of Mrs. Otis, was	....	....
(d) extremely annoying, but what really distress him most was that he had been unable to wear the suit of mail.	....	....

	Incorrect	Correct
13. Students are generally immature in his mental	his	their
(a) faculties. They are rash and hot-blood.	....	....
(b) They are not suppose to be wise and balanced	....	....
(c) in their judgment. His active participation in	....	....
(d) politics can lead in dangerous consequences.	....	....

	Incorrect	Correct
14. (a) Researchers from a universities of	....	....
(b) Bonn and Toulose on Germany	....	....
(c) had identified mutations in three genes	....	....
(d) that ought to cause what is	....	....
(e) known for "uncombable hair	....	....
(f) syndrome". These affected tend to	....	....
(g) have fair hair those is dry, frizzy,	....	....
(h) thin and resistant to be brushed or combed.	....	....

	Incorrect	Correct
15. Trying to achieve your goals without an		
(a) action plan is like trying for drive across	....	....
(b) the country within a map. The wasted	....	....
(c) time, energy or money will probably	....	....
(d) make you give in travelling before you	....	....

(e) go very far. Such goals is not goals at all ....
(f) They are merely fantasies. Success people
(g) find out what it costs to make his dream
(h) come true. They don't complain when the effort made.

16. While climbing up a mountain	**Incorrect**	**Correct**
(a) a groups of young boys saw	....	....
(b) an bear walking towards them	....	....
(c) One of them suggests that they	....	....
(d) should climbed up a tree.	....	....
(e) The boys quick followed his	....	....
(f) instructions. They felt safe as he	....	....
(g) watched a bear walk past	....	....
(h) the tree. They climbed down only while the bear had disappeared in the woods.	....	....

17. My father became Chief Secretary of Tamil Nadu	**Incorrect**	**Correct**
(a) on 1962. Soon after, he told my cousin and me,	....	....
(b) whenever we accompanied him to any functions,	....	....
(c) we were to sit on the car beside him	....	....
(d) and gave him a nudge if we saw a policeman	....	....
(e) salute him which he was preoccupied in studying	....	....
(f) his notes. He said so that he was concerned	....	....
(g) of the policemen standing in the hot Sun.	....	....
(h) He felt that he would return their greetings.	....	....

18. The passengers were waiting at the	**Incorrect**	**Correct**
(a) station when five policemen rushing	....	....
(b) into difference compartments of a	....	....
(c) train. After some times, one of them	....	....
(d) comes out with two young men	....	....
(e) and soon the other policemen joined her.	....	....
(f) The men which had been arrested	....	....
(g) was been caught for a theft.	....	....
(h) They had stealed two cars and a motorcycle.	....	....

	Incorrect	**Correct**
19. (a) Kodaikanal or Kodai Hills is a serene hill station who remains still	....	....
(b) unspoilt by the evils of urbanisation. Set high to the Palani Hills at an	....	....
(c) altitude of over 2100 metres, Kodai Hills is a 120 km drive to Madurai	....	....
(d) Surrounded by natural forests, it has a lake who is spread out in a star	....	....
(e) shape over sixty acres. Kodai is endows with thickly wooded slopes with waterfalls.	....	....

20. (a) It was an fine sunny morning when we set
(b) out to cover a last seven miles to the glacier.
(c) We had expected this to be a stiffest climb,
(d) but the ascent was fair gradual.
(e) The snow peaks was very close.

	Incorrect	Correct
(a)	....	....
(b)	....	....
(c)	....	....
(d)	....	....
(e)	....	....

21. We left after a mid-day heat.
(a) As we climb, the forest grew
(b) thick in bamboo trees. The Sun filtered
(c) through brief and gave us a
(d) pure delight. We are thrilled and
(e) soon our destination come in sight.

	Incorrect	Correct
e.g.	a	the
(a)	....	....
(b)	....	....
(c)	....	....
(d)	....	....
(e)	....	....

22. When he is eighteen Velan left
(a) home. His father slap his face
(b) one day on coming late with the
(c) mid-day meal, and he did this
(d) in the presence of others in a
(e) room. Velan glared on his father and left the place.

	Incorrect	Correct
e.g.	is	was
(a)	....	....
(b)	....	....
(c)	....	....
(d)	....	....
(e)	....	....

23. Lying on bed Swami realised with
(a) a shudder that it is Monday
(b) morning. It looked as though only an
(c) moment ago it has been the last
(d) period over Friday. He hoped that an
(e) earthquake will reduce the school to dust.

	Incorrect	Correct
e.g.	on	in
(a)	....	....
(b)	....	....
(c)	....	....
(d)	....	....
(e)	....	....

24. Stirred from the smell of food
(a) the dog stands before the blind
(b) man wagging his tail and gazing on
(c) the bowl. A blind man asked, "Who
(d) is there?" At whom the dog went up
(e) for him and licked his hand.

	Incorrect	Correct
e.g.	from	by
(a)	....	....
(b)	....	....
(c)	....	....
(d)	....	....
(e)	....	....

Type III : Omission

Directions (Q. Nos. 1 to 29) In the following passages, one word has been omitted in each line, against which a blank is given. Write the missing word along with the words that come before and after it in the space provided in any four lines.

1. (a) Wetlands are wold's most productive environment.
(b) Wetlands stretch mountains to seas.
(c) Wetlands provide a barricade the sea and land.
(d) They are found all the world.

	Before	Missing	After
(a)	....	....	....
(b)	....	....	....
(c)	....	....	....
(d)	....	....	....

	Before	Missing	After
2. I ten minutes late	e.g. I	was	ten
(a) for work morning. The exhaust pipe	....	....	....
(b) fell the bus. Mr. Brown was entirely	....	....	....
(c) unsympathetic. He said, 'You get	....	....	....
(d) yourself bicycle, Robin.'	....	....	....

	Before	Missing	After
3. The science is clear: to avoid worst	e.g. with	the	fact
(a) impacts of climate change, emission to be	....	....	....
(b) reduced by almost half by 2030 and net-zero	....	....	....
(c) by 2050. Achieve this, we need to end our reliance on fossil fuels and invest in alternative source of energy	....	....	....
(d) that clean, accessible, affordable, sustainable, and reliable.	....	....	....

CBSE SQP 2024

	Before	Missing	After
4. (a) The planets celestial bodies that manifest	....	....	....
(b) their powers human beings and other	....	....	....
(c) organic lives. Astrologers pandits worldwide are	....	....	....
(d) of opinion that planets have influence on	....	....	....
(e) various aspects our lives, such as love,	....	....	....
(f) personality, intelligence, career finance.	....	....	....
(g) The planets in solar system radiate a	....	....	....
(h) cosmic energy various degrees, which affects the minds and activities of humans.	....	....	....

	Before	Missing	After
5. (a) At the time I driving near Ohio, I suddenly	....	....	....
(b) felt need to stretch my legs. As I parked the	....	....	....
(c) car strolled down the pavement, feelings of	....	....	....
(d) self-pity enshrouded mind. I loved the lord	....	....	....
(e) and my ministry, I felt drained and burdened.	....	....	....
(f) My cup empty. Suddenly the impatient	....	....	....
(g) ringing of telephone nearby caught my	....	....	....
(h) attention. It was coming a phone booth at a service station on the corner.	....	....	....

	Before	Missing	After
6. (a) Vigilance is guard of all the faculties	....	....	....
(b) and powers the mind. It is the detective	....	....	....
(c) that prevents the entrance any	....	....	....
(d) violent destructive element. It is the	....	....	....
(e) close companion protector of all success,	....	....	....
(f) liberty and wisdom. The lack vigilance	....	....	....
(g) is shown in thoughtlessness a	....	....	....
(h) general looseness in the common details life.	....	....	....

	Before	Missing	After
7. (a) We live only what we do. Earnest	....	....	....
(b) people are dissatisfied anything short	....	....	....
(c) of highest excellence in whatever they do,	....	....	....

(d) and they always reach that excellence. Whatever are,
(e) whether a shopkeeper saintly teacher, you
(f) can safely give very best to the world without
(g) any doubt misgiving. If the indelible impress
(h) of your earnestness be on your goods the one case or on your words in the other, your business will flourish.

Before	Missing	After
....	....	....
....	....	....
....	....	....
....	....	....
....	....	....

8. (a) The temple had to slightly remodelled by the British
(b) when began repairs. During Aurangzeb's
(c) attack, his demolition men begun from
(d) the roof and worked way downwards.

Before	Missing	After
....	....	....
....	....	....
....	....	....
....	....	....

9. (a) All living things to breathe
(b) to survive, each species has
(c) its peculiar way. Some
(d) breathe lungs while others through skin.

Before	Missing	After
....	....	....
....	....	....
....	....	....
....	....	....

10. When thinking of the first ever iPod
(a) more a decade ago, Jobs realised that
(b) what would increase the attraction such a device to
(c) the consumers was a way for to buy
(d) music in seamless way.

Before	Missing	After
....	....	....
....	....	....
....	....	....
....	....	....

11. (a) Kerala a state in South
(b) India. Kerala became first
(c) state be recognised as a completely literate state. Kerala's
(d) net enrolment primary education is almost 100 per cent.

Before	Missing	After
....	....	....
....	....	....
....	....	....
....	....	....

12. (a) Gone the days when wedding
(b) gifts meant anything was readily available. Today
(c) people tend to spend effort to choose the right gift–a gift
(d) that only has aesthetic appeal but also has a high usability.

Before	Missing	After
....	....	....
....	....	....
....	....	....
....	....	....

13. (a) The Supreme Court made it
(b) compulsory cinema theatres
(c) to play National Anthem with
(d) the image of the National Flag prior screening.

Before	Missing	After
....	....	....
....	....	....
....	....	....
....	....	....

14. I went to my friend last week at 9 AM and returned after
(a) two hours. Actually, I wanted his scooter a day. But
(b) I was shocked he politely refused to oblige me. I did not
(c) speak even a single word on subject and hastened to be
(d) back. Whenever I think the matter, I feel ashamed of my
(e) inability own a scooter when all my friends own a car.
(f) Perhaps, I mistaken in assessing what true friendship is.
(g) It a lesson in my life and I was determined
(h) not forget it if I wanted success.

Before	Missing	After
....	....	....
....	....	....
....	....	....
....	....	....
....	....	....
....	....	....
....	....	....
....	....	....

		Before	Missing	After
15.	There are various entry points			
	(a) to India. Most foreigners land in Delhi, a	....	....	....
	(b) good proportion of head for	....	....	....
	(c) the main bazaar, is India's	....	....	....
	(d) craziest street. It situated close to the Delhi Railway Station.	....	....	....
	(e) The main bazaar is packed foreigners	....	....	....
	(f) from all the world. Frequent	....	....	....
	(g) power-cuts affect area and the	....	....	....
	(h) ugly sound growling generators is a common phenomenon.	....	....	....

		Before	Missing	After
16.	When in the evening Hari Ram's son did not come, he			
	(a) and his wife very much sad and worried. The son	....	....	....
	(b) arrived three days. When Hari Ram asked him where	....	....	....
	(c) he was for three days, he replied that he had to Goa	....	....	....
	(d) and not return due to the late running of the train .	....	....	....
	(e) Hari Ram asked him to inform him he went out again.	....	....	....
	(f) The son told him that he do so in future. He	....	....	....
	(g) stuck his promise and never	....	....	....
	(h) gave chance of complaint to anybody.	....	....	....

		Before	Missing	After
17.	I went to the hospital yesterday evening at about			
	(a) 6 PM see my uncle there. Last week, he had sustained	....	....	....
	(b) an injury in his leg in fall from the outer wall and	....	....	....
	(c) to be hospitalised. I asked him how he was feeling and	....	....	....
	(d) he told that he was okay except for some pain in leg.	....	....	....
	(e) However, he looked cheerful and hoped that he come	....	....	....
	(f) home some time. I felt much relieved after	....	....	....
	(g) meeting him. I think that a visit to a hospital always	....	....	....
	(h) fraught sadness as its ambience is like this.	....	....	....

		Before	Missing	After
18.	When I stood up and looked around I saw a beautiful scene.			
	(a) I confess that I have never beheld such a beautiful scene.	....	....	....
	(b) The country appeared like a vast garden greenery all	....	....	....
	(c) around. The enclosed fields about forty square feet wide.	....	....	....
	(d) They resembled many beds of flowers. These fields	....	....	....
	(e) intermingled with woods the tallest trees appeared to be	....	....	....
	(f) seven feet high. The town situated on my left side and looked like a painted scene. I had a feeling of	....	....	....
	(g) utter disbelief I had never seen such things before,	....	....	....
	(h) but these there and I couldn't forget them.	....	....	....

		Before	Missing	After
19.	(a) A policeman responded promptly a burglary report at	....	....	....
	(b) a house. The policeman sat down the sofa to take a	....	....	....
	(c) statement the house owner, not realising that the burglar	....	....	....
	(d) was hiding under it. The house owner looked down saw	....	....	....
	(e) the burglar lying flat his stomach half under and behind	....	....	....
	(f) the sofa. His head was right under policeman's legs.	....	....	....
	(g) The policeman jumped the sofa and caught the burglar	....	....	....
	(h) with some stolen jewellery his hand.	....	....	....

20. (a) The major types environmental pollution are air pollution, water pollution,
(b) noise pollution, thermal pollution, soil pollution, light pollution. During the last 10
(c) years, the world has witnessed a severe rise environmental pollution. Household
(d) and commercial waste pollutes the environment when disposed of properly.

	Before	Missing	After
(a)	....	....	....
(b)	....	....	....
(c)	....	....	....
(d)	....	....	....

21. I ten minutes late
(a) for work morning. The exhaust pipe
(b) fell the bus, Mr. Brown was entirely
(c) unsympathetic, He said, 'You get
(d) yourself bicycle, Robin.'

	Before	Missing	After
e.g.	I	was	ten
(a)	....	....	....
(b)	....	....	....
(c)	....	....	....
(d)	....	....	....

22. Most the people
(a) are annoyed passwords.
(b) They have many remember.
(c) On any given day are
(d) bound forget them
(e) This creates difficulties the people.

	Before	Missing	After
e.g.	Most	of	the
(a)	....	....	....
(b)	....	....	....
(c)	....	....	....
(d)	....	....	....
(e)	....	....	....

23. Do you remember last time you laughed
(a) loudly? For most us laughing out loud is an
(b) uphill task. More often not people think
(c) that they no time to laugh. There are more
(d) important things do. Says Sudha Chandra,
(e) "Hiring laughter coach is my aim here."

	Before	Missing	After
e.g.	remember	the	last
(a)	....	....	....
(b)	....	....	....
(c)	....	....	....
(d)	....	....	....
(e)	....	....	....

24. In 2018, Indian Women's cricket team a
(a) T-20 match Pakistani team.
(b) India won toss and
(c) chose field first. The Pakistani team
(d) lost three wickets no time.
(e) The fourth wicket tried level best to save the match.

	Before	Missing	After
e.g.	team	played	a
(a)	....	....	....
(b)	....	....	....
(c)	....	....	....
(d)	....	....	....
(e)	....	....	....

25. Police have launched special teams catch
(a) the snatchers. Each the teams will move into
(b) the crime affected areas. The teams directly
(c) report the district unit.
(d) police teams residents will work together
(e) to catch snatchers.

	Before	Missing	After
e.g.	teams	to	catch
(a)	....	....	....
(b)	....	....	....
(c)	....	....	....
(d)	....	....	....
(e)	....	....	....

CBSE 2020

26. Ever wondered what sleep deficit is? Well,

(a) sleep deficit a common problem among teenagers today, with many staying up late
(b) to use electronic devices. This lead to
(c) difficulty in concentrating mood swings
(d) It's important for teens to prioritise sleep to ensure their overall health and well-being.

Before	Missing	After
....	....	....
....	....	....
....	....	....
....	....	....

CBSE SQP 2023

Type IV : Sentence Reordering

I. Directions (Q. Nos. 1 to 5) Rearrange the following jumbled words/phrases in the given dialogue to create a meaningful sentence.

1. The King summoned his ministers who were whispering to each other and said to them.

The King What are you whispering about?

Minister 1 Your highness, we were talking about the new education policy in the country.

Minister 2 education experience/a more dynamic/for a holistic/the NEP is/and wholesome/pave the way/approach/which will **CBSE 2025**

2. Did you know that the lack of hydrological resources affects more than 40% of the world population?

No, I didn't. What are hydrological resources?

water resources/survival/and plant/to human/animal/refer to/which/are vital/hydrological resources **CBSE SQP 2023**

3. A : Do you have an idea that India is the sunny belt of the world.

B : What do you mean by sunny belt ?

Energy/Receives/Solar/Energy/Country/The/Far/Tha n/More/ Total/Annual/Consumption/Its/is/the

4. **Mohan :** Do you know why many people, now-a-days, do not like the concept of zoo?

Lalit :

Mohan : like/zoos/animals in cages/many/do not/zoo/concept of/people/ this /keep/as

5. **Person X :** We, as a nation are integrated into one unit. You know this, right?

Person Y : Er .... I do but I,d appreciate knowing a little more please. **CBSE SQP 2024**

Person X : (i) A NATION INTO /NATIONAL INTEGRATION,/ UNIFYING DIVERSE COMMUNITIES/A COHESIVE WHOLE, /REFERS TO/IS ESSENTIAL FOR/WITHIN/FOSTERING SOCIAL HARMONY/THE PROCESS OF/AND STABILITY /WHICH/

6. The earthworm is the worm we know best. An earthworm wriggles like most worms do. Some worms have no legs but they can swim. Earthworms live in the ground.

rainy/season/come/during/in/large/numbers/they/out

II. Directions (Q. Nos. 1 to 30) Rearrange the following words and phrases to form meaningful sentences.
The first one has been done for you in some questions as examples.

1. (a) had all their/bright condition/they still/classroom in
(b) they/gone/have/to/match/a/see
(c) real mother/suffering found/the love and affection/the sick and the/in Mother Teresa/of a
(d) that it/its knowledge/of our civilisation/does not know/with/the great defect/is/what to do

2. (a) watching TV/while you are/the following ways/the American Council/suggests/to exercise
(b) the remote/the channel/to change/get up/from the couch/instead of using
(c) the room during/walk up/the stairs/or around/and down/commercial breaks
(d) a treadmill/use/you watch/while/you can/TV

3. (a) Linda/London/go/will/tomorrow/after/day/to
(b) rarefied/the/there/is/air
(c) to exert/it/first 24 hours/advisable/for the/is not
(d) common/for/or two/breathlessness/is/a day

4. (a) emotional state/anger/accompanied/changes/is an/biological/by
(b) disability/common/congenital/a/it is/physical
(c) Shafique's foot/twisted inward/have/would
(d) every/entire/is/the/cosmos/changing /moment

5. (a) something positive/anger/can/be/by focusing/suppressed/on
(b) Shrifan/killed/Maoists/by/was/train/the/in/the
(c) one/of our time/of the/Mother Teresa/is/missionaries/greatest
(d) feelings of/deserted by everybody/those who were/she cared for/unwanted/the/uncared for/and

6. (a) for example/for long/it is not easy/to any one person/ to listen
(b) conversation/only a/in company/to take/try/of the/fair share

(c) keep quiet/to say something/when/a little/you have said/and give/a chance/your friend

(d) resistance band/while watching/use a/television

7. (a) those who/in life/get glory/only/work hard/and success

(b) effort/great/without/nothing/achieved/can be

(c) worked hard/never come out/unless he has/throughout the year/a student/can/with flying colours

(d) service/the/of mankind/God/the service/of/is

8. (a) does not/to mankind/there is/the ideal of/not a single religion/service/which/preach

(b) in his poem/that God loves/love their fellowmen/the famous poet Leigh Hunt/the idea/those who/is rightly brought/Abou Ben Adhem/out by

(c) like small children/given us/yet we/fit for/science has/Gods/powers/use them

(d) manage/machines/we/how to/don't know/our

9. (a) the body/fasting/removes/from/also/poison

(b) four hours/the fast/liquids/during/every/take

(c) the fast/grapes/is recommended/and oranges/during/juice of lemons

(d) the leisure hours/the majority of/of the TV/today/are spent/in front

10. (a) of most/now a days/the attitude/parents is/different

(b) work and play/different things/they see/as two

(c) thirst-quenchers/one of the best/watermelon/in summer/is

(d) cultivated /96 countries/it is/around/in the world/in

11. (a) is heard/is dialled/when/the dial tone/required/the/number

(b) at/end/picked up/the receiver/is/the/other

(c) go/as/can/the/conversation/long/as one likes/on for

(d) grown/about 5000 years/first/ago/it was/in Africa

12. (a) Kali/Ram's/prayers/sincere/heard/mother

(b) she/before/him/in/appeared/glory/all her

(c) was filled/he/when/saw her/he/with amazement

(d) race/slow/wins/steady/the/and

13. (a) in rural areas/is/employment opportunities/there/of/lack

(b) come to cities/in/people/so/of work/search

(c) appalling conditions/cities/they/in/live/in

(d) other amenities/they/running water/and/sanitation/proper/lack

14. (a) that/used/he said/in his childhood/to be celebrated/his birthday/differently

(b) distribute sweets/instead of/they/cutting a cake/used to

(c) blow out/but/used to/they/we/candles/light a lamp

(d) are killed/accidents/daily/ in/road/many people

15. (a) communication/not matter/was slow/it did/between different/when the/parts of the world

(b) for a/people/felt/our times/the need/in/common language

(c) unconnected with/creation of/the first solution/an/artificial language/was the/any existing language

(d) a great rush/there is/in the/on the road/morning time

16. (a) not/children/below/of/the age/must/drive/eighteen years

(b) protection/our/we/must/helmets/own/wear/for

(c) phones/must/used/not/mobile/be/driving/while

(d) traffic police/making/efforts/is/to increase/on the roads/safety

17. (a) an antidote/and pain/it is/to stress

(b) for toning/a good exercise/up/it is/facial muscles

(c) are stabilised/is improved/body functions/and blood circulation

(d) makes one/of friends/feel good/in making/a lot/laughter/and helps

18. is / Devprayag / town / beautiful / a

e.g. Devprayag is a beautiful town.

(a) it / sparsely populated / a / is / in Uttarakhand/ town

(b) an average / has / literacy rate / it / 77% / of

(c) Devprayag / *Pandas* / Badrinath Dham / the / is / seat of

(d) Alaknanda / confluence / town lies / at the confluence / the / and Bhagirathi / rivers / of the

19. (a) to/very/deforestation/can/to be/prove/ damaging/Mother Earth

(b) should/individual/his/Every/a/on/plant/ tree/birthday

(c) must/we/live/that/we/understand/trees/ cannot/without

(d) if/we/to/encourage/we/must/afforestation /the/want/keep/Earth/green

20. ideal citizen / the nation / an / to / an asset / is

e.g. An ideal citizen is an asset to the nation.

(a) makes / he / a valuable contribution / nation building / to / activities

(b) he / his / knows / and / rights / responsibilities

(c) his country / of / he abides / the / by / laws

(d) instrumental / nation / thus / development of / he is / in / the

21. Rearrange any four of the following word clusters to make meaningful sentences.

(a) very exciting/can be/new country/travelling to/a

(b) it/a lot of/before/actually requires/the visit/preparation

(c) option/is/light/travelling/best/the

(d) also need/we/the local weather/in mind/to/keep

(e) always/enriched/we/return/experience/the/with

22. (a) an / are / good citizens / asset / a nation / to

(b) rights / they are / respect / law abiding / others' / and

(c) good citizens / about others / and try / are concerned / help them / to

(d) socially useful/they / activities/ in / are / involved

(e) depends / strength / on / responsible / citizens / a nation's

23. (a) to the / and / was/winding / the way/ market/ long

(b) could / walking / get / boring / alone / quite

(c) a/ for / good time / it was / day / the / to plan

(d) walk keeps/ the day/ for/ fit and healthy/ you / the

(e) for / advisable/ distances / is / short / it / to walk

24. (a) stormy/scary / a / was/ and / night / dark /it

(b) to / the visibility / road / drive/ on the / was / too poor

(c) way/ fallen/ obstructing/ a/the / tree / was

(d) to/ the / be / driver/ needed / careful/ very

(e) succeed / only/ driver/ an/ would / experienced

25. (a) not/ be / student / it / easy/ a /is/ to

(b) are/ these / they / under/ days/ pressure

(c) need/ be / the / parents / to/ supportive/ very

(d) can't / be judged / academic / on their / only / students / performance

(e) provide/ we/ them / more/ should/ opportunities.

Type V : Sentence Transformation

1. Report the dialogues to complete the paragraph that follows.

The King summoned his ministers who were whispering to each other and said to them:

The King How will the new policy benefit college students?

Minister 2 The policy will provide for an interdisciplinary education that has flexible study plans.

The King asked Minister 2 how would the new education policy benefit college students?

Minister 2 told the king that the new education policy .... interdisciplinary education .... flexible study plans.

CBSE 2025

2. Study the notes given below and complete the paragraph that follows by filling in the blanks suitably.

Mrs. Gupta -alone-flat-a man knocked	opens-three men enter-revolvers
tied up -Jewellery worth ₹ 50000	disconnect telephone

Mrs. Gupta was **(a)** .... A man knocked at her front door. When she opened the door **(b)** .... At gunpoint, they **(c)** .... Mrs. Gupta, disconnected the telephone and **(d)** .... worth ₹ 50000.

3. Study the conversation between two persons given below and complete the paragraph that follows by filling in the blanks suitably.

CBSE SQP 2023

Photographer I want to use a drone for photographing your event.

Customer Really! Do you usually offer this advice?

Photographer No, I don't. Your event is in an open and picturesque area and I want to capture the complete scene.

The photographer told the customer that she wanted to use a drone for photographing his event. The customer exclaimed in suprise and asked **(a)** .... The photographer replied in the negative and shared that **(b)** .... as his event was in an open and picturesque area.

4. Report the dialogues to complete the paragraph that follows.

Rohit	I have bought a new DSLR camera.
Mohit	What will you do with this?
Rohit	I will click beautiful pictures with this camera.

Rohit told Mohit that *(a)* .... As Mohit was not aware of it, so he asked *(b)* .... To this, Rohit, answered that he would click beautiful pictures with that camera.

5. Study the conversation between two friends given below and complete the paragraph that follows by filling in the blanks suitably.

Anil	Why is there such a big crowd on that street?
Ravi	A new shop selling sports goods is opening today.
Anil	Is a film star doing the opening ceremony?
Ravi	I heard that Sachin Tendulkar is inaugurating it.

Anil asked Ravi *(a)* .... Ravi replied that a new shop *(b)* .... Anil enquired *(c)* .... Ravi replied that he had heard that *(d)* .... it.

6. Read the following conversation and then report what was said by completing any four of the blanks in the following passage.

Boy	Mom, I want to buy some new colours for myself.
Mother	You don't keep your things properly. Last month only I bought you two new packs of colours.
Boy	Mom, I have used them all. You know I love drawing and colouring.
Mother	You can buy one colour box for yourself and after going home I would love to see what all you have drawn and coloured.

A boy said to his mother that **(a)** .... The mother angrily replied that he did not keep his things properly and that **(b)** .... To this, the boy replied that he has used them all and further told his mother that **(c)**............. . The mother told the boy that **(d)** .... and that after going home **(e)** ....

7. Read the following conversation and then report what was said by completing the following passage.

Sameer	Neha, why do you keep on wasting time in useless pursuits?
Neha	It's not a useless job, I am trying to make an angel with this waste material.
Sameer	What is the need to do all this, when you have so many important things to do?
Neha	I am making an angel to bless my family.

Sameer asked Neha **(a)** .... Neha told Sameer that it was not a useless job and that **(b)** .... Sameer asked **(c)** .... To which Neha replied **(d)** ....

8. Report the dialogues to complete the paragraph that follows. **CBSE SQP 2024**

Student 1	I've decided to become a mathematician.
Student 2	Really? Why?
Student 1	Because I already excel at dividing my attention between homework and video games!

Student 1 told student 2 that they wanted to become a mathematician. Student 2 was taken by surprise and **(a)** .... Student 1 exclaimed **(b)** .... their attention between homework and video games.

9. Read the following conversation and then report what was said by completing the following passage.

Mother	Tomorrow is Diwali, so I am going to the market to buy a few things.
Daughter	Shall I come along, mother?
Mother	No, Shreya I want you to do some cleaning.
Daughter	Fine mom, I will stay at home and do the cleaning.

The mother said to her daughter that **(a)** .... The daughter asked **(b)** .... To this the mother replied **(c)** .... The daughter **(d)** ....

10. Read the following conversation and then report what was said by completing the following passage.

Tanmay	How did you spend your vacation?
Astha	I visited Kashmir with my parents.
Tanmay	Have you been there earlier too?
Astha	No, it was my first trip.

Tanmay asked Astha **(a)** .... Astha replied that **(b)** .... Tanmay further asked her **(c)** .... too. Astha replied in the negative, saying that **(d)** ....

11. Read the following conversation and then report what was said by completing the following passage.

Teacher	Why are you late?
Sumit	I missed my school bus.
Teacher	Why didn't you leave in time?
Sumit	Sorry, I will do so from tomorrow.

The teacher asked Sumit **(a)** .... Sumit replied that **(b)** .... school bus. When the teacher asked him why **(c)** .... in time, Sumit apologetically replied that **(d)** ....

12. Read the conversation given below and complete the paragraph that follows.

Pramod	Did you learn anything at the NCC camp?
Sarvesh	We learned a lot, including pitching a tent and lighting a fire.
Pramod	Can you teach me tent pitching?
Sarvesh	Yes, but first get yourself registered for the camp.

Pramod asked Sarvesh **(a)** .... Sarvesh replied **(b)** .... including tent pitching and lighting a fire. Then Pramod asked Sarvesh **(c)** .... Sarvesh agreed and **(d)**.............. for the camp.

13. Read the conversation given below and complete the paragraph that follows.

Wife	Our new servant has run away.
Husband	Is anything missing?
Wife	Yes, I can't locate my watch.
Husband	Where did you keep it?
Wife	Near the kitchen sink.

The wife informed her husband that **(a)** .... He asked her **(b)** .... She replied in the affirmative and added that **(c)** .... He asked her **(d)** .... She replied that she had kept it near the kitchen sink.

14. Read the conversation given below and complete the paragraph that follows.

Anika	What are you doing here, Arya? I haven't seen you since December.
Arya	I have just come back from my holiday in Scotland.
Anika	Did you enjoy it?
Arya	I love Scotland. And the Scottish people were so friendly.

Anika asked Arya **(a)** .... She added that she had not seen her since December. Arya explained **(b)** .... from her holiday in Scotland. Anika wondered **(c)** .... Arya told her that **(d)** .... very friendly.

15. Read the conversation given below and complete the paragraph that follows.

Mrs. Grover	Where are the memos I had left yesterday?
Kundan	I am sorry! I have thrown them away by mistake.
Mrs. Grover	What a silly thing to do! Have you taken any photocopies of them at least?
Kundan	Yes, I have put them in a file.

Mrs. Grover asked Kundan **(a)** .... Kundan answered that he was sorry **(b)**, ... Mrs. Grover told him that was a silly thing to do. She also asked **(c)** .... Kundan replied that he had and **(d)** ....

16. Read the conversation given below and complete the paragraph that follows.

Nishant	Mr. Verma, what's happened to Shyam?
Mr. Verma	He has left the company.
Nishant	Why has he done that?
Mr. Verma	He asked me for a salary rise but I didn't give it to him.

Nishant asked Mr. Verma **(a)** .... Mr. Verma replied **(b)** .... Nishant wondered **(c)** ...., to which Mr. Verma replied **(d)** .... refused to give it to him.

17. Report the dialogues to complete the paragraph that follows.

Daughter	Read me a story, Mom.
Mom	Give me a few minutes to relax and unwind.
Daughter	I will go out to play.

The daughter requested her mother **(a)** .... The mother replied and told her **(b)** ....

18. Read the conversation given below and complete the paragraph that follows.

Raj	Our school is celebrating its Annual Day tomorrow.
Sujay	Who is your Chief Guest?
Raj	Our Chief Guest is the honourable President himself.
Sujay	That is quite incredible.

Raj told Sujay **(a)** .... Sujay wanted to **(b)** .... Raj replied that the **(c)** .... Sujay was surprised and commented that it **(d)** ....

19. Read the conversation given below and complete the paragraph that follows.

Rejula	Madam, may I borrow a dictionary? I didn't bring mine.
Teacher	How can you be forgetful? Didn't I remind you yesterday?
Rejula	Yes ma'am. I am sorry. I will not repeat the mistake.
Teacher	Borrow it for today.
Rejula	Thank you ma'am.

Rejula requested the teacher **(a)** .... since she **(b)** .... The teacher chided her for being forgetful and asked her **(c)** .... When Rejula promised not to repeat the mistake the teacher permitted her **(d)** .... Rejula was relieved and thanked the teacher.

20. Read the conversation given below and complete the paragraph that follows.

Ritu	Hello Reena! Do you know that the school trip to Mussoorie has been cancelled?
Reena	No, I didn't know that. Why has the trip been cancelled?
Ritu	Our school Principal is a little worried about our safety.
Reena	Why is she worried?
Ritu	It has been raining heavily for the past four weeks in Mussoorie. Our Principal feels that a landslide could occur in that area.

Ritu met Reena and asked her **(a)** .... cancelled. Reena replied that she didn't know that. She asked Ritu **(b)** .... Ritu told her that **(c)** .... Reena asked her why she was worried. Ritu told her **(d)** .... for the past four weeks over there and their Principal felt that a landslide could occur in that area.

21. Read the conversation given below and complete the paragraph that follows.

Hemant	How long have you been living in Delhi?
Prateek	I have been living here for the last three years. My parents and I shall be leaving for Mumbai soon as my father is posted there.
Hemant	When will you all be leaving?
Prateek	We will be leaving by the first week of next month.

Hemant asked Prateek **(a)** .... Delhi. Prateek replied **(b)** .... He further added that his parents and he **(c)** .... as his father was posted there. Hemant asked him **(d)** .... Prateek replied that they would be leaving by the first week of the following month.

22. Read the conversation given below and complete the paragraph that follows.

Raghav	Hi Ravi, Varun and I are going to watch the cricket match tomorrow. Would you like to join us?
Ravi	I would love to but I have to take my father's permission first.
Raghav	You must let me know by this evening because I have to arrange for the passes.
Ravi	I will do so.

Raghav informed Ravi that Varun and he were going to watch the cricket match the next day. He asked Ravi **(a)** .... Ravi replied **(b)** .... permission first. Raghav told him **(c)** .... for the passes. Ravi said **(d)** ....

23. Complete the dialogue by choosing the correct option from those given below. Write your answers against the correct blank numbers.

Waiter	What would you like to order, ma'am?
Shruti	A coffee.
Waiter	Anything else, ma'am.
Shruti	Nothing, thanks.

The waiter asked Shruti **(a)** .... Shruti replied that **(b)** .... a coffee. The waiter inquired if **(c)** .... Shruti replied **(d)** ....

(a) (i) what she would like to order
(ii) what would you like to order
(iii) what did she order
(iv) what she would have ordered

(b) (i) she ordered
(ii) she would like
(iii) she wanted
(iv) she would have liked

(c) (i) anything else
(ii) she wanted anything else
(iii) she wanted more
(iv) she wants anything else

(d) (i) negatively and thank him
(ii) in the negative and thank him
(iii) negatively and thanking him
(iv) in the negative and thanked him

ANSWERS

Type I : Gap Filling

1. (a) (i) had acquired (b) (i) seems
(c) (iii) is
2. (a) (iii) could (b) (ii) Taking
(c) (ii) than
3. (a) (ii) the (b) (iii) with
(c) (i) is (d) (iv) during
4. (a) (ii) should (b) (ii) engage
(c) (iii) any
5. (a) (ii) at (b) (i) the
(c) (iii) took (d) (iv) did
6. (a) was (b) is
(c) waits (d) was
(e) has (f) was
(g) has (h) help
7. (a) (i) a (b) (iii) descended
(c) (ii) on (d) (iv) were
8. (a) could (b) allowing
(c) many
9. (a) as (b) sat
(c) staring (d) were
(e) who (f) a
(g) while (h) a
10. (a) the (b) the
(c) decaying (d) the
11. (a) (ii) was accused (b) (ii) the
(c) (iv) that
12. (a) (iv) Very (b) (ii) the
(c) (iii) the (d) (ii) could
13. (a) (iii) an (b) (iii) may
(c) (ii) your (d) (iii) view
14. (a) (iv) Why (b) (ii) which
(c) (iii) mean (d) (i) most
15. (a) is (b) a
(c) to (d) the
16. (a) are (b) burning
(c) cutting (d) causes
17. (a) (ii) when (b) (iii) the
(c) (iii) someone (d) (iv) him
18. (a) to cross the English Channel
(b) successful at her first attempt
(c) see the land due to the fog
(d) determination to succeed
19. (a) (iv) helped (b) (i) depends
(c) (iii) changes (d) (iii) been
(e) (i) has
20. (a) (ii) with (b) (iv) had
(c) (ii) would (d) (ii) had
(e) (i) the
21. (a) (iii) to (b) (i) grew
(c) (iii) fewer (d) (iv) the
(e) (ii) into
22. (a) (iii) are (b) (i) received
(c) (iii) has (d) (iii) to
(e) (iv) has been
23. (a) (iv) to (b) (ii) a
(c) (iii) had (d) (i) between
(e) (iii) sprung
24. (a) (iii) from (b) (ii) looked
(c) (i) the (d) (ii) for
(e) (iv) turned
25. (a) (ii) be (b) (iii) greatest
(c) (i) have (d) (iv) for
(e) (i) give

26. (a) (i) has acquired (ii) seems (iii) is

Type II : Editing

	Incorrect	Correct
1.	(a) over	on
	(b) knew	know
	(c) their	his
	(d) the	a
2.	(a) was	is
	(b) to	in/ of
	(c) establishment	established
	(d) primary	primarily
3.	(a) in	under
	(b) an	the
	(c) replace	replaced
	(d) through	by
4.	(a) is	was
	(b) the	a
	(c) the	a

	Incorrect	Correct
	(d) And	But
	(e) place	placed
	(f) which	where
	(g) can't	couldn't
	(h) in	for
5.	(a) the	a
	(b) this	that
	(c) was	is
	(d) the	a
	(e) could	can
	(f) our	your
	(g) for	to
	(h) possesses	possess
6.	(a) his	her
	(b) for	about
	(c) to	for
	(d) the	a
	(e) the	a
	(f) says	said
	(g) swallow	swallowed
	(h) couldn't	can't
7.	(a) me	us
	(b) enjoy	enjoyed
	(c) who	how
	(d) in	of
8.	(a) was	is
	(b) at	in
	(c) functions	function
	(d) to	of
	(e) had	has
	(f) much	more
	(g) was	is
	(h) was	is
9.	(a) emerge	emerged
	(b) were	was
	(c) a	an
	(d) fact	facts
10.	(a) An	A
	(b) through	by/ in
	(c) him	his
	(d) Anyone	Someone
11.	(a) spoke	speak
	(b) in	of
	(c) being	are
	(d) those	they
	(e) hostile	hostility
	(f) seeming	seems
	(g) being	be
	(h) the	a

	Incorrect	Correct
12.	(a) for	to
	(b) those	the
	(c) was	were
	(d) distress	distressed
13.	(a) hot-blood	hot blooded
	(b) suppose	supposed
	(c) His	Their
	(d) in	to
14.	(a) a	the
	(b) on	in
	(c) had	have
	(d) ought to	can
	(e) for	as
	(f) These	Those
	(g) those	that
	(h) be	being
15.	(a) for	to
	(b) within	without
	(c) or	and
	(d) in	up
	(e) is	are
	(f) Success	Successful
	(g) his	their
	(h) when	despite

16.	(a) groups	group
	(b) an	a
	(c) suggests	suggested
	(d) climbed	climb
	(e) quick	quickly
	(f) he	they
	(g) a	the
	(h) while	when
17.	(a) on	in
	(b) accompanied	accompany
	(c) on	in
	(d) gave	give
	(e) which	while
	(f) that	because
	(g) of	about
	(h) would	should
18.	(a) rushing	rushed
	(b) difference	different
	(c) times	time
	(d) comes	came
	(e) her	him
	(f) which	who
	(g) was	had
	(h) stealed	stolen

	Incorrect	Correct
19.	(a) who	which
	(b) to	in
	(c) to	from
	(d) who	which
	(e) endows	endowed
20.	(a) an	a
	(b) a	the
	(c) a	the
	(d) fair	fairly
	(e) was	were
21.	(a) climb	climbed
	(b) in	with
	(c) brief	briefly
	(d) are	were
	(e) come	came
22.	(a) slap	slapped
	(b) on	for
	(c) this	it
	(d) a	the
	(e) on	at
23.	(a) is	was
	(b) an	a
	(c) has	had
	(d) over	on
	(e) will	would
24.	(a) stands	stood
	(b) on	at
	(c) A	The
	(d) whom	which
	(e) for	towards

Type III : Omission

	Before	Missing	After
1.	(a) stretch	from	mountains
	(b) support	a	variety
	(c) a	from	the
	(d) all	around	the
2.	(a) work	this	morning
	(b) fell	on	the
	(c) you	should	get
	(d) yourself	a	bicycle
3.	(a) emissions	need	to
	(b) and	reach	net-zero
	(c) 2050	To	achieve
	(d) that	are	clean
4.	(a) planets	are	celestial
	(b) powers	over	human
	(c) Astrologers	and	pandits
	(d) of	the	opinion
	(e) aspects	of	our
	(f) career	and	finance
	(g) in	the	solar
	(h) energy	in	various
5.	(a) I	was	driving
	(b) felt	the	need
	(c) car	and	strolled
	(d) enshrouded	my	mind
	(e) ministry,	but	I
	(f) cup	was	empty
	(g) of	a	telephone
	(h) coming	from	a
6.	(a) is	the	guard
	(b) powers	of	the
	(c) entrance	of	any
	(d) violent	and	destructive
	(e) companion	and	protector
	(f) lack	of	vigilance
	(g) thoughtlessness	and	a
	(h) details	of	life
7.	(a) only	in	what
	(b) dissatisfied	with	anything

	(c)	of	the	highest
	(d)	Whatever	you	are
	(e)	shopkeeper	or	saintly
	(f)	give	the	very
	(g)	doubt	or	misgiving
	(h)	goods	in	the
8.	(a)	to	be	slightly
	(b)	when	they	began
	(c)	men	had	begun
	(d)	worked	their	way
9.	(a)	things	have	to
	(b)	survive	but	each
	(c)	its	own	peculiar
	(d)	breathe	through	lungs
10.	(a)	more	than	a
	(b)	attraction	of	such
	(c)	for	them	to
	(d)	in	a	seamless
11.	(a)	Kerala	is	a
	(b)	became	the	first
	(c)	state	to	be
	(d)	enrolment	in	primary
12.	(a)	Gone	are	the
	(b)	anything	that	was
	(c)	spend	more	effort
	(d)	that	not	only
13.	(a)	Court	has	made
	(b)	compulsory	for	cinema
	(c)	play	the	National
	(d)	prior	to	screening
14.	(a)	scooter	for	a
	(b)	shocked	when	he
	(c)	on	the	subject
	(d)	think	over	the
	(e)	inability	to	own
	(f)	I	was	mistaken
	(g)	It	was	a
	(h)	not	to	forget
15.	(a)	India	When	most
	(b)	of	them	head
	(c)	bazaar	which	is
	(d)	It	is	situated
	(e)	packed	with	foreigners
	(f)	all	over	the
	(g)	affect	the	area
	(h)	sound	of	growling

16.	(a)	wife	were	very
	(b)	arrived	after	three
	(c)	had	been	to
	(d)	and	could	not
	(e)	him	when	he
	(f)	he	would	do
	(g)	stuck	to	his
	(h)	gave	any	chance
17.	(a)	PM	to	see
	(b)	in	a	fall
	(c)	–	had	to
	(d)	in	the	leg
	(e)	he	would	come
	(f)	home	after	some
	(g)	hospital	is	always
	(h)	fraught	with	sadness
18.	(a)	I	must	confess
	(b)	garden	with	greenery
	(c)	fields	were	about
	(d)	fields	were	–
	(e)	woods	and	the
	(f)	town	was	situated
	(g)	disbelief	as	I
	(h)	these	were	there
19.	(a)	promptly	to	a
	(b)	down	on	the
	(c)	statement	from	the
	(d)	down	and	saw
	(e)	flat	on	his
	(f)	under	the	policeman's
	(g)	jumped	off	the
	(h)	jewellery	in	his
20.	(a)	types	of	environmental
	(b)	pollution	and	light
	(c)	rise	in	environmental
	(d)	when	not	disposed
21.	(i)	work	this	morning
	(ii)	fell	on	bus
	(iii)	you	should	get
	(iv)	yourself	a	bicycle
22.	(a)	annoyed	at	passwords
	(b)	many	to	remember
	(c)	day	they	are
	(d)	bound	to	forget
	(e)	difficulties	for	the
23.	(a)	most	of	us
	(b)	often	than	not

	(c) they	have	no
	(d) things	to	do
	(e) Hiring	a	laughter
24.	(a) match	against	Pakistani
	(b) won	the	toss
	(c) chose	to	field
	(d) wickets	in	no
	(e) tried	its	level
25.	(a) Each	of	the
	(b) teams	will	directly
	(c) report	to	the
	(d) teams	and	residents
	(e) catch	the	snatchers
26.	(a) deficit	is	a
	(b) This	can	lead
	(c) concentrating	and	mood
	(d) prioritise	their	sleep

Type IV : Sentences Reordering

I. **1.** The NEP is a more dynamic and wholesome approach which will pave the way for a holistic education experience.

2. Hydrological resources refer to water resources, which are vital to human, animal and plant survival.

3. The Solar Energy the country receives is far more than its total annual energy consumption.

4. Many people do not like this concept of zoo as zoos keep animal in cages.

5. (i) NATIONAL INTEGRATION, WHICH REFERS TO THE PROCESS OF UNIFYING DIVERSE COMMUNITIES WITHIN A NATION INTO A COHESIVE WHOLE, IS ESSENTIAL FOR FOSTERING SOCIAL HARMONY AND STABILITY.

6. During rainy season, they come out in large numbers.

II. **1.** (a) They still had all their classroom in bright condition.

(b) They have gone to see a match.

(c) The sick and the suffering found the love and affection of a real mother in Mother Teresa.

(d) The great defect of our civilisation is that it does not know what to do with its knowledge.

2. (a) The American Council suggests the following ways to exercise while you are watching TV.

(b) Get up from the couch instead of using the remote to change the channel.

(c) Walk up and down the stairs or around the room during commercial breaks.

(d) You can use a treadmill while you watch TV.

3. (a) Linda will go to London day after tomorrow.

(b) The air there is rarefied.

(c) It is not advisable to exert for the first 24 hours.

(d) Breathlessness is common for a day or two.

4. (a) Anger is an emotional state accompanied by biological changes.

(b) It is a common congenital physical disability.

(c) Shafique's foot would have twisted inward.

(d) Every moment the entire cosmos is changing.

5. (a) Anger can be suppressed by focusing on something positive.

(b) Shrifan was killed by the Maoists in the train.

(c) Mother Teresa is one of the greatest missionaries of our time.

(d) She cared for the feelings of those who were unwanted, uncared for and deserted by everybody.

6. (a) It is not easy, for example, to listen to any one person for long.

(b) In company, try to take only a fair share of the conversation.

(c) When you have said a little, keep quiet and give your friend a chance to say something.

(d) Use a resistance band while watching television.

7. (a) Only those who work hard get glory and success in life.

(b) Nothing great can be achieved without effort.

(c) A student can never come out with flying colours unless he has worked hard throughout the year.

(d) The service of mankind is the service of God.

8. (a) There is not a single religion which does not preach the ideal of service to mankind.

(b) The idea that God loves those who love their fellowmen is rightly brought out by the famous poet Leigh Hunt in his poem Abou Ben Adhem.

(c) Science has given us powers fit for Gods, yet we use them like small children.

(d) We don't know how to manage our machines.

9. (a) Fasting also removes poison from the body.

(b) Take liquids every four hours during the fast.

(c) Juice of lemons, grapes and oranges is recommended during the fast.

(d) Today, the majority of the leisure hours are spent in front of the TV.

10. (a) The attitude of most parents is different nowadays.

(b) They see work and play as two different things.

(c) Watermelon is one of the best thirst-quenchers in summer.

(d) It is cultivated in around 96 countries in the world.

11. (a) When the dial tone is heard, the required number is dialled.

(b) The receiver is picked up at the other end.

(c) The conversation can go on for as long as one likes.

(d) It was first grown in Africa about 5000 years ago.

12. (a) Mother Kali heard Ram's sincere prayers.
(b) She appeared before him in all her glory.
(c) He was filled with amazement when he saw her.
(d) Slow and steady wins the race.

13. (a) There is lack of employment opportunities in rural areas.
(b) So, people come to cities in search of work.
(c) They live in appalling conditions in cities.
(d) They lack proper sanitation, running water and other amenities.

14. (a) He said that in his childhood, his birthday used to be celebrated differently.
(b) Instead of cutting a cake they used to distribute sweets.
(c) We blow out candles but they used to light a lamp.
(d) Many people are killed daily in road accidents.

15. (a) It did not matter when the communication between different parts of the world was slow.
(b) In our times, people felt the need for a common language.
(c) The first solution was the creation of an artificial language unconnected with any existing language.
(d) There is a great rush on the road in the morning time.

16. (a) Children below the age of eighteen years must not drive.
(b) We must wear helmets for our own protection.
(c) Mobile phones must not be used while driving.
(d) Traffic police is making efforts to increase safety on the roads.

17. (a) It is an antidote to stress and pain.
(b) It is a good exercise for toning up facial muscles.
(c) Body functions are stabilised and blood circulation is improved.
(d) Laughter makes one feel good and helps in making a lot of friends.

18. (a) It is a sparsely populated town in Uttarakhand.
(b) It has an average literacy rate of 77%.
(c) Devprayag is the seat of Badrinath Dham pandas.
(d) The town lies at the confluence of the Alaknanda and Bhagirathi rivers.

19. (a) Deforestation can prove to be very damaging to Mother Earth.
(b) Every individual should plant a tree on his birthday.
(c) We must understand that we cannot live without trees.
(d) If we want to keep the Earth green we must encourage afforestation.

20. (a) He makes a valuable contribution to nation building activities.
(b) He knows his rights and responsibilities.
(c) He abides by the laws of his country.
(d) Thus he is instrumental in development of the nation.

21. (a) Travelling to a new country can be very exciting.
(b) The visit actually requires a lot of preparation before it.
(c) The best option is travelling light.
(d) We also need to keep the local weather in mind.
(e) We always return enriched with the experience.

22. (a) Good citizens are an asset to a nation.
(b) They are law abiding and respect others' rights.
(c) Good citizens are concerned about others and try to help them.
(d) They are involved in socially useful activities.
(e) A nation's strength depends on responsible citizens.

23. (a) The way to the market was long and winding.
(b) Walking alone could get quite boring.
(c) It was a good time to plan for the day.
(d) The walk keeps you fit and healthy for the day.
(e) It is advisable to walk for short distances.

24. (a) It was a dark, stormy and scary night.
(b) The visibility on the road was too poor to drive.
(c) A fallen tree was obstructing the way.
(d) The driver needed to be very careful.
(e) Only an experienced driver would succeed.

25. (a) It is not easy to be a student.
(b) These days they are under pressure.
(c) The parents need to be very supportive.
(d) Students can't be judged only on their academic performance.
(e) We should provide them more opportunities.

Type V : Sentence Transformation

1. would provide, that has

2. (a) alone in her flat
(b) three men entered with revolvers
(c) tied up
(d) stole jewellery

3. (a) if she usually offered that advice
(b) she wanted to capture the complete scene

4. (a) he had bought a new DSLR Camera
(b) what he would do with that

5. (a) why there was such a big crowd on that street
(b) selling sports goods was opening that day
(c) whether a film star was doing the opening ceremony
(d) Sachin Tendulkar was inaugurating

6. (a) he wanted to buy some new colours for himself
   (b) she had bought him two new packs of colours the previous month only
   (c) she knew he loved drawing and colouring
   (d) he could buy one colour box for himself
   (e) she would love to see what all he had drawn and coloured
7. (a) why she kept on wasting time in useless pursuits
   (b) she was trying to make an angel with that waste material
   (c) what was the need to do all those things when she had so many important things to do
   (d) that she was making it to bless her family.
8. (a) asked why/enquired the reason
   (b) that was because they already excelled at dividing
9. (a) it was Diwali the next day, so she was going to the market to buy a few things
   (b) if she could come along with her
   (c) in the negative and said she wanted her to do some cleaning
   (d) agreed to it and said that she would stay at home and do the cleaning
10. (a) how she had spent her vacation
   (b) she had visited Kashmir with her parents
   (c) if she had been there earlier
   (d) it had been her first trip
11. (a) why he was late
   (b) he had missed his
   (c) he had not left
   (d) he would do so from the next day
12. (a) about what he learnt at the NCC camp
   (b) that they had learned a lot
   (c) if he could teach him tent pitching
   (d) asked him to first get registered
13. (a) their new servant had run away
   (b) if anything was missing
   (c) she could not locate her watch
   (d) where she had kept it
14. (a) what she was doing there
   (b) that she had just come back
   (c) whether she had enjoyed it/if she had enjoyed it
   (d) she loved Scotland and the Scottish people had been
15. (a) where the memos she had left on the previous day were
   (b) but he had thrown them away by mistake
   (c) if he had taken any photocopies of them at least
   (d) that he had put them in a file
16. (a) what had happened to Shyam
   (b) that he had left the company
   (c) why he had done so
   (d) that he had asked him for a salary rise but he had
17. (a) to read her a story
   (b) to give her a few minutes to relax and unwind
18. (a) that their school was celebrating its Annual Day the next day
   (b) know who their Chief Guest was
   (c) Chief Guest was the honourable President himself
   (d) was quite incredible
19. (a) to allow her to borrow a dictionary
   (b) had forgotten to bring hers
   (c) if she hadn't reminded her a day in advance
   (d) to borrow it for that day
20. (a) if she knew that the school trip to Mussoorie had been
   (b) why the trip had been cancelled
   (c) their school Principal was a little worried about their safety
   (d) that it had been raining heavily
21. (a) how long he had been living in
   (b) that he had been living there for the last three years.
   (c) would be leaving for Mumbai soon
   (d) when they all would be leaving
22. (a) if he would like to join them
   (b) that he would love to but he had to take his father's
   (c) that he must let him know by that evening because he had to arrange
   (d) that he would do so
23. (a) (i) what she would like to order
   (b) (iii) she wanted
   (c) (ii) she wanted anything else
   (d) (iv) in the negative and thanked him

Section D : Literature
Textbook : Interact in English *(Prose)*

Two Gentlemen of Verona

by A.J. Cronin

CHAPTER 1

CHAPTER SUMMARY The story is set in Verona, Italy, after the Second World War. The story begins with the narrator driving down the foothills of the Alps where he encounters the two brothers, Nicola and Jacopo. The story recounts the hard life chosen by two young boys so that they could pay for the treatment of their sister afflicted with tuberculosis. The boys' sacrifice, their sincerity and devotion to the cause, and the maturity they display in their actions gives a new hope for humanity.

The Narrator Meets the Two Small Brothers

When the narrator and his companion were driving through the foothills of the Alps, two small boys stopped them just outside the city of Verona. The two boys wanted to sell wild strawberries but their driver Luigi, warned the narrator against purchasing the fruits. According to Luigi, the narrator and his companion could get much better quality fruits in Verona. Further, he felt that both the boys were not dressed properly. One of them was wearing an old jersey and *khaki* pants. The other boy had put on an uncomfortable old army tunic which had also been shortened.

The Narrator Found the Two Boys Interesting

The two brown-skinned boys had tangled messy hair and dark earnest eyes which seemed thoughtful and sincere. In spite of their appearance, the narrator and his companion found the boys interesting and strangely fascinating. The narrator's companion talked to the boys and found out that they were brothers. The elder one, Nicola was 13 years old. The younger one, Jacopo was shorter and almost 12 years old. The narrator and his companion left for the town of Verona after buying the fruit basket from the boys.

The Narrator Found the Boys Again

Next morning when the narrator and his companion came out of their hotel room to the public square, they saw the same boys polishing people's shoes near the fountain. They were very busy in their work.

The narrator and his companion waited till the boys were free to go to them. As they reached them, the boys greeted the two men with a friendly smile. Then, the narrator curiously told them that he thought that they picked fruit from somewhere and sold it to earn their livelihood.

The Boys did Many Odd Jobs for a Living

Nicola informed the narrator that they performed many odd jobs to earn money. He said that they often took tourists around the town to show them places of interest like Juliet's Tomb. The narrator asked the boys to be their guide and take them around the town. Sincere and devoted, Nicola and Jacopo made themselves useful to the narrator. They provided them with information about good restaurants. They also got them packets of American cigarettes and seats for the opera.

As the narrator got to know the boys, he was impressed by their remarkable nature. Inspite of their innocence, the two boys were quite lively and active. Nicola's smile was steady and engaging while Jacopo was lively. At the same time, both the boys showed a seriousness and maturity.

The narrator was further impressed by the boys' willingness to work. Even in summer, they continued to shine shoes, sell fruits, hawk newspapers, conduct tourists around and did all odd jobs eagerly without paying attention to the heat.

The Positive Outlook of the Boys

One night, the narrator and his companion found the boys in the deserted square. They were resting on the stone pavement beneath the lights. Nicola sat upright while Jacopo, with his head resting on Nicola's shoulders, was asleep. When the narrator asked Nicola why he was there so late, the boy informed him that they wished to sell off their unsold newspapers to the passengers of the last bus from Padua. The narrator asked Nicola why they worked so hard. The boy simply said that they were not complaining about it.

The Narrator Offered to do Something for the Boys

Next morning, the narrator went over to the fountain to get his shoe shined and find out what ambitious plan made them work so hard. However, the little boys did not want to answer in clear terms. Observing their attitude, the narrator thought it better not to ask them the question. However, the narrator still offered to do something for them before leaving Verona.

Jacopo told him to favour them with a 30 km ride to Poleta in his car. Otherwise, like every Sunday, they would have to hire bicycles and pedal all the way through the countryside. On the other hand, Nicola did not wish to take anyone's favour to make things easier for them. The narrator assured the boys that he would drive them there himself.

The Narrator Followed the Boys

Nicola and Jacopo went to Poleta the next afternoon. The narrator thought the boys would be going to some ordinary locality but Jacopo directed him to a large red-roofed villa. The narrator felt surprised. The boys told him that they would not take more than an hour and suggested him to go to a cafe in the village while he waited. Instead, the narrator followed the boys.

The Boys' Secret

As he entered the premises, he was greeted by a uniformed trained nurse as that villa was actually a hospital. The nurse guided the narrator through the lobby to a small room and showed him where the two boys were sitting. Through the glass partition, the narrator could see that the boys were sitting by the bedside of a girl. Anyone who looked at the three of them could see a close similarity in their looks and easily tell that she was their sister. The nurse suggested him to go inside but he declined as he didn't want to intrude upon their privacy. Moreover, he wanted the boys to be happy with the thought that their secret remained a secret.

The Boys' Terrible Past

The narrator requested the nurse to tell him all she knew about them. The nurse willingly told the narrator that Lucia was their sister and was suffering from tuberculosis of the spine. The children had always known a comfortable and a cultured life. However, the war not only orphaned them but also destroyed their home and exposed them to a life of hardship and misery.

The nurse informed the narrator that Lucia at one time was being trained to be a singer. Their father, too, had been a well-known singer in his time. However, war deprived Lucia of all the comforts of life and threw her into the streets, separating her from her brothers. The boys joined the resistance movement against the Germans who had ruined their family. Later, Lucia developed tuberculosis of the spine. By good luck, the two brothers found Lucia and started trying to restore her good health. Both of them struggled hard to pay for her treatment. Lucia, thus, was hopeful and thought that happy days were not far away.

The Two Boys Gave a New Hope for Humanity

The story of the two brothers touched the narrator deeply. When the boys came out after meeting their sister, he drove them back to the city. The narrator kept quiet as he didn't wish to deprive these two 'gentlemen' of the pleasure of keeping their secret a secret.

The narrator thought about how Nicola and Jacopo took the hardships of life in a positive way. They put in all their resourcefulness and energy to face all the challenges that came their way. According to the narrator, they were real heroes and gentlemen. They showed the meaning of true humanity to the world.

Word Meaning

Word	Meaning	Word	Meaning
outskirts	the parts of a city or town that are farthest from the centre	far beyond their years	of someone much older
Verona	a city in Northern Italy	ran errands	made short trips for particular purposes
shabby	untidy, disordered	deserted	uninhabited
worn	old and damaged as a result of much use	emigrate	leave one's own country in order to settle permanently in another
earnest	serious, sincere	vexation	annoyed
slackened	decreased in speed or intensity	put out	annoyed or offended
Juliet's tomb	the place where Juliet, the heroine of Shakespeare's play 'Romeo and Juliet' was buried	vestibule	a hall or lobby
demeanour	appearence and behaviour	cubicle	a small partitioned area of a room, for example a desk in an office
artless	simple, innocent	intrude upon	disturb
engaging	charming and attractive	scarce	insufficient, not enough
		dear	expensive

Textbook FOLDER

Here, we have covered questions given in the CBSE Textbook along with their answers.

ON PAGE 8

Q.4 Based on your reading of the story, answer the following questions by ticking the correct options.

(i) The driver did not approve of the narrator buying fruit from the two boys because

(a) the boys were untidy and poorly dressed
(b) the strawberries were not fresh
(c) they were asking for a heavy price
(d) the driver did not approve of small boys who worked

Ans. (a) the boys were untidy and poorly dressed

(ii) The narrator was most impressed by boy's ....

(a) desire to earn money
(b) willingness to work
(c) ability to perform many tasks
(d) sense of fun

Ans. (b) willingness to work

(iii) Nicola was not pleased when Jacopo asked the narrator to drive them to poleta as he

(a) did not want a stranger to become involved with their plan
(b) preferred going to Poleta by train so that he could enjoy the scenery
(c) did not want to ask anyone for favours
(d) did not want to take help from someone he did not know well

Ans. (c) did not want to ask anyone for favours

(iv) The narrator did not go inside Lucia's room as

(a) he did not want to intrude into their privacy
(b) he thought that the boys would object
(c) Lucia would not welcome a stranger
(d) the boys would feel he was spying on them

Ans. (a) he did not want to intrude into their privacy

(v) The boys were the first to join the resistance movement against the Germans because

(a) the Germans had hurt their sister
(b) the Germans ruled the city
(c) the Germans ruined their family
(d) the Germans had destroyed their home

Ans. (c) the Germans ruined their family

(vi) The author did not speak to the boys on their return journey because

(a) because he thought the boys would prefer to keep their secret
(b) because he thought the boys were ashamed of their sister's condition

(c) he thought they wouldn't tell him the truth

(d) because he thought the boys might ask him for money for their sister

Ans. (a) because he thought the boys would prefer to keep their secret

ON PAGE 9

Q.5 What do you understand by the following statements?

(a) "We do many things, sir" Nicola answered seriously. He glanced at us hopefully.

Ans. Nicola informed the narrator and his companion that they did many jobs to earn money. He told them that they took visitors for a tour around the city, shined shoes, sold fruit, hawked newspapers and ran errands. Nicola looked at the two of them with the hope of getting more work from them so that they would be able to earn more money.

(b) He coloured deeply under his sunburn, then grew pale.

Ans. When the narrator asked Nicola that they worked very hard and earned enough money but neither they spent it on clothes nor on good food, Nicola blushed red with anxiety and confusion. Further, Nicola became pale as he feared that now their secret that they saved money for the medical treatment of their sister who was suffering from tuberculosis of the spine, was at the verge of being leaked out.

(c) He smiled uncomfortably. "Just plans, sir," he answered in a low voice.

Ans. This statement shows that Nicola behaves like an intelligent and mature boy. He does not like to reveal his secret plans to others.

(d) Yet, in both these boyish faces, there was a seriousness which was far beyond their years.

Ans. Life treated Jacopo and Nicola very harshly. They had to work for a living and their sister's treatment. They forgot all the joys of childhood. With the responsibility of their sister, the two were forced into adulthood prematurely. Hence, we can find a maturity and seriousness in the innocent and boyish faces of the boys.

ON PAGE 9

Q.6 Answer the following questions briefly.

(a) Why didn't Luigi, the driver, approve of the two boys?

***Or* Why do you think Luigi did not approve of the boys?** **CBSE 2024 C**

Ans. Luigi, the driver, did not approve of the two boys because he thought they were untidy and poorly dressed: The boys, Nicola and Jacopo, were shabbily dressed in worn-out clothes, and their hair was tangled. Jacopo wore a shortened army tunic, while Nicola wore an old jersey and cut off khaki pants.

(b) Why were the narrator and his companion impressed by the two boys?

Ans. The narrator and his companion were impressed by the two boys because of their hard work, determination, and selfless nature. The boys were willing to do any odd job, such as selling fruit, running errands and working as tourist guides, even in the hot Sun. They were resourceful and dogged in their determination to do useful work. Further, the boys were also helpful to the narrator in many ways, such as arranging seats for the opera, taking him around Juliet's Tomb, and providing him with the name of a good restaurant.

(c) Why was the author surprised to see Nicola and Jacopo working as shoeshine boys?

Ans. The narrator was astonished to see the two boys at the public square because they were shining people's shoes. The narrator thought that the boys only sold fruit to earn their livelihood as he had earlier seen them selling strawberries. The narrator could not stop himself from being curious to understand why they were engaged in so many professions.

(d) How were boys useful to the author?

Ans. The boys were useful to the narrator because he was new to the place and the boys provided him information about good restaurants, got him seats for the opera and found packs of American cigarettes for him. They also showed him places like Juliet's tomb.

(e) Why were the boys in the deserted square at night? What character traits do they exhibit?

Ans. The boys were in the deserted square at night as they were waiting for the last bus from Padua. They wanted to sell newspapers to the passengers of that bus and earn some more money. The character traits exhibited by the boys here are dedication and perseverance.

(f) The narrator asks the boys, "Must you work so hard? You both look rather tired." The boys reply, "We are not complaining, sir." What do you learn about the boys from their reply?

Ans. The given lines tell us that the boys were mature. They understood that ups and downs are a part and parcel of every human life. Complains and hatred serve no purpose. Only dedication, hard work and constant pursuit of one's goal can bring about desired changes in one's life.

(g) **When the narrator asked Nicola and Jacopo about their plans, they were evasive. Why?**

Or **When the narrator asks the boys about their plans, they are evasive. Why don't they disclose their problems?**

Ans. Nicola and Jacopo had an acute sense of self-respect and they believed in fighting their own battle in life. They did not like to take the help or support of anybody. Therefore, they did not disclose their plans or problems to the narrator.

ON PAGE 9

Q.7 Discuss the following questions and write the answers in your notebook.

(a) **Appearances are deceptive. Discuss with reference to the two boys.** **Competency Based**

Ans. A casual look at the two boys would hardly arouse any interest in them. However, their appearance proved to be misleading because their sense of responsibility, devotion to work, noble heart and sacrifices were hidden behind their shabby get-up. War had made them helpless and orphaned but it could not snatch away the richness of their hearts. They stood as a symbol of hope for humanity.

(b) **Do you think the boys looked after Lucia willingly? Give reasons for your answer.**

Ans. Yes, I think the boys looked after Lucia willingly because no one was forcing them to work so hard to earn money. They sacrificed their own needs to save the money for the treatment of their sister.

(c) **How does the story 'Two Gentlemen of Verona' promise hope for society?**

Or **What message does the story 'Two Gentlemen of Verona' give?**

Ans. If we take a glance at our society, we shall find that most people work only for their own interests. Nobody cares about others. Each one of us only cares for our own selfish needs. This tendency of the people will kill any hope for humanity. In this light, 'Two Gentlemen of Verona' is a story of hope for society. The two boys, Nicola and Jacopo, are mature beyond their age. They work for the well-being of their sister Lucia, who is suffering from tuberculosis of the spine. They do many odd jobs to earn money for her treatment. They don't fear the difficulties that come in their way. They bear their hardships themselves and don't seek help from others. To achieve their goal, they never adopt any wrong way. They are honest, loving, brave and sincere. They believe in sacrifice, sincerity and devotion. The story, thus, conveys the message of sacrifice, sincerity and devotion that gives a new hope for society.

ON PAGE 9-10

Q.8 Look at the italic words in the following examples.

(a) **We bought their biggest basket, then *set off* toward town.**

(b) **One night we *came upon* them in the windy and deserted square.**

(c) **He bit his lip, then in a rather *put out* tone he said, 'Very well.'**

(d) **I shook my head and *turned away*.**

Here are a few more. Match the phrases to their meanings.

Phrases	Meanings
set up	to start on a journey
break down	to tolerate a situation or a person
set off	to lose control of your feelings and start crying
put up with	to enter
put off	to be faced with or opposed by
put on	to start/establish a company
come in	to refuse/reject
come across	to postpone
come up against	to try to get help/advice/sympathy from someone
turn down	to wear
turn in	to meet or find by chance
turn to	to inform on or deliver up

Now use the phrases given above to complete the following sentences.

1. **The landlord was suspicious of the two men staying in his flat so he called the police and .... them ....**
2. **Early in the morning we packed our bags and .... for a hike over the mountain.**
3. **Janvi .... some photographs of her grandfather in the old trunk.**
4. **My father .... his own business 10 years ago.**
5. **The Bank .... Paul's request for a loan.**
6. **The Corporation's decision to reduce the leave of the employees .... a lot of opposition.**

Ans.
- set up-to start/establish a company
- break down-to lose control of your feelings and start crying
- set off- to start on a journey
- put up with- to tolerate a situation or a person
- put off- to postpone
- put on- to wear
- come in- to enter
- come across- to meet or find by chance
- come up against- to be faced with or opposed by
- turn down - to refuse/reject
- turn in- to inform on or deliver up
- turn to- to try to get help/advice/sympathy from someone

1. turned, in	2. set off
3. came across	4. set up
5. turned down	6. came up against

ON PAGE 10-11

Q.9 Two Gentlemen of Verona is written in the first person. A story written in the first person is a first-hand account of events told or narrated through the eyes of a single character, typically the main character. Stories written in the first person are easily identified by the use of the pronoun 'I' rather than 'he or she'.
The reader will see phrases such as "I said, I thought," rather than "he said, she thought." Everything is experienced through the eyes of a single character, and all thoughts and observations are limited to that one person. There can be no outside observer. If the narrator does not see or experience an event first-hand, it cannot be a part of the story. All scenes in the story are filtered through this person's unique perception.
The third-person is a narrative mode in which both the reader and author observe the situation either through the senses and thoughts of more than one character, or through an overarching godlike perspective that sees and knows everything that happens and everything the characters are thinking. In this mode of narration, the narrator can tell the reader things that the main character does not know, or things that none of the characters know.
Rewrite, in third person, any part of story you like.

Ans. Refer to Summary of the Chapter

ON PAGE 11

Q.10 The narrator realises why Nicola and Jacopo work so hard. Yet he does not go in to meet their sister nor does he speak to them about what he learns from the nurse. Working in groups, discuss the following aspects of the story and share your views with the class.

(a) The love, devotion and the family values Nicola and Jacopo display.

Ans. Nicola and Jacopo display that they are family oriented people. They not only return to find their sister after the war but also make sure that she is receiving treatment.

(b) Their pride in themselves and their family.

Ans. We are told in the end of the lesson that both the boys belong to a cultured family who were ruined by the Germans and the War. The boys, thus, did not forget the background of their family and take pride in it. Hence, it could be one of the reasons why they did not like to share their problems or ask for help.

(c) The trust they place in the narrator.

Ans. The boys have started to trust the narrator as an acquaintance for they had been in his company for some days. However, they still do not trust him completely to share their secret.

(d) The reason the narrator does not disclose to them that he knows their secret.

Ans. The narrator knows that the boys do not wish to oust their secret and hence, even though he knows it, he does not talk about it to the boys. This shows that he was kind and sensitive.

WRITING TASK

Q.11 As the narrator, write an article on the lesson of love, faith and trust that you have learnt from the two young boys of Verona.

Ans. **Two Gentlemen of Verona : A Hope for Humanity**

by XYZ

The power of love, faith and trust not only rewards an individual but also the entire human society with optimism, hope and inspiration. A recent encounter with two small orphaned boys, Nicola and Jacopo, revealed how their immense love for their sister sustained them through all hardships and gave them power, energy and capability to face all the challenges of life without indulging in any self-pity.

These two boys held on to their values in difficult circumstances when even adults would often give up or lose hope. We learn through them the virtues of love, faith and trust that are the source of hope. They help one overcome all the obstacles and impediments of life with a wonderful sense of achievement of one's goal.

Q.12 After her brothers' visit, Lucia writes a page in her diary about her past life and her present situation. As Lucia, write the diary entry in about 150 words.

Ans. Tuesday, 11th August, 20XX 9:00 pm

Dear Diary

Today Nicola and Jacopo, my two lovely brothers, paid their weekly visit to me in the hospital. Though they were trying to show me that they were happy in their current state, I know about the difficulties they are facing in paying for my treatment.

I did not feel comfortable seeing them in such a situation. Their visits always make me happy but gone are the days when we would enjoy life with our parents in our home. In those days, both Nicola and Jacopo were quite choosy about their food and clothes. They would always prefer the best.

But things have changed drastically for us. The boys have to work very hard so that they can pay my hospital bills. They cannot even afford decent clothes and healthy food for themselves. I want to work for them but cannot do so because of my illness. I can only wish for their healthy future.

Lucia

REVIEW EXERCISE

Including Previous Years' and Practice Questions

Extract Based Questions

Read the following extracts carefully and answer the questions that follow.

1. They greeted us with friendly faces. "I thought you picked fruit for a living", I said.

(a) What do you mean by 'a living'?

Ans. 'A living' means 'livelihood or a means of earning money.'

(b) How did 'they' greet the narrator?

Ans. The boys greeted him with a smile.

(c) What did the narrator think 'they' did for a living?

Ans. The narrator thought that the boys sold fruit for a living.

(d) Who are 'they' and why did 'they' greet the narrator with friendly faces?

Ans. 'They' are the boys Nicola and Jacopo. They greeted the narrator in a friendly manner because they had sold their berries to him and were expecting some more business.

2. "We do many things, Sir", Nicola answered seriously. He glanced at us hopefully. "Often we show visitors through the town ....to Juliet's tomb.... and other places of interest." **CBSE 2016, 15**

(a) To whom is Nicola speaking?

Ans. Nicola is speaking to the narrator.

(b) What things did Nicola and his brother do ?

Ans. Nicola and his brother did many things such as selling wild strawberries, shining people's shoes, selling newspapers, working as tourist guides along with doing odd jobs to earn their living.

(c) What does the word 'glanced' mean?

Ans. The word 'glanced' means 'to look quickly.'

(d) Why was Nicola serious?

Ans. Nicola was serious because he did not want to share the details of his personal life with a stranger.

3. As we made the rounds, my interest was again provoked by their remarkable demeanour. They were childish enough and in many ways quite artless. Jacopo was as lively as a squirrel. Nicola's smile was steady and engaging. Yet in both their boyish faces there was a seriousness which was far beyond their years. In the week which followed we saw them frequently, for they proved extremely useful to us.

(a) What can we say about the demeanour of the two boys?

Ans. We can say that the demeanour of the two boys was remarkable because they were lively but serious.

(b) **What does the writer wish to imply via the comparison of Jacopo to a squirrel?**

Ans. Through the comparison of Jacopo with a squirrel, the writer implies that in comparison to his brother Nicola, Jacopo was much more childlike and lively.

(c) **Why did they see them frequently?**

Ans. The narrator and his companion saw the boys frequently because the two boys helped them in various ways during their stay in Verona.

(d) **Select a phrase from the extract that means the same as, 'to circulate'.**

Ans. 'Made the rounds'.

4. One night, we came upon them in the windy and deserted square, resting on the stone pavement beneath the lights. Nicola sat upright, tired. A bundle of unsold newspapers lay at his feet. Jacopo, his head resting upon his brother's shoulder, was asleep. It was nearly midnight. "Why are you out so late, Nicola?". "Waiting for the last bus from Padua. We shall sell all our papers when it comes in.". "Must you work so hard? You both look rather tired."

(a) **The word .... in the extract is an antonym of 'leaving.'**

Ans. waiting

(b) **At which place were the boys waiting for the last bus?**

Ans. The two boys waited in the public square at night.

(c) **Why were the two boys waiting for the last bus?**

Ans. They were waiting to sell all their remaining newspapers to the passengers of the last bus.

(d) **What impression does the narrator get about the two boys from this meeting and their conversation?**

Ans. The narrator gets the impression that they are willing to do any work which earns money.

5. I said, "Nicola, the way you and Jacopo work, you must earn quite a bit. You spend nothing on clothes. You eat little enough... when I see you have a meal it's usually black bread and figs. Tell me, what do you with your money?" He coloured deeply under his sunburn, then grew pale. He looked to the ground. "You must be saving up to emigrate to America," I suggested. He looked at me sideways, spoke with an effort.

(a) **What does the narrator's remark '... the way you and Jacopo work...' refer to?**

Ans. The given remark indicates that the boys were open to doing odd jobs..

(b) **How did the narrator's question impact Nicola? What does the sunburn help you deduce about Nicola?**

Ans. The narrator's question embarrassed Nicola. Nicola's sunburn shows that he used to stay or work under the scorching heat of the Sun.

(c) **State one aspect that might have led the narrator to think that the boys must be saving to emigrate to America.**

Ans. The narrator thought that the boys must be saving to emigrate to America because the boys worked day and night doing odd job to earn money and yet did not eat much. They only ate black bread and some figs.

(d) **Why was the smile of the boy combined with a sign of discomfort?**

Ans. The smile of the boy was combined with a sign of discomfort because he did not want to reveal his plans to the narrator.

6. "Well," I said, "we're leaving on Monday. Is there anything I can do for you before we go?" Nicola shook his head, but suddenly Jacopo said, "Sir," he burst out, "every Sunday we make a visit to the country, to Poleta, 30 kilometres from here. Usually we hire bicycles. But tomorrow, since you are so kind, you might send us in your car." I had already told Luigi he might have the Sunday off. However, I answered, "I'll drive you out myself." There was a pause. Nicola was glaring at his young brother in vexation. "We could not think of troubling you, sir." "It won't be any trouble." **CBSE SQP 2023**

(a) **Identify the phrase that indicates that the visit to Poleta on Sundays is significant as a routine or tradition.**

Ans. The phrase 'every Sunday' indicates that the visit to Poleta on Sundays is significant as a routine or tradition.

(b) **What does the narrator's offer to drive the brothers to Poleta reveal about his character?**

Ans. The narrator's offer to drive the brothers to Poleta reveals his kindness and generosity.

(c) **Why was there a pause after the narrator's offer?**

Ans. There was a pause after the narrator's offer because Nicola was taken aback by Jacopo's request and needed a moment to process it. Nicolo was hesitant to accept help from the narrator, possibly due to pride.

(d) **State one reason why Jacopo might have wanted a car ride despite the choice of hired bicycles?**

Ans. Jacopo wanted a car ride despite the choice of hired bicycles because a car ride would be more efficient and less tiring than cycling for 30 kilometres. Furthermore, it is an opportunity to experience something different and more comfortable.

7. "We shall not be long, sir. Perhaps only an hour. May be you'd like to go to the cafe in the village for a drink?"

(a) Where did the boys take the narrator?

Ans. The boys took the narrator to a hospital in the village of Poleta, 30 kilometres from Verona.

(b) What do you mean by the expression "we shall not be long"?

Ans. The given expression means that they won't take a long or a great amount of time.

(c) Why did they suggest that the narrator should go to the village cafe?

Ans. They suggested it as they did not want the narrator to know about what they came to Poleta for.

(d) Did the narrator follow their advice?

Ans. No, the narrator did not follow their advice but tried to find out the reason for their visit secretly.

8. The two boys were seated at the bedside of a girl of about twenty, who, propped up on pillows, wearing a pretty lace jacket, was listening to their chatter, her eyes soft and tender. One could see at a glance her resemblance to her brothers.

(a) Who was seeing the scene described here?

Ans. The narrator was seeing the scene described here.

(b) What is the relation between the girl and the two boys?

Ans. The girl was the elder sister of the two boys.

(c) What was the villa being used as?

Ans. The villa was being used as a hospital.

(d) The word .... in the extract means, 'sensitive.'

Ans. 'tender'

9. "Won't you go in?" the nurse murmured. "Lucia will be pleased to see you." I shook my head and turned away. I felt I could not bear to intrude upon this happy family party. But at the foot of the staircase I drew up and begged her to tell me all she knew about these boys. She was eager to do so. They were, she explained, quite alone in the world, except for this sister, Lucia.

(a) The word .... in the extract means "to ask someone humbly for something."

Ans. begged

(b) Who is 'I' speaking to?

Ans. 'I', the narrator, is speaking to the nurse who was taking care of Lucia, the sister of the two boys.

(c) Why was the speaker so inquisitive about 'these boys'?

Ans. The speaker was inquisitive (curious) about the boys as he found them doing all kinds of odd jobs and he wanted to know why they needed to toil so hard.

(d) In which building is the staircase mentioned in the extract?

Ans. The staircase is in the villa which functions as a hospital.

Short Answer Type Questions

Answer the following questions in 30-40 words.

1. What impression did the narrator get on his first meeting with the two boys?

Ans. The narrator and his friend met Nicola and Jacopo at the outskirts of Verona. The two boys were selling wild strawberries. Though shabbily dressed, the narrator and his companion felt strangely attracted to them.

2. What different jobs did Nicola and Jacopo perform to make a living?

Or **"We do many things, sir", Nicola answered. Describe the difficult jobs undertaken by the boys for their livelihood.**

Or **Nicola says, "We do many things, sir". What are the things that he and his brother do?**

Or **What all errands did Nicola and Jacopo run for their living?**

Ans. The two boys did various odd jobs. They sold wild strawberries on the outskirts of Verona. They polished shoes, hawked newspapers and even acted as tourist guides. They also arranged opera tickets and American cigarettes for the narrator.

3. Despite such a tender age, what made the two boys–Nicola and Jacopo work so hard? CBSE 2025

Ans. Despite being so young, Nicola and Jacopo worked hard because they loved their sick sister, Lucia. They took on tough jobs to earn money for her treatment. Their goal was to help her get better, so they were willing to work tirelessly.

4. "They were childish enough and in many ways quite artless." Who says it and why?

Ans. The narrator says these words for the two young brothers. The narrator finds the behaviour and attitude of the two boys quite interesting. They are wise but innocent. The younger one is full of life and the elder one keeps a charming smile on his face.

5. What was the difference between the personality of Jacopo and Nicola?

Ans. Jacopo was very lively; in fact, as lively as a squirrel. On the other hand, we find a seriousness and maturity in Nicola. Jacopo was frank by nature whereas Nicola was sober and reserved.

6. What favour did Jacopo ask from the narrator when he volunteered to do something for the two brothers?

Ans. The narrator was going to leave Verona on Monday. He asked the two brothers if he could do something for them. Jacopo told the narrator that him and his brother Nicola went to a village in the countryside every Sunday. Jacopo asked him if he could take them there in his car.

7. What were the hardships faced by Nicola and Jacopo?

Ans. Nicola and Jacopo faced many hardships in their little life. The war destroyed their lives completely as their father, a widower, died and their house was destroyed by a bomb. They lost everything. To look after their sister and themselves, they had to do all kinds of odd jobs.

8. The nurse suggested to the narrator to go inside Lucia's room in the hospital. Why did he reject her suggestion?

Ans. The narrator rejected the nurse's suggestion because he did not want to disturb the family reunion. Moreover, he also did not want to hurt the feelings of the two boys. He wanted them to believe that their secret was safe.

9. What did the nurse tell the author about Nicola and Jacopo's father?

Ans. The nurse told the author that Nicola and Jacopo came from a well-off family. She told him that their father, a widower and a well-known singer, had been killed in the early part of the war.

10. Why did Nicola and Jacopo go to Poleta every Sunday?

Ans. Nicola and Jacopo went to Poleta every Sunday to meet their elder sister. Their sister, Lucia, was suffering from the tuberculosis of the spine and was admitted in a hospital in Poleta.

11. Draw the contrast between 'childish' and 'artless' faces and the 'seriousness' beyond their years visible on them in the story 'Two Gentlemen of Verona'.

Ans. At the first glance, the two boys seem to be 'childish' and 'artless' but there is a very deep and serious side to them. The terms 'childish' and 'artless' suggest innocence and immaturity whereas seriousness indicates maturity. The hardships of their lives had matured the boys beyond their years.

12. Who are called the two gentlemen in the story 'Two Gentlemen of Verona?' Why?

Or **Though, Nicola and Jacopo are two young boys, the narrator addresses them as two gentlemen. What special qualities make them fit to be called gentlemen?**

Ans. Nicola and Jacopo display the qualities of hard work and sincerity. They do their duties and understand their responsibilities towards their sister, who is suffering from tuberculosis of the spine. Moreover, they never let the world know about their hardships. Hence, they have rightly been addressed as gentlemen.

13. How did Nicola and Jacopo face the hardships of life?

Ans. Nicola and Jacopo took the hardships of life in their stride. They put in all their resourcefulness and energy to face all the challenges that came their way. They neither indulged in any self-pity nor tried to arouse other people's sympathy to get favours from them.

14. The story is full of surprises. Briefly mention any two such instances.

Ans. Yes, it is true that the story is full of surprises. First, we are shocked to see the two innocent young boys doing many odd jobs like selling fruits and newspapers, polishing shoes, etc.

Second, we are surprised to know the terrible past of the boys, the condition of their sister and how, even in their conditions, they move ahead with a positive outlook in life.

15. Support the opinion that the narrator was kind and sensitive.

Ans. It is true that the narrator was kind and sensitive. He keenly observes the boys and is worried for them. Later, when he realises the boys' secret, he doesn't tell the boys about it. He does not want the boys to feel embarrassed at the revelation of their secret which they don't discuss with anyone.

16. Justify the title of the story 'Two Gentlemen of Verona.'

Ans. The story 'Two Gentlemen of Verona' is based on two brothers, Nicola and Jacopo, who have devoted all they had to restore their sister's good health. They toil (work hard) day and night, sacrificing their comfort, sleep and other basic needs. They don't want sympathy from others and wish to keep their mission secret. Their gentlemanly qualities fully justify the title.

17. How do Jacopo and Nicola show their dedication and love for their family member in Two Gentlemen of Verona? **CBSE SQP 2024**

Ans. Jacopo and Nicola show their dedication and love for their family by working tirelessly to support their sister, Lucia, who is in a hospital for tuberculosis. Despite their young age, they take on various jobs, like shining shoes, selling fruit, guiding tourists, and running errands.

Their consistent Sunday visits to the village of Poleta to see and support their sister show their devotion and commitment to their sister's well-being. This illustrates their sense of responsibility and sacrifice for family.

Long Answer Type Questions

Answer the following questions in 150 words.

1. "One can overcome all odds in life through will and determination." Discuss with reference to the story, 'Two Gentlemen of Verona.'

Ans. The two boys, Nicola and Jacopo, suffered all kinds of problems in life. The war completely ruined their family, orphaned them and destroyed their home. The children, who had once known the comforts of a warm home, were now left homeless and lonely. Their sister Lucia, whom they loved dearly, was also stuck to her bed in the hospital due to her disease.

However, Nicola and Jacopo did not give up. They worked very hard, took up all sorts of jobs and worked till late at night.

Even though they were tired, they worked willingly and cheerfully, and never complained. It was through the values of strong will and determination that they got their sister admitted in the hospital and even managed to pay for her treatment. Lucia was making good progress and was sure to completely recover one day. Therefore, Nicolo and Jacopo teach us that we can overcome all odds in life through will and determination.

2. "When you live for a strong purpose, then hard work isn't an option. It is a necessity." Both Nicola and Jacopo were hardworking and uncomplaining. You too realise the importance of hard work after reading their story. Write an article on 'Virtues of Hard Work.'

Ans. **Virtues of Hard Work**

by Sahil Sharma

When you live for a strong purpose, then hard work isn't an option. It is a necessity. Nicola and Jacopo spared no effort to grab every single opportunity to work. Their willingness to work and to work with full devotion never left them jobless. Both of them were hardworking and uncomplaining.

We live in an age when many people do not want to exert the necessary effort and work hard to succeed. Then, these people wonder why others manage to excel while they do not. Recognising the importance of hard work and determination has been well known for a long time.

Hard work is the key to success. Nothing in life comes easy. In order to achieve success, one needs the strength of mind and body to struggle and work hard to reach one's full potential. There is no substitute for hard work. Moreover, one can overcome all challenges and progress in life through hard work.

3. "Their selfless action brought a new nobility to human life, gave promise of a greater hope for human society."

After reading the above lines from the story, 'Two Gentlemen of Verona' you get motivated. You understand that sacrifice and devotion make a person a complete human being. Write a letter to your friend telling him about the value of sincerity and hard work.

Ans. I5, DXY Colony

Meerut City – 250001

10th May, 20XX

Dear Anirudh

How are you? I am good here too. Your previous letter regarding the death of the man and hopelessness for the future of mankind got me thinking. Contrary to your belief, I still find hope for our society. My belief was furthered by a story I read a few days ago.

The story titled 'Two Gentlemen of Verona' teaches the values of sacrifice and devotion that give hope for the entire humanity.

In the story, two young brothers, Nicola and Jacopo, perform many odd jobs to earn their livelihood. They work day and night to collect money for the treatment of their sister, Lucia, who is suffering from tuberculosis of the spine.

They don't spend money on themselves or their hobbies. They don't care for themselves and only think about the treatment of their sister. They believe in hard work and sincerity; these qualities raise their personalities above those of normal people. They are full of moral values. We, thus, learn how selfless actions can bring a hope for human society.

I suggest you to read the story as it inspires us to be more devoted to our work.

Yours affectionately

Ashok

4. "If we have no peace, it is because we have forgotten that we belong to each other."— Mother Teresa. Both Nicola and Jacopo are perfect examples of selflessness. Motivated by these two young boys, you decide to do something for the poor and join an NGO. Write a letter to a friend describing your experience of working with the NGO.

Ans. A-21, Panchsheel Park
New Delhi-110017

30th October, 20XX

Dear Sonal

How are you? I am good too. Do you remember the story 'Two Gentlemen of Verona'? If not, please read it. It will inspire you, just like it motivated me.

After reading the selfless story of Nicola and Jacopo in 'Two Gentlemen of Verona', I too decided to do something for the poor and joined an NGO. It was a unique experience for me. It gave me immense satisfaction and inner peace.

Every morning, we traveled to a village to educate the people there about healthy habits, proper sanitation, efficient use of gadgets and electrical appliances besides conducting adult literacy classes in the only school in the village.

The atmosphere there was truly amazing, as we were close to nature and felt peaceful. I got acquainted with people who have devoted their whole lives for the betterment of society with no self-gain or greed behind it. They chose that work for the satisfaction from the joy of giving.

Each day is a new day, with new targets and different challenges. I am truly enjoying this selfless experience.

Yours affectionately

Shilpi

5. The story of the two boys, as revealed by the nurse, deeply impacts the narrator. He decides to write a diary entry, recording how he feels inspired by the grit, determination and selfless actions of the two gentlemen of Verona. As the narrator, write the entry.

Ans. Monday, 11th August, 20XX 9:30 p.m.

Dear Diary

Life is a revelation. Each and every day, it teaches us something new and brings new hope. I also realised this hope when I met those young boys Nicola and Jacopo. Such young boys and such great grit, determination and selfless actions. The boys, I thought, were born poor but in reality it was their circumstances that made them so. They suffered so much by the hand of fate and yet today they proudly stand before us all. They work hard without any complaints and then give away all their hard-earned money to save their sister.

What impresses me most is that they can easily get help by people like me. When I told them that I wanted to help them, they refused. They did not want to share their problems or want any favours. The two gentlemen of Verona filled me with optimism and hope for our society.

I can go on and on about the boys if asked to. But for now, I'll stop.

A.J. Cronin

6. When Lucia gets well she writes a letter to Nicola and Jacopo to express her feelings of gratitude and admiration for them. As Lucia, write the letter.

Ans. XYZ, City
ABC Street

12th August 20XX,

Dear Nicola and Jacopo

How are you both? By the grace of God and my two little angels, I am in good health having recovered from the tuberculosis of the spine. I really don't know where to start. Thank you for being there and making sure that I was recovering. Thank you for always being optimistic and for paying for my recovery although it should not have been you two.

I am so happy to have recovered. Now, I can take care of you both. Come back home boys. I will work and send you to school where you should have been in the first place.

I will be eagerly waiting for you both.

Yours dearly

Lucia

ASSESSMENT EXERCISE

Extract Based Questions

Read the following extract carefully and answer the questions that follow.

1. I waited outside until the boys rejoined me, then drove them back to the city. They sat beside me, not speaking. For my part, I did not say a word .... I knew they would prefer to feel that they had safely kept their secret.

(a) Whom did they go to meet?

(b) Why did the narrator go with them?

(c) Where did they go and where are they returning to?

(d) Why were the boys not speaking?

2. "Well," I said, "we're leaving on Monday. Is there anything I can do for you before we go?" Nicola shook his head, but suddenly Jacopo said, "Sir," he burst out, "every Sunday we make a visit to the country, to Poleta, 30 kilometres from here. Usually we hire bicycles. But tomorrow, since you are so kind, you might send us in your car." I had already told Luigi he might have the Sunday off. However, I answered, "I'll drive you out myself." There was a pause. Nicola was glaring at his young brother in vexation. "We could not think of troubling you, sir." "It won't be any trouble."

(a) Who is referred to as 'sir' here?

(b) Why did Nicola glare at his younger brother?

(c) What offer was made by 'sir'?

(d) Select the expression from the text that shows Nicola angry at Jacopo.

Short Answer Type Questions

Answer the following questions in 30-40 words.

1. Why were Nicola and Jacopo not complaining?

2. What meal did the two brothers usually have? Why?

3. Why did Jacopo ask the narrator for a favour?

4. What do we get to know about the narrator's driver, Luigi, after reading the story?

5. Describe the place where Jacopo led the narrator to. Why did it surprise the narrator?

6. Who greeted the narrator at the door to the villa? Describe his/her appearance.

7. Why did the woman's face light up on the mention of the two small boys?

8. What sight did the narrator see through the glass partition?

Long Answer Type Questions

Answer the following questions in 150 words.

1. There is an age-old English saying—'Where there is a will, there is a way.' How did the two brothers, Nicola and Jacopo, prove this saying?

2. No work is ever small or low. What lessons regarding dignity of labour do we learn from the story 'Two Gentlemen of Verona'?

Mrs. Packletide's Tiger

by Saki

CHAPTER 2

CHAPTER SUMMARY The story 'Mrs. Packletide's Tiger' is a humorous satire that exposes how a woman belonging to high society can play a false game to earn fame among the people. Mrs. Packletide is one such character who wants to kill a tiger just to let down Mrs. Loona Bimberton, her arch rival. However, she has to pay a huge price for it.

Mrs. Packletide Plans to Shoot a Tiger

Mrs. Packletide is full of jealousy and bitterness against her arch rival (main competitor) Loona Bimberton who had gained popularity because she was flown eleven miles in an aeroplane by a pilot from Algeria. Thus, she decided to earn fame by doing something adventurous and decides to hunt a tiger. She felt that a collection of press photographs with a personally procured tiger skin would help her gain fame.

In her mind she had already arranged the lunch she would give at her house in Curzon Street, supposedly in honour of Loona Bimberton. She believes that the tiger skin rug would be the most talked about thing in the lunch. Mrs. Packletide had also decided that she would gift the tiger claw brooch to Loona Bimberton on her next birthday.

Mrs. Packletide Offered a Reward for Tiger Hunt

Mrs. Packletide had offered a reward of a thousand rupees to anyone who would provide her with the opportunity of shooting a tiger without much risk. Circumstances proved to be favourable because an old and weak tiger was roaming in a nearby village in search of food. The villagers were tempted as one thousand rupees was a lot of money in those days. The villagers posted children day and night on the boundary of the local jungle to keep an eye on the tiger in their area. The villagers were also doubtful that the old tiger might not survive till the decided day for the hunt. Thus, necessary precautions were taken so that the tiger would not get disturbed by any kind of irrelevant noise.

A Tiger Hunt was Arranged

Finally, the night of the hunt arrived. A platform had been built on an appropriate tree. Mrs. Packletide had paid Louisa Mebbin to assist her and both of them sat together on the platform.

A goat which bleated loudly was chosen and tied to attract the tiger. As they awaited the coming of the tiger, Louisa Mebbin told Mrs. Packletide that they were in danger. However, Mrs. Packletide told her that she wasn't in any kind of danger as the tiger was very old. On knowing this, Louisa Mebbin said that if it was an old tiger, then she should have gotten it cheaper because a thousand rupees for it was a lot of money.

Mrs. Packletide Shot the Tiger

After waiting a little, the tiger came, saw the tied up goat and lay down on the ground. At that position, Mrs. Packletide fired a shot from her rifle and the tiger fell down to one side. The excited crowd sprang up after hearing the noise and carried the glad news to the village. Mrs. Packletide started dreaming of the party she would now throw at Curzon Street.

The old tiger's death was actually caused by heart failure due to the sudden loud sound of the gun. It was Louisa Mebbin who disclosed that the bullet had, in fact, hit the goat and not the tiger. Mrs. Packletide was very angry at this discovery but she became the owner of a dead tiger. The villagers were happy for their thousand rupees and Louisa Mebbin, being a paid companion, kept quiet over the matter at that time.

Mrs. Packletide was Happy with her False Image

In spite of knowing the fact, Mrs. Packletide was happy with the false image. She happily posed in front of the cameras. *Texas Weekly Snapshot* and *Novoe Vremya* magazines published her photographs. As for Loona Bimberton, she refused to see any illustrated paper for weeks and though she wrote a letter of thanks for the gift of a tiger-claw brooch, she nevertheless declined the luncheon party organised by Mrs. Packletide.

Mrs. Packletide's Joy Turned into Sorrow

Mrs. Packletide was very happy after achieving fame in society, but her joy was interrupted by her paid companion. Louisa Mebbin was a cunning woman. She did not leave any opportunity which she could use to her advantage. After knowing about the jealous chemistry between Loona Bimberton and Mrs. Packletide, she blackmailed Mrs. Packletide saying that Loona Bimberton would be very amused and happy if she came to know how the tiger actually died.

Mrs. Packletide Paid Heavily for the Tiger Hunt

Mrs. Packletide was taken aback by this statement and begged Louisa Mebbin not to reveal that fact. She agreed to do so but, in return, she said that she would like to possess a week-end cottage which she had seen near Darking. The cost of cottage was six hundred and eighty pounds, freehold. She could do so only with the help of Mrs. Packletide. Thus, she managed to bargain for the house to keep her mouth shut and Mrs. Packletide had no choice but to agree to this condition.

Louisa Mebbin named the cottage 'Les Fauves'. She also started to plant tiger-lilies as a reminder about Mrs. Packletide and her tiger hunt. People were no doubt surprised when Louisa Mebbin, a humble paid companion, suddenly became a homeowner. At the same time, they were full of admiration for her taste. Then onwards, Mrs. Packletide decided not to indulge in big game shooting because the incidental expenses were very heavy.

Word Meaning

Word	Meaning
lust	desire, passion, intent
deviation	change
Nimrod	a Biblical character (Noah's great-grandson), depicted as a man of power and a great hunter
aviator	pilot
ostensibly	apparently, seemingly, supposedly
brooch	an ornamental pin fastened to clothing
propitious	auspicious, favourable
rendezvous	a place for a meeting
antecedents	ancestors
infirmities	weaknesses
stimulated	encouraged, motivated
venerable	respected, especially because of age, wisdom or character
tethered	tied
thumb-nail pack of patience cards	a pack of small-sized cards for playing solitaire
dissipating	wasting away, squandering
rouble, francs	the currencies of Russia and France respectively

Word	Meaning
centimes	a monetary unit equal to one hundredth of a franc (used in France, Belgium and Luxembourg until the introduction of Euro)
depreciation	reduction in value
remnants	remains
ambush	hiding
ambling	walking casually
tawny	brownish
immeasurably	considerably, extremely
death-throes	the final stage before dying
succumbed	gave in to
senile	caused by old age
connived at	gave silent approval to; promoted
book of patterns	a book depicting the colour patterns of horse racing, including colours worn by jockeys
post time	the specific time when a horse race begins and the deadline for placing a bet
christened	named
Les Fauves	French term for 'the wild beasts'
incidental	secondary; related

Textbook FOLDER

Here, we have covered questions given in the CBSE Textbook along with their answers.

ON PAGE 12

Q.2 Read these lines and guess the answers to the questions given below.

It was Mrs. Packletide's pleasure and intention that she should shoot a tiger .... The compelling motive .... was the fact that Loona Bimberton had recently .... personally procured tiger-skin and a heavy harvest of press photographs could successfully counter that sort of thing.

(a) Why did Mrs. Packletide want to kill a tiger?

Ans. Mrs. Packletide was jealous of the fame received by Mrs. Loona Bimberton. She also wanted to achieve a similar fame and thus, made a plan to kill a tiger in any possible way.

(b) What does it tell you about her?

Ans. The plan to kill a tiger just for the sake of achieving fame, like Mrs. Loona Bimberton, clearly reveals Mrs. Packletide's jealous nature. She did not have the talent to hunt but she went out of her way to achieve her target. This tells about her nature to create false impressions.

(c) What is the tone of the storywriter?

Ans. The tone of the writer is very entertaining and satirical. The whole story is narrated in a very humorous way.

(d) Do you think she was successful in her mission?

Ans. No, she wasn't successful in killing the tiger although the tiger died due to her shot. However, her aim behind this desire was certainly achieved as she did manage to outshine her rival Loona Bimberton in popularity.

(e) What do you think the story is all about?

Ans. The story is about a jealous woman who, in order to receive fame and outshine her rival, engages in a tiger hunt and in the process suffers a huge loss of money.

ON PAGE 16-17

Q.4 Answer the following questions in your own words.

(a) Why did Mrs. Packletide wish to kill a tiger?

Ans. Mrs. Packletide's arch rival, Loona Bimberton, had gained popularity because she was flown 11 miles in an aeroplane by an Algerian pilot.

Mrs. Packletide felt jealous of her. She wanted to prove that she was braver and more adventurous than her rival. Hence, she wanted to kill a tiger.

(b) What made her decide to give a party in Loona Bimberton's honour? What did she intend to give Loona on her birthday?

Or **What had Mrs. Packletide already arranged in her mind for Loona Bimberton?**

Ans. Outwardly, Mrs. Packletide wanted to give a party in Loona Bimberton's honour for her plane ride. However, she wanted to display a tiger rug made from the tiger she would shoot so that her deed would overshadow Loona Bimberton's achievement. In addition to press her point home, she wanted to gift Loona Bimberton on her next birthday a tiger-claw brooch made from a claw of the tiger she would shoot.

(c) How was the tiger shooting arranged? What kind of a tiger was chosen for the purpose?

Ans. To arrange for the tiger shooting, Mrs. Packletide offered a thousand rupees to villagers who would arrange an opportunity to shoot a tiger without much risk or exertion. An old tiger that had given up hunting and confined himself to eating domestic animal was chosen for this purpose.

(d) In what way did the villagers help Mrs. Packletide shoot the tiger?

Ans. It was only due to the villagers' help that Mrs. Packletide could shoot the tiger. They posted children to see that the tiger did not move away to other grounds. Women passing through the jungle sang softly so that the noise would not disturb the tiger. A goat was also tied at the scene to attract the tiger to a particular place.

(e) Who was Miss Mebbin? Was she really devoted to Mrs. Packletide? How did she behave during the tiger shooting?

Or **Do you think that Louisa Mebbin was devoted to Mrs. Packletide? Give reasons for your answer.**

Ans. Miss Mebbin was Mrs. Packletide's paid companion who would assist her during the tiger hunt. Miss Mebbin was not at all devoted to Mrs. Packletide. She behaved like a professional companion who was just concerned about her payment and intended to save as much as possible. On the whole, her attitude was money-minded and arrogant.

(f) Mrs. Packletide was a good shot. Discuss.

Ans. Mrs. Packletide was not at all a good shot. Her aim went wrong as she killed the goat instead of the tiger.

(g) What comment did Louisa Mebbin make after Mrs. Packletide had fired the shot? Why did Louisa make this comment? How did Mrs. Packletide react to this comment?

Ans. Louisa Mebbin revealed that Mrs. Packletide had killed the goat instead of the tiger. The tiger had simply died due to heart failure. She made this comment to make Mrs. Packletide realise that she was unsuccessful in her mission. Mrs. Packletide was very annoyed after knowing the fact.

(h) How did the villagers react to the tiger's death?

Ans. The villagers were very happy after the tiger's death. All of them gathered on the scene and the message was carried to the rest of the villagers. They were only bothered for their thousand rupees. They did not pay any heed to Miss Mebbin's revelation that Mrs. Packletide had not killed a tiger.

(i) Did Mrs. Packletide achieve her heart's desire? Give reasons for your answer.

Ans. Mrs. Packletide was only partly able to achieve her heart's desire. Although her photographs were published in the magazines, Loona Bimberton declined her offer for the luncheon party, which was Mrs. Packletide's main motive behind the tiger shoot. Moreover, she suffered a huge loss in the hunt due to Miss Mebbin blackmailing her.

(j) How did Miss Mebbin manage to get her week end cottage? Why did she plant so many tiger-lilies in her garden?

Ans. Louisa Mebbin blackmailed Mrs. Packletide to get her week end cottage to keep her mouth shut about the fact that the tiger had not actually been killed by her and had died due to heart failure. She planted tiger-lilies in the garden because they were symbolic of how she had managed to get the cottage, i.e. due to a tiger.

(k) "The incidental expenses are so heavy", she confides to inquiring friends.

Who is the speaker? What is she referring to here?

Ans. The given lines have been spoken by Mrs. Packletide. She is referring to the heavy expenses she had to bear for the tiger hunt. She had willingly paid the villagers to arrange for the hunt but she had to pay Louisa Mebbin at the end to keep her mouth shut about what actually killed the tiger. This put a heavy burden on her pocket.

ON PAGE 17

Q.5 Discuss the following questions in detail and write the answers in your notebook.

(a) Do you think the tiger shooting organised by the villagers was a serious affair? Give reasons for your answer.

Ans. The tiger shooting organised by the villagers was a serious affair as they were very keen to earn their thousand rupees. They posted children at the outskirts (boundary) of the jungle to keep a watch on the tiger in case it wandered off to new hunting grounds. Some cheaper kind of goats were left out to keep him satisfied and to prevent him from starving.

Mothers with babies walked quietly through the jungle so as not to disturb its sleep. The villagers had only one worry that the tiger should not die of old age before the day of the shoot.

(b) Do you think the writer is trying to make fun of the main characters in the story, i.e. Mrs. Packletide, Louisa Mebbin and Loona Bimberton? Pick out instances from the story that point to this fact.

Ans. Yes, the writer is making fun of the main characters. Some instances are given in quotes against the names of the characters.

Mrs. Packletide

"Not that the lust to kill .... per million of inhabitants."

"was an exception; her .... dislike of Loona Bimberton."

"already that luncheon party ...... immeasurably nearer".

Louisa Mebbin

"She had a morbid dread .... she had been paid for."

"adopted a protective elder sister attitude ...... headlong from less sympathetic hands."

Loona Bimberton

"Had recently been carried eleven miles .... talked of nothing else."

"She refused to look at an illustrated paper .... was a model of repressed emotions."

(c) A person who is vain is full of self-importance and can only think of himself/herself and can go to great lengths to prove his/her superiority. Do you think Mrs. Packletide is vain? Give reasons in support of your answer.

Ans. Mrs. Packletide was essentially vain by nature. She actually went to great lengths just to prove herself superior to Loona Bimberton.

To arrange for the tiger hunt and then to keep Louisa Mebbin's mouth shut, she paid heavily. She threw a luncheon party to actually honour herself and not Loona Bimberton, which indicated how much importance she attached to herself. She posed before the cameras with pride even when she had not shot the tiger and managed that the news and photographs of her adventure were published in newspapers and magazines. This shows her self-obsessed nature.

(d) **Sometimes, writers highlight certain negative aspects in society or human beings by making fun of them. This is called satire. In your groups discuss whether you would classify this story as a satire. Give reasons to support your answer.**

Ans. Satire is a light form of literary work which aims at attacking the prevailing human vices, follies and shortcomings through the use of irony, sarcasm and ridicule. The intention of satire is to bring about improvement in individuals or in society.

'Mrs. Packletide's Tiger' is a complete satire on the elite (high) society of the time it describes.

Here, the writer has shown the negative aspects of vanity in a way which is humorous. The whole story revolves around the intentions of three women characters, who are suffering from complexities and wrong attitudes. Mrs. Packletide's jealous and hollow nature, the hypocrisy of Loona Bimberton and the greed of Louisa Mebbin are all expressed through satire.

(e) **How does the writer create humour in this story?**

Or **Humour plays a major role in the chapter, 'Mrs. Packletide's Tiger'. Prove this statement with the instances of humour.** **CBSE 2024**

Ans. The writer creates humour in the story through various situations and mainly through the use of language and satirical tone. The whole scene of the hunting ground and the exchange of dialogues between Louisa Mebbin and Mrs. Packletide are humorous.

We are amused how the villagers manipulate the situation to their advantage. Then, the killing of the goat by the bullet and the death of the tiger due to heart failure caused by the noise of the rifle-bullet is also quite amusing.

Louisa Mebbin's protective 'elder sister attitude' towards money and her "morbid dread of performing, even a bit more than she was paid for" add a pleasant twist to the humour.

At the end, when Mrs. Packletide mentions about the incidental expenses of big-game shooting being too much, we are also left with a message given in a humorous manner.

ON PAGE 18

Q.6 Choose extracts from the story that illustrate the character of the people listed in the table given below. There are some words given to help you. You may add words of your own. One has been done as an example:

vain jealous competitive shrewd manipulative stingy materialistic spiteful

Character	Extract from the story	What this tells us about the character
Mrs. Packletide	(i) The compelling motive for her sudden deviation towards the footsteps of Nimrod was the fact that Loona Bimberton had recently been carried eleven miles in an aeroplane by an Algerian aviator and talked of nothing else; only a personally procured tiger-skin and a heavy harvest of press photographs could successfully counter that sort of thing. (ii) Mrs. Packletide had offered a thousand rupees for the opportunity of shooting a tiger without over-much risk or exertion. (iii) Mrs. Packletide faced the cameras with a light heart, and her pictured fame reached from the pages of the Texas Weekly Snapshot to the illustrated Monday supplement of the Novoe Vremya.	Competitive
Louisa Mebbin	(i) "If it's an old tiger I think you ought to get it cheaper. A thousand rupees is a lot of money." (ii) Louisa Mebbin adopted a protective elder-sister attitude towards money in general, irrespective of nationality or denomination. (iii) "How amused everyone would be if they knew what really happened," said Louisa Mebbin a few days after the ball. (iv) Louisa Mebbin's pretty week-end cottage, christened by her "Les Fauves" and gay in summer-time with its garden borders of tiger-lilies, is the wonder and admiration of her friends.	
Loona Bimberton	(i) As for Loona Bimberton, she refused to look at an illustrated paper for weeks and her letter of thanks for the gift of a tiger claw brooch was a model of repressed emotions. (iii) There are limits beyond which repressed emotions become dangerous.	

Ans. **Mrs. Packletide**

(ii) shrewd (iii) vain

Louisa Mebbin

(i) stingy (ii) materialist

(iii) manipulative (vi) witty

Looma Bimbertion

(i) jealous (ii) spiteful

ON PAGE 19

Q.7 There are many amusing lines in the story. Here are a few of them. Rewrite each one in ordinary prose so that the meaning is retained. One has been done for you as an example.

(a) It was Mrs. Packletide's pleasure and intention that she should shoot a tiger.

Ans. Mrs. Packletide wanted to shoot a tiger.

(b) Mrs. Packletide had already arranged in her mind the lunch she would give at her house on Curzon Street, ostensibly in Loona Bimberton's honour, with a tiger-skin rug occupying most of the foreground and all of the conversation.

Ans. Mrs. Packletide had arranged a lunch at her house on Curzon Street to display her tiger rug in the guise of honouring Loona Bimberton.

(c) Mothers carrying their babies home through the jungle after the day's work in the fields hushed their singing lest they might curtail the restful sleep of the venerable herd-robber.

Ans. Mothers carrying their children silently returned home so as to not disturb the tiger.

(d) Louisa Mebbin adopted a protective elder-sister attitude towards money in general, irrespective of nationality or denomination.

Ans. Louisa Mebbin was stingy.

(e) Evidently, the wrong animal had been hit, and the beast of prey had succumbed to heart-failure, caused by the sudden report of the rifle, accelerated by senile decay.

Ans. The tiger had died of heart failure.

(f) As for Loona Bimberton, she refused to look at an illustrated paper for weeks and her letter of thanks for the gift of a tiger claw brooch was a model of repressed emotions.

Ans. Loona Bimberton was jealous and refused to see the illustrated paper and her letter of thanks showed her jealousy.

ON PAGE 19-20

Q.8 An oxymoron is a figure of speech that combines normally-contradictory terms. The most common form of oxymoron involves an adjective-noun combination of two words like- failed success.

Writers often use an oxymoron to call attention to an apparent contradiction. For example, Wilfred Owen's poem, The Send-off refers to soldiers leaving for the front line, who "lined the train with faces grimly gay." The oxymoron 'grimly gay' highlights the contradiction between how the soldiers feel and how they act: though they put on a brave face and act cheerful, they feel grim. Some examples of oxymorons are- dark sunshine, cold sun, living dead, dark light, almost exactly, etc.

The story Mrs. Packletide's Tiger has a number of oxymorons. Can you identify them and write them down in your notebooks?

Ans.
- Elaborate carelessness
- Venerable herd robber
- Disagreeably pleasant laugh
- Over-much risk
- Immeasurably nearer
- Gladly connived
- Pardonably annoyed

ON PAGE 20

WRITING TASK

Q.9 (a) Years later, Mrs. Packletide writes her autobiography. As Mrs. Packletide, write about the tiger episode with the help of the clues given below.

jealous of the applause Loona was getting-thought of tiger hunt-all arranged- Louisa Mebbin accompanied; turned out to be a blackmailer-huge price to pay to outdo a rival.

Ans. It was a time when I was jealous of the applause Loona got. She was carried home by an Algerian aviator and I, very much wanted to outrun her. I wanted fame and thus, thought of going on a tiger hunt. I made all the arrangements and was going to pay anyone who helped me in the task ₹ 1000. An entire village came to help me along with Miss Louisa Mebbin. An innocent looking companion who was nothing but a blackmailer. She knew that I missed the shot. I killed the goat and not the tiger and she used it to get what she wanted.

My desire of fame led me to give away a huge amount of money to her. To outdo Loona and to keep my secret, I had to bribe Miss Mebbin.

(b) In groups of four, construct the dialogues and enact the following situations from the story.

1. **Mrs. Packletide and the headman of the village/other villagers discussing the details of the tiger shooting.**
2. **Miss Mebbin blackmailing Mrs. Packletide into gifting her a cottage.**
3. **Loona Bimberton and a lady-friend discussing Mrs. Packletide's hunting success.**

Ans. 1. **Mrs. Packletide** I want to shoot a tiger. I will give you a thousand rupees to make the necessary arrangements for tiger hunting. I want to shoot a tiger but without any risk or exertion.

Village Headman There is an old tiger in the jungle that has given up hunting because of old age. He will be right for this hunt.

Mrs. Packletide That will be perfect! I will make other arrangements. You let me know when the time is right.

2. **Miss Mebbin** What would everyone say if they got to know the truth?

Mrs. Packletide What do you mean?

Miss Mebbin The truth, Mrs. Packletide! How you shot a goat and frightened the tiger to death!

Mrs. Packletide (shocked) No one would believe it!

Miss Mebbin Loona Bimberton would.

Mrs. Packletide You wouldn't tell the truth to Loona.

Miss Mebbin I wish to buy a week end cottage at Darking. It is just that I don't have the money.

Mrs. Packletide If I buy you the cottage, would you promise not to tell our little secret to Loona Bimberton?

Miss Mebbin Oh, yes! Yes!

3. **Lady-friend** Did you see the newspapers today?

Loona Bimberton Why? What happened?

Lady-friend Didn't you see pictures of Mrs. Packletide with a dead tiger?

Loona Bimberton Oh, that! Yes, I glanced at it.

Lady-friend Isn't it amazing!

Loona Bimberton Yes, yes, of course. Did I tell you about my experience in the Algerian aviator?

REVIEW EXERCISE

Including Previous Years' and Practice Questions

Extract Based Questions

Read the following extracts carefully and answer the questions that follow.

1. In a world that is supposed to be chiefly swayed by hunger and by love, Mrs. Packletide was an exception; her movements and motives were largely governed by dislike of Loona Bimberton.

(a) By why were Mrs. Packletide's movements and motives governed?

Ans. Mrs. Packletide's movements and motives were mostly governed by her dislike of Loona Bimberton.

(b) Why was Mrs. Packletide different from other people?

Ans. Mrs. Packletide was different from other people because their movements and motives were governed by hunger and love.

(c) What had Mrs. Packletide planned to outshine Loona Bimberton's achievement?

Ans. Mrs. Packletide had planned to shoot a tiger and display its skin in a party to outshine Loona Bimberton's achievement.

(d) The word .... in the extract is a synonym of 'influenced'.

Ans. swayed

2. The prospect of earning the thousand rupees had stimulated the sporting and commercial instinct of the villagers;

(a) The word..........in the extract is an antonym of 'discouraged.'

Ans. stimulated

(b) Why was the money offered?

Ans. The money was offered for arranging a tiger for Mrs. Packletide to shoot without any risk or exertion.

(c) **What was the reaction of the villagers to the offer?**

Ans. This (₹ 1000) was a big amount of money for the villagers. So, they readily accepted it and helped Mrs. Packletide in her mission to shoot a tiger.

(d) **'Money provokes'. Justify the statement in the light of the extract.**

Ans. Money makes the things done. It really provokes the desire of people. Villagers were keen on getting that sum for getting the tiger killed.

3. Mothers carrying their babies home through the jungle after the day's work in the fields hushed their singing lest they might curtail the restful sleep of the venerable herd-robber.

(a) **Who is the herd-robber?**

Ans. The old tiger in the jungle is the herd-robber.

(b) **Why did the mothers not want to disturb the herd-robber?**

Ans. The mothers did not want to disturb the herd-robber, i.e. the tiger because he was very old and ill. They did not want the tiger to die before the actual shoot took place.

(c) **What ultimately happened to the herd-robber?**

Ans. The tiger died due to heart failure on hearing the loud noise of Mrs. Packletide firing her gun.

(d) **The word .... in the extract means the same as 'highly respected due to age'.**

Ans. venerable

4. Louisa Mebbin adopted a protective elder-sister attitude towards money in general, irrespective of nationality or denomination.

(a) **Who was Louisa Mebbin?**

Ans. Louisa Mebbin was Mrs. Packletide's paid companion who was supposed to assist her during the tiger shoot.

(b) **What was Louisa Mebbin's attitude towards money?**

Ans. Louisa Mebbin adopted a protective elder-sister attitude towards money and could go to any length to earn it in any form.

(c) **The word .... in the extract is a synonym of 'citizenship'.**

Ans. nationality

(d) **Justify the usage of 'protective' for Louisa Mebbin.**

Ans. 'Protective' is the right usage for Louisa Mebbin for she could go to any length to get money despite the methods she adopted being unusual.

5. "It was Louisa Mebbin who drew attention to the fact that the goat was in death throes from a mortal bullet-wound, while no trace of the rifle's deadly work could be found on the tiger. Evidently the wrong animal had been hit and the beast of prey had succumbed to heart-failure, caused by the sudden report of the rifle, accelerated by senile decay. Mrs. Packletide was pardonably annoyed at the discovery; but, at any rate, she was the possessor of a dead tiger and the villagers anxious for their thousand rupees, gladly connived at the fiction that she had shot the beast. And Miss Mebbin was a paid companion.

(a) **Which line from the extract supports the idea that people had no doubts about Mrs. Packletide missing her mark?**

Ans. '… villagers anxious for their thousand rupees, gladly connived at the fiction that she had shot the beast.'

(b) **Characterise Mrs. Packletide using 3 adjectives.**

Ans. Mrs. Packletide is greedy, pretentious and vain.

(c) **State the reason for Mrs. Packletide's brief annoyance.**

Ans. The reason for Mrs. Packletide's brief annoyance is that she had not killed the tiger. She had actually shot the goat while the tiger died of heart failure.

(d) **Identify the writer's tone in this extract.**

Ans. In the given extract, the writer has taken an objective as well as a satirical tone in presenting how a rich lady can manipulate people with the power of money.

6. As for Loona Bimberton, she refused to look at an illustrated paper for weeks and her letter of thanks for the gift of a tiger claw brooch was a model of repressed emotions.

(a) **Why did Loona Bimberton not look at the papers for weeks?**

Ans. The newspapers were full of news about Mrs. Packletide's tiger hunt. Mrs. Loona Bimberton probably couldn't stand the sight of Mrs. Packletide being praised so much.

(b) **The word......in the extract means 'restrained'.**

Ans. repressed

(c) **Why were her emotions 'repressed'?**

Ans. Loona Bimberton was jealous of the attention Mrs. Packletide was getting but she couldn't do anything about it. Hence, her emotions were repressed.

(d) **State the motive behind presenting a tiger claw brooch to Loona Bimberton.**

Ans. Mrs. Packletide wanted to present a tiger claw brooch to Loona Bimberton just to satisfy her own vanity and tell her rival that she was also an achiever.

7. "How amused everyone would be if they knew what really happened," said Louisa Mebbin a few days after the ball.

"What do you mean?" asked Mrs. Packletide quickly.

"How you shot the goat and frightened the tiger to death," said Miss Mebbin, with her disagreeably pleasant laugh. **CBSE SQP 2024**

(a) What impact did Louisa Mebbin wish to create on Mrs. Packletide, with her statement, "How amused everyone would be if they knew what really happened"?

Ans. By making such a statement, Louisa Mebbin wanted to make Mrs. Packletide upset by implying that she knew the truth about the tiger hunt.

(b) Why did Mrs. Packletide ask Louisa Mebbin what she meant by her comment?

Ans. Mrs. Packletide asked Louisa Mebbin what she meant by her comment because the comment suggested that Mebbin knew something about the real circumstances of the tiger hunt, which made Mrs. Packletide nervous.

(c) What feelings did the speed of Mrs. Packletide's response reflect? (any two)

Ans. The speed of Mrs. Packletide's response shows her anxiety and uneasiness about the matter.

(d) What does the writer mean by 'disagreeably pleasant laugh?

Ans. The writer means that even though her laugh is pleasant, it is annoying due to the given circumstances. Louisa Mebbin's laugh makes Mrs. Packletide uncomfortable because of its hidden intent.

8. "I've seen a week-end cottage near Darking that I should rather like to buy," said Miss Mebbin with seeming irrelevance. "Six hundred and eighty, freehold. Quite a bargain, only I don't happen to have the money."

Louisa Mebbin's pretty week-end cottage, christened by her "Les Fauves" and gay in summer-time with its garden borders of tiger-lilies, is the wonder and admiration of her friends.

(a) Why did the speaker say these words?

Ans. Louisa Mebbin said these words to blackmail Mrs. Packletide into giving her the amount of money required for buying a cottage in England.

(b) Which characteristic of Louisa Mebbin is highlighted in the above extract?

Ans. It reveals that she is an opportunist and had a keen sense of observation.

(c) What lesson does Mrs. Packletide learn during the big game hunting?

Ans. Mrs. Packletide had suffered a huge loss in her attempt to outdo her rival and thus dropped the idea of indulging in big game hunting in future.

(d) How would you assess the heavy expenses mentioned in the extract?

Ans. Mrs. Packletide's heavy expenses are an example of an unplanned and fame seeking act. She should have thought of all possibilities of the tiger hunt before venturing into it.

Short Answer Type Questions

Answer the following questions in 30-40 words.

1. What motivated Mrs. Packletide to deviate towards the footsteps of Nimrod?

Ans. Like any other woman of high society, Mrs. Packletide was an ordinary housewife. The news of Loona Bimberton being flown 11 miles by an Algerian pilot aroused her jealousy and the bitterness of her heart compelled her to resort to hunting a tiger in order to outshine her. This desire motivated her to deviate towards the footsteps of Nimrod (a famous hunter in the old testament of the Bible).

2. What traits of Mrs. Packletide's character does the idea of hosting the lunch bring out?

Ans. Mrs. Packletide wanted to throw a lunch party to honour Loona Bimberton. However, her actual motive was to display a tiger skin rug made from the tiger she would shoot. This shows that she is an envious woman who wants to outshine her rival and gain the attention of the people.

3. How did the dislike for Loona Bimberton affect Mrs. Packletide's life? **Competency Based**

Ans. Mrs. Packletide's activities were guided by her great dislike for Loona Bimberton. Whatever she planned and implemented was a result of this hatred. Her wish to outshine Loona pushed her into actions like big game hunting, sending her a tiger claw brooch and planning a luncheon party to outshine Loona.

4. What does the writer mean by "the world is swayed by hunger and love"?

Ans. By the given line, the writer means that the world takes action according to its needs related to hunger and feelings of love. On the other hand, Mrs. Packletide's actions were controlled by dislike of and jealousy against Loona Bimberton.

5. How did the circumstances prove favourable for the tiger hunt by Mrs. Packletide in 'Mrs. Packletide's Tiger'? **CBSE 2019**

Ans. The circumstances proved to be favourable for the hunt by Mrs. Packletide because a neighbouring village which was a famous point where a lot of tigers were found, had recently reported the presence of an old tiger.

6. Mention three clues from the story which definitely show that Mrs. Packletide's adventure took place in India.

Ans. The story is certainly set in India. There are some clues given in the story regarding it. Some words like 'India', 'Hindustani' and 'a thousand rupees' have been used in the story. Hence, we can say that the adventure of Mrs. Packletide took place in India.

7. What do you understand by the expression "a ready echo in the heart of Mrs. Packletide"?

Ans. Mrs. Packletide was overconfident about her ability to shoot a tiger. Hence, the phrase "a ready echo in the heart of Mrs. Packletide" here means that she was confident that her bullet had killed the tiger and was happy that her plan of hunting a tiger was successful.

8. Why did the villagers and Miss Mebbin hide the fact that Mrs. Packletide had not killed the tiger? **CBSE 2019**

Ans. The villagers and Miss Mebbin hid the fact that Mrs. Packletide had missed the shot and killed the goat to get the money. The villagers were getting ₹ 1000 while Miss Mebbin was also getting a financial reward.

9. "Mrs. Packletide faced the cameras with a light heart." What made her feel so relaxed?

Ans. Mrs. Packletide was quite confident while facing the cameras because she thought that the villagers were sure not to reveal the truth behind the tiger hunt as they wanted the thousand rupees. Also, Louisa Mebbin was a paid companion. So, she had no fear of her secret being revealed.

10. How did Loona Bimberton react to Mrs. Packletide's invitation to the luncheon party in her honour? Why did she react that way?

Ans. Angered and irritated by Mrs. Packletide's achievement of killing a tiger, Loona Bimberton declined the invitation. Mrs. Packletide's achievement had made her own adventure into insignificant and she couldn't bear to see her rival in the limelight.

11. What advantage did Louisa Mebbin take from Mrs. Packletide? Why?

Or **How does Louisa Mebbin blackmail Mrs. Packletide into gifting her a cottage?**

Ans. Louisa Mebbin knew that Mrs. Packletide had actually not shot the tiger. She was a cunning woman and decided to use this to her advantage. She threatened and blackmailed Mrs. Packletide by demanding a big amount to buy a week end cottage for not letting out her secret.

12. Miss Mebbin was a clever opportunist. Substantiate with reference to 'Mrs. Packletide's Tiger'. **CBSE 2019**

Ans. It is true that Miss Mebbin was a petty and clever opportunist who found ways to save and earn money. She is introduced to us as a miser who saved money wherever possible. Her opportunist nature comes forward when she not only hides the truth of the hunt to get money but later also blackmails Mrs. Packletide to buy her a cottage.

13. Why did Mrs. Packletide give up big-game shooting?

Ans. Mrs. Packletide gave up big-game shooting because she had to pay a really heavy price for indulging in the sport. She had paid the villagers for organising the shoot. Moreover, she had to pay Louisa Mebbin a considerable sum for keeping her secret. The cunning woman had blackmailed Mrs. Packletide into gifting her a cottage.

14. How was the tiger hunt more beneficial to others than to Mrs. Packletide?

Ans. Mrs. Packletide's main objective behind the tiger hunt was to demoralise Mrs. Loona Bimberton. She failed in her mission miserably because Mrs. Loona Bimberton declined her invitation to the luncheon party she had thrown to show off. On the other hand, she had to spend a huge sum of money due to being blackmailed by Miss Mebbin. Further, she had already paid the villagers for aiding her in the hunt. Thus, the hunt was more beneficial to others than to Mrs. Packletide.

15. What message is conveyed through the story 'Mrs. Packletide's Tiger'?

Ans. The story conveys the message that those who consider themselves smart enough to outshine others often get outsmarted themselves. The actions of these manipulative people can backfire and recoil on them.

16. Briefly comment on the behaviour of the villagers throughout the story.

Ans. The behaviour of the villagers in the story is driven by their need for money for their survival. Hence, as soon as they heard about getting ₹ 1000 for hunting a tiger, they took the chance. They even made sure that the tiger was unharmed for the purpose. Further, to get the money, they accepted that Mrs. Packletide had shot the tiger and killed it.

17. Do you think the silent figure of Loona Bimberton, in the background, plays a crucial role in the story? Explain. **Competency Based**

Ans. Yes, the silent figure of Loona Bimberton in the background plays a crucial role in the story. The main action of the story is driven by Mrs. Packletide's desire to out-run Loona Bimberton's fame. Later, the fear of revelation of the truth to Loona Bimberton puts Mrs. Packletide in a bad spot and she not only has to buy a cottage for Miss Mebbin but she also gives up hunting.

18. **"The incidental expenses are so heavy." Why do you think Mrs. Packletide felt so after killing the tiger?** **CBSE 2024 C**

Ans. It is true to say that "the incidental expenses are so heavy" For Mrs. Packletide. This is so because apart from Rs 1000 promised to the villagers, Mrs. Packletide had to pay 680 pounds (English currency) for Louisa Mebbin's week-end cottage due to being blackmailed. This made the incidental expenses too heavy for Mrs. Packletide.

Long Answer Type Questions

Answer the following questions in 150 words.

1. **"Before targeting anyone, one must not forget that even a biter can be bit." Explain how Mrs. Packletide's false values brought this saying out in the story.**

Ans. It is Mrs. Packletide's vanity that had made her enact the tiger hunting drama. Her urge to outshine Loona Bimberton was nothing but an attempt to satisfy this vanity. Her posing for photographs and throwing a luncheon party with the tiger skin prominently spread in her drawing room reflects her efforts to prove her superiority and become a celebrity.

Mrs. Packletide targeted Loona Bimberton but she herself was targeted by Miss Mebbin. The manipulative Miss Mebbin started blackmailing Mrs. Packletide. To keep her mouth shut and not reveal the fact that Mrs. Packletide had killed the goat and not the tiger, she had to pay an exorbitant price.

Thus, the people who consider themselves smart enough to outshine others often get outsmarted themselves. We should try to get name and fame by our good deeds, not by insulting and having rivalry with others.

Our manipulative actions can backfire and recoil on ourselves. Thus, Mrs. Packletide's false values have been brought out in this story.

2. **Show that Miss Mebbin is greedy and Mrs. Packletide is jealous.** **CBSE 2020**

Ans. It is true that Miss Mebbin is greedy and Mrs. Packletide is jealous. The premise of the story is a result of Mrs. Packletide's jealousy towards Loona Bimberton and her achievement/ fame. She wants to hunt a tiger to outrun Loona Bimberton and later even plans to make her rival jealous by throwing a luncheon in her honour and gifting her a brooch made of tiger claw.

Miss Mebbin is a greedy miser who looks for ways to save money wherever she can. She tells Mrs. Packletide how she had overpaid for the goat and for the hunt so that she could get more money. She later not only hides the truth of the hunt but also blackmails Mrs. Packletide to buy a cottage.

3. **"The incidental expenses are so heavy", she confides to inquiring friends. Later on, Mrs. Packletide understands that trying to make a false image is certainly not right and can cause more harm than providing attention and praise. Now, write an article keeping the sense of the words given above.** **Competency Based**

Ans. **Don't Portray What You Are Not**

by Rashmi Kaushik

The story 'Mrs. Packletide's Tiger' is a very apt depiction of how things can backfire if we try to portray ourselves as someone we are not.

Mrs. Packletide incurred huge losses in her bid to outdo her arch rival. Whenever you try to emulate someone else's behaviour or manifest some image of how you think you should be but actually are not, it will end in loss. Mrs. Packletide wanted to impress everybody including Loona Bimberton but what happened? Loona Bimberton did not attend the party where Mrs. Packletide displayed the tiger skin rug. In addition, Mrs. Packletide had to pay a lot of money to keep Miss Mebbin quiet. Thus, Mrs. Packletide lost a large amount of money but gained hardly anything.

Similarly, we should not put on false pretences to portray what we are not. Instead we should display our true selves and try to become better human beings.

4. **Imagine that the Mariner hears of Mrs. Packletide's hunt and decides to share some advice with her about the impact of wilfully killing creatures. As the Mariner, write this letter, in about 150 words, to Mrs. Packletide,based on the consequences following your own experience of having killed a creature intentionally.** **CBSE 2020**

Ans. House-No. 1, Curzon Street

London-XXXX

22nd June, 20XX

Dear Mrs. Packletide

I have written this letter to advise you against killing any creature. Recently, I heard about your vain hunt and was shocked at the meaningless reason for which you took the life of that innocent tiger. I must tell you that such vain killings are always disastrous. I myself have suffered the horrible consequences of such killings. I killed an albatross and brought down a curse upon myself and my crew. I learned the hard way that there are often unintended consequences to our actions.

Thus, we need to respect life in all its forms and refrain from hunting wild animals for pleasure. Remember, that the tiger you killed was a majestic creature that deserves to be appreciated and respected, rather than to become a trophy to be mounted on your wall.

Your actions create a resonance in the world. Reflect on how killing the tiger revealed your disrespect for life and nature. As a famous figure now, enlighten people against killing any creature and you will find peace within yourself.

Hope my words leave a positive impact on you.

Warm regards
Mariner

5. Both, the poem 'The Frog and The Nightingale' and the story 'Mrs. Packletide's Tiger', reflect themes of exploitation of others in pursuit of personal benefit. How, according to you, do each of these literary works manipulate situations to attain their personal desires and with what consequences? **CBSE 2025**

Ans. Both 'The Frog and the Nightingale' by Vikram Seth and 'Mrs. Packletide's Tiger' by Saki explore exploitation, where individuals manipulate situations for personal gain, leading to ironic or tragic consequences. In 'The Frog and the Nightingale', the frog, an arrogant singer, exploits the nightingale's innocence. He convinces her she needs his training, imposes harsh demands, and charges fees, ultimately breaking her spirit. His relentless pressure leads to her untimely death, ensuring he remains the sole singer of the bog. This highlights how power and manipulation can crush true talent.

Similarly, in 'Mrs. Packletide's Tiger', Mrs. Packletide, driven by jealousy, arranges a staged tiger hunt for social prestige. She bribes villagers to present her with a weak, old tiger, hoping to claim false glory. However, her deception backfires when Miss Mebbin, her companion, blackmails her, forcing her to pay a heavy price to maintain her reputation. Though she achieves her goal momentarily, she ultimately suffers financial loss and humiliation, proving that manipulation often leads to downfall.

Both works caution against exploiting others for selfish gains. While the frog's greed leads to the tragic loss of talent, Mrs. Packletide's vanity results in embarrassment. In the end, deception and selfishness bring irony and regret rather than success.

ASSESSMENT EXERCISE

Extract Based Questions

Read the following extracts carefully and answer the questions that follow.

1. "The compelling motive for her sudden deviation towards the footsteps of Nimrod was the fact that Loona Bimberton had recently been carried 11 miles in an aeroplane by an Algerian aviator and talked of nothing else; only a personally procured tiger skin and heavy harvest of press photographs could successfully counter that sort of thing."
   (a) For whom is the pronoun 'her' used in this context?
   (b) What was the sudden deviation being referred to in the extract?
   (c) Who is Nimrod?
   (d) Why is his reference made here?
2. "The rifle flashed out with a loud report and the great tautly beast sprang to one side and then rolled over in the stillness of death. In a moment, a crowd of excited natives had swarmed on the scene and their shouting speedily carried the glad news to the village..."
   (a) What is the glad news?
   (b) Why were the natives excited and shouting?
   (c) Select the expression used for the tiger.
   (d) Describe the scene.

Short Answer Type Questions

Answer the following questions in 30-40 words.

1. What did Mrs. Packletide intend to do with the tiger skin and claws?
2. What was the 'one great anxiety' of the villagers?
3. Why did Louisa Mebbin name her week end cottage 'Les Fauves'?
4. How did the circumstances prove propitious (likely to produce a successful result) for Mrs. Packletide?
5. Which newspaper featured the news of Mrs. Packletide's feat? Why?
6. What kind of goat was chosen for the hunt? Why?
7. Why did the tiger lie down flat on the earth after it saw the goat?
8. What could the neighbouring village boast of?

Long Answer Type Questions

Answer the following questions in 150 words.

1. Do you think ruthless killing of tigers for their skin and claws is right? Why/Why not? According to you, what steps can be taken to educate schoolchildren about the need to save tigers?
2. 'Vanity blossoms but bears no fruit.' Throw light on the characters of Mrs. Packletide and Loona Bimberton with respect to the above statement. Why do you think we should keep vanity at bay?
3. There is an old Latin proverb – 'A jealous woman will set a whole house on fire.' Discuss the evils of jealousy that can be learnt from Saki's story 'Mrs. Packletide's Tiger.'

CHAPTER 3

The Letter

by Dhumaketu

CHAPTER SUMMARY 'The Letter' is a story of an old coachman, Ali. He suffered the pain of separation when his daughter Miriam left him alone after her marriage. The story reveals the careless attitude of the younger generation towards their old parents. The insensitive behaviour of the post office employees shows the hollowness of society.

The Early Morning Scene

It was a cold early winter morning and the sky was still grey. An old man was walking through the town, trying to protect himself from biting cold wind. Most of the people were still asleep as there was silence all around. This silence was broken occasionally by the sound of grinding mills from some houses, women singing, dogs barking, a workman going to work and a bird making a loud and unpleasant sound.

The Post Office—A Place of Pilgrimage for Ali

This old man was Coachman Ali, who never forgot his routine of going to the post office every morning. Neither winter nor summer could deter his firm determination. His strong hope made his legs carry him every day to the post office. His daughter had gone far away after her marriage and he wished to get news of her well-being. It was difficult to imagine that he had been going to the post office regularly for the last five years. The post office was like a place of pilgrimage for Ali.

No Relief for Poor Ali

Though Ali had been going to the post office for the past five years regularly, he did not receive any letter from his daughter. However, he did not give up hope and very regularly went to the post office early in the morning. Sitting in the veranda of the post office, he would hear the voice of the people working there doing their routine work.

Post Office Clerks Regarded Ali as a Madman

While waiting, Ali would hear the peons of various companies gossiping about their bosses. People there had become aware of his habit and considered him mad. They made fun of him by calling out his name even though there was no letter for him. They just wanted to see him jump eagerly to receive the letter which was not there at all. Thus, they insulted and laughed at the poor old man. They used to tell the postmaster that the man sitting outside was mad and troubled them everyday.

One day, the postmaster enquired about Ali, as he had been seeing him sitting there regularly. He was told by the clerk that Ali has been coming there for the past five years in the hope of a letter. The postmaster was convinced that Ali was mad.

Ali-A Seasoned Hunter

Ali was a skilled shikari at one time. As his skill improved, so did his love for hunting. He was unable to pass even a single day without hunting. The earth-brown partridge (a kind of bird), almost invisible to other eyes, was easily spotted by him. He could easily spot a rabbit even when the dogs failed to do so. Besides this, he would often go out with his friends, who were fishermen.

Separation Made Ali Change His Ways

Ali changed his ways in his old age. This was due to the marriage of his only child, Miriam, with a soldier who was posted in Punjab. Ever since she had gone away, Ali had not heard from her. He became a very unhappy man. He now realised the meaning of love and separation.

He lost all interest in hunting. He had now become a very lonely man. He sat under a tree and wept bitterly. He rose each morning at four to walk to the post office and would wait for his letter patiently.

The Postmaster's Rude Behaviour

For many days, Ali did not go to the post office. While none of the people in the post office cared, they were all anxious and eager to know the reason. After a few days, when he came again, he was very sick and was breathing with difficulty.

He was too old and it looked like he was not going to live long. That day, he could not hold back his emotions. He walked up to the postmaster to enquire if there was a letter for him from his daughter, Miriam. The postmaster, who was in a hurry to go out, called him a pest and shouted at him, saying that if his letter came, they would give it to him.

Ali's Request to Lakshmi Das

Helpless and impatient, Ali heard one of the clerks coming up behind him. The clerk's name was Lakshmi Das. Ali gave him five golden guineas (coins) requesting him that whenever his daughter Miriam's letter came, he should forward it to him at his grave.

Ali was aware of his approaching death. He told the clerk that it was his last day. After that, no one ever saw Ali again, nor did anyone bother to enquire about the reason for his not coming to the post office.

Postmaster Felt Remorse

One day, the postmaster was troubled and restless. His daughter, who lived in another town, was ill and he was anxiously waiting to hear from her that day. When the post was brought, he eagerly rushed towards it. He snatched at an envelope which looked like the one he was expecting from his daughter. He was shocked when he read the name on the envelope. It was addressed to Coachman Ali. He, at once, dropped the letter and realised that it was the letter for which Ali had been waiting for five years.

The postmaster called out to the clerk to whom Ali had given the gold coins and enquired from him about Ali. The clerk promised to find out about Ali. The postmaster, who was now regretting his behaviour towards Ali, thought of giving the letter to Ali himself when he would come at four the next morning.

The Postmaster Understood the Feelings of a Father

The postmaster did not receive the letter which he had been waiting for. His worry for his daughter made him understand the anxiety felt by Ali for the past five years. That night, the postmaster got up at three in the morning and went to the post office. At five in the morning, the postmaster heard someone knocking at the door.

Feeling sure that it must be Ali, the postmaster eagerly got up from his chair, opened the door and asked Ali to enter. Then, he handed the letter to Ali. The postmaster felt that Ali had doubled with age and his face was wet with tears while he leaned on his stick. His face looked gentle but there was an unearthly (very strange) light in his eyes. The postmaster moved back in fear.

The Essential Human Worth of a Letter

Suddenly, Lakshmi Das came towards the postmaster. The postmaster told Lakshmi Das that he had just been speaking to Ali. Lakshmi Das told him that Ali had died three months ago. The postmaster was surprised when he heard about Ali's death. He saw Miriam's letter lying on the floor. Soon, the postmaster followed his daily routine but now he did not consider the envelope as just a thing on which something was written. He understood the essential human worth of a letter.

That evening after office, he went along with Lakshmi Das to Ali's grave and laid the letter on it. The postmaster's newly awakened father's heart was making him regret his behaviour of not being able to understand the anxiety of a father.

Word Meaning

Word	Meaning
screech	a loud, harsh, piercing cry
sway	influence
caressing	expressing affection
plodded	walked heavily or laboriously
crevices	cracks
beholding	looking at, seeing
squatted	sat in a low or crouching position with legs drawn up closely beneath or in front of the body
jesting	joking
calling	visiting
partridge	a brown short-tailed bird
dragged along	slowly carried on
bewildered	confused
bereft	deprived of

Word	Meaning
instinct	inborn pattern of behaviour
inescapable	unavoidable
serenity	calmness
persevered	continued even in the face of difficulty, or without any indication of success
boundless	unlimited
animation	liveliness
relic	an object surviving from an earlier time
chimed in	broke into a conversation, usually to express an opinion
lunacy	insanity, madness
contain	control
startled	shocked
brimming	filled up completely
reproaching	accusing, scolding

Textbook FOLDER

Here, we have covered questions given in the CBSE Textbook along with their answers.

ON PAGE 29-30

Q.4 Answer the following questions by selecting the correct options.

(a) Ali's walking to the Post Office daily even in biting cold weather shows his

(i) courage (ii) optimism
(iii) foolishness (iv) strength of will

Ans. (ii) optimism

(b) The Post Office is referred to as Ali's 'place of pilgrimage' as he

(i) visited it daily.
(ii) came there to pray for a letter from his daughter.
(iii) went there with faith and hope.
(iv) believed God would bless him if he went there.

Ans. (iii) went there with faith and hope.

(c) The Post Master's rudeness towards Ali reveals his ....

(i) lack of empathy
(ii) preoccupation with his work
(iii) preconceived notions
(iv) sensitivity

Ans. (i) lack of empathy

(d) Ali did not come to the Post Office for several days as

(i) he had given up hope
(ii) he was upset by the Post Master's rebuke
(iii) he was unwell and unable to walk to the Post Office
(iv) he was busy hunting

Ans. (iii) he was unwell and unable to walk to the Post Office

(e) "Tortured by doubt and remorse, he sat down in the glow of the charcoal sigri to wait." The Post Master was waiting for ....

(i) a letter from Miriam
(ii) a letter from his own daughter
(iii) a letter from Ali
(iv) Ali to deliver Miriam's letter to him.

Ans. (ii) a letter from his own daughter

ON PAGE 30

Q.5 Answer the following questions briefly.

(a) Who was Ali? Where did he go daily?

(b) "Ali displays qualities of love and patience." Give evidence from the story to support the statement.

***or* "Ali displays qualities of love and patience." Elaborate.**

(c) How do you know Ali was a familiar figure at the post office?

(d) Why did Ali give up hunting?

***or* Why did Coachman Ali give up his favourite sport?**

***or* What were Ali's old ways and when did his life take a new turn?**

(e) What impression do you form of the postmaster after reading the story 'The Letter'?

(f) The postmaster says to Ali "What a pest you are, brother!" Do you agree with the statement? Give reasons for your answer.

***or* In the story 'The Letter', the postmaster called Ali a pest. Do you find this comment justified? Explain.**

(g) "Ali came out very slowly, turning after every few steps to gaze at the post office. His eyes were filled with tears of helplessness, for his patience was exhausted, even though he still had faith." Why were Ali's eyes filled with tears of helplessness? What had exhausted his patience, but not his faith?

(h) "Tortured by doubt and remorse, he sat down in the glow of the charcoal *sigri* to wait." Who is tortured by doubt and remorse? Why? What is he waiting for?

Ans. (a) Ali is an old a coachman and a hunter. He went to the post office every day to wait for a letter from his daughter, Miriam.

(b) There are many instances given in the story of Ali displaying qualities of love and patience. He visited the post office every single day during the last five years to enquire about a letter from his daughter Miriam, although no letter came. This shows his patience and love for his daughter.
He bore the taunts and insults hurled at him by the staff of the post office. Finally, when he was dying, he gave a post office employee a large amount of money to ensure that if his daughter's letter came after his death, it would be delivered to his grave.

(c) Ali was a familiar figure at the post office for the past five years because he went there every day in the hope of receiving a letter from his daughter. He was always the first one to reach there.

(d) Ali was a seasoned (experienced) hunter. He could not live without hunting. However, when his daughter got married, he understood the grief (pain) of separation and the meaning of love. This brought about a change in him. He could no longer enjoy hunting and gave it up for good.

(e) The postmaster was a proud and arrogant man. He was a very cold person with no compassion. This is seen is his rude and unsympathetic remark towards Ali. However, a change came over him when he found himself in the same situation. Then, he was able to appreciate Ali's feelings.

(f) No, Ali was not a pest as called by the postmaster, who himself was a person without compassion (kindness). He failed to understand the feelings of an anxious father. He considered him a pest because Ali came every day for a letter from his daughter Miriam.

(g) Ali's eyes were filled with tears of helplessness because he knew his end was imminent. He had grown quite old and his loneliness and suffering had further affected his health. The time was running out fast for him. He knew Miriam would certainly write to him, but he didn't have much time left with him.

(h) It is the postmaster who is tortured by doubt and remorse. He was waiting for news from his ill daughter who lived in another town. He spent a whole night in suspense and anxiety.

ON PAGE 31

Q.6 The writer carefully builds up an atmosphere of loneliness and grief in the story. Working in groups, pick out words/ phrases from the story that build up the atmosphere. Copy the following table in your notebook and complete it.

Loneliness	Grief
An old man was walking through the town, now and again drawing his tattered clothes tighter to shield his body from the cold and biting wind his lonely way	the whole town was wrapped in deathly silence

Ans.

Loneliness	Grief
and for the last five years he had no news of this daughter for whose sake alone he dragged along a cheerless existence. Now he understood the meaning of love and separation.	He reflected deeply, and came to the conclusion that the whole universe was built up through love and that the grief of separation was inescapable. And understanding this, he sat down under a tree and wept bitterly.

Q.7 Complete the table by explaining the following phrases/sentences in your own words.

Phrases	Meanings
happy memories light up a life that is nearing its close	
the sounds helped him along his lonely way	
the cold used sleep to extend its sway over all things even as a false friend lulls his chosen victim with caressing smiles	
when the evening of his life was drawing in, he left his old ways and suddenly took a new turn	
the whole universe is built up through love and that the grief of separation is inescapable	
the post-master, a man with a face as sad and as inexpressive as a pumpkin, would be seen sitting on his chair inside	
And so the clerk, like a worshipper of Lord Vishnu, repeated his customary thousand names	
The haughty temper of the official had quite left him in his sorrow and anxiety, and had laid bare his human heart	

Ans.
- Happy memories of the past make a dying man happy.
- The sounds entertained him on his way.
- Each and every individual was sleeping in the cold weather.
- As he got old, he left his old lifestyle.
- Love and grief of separation are essential parts of the living world.
- The arrogant post master was sitting in his chair.
- And so the clerk remembered his God.
- The post-master was suffering and was in emotional pain.

ON PAGE 32

WRITING TASK

Q.9 Tortured by doubt and remorse, the postmaster sits in the glow of a charcoal *sigri* that night, waiting for news of his daughter. As he sits, he writes his diary.

As the postmaster, write a diary entry in about 150 words outlining your feelings about the day's events.

Ans. Wednesday, 9th January, 20XX 11:00 pm

Dear Diary

I am very worried today as there is no letter from my daughter who is sick in another town far away from here. I am very worried about her well-being.

I remember some days ago, I had scolded the old Coachman Ali, who was coming every day to enquire about a letter from his daughter Miriam. Now, I am having a similar worry and so am feeling remorse for having scolded Ali. I can now understand his fatherly feelings of love for his daughter, who has not written any letter to him for so many years after she got married and went away. Ali was a really patient and persistent person. He also displayed a lot of hope. I can now understand Ali's pain of separation from his daughter for so many years. He was a model of affection for his daughter. I feel sad now that I could not apologise to him for my harsh words.

Postmaster

SPEAKING TASK

Q.10 (a) The postmaster believes that he had seen Ali. What do you think? Discuss with your partner and present your views in front of the class.

(b) The postmaster was anxiously waiting for his ailing daughter's news. On not getting any news, he visits his daughter's town. Now create a dialogue between the postmaster and his daughter and enact it.

Ans. (a) I think that the postmaster saw Ali simply because the latter had a great faith that his daughter would write a letter to him. Hence, even after his death, he came to see the fulfillment of his faith or the receiving of his daughter's letter.

One can refute the postmaster's apparent seeing of Ali as the manifestation of his own guilt for having treated a worrisome father wrongly. Now that the postmaster himself is suffering from paternal pain, he can understand Ali's pain. Now, he regrets treating Ali wrongly and wants to correct his wrong by giving the letter to Ali himself. Therefore, he imagines Ali coming to take the letter.

(b) **Postmaster** How are you, my girl? I have been worried sick for you. When I did not hear about your condition, I was so worried. I couldn't eat, sleep or pay attention to anything.

But by the grace of God, you are safe and healthy.

Postmaster's daughter Dad, I am doing good. I am sorry for not writing sooner. I just did not have the time or energy to do anything.

Postmaster It is all good now. You are fine. But next time, please make sure that someone informs me about anything related to you at the earliest. God, I was so worried and it was just a few days. I cannot imagine the worry that Coachman Ali has.

Postmaster's daughter Coachman Ali? Who is he, dad?

Postmaster He was an old man. He came to the post office everyday to see if he had got a letter from his daughter, Miriam. At that time, I also couldn't understand him. I used to get so irritated that he came everyday and one day even shouted at him. Only when you were ill, I realised the worry and pains he had suffered. For five years he came to the post office to get to know about the well-being of his daughter and what did I do? I shouted on him.

Postmaster's daughter It's okay, dad. He is in a better place now.

Postmaster You know his letter came 3 months late. He was dead by the time and I could not do anything but keep it at his grave.

Postmaster's daughter Now, he knows that his daughter is well, dad.

Postmaster I hope so.

REVIEW EXERCISE

Including Previous Years' and Practice Questions

Extract Based Questions

Read the following extracts carefully and answer the questions that follow.

1. The old man, shivering at times but fixed of purpose, plodded on till he came out of the town gate on to a straight road. Along this he now went at a somewhat slower pace, supporting himself on his old staff.

(a) Who was the old man and why was he shivering?

Ans. The old man was Coachman Ali. He was shivering because it was a cold winter morning.

(b) Where was he going so early?

Ans. He was going to the post office so early.

(c) What does the phrase, 'plodded on' mean?

Ans. It means to walk with great effort or laboriously.

(d) Why did the old man slow down?

Ans. The old man slowed down as he was tired from walking the long distance.

2. Beholding the wooden arch of this building, the old man was filled with the joy that the pilgrim feels when he first sees the goal of his journey. On the arch hung an old board the verandah. The voices of two or three people busy and their routine work could be faintly heard through the wall. "Police Superintendent," a voice called sharply. The old man started at the sound, but composed himself again to wait. But for the faith and love, that warmed him, he could not have borne the bitter cold.

(a) Why did he go to the building?

Ans. He went to the post office in the hope of getting a letter from his daughter, Miriam.

(b) Why is the old man compared to a pilgrim?

Ans. The old man is compared to a pilgrim because the post office is like a place of pilgrimage for him, as he visits it every day to enquire for a letter from his daughter.

(c) Why was 'he' in the bitter cold? Was he rewarded for his faith and love?

Ans. 'He', *i.e.*, Ali, was in the bitter cold because he was waiting outside the post office in early morning. No, he was not rewarded as he did not receive any letter from his daughter.

(d) How was he able to gain strength to bear the bitter cold?

Ans. The hope of getting a letter from his daughter gave him strength to bear the bitter cold.

3. "It's a mad man, sir, who worries us by calling every day for letters that never come", said the clerk to the postmaster.

(a) Who is referred to as a 'mad man'?

Ans. Coachman Ali is referred to as a mad man here.

(b) The word .... in the extract means 'insane.'

Ans. mad

(c) What is the attitude of the clerk and the postmaster towards the mad man?

Ans. Their attitude is cruel and insensitive.

(d) What had the 'mad man' done to get this response from the clerk?

Ans. The 'mad man' had requested the clerk to give the letter addressed to him, as the clerk had announced his name jokingly, although no letter was there for him.

4. ...... that now, forgetting his sport, he would become lost in the admiration of the green cornfield. He reflected deeply, and came to the conclusion that the whole universe was built up through love and that the grief of separation was inescapable. **CBSE 2025**

(a) Why has Ali forgotten his sport?

Ans. Ali has forgotten his sport because he has become deeply absorbed in the beauty of the green cornfield. As he observes the field, he is moved by its peacefulness and harmony, which seem to stir a profound reflection within him.

(b) What do the above lines tell you about Ali's attitude towards nature?

Ans. The lines suggest that Ali has a deep and contemplative attitude towards nature. His reaction to the green cornfield shows that he is not just appreciating its beauty on the surface but is also moved by it in a way that triggers profound thoughts.

(c) What did his deep reflection of life make him realise?

Ans. This deep reflection on life made Ali realise that the entire universe is built on the foundation of love, and that the grief of separation is an inevitable part of life.

(d) What does the writer mean by 'grief of separation'?

Ans. By 'grief of separation', the writer refers to the inevitable pain and sorrow that comes when people or even aspects of life, are parted from each other.

5. The post office, one of the most uninteresting buildings in the world, became his place of pilgrimage. He always occupied a particular seat in a particular corner of the building, and when the people got to know his habit, they laughed at him. The postmen began to make a game of him. Even though there was no letter for him they would call out his name for the fun of seeing him jump up and come to the door. Still with boundless faith and infinite patience, he came every day, and went away empty-handed.

(a) Identify any two characteristics of the postmaster that are revealed via their behaviour towards Ali.

Ans. The postmaster is a proud and an arrogant man who lacks empathy. He cannot understand Ali's emotions and fears regarding his daughter until he himself suffers it.

(b) Give one reason why the writer refers to the post office as "one of the most uninteresting buildings in the world".

Ans. The writer refers to the post office as 'one of the most uninteresting buildings in the world' as people come here to collect their letters and mails and leave. They do not stay here for more than they are required to.

(c) State Ali's thoughts as he walks out of the post office.

Ans. I am sure that Miriam will write to me some day. I will wait till then.

(d) Identify two words from the extract that imply 'without limits'.

Ans. Boundless and infinite

6. The postmaster was beginning to lose his temper. "Have you no sense?" he cried. "Get away! Do you think we're going to eat your letter when it comes?" and he walked off hastily. Ali came out very slowly, turning after every few steps to gaze at the post office.

His eyes were filled with tears of helplessness, for his patience was exhausted, even though he still had faith. Yet how could he still hope to hear from Miriam?

(a) Select the expression that means to get angry.

Ans. to lose his temper.

(b) How was Ali feeling?

Ans. Ali was feeling helpless and sad.

(c) What made him feel so?

Ans. Ali felt very sad because the postmaster had behaved rudely with him.

(d) Why was Ali repeatedly looking back at the post office?

Ans. Ali was repeatedly looking back at the post office because he realised that this was his last visit there, as he understood that he would die soon. He looked back repeatedly in the hope that somebody would call him back and give him a letter from his daughter.

7. "They will be useful to you and they can never be to me. But will you do one thing?" "What?"

"What do you see up there?" said Ali, pointing to the sky. **CBSE 2019**

(a) Identify the person being spoken to.

Ans. Lakshmi Das, the post office clerk, is the person being spoken to or the listener here.

(b) What does the word 'they' refer to?

Ans. 'They' refers to 'five golden guineas' (gold coins) which Ali gave to Lakshmi Das.

(c) Why did Ali say 'they' can never be useful to him?

Ans. 'They', the coins, could never be useful to Ali, because he realised that he was going to die soon.

(d) What opinion do you form of Ali on the basis of the given extract?

Ans. The given extract tells us that Ali was a worldly, sensitive man who was desperate for something. He knew his death was near and so used his money to fulfill his last desire, i.e. to get his daughter's letter.

Short Answer Type Questions

Answer the following questions in 30-40 words.

1. How does the author describe the early morning in the story?

Ans. The author describes the early morning in a very beautiful manner. We are told that it was the time of dawn (sunrise/early morning) and the stars could still be seen in the sky. It was winter season and a cold wind was blowing. A deathly silence spread all around, which was occasionally broken by some normal sounds for this time of the morning.

2. How does the author describe the place near the post office?

Ans. The author describes the place in an impressive way. The trees stood in a line on one side of the road and on the other side was the public garden of that town. At the end of the garden, there was a building in the newest style. It was the post office.

3. Ali, in the story 'The Letter', is a lonely man. How does the author bring out his loneliness?

Ans. Being a devoted father, Ali got up at 4 am every day and went to the post office in the hope of getting a letter from his daughter who lived in Punjab after her marriage with a soldier. Thus, he was a lonely man without any companion. Further, Ali gave up hunting and did not engage himself in any other activity either.

4. The post office became a place of pilgrimage for Ali. How?

Ans. Ali was suffering from the pain of separation from his daughter who had gone away after marriage. He was so anxious (worried) about her well-being that he would visit the post office every day, expecting a letter from her. Thus, the post office became a place of pilgrimage for the old man.

5. "Mad men are strange people", the postmaster said. Comment.

Ans. The postmaster was told by a clerk that the old man was mad because he came to the post office every day for the past five years without bothering about the weather. Thus, the postmaster made this comment without realising why the 'mad man', i.e. Ali, had been coming to the post office every day.

6. "The haughty temper of the official had quite left him in his sorrow and anxiety, and had laid bare his human heart." In the lesson 'The Letter', who is the official referred to? Give an example of his haughty behaviour. **Competency Based**

Ans. The official referred to is the postmaster. When Ali asked him about the letter from his daughter for the last time, the postmaster became angry and started shouting at him. He called Ali 'a pest' and 'a man with no sense', showing his haughty behaviour.

7. What is your impression of the postman and the postmaster in the story, 'The Letter'?

Ans. The postman as well as the postmaster were very rude towards Ali. The postman used to ridicule him and called him mad. They were insensitive and cruel. The postmaster was haughty, arrogant and emotionless. He was ill-tempered and called Ali 'a pest'.

8. Why was Ali impatient when he visited the post office after many days?

Or **Why did Ali not come to the post office for several days? Why was he impatient when he finally returned to the post office?**

Ans. It had been Ali's regular routine for the past five years to visit the post office, as he hoped to receive a letter from his daughter. However, his bad health interrupted this routine. He had realised that his life was close to its end. Hence, he became impatient to know about his daughter's letter.

9. Ali's patience was exhausted. Why?

Ans. Ali had been showing his patience by waiting for his daughter's letter. Every morning, for the past five years he had been regularly visiting the post office and enquiring for Miriam's letter. His patience was now giving way because he could foresee his approaching death.

10. What request did Ali make to Lakshmi Das?

Or **What was Ali's request to the clerk?**

Ans. Ali requested Lakshmi Das to deliver his daughter's letter to him whenever it came. For this, Ali gave five gold coins to the clerk. When the clerk asked him where he was to deliver the letter, the old man told him to leave the letter at his grave as he realised that he would die soon.

11. What made the postmaster understand Ali's pain later on in the story 'The Letter'? **CBSE 2020**

Ans. The postmaster understood Ali's pain when he himself faced a similar situation that Ali had been facing for the past 5 years. The postmaster's daughter was ill and he had no news of her. Just like Ali, he also had to wait for the letter from his daughter informing about her health and well being.

12. How did the postmaster become a changed man?

***Or* What brings about a change in the postmaster?**

Ans. At first, the postmaster was a man devoid of compassion (kindness). However, one day, he faced the same situation that Ali had faced for five years. Now, he realised Ali's painful mental situation. As a result, the postmaster grew remorseful and became a changed man.

13. Why was the postmaster so keen to deliver the letter to Ali himself?

Ans. The postmaster was very worried all night as he did not receive any news about his ill daughter. This made him understand Ali's agony (pain). Afflicted with regret, he scolded himself for his insensitivity. His own worry and anxiety made him identify himself with Ali. So, he decided to deliver the letter to Coachman Ali personally.

14. What is the importance of 'The Letter' in the story?

***Or* What is the role of 'The Letter' in the story by Dhumaketu?**

Ans. For five years, Ali waited for 'The Letter' from his daughter. The postmaster understood Ali's feelings only after he found himself in a similar situation. He realised the essential human worth of 'A letter'. Hence, 'A letter' plays a very important role in the story.

15. "Ali is a true example of love, faith and sacrifice." Elaborate.

Ans. It is true that Ali is a true symbol of faith, love and sacrifice. Owing entirely to his deep love for his daughter, Ali gave up his passionate sport, hunting, and accepted the life of an ascetic but he had firm faith in providence. He thought that his daughter would write to him one day asking his well-being and telling her own. For this, he went to the post office everyday braving biting cold and scorching heat.

16. What does the writer wish to convey via the use of the metaphor for a false friend in the given line from 'The Letter'? **CBSE SQP 2023**

...... the cold used sleep to extend its sway over all things even as false friend lulls his chosen victim with caressing smiles.

Ans. The metaphor of false friend is used to describe the winter cold, which is depicted as a treacherous and sneaky force that gradually extends its sway over all things. Like a false friend, the cold initially seems harmless and even welcoming, as it lulls its victims into a false sense of security with its 'caressing smiles'. However as the metaphor suggests, the cold is not a friend at all, but a deceiver who ultimately seeks to harm and control its victims.

17. Evaluate how The Letter by Dhumaketu portrays the impact of separation on human emotions. **CBSE SQP 2024**

Ans. 'The Letter' by Dhumaketu portrays the impact of separation on human emotions poignantly. It truly captures the emotional turmoil caused by separation. The story revolves around Ali, an old man who longs for a letter from his daughter, Miriam. His daily visits to the post office and eventual death without receiving the letter highlight the profound loneliness and yearning that separation can cause.

Long Answer Type Questions

Answer the following questions in 150 words.

1. "But when the evening of his life was drawing in, he left his old ways and suddenly took a turn." What was the change in Ali's nature towards the end of his life? What was the reason for this transformation? What values do we learn from his story? **Competency Based**

Ans. Ali was a clever hunter in his youth. He killed many birds and animals, and left their families bereft of their loved ones. However, when his daughter, Miriam, got married and went far away from him, he too suffered the pangs (pain) of separation. He realised that it was really difficult to live without our near and dear ones. He gave up hunting. His heart was completely changed after the separation from his only child.

He understood the real meaning of love and the acute pain of separation. He could not bear this pain and even cried. He became lonely and his journey to the post office began. The story teaches us that everyone in this world needs to love and be loved, but everyone has to bear the grief (pain) of separation from the loved ones.

2. Do you think Ali's misery is a result of his past deeds? Give reasons to justify your answer.

Ans. Ali had been a clever and skilled hunter in his youth, and he never cared to think of the pain he caused to the birds and animals he hunted, or to the young ones who were orphaned. However, after Ali's daughter went away from him, he realised the true meaning of love and separation. This made him give up hunting. Ali's present misery, that he suffers from the pangs (pain) of separation from his daughter Miriam, can be seen as a result of his past deeds. He has to pay a really heavy price for the cruelty he so enjoyed in the past. However, this turns out to be too harsh a punishment for the old man. He had already realised his mistake and had given up the cruel sport. In my opinion, this suffering is too much for him in his old age.

3. One feels other's pain only when one goes through it oneself. Explain the postmaster's change of heart in the chapter 'The Letter' and why it took place.

Or **You can feel others pain only when you go through it yourself. Validate this statement with reference to the story 'The Letter' and why it took place?** CBSE 2024

Ans. At the beginning of the story, the postmaster appeared to be a haughty, high-headed and ill-tempered official. His behaviour towards Ali, when the latter asked him if he had a letter from his daughter, was quite rude.

Once the postmaster's daughter fell ill in another town, he anxiously awaited news from her. It was at this point that his suffering father's heart realised the pain of separation in Ali's heart for Miriam. He was no longer a haughty official but a loving father, full of respect for Ali's feelings. Thus, it was only when the postmaster himself underwent a similar experience that he was able to feel Ali's pain. We should, thus, be good to others and never treat anyone harshly.

4. Lakshmi Das, the clerk, to whom Ali had given the money, writes a diary entry regretting his misbehaviour with Ali when he pestered him. Imagine you are Lakshmi Das and make the diary entry. Also mention what Lakshmi Das learned from his mistake.

Ans. Monday, 17th December, 20XX 10 p.m.

Dear Diary

Today, I have realised that we must not misbehave with anybody for any reason.

Ali loved his daughter and waited for her letter for a long time. He was suffering from loneliness and I should have understood his situation.

The postmaster insulted him and others used to make fun of him. Ali knew that he would not live long and so he offered me five gold coins as he wanted me to place his daughter's letter on his grave.

The poor soul died waiting for the letter. I regret not being compassionate enough towards him. It taught me a great lesson that what goes around comes around. We must not treat anyone harshly, otherwise others may also treat us harshly. I pray to God to forgive me for my rude behaviour towards Ali.

Lakshmi

5. Both the stories 'Two Gentlemen of Verona' and 'The Letter' teach us not to lose hope and courage even in adverse situations. Write a letter to a friend justifying the statement with reference to the stories. CBSE 2024

Ans. 15, Shastri Colony
Kolkata, 244573

10th March, 20XX

Dear Pratiksha

How are you? I am good here too. Your previous letter about feeling sad about not achieving good scores in Science competition got me thinking. I believe that we shouldn't give up and be upset because of failures and difficult conditions but we should be brave and courageous. I learned this lesson when I read two stories, 'Two Gentlemen of Verona' and 'The Letter'.

In the first story, two brothers, Nicola and Jacopo, perform many odd jobs to earn money for their sister's treatment. Even after losing their parents and their home, they do not give up and work hard so that they can help their sister get better. 'The Letter' is another story with the same message where an old man visits a post office regularly for five years in hopes that he would receive his daughter's letter addressed to him. He goes early in the morning daily just because he didn't want to miss the chance of hearing from his daughter.

So, I suggest you read these stories because they'll inspire you to work harder and not be sad about failed attempts.

Yours affectionately
Prachi

6. Love and pain are two emotions which can transform people. Write an article in around 150 words about the values you have learnt from Ali (The Letter) and Nicola and Jacopo from 'Two Gentlemen of Verona'.

Ans. **Love and Pain-Keys to Transformation**

Life is an intricate tapestry woven from myriad emotions, experiences, and relationships. Among the most profound of these are love and pain, two forces that, while seemingly opposing, often intertwine to shape, transform, and elevate the human experience. Individually, love can be a source of joy and fulfillment, while pain can lead to suffering and despair. However, when these two forces merge, they have the remarkable ability to transform people in profound and lasting ways.

We can find two instances of this transformative power in the stories 'Two Gentleman of Verona' and 'The Letter'. In 'Two Gentleman of Verona', the two boys Nicola and Jacopo enter the world of war against Germans who destroyed their families. However, they undergo a change when they found that their sister was ill. Hence, they decided to word hard to make sure that their sister was treated.

In 'The Letter', this is true for the postmaster who had initially being rude and angry at Ali. However, when he faced a situation similar to that of Ali, he realised his mistake. He transformed into a man who sympathised with Ali.

Thus, love and pain are intertwined forces that have the power to transform individuals in profound ways.

ASSESSMENT EXERCISE

Extract Based Questions

Read the following extracts carefully and answer the questions that follow.

1. "But when the evening of his life was drawing in, he left his old ways and suddenly took a new turn. " His only child, Miriam married and left him. She went off with a soldier into his regiment in the Punjab.
   (i) What does the expression 'evening of life' mean?
   (ii) What does 'old ways' refer to here?
   (iii) Whose life is being referred to in the above lines?
   (iv) Why has Ali's life taken a new turn?
2. "Master Sahib", he begged the post-master, "Have you a letter from my Miriam?"
   The Postmaster wanted to get out to the country, and was in a hurry.
   "What a pest you are, brother!" He exclaimed.
   "My name is Ali", answered Ali absent-mindedly.
   (i) Who is the speaker of the first line?
   (ii) Why does he call Ali a pest?
   (iii) What light does it throw on the character of the speaker?
   (iv) What does it tell us about the listener?

Short Answer Type Questions

Answer the following questions in 30-40 words.

1. How did loneliness start haunting Ali?
2. What kind of childhood do you think Miriam had?
3. Why does the author describe Ali as 'a pitiable figure a century behind his time'?
4. Describe the daily routine of the post office clerks.
5. Which instinct was still in Ali's blood and bones? Why?
6. 'The postman began to make a game of him'. Explain.
7. Why did the young peons come to the office? What did they discuss?
8. What kind of men usually prove to be village schoolmasters, office clerks or postmasters? Why?

Long Answer Type Questions

Answer the following questions in 150 words.

1. The 'empty nest syndrome' refers to feelings of loneliness and helplessness experienced by elderly persons when their children move out of home for various reasons. Give some reasons that lead to the 'empty nest syndrome'. Do you think the children should understand their responsibility towards their parents and not leave them alone in the final stage of their lives? Support your answer with reasons.
2. There is an old English proverb 'What goes around comes around'. Discuss this proverb with respect to both Ali and the postmaster from the story 'The Letter'. What lesson do we learn from their examples?
3. It is often said that 'Patience is a virtue'. Discuss how the quality of 'patience' can help us lead better and more enriched lives. How can we develop this quality?
4. Love can move mountains. In the story 'The Letter', Ali's intense love for his daughter makes him go to the post office every day for her letter. Discuss the value of love and devotion highlighted in the story. How can love motivate us to bring a positive change in our lives?

A Shady Plot

CHAPTER 4

by Elsie Brown

CHAPTER SUMMARY This story is about a man named John Hallock who has to write a ghost story for the publication. Searching for inspiration for the story, he encounters the ghost of a woman named Helen, who answers his questions and makes a demand to stop the use of Ouija Boards. Later, Hallock's wife comes to know about Helen and suspects him of cheating on her. However, when she comes to know the truth, she forgives him. Matters end in a cordial manner between the couple and John Hallock gets an excellent plot to write his ghost story.

Demand for a Ghost Story

Jenkins (owner of the magazine) demands another story on supernatural powers from John Hallock. He wants something which can give horror to the readers because that is what the public wants. He thinks that Hallock is good at writing ghost stories because his ghosts seemed real to the readers. The first fiction written by Hallock is also a ghost story. Hallock does not turn down the demand as he knows that this is the only magazine in which his writing is published. Therefore, Hallock agrees to write the story although he does not have any plot in his mind. He returns home and sits down to write, hoping that some idea will cross his head.

Hallock's First Encounter with the Ghost

When Hallock sits down to write, his mind begins to wander off to other matters. He thinks of his wife's shopping and wonders how on Earth he would cure her of her alarming tendency to spend money on the latest fashions and trends. Then, he starts staring at the ceiling. He next starts talking aloud to himself when, suddenly, a voice answers him.

The person behind the voice then starts taking shape in pieces. First an arm becomes visible, then a sleeve, then a leg and in the end, there stands a complete figure of a woman. She is tall and angular, with enormous fishy eyes behind big bone-rimmed spectacles, with her hair in a tight wad at the back of her head. The entire figure starts looking absolutely real. She comes over and stands in front of him, staring at him.

The Conversation Between the Ghost and Hallock

The ghost named Helen tells Hallock that she too used to write in the other world. Later, she became a reader but faced many problems. Therefore, she and other ghosts like her decided to form 'The Writer's Inspiration Bureau'. They roam here and there, and help the writers, who don't have sufficient ideas, to write their stories. They give the writers' thinking a shape and when their work is done, they have to report to their main office. She claims that she has helped him with ideas and inspiration on many occasions in the past. The ghost further tells him that now he would have no more assistance from them as they were going on a strike.

She tells him that the ghosts have stopped wandering and now, sit at one place to answer questions. This is because of the Ouija Board fanatics. She, thus, tells him to ask his friends and acquaintances to stop using Ouija Boards.

Lavinia Interrupts the Scene

Lavinia, Hallock's wife, listens to loud voices coming from the room. When she questions Hallock, he refuses to answer. She tells him that she had bought an Ouija Board for him to help him write ghost stories. However, she bought it only because of her fascination for new trends. John asks Lavinia to sell the Ouija board and buy something else. She refuses and gets angry. Next day, John went to his job as a bookkeeper and forgot all about ghost and stories. When he later returned home, he found that his wife had called for an Ouija board party. Hallock refuses to attend it initially. Later, when he attends the party, Lavinia pairs him with Laura Hinkle who is a flirtatious woman.

Hallock is Called a Traitor

At the party, when the Ouija Board is used, it takes the name of Hallock as a traitor (cheater). Everyone is surprised. Hallock sees that the board was going round faster than ever. He tries to get up but his fingers seemed stuck to the board. Laura Hinkle asks the board who was talking. The board spells 'H-E-L-E-N'. Hinkle asks Lavinia if she knows anyone by the name of Helen. Hinkle tells her that someone with the name Helen has been trying to communicate with her husband. Very soon, others people begin to report that their boards too are taking Hallock's name. At the party, John asks everyone not to use the Ouija Board but nobody listens to him.

Turmoil in the Couple's Relationship

At the party, Lavinia could handle the situation but looks towards Hallock with suspicion as she had done in the library the evening before. Hallock does not know when the party ends so he goes to his room and falls asleep. Next morning, he cannot find his wife and when he is sitting in his library, trying to make another try for his story, a slip of paper slides under the door. It reads, "Dear Hallock, I am going back to my grandmother. My lawyer will communicate with you later." After reading this, Hallock wishes that he were dead.

The Ghost Reappears

Suddenly, the voice of the ghost is heard again. She agrees that he should be dead. Hallock asks the ghost why she appears in parts. She replies that if he gives her time, she would appear in full. She is now too tired to materialise. She has come back again just to know when his wife is going to get rid of the Ouija Board.

Hallock blames the ghost for disturbing his relationship with his wife. It is due to her that Lavinia has decided to leave. Meanwhile, Gladolia, the cook, comes at the door and remarks that she does not like hoodoos (black magic) and Ouija Boards. Thus, she is leaving her job. Hallock again blames the ghost for this.

Hallock, Lavinia and the Ghost

Then, the door opens and Lavinia enters, ready to leave with her suitcase. Hallock behaves strangely on hearing her decision and tries his best to conceal the ghost from Lavinia. This arouses Lavinia's suspicions further.

She is clearly able to make out that Hallock is hiding something from her. She is now wants to know what is actually going on and why he is being so mysterious.

Hallock thinks that Lavinia would faint if she sees a ghost because she fears even a mouse.

The Truth is Revealed

Lavinia argues with Hallock over flirting at the Ouija Board party. While they are arguing, she notices someone behind Hallock and then, the ghost herself reveals that she is Helen. Lavinia is shocked to see the ghost.

Lavinia asks her whether she was Helen of Troy and the ghost agrees that she was Helen of Troy, New York and disappears after saying goodbye. This revelation calms Lavinia down and she realises her mistake of unnecessarily suspecting her husband of cheating on her with the ghost of Helen of Troy.

She, thus, forgivingly falls into his arms and regrets misunderstanding him. Hallock now feels a strong desire to write. He claims that now he has an idea for a ghost story.

Word Meaning

Word	Meaning
uncanny	strange
pestering	annoying
dunned	persistently ask for something that is overdue
cocky	overconfident
fad	craze
sarcastically	mockingly
imbecility	stupidity
shirtwaist	a woman's blouse shaped like a man's shirt
plaid skirt	chequered design skirt
wad	hair rolled and tied neatly
glared	stared in an angry or fierce way
crisped	said in an abrupt but polite way
drivelling	speaking nonsense
draped	spread
reminiscent	with one's mind full of memories
purgatory	a place or state of suffering
patronisingly	scornfully
Ouija Board	a board on which are marked the letters of the alphabet. Answers to questions are spelt out by a pointer or glass held by the fingertips of the participants, and are supposedly formed by spiritual forces
fanatics	people obsessive about something
brogans	a heavy ankle-high work boot with laces
affection	(here) condition, state of being affected
disintegrate	to split
vestige	traces
lingered	remained
hysterics	fits
speck	fragment
premonitory	a foreboding
a darn sight	much
huffily	haughtily
bookkeeper	accountant

Word	Meaning
argify	(here) argue
mournful squeak	sound of sadness
gasped	huffed
coyly	flirtatious but pretending to be shy or modest
tugging	pushing
cooed	made a soft murmuring sound
hovered	hung around
traitor	cheater
apparently	it seems that
inexorable	unstoppable
simpered	smiled in a silly, often coy manner
crimson	red
wretched	miserable
semblance	appearance
sly	cunning
gurgled	babbled
prickle	sting
protruding	projecting
hoodoos	putting curses and charms to bring bad luck on someone
brassily	rudely, insolently
staccatoed	spoke in an abrupt, detached manner
queerly	weirdly
contraptions	devices
skeered	scared
coon	(here) the one doing a menial job
waspishly	in an irritated manner
dratted	damned
lithely	gracefully
apparition	ghost
swoon	faint
fervently	passionately
bulliest	best, excellent

Textbook FOLDER

Here, we have covered questions given in the CBSE Textbook along with their answers.

ON PAGE 46-47

Q.4 Based on your reading of the story above, answer the following questions by selecting the correct options.

(i) The narrator earns his living by ....

(a) writing moral and ethical stories

(b) working as a reader for a magazine

(c) working as a stenographer

(d) working as an accountant in a lumber company

Ans. (d) working as an accountant in a lumber company

(ii) The writer was overconfident about his ability to write ghost stories because

(a) whenever magazines wanted a ghost story, they got in touch with him

(b) he was always able to write a ghost story whenever he had to write one.

(c) he had an Ouija board.

(d) he knew the ghost lady would help him write a good ghost story.

Ans. (b) he was always able to write a ghost story whenever he had to write one.

(iii) The sight of the ghost materialising in his room filled the narrator with ....

(a) fear (b) excitement

(c) joy (d) anticipation

Ans. (d) anticipation

(iv) The ghost wanted John to ....

(a) stop his wife from using the Ouija board

(b) stop using the Ouija board himself

(c) stop his guests from using the Ouija board

(d) stop people from using the Ouija board

Ans. (d) stop people from using the Ouija board

(v) John wants the ghost to disappear before his wife enters the room and waves his arms at the ghost with something of the motion of a beginner when learning to swim.

His movement shows his ....

(a) fear (b) amusement

(c) desperation (d) anxiety

Ans. (c) desperation

(vi) When the narrator says his wife is never so pretty as when she's doing something she knows he disapproves of, his tone is ....

(a) amused (b) ironic

(c) angry (d) irritated

Ans. (b) ironic

(vii) The ghost says, "It's all your fault." 'It' here refers to the ....

(a) narrator's wife's anger

(b) ghost's anger

(c) narrator's wife leaving him

(d) ghost materialising in sections

Ans. (d) ghost materialising in sections

(viii) Gladolia wishes to leave the narrator's house as ....

(a) she does not like the Ouija boards

(b) she is afraid of the ghost

(c) she is afraid of magic and hoodoo

(d) she likes Ouija boards and hoodoo

Ans. (c) she is afraid of magic and hoodoo

ON PAGE 48

Q.5 Answer the following questions briefly.

(a) What genre of stories does Jenkins want the narrator to write? Why?

Ans. Jenkins wants the narrator to write ghost stories or stories on supernatural elements because the public likes such stories and also because he thinks that John is good at writing such stories as his ghosts are very realistic and scary.

(b) Does the narrator like writing ghost stories? Support your answer with evidence from the story.

Ans. The narrator likes to write ghost stories but probably not every time. He himself says that he could not contradict Jenkins because his magazine had been the only one to print his stuff. Thus, we can say that he has no choice but to give in to Jenkins' demand to write ghost stories.

(c) What makes Helen, the ghost, and her other co-ghosts organise 'The Writer's Inspiration Bureau'?

Ans. When Helen was alive, she used to write and later on she became a reader in a magazine. She remembers those days as the most terrible ones as they used to read horribly written stories.

When she became a ghost after her death, she planned to do something for all those who have suffered in the same way. It was this inspiration that led her and her co-ghosts to organise 'The Writer's Inspiration Bureau'.

(d) Why had Helen, the ghost, been helping the narrator write ghost stories? Why was she going on strike? What condition did she place for providing continued help?

Ans. Helen, the ghost, helped the narrator to write ghost stories because he did not have ideas to write a story. She was going on strike because she and her other co-ghosts were always occupied because of the Ouija Boards. They had to sit at a desk and answer questions which was tiring. She said she would help the narrator further only if he would stop all his friends and acquaintances from using the Ouija Board.

(e) How does the ghost undermine the narrator's faith in his ability to write ghost stories?

Ans. The ghost undermines the narrator's faith in his ability to write ghost stories by telling him that it was she who helped him write ghost stories. She added that she would continue to help him only if he stops his friends and acquaintances from using the Ouija Board.

(f) Why does John want the ghost to disappear before his wife appears on the scene? What impression of his wife's character do you form from his words?

Or **Why does Hallock want the ghost to disappear before his wife appears on the scene?**

Ans. Hallock does not want to lose his wife's faith in him and neither does he want his wife to get scared by seeing a ghost because like all sensitive women, Lavinia was a subject to hysterics (going crazy). This is the reason why he wants the ghost to disappear before his wife appears on the scene.

(g) Why does the narrator hesitate to be a partner to Laura Hinkle during the Ouija Board party?

Ans. The narrator hesitates to be a partner to Laura Hinkle during the Ouija Board party because neither did he wish to use the Ouija Board, because of the ghost's warning, nor did he like the flirtatious behaviour of Laura Hinkle.

(h) What message does the ghost convey to the group that had assembled in the narrator's house? What is their reaction to the message?

Ans. The ghost conveys the message that John has been a traitor as he could not prevent people in the room from playing the Ouija Board. However, all the ladies misunderstand it by thinking that someone named Helen was trying to contact John. The ladies begin to doubt John's loyalty to his wife Lavinia. Most of the ladies are amused but John's wife is annoyed.

(i) Do you agree with the narrator calling the assembly of women 'manipulators'? Give reasons. **Competency Based**

Ans. The word 'manipulators' refers to people who skilfully control anyone or anything. In the story, all the ladies were trying to force John into an uncomfortable situation. The author felt that the ladies were controlling the Ouija Board indicator to spell out his name purposely and so he called them manipulators.

(j) Why is John's wife angry? What does she decide to do?

Ans. John's wife is angry because the Ouija Board was conveying a message from Helen to her husband, which filled her with suspicion about his unfaithfulness to her. She could not tolerate her husband's supposed infidelity and decided to leave him.

(k) Why does John wish himself to be dead.

Ans. John's wife decided to leave him after she suspected him of having an affair with another woman. She wrote a message that she had decided to leave him. Hallock was humiliated by the incident and he felt totally helpless. The utter chaos in his life made him wish that he were dead.

(l) When confronted by Lavinia about his flirtations over the Ouija Board, John insists that 'the affair was quite above-board, I assure you, my love.' Bring out the pun in John's statement.

Ans. A pun is a use of words for double meaning. In Hallock's statement, the pun is on the phrase 'above-board', which means in the open, i.e. without any dishonesty. This is true, as he is not flirting with Helen, the ghost. The other meaning of 'above-board' here relates to the fact that in the party, John and Laura Hinkle were moving the Ouija Board indicator above (on top of) the board.

(m) John's apprehensions about his wife's reaction to her encounter with the ghost are unfounded. Justify.

Or **John was worried and concerned about his wife's response after meeting the ghost. But it proved to be baseless. Justify.** **CBSE 2024**

Ans. Hallock was trying to hide the ghost from Lavinia because he thought she would get scared and faint. After seeing Lavinia's reaction, his apprehensions get diluted because she did not faint; rather she had a broad, satisfied smile over her face. So, his apprehensions turned out to be unfounded.

ON PAGE 48

Q.6 Answer the following questions in detail.

(a) After her reconciliation with her husband, John Hallock, Lavinia writes a letter to her friend expressing how her relationship with him had almost been on the verge of breaking and what saved it. Write her letter.

Ans. 1826, Carnival Road
Camden, New Jersey
15th October, 20XX

My Dear Pamela

How are you? It seems you have been praying for my well-being because the miraculous way in which I have passed the recent crucial phase in my life is surely due to some blessing.

One day, I gifted John an Ouija Board which he did not want to use. He even refused to attend the Ouija Board party which was later arranged. He came later, where I partnered him with Laura Hinkle. To my surprise, the Ouija Board started calling him a 'traitor'. When we asked the Ouija to tell us the name of the ghost, it said it was 'Helen'. I believed that John had been having an affair with the ghost of Helen of Troy. I had enough reasons to leave him.

I regretted doubting John when I learned how I had misunderstood him. There was a ghost who was helping him to write horror stories for a magazine. And it wasn't the ghost of Helen of Troy! It was the ghost of an ordinary Helen who had lived in New York and who had been a writer when she was alive. John was just trying to save me from seeing a ghost. I asked him to pardon me and now we both are happy again.

I am content now because my life has been saved from turmoil.

With love
Lavinia

(b) John Hallock reflects upon his experience with Helen's ghost and in retrospect he finds it quite amusing. All the same he is relieved that he is no longer plagued by it. Ironically, the same ghost inspires his creativity and he writes a diary entry reflecting upon the comical aspect of his experience. Write his diary entry.

Ans. Monday, 15th October, 20XX 9:00 p.m.

Dear Diary

What an experience it was! Seeing a ghost, being embarrassed, my wife wanting to leave me and finally finding a plot for my story. My domestic life was also rescued from turmoil in the bargain.

Helen the ghost gave me some details about herself and it was quite interesting to know that the ghosts had a 'Writer's Inspiration Bureau'. She then asked me to stop my friends and acquaintances from using the Ouija Board as the ghosts had to work hard to answer the questions raised by people using their Ouija Boards.

However, Lavinia gifted me an Ouija Board and called for an Ouija Board party. But the boards started calling me a 'traitor' at the party. My wife started doubting me and decided to leave me. But when she saw Helen in reality, she realised the truth that Helen was only a ghost and not woman. Finally, my purpose has been solved as I now have an excellent plot to write a ghost story.

John

ON PAGE 49-50

Q.7 The narrator and his wife reveal something about their character through their words and actions. We also learn about them from what other people say. Can you pick out the words that describe them from the box given below? Also, pick outlines and instances from the story to illustrate your choice.

shy arrogant loyal clever overconfident manipulative protective self-disparaging suspicious sceptical jealous fearless firm shrewd strong gullible sly creative loves novelty and thrills

Person	Extract from story	What it tells us about the character
John Hallock	1. ...in the end things had always come my way..... somehow I'd always been able to dig one (plot) up for him, so I'd begun to get a bit cocky as to my ability (to write stories).	1. ....
	2. "But my ghosts aren't a bit like you .....".	2. Sceptical
	3. We scout around until we find a writer without ideas and with a mind soft enough to accept impression.	3. gullible
	4.	4. creative
	5.	5. protective
Lavinia Hallock	1.	1. loves novelty and thrills
	2.	2. Spendthrift
	3.	3. Suspicious
	4.	4. Jealous
	5. Buys the Ouija board but says it is for John's research	5. manipulative
	6. Does not flinch when she meets the ghost but talks to her casually	6. strong

Ans. John Hallock

(1) Overconfident

(4) I had often been like that before and in the end things had always come my way… . I didn't in the least know how or why. It had all been rather mysterious.

(5) I threw a protective husband's hand around her to catch her if she fainted.

Lavinia Hallock

(1) "John Hallock," she said distinctly. "I don't propose to do anything of the kind. In the first place they won't exchange things bought at a bargain sale and in the second, if you aren't interested in the other world I am. So there!"

(2) you know I bought the loveliest thing this afternoon.

(3) Lavinia stopped and began to look at me through narrowed lids much as she had done in the library the evening before.

(4) "John," Lavinia demanded like a ward boss, "you are hiding somebody in here! Who is it?" I only waved denial and gurgled in my throat. She went on, "It's bad enough to have you flirt over the Ouija board with that hussy......"

ON PAGE 50-51

Q.8 Gladolia, the narrator's cook, is an African woman. The language she speaks is different from that of the others. This is known as Dialect. A dialect consists of words or phrases that reflect the regional variety of a language. An author often uses a dialect to make the dialogue more authentic. Initially, a dialogue may seem a little difficult to understand. However, as you continue reading, the language becomes more comprehensible. Working in groups, write what Gladolia's words mean as shown.

Column A	Column B
• Misto Hallock	Mister Hallock
• de Missus	
• sho t'inks you's lost!	
• she done 'phone you dis mawnin'	
• fo' de lawd's sake	
• not to stop to argify now	
• I's gwine t' quit.	
• I don't like no hoodoos.	
• I'se done lef' dis place	
• I is	

Ans. 1. the Mrs.
2. she thinks that you are lost
3. she phoned you this morning
4. for the lord's sake
5. do not stop to argue now
6. I am going to quit
7. I don't like hoodoos/ hoodoo magic
8. I am done with this place and I am going to leave this place
9. I am

Q.9 Read and understand the following ghost phrases and expressions.

(a) **To give up the ghost**-to die or to stop trying
(b) **A ghost of a chance**-a poor chance, not likely to happen
(c) **The ghost at the feast**-something or someone that spoils your enjoyment by reminding you of something unpleasant
(d) **Ghost town**-a town which most people have left, abandoned and deserted
(e) **Ghost-write**-to write for someone else
(f) **Lay the ghost of something/somebody (to rest)**-to finally stop being worried or upset by something or someone that has worried or upset you for a long time
(g) **Ghost image**-secondary image, especially, one appearing on a television screen as a white shadow, caused by poor or double reception or by a defect in the receiver
(h) **the ghost of a smile**-faint trace of a smile
(i) **As white as a ghost**-very pale or white in the face

Now, complete the following story by using the appropriate phrases in the blanks given below.

I was alone in a place that bore a deserted look like that of a .... I increased the pace of my footsteps as I walked through the dark forest. I felt someone walking behind me. I turned immediately and spotted the contour of a figure in the form of a .... It smiled at me wickedly. I started shaking with fear and perspiring profusely when I felt its skeletal hand upon my neck. I woke up with a start, relieved that it was only a nightmare.

This was not the first time I had had one. It had all started when I had watched the horrendous horror film with an eerie ghost character that had a scary ghost of a smile on its face. It had been almost a month. The strange thing was that I saw a similar face at the station the next morning. That was uncanny.

I was to attend a dinner at my friend's at Northanger Abbey that night. I had decided to narrate my experience to the group that would assemble there. Although I knew, there was ...... that they would be convinced.

After everyone had finished pouring their drinks to themselves, I cleared my throat and started narrating my spooky experience. However, every one of the group started accusing me of being .... and held me responsible for spoiling the spirit of revelry. I gave up the ghost and sat quietly waiting for the party to be over. Back at home, the fears returned. I knew I had to talk about my experience to somebody to feel better. I have now decided to .... and publish my experience under a pseudonym. Only then can I ....

Ans.
- ghost town
- ghost image
- a ghost of a chance
- the ghost at the feast
- lay the ghost to rest
- ghost write

ON PAGE 52-53

WRITING

Q.11 Do you think a story has an atmosphere? Complete the following blanks to make up your ghost story by choosing the correct options.

A Ghost Story

She opened the......... (secret door/ spaceship's hatch/door of the cottage/cemetery gate/door of the castle/ cockpit)......... (brashly/loudly/silently/ stupidly/ fearfully/ joyously). Standing in front of her was a ....(terrifying/handsome/smelly/ anonymous/ tiny/huge/bossy) ....(policeman/spy/ apparition/ witch/prince/ wizard) with a ....(wand/ rose/rod/ knife/scythe/coded message) in his/her (its) .... (ghoulish /bony/beautiful/fair/manly /gloved/ magical)/hand.

Ans. She opened the secret door fearfully. Standing in front of her was a terrifying apparition with a rose in her bony hand.

REVIEW EXERCISE

Including Previous Years' and Practice Questions

Extract Based Questions

Read the following extracts carefully and answer the questions that follow.

1. So I sat down to write a ghost story. Jenkins was responsible.

"Hallock," he had said to me, "give us another on the supernatural this time. Something to give 'em the horrors; that's what the public wants, and your ghosts are live Propositions." Well, I was in no position to contradict Jenkins.

(a) Who does 'he' refer to?

Ans. 'He' refers to Jenkins.

(b) What did 'he' want from Hallock?

Ans. Jenkins wanted Hallock to write a ghost story for his magazine.

(c) Why had 'he' stressed that he wanted only a 'supernatural'?

Ans. He had made this request because Hallock's ghost stories were very lively and quite popular with the readers.

(d) Why was the narrator not in a position to refuse Jenkins' request?

Ans. Jenkins' magazine had been the only one to print the narrator's stories. So, he could not refuse Jenkins' request to write a ghost story for his magazine.

2. I hadn't the shade of an idea, but at the time that didn't worry me in the least. You see, I had often been like that before.

(a) Who is 'I'? What did he not have an idea about?

Ans. 'I' here refers to John Hallock, the narrator. He did not have any idea about writing a new ghost story for Jenkins.

(b) Why was he not worried?

Ans. He was not worried because whenever he sat down to write a ghost story, ideas came to him naturally.

(c) Which word in the above extract means the same as 'distress'?

Ans. The word 'worry' means the same as 'distress'.

(d) Who does 'you' refer to in the concluding sentence?

Ans. In the concluding sentence, 'you' refers to the reader of this story.

3. Even now whenever Jenkins wanted a ghost, he called on me. And I had never found it healthy to contradict Jenkins. Jenkins always seemed to have an uncanny knowledge as to when the landlord or the grocer was pestering me, and he dunned me for a ghost.

(a) Why is Jenkin's knowledge uncanny ?

Ans. Jenkins always knew, as if through some mysterious powers, when the narrator needed money. Thus, he asked John for a story at that time.

(b) Explain 'he dunned me for a ghost'.

Ans. The phrase means that the editor persistently asked the narrator to write a ghost story for the magazine.

(c) Why was Jenkins confident that he will be able to get a story written by John?

Ans. Jenkins was confident because in the past, John had always been able to write a ghost story when asked by Jenkins.

(d) How did Jenkins trap Hallock to write a story?

Ans. Jenkins trapped Hallock to write a story as Hallock needed money for his basic needs and Jenkins offered him the money for writing a ghost story.

4. '...... such as my wife's shopping and how on Earth I was going to cure her of her alarming tendency to take every new fad that came along and work it to death.'

(a) Who is the speaker here?

Ans. The speaker of these lines is John Hallock.

(b) What does the speaker want to cure his wife of?

Ans. John wants his wife to drop her habit of pursuing every new fad.

(c) What does the phrase 'work it to death' mean?

Ans. The phrase means to follow something to the point of exhaustion.

(d) What was the speaker doing when he said this?

Ans. John was thinking about the plot for writing a ghost story when he said this.

5. 'I sat staring at it and presently noticed something just taking shape. It was exactly like watching one of these moving picture cartoons being put together.'

(a) What was the narrator staring at?

Ans. Hallock was staring at the shadow that started taking a definite shape at the far end of the room.

(b) How was the figure taking shape?

Ans. The shape was forming exactly like moving picture cartoons put together.

(c) Which expression is used for the movement described in these lines?

Ans. 'Moving picture cartoons'.

(d) Why has the phrase 'being put together' been used here and why is it used?

Ans. 'Being put together' means to make something by joining all its parts. The narrator has used it because the view seemed like many small cartoons who were forming a bigger picture of a ghost.

6. We scout around until we find a writer without ideas and with a mind soft enough to accept the impression. The case is brought to the attention of the main office, and one of us is assigned to it. When that case is finished we bring in a report.

(a) What does 'we' refer to in the above lines?

Ans. 'We' in the given extract refers to the members of the Writer's Inspiration Bureau.

(b) How does the context of the given extract fit John Hallock?

Ans. The context of the given extract fits John Hallock as he is one of the writers scouted by 'we'.

(c) Which character of the speaker is highlighted in the extract? State in one word.

Ans. Creative

(d) 'We scout around...' What purpose does the scouting serve?

Ans. The purpose of the scouting is to look for writers who don't have sufficient ideas to write their stories. Then, 'we' help these writers in giving shape to their thought so that interesting stories could be written.

7. "Get all your friends and acquaintances to stop using the Ouija board, and then we'll start helping you to write."

(a) Identify the speaker of the above lines.

Ans. The speaker of the given lines is a ghost named Helen.

(b) To whom has this request been made?

Ans. The request has been made to John Hallock, a ghost story writer.

(c) Why had the speaker made this request?

Ans. The speaker had made this request because she and her companions have to answer the questions asked through Ouija Boards and thus have no time to help writers.

(d) How has the speaker been 'helping you to write'?

Ans. The speaker had been helping the writer by giving shape to his ideas regarding ghost stories.

8. "Madam, I must ask you to leave, and at once. Consider the impression if you were seen here ...."

The ghost nodded, and began, very sensibly, I thought, to demobilise and evaporate.

First the brogans on her feet grew misty until I could see the floor through them, then the affection spread to her knees and gradually extended upward. By this time my wife was opening the door.

(a) Who does the narrator address as 'Madam' in the extract?

Ans. The narrator addresses the ghost of Helen as 'Madam'.

(b) Why does the speaker want the listener to leave immediately?

Ans. John wants the ghost of Helen to leave immediately as he doesn't want his wife to see them together.

(c) What might happen if the listener is seen?

Ans. John thought that his wife might faint out of fear or become hysterical on seeing the ghost.

(d) What do you mean by 'impression'?

Ans. The word 'impression' means 'effect'.

9. 'I don't propose to do anything of the kind. In the first place they won't exchange things bought at a bargain sale, and in the second, if you aren't interested in the other world I am, so there!"

(a) What does the speaker refer to by saying "anything of the kind"?

Ans. John wanted Lavinia to get rid of the Ouija Board by returning it to the shop and buying something else in exchange. Lavinia refers to this as "anything of the kind."

(b) What has been bought at a bargain sale?

Ans. An Ouija Board has been bought by Lavinia at a bargain sale.

(c) **What does "the other world" refer to?**

Ans. 'The other world' refers to the supernatural world, the world of ghosts and spirits.

(d) **Why does Lavinia not want to exchange the Ouija Board?**

Ans. Lavinia does not want to exchange the Ouija Board because she is interested in the world of spirits and ghosts.

10. 'I had hardly seated myself at the desk when there came a tap at the door and a white slip of paper slid under it. I unfolded it and read.....' Dear John "I am going back to my grandmother. My lawyer will communicate with you later."

(a) **Who had written the slip of paper? What was written on it?**

Ans. John's wife, Lavinia, had written the slip of paper. Lavinia wrote that she was going back to her grandmother and her lawyer would communicate with John later.

(b) **Why had Lavinia written the slip of paper?**

Ans. Lavinia had written the slip of paper to Hallock because she doubted John's marital fidelity, so she wanted to divorce him.

(c) **Describe the mood of the writer of the message and the reason behind her mood.**

Ans. The writer, Lavinia, was angry with her husband, Hallock, as she felt that he was cheating on her.

(d) **Why is the writer going back?**

Ans. The writer (Lavinia) is going back to her maiden home and is going to file papers for a divorce as she thinks that John is having a secret love affair.

11. That suitcase had an air of solid finality about it, and its lock leered at me brassily.
I leaped from my chair with unaccustomed agility and sprang in front of my wife.
I must conceal that awful phantom from her, at any risk!

(a) **Why did the narrator spring in front of his wife?**

Ans. The narrator sprang in front of his wife so that she would not be able to see the ghost standing behind him.

(b) **Why did he take such a risk ?**

Ans. He took the risk because his wife, being sensitive and scared even of a mouse, would be terrified of the ghost and become hysterical or faint.

(c) **What do you mean by 'brassily'?**

Ans. The word 'brassily' means 'rudely'.

(d) **Whom does the narrator address as 'phantom' here?**

Ans. The narrator addresses Helen, the ghost, as 'phantom' here.

Short Answer Type Questions

Answer the following questions in 30-40 words.

1. John Hallock could never displease Jenkins. Why?

Ans. John Hallock could never displease (make angry) Jenkins because he was the only publisher who published his stories and was a source of income. Moreover, he could not risk Jenkins getting angry and withdrawing the offer or not giving him any work in the future.

2. Hallock's 'ghosts' were 'live propositions'. How could he pen down ghost-special stories?

Ans. Hallock never considered himself as a specialist at writing ghost stories. However, mysteriously, every time he needed some inspiration for a story, an idea would come to his mind. Actually, Helen, a ghost, was helping him write such realistic ghost stories although he was not aware of it.

3. Bring out the irony in the statement: 'I did not specialise in ghost stories, but more or less, they seemed to specialise in me.'

Ans. Though John Hallock did not consider himself a good writer of ghost stories, as expressed in this statement, the readers of the magazine loved it because the stories were very good.

4. In what sense does Hallock claim that ghosts had specialised in him?

Ans. Hallock did not write ghost stories out of choice. However, it was his ghost stories that were popular among the readers. Hallock believed that ghosts had specialised in him because whenever he thought of writing a ghost story, he could easily get ready inspiration.

5. What happened when Hallock sat down at his desk and waited for ideas for his story?

Ans. When Hallock sat down at his desk, he could not think of any plot. He stared at the ceiling and said to himself, "This writing business is delightful, isn't it?" As if in response, the ghost of Helen appeared and answered his question, saying, "Yes ... I should say it is."

6. How did the narrator react to the gradual appearance of the ghost?

Ans. John was trying to write a ghost story but got distracted and was thinking about something else when the ghost of Helen gradually appeared before him. He was initially scared of the ghost taking shape before him. However, his fear was shortlived and he faced the ghost quite boldly.

7. What did the ghost tell about herself before she became a ghost?

Ans. Helen appeared before John and told him that she was a ghost from the Writer's Inspiration Bureau. However, before that, in her human life, she used to write and later, worked as a reader in a magazine. As she knew the work was quite tiresome, she along with other ghosts formed the Writer's Inspiration Bureau.

8. What was the purpose behind organising the Writer's Inspiration Bureau? How does this bureau function?

Ans. The Writer's Inspiration Bureau was an organisation formed by some ghosts to provide inspiration to struggling writers. As a rule, the bureau members helped writers without ideas to write successfully by giving ideas and inspiration to their soft and impressionistic minds.

9. Why did the ghost want people to stop using the Ouija board?

Or Why were the ghosts angry with the Ouija Board fanatics?

Or Why is Helen the ghost, upset with people using Ouija boards?

Ans. Helen, the ghost, wanted to stop the people from using Ouija boards because all of the ghosts were overworked and tired from answering the queries of people all the time. Now, they had no time for amusement or rest. They didn't even have enough energy to properly do their work, as evidenced with how difficult it was for Helen to materialse after the Ouija board party. This is why they were very angry with the Ouija board fanatics and wished for them to stop using the Ouija boards.

10. Lavinia felt that her husband's problems could be solved with help of the Ouija Board : Do you agree? CBSE 2024 C

Ans. Yes, I believe that Lavinia felt that the Ouija Board would help her husband write his stories. Now, he would not have to research old books in the public library. He could have a face-to-face talk with legendary characters like William the conqueror, Napoleon or Helen of Troy. With the help of an Ouija Board, he could write whatever he needed without any trouble.

11. What does Ouija board in 'A Shady Plot' symbolise ? CBSE 2025

Ans. In 'A Shady Plot', the Ouija board symbolises the characters' curiosity about the supernatural and their desire to communicate with spirits. It represents both their fascination with the unknown and the potential dangers of trying to control or connect with forces beyond their understanding.

12. Why couldn't John Hallock give his whole time to writing?

Ans. John had a family to provide for and was not a renowned writer. There was only one magazine which published his work. Obviously, this couldn't provide him with the money to meet all his needs. Hence, he worked as a bookkeeper in a lumber company.

13. Why did John Hallock run away from the party before it was over?

Ans. During the Ouija Board game, everyone in the hall using the Ouija Board received a similar message. A ghost named Helen called John a traitor. All the ladies were curious that someone named Helen was trying to give a message about John. The ladies begin to doubt John of having some affair with Helen. Thus embarrassed and ashamed, and seeing his wife Lavinia growing suspicious about him, John ran away from the hall.

14. Why did John's wife want to go to her grandmother's house?

Ans. Lavinia was furious with John. She thought that John was having a clandestine (secret) affair, after the Ouija Board announced that a woman named Helen was calling her husband a traitor. She was deeply hurt due to his supposed infidelity and wanted to leave him. As a result, she wanted to go back to her grandmother's house.

15. What problems did Helen, the ghost, cause in John Hallock's life?

Ans. The ghost of Helen disrupted Hallock's relationship with his wife. Lavinia suspected Hallock of having a secret affair with a woman named Helen. She also called Hallock 'traitor' on the Ouija Board. Thinking that her husband had been a traitor, Lavinia became hysterical and decided to get separated from Hallock for his betrayal of her trust.

16. How did Lavinia react on seeing the ghost of Helen of Troy? Why was it contrary to what Hallock expected?

Or How did Lavinia react when she saw Helen the ghost? CBSE 2017

Ans. Lavinia reacted quite normally and was not worried on seeing the ghost inside John's room. In fact, she was relieved to see a ghost and not a real woman. John, on the contrary, had feared that she would faint or become hysterical on seeing a real ghost in front of her.

17. What impression do you form about Lavinia?

Or What kind of woman is Lavinia?

Ans. Lavinia is a jealous, possessive and sensitive woman who is subject to hysterics. She is also impulsive and takes decisions without considering the overall scenario. She is also extravagant and spends a lot of money on the latest fashions and trends.

18. Why was John Hallock eager to burn the Ouija Board?

Ans. John Hallock was eager to burn the Ouija Board because it created many problems in his life. His wife started doubting him because of the misunderstanding due to the board. Also, the maid was scared of the board and had announced her departure. Thus, the board was the root cause of the entire problem.

19. Comment on Elsie Brown's writing style in the story 'A Shady Plot'. **CBSE SQP 2023**

Ans. Elsie Brown's writing style in the story is characterised by its light and humorous tone. The story is written from the first person point of view of the protagonist, John Hallock. Brown's writing style is concise and clear, with a good use of dialogue and description to create vivid scenes and characters. She uses irony and satire to poke fun at the publishing industry and its practices. Overall, her writing style effectively conveys the story's humour and underlying message, making it an enjoyable and thought provoking read.

Long Answer Type Questions

Answer the following questions in 150 words.

1. How does the lesson 'A Shady Plot' remind us that man has no right to invoke the supernatural through Ouija Boards, Tarot cards, etc to solve his problems, and that one should face life boldly and overcome difficulties using wit and intelligence?

Ans. The world of the supernatural is something meant to be beyond the reach of humans. However, man, in his quest for the unknown, has explored this forbidden realm and has devised various means to communicate with supernatural beings. There are innumerable people who claim to use Ouija Boards, Tarot cards, planchette, etc. and invoke the help of supernatural elements.

The lesson 'A Shady Plot' too deals with this fact as one of its major themes. Though the story shows a ghost willingly offering help to a writer, this ghost does object to the use of Ouija Boards for any such communication or invocation. We see the turmoil that the narrator and his wife experience when she brings home an Ouija Board and throws an Ouija Board party. This is a reminder that man should not try to mess with the forbidden land of the spirits and rely upon his own wit and intelligence to solve his problems.

2. Lavinia suspects Hallock of cheating on her and threatens to leave him. She behaves like a wife who does not try to find out details before taking an extreme step. Do you think she was justified in taking such a step? What do you learn from her behaviour?

Ans. Lavinia, John Hallock's wife, is possessive of her husband. She cannot tolerate the idea of him having an affair with another woman as she concluded from his peculiar behaviour and the message the Ouija Board gave at the party. She suspects Hallock of infidelity and is full of jealousy and anger. Thus, she takes an irrational decision of leaving him and filing for a divorce. However, she is not justified in taking such a step, as she should first have confronted her husband and confirmed what her observations had made her conclude.

From her behaviour, we learn that relationships are dependent upon trust and her trust was overcome by jealousy. Moreover, when the actual truth is revealed, and she understands that it is only a female ghost who is trying to give him some ideas for a horror story, she realises her folly of unnecessarily suspecting her husband and she apologises by going back into his arms. Lavinia should have tried to find out the details before taking such an extreme step.

3. Relationships are dependent upon trust. However, small misunderstandings, if not cleared soon, destroy the best of relationships. John's marriage was on the verge of a dreadful end. What mistakes did the Hallocks make in their relationship?

Ans. Trust in a relationship has to be from both sides. One cannot try to hide things and think of being trusted. The Hallocks made two grave mistakes which led to some sourness in their relationship.

First, John tried to conceal facts from Lavinia, although she was his wife and had every right to know what the real story was. The first time when the ghost of Helen was in his presence, he did not tell his wife about it. Though this was due to his concern for his wife's well-being, as she might have become hysterical on hearing about a ghost. However, his fear was misplaced, as proved near the end of the story, when Lavinia actually sees the ghost.

Second, Lavinia doubted her husband and considered him a cheater without going into the details of what was happening. Her trust was overcome by jealousy. All this would not have happened if John had told Lavinia the truth and Lavinia would have trusted her husband enough to find out the real truth before deciding to leave him.

4. The story, 'A Shady Plot' triggers the age old debate on superstitions and the supernatural. Is it good to believe in superstitions ? What impact does it have on human health? How can one get rid of superstitions? **Competency Based**

Ans. The story, 'A Shady Plot' triggers the age old debate on superstitions and the supernatural. It questions whether ghosts do exist and whether supernatural events happen and whether spirits like Helen control our lives.

No, it is not good to believe in superstitions. Superstitions can lead to unnecessary troubles and misunderstandings. Just as in the case of Lavinia, who believed the message given by the Ouija Board and suspected her husband of having an affair with a woman named Helen. It is when she threw away the Ouija Board did all the misunderstandings get cleared and their life went back to normal.

Superstitions can affect one's mental health adversely. One forgets to think rationally and practically. Superstitions exploit one's innocence and ignorance and ruin one's domestic life. Thus, one should get rid of such superstitious beliefs and instead conquer such fears by having knowledge about the world around.

5. The story of 'A Shady Plot' is woven around the theme of conjuring up the spirits of dead people in order to know the unknown. Do you think it is moral to conjure up spirits and expect them to solve our problems?

Ans. The world of the supernatural is something that is supposed to be beyond the reach of humans. Man, in his quest of the unknown, has time and again explored this forbidden realm. He has devised various means to communicate with supernatural beings. There are innumerable people, who claim to use Ouija Boards, Tarot cards, etc. and invoke the help of supernatural elements. However, sometimes such communication or invocation can have a negative impact as well. Supernatural forces are much stronger than humans and, if disturbed, can create havoc resulting into a loss of life. Thus, it is immoral to conjure up spirits and disturb them. In the story, the ghost of Helen raises a strong objection to the use of Ouija Boards. Man should, thus, not encroach upon the forbidden land of the spirits and rely upon his own wit and intelligence to solve his problems.

ASSESSMENT EXERCISE

Extract Based Questions

Read the following extracts carefully and answer the questions that follow.

1. I hadn't the shade of an idea, but at the time that didn't worry me in the least. You see, I had often been like that before and in the end things had always come my way– I didn't in the least know how or why. It had all been rather mysterious. You understand I didn't specialise in ghost stories, but more or less they seemed to specialise in me.
   (a) In which shade does the passage show the narrator ?
   (b) In which field is the narrator a specialist?
   (c) What does the narrator mean by the last sentence in the extract?
   (d) Write the synonym of 'shade' in the first sentence.
2. I found others who had suffered similarly and between us we organised the 'Writer's Inspiration Bureau'. We scout around until we find a writer without ideas and with a mind soft enough to accept impression.
   (a) Who founded the 'Writer's Inspiration Bureau'?
   (b) Why was the Bureau formed?
   (c) What do you mean by 'scout around'?
   (d) Why do writers have to be ones with 'a mind soft enough to accept impression'?

Short Answer Type Questions

Answer the following questions in 30-40 words.

1. What did Hallock tell himself when his mind had reached a state of imbecility ? Who answered his question?
2. How did John conclude that the woman in his room was a real ghost?
3. Hallock's meeting the ghost was by chance. What chanced this meeting?
4. What kind of works were ghosts in the past assigned to?
5. What was Hallock's premonitary chill?

Long Answer Type Questions

Answer the following questions in 150 words.

1. "Why she says it's you, Mr Hallock. What does she mean? ... Lavinia stopped and began to look at me through narrowed lids.
   Do you think Lavinia is justified in basing her suspicions on the Ouija Board? Give reasons for your answer.
2. "You'd never guess in the world. It's the duckiest, darlingest Ouija Board, and so cheap! I got it at a bargain sale. Why, what's the matter, John ?"
   Why are some people crazy for new and unusual things? Is there any intrinsic or perennial value of fads in life ? Write your answer in 150 words.
3. Jenkins always seemed to have an uncanny knowledge as to when the landlord or the grocer was pestering me, and he dunned me for a ghost. And somehow I'd always been able to dig one up for him, so I'd begun to get a bit cocky as to my ability.
   Why do people write ? Do you think they are exploited by publishers? If yes, how? Respond to all these questions in a letter to your younger brother who wants to take up writing as a career.
4. Family relationships sometimes undergo checks and trials. The best way to overcome such trials is to be frank with each other. Discuss.

Patol Babu, Film Star

by Satyajit Ray

CHAPTER 5

CHAPTER SUMMARY

'Patol Babu, Film Star' is a story about Patol Babu, an old man, who once had been in great demand for stage shows. However, after losing his job, he had to struggle for a living and had to start doing various odd jobs. When finally his friend offers him a role in a film, he gets very excited about it.

However, when he comes to know that he has just one word to say in the film, he gets very disappointed in the beginning. However, he controls his emotions and remembers what he had been taught by his mentor. He puts all his heart and soul into his performance and performs his role with great ease and perfection.

Patol Babu and His Theatre Days

Patol Babu was a 52 year old, short and bald-headed man who lived in Calcutta with his wife. At one time, he had a real passion for the stage and was always in demand. He had performed in *Jatras*, amateur theatricals and plays. His name had appeared in handbills on countless occasions. There was a time when people bought tickets especially to see his performance. That was when he used to live at Kanchrapara. He used to work in a railway factory there. However, he left the job in 1934 when he was offered a higher salary in a clerical post with Hudson and Kimberley in Calcutta.

Patol Babu's Struggle to Earn a Living

Life was running quite smoothly for some time till Patol Babu lost his nine year old job due to the war. Ever since then, Patol Babu had struggled to make a living. He tried every means of earning a livelihood without ever succeeding in improving his lot.

Nishikanto Ghosh Makes an Offer to Patol Babu

Nishikanto Ghosh lived three houses away from Patol Babu. He was a friendly person. One day, he visited Patol Babu early in the morning and told him that he had recommended his name to his youngest brother-in-law, Naresh Dutt, who was looking for an actor for a scene in a film they were shooting. Patol Babu's appearance matched with that of the character, a man in his fifties, short and bald-headed. They would also pay him for his part.

Patol Babu Accepts the Offer

Patol Babu did not expect such an offer would come to him at the beginning of the day. He was so excited at the prospect of acting in a film that he willingly accepted the offer without even asking about the payment. Naresh Dutt came to meet Patol Babu the next day and explained to him that he had to play the part of an absent-minded, short-tempered pedestrian. He told him the venue for the shot along with details about his attire and then, left.

Patol Babu Reaches the Location on Time

After Naresh Dutt left, Patol Babu gave the news to his wife. He was reminded of his past days when he worked on the stage. He wished this offer would be his first step to rise to fame and fortune. His wife warned him not to count the chickens before they were hatched.

On the day of the shooting, Patol Babu was quite punctual to reach the shooting venue. There he saw that a big crowd had gathered. He waited there for Naresh Dutt because he was the only one whom he knew. He stood in the shade of a paan shop and waited till he was called for his turn. Soon, Naresh, who was standing at the entrance of the building, called out to him. The man had got his name wrong and addressed him as 'Atul Babu'. He, then, commented on Patol Babu's punctuality.

Patol Babu Gets His Dialogue

Patol Babu was working in a film in which the main lead was Chanchal Kumar and the director was Baren Mullick. Patol Babu was made to wait for a long time. This made him very impatient as he could not wait for his turn to act and show his talent. After waiting for long, Patol Babu thought about his dialogue. He did not know what he was suppossed to say.

It didn't matter if the part was small but he had to make the most of it and had to learn his lines beforehand. In vain, he requested Naresh Dutt a number of times to let him have his dialogue so that he could rehearse it. Every time he was asked to wait. Finally, his dialogue was given to him written on a piece of paper.

Patol Babu is Shocked and Disappointed

Patol Babu was shocked and disappointed when he read his dialogue which comprised only one word, 'Oh!'. He felt that these people were making fun of him. The members of the film unit tried to convince him that his role was a crucial one in the film. However, Patol Babu thought that he had been fooled by the film unit.

Then, the whole thing was explained to him by saying that there were hundreds who didn't have even a word to say in the film. They just had to walk past the cameras and some didn't even walk; they just stood at a spot. He could not stand in one place any more as his legs felt heavy. So, he moved ahead to the office beyond the paan shop and sat down on the stairs. He thought that he should not waste his time on an insignificant role like that. The thought of going to an acquaintance Karali Babu's house to listen to Kali hymns appealed to him better.

Patol Babu Remembers His Mentor

Initially, Patol Babu was much stressed to play this part. However, soon, he settled down because it had become a routine for him to accept things as they came. His thoughts went back to his theatre days. Then he recalled the words of his mentor, Mr. Gogon Pakrashi, who was a wonderful actor with no trace of vanity in him.

He was a saintly person and a very good actor. He often used to say that an actor must never consider a part beneath his dignity, however small it is. Instead, he should make the most of the opportunity. It is the duty of the actor to get the essence of his role and serve it up to the audience for their edification.

Patol Babu Practises His Dialogue Many Times

The memory of his mentor made him bow his head in obedience. Now, he started practising his one word dialogue and made an amazing discovery that this one word, when spoken in different ways, carried different shades of meaning. He suddenly felt that a true actor could make a mark with this simple exclamation. He kept rehearsing his role all alone for a long time till he was called for his shot.

Patol Babu Gets Ready for the Shot

At last, Patol Babu's turn came. Now, he had settled well into his role. The real artist had taken him over. He was briefed about his role by the director. In the scene, he had to collide with Chanchal Kumar who was in a hurry to move ahead. On being hurt due to the collision, he had to remark 'Oh!'.

Before the shot, he told the director that if he had a newspaper in his hand while colliding, the scene would look more real as he would appear busy and absent-minded, as required by the role. The director agreed immediately and he was also given a moustache which suited him a lot.

Before the shot, Patol Babu carefully calculated the number of steps to be taken, the speed at which he was to walk, the emotions he had to portray. He mixed the emotion of irritation and surprise in his dialogue and the collision took place at the most appropriate time. The shot was okayed in a single take and everyone appreciated Patol Babu's performance.

Patol Babu Disappears without Being Paid

After the shoot, Patol Babu went back to the paan shop and felt immensely satisfied. He had done his job really well.

Even after all these years of struggle, he had not lost his acting talent. He was asked to wait a little for the payment but he left the location without waiting to be paid. It is true that he needed money very badly, but what was twenty rupees when measured against the intense satisfaction of a small job done with perfection and dedication.

Ten minutes later when Naresh Dutt came looking for him, he could not find him and was surprised that the actor had left the location without getting his payment.

Word Meaning

Word	Meaning
genial	amiable, friendly
nonentity	insignificant person
beyond his wildest dreams	in a way he had not imagined
strapping	well built
aubergines	garden egg (brinjal)
verged on obsession	could not think of anything else
amateur	non-professional
smooth sailing	having no problems
toying with the idea	considering an idea
retrenchment	cutback in employees
recalls at times with a sigh	sometimes remembers past events and experiences fondly
thunderous twang	deafening sound
diffidence	shyness
cast an appraising look	to consider or examine somebody or something and form an opinion about that person or thing
rise to fame and fortune	becoming famous and wealthy
counting your chickens again before they're hatched	thinking of success again before it has actually happened
make a go of it	become successful

Word	Meaning
oblong	diamond shaped
muffed	messed up
hubbub	noise made by many people talking at the same time
gigantic hoax	huge prank
embezzlement	cheating
stifling	suffocating
pompous	spectacular
trivial	unimportant
tract of vanity	trace of pride
edification	enlightenment
obeisance	respect
inflection	tone
enunciating	uttering, pronouncing
apathy	indifference
strides	steps
perspicacity	ability to understand somebody or something quickly and accurately
excruciating	awful
blunted his sensibility	reduced his acting talent

Textbook FOLDER

Here, we have covered questions given in the CBSE Textbook along with their answers.

ON PAGE 67

Q.3 Answer the following questions briefly.

(a) What was the news that Nishikanto Ghosh gave Patol Babu?

Ans. The news that Nishikanto Babu gave to Patol Babu was regarding a role in a film. He told Patol Baby that his brother-in law, who was in the film business, was looking for an actor for a film they were shooting. The character he described reminded Nishikanto Babu of Patol Babu so he gave him his address and asked him to get in touch with him.

(b) How did Patol Babu react? Why?

Ans. Patol Babu was very excited. Going through a mundane life and a routine existence, he never expected such news at the age of fifty-two, when he had given up acting twenty years ago and was living life like a common man.

(c) Why did Patol Babu lose his first job in Calcutta?

***Or* Why did Patol Babu come to Calcutta?**

***Or* What job did Patol Babu have in Calcutta and why did he leave it?**

Ans. Patol Babu had to leave his first job in Calcutta because there was a sudden retrenchment (cut back in employees) in his office due to the war.

(d) How does Patol Babu reconcile to the dialogue given to him?

Ans. Patol Babu initially lost his temper when he came to know about his dialogue. He later regained composure when he remembered the advice of his mentor and guru Mr. Gogon Pakrashi. The advice helped Patol Babu reconcile to the dialogue given to him.

(e) Who was Mr. Pakrashi? How do his words help Patol Babu in enacting his role?

***Or* What made Patol Babu remember Mr. Pakrashi?**

***Or* What changed Patol Babu's mind about the small role allotted to him?**

Ans. Mr. Pakrashi was Patol Babu's mentor and guru. His words proved to be a source of inspiration to Patol Babu at the time of the shooting. After remembering his words, he was able to fight with his initial apprehensions and go ahead with enacting his role.

(f) Patol Babu was a meticulous man. Elucidate.

Ans. Patol Babu was a meticulous man because he rehearsed well before his shot. Although his part was very small, he wanted to deliver it with perfection and at one go. He rehearsed his dialogue in various ways with different emotions in order to come out with the best one.

(g) Why did Mr. Mullick turn down Patol Babu's request for a rehearsal?

Ans. Mr. Mullick turned down Patol Babu's request for a rehearsal because they had to perform the scene in sunlight and there was a large patch of cloud approaching. To finish the shot off fast, he turned down his request.

(h) What were the special touches that Patol Babu gave to his role to make it more authentic?

Ans. Patol Babu practised his dialogue in different ways. He discovered that when 'Oh!' was uttered in different ways, it could express various emotions. He gave it various attempts to come out with the best one, which was his way to make his role authentic. Also, he persuaded the director to allow him to hold a newspaper in his hand, as it would make the collision more authentic.

ON PAGE 67-68

Q.4 Discuss the following questions in detail and write the answers in your notebooks.

(a) 'I hope the part calls for some dialogue'. Who says this? Why does he/she ask this question?

Ans. Patol Babu says these words to Naresh Dutt. He asks this question because he was overwhelmed at the proposal of acting in a film. He took this very seriously and desired for a proper preparation. He wanted to practise his part before the shooting so that he could do full justice to it.

(b) "Were these people pulling his legs? Was the whole thing a gigantic hoax? A meek, harmless man like him and they had to drag him into the middle of the city to make a laughing stock out of him. How could anyone be so cruel?" Why does Patol Babu have these thoughts?

Ans. When he came to know what his dialogue and role was, Patol Babu was taken aback. He felt humiliated because at one time he had been a very famous amateur stage actor. After having been an actor in demand, it was very difficult for him to accept such a short and insignificant role. Thus, he comes up with these thoughts in his anger and irritation.

(c) Patol Babu is an amateur actor for whom a walk-on part in a movie turns into an ultimate challenge. Discuss.

Ans. It is true to say that Patol Babu is an amateur actor for whom a walk-on part in a movie turns into an ultimate challenge. When Patol Babu got his role, he was very upset for getting such a small insignificant role when he had, a few years ago, been a popular amateur artist. Thus, the first challenge for him was to accept the role. He was able to do so when he remembered the words of his mentor, who had told him that no role was small. Therefore, he took this role as a challenge and practiced to deliver his single worded dialogue in the best way possible.

(d) Do you agree with the statement that Patol Babu is a practical man who comes to terms with whatever life has to offer? Give reasons for your answer.

***Or* Patol Babu is a practical man who comes to terms with whatever life has to offer. Support your answer quoting examples from the text.**

***Or* One must accept life as it comes and not grumble about it. Explain this statement with reference to the story of Patol Babu, Film Star.**

Ans. Patol Babu was a practical man who took the ups and downs of life in a positive way. During his youth, he was a popular amateur stage actor when he worked in the railway factory at Kanchrapara. When he was offered a clerical job in a British company in Kolkata at a higher salary, he shifted there. Unfortunately, due to sudden retrenchment in his office due to the war, he lost his job. Since then, he had struggled hard to make a living but never gave up. He tried his hands at many odd jobs but in vain. Then, he accepted the offer of working for a small role in a film being made. Though it was just a one word dialogue, he worked hard to rehearse his part so that he could do justice to it. He did not grumble that the role was too small for him.

Thus, it is true that one must accept life as it comes and not grumble about it. One should be practical enough to move ahead in life despite the struggles.

(e) Why does Patol Babu walk away before he can be paid for his role? What does this reveal about his character?

***Or* Why couldn't Naresh Dutt find Patol Babu to make the payment for the role he had played?**

***Or* Patol Babu doesn't collect his payment after his role is over. Why?**

Ans. Patol Babu had walked away after the shot without taking the payment because he knew that the money he would be paid could not match the satisfaction that he had got from giving his best to the role. Material gain had lost its sheen in comparison to his immense satisfaction in his performance. This shows that Patol Babu was a high-value person who gave priority to his self-respect the most. He acted in his part of the film perfectly by putting all his efforts. So, he thought it would be disrespecting his art and acting skills by taking money.

(f) Do you think making a movie is an easy job? Discuss with reference to the story.

Ans. Movie-making is extremely tiring, painful and a long process. It involves extreme hard work. The unit of a movie needs hundreds of staff who have to carry out different tasks. Arrangements for shooting at a particular location can be cumbersome (difficult) and time consuming. In case of an outdoor shoot, crowd management is another headache.

ON PAGE 68

Q.5 Here are some lines from the lesson. What do they tell us about Patol Babu's character? You may take help from the words given in the table below or find some of your own from the dictionary. The first one has been done for you.

passionate actor, diligent, unassuming, talented genial, mercenary, short-tempered, introvert, meticulous, modest, humble, arrogant

(a) That an offer to act in a film could come to a 52-year-old nonentity like him was beyond his wildest dreams unassuming; modest

(b) Indeed, there was a time when people bought tickets especially to see him ....

(c) 'I was with Hudson and Kimberley for nine years and wasn't late for a single day.' ....

(d) It didn't matter if the part was small, but, if he had to make the most of it, he had to learn his lines beforehand. How small he would feel if he muffed in the presence of so many people ....

(e) Patol Babu cleared his throat and started enunciating the syllable in various ways. Along with that he worked out how he would react physically when the collision took place-how his features would be twisted in pain, how he would fling out his arms, how his body would crouch to express both pain and surprise-all these he performed in various ways in front of a large glass window ....

(f) It is true that he needed money very badly, but what was twenty rupees when measured against the intense satisfaction of a small job done with perfection and dedication? ....

Ans. (b) passionate actor (c) diligent

(d) meticulous (e) talented

(f) modest, humble

ON PAGE 68-69

Q.6 **Here are some lines from the lesson. Match the meanings of the underlined words with their meanings listed below.**

(a)	Then he had a job in a Bengali firm which he <u>gave up</u> in disgust when his boss began to treat him in too high-handed a fashion	stimulate the imagination
(b)	A faint memory was <u>stirred up</u> in Patol Babu's mind.	to surrender or relinquish
(c)	At first he opened a variety store which he had to <u>wind up</u> after five years.	staged
(d)	In Jatras, in amateur theatricals, in plays <u>put up</u> by the club in his neighbourhood, Patol Babu was always in demand	to gain control over one's actions
(e)	Patol Babu was about to step forward when he was <u>pulled up</u> short by a voice shouting 'Silence!'	shut down
(f)	Patol Babu <u>pulled himself together</u>	stopped

Ans. (a) to surrender or relinquish

(b) stimulate the imagination

(c) shut down (d) staged (e) stopped

(f) to gain control over one's actions

Q.7 **After Patol Babu returns home he recounts his experience in front of the camera to his wife. In pairs write out the exchange in the form of a dialogue and enact it before the class. You may start like this....**

Patol Babu's wife So, what happened at the shooting today? Did you get to do your role?

Patol Babu Oh, yes, I had the time of my life................

Ans. **Patol Babu's wife** So, what happened at the shooting today? Did you get to do your role?

Patol Babu Oh, yes. I had the time of my life. I have got another experience in film making for my acting skills today.

Patol Babu's wife Oh, really! How exciting you found film making journey?

Patol Babu Film making is a collaboration work where the entire team works their individual parts. All members including technicians, editors, director, actors, makeup man, camera man, etc. work hard to make a beautiful movie. Director constantly gives instruction to present everything in a perfect way and he takes multiple shots of actors until he feels satisfied with a final one.

Patol Babu's wife That's great! Who was the director of that film?

Patol Babu He is Baren Mullick.

Patol Babu's wife Okay, fine. Now, tell me about your role, what was it and how you did it?

Patol Babu It was a short role in a big situation with some minimum dialogue. However, I tried to give my best to create the situation beautifully.

Patol Babu's wife Amazing! Will you have dinner now?

Patol Babu Yes, let's have our dinner together.

WRITING TASK

Q.9 **Patol Babu writes a letter to Nishikanto Ghosh to thank him for being instrumental in his getting a role in a film. He also shares his experience at the film shoot including the excitement and deep satisfaction that he derived from the same. Write the letter in about 200 words.**

Ans. 1504, Nepal Bhattacharji Lane, Kalighat

Kolkata-700026

15th September, 20XX

My Dear Nishikanto Babu

How are you? I am writing you this letter to express my sincere gratitude. I would like to thank you for the chance you gave me, the chance which has left me with a great sense of satisfaction.

I had initial apprehensions when you offered me the role. When I reached the shot I came to know that I hardly had a dialogue in the film. I just had to collide with Chanchal Kumar, the famous actor and on being hurt, had to say 'Oh!'.

I was very disappointed and felt humiliated to get such a trivial role, but later I was reminded of my guru's words.

He had taught me that it is the actor's duty to squeeze the last drop of meaning out of his lines for the audience.

Due to his words, I was infused with a new vision and youthful energy. First, I rehearsed my dialogue by speaking 'Oh!' differently. I gave different inflections to it and added emotions to it for the required purpose. Then, with full vigour I gave my shot at one go. Everybody was impressed and I was highly satisfied.

This small role helped me to bring out my talent. I didn't feel necessary to take any payment for the role as my biggest payment was the satisfaction I had derived and the monetary payment would interfere with it.

I am very thankful to you for recommending me for the role.

With best wishes

Patol Babu

REVIEW EXERCISE

Including Previous Years' and Practice Questions

Extract Based Questions

Read the following extracts carefully and answer the questions that follow.

1. He said he was looking for an actor for a scene in a film they're now shooting. The way he described the character- fiftyish, short, bald-headed-it reminded me of you. So I gave him your address and asked him to get in touch with you directly. I hope you won't turn him away. They'll pay you, of course.'

(a) What is meant by the phrase 'to get in touch'?

Ans. The phrase means 'to contact'.

(b) To whom does 'him' refer to?

Ans. 'Him' refers to Nishikanto Babu's youngest brother-in-law, Naresh Dutt.

(c) Why would they pay the listener?

Ans. They would pay Patol Babu for acting out a role in a movie.

(d) What is the significance of using 'of course' in the end?

Ans. 'Of course' is suggestive of the emphasis on the idea that the listener will be paid for his services to them.

2. 'Well, yes or no?' asked Nishikanto Babu. 'I believe you did some acting on the stage at one time?' 'That's true,' said Patol Babu. 'I really don't see why I should say no. But let's talk to your brother-in-law first and find out some details. What's his name?' 'Naresh. Naresh Dutt. He's about thirty. A strapping young fellow. He said he would be here around ten-thirty.'

(a) Who is the speaker of these lines and to whom is he speaking?

Ans. Nishikanto Ghosh is the speaker and he is speaking to Patol Babu.

(b) Explain the meaning of the word 'stage'.

Ans. 'Stage' here means the play acting profession.

(c) Why has the speaker come to the listener?

Ans. The speaker Nishikanto Ghosh has come to Patol Babu because he has an acting opportunity for him.

(d) The speaker said , "I believe ...." What is the reason behind his belief?

Ans. The reason behind his belief is that he was told earlier about Patol Babu's acting on the stage.

3. In Jatras, in amateur theatricals, in plays put up by the club in his neighbourhood, Patol Babu was always in demand. His name had appeared in handbills on countless occasions. Once it appeared in bold type near the top: 'Sitalakanto Ray (Patol Babu) in the role of Parasar'. Indeed, there was a time when people bought tickets especially to see him.

(a) Who is 'him' in the above lines?

Ans. 'Him' here refers to Patol Babu.

(b) Why did people buy tickets to see him?

Ans. Patol Babu was a very popular actor and thus people bought tickets especially to see him.

(c) What is the significance of the word 'indeed' used here?

Ans. The use of the word 'indeed' here is to emphasise the fact stated earlier that Patol Babu was always in demand.

(d) What does the phrase 'there was a time' signify?

Ans. The phrase signifies that, in the past, Patol Babu was a popular theatre artist. Now, he has left acting as a profession.

4. 'Come in, come in, sir!' Patol Babu almost dragged the young man in and pushed the broken-armed chair towards him. 'Do sit down.'

'No, thanks. I.........

'Oh yes. I must say I was quite taken aback. After so many years.'

'I hope you have no objection?'

(a) Who is the speaker of these lines?

Ans. Patol Babu is the speaker of these lines.

(b) Explain the meaning of 'taken aback'.

Ans. The phrase 'taken aback' means 'shocked' or 'surprised'.

(c) Why was the speaker taken aback?

Ans. Patol Babu was taken aback because he had been asked to act after many years. He never expected this opportunity.

(d) Do you find anything unusual in Patol Babu's being taken aback?

Ans. No, there is nothing unusual. He had not been acting for many years and so when he got a chance suddenly he was taken aback.

5. Patol Babu suddenly thought of a crucial question.

'I hope the part calls for some dialogue?'

'Certainly. It's a speaking part. You have acted before, haven't you?'

'Well, as a matter of fact, yes.'

'Fine. I wouldn't have come to you for just a walk-on part. For that we pick people from the street. Of course there's dialogue and you'll be given your lines as soon as you show up tomorrow.' **CBSE SQP 2024**

(a) Why was the question about dialogue "crucial" for Patol Babu?

Ans. The question was crucial for Patol Babu because it reflected the importance of the role he was being offered.

(b) How does Patol Babu's previous acting experience play a role in the casting decision?

Ans. Patol Babu's previous experience gets him a positive response from the person casting him and implies that his experience contributed towards his selection.

(c) What does the casting director's statement, 'I wouldn't have come to you for just a walk-on part,' reveal about his opinion of Patol Babu's acting skills?

Ans. The casting director's statement suggests that he respects Patol Babu's acting abilities and considers him suitable for bigger roles that have more substance and dialogue.

(d) What type of conversation do Patol Babu and the casting director have?

Ans. Patol Babu and the casting director have a professional conversation.

6. Remember? This is only the first step on the ladder, my dear better-half! Yes...... the first step that would ...... God willing-mark the rise to fame and fortune of your beloved husband!'

'Counting your chickens again before they're hatched, are you? No wonder you could never make a go of it .'

(a) Identify the speaker of these lines.

Ans. Patol Babu's wife is the speaker of these lines.

(b) What is the tone of the speaker here?

Ans. The speaker is ridiculing Patol Babu for his daydreaming.

(c) Explain the statement 'Counting your chickens before they're hatched'.

Ans. The phrase means to talk of success even before it has happened.

(d) Why had the speaker used 'again' in the statement?

Ans. The speaker had used 'again' because Patol Babu had day dreamt about getting acting roles before too.

7. Counting your chickens again before they're hatched, are you ? No wonder you could never make a go of it.'

'But it' s the real thing this time! Go and make me a cup of tea, will you? And remind me to take some ginger juice tonight. It's very good for the throat.' (Patol Babu) **CBSE 2024**

(a) Identify the phrase that gives an impression that the speaker does not have any faith in Patol Babu.

Ans. The phrase 'counting your chickens again before they're hatched' gives an impression that the speaker doesn't have any faith in Patol Babu.

(b) How does Patol Babu try to convince his wife?

Ans. Patol Babu tries to convince his wife by saying that the opportunity is different and real this time.

(c) What does the phrase 'Counting your chickens again before they're hatched' mean?

Ans. The phrase means to be overoptimistic in acting on expectations which are not yet fulfilled.

(d) Why was Patol Babu not successful, according to his wife?

Ans. According to his wife, Patol Babu wasn't successful because he has the habit of putting too much faith in opportunities that might not be fruitful in the end.

8. He moved up to the office beyond the pan shop and sat down on the steps. It was nearly half-past nine. On Sunday mornings, songs in praise of goddess Kali were sung in Karali Babu's house. Patol Babu went there every week and enjoyed it. What if he were to go these useless people, and be made to look foolish on top of that? 'Silence'! Stuff and nonsense! To hell with your 'silence'! They had put up this pompus show for something so trivial! Things were much better on the stage.

(a) What was the trigger for Patol Babu's chain of thought that made him question his presence at the film shoot?

Ans. The trigger for Patol Babu's chain of thought that made him question his presence at the film shoot was the fact that he was wasting a great Sunday on doing something so small and insignificant.

(b) Why did Patol Babu think things were much better on the stage?

Ans. Patol Babu thought that Things were much better on the stage, because he delivered long dialogues and got important roles.

(c) Infer Patol Babu's tone as reflected in the extract.

Ans. Angry and regretful

(d) The writer uses questions in his writing. Comment on the purpose of this style.

Ans. The writer uses questions in his writing style to present the intense emotions felt by the central character Patol Babu.

9. "Each word spoken in a play is like a fruit in a tree. Not everyone in the audience has access to it. But you, the actor, must know how to pluck it, get at its essence, and serve it up to the audience for their edification."

(a) What is the duty of an actor ?

Ans. An actor should understand the role by going deep into the character and present it with perfection to the audience.

(b) What was the impact of the above mentioned words on the listener?

Ans. The given words had a positive impact on the listener. It resulted in the small role being taken as a challenge and being performed with precision by Patol Babu.

(c) What do you mean by 'edification'?

Ans. The word 'edification' means 'enlightenment'.

(d) Who said these lines?

Ans. Mr. Gogon Pakrashi, guru of Patol Babu, said these lines.

10. "Oh, oh, oh, oh, oh ....." Patol Babu began giving the exclamation a different inflection each time he uttered it. After doing it a number of times he made an astonishing discovery.

(a) Why did Patol Babu repeat the word, 'Oh' over and over again?

Ans. Patol Babu repeated the word, 'Oh' over and over again to give the exclamation 'Oh!' a different inflection each time he spoke it.

(b) What 'astonishing discovery' did he make?

Ans. He made an astonishing discovery that this one word, when spoken in different ways, carried different shades of meaning.

(c) What does the word, 'uttered' mean?

Ans. The word 'uttered' means 'spoke'.

(d) What does the practice of the word "oh" tell you about Patol Babu?

Ans. The practice of the word 'Oh!' was the justification of the dedication of Patol Babu towards acting.

11. Patol Babu suddenly felt that he could write a whole thesis on that monosyllabic exclamation. Why had he felt so disheartened when this single word contained a gold-mine of meaning?

(a) Why had Patol Babu been disheartened?

Ans. Patol Babu had been disheartened because not only was his part short and unimportant, the dialogue that he had to utter was only a monosyllabic exclamation 'Oh!'.

(b) Which was the word that contained a 'gold-mine'?

Ans. The word 'Oh!', a monosyllabic exclamation of pain, despair or surprise, contained a 'gold-mine.'

(c) What does the word 'monosyllabic' mean?

Ans. The term 'monosyllabic' means a word having a single syllable.

(d) **What made him (Patol Babu) feel that he could write a whole thesis on the word?**

Ans. When Patol Babu was practising to speak the word 'oh', he got various shades of meaning of that word by speaking it in different ways. That's how he felt that he could write a whole thesis on it.

12. It is true that he needed money very badly, but what was twenty rupees when measured against the intense satisfaction of a small job done with perfection and dedication?

(a) **Why did Patol Babu need money?**

Ans. Patol Babu badly needed money because his household finances were in shambles and any money would have helped.

(b) **What was the 'small job'?**

Ans. The small job was to play the part of an extra who utters just one dialogue upon a collision with the hero of the film on the street.

(c) **What do you mean by the word 'measured' as used in the above lines?**

Ans. The word 'measured' means 'compared to' in this context.

(d) **What was the source of satisfaction for Patol Babu?**

Ans. The source of satisfaction for Patol Babu was his performing the role with perfection and dedication.

Short Answer Type Questions

Answer the following questions in 30-40 words.

1. Why did Patol Babu get excited when Nishikanto Babu met him?

Ans. Patol Babu got excited when Nishikanto Babu told him that his brother-in-law was looking for a man to play a part in a film and Nishikanto suggested that Patol would suit the description. Patol Babu had never seen this coming and was excited to act again.

2. Nishikanto's offer stirred Patol Babu to the core. Comment.

Ans. It is true that Nishikanto's offer stirred Patol Babu to the core. Nishikanto Ghosh, a neighbour of Patol Babu came to him to inform that his brother-in-law was in search of some actor and that he had referred him for the role. This shocks Patol Babu as he had been an actor in his younger days and had almost given up acting. Now, he was going to get an opportunity to act again.

3. Even at the age of 52, Patol Babu cherished dreams. What were his dreams?

Ans. Even at the age of 52, Patol Babu cherished his fondest dreams of rising to fame as an actor. He wanted to bring back his glorious days as an actor before coming to Calcutta. He wanted to be popular once again and his name to be the talk of the town.

4. What do you know about Patol Babu's days as a stage performer?

Or **What was Patol Babu's previous experience as an actor?**

Ans. At one time, Patol Babu was a well-known stage actor. He was passionate about acting and could not think of anything but acting. He was always in demand in *Jatras*, amateur theatricals and in plays put up by the club in his neighbourhood. On countless occasions, his name appeared in handbills. There was a time when people used to buy tickets especially to see him.

5. Why, according to you, did Patol Babu long to act? Cite reasons from the story. **CBSE 2025**

Ans. Patol Babu longed to act because it was his lifelong passion. Once a talented stage actor, he missed the joy of performing. The film role rekindled his excitement, and despite its small size, he embraced it with dedication, proving his love for acting was driven by fulfillment, not fame.

6. Patol Babu struggled to make a living after he lost his job in Calcutta. Elaborate.

Or **What did Patol Babu do after losing his job with Hudson and Kimberley?**

Ans. After the retrenchment from Hudson and Kimberley, Patol Babu opened a variety store which got wound up after five years. He gave up his job in a Bengali firm in disgust. For ten long years, he worked as an insurance salesman but never made good of anything.

7. How did Patol Babu's dream come true?

Ans. Patol Babu was an actor by heart. In his young days, he was a very famous stage actor. However, at the age of fifty two, he found himself struggling to meet his daily requirements. However, his dream came true when he got an acting role when Nishikanto Babu approached him with a small side role for a film.

8. How did Patol Babu's wife react on her husband being offered a chance in a film?

Ans. Patol Babu's wife was not much excited about his chance to work in a film. It was because she had lost trust in his promises of rising to a star. Moreover, she knew from her previous experiences that it was his habit to talk about his achievements before he actually accomplished them.

9. What does the expression 'Counting your chickens before they're hatched' mean? In what context was it spoken in the chapter 'Patol Babu'?

Ans. The expression means to get excited about the happening of something even before it has actually happened. These words were rightly said by Patol Babu's wife when he started imagining his role and rise to fame.

10. Why was Patol Babu so anxious to know his lines?

Ans. Patol Babu had expected his character to have some important dialogues as he wanted to express his acting skills. He was anxious to know his lines so that he could learn his dialogues well, rehearse his part and give his best performance when the actual shooting took place.

11. How can you say that Patol Babu was a very punctual man?

Ans. Punctuality was Patol Babu's virtue. He worked with Hudson and Kimberley for nine years but wasn't late for a single day. He also reached the shooting location before time, due to which Naresh Dutt praised him for his punctuality.

12. What information was gathered by Patol Babu on the sets of the shot?

Ans. The information gathered by Patol Babu was that the film in which he was playing a role was directed by Baren Mullick, a director who had three smash hits in a row. He had also come to know that Chanchal Kumar, who was playing the lead in the movie, was a lead in four movies.

13. How did Patol Babu feel when he was mistaken as Atul Babu by Naresh Dutt?

Ans. When Naresh Dutt mistakably called Patol Babu as Atul Babu, Patol felt awkward. For Patol, his name was much more than just a name as he was once a well-known name associated with acting and drama in Kanchrapara.

14. Who gave Patol Babu his lines and how did he react after receiving them?

Or **What were Patol Babu's dialogues and what was his reaction on seeing them?**

Or **How did Patol Babu initially react to the role allotted to him?**

Ans. Sosanko handed over the 'lines' that Patol Babu needed to speak. However, upon receiving his dialogue, Patol Babu was shocked. His dialogue was just a monosyllabic exclamation 'Oh'. He felt insulted and dejected that he had only one word as a dialogue.

15. Why did Sosanko, script in charge, say that Patol was the luckiest of actors?

Ans. According to Sosanko, Patol Babu was the luckiest of actors that day because he was the only one who had any dialogue to deliver in the scene that was shot. Moreover, there had been over a hundred actors in that film who played their roles without any dialogue. Most actors played their roles without having to walk or show their faces.

16. What idea did Patol Babu have while rehearsing? Did the director approve of the idea?

Ans. While rehearsing his dialogue and the scene, Patol Babu thought that if he had a newspaper in his hand then the collision would look much more realistic. The director, Baren Mullick, was quite impressed with the thought and he readily agreed.

17. How was Patol Babu feeling right before his shot?

Ans. Patol Babu was a bit nervous and excited right before his shot. He wanted to give his best shot at it. He was no stranger to such feelings because he had experienced them every time he stepped on to the stage in earlier days.

18. What was the greatest reward that Patol Babu received for his role in the film?

Ans. Patol Babu performed so well that he received praises from Chanchal Kumar, who praised his amazing timing. Baren Mullick, the director acclaimed the performance and went on to say that Patol Babu was quite an actor. Patol Babu himself was so pleased with his performance that he felt immense joy and complete satisfaction.

19. Baren Mullick was brilliant at his work. Do you agree? Give reasons.

Ans. Baren Mullick indeed was brilliant at his work. He suggested that Patol Babu have a moustache for authenticity. He did not want to waste time on unimportant issues but still paid attention to every minute detail. He even accepted Patol Babu's suggestion of a newspaper.

20. In Patol Babu, Film Star, how is Patol Babu's character a commentary on the struggling actors in the film industry? CBSE SQP 2023

Ans. Through Patol Babu's character, Satyajit Ray highlights the plight of the struggling actors who often go unnoticed and the difficulties they face in getting even small roles. Patol Babu's dedication to his craft and his ability to turn even a minor role into a memorable one is a testament to the hard work and determination of many such individuals in the industry.

21. Money and satisfaction are like parallel banks of a stream. How does this statement correspond to Patol Babu's emotion, after the shot was over? Competency Based

Ans. After the shot of Patol Babu was done, he became depressed and regretful that he was questioning his small acting part. At this moment, he realised that 'money and satisfaction are like parallel banks of a stream'. He remembered his old acting days when he found happiness through acting. He felt that same joy and satisfaction in playing the small role and thus, left without taking the money. For him, money could not measure up to the satisfaction he felt.

Long Answer Type Questions

Answer the following questions in 150 words.

1. Who was Mr. Pakrashi and how did he instil the value of being true to one's work in Patol Babu?

Mr. Pakrashi was the force behind Patol Babu's brilliant performance as an absent-minded pedestrian. Substantiate with reference to 'Patol Babu, Film Star'.

Or 'Patol Babu, Film Star', by Satyajit Ray emphasises the valuable contribution of a mentor on changing a negative mind-set into a positive one. Describe how Mr. Pakrashi's advice helps Patol Babu in performing his role. Competency Based

Ans. Mr. Gogon Pakrashi was the mentor and guru of Patol Babu during his theatre days. He was a wonderful actor with no trace of vanity in him. He instilled the value of being true to one's work in Patol Babu. He advised Patol that no part was beneath an actor's dignity to accept and that an actor should make the most of the opportunity and do full justice to the role. He would also advise him to get at the essence of every role and enlighten the audience with its true performance. This helped Patol Babu in enacting his small role, which he thoroughly rehearsed, carefully planned and even improvised, like a true actor.

He, thus, turned his small and insignificant role into a masterpiece of a performance by using a newspaper as a prop to look absent-minded. He cleverly brought out the irritation, surprise and anguish of his role. Thus, his performance won him the admiration of both the film director and the male lead of the film.

2. 'Patol Babu had an important quality, that of being very meticulous.' What values does it highlight about his character?

Or Dedication and hard work are essential for success. Explain how these qualities enable Patol Babu to perform his small role to perfection.

In the lesson 'Patol Babu, Film star', what kind of values are being upheld by Patol Babu? Quote instances to show his sincerity and dedication. CBSE 2020

Ans. Patol Babu was indeed a meticulous man. When he got a role in a film, although the role was very small, he kept inquiring about different aspects of his role and was eager to know his dialogues. He rehearsed his one dialogue over and over again. He practised saying the word 'Oh!' in many different ways. He also worked out how he would react physically when he would collide with the lead actor and utter his dialogue.

Just before the shot was about to be taken, he suggested an improvisation that he should carry a newspaper to make the collision appear more real. This shows how meticulous a man Patol Babu was. It also highlights his passion and dedication towards his work. He performed his role with perfection to the satisfaction of the director.

3. No work is small or petty. How has Satyajit Ray exemplified this in his story- 'Patol Babu'?

Ans. We should never undermine or reject a work opportunity regarding it as small, petty or insignificant. Whatever we do, we should give our best at it. This is what Satyajit Ray has exemplified through the character of Patol Babu in his story.

Patol Babu had been a renowned stage actor in his youth, but he could not continue with his acting due to financial constraints. He gets an opportunity to work in a movie when he is in his fifties. However, he is totally disappointed to know that he has to play a short, insignificant part, and his dialogue would comprise of a single utterance, the monosyllabic exclamation, 'Oh!'. He then remembers his mentor, Mr. Pakrashi, who used to say that no role was unimportant in a play, nor was any dialogue insignificant, even if it was only one word. Patol Babu rehearsed his one word dialogue and gave a wonderful performance. He had realised that no work is small or petty.

4. The character of Patol Babu draws respect from time to time. He is an inspiration. What are the values that draw the reader towards him?

Ans. Patol Babu is indeed an inspiration. The hardships of his professional life didn't make him depressed. He is a practical and a persistent man. When he was retrenched from his job due to the war, he kept on trying his hand at different occupations like opening a shop, becoming an insurance agent and so on.

He is also an epitome of punctuality. For the full nine years that he worked at Hudson and Kimberley, he was not late even for a single day. He also arrived well in advance for the time of the film shooting. Although he was told to come at half past eight, he had reached the venue of the shooting at seventeen minutes past eight.

Another very good quality about him is that he is a perfectionist, a quality much needed for a film star. He rehearsed the various ways of speaking 'Oh!' to decide the best method of doing so.

Finally, he didn't accept the wages for his part, because, as he thought, 'work satisfaction is more important than monetary gain'.

5. "Remember one thing Patol; however small a part you're offered, never consider it beneath your dignity to accept it. As an artist, your aim should be to make the most of your opportunity and squeeze the last drop of meaning out of your lines. A play involves the work of many and it is the combined effort of many that makes a success of the play."
The above lines made you write a letter to your brother who is upset over the fact that he was given the duty of designing dresses for a play rather than playing a role. Write the letter advising him that no work is little or big.

Ans. 15, Daryaganj
Delhi–110002

20th July, 20XX

Dear Mukesh

How are you keeping? I am fine here. Mother wrote that things are not going good with you. She also mentioned that you were upset as you couldn't get a part in a school play. However, you got an important role; that of designing the dresses that the characters in the school play will be wearing.

Let me tell you a secret. 'The secret to a happy life is not to do what you like, but to like what you do.' I think that you failed to realise what an important part you will play! All the characters in the play will look their part due to the dresses that they will wear. The entire audience will see the costumes designed by you. They literally will give life to the whole play. So, don't think that your part is any less important than that of the others.

Always remember that people will only appreciate true talent. Hence, you should always give your best in whatever you do.

Convey my regards to all.

Your loving brother
Sanjay

6. Patol Babu always remembered the words of his mentor that one has to accept whatever is offered and make the best of any opportunity. Write a letter to a friend telling him about the value of hard work and the art of putting in your best. Write the answer in 150 words.

Ans. H.No. 7/A, WEA, Karol Bagh
New Delhi-110005

21st December, 20XX

Dear Tarasha

How are you? I am good here. I have written this letter to tell you the value of hard work. Recently, I read a story that taught me that one should accept whatever is offered and make the best of any opportunity. We should take every task as a challenge and perform it with perfection. It is very important to work hard in order to achieve our goals. Hard work is the key to success.

Moreover, one should put in one's best efforts to excel in life. To achieve that one needs strength of mind and body. One needs to have the right attitude, self-discipline and the ability to put one's goal before one's own needs. There is after all no substitute for hard work. Intense hard work along with great skills can help anyone to be successful. One should never give up and keep struggling until one perfects one's art.

Indeed, success is not measured by the position that one is in today but the amount of hard work you put in and the number of obstacles that you overcome to reach your goal.

Yours faithfully
Kaira

ASSESSMENT EXERCISE

Extract Based Questions

Read the following extracts carefully and answer the questions that follow.

1. Patol Babu hadn't expected such news at the start of the day. That an offer to act in a film could come to a 52-year-old nonentity like him was beyond his wildest dreams.

(a) Who had brought the unexpected news?

(b) What had Patol Babu not dreamed?

(c) What is a synonym of 'nonentity'?

(d) Why was the offer 'beyond his wildest dreams'?

2. In 1943, when he was just toying with the idea of starting a club in his neighbourhood, sudden retrenchment in his office due to the war cost him his nine-year-old job.

(a) Who was toying with the idea?

(b) In which office did 'he' work?

(c) What is meant by 'retrenchment'?

(d) What can you say about 'he' regarding the idea of opening a club in neighbourhood?

Short Answer Type Questions

Answer the following questions in 30-40 words.

1. For what was Patol Babu wanted by the film production company? Why did Nishikanto Babu suggest his name?

2. What did Patol Babu do for a living after having been retrenched?

3. How did Patol Babu disclose his pleasure for being offered the film role before his wife?

4. What did Patol Babu hear standing near the *paan* shop and how did he react to it?

5. What did Jyoti tell Patol Babu about his role before it was to be shot?

Long Answer Type Questions

Answer the following questions in 150 words.

1. Patol Babu glanced at the paper and found a single word had been scrawled on it—'Oh'...
Sosanko said, "What's the matter Grandpa? You don't seem too pleased."

Inspite of his initial disappointment, Patol Babu came to terms with what was offered to him and finally achieved satisfaction and happiness. Write an article for your school magazine entitled, 'Take Challenges in your Stride'.

2. After reading the lesson you begin to think that practice makes man perfect. A man becomes perfect only when he does a thing repeatedly. Explain this in a letter to your younger brother/ sister in 150 words.

3. At the end it was not money which would have given as much happiness as the happiness he got from playing his role well. Motivated by his story, write a paragraph highlighting the value of putting in one's best in everything one does, be it at work, home or play, because the quality of one's work is a measure of the quality of the person.

Virtually True

by Paul Stewart

CHAPTER 6

CHAPTER SUMMARY 'Virtually True' is a science fiction story based on interactive psycho-driven games. It is a story about Michael Dawson and Sebastian Shultz. Both of them are connected in the virtual world through a computer game. It is an interesting story because this virtual world has certain real connections which are discovered by the two boys. Sebastian's consciousness gets transferred to his games which land into Michael's hands. Michael then encounters him in the games and somehow manages to save him.

Miraculous Recovery of a 14-year-old Boy

The narrator was travelling in a train when his eyes saw an article in a newspaper which a big woman opposite him was reading. It talked about the miraculous recovery of a boy named Sebastian Shultz from coma. It was this name that particularly struck the narrator and he leant forward to read the whole article.

The 'miracle recovery' story which Michael read stated – 'Sebastian Shultz, a 14-year-old boy from South London, awoke from a coma that doctors feared might last forever.' Michael recollected the name and thought that he had somewhere met a person with this name.

Six weeks ago, Sebastian Shultz was badly injured in a motorway accident. His condition on arrival at the General Hospital was described as critical though stable. In spite of the doctor's efforts, the boy could not regain consciousness. He went into a coma. Only a miracle could have saved him.

Michael Runs Through the Events

Michael was shocked to read the article. When he saw the picture of Sebastian, he realised that he was the same person whom he had met in the virtual world and was trying to rescue. Michael could not understand how he could have met Sebastian if he was in a coma.

Michael thought back to the events in his memory and realised that Sebastian had been in a coma all this time. He felt nervous as to how it had happened. Michael recollected that a month ago, he and his father had spent one entire Saturday afternoon at the Computer Fair. His dad was crazy about computer gadgets and possessed all the latest ones. At the computer fair, they bought a number of attachments and the latest interactive psycho-drive games. The games were unique as they were driven by mental power. Although the games were second-hand, Michael was happy to have them.

Michael Plays the Psycho-Drive Games

On reaching home, Michael started playing a game called Wildwest, which was a strategy game. He was the Sheriff of the town and as he burst into a saloon, he was challenged to a fight by Black-Eyed Jed.

Before he could go out, Michael saw another sheriff come inside. He did not move like a computer image and ordered Michael to follow him and they both ran out. They were followed by gunmen and the other sheriff was shot at. Suddenly, Michael could see the sign 'Game Over' on his screen.

A Message from Sebastian Shultz

After the game was over, Michael received a message from Sebastian. It read : 'I'M STUCK. PLEASE HELP TO RETRIEVE ME. TRY 'DRAGONQUEST'. Michael played the game as suggested the next morning. The aim of the game was to rescue the fair Princess Aurora from a wicked Dragon and to collect the treasure. While he was rescuing the princess, he heard another cry from a second knight for rescuing him.

He, at once, recognised him to be Sebastian. Michael tried his best to save him from the dragon but failed again. Now, he was invited for another attempt named 'Jailbreak'. The message also requested Michael not to give up, otherwise Sebastian would have to stay there forever.

Michael Plays Games to Rescue Sebastian

Michael hurriedly started playing the game. In this game, Sebastian was his cellmate. They broke the jail and raced down the corridors and up to the roof with guards and their dogs following behind. Michael was surprised to know that Sebastian had arranged a helicopter to rescue them. Just then, the guards and their dogs arrived on the roof. Sebastian mistakenly stepped off the roof and fell down to the concrete ground. Once again, Michael failed to rescue Sebastian and the game was over. Sebastian requested Michael for a last try.

The Final Game to Rescue Sebastian

Michael played the game 'Warzone' which looked like a real war zone with gunfire all around. Both the boys ran towards a nearby jeep and drove away. Michael jumped off the jeep into the helicopter but Sebastian could not. As the helicopter started moving, Michael saw a tank crashing into the jeep, sending Sebastian upwards. Michael pulled him up and rescued him. Thus, Michael was finally able to save Sebastian and hit a jackpot score of 40000000.

He now knew that Sebastian, the boy from the game, did exist in real life. He had seen the proof in the newspaper.

Michael Correlates the Virtual and the Real

Michael wanted to know more about the miracle recovery story because he thought that the Sebastian, who had recovered, was the one whom he had rescued in the game. Upon doing some research on the internet, he learnt that Sebastian had been playing the same psycho-drive game like him when he had an accident and went into a coma. He thought that Sebastian would have been plugged into the computer when his head banged against the computer, and the computer might have stored his memory in its own. He remembered that his father always said that nothing is ever lost in a computer.

The Virtually True Experience

Michael remembered that Sebastian's father had mentioned in the recovery story that they had lost their stock of games. This stock of games might have landed in the Computer Fair, from where Michael purchased the games. He, then, checked his e-mail, where he had received one mail from Sebastian in which he had thanked Michael for saving his life. He offered to meet him and asked Michael to keep the games with him as he had earned them. It was a real message from the real Sebastian. They both knew that in reliving the accident something wonderful had happened. He now knew that whatever he had experienced was 'Virtually True'.

Word Meaning

Word	Meaning
wheezy	to breathe with an audible whistling sound or with difficulty
coma	a prolonged state of deep unconsciousness
nutty	crazy about, has a passion for
Mhz-megahertz	one million hertz (the unit of frequency equal to one cycle per second)
RAM	Random Access Memory
CD ROM	Compact Disk Read Only Memory
Sheriff	(In the US) an elected officer in a town who is responsible for maintaining peace.
gizmos	gadgets, especially mechanical or electrical devices
virtual	computer generated, unreal
visor	a movable part of a helmet that can be pulled down to cover the face
psycho-drive	driven by mental power
strode	walked
sarsaparilla	a carbonated drink flavoured with sarsaparilla root
silhouetted	casting a dark shape
drawled	to speak in a slow and lazy way

Word	Meaning
posse	gang
studded	decorated
plaits	braided hair
squealed	screamed
tapestry	wall-hanging
dungeons	cells
skeleton swipe-card	a plastic card on which data has been stored magnetically that can be read by an electronic reading device
wailed	cried
vicious	nasty
hurtling	crashing
tumbling	falling
riddled	making a large number of small holes in something
raked	scratched
sniper fire	gunshots fired by somebody in a concealed position
scuttling	rushing
revved	increased speed sharply

Textbook FOLDER

Here, we have covered questions given in the CBSE Textbook along with their answers.

ON PAGE 78

Q.1A Answer the following questions.

(i) According to the newspaper, what had happened to Sebastian Shultz?

Ans. According to the newspaper, Sebastian Shultz, a 14-year-old schoolboy from South London, had awoken from a coma which doctors had feared would last forever. Six weeks ago, he was badly injured in a motorway accident and was brought to the hospital in critical condition.

(ii) 'Dad's nutty about computers'. What evidence is there to support this statement?

***Or* How do we know that Michael's father was fascinated by computers?**

Ans. Michael's dad was crazy about computers. He had a Pentium 150 Mhz processor, with 256 MB of RAM, a 1.2 Gb hard disk drive and 16X speed CD-ROM, complete with speakers, printers, modem and scanner, which could probably do everything. He could not resist any of the new gadgets or gizmos that came to the market.

(iii) In what way did the second game seem very real?

Ans. In the second game called 'Dragonquest', the players assumed the role of a knight and tried to save the princess. It seemed real because the narrator received a message from Sebastian to help him. Moreover, it was in continuation of the first game 'Wildwest'. All through the game the narrator could feel, hear and even smell the evil dragon following in close pursuit.

(iv) The last game has tanks, jeeps, helicopters and guns. What heading would you put this and the other games under?

Ans. The last game and other games can be put under the heading of action, adventure, first-person shooter, strategy and RPG (Role Playing Games). In these games, the player becomes a part of the action and usually plays the part of a hero or a good guy whose job is to eliminate the evil forces and rescue someone from such forces.

(v) What was Michael's theory about how Sebastian had entered the games?

Ans. Michael believed that at the time of the accident, Sebastian was using his laptop to play one of the same psycho-drive games that the narrator had. He was plugged into the computer when he banged his head in the accident, and the computer saved his memory into its own. Moreover, the computer games that narrator bought at the computer fair belonged to Shultz and were stolen from the hospital.

ON PAGE 78-79

Q.3 Answer the following questions briefly.

(a) Why did the news of the 'miracle recovery' shock Michael?

Ans. Michael was shocked after reading the 'miracle recovery' story because the name of the person who recovered was Sebastian Shultz, whom he thought he knew. Sebastian was his companion in the psycho-drive games.

As Michael succeeded in saving him, Sebastian also recovered. Michael realised that Shultz in the game and Shultz in the hospital were actually the same person.

(b) Michael's meeting with Sebastian Shultz had been a chance meeting. Where had it taken place and how?

Ans. Michael and Sebastian met in a psycho-drive computer game, 'Wildwest'. It had been a chance meeting because Sebastian's memory was saved to that game. They would probably never have met if Sebastian had not met with the accident.

Furthermore, in the game Micheal played the role of a sheriff who has an altercation with black-eyed Jed when he was going to meet him out of saloon. Before he could go, he saw another sheriff but different from computer images. This situation also shows that it was a chance meeting.

(c) What kind of computers fascinated Michael and his dad? Why?

Ans. Michael and his dad were fascinated with computers which had the latest updates and could do almost everything like paint, play music, create displays and many more. They liked such software because they were crazy about it.

(d) Describe the first place where Michael was virtually transported.

Ans. The first place where Michael was virtually transported was a completely dusty track through the centre of a town. He had a sheriff's badge pinned to his shirt. It was the virtual reality game 'Wildwest'. There he went to the saloon and was challenged to a duel by 'Black-Eyed Jed'.

(e) What help did Sebastian Shultz ask Michael for? How did he convey this message?

Ans. Sebastian Shultz sent a message through a computer printout to Michael. It read, 'I'M STUCK. PLEASE HELP TO RETRIEVE ME. TRY 'DRAGONQUEST'. Sebastian Shultz.' He was stuck in the games and asked Michael to play further to help him out from there.

(f) Why did Michael fail in rescuing Sebastian Shultz the first time?

Ans. Michael was unable to save Sebastian the first time because, when both of them were trying to escape the chase on a horse, Sebastian was shot dead by the enemies.

(g) The second attempt to rescue Sebastian Shultz too was disastrous. Give reasons.

Ans. The second attempt made by Michael to save Sebastian went in vain. Shultz and Michael went down the staircase and secret passages with sword drawn and hid in a dungeon. This turned out to be a fatal mistake as all of a sudden a dragon appeared at the end of the corridor and jumped on Sebastian. Sebastian tried his best to kill it but failed and got killed.

(h) Narrate the accident that injured Sebastian Shultz.

Ans. Six weeks before the 'miracle recovery' story was published, Sebastian Shultz was badly injured in a motorway accident. Apparently, the motorcar had skidded and spun off the road when the driver suddenly applied brakes. His condition was declared to be critical though stable by the doctors. Despite the doctor's efforts, he was unable to gain consciousness and had slipped into a state of coma.

(i) How had Sebastian Shultz entered the games?

Ans. Sebastian was playing psycho-drive games on his laptop when the motorway accident occurred. His head hit the laptop when he was being tumbled around in the car and the computer saved his memory into its own. After that, he appeared in the games which he himself had been playing on his laptop before the accident.

(j) How was Sebastian Shultz's memory stored on Michael's disk? How did Michael discover that?

Or **How did Sebastian's memory stored on a disk end up on Michael's computer? How had Sebastian Shultz entered the games?**

Ans. Sebastian had been plugged into the computer when he banged his head during the accident on the motorway and the computer had saved his memory in its own memory. Michael discovered the fact when Mr. Shultz stated that they were going to stock up on some games and while they were in the hospital, the games were stolen, These games landed in a computer fair from where Michael and his dad had purchased them. The games had Sebastian's consciousness stored in them.

Michael also discovered that the weird versions of the games he was drawn into had been attempts to retrieve Sebastian's memory. He had to play four games to save Sebastian and was lucky only in the fourth one.

ON PAGE 79

Q.4 Sebastian Shultz had a close brush with death. After he recovers, he returns to school and narrates his experience to his classmates. As Sebastian Shultz, narrate your experience. Competency Based

Ans. Hello everybody! I am back and I am very happy to see all of you once again.

It's been six weeks but for me it seems a matter of yesterday. I understand that all of you would like to know what actually happened. I was being driven in my car on a motorway. I was as usual busy on my computer, playing games. Therefore, I could not observe the road and the traffic, relying totally on my driver.

He was driving smoothly when suddenly a lorry overtook us and was rushing at a great speed. The accident actually occurred when another lorry, in a bid to overtake the lorry going ahead, hit my car.

There was a big bang and my driver lost control for a second. The car skidded and spun off the road when the driver suddenly applied brakes. After that, I don't remember anything. It's only after I recovered that I came to know how I was brought to the hospital.

I was told that I had slipped into a coma and only a miracle had brought me back. Another miraculous thing happened to me. Accidentally, my memory entered my games when I banged my head on my laptop.

The games were stolen from the hospital and landed in the Computer Fair. Michael, who bought them, rescued me.

He is my saviour. I am planning to meet him soon. It's great to be back after the harrowing time spent virtually.

Q.5 Continue the story.

Will Michael and Sebastian Shultz meet in real life? Will they be friends? Will they try to re-enter the virtual world together? You may use the following hints

- How the accident occurred
- Transfer of memory
- Meeting with Michael
- Appeals for help
- Rescue and recovery

Ans. Well, Michael and Sebastian will meet in real life. After reading the 'miracle recovery' story and realising Sebastian is the same person with whom he had been playing, Michael took Sebastian's address from the authorities of the hospital where Sebastian was admitted.

A meeting was fixed up where Michael and Sebastian became friends. Michael at that meeting let Sebastian know what he had gone through. After listening to Michael, Sebastian could connect his recovery through Michael's win in the computer game and became obliged to him. Now, they will try to enter the virtual world together and experience other games and levels which will also help them to strengthen their relationship.

ON PAGE 79-80

Q.6 Put the following sentences in a sequential order to complete the story.

(a) Sebastian Shultz was badly injured in a motorway accident and went into a coma.

(b) Sebastian's memory was saved in the computer when he banged his head on it during the accident.

(c) When Michael played the game, he entered Sebastian's memory.

(d) Michael bought the latest psycho-drive games from the Computer Fair.

(e) Sebastian Shultz was the second sheriff in the game 'Wildwest'.

(f) Michael pulled Sebastian into the helicopter and the screen flashed a score of 40,000,000.

(g) Sebastian requested Michael to try 'Jailbreak'.

(h) Michael failed to save the boy who fell through the air.

(i) Sebastian thought the helicopter was the right idea and they should go into 'Warzone'.

(j) The games were stolen from Shultz's house.

(k) Sebastian thanks Michael for saving his life and asks him to keep the games.

Ans. The correct sequential order for the complete story is a, b, j, d, c, e, g, h, i, f, k

WRITING TASK

Q.7 Do you think it is a true story? Could it happen to you one day? Here are some opinions about computer games in general.

- Encourage sedentary lifestyle
- Too much time is wasted
- Negative impact on health
- Psychological imbalance
- The games are addictive
- Reduce social skills
- Promote violence and aggression
- Detach one from reality

Ans. No, I do not believe it to be a true story because in real life your memory can never be transferred to a computer after banging your head with it. All this is simple imagination, where a person wants to see and do what he wishes to do, overlooking the reality.

Q.8 Do you think these opinions are biased? Write an article entitled 'Virtual games are a reality'.

Ans. **Virtual Games are a Reality**

by XYZ

The virtual world or cyberspace is an environment using computer technology to create a simulated, three-dimensional world that a user can explore while feeling as if he were in that world. In a virtual reality environment, the user experiences the feeling of being inside and a part of that world. He/She is also able to interact with the environment in meaningful ways.

However, some psychologists are concerned that virtual reality games could psychologically affect a player. They suggest that these games place a player in violent situations, particularly as the perpetuator of violence, and could result in the user becoming desensitised to violence.

Some psychologists also believe that these games can lead to cyber addiction. Another rising concern is about criminal acts. Studies indicate that people can have real physical and emotional reactions to stimuli within a virtual game. Thus, it is quite possible that a victim of a virtual attack could feel real emotional trauma. Can the attacker be punished for causing real-life distress? We don't have answers to these questions yet.

REVIEW EXERCISE

Including Previous Years' and Practice Questions

Extract Based Questions

Read the following extracts carefully and answer the questions that follow.

1. MIRACLE RECOVERY, the headline said. Sebastian Shultz, a 14 year-old schoolboy from South London, awoke yesterday from a coma that doctors feared might last forever. It couldn't be the Sebastian Shultz I'd met. I leant forward to read the rest of the article.

(a) Identify the speaker.

Ans. Michael Dawson is the speaker.

(b) Who is Sebastian Shultz?

Ans. Sebastian Shultz is a 14-year-old schoolboy from South London who had recovered from a coma.

(c) Why did the speaker lean forward to read the remaining part of the article?

Ans. The speaker had to lean forward because the article had come out in a newspaper being read by a woman sitting opposite the speaker in a train.

(d) In one word, state the tone of the given extract.

Ans. Surprise.

2. Six weeks ago, Sebastian Shultz was badly injured in a motorway accident. His condition, on arrival at the General Hospital, was described as critical though stable. Despite doctors' hopes, the boy did not regain consciousness. His parents were informed that their son was in a coma. At a press conference, Mrs Shultz said, "The doctors were doing all they could, but in our hearts we knew we needed a miracle."

(a) Who is the boy referred to here? What had happened to him?

Ans. The boy referred to here is Sebastian Shultz. Sebastian had met with a road accident and was in coma ever since.

(b) Why did they need a miracle?

Ans. They needed a miracle to bring out Sebastian from a coma.

(c) What had happened to make them require a miracle?

Ans. Mrs. Shultz's son, Sebastian, had met with an accident on the motorway and his head had been badly injured in the accident due to which he had gone into a coma.

(d) Which word in the extract is a means the same as 'an extraordinary and welcome event'

Ans. The word 'miracle' means the same as 'an extraordinary and welcome event'.

3. Technology was advancing every day, and Dad couldn't resist any of the new gadgets or gizmos that came on the market. That was why we went to the Computer Fair. We came away with a virtual reality visor and glove, and a handful of the latest interactive psycho-drive games. They're terrific. **CBSE 2024 C**

(a) Explain the usage of the word 'terrific' in the above lines.

Ans. The use of the word 'terrific' in the given lines shows the narrators' amazement at the new pschyo-drive games. They show the level to which technology had advanced to such an extent that it can store human memory.

(b) What did they purchase from the Computer Fair?

Ans. They purchased things like the virtual reality visor and glove and a few of the latest interactive psycho-drive games.

(c) Identify the phrase which reflects Dad's interest in technology.

Ans. 'Dad couldn't resist any of the new gadgets or gizmos that came on the market.'

(d) What are pschyo-drive games?

Ans. Psycho-drive games are interactive games that are powered by mental power. In these games, the player and a computer interact, and the player can control the action with their thoughts or use a virtual reality visor and glove to change what they see.

4. 'That was my idea' said Sebastian excitedly. If only it would go a bit faster.

(a) Where was Sebastian when he spoke these words?

Ans. Sebastian was on the roof of the prison he had broken out of when he spoke these words.

(b) What was his idea and what was he referring to?

Ans. His idea was to be rescued from there only by a helicopter. He was referring to a helicopter that was coming to their rescue.

(c) Was the idea a good one and did it eventually succeed? How?

Ans. The idea was quite good but it did not succeed. Sebastian had slipped and came tumbling down from the roof to the concrete below in the first try. However, in the second try, Sebastian was able to board the helicopter and was rescued.

5. As I burst in through the swing doors of the saloon, everyone went silent and glared at me.
I strode over to the bar. 'Sarsaparilla!' I said and a glass of fizzy red stuff came sliding along the bar towards me. As I took a sip, I heard a loud crash.
I spun round. There, silhouetted in the doorway, was Black-Eyed Jed, the fastest gun in the west.
'This town ain't big enough for the both of us, Sheriff Dawson,' he drawled, and fingered his guns lightly. 'Outside. Just you and me.'

(a) Identify the speaker of these lines.

Ans. Michael Dawson is the speaker here.

(b) What is the meaning of 'saloon' here?

Ans. The word 'saloon' here means a pub.

(c) What does the reaction of others reflect about the situation?

Ans. The reaction of other people suggests that they were annoyed and perhaps not friendly.

(d) Where was the speaker when he spoke these lines?

Ans. Michael, the speaker, was playing a game called 'Wildwest' on his computer, which he had bought at the Computer Fair.

6. I didn't even bother to read the rules of Jailbreak before going in. I knew that my task would be to rescue the boy. And sure enough, my cell mate was prisoner 02478: Shultz. 'I've got to get out of here,' Sebastian sighed. 'Are you going to help?'

'Of course,' I said. 'Have you got a plan?'

Stupid question. With the help of a skeleton swipe-card, we were soon out of the cell and racing down the corridors. Sirens wailed, guard dogs howled, boots came tramping. Behind us, steel-barred doors slammed shut. We dodged the guards, we fled the dogs, we made it to a staircase and pounded upwards.

(a) What can be inferred about Michael from his words, 'I knew my task'? State in one word.

Ans. Confidence

(b) What is the given extract about? Why didn't the speaker bother to read the rules of Jailbreak?

Ans. The given extract is about the progression of an escape. The speaker didn't bother to read the rules because he knew that, just like in the other games, he would have to rescue Sebastian Shultz.

(c) What is Jail break?

Ans. Jailbreak is a computer game which Sebastian had asked Michael to play.

(d) What does the expression 'going in' mean?

Ans. 'Going in' here refers to launching or starting of the computer game.

7. Better luck next time. Please don't give up, Michael. Otherwise I'll have to stay in here forever. Try 'Jailbreak'. I think it might just work!

(a) By whom was this message given?

Ans. This message was given by Sebastian Shultz.

(b) Where was 'I' stuck?

Ans. Sebastian's consciousness was stuck in games which he was playing at the time of the accident.

(c) What do you understand by 'Jailbreak' here?

Ans. 'Jailbreak' is the name of a game in which Sebastian's consciousness was imprinted.

(d) What does 'don't give up' mean?

Ans. The phrase 'don't give up' means 'don't stop trying'.

8. 'I've got to get out of here,' Sebastian sighed. 'Are you going to help?'
'Of course,' I said. 'Have you got a plan?' Stupid question. With the help of a skeleton swipe-card, we were soon out of the cell and racing down corridors. Sirens wailed, guard dogs howled, heavy boots came tramping.

(a) Who is 'I' referred to in the last line?

Ans. 'I' in the last line refers to Michael.

(b) What do you understand about the mentality of the second person?

Ans. The second person is ready to help Sebastian.

(c) Which word in the extract is a synonym of 'moaned'?

Ans. The word 'sighed' is a synonym of 'moaned'.

(d) From where does the second person want to get out?

Ans. The second person, Sebastian Shultz, wants to get out from the prison in the game 'Jailbreak'.

9. At least, that was what I thought then. Now I knew that Sebastian Shultz, the boy from the game, really did exist. I'd seen the proof in the newspaper. **CBSE 2013**

(a) What had Michael thought earlier?

Ans. Michael had thought earlier that Sebastian Shultz was just a character in the game.

(b) What had Michael seen in the newspaper?

Ans. Michael had seen the proof of the existence of the boy from the game in the newspaper. There was an article on his miraculous recovery.

(c) Which word in the extract means the same as 'validation'?

Ans. The word 'proof' means the same as 'validation'.

(d) After what event did Michael start thinking these thoughts?

Ans. Michael started thinking these thoughts after he had cracked the game and rescued Sebastian.

10. After all, Dad always says about the computer's memory-'It can never forget, Michael. Nothing ever gets lost.'
But, even if it was possible that Sebastian's memory had been stored on disk, how had it ended up on my computer? Scrolling down the article I found a possible explanation.

(a) Who is 'I' in the given extract?

Ans. 'I' in the given extract refers to Michael Dawson.

(b) Which article is mentioned here?

Ans. The article mentioned here is the newspaper article describing the recovery of Sebastian Shultz from coma.

(c) What do you mean by 'scrolling'?

Ans. Scrolling is the action of moving the eyes up or down.

(d) Where was 'I' when he found the 'possible explanation'?

Ans. Michael was browsing the internet on his computer in which the article on Sebastian Shultz's miraculous recovery from coma had been reported.

11. I said quietly. 'They ended up at the Computer Fair. And we bought them.'
I left the Net and checked my email. There was one from Sebastian. With trembling fingers I clicked in, and read the message.

(a) What do you mean by 'ended up'?

Ans. The phrase 'ended up' means 'finally reached'.

(b) **What are 'they' referred to here?**

Ans. 'They' are the psycho-drive games which Michael and his father had bought from the Computer Fair.

(c) **How did 'they' end up at the Computer Fair?**

Ans. Someone stole the CDs of the psycho-drive games from the hospital where Sebastian was lying in a coma and they were then sold at the fair.

(d) **Who is the speaker here?**

Ans. The speaker here is Michael Dawson, who rescued Sebastian Shultz in the computer game and brought him out from a coma.

Short Answer Type Questions

Answer the following questions in 30-40 words.

1. What news about Sebastian Shultz did Michael see in the newspaper?

Ans. The news was that Sebastian Shultz, a 14-year-old boy from South London, had been badly injured in a motorway accident and had gone into a coma six weeks ago. His mother hoped that one day her son would be well and only a miracle could save him. According to the newspaper, Sebastian Shultz had now awoken from coma.

2. What did Mrs. Shultz say at a press conference? Did that miracle happen?

Ans. Despite doctor's efforts, Sebastian Shultz could not regain consciousness. The doctors feared that he would forever remain in coma. At a press conference, Mrs. Shultz said that she hoped that a miracle would save their son Sebastian. Yes, that miracle took place. Sebastian Shultz came out from his coma.

3. Why was Sebastian Shultz's recovery called a miracle?

Ans. Sebastian Shultz's recovery was called a miracle because doctors feared that he would remain in coma forever due to the accident. So, when he regained consciousness and his memory, it was called a miracle.

4. Why had Michael and his father gone to the Computer Fair?

Ans. Michael and his father had gone to the Computer Fair as technology was advancing everyday and Michael's dad could not resist any of the new gadgets or gizmos that came in the market. Both of them were fascinated by the latest and fastest computers available.

5. How did Michael equip himself for the game experience at the 'Powerbase'?

Ans. Michael had the latest Pentium 150 MHz computer with 256 MB RAM, 1.2GB hard disk and 16 speed CD ROM. To add to his game experience, he had a virtual reality visor and glove with which he was able to experience the game very realistically. Besides, the computer was connected to the internet and a printer that printed messages from the characters in the game.

6. Why did Michael enjoy playing the psycho- drive games?

Ans. Michael enjoyed them because the big screen with the loud volume made him feel like he was inside the game, battling it out. They were games played with a virtual reality visor and glove, which have the ability to change what a person can see.

7. In the story, Virtually True, Michael said, "That's what I like about computers. The more futuristic they get, the better you can understand the past." Explain what he meant. **CBSE SQP 2023**

Ans. Michael is expressing his enthusiasm for the capabilities of modern technology such as computers, to help him experience and understand historical events and settings in a better way. He is suggesting that as technology advances and becomes more futuristic, it can allow people to have more vivid and realistic experiences that bring the past to life. This could include using virtual reality technology to explore historical sites or playing interactive games that simulate historical events.

8. When did the first video game come to an end and with what?

Ans. In the first game, Wildwest, Michael played the character of Sheriff Dawson who was challenged by Black-Eyed Jed, the fastest gun in the West. In order to escape, the narrator and the second sheriff went ahead on horseback being chased by the horsemen. At that moment, the sound of a gunshot echoed in the air. The second sheriff groaned and slumped back against him. At this, the game was over.

9. What was the aim of the game, 'Dragonquest'?

Ans. The aim of the game Dragonquest was to rescue the fair princess' princess, Aurora, from the wicked dragon. She was imprisoned at the top of a tall tower. The players also had to collect treasures along the way.

10. How did Sebastian and Michael run away from the dragon? Why was their attempt not successful?

Ans. To run away from the dragon, Sebastian chopped off the princess' two long plaits and tied them together, fixed one end round the bedpost and threw the other end out of the window. They jumped out of the window with the dragon behind them in close pursuit. They could not escape from the dragon as it suddenly appeared in front of them and sprang upon Sebastian.

11. Why was Michael disappointed at the close of 'Jailbreak' and how did he reconcile himself?

Ans. After the game 'Jailbreak' was over, Michael was very disappointed. He felt very bad as he could not save Sebastian Shultz. It was only later that he realised that the Sebastian, who could not be rescued was not real. He thus, reconciled himself as Sebastian Shultz was just a character in the game.

12. How did Michael save Sebastian in the last game?

***Or* How did the narrator happen to crack the video game?**

***Or* How was Shultz finally rescued by Michael?**

Ans. Michael's success in the last game was a matter of luck as well as quick responses. The force caused by the crash between the tank and the jeep threw Sebastian out of the jeep just below the hatch of the helicopter, from where he was pulled up by Michael. Therefore, Michael was finally successful in saving Sebastian Shultz in the game 'Warzone'. After the game was over, the screen flashed a score of 40000000.

13. How did Sebastian Shultz communicate with Michael? What did he say in his last message?

***Or* What did Sebastian write in the final e-mail he sent to Michael?**

Ans. Sebastian Shultz communicated with Michael through computer printouts. His last message was sent through an e-mail. In it, Sebastian had thanked Michael for saving his life. He also expressed a wish to meet Michael soon in real life. Besides, he wanted Michael to keep the games as he had earned them.

14. 'A real message from the real Sebastian Shultz', says Michael. What does he mean by this?

Ans. Michael had always met Sebastian as a character in his games. All his messages so far had also been in the form of computer printouts. However, his last message to Michael was an e-mail sent by the real Sebastian, not a character in the virtual world of psycho-drive computer games.

15. How, according to you, did Sebastian's normal life get revived? Give an argument in support of your answer. **CBSE 2025**

Ans. Sebastian's normal life was revived when Michael successfully rescued him from the virtual world by completing *Warzone*. This is confirmed by a newspaper article stating Sebastian had recovered from his coma. The story suggests a mysterious connection between virtual reality and real life, where Michael's actions influenced Sebastian's survival.

Long Answer Type Questions

Answers the following questions in 150 words.

1. How was Michael able to rescue Sebastian in the end? Describe the values you could identify from this act of rescuing.

Ans. In the last game 'Warzone', Michael finds himself in a war zone in a city. He along with Shultz had to make it to the helicopter safely amidst gunfire and bomb explosions. Braving a tank fire they attempt to escape. They found a jeep on the road side, boarded it and headed for the helicopter. Just then, a tank came hurtling towards them. Sebastian suddenly applied the brakes and the jeep skidded into a spin. While Michael leapt clear out of the jeep and jumped into the helicopter, Shultz failed to make it.

The tank crashed into the jeep, throwing Shultz into the air. He tumbled round and round and landed just below the helicopter hatch. Michael pulled him up and the helicopter soared into the sky. Thus, Michael succeeded in saving Sebastian at last. This act of rescuing Sebastian displayed the boys' determination to be successful. Through this we learn the value of unity. Their success was a result of systematic planning and execution, teamwork and dedication towards a common goal.

2. In what sense can we call Michael a true gentleman?

Ans. Michael was a true gentleman by nature and temperament. Although he loved playing violent games like 'Warzone', 'Wildwest' and 'Jailbreak', he was in fact a child at heart who loved adventure and was mesmerized by the evolving technology.

Even though he was eager to play the psycho-drive games he had recently bought at the fair, he puts aside his feelings on the matter and immediately begins helping Sebastian without even having understood the situation. Even after repeated failures and his own limited information on the true situation of Sebastian, he never stops trying. He continues his attempts to save Sebastian just because the other boy had asked for help. Hence, through his actions Michael turns out to be a real gentleman.

3. What was the real message to Michael by the real Sebastian Shultz? Briefly describe how the writer has tried to convey certain values through this message.

Ans. The real Sebastian Shultz communicated with Michael through an e-mail. Sebastian thanked Michael for saving his life. He expressed his wish to meet Michael soon in real life. Besides that, he wanted Michael to keep the games since he had earned them.

Through this communication the writer has tried to convey the value of being grateful towards others. Sebastian's rescue from the games was only possible due to the teamwork and coordination that both Michael and Sebastian show while playing the game. It was their teamwork that had won.

Moreover, it led to the beginning of a new friendship. There developed a bond between themselves and Sebastian was ready to share his games with Michael. Though the games belonged to Sebastian Shultz, he did not want them back and instead asked Michael to keep them as he had earned them. This shows his selfless nature. The writer, thus, brings out the values of gratitude, teamwork and selflessness through the characters in the story.

4. Will power and determination bring success against all odds. Elaborate with reference to the lesson 'Virtually True'.

Or **Will power and determination bring success against all odds. Comment with reference to 'Virtually True'?** **CBSE 2024**

Ans. The story 'Virtually True' teaches us the value of perseverance. It shows how will power and determination brings success against all odds. They help us to achieve our goal successfully.

In the story, Sebastian Shultz meets with an accident while playing one of the psycho-driven games on his laptop. He bangs his head on his laptop and loses consciousness. In the hospital, despite the doctor's hopes, he goes into a coma.

When Michael starts playing the game, 'Wildwest', Sebastian contacts him and requests Michael to rescue him. The rescue efforts happen in the games Wildwest, Dragonquest and Jailbreak but in all attempts, Michal sees failure. However, he does not lose hope. Moreover, it is Sebastian who keeps on cheering him and instilling confidence in him. Both the boys keep fighting and never give up.

It is in the last game, 'Warzone', that their will power and determination finally pays off and Michael is able to rescue Sebastian and help him retrieve his memory, which brings him out of the coma. Thus, it is their perseverance that helps them succeed in their endeavour.

5. I shook my head. A real message from the real Sebastian Shultz. We both knew that by reliving the accident, something wonderful had happened. But then again, now that there are two advanced intelligences on earth, who can say what is and what isn't possible.
What I know is this. Everything that I've described is true-Virtually!
You feel that the youth of the country is an asset and should not waste too much time enjoying the virtual world. They should be ambitious, industrious and must try to face the challenges of the real world. Write an article highlighting the strengths of the youth and how they can be supported to be able to use their potential to the maximum. **Competency Based**

Ans.

Virtual v/s Real

The youth of the country is an asset and should not waste too much time enjoying the virtual world. They should learn to be practical in their approach and be prepared for the challenges that are thrown up by life. In today's world, there are a lot of distractions such as the mobile phones, computers, etc. As a result, the youth is not focused.

The young generation needs to be more ambitious and should channelise its energy in the right direction. In the story, 'Virtually True', the way Michael rescued Sebastian in the game and saved his life shows that our youth definitely has the potential to put technology to good use when needed.

Today's world provides a lot of exposure and learning which the youth can use for helping humanity and make the nation progress. What they can do virtually can be experienced in the real world. They should learn to share their learning and put in their best efforts to bring about a change in the country. The older generation needs to guide the youth in the right direction. They should help imbibe good values in them. With proper guidance and support, the youth can help the country to prosper.

6. The story Virtually True has elements of virtual reality and advanced technology that contrast with the traditional ghostly occurrences in Shady Plot. How do these contrasting themes and narrative styles contribute to the overall tone and meaning of each story? **CBSE SQP 2024**

Ans. The contrasting themes and narrative styles in Virtually True and Shady Plot significantly contribute to the tone and meaning of each story. They highlight the ways in which technology and traditional ghostly occurrences evoke different emotional responses and reflections on the nature of reality, the supernatural, and human experience.

The contrast between these two stories lies primarily in their approach to the supernatural and the emotional reactions they provoke in the reader. Virtually True explores how technology and virtual reality can create disorienting and unsettling experiences that challenge perceptions of reality. The tone is more modern, focused on the dangers of the future and the complexities of living in a world where the digital and physical worlds are increasingly intertwined.

In contrast, Shady Plot draws from a rich tradition of ghost stories, using the supernatural as a way to explore timeless human fears, such as death, the unknown, and the consequences of past actions. Its slower-paced, more atmospheric tone emphasizes a sense of mystery and dread that is both intellectual and emotional.

The contrasting themes in these stories contribute to different interpretations of what it means to confront the unknown. In Virtually True, the unknown is represented by technology's potential to distort reality. Meanwhile, Shady Plot uses the traditional ghost story to explore the human condition, specifically the idea of unfinished business, guilt, and the unresolved nature of human existence. In summary, the contrasting themes and narrative styles of Virtually True and Shady Plot, serve to evoke different emotional tones and offer distinct reflections on the nature of reality, the unknown, and the human experience.

ASSESSMENT EXERCISE

Extract Based Questions

Read the following extracts carefully and answer the questions that follow.

1. I suddenly saw the photograph that went with the story and gasped. The boy in the picture was Sebastian. There was no doubt. "But how?" I muttered.
   (i) Who is 'I'?
   (ii) Whose photograph did he see?
   (iii) What was the story about?
   (iv) What had happened to him?

Short Answer Type Questions

Answer the following questions in 30-40 words.

1. What had happened to Sebastian Shultz? How was he at present?
2. When did the first video game Wildwest become complicated?
3. Who was the second sheriff? How does the narrator describe him?
4. How did the second game appear to be more real than virtual?
5. What did Shultz suggest to Michael to save him? What happened when the narrator swiped a skeleton's e-card?

Long Answer Type Questions

Answer the following questions in 150 words.

1. 'Virtual' means something which does not really exist but only seems to exist. It has no reality in real time and space but only exists in cyber space. The story written by Paul Stewart highlights the story of Michael who plays psycho-drive interactive games. You are a student of class 10th. After reading this lesson, write an article on 'The Future of Virtual Reality'.
2. Answering a reporter's question as to what the family was going to do next, Mr. Shultz said that they were off to stock up on some games.
   Computers, especially computer games, are a rage with children as well as adults. They play an important role in our lives but they are also a major distraction and have their hazards. In 150 words, write an article on the hazards of addiction and how to overcome them.
3. The story 'Virtually True' depicts a world of immense possibilities, resulting out of a synthesis of human intelligence and the artificial intelligence of computers. Write a short note on how computer games enhance and promote values like goal selling and achievement, problem solving, meeting challenges, etc.

Section D : Literature
Textbook : Interact in English, (Poetry)

The Frog and The Nightingale

by Vikram Seth

CHAPTER 1

Introduction 'The Frog and the Nightingale' revolves around the two main characters - the Nightingale and the Frog. It tells us how the cruel frog pushes the innocent nightingale towards death.

In this poem, the poet tells us the importance of self-confidence and moral courage. The poem highlights the situation of those innocent people whose simplicity and trustful nature makes them complete misfits in the world of manipulation. In order to survive in this manipulative world, it is important to have worldly wisdom.

Stanzawise Explanation

Stanza 1 (Lines 1-14)

Once upon a time a frog
Croaked away in Bingle Bog
Every night from dusk to dawn
He croaked awn and awn and awn.
Other creatures loathed his voice,
But, alas, they had no choice.
And the crass cacophony
Blared out from the sumac tree
At whose foot the frog each night
Minstrelled on till morning light.
Neither stones nor prayers nor sticks,
Insults or complaints or bricks
Stilled the frog's determination
To display his heart's elation.

Explanation Once upon a time, there lived a frog in a place named Bingle Bog. He would sing every night from dusk to dawn (throughout the night).

The other creatures of the bog hated his loud and unpleasant voice. However, they had no option but to listen to him sing. Sitting at the foot of the sumac tree, the frog sang constantly each night till the next morning.

The creatures of the bog tried every trick to stop the frog from singing. They pelted stones at him, requested him, hit him with sticks and bricks, and even insulted him. However, nothing could deter the frog from singing. He was determined to display his heart's pride and joy, and continued singing loudly.

Stanza 2 (Lines 15-32)

But one night a nightingale
In the moonlight cold and pale
Perched upon the sumac tree
Casting forth her melody.
Dumbstruck sat the gaping frog.
And the whole admiring bog
Stared towards the sumac, rapt,
And, when she had ended, clapped,
Ducks had swum and herons waded
To her as she serenaded
And a solitary loon
Wept, beneath the summer moon.
Toads and teals and tiddlers, captured
By her voice, cheered on, enraptured:
"Bravo!" "Too divine!" "Encore!"

So the nightingale once more,
Quite unused to such applause,
Sang till dawn without a pause.

Explanation One night, a nightingale came to the Bingle Bog and sat upon the branch of the sumac tree. In the cold and dim moonlight, she started singing in her sweet voice. Every creature in the bog was pleasantly surprised to hear such a sweet song. The frog was so surprised that he sat with an open mouth.

All the creatures in the bog listened to the song and looked towards the sumac tree with attention. They cheered and clapped when the song ended. Duck swum and the herons walked through water only to listen to the beautiful song of the nightingale.

The loon, a large water bird, was so impressed by the beauty of the song that he started weeping. Other creatures like toads, tiddlers, teals, etc. were also captivated by her voice and appreciated her song.

All the creatures of the bog requested her to sing the song once more. The nightingale, who was not used to such kind of appreciation, got excited and sang her song continuously till dawn.

Stanza 3 (Lines 33-46)

Next night when the Nightingale
Shook her head and twitched her tail,
Closed an eye and fluffed a wing
And had cleared her throat to sing
She was startled by a croak.
"Sorry - was that you who spoke?"
She enquired when the frog
Hopped towards her from the bog.
"Yes", the frog replied. "You see,
I'm the frog who owns this tree.
In this bog I've long been known
For my splendid baritone
And, of course, I wield my pen
For Bog Trumpet now and then."

Explanation Next night, when the nightingale shook her head and pulled her tail, closed an eye, fluttered a wing and cleared her throat to sing, she was stopped by the sudden croaking of the frog. The nightingale asked the frog if it was he who had spoken just then to which the frog affirmed. Then, the frog told the nightingale that he owned the sumac tree and was well-known for his singing in the bog. He added that because of his talent he also wrote songs/columns for the magazine 'Bog Trumpet'.

Stanza 4 (Lines 47-56)

"Did you… did you like my song?"
"Not too bad - but far too long.
The technique was fine of course,
But it lacked a certain force."
"Oh!" the nightingale confessed.
Greatly flattered and impressed
That a critic of such note
Had discussed her art and throat:
"I don't think the song's divine.
But - oh, well - at least it's mine".

Explanation The nightingale was impressed and believed that the frog was a great singer and critic. So, she asked the frog if her song had impressed him. Intentionally, the frog did not praise her song. Instead, he called it 'too long' and said that it lacked force.

The nightingale felt disappointed that a talented critic like the frog had not liked her song. However, she was happy that the frog had discussed her art of singing. Accepting the frog's opinion, the nightingale told the frog that her song was original and she had not copied anyone.

Stanza 5 (Lines 57-68)

"That's not much to boast about".
Said the heartless frog. "Without
Proper training such as I
-And few others - can supply.
You'll remain a mere beginner.
But with me you'll be a winner".
"Dearest frog", the nightingale
Breathed: "This is a fairy tale -
And you're Mozart in disguise
Come to earth before my eyes".
"Well I charge a modest fee.
Oh!... But it won't hurt, you'll see"

Explanation The frog told the nightingate that her song was not so good that she could boast about it. According to him, the nightingale was a beginner and still needed some well-planned training, which only he could provide. He told her that he could turn her into a winner. The nightingale said that it was like a dream come true that such a great musician like him was offering to train her. She was thinking that it was Mozart who had come in disguise of the frog to teach her. The frog immediately stated his demand. He wanted to train her for a modest fee.

Stanza 6 (Lines 69-84)

Now the nightingale inspired,
Flushed with confidence, and fired
With both art and adoration,
Sang - and was a huge sensation.
Animals for miles around
Flocked towards the magic sound,
And the frog with great precision
Counted heads and charged admission.
Though next morning it was raining,
He began her vocal training.
"But I can't sing in this weather".
"Come my dear - we'll sing together.
Just put on your scarf and sash,
Koo-oh-ah! ko-ash! ko-ash!"
So the frog and nightingale
Journeyed up and down the scale

Explanation After hearing the frog's words, the nightingale was inspired and gained confidence. She sang with great adoration (love). Her voice was so melodious that many animals came from far off places towards that sumac tree only to listen to the song of the nightingale. The frog was very greedy. He started charging admission fee from all the animals after counting them.

The frog started the vocal training of the nightingale. As it was raining heavily the next morning, the nightingale did not want to sing. She told him that she could not sing in that weather. However, the frog gently convinced her to continue her training by accompanying him in singing. He asked her to wear her scarf and sash. Then, they started singing together in high and low notes.

Stanza 7 (Lines 85-98)

For six hours, till she was shivering
And her voice was hoarse and quivering.
Though subdued and sleep deprived,
In the night her throat revived,
And the sumac tree was bowed,
With a breathless, titled crowd:
Owl of Sandwich, Duck of Kent,
Mallard and Milady Trent,
Martin Cardinal Mephisto,
And the Coot of Monte Cristo,
Ladies with tiaras glittering
In the interval sat twittering -
And the frog observed them glitter
With a joy both sweet and bitter.

Explanation For six hours without a break, the frog and the nightingale sang together in different notes and pitch. Continuous singing in the rainy weather resulted in the nightingale's voice becoming rough and unclear. She was also sleep deprived because she used to practice during the day and gave her performance at night.

Many creatures came to listen to the sweet and melodious song of the nightingale. They were so many in number that even the sumac tree bowed under their weight. Distinguished personalities from the royalty like the Owl of Sandwich, Duck of Kent, the Coot of Monte Cristo and even the royal ladies wearing glittering crowns came to attend her concert and listen to her songs.

The frog was observing all that and felt bitter that they did not like his singing. However, at the same time, he was happy because he had charged admission fee from so many animals and had raised a good amount.

Stanza 8 (Lines 99-122)

Every day the frog who'd sold her
Songs for silver tried to scold her:
"You must practice even longer
Till your voice, like mine grows stronger.
In the second song last night
You got nervous in mid-flight.
And, my dear, lay on more trills:
Audiences enjoy such frills.
You must make your public happier:
Give them something sharper, snappier.
We must aim for better billings.
You still owe me sixty shillings."
Day by day the nightingale
Grew more sorrowful and pale.
Night on night her tired song
Zipped and trilled and bounced along,
Till the birds and beasts grew tired
At a voice so uninspired
And the ticket office gross
Crashed, and she grew more morose -
For her ears were now addicted
To applause quite unrestricted,
And to sing into the night
All alone gave no delight.

Explanation The frog trained the nightingale and scolded her for not singing properly. He told her that she had got nervous while singing the song the previous night and commanded her to practice singing till her voice grew as strong as the voice of the frog.

The innocent nightingale could not understand the bad intentions of the frog and kept on practising the way the frog guided her.

The frog told her to lay stress on musical notes as it was important to keep her audience happy. He added that she must give her audience something sharper so that they kept coming to the sumac tree to listen to her song. He, further, informed her that they should aim for better performance to get more money as the nightingale still owed sixty shillings to the frog.

After being ill-treated and exploited for days, the nightingale grew pale and sorrowful. All the originality and energy in her songs vanished and her songs became stale, old and mechanical. Now, her songs did not bring a divine joy to the creatures of the bog. So, gradually, the audience stopped going to her concerts. The nightingale had become addicted to singing in front of a large crowd along with the applause she received. As a result, singing all alone in night did not delight her.

Stanza 9 (Lines 123-140)

Now the frog puffed up with rage.
"Brainless bird - you're on the stage -
Use your wits and follow fashion.
Puff your lungs out with your passion."
Trembling, terrified to fail,
Blind with tears, the nightingale
Heard him out in silence, tried,
Puffed up, burst a vein, and died.
Said the frog: "I tried to teach her,
But she was a stupid creature -
Far too nervous, far too tense.
Far too prone to influence.
Well, poor bird - she should have known
That your song must be your own.
That's why I sing with panache:
"Koo-oh-ah! ko-ash! ko-ash!"
And the foghorn of the frog
Blared unrivalled through the bog.

Explanation The frog was annoyed as the audience stopped coming to the concert. He got so angry that he called the nightingale 'a brainless bird'. He reminded her that she was a stage performer, so she should perform what the audience liked or what the trend was. He asked her to be passionate about her singing. Hearing the frog, the nightingale feared failure. Following his instructions, she put in more force in her song. Tired, humiliated, exploited and sleep-deprived, the nightingale burst a vein and died.

The frog clarified to the creatures of the bog that he was her helper and tried to train her in the best possible manner. However, the nightingale was a very tense and nervous creature. He called her a 'poor bird', showing false sympathy.

The frog then, added that one should have originality in songs. He cited himself as an example and said that he always sang with a confident style of his own. So, just like before, the frog started singing in a loud, jarring tone and he once again became the undisputed singer of Bingle Bog.

Poetic Devices Used in the Poem

Alliteration Repetition of initial consonant sounds in the same line.

- Bingle bog
- Dusk to dawn
- Brainless bird
- Crass cacophony
- Something sharper, snappier
- Better billings

Imagery It is the literary term used for language and description that appeals to our five senses.

Moonlight cold and pale

Metaphor A device which compares two things or qualities which are unlike.

This is a fairy tale - and you're Mozart in disguise

Onomatopoeia Using a word which suggests the meanings by its sound.

- awn and awn and awn
- ko-ash, ko-ash

Personification A figure of speech which is used for an inanimate object or animals/birds that look or feel human qualities.

Symbolism Where an object, person or situation has another meaning other than its literal meaning.

- The frog symbolises cunning and opportunistic people
- The nightingale symbolises innocent, gullible and naturally talented artists

Parody It is a piece of writing that intimates another piece of writing or an author's style, to produce humor.

- Owl of Sandwich
- Duck of Kent
- Mallard and Milady Trent
- Martin Cardinal Mephisto
- The Coot of Monte Cristo

Word Meaning

Word	Meaning
Stanza 1	
croaked	gave out low and sharp sounds
awn	on; spelt thus to make it rhyme with dawn.
loathed	hated, disliked greatly
alas	at last
crass	coarse, rough
cacophony	a harsh discordant mixture of sounds
blared out	sounded loudly
minstrelled	sang; minstrels were medieval entertainers, who travelled from place to place to sing or recite poetry
Stanza 2	
pale	herein quiet
perched	settled
casting forth	delivering, singing to a gathering
dumbstruck	speechless due to shock
gaping	looking at something with an expression of shock
rapt	fascinated, enraptured
waded	walked through water
serenaded	sang beautifully
solitary	herein single in number
loon	a short-tailed, fish-eating water bird
teals	small freshwater ducks
tiddlers	small fish
enraptured	charmed, pleased greatly
Stanza 3	
twitched	moved or jerked suddenly
fluffed	made to appear fuller by shaking or brushing
baritone	an adult male singing voice, usually deep or heavy
wield my pen	write effectively
Stanza 4	
flattered	praised, complimented

Word	Meaning
critic	analyser, person who expresses opinion
divine	delightful, very pleasing, related to God
Stanza 5	
breathed	said
Mozart	W. Mozart was an influential German music composer of the classical era
disguise	different appearance to conceal one's identity
modest	small amount
Stanza 6	
flushed	excited or elated by something
sash	a long strip of cloth worn over one shoulder or round the waist, as a badge of honour or as part of an official dress
scale	a set of musical notes
Stanza 7	
hoarse	sounding rough and harsh
quivering	shaking, trembling
subdued	quiet, with little energy or spirit
tiaras	semi-circular metal bands decorated with jewels and worn by wealthy women on formal social occasions
Stanza 8	
trills	repeated short high sounds
frills	an extra feature or embellishment
snappier	sharper, more catchy
billings	publicity or promotion
zipped	sang at high speed
morose	ill-tempered, miserable
Stanza 9	
puffed up	filled up
wits	intelligence
panache	confident style or manner
foghorn	a loud, deep, unpleasant sound
unrivalled	having none to match

Textbook FOLDER

Here, we have covered questions given in the CBSE Textbook along with their answer

ON PAGE 91

Q.5 The following is a summary of the poem, but it is jumbled up. Write out the events in their correct order to form a continuous paragraph.

(a) As a result, her voice lost its beauty, and the other creatures stopped coming to hear her sing.

(b) Soon, the nightingale became famous and creatures from miles around came to hear her sing.

(c) All the creatures in the bog cheered and clapped at her beautiful song.

(d) He offered to train the nightingale so that she could sing even more beautifully.

(e) So the frog could sing unrivalled in the bog once more.

(f) The next night, the frog introduced himself.

(g) The frog charged an admission fee and earned a lot of money from these concerts.

(h) A frog croaked all night in a bog in an unpleasant voice.

(i) But the frog made the nightingale rehearse continuously in the rain.

(j) One night, a nightingale began to sing in a melodious voice.

(k) Finally, the nightingale burst a vein and died.

Ans. (h) A frog croaked all night in a bog in an unpleasant voice.

(j) One night, a nightingale began to sing in a melodious voice.

(c) All the creatures in the bog cheered and clapped at her beautiful song.

(f) The next night, the frog introduced himself.

(d) He offered to train the nightingale so that she could sing even more beautifully.

(b) Soon, the nightingale became famous and creatures from miles around came to hear her sing.

(g) The frog charged an admission fee and earned a lot of money from these concerts.

(i) But the frog made the nightingale rehearse continuously in the rain.

(a) As a result, her voice lost its beauty and the other creatures stopped coming to hear her sing.

(k) Finally, the nightingale burst a vein and died.

ON PAGE 91-92

Q.6 Now that you have read the poem, add more personality traits to the word-web of the frog and the nightingale as depicted in the poem. Then complete the table given below. (Some of the words in the box below the table may help you. You may also use the word given in Q.1.)

Character	*Extract*	*Personality Traits*
Nightingale	Sorry- was that you who spoke?	(a) Polite, Timorous
Frog	Yes,......you see, I'm the frog who owns this tree. In this bog I've long been known For my splendid baritone.	(b)
Nightingale	Did you....did you like my song?	(c)
Frog	Not too bad-but far too long. The technique was fine, of course But it lacked a certain force.	(d)
Frog	Without proper training such as I And a few others can supply You'll remain a mere beginner, But with me you'll be a winner.	(e)
Nightingale	But I can't sing in this weather.	(f)

Nightingale	......This is a fairy tale – And you're Mozart in disguise Come to Earth before my eyes.	(g)
Frog	Come, my dear-we'll sing together.	(h)
Frog	We must aim for better billings. You still owe me sixty shillings.	(i)
Frog	Brainless bird - you're on the stage Use your wits and follow fashion. Puff your lungs out with your passion.	(j)
Frog	......I tried to teach her, But she was a stupid creature.	(k)

Dismissive	Nervous	Timid
Presumptuous	Superior	Fawning
Shy	Polite	Meek
Possessive	Dominating	Mercenary

Ans. (b) Territorial, boastful, proud
(c) Hesitant, modest
(d) Dismissive, superior, patronising
(e) Dominating, superior, haughty, boastful
(f) Timid, nervous
(g) Eager to please, flattering
(h) Polite, possessive, hypocrite
(i) Crafty, selfish, mercenary
(j) Arrogant, overbearing, authoritative
(k) Dismissive, deceitful, clever, arrogant

ON PAGE 93

Q.8 On the basis of your understanding of the poem, complete the sentences given below by choosing the most appropriate options.

(i) The frog's aim was to
(a) make the nightingale a sensation.
(b) make the nightingale as good a singer as him.
(c) maintain his supremacy in the bog.
(d) make a lot of money.

Ans. (c) maintain his supremacy in the bog.

(ii) The animals reacted to the nightingale's song with
(a) hatred
(b) admiration
(c) indifference
(d) suggestions for improvement

Ans. (b) admiration

(iii) The nightingale accepted the frog's tutelage as she
(a) was not confident of herself.
(b) wanted to become as good a singer as the frog.
(c) wanted to become a professional singer.
(d) was not a resident of Bingle Bog.

Ans. (a) was not confident of herself.

ON PAGE 94

Q.9 Read the stanza given below and complete the sentences by choosing the most appropriate option.

Day by day the nightingale
Grew more sorrowful and pale.
Night on night her tired song
Zipped and trilled and bounced along,
Till the birds and beasts grew tired
At a voice so uninspired
And the ticket office gross
Crashed, and she grew more morose –
For her ears were now addicted
To applause quite unrestricted,
And to sing into the night
All alone gave no delight.

I. The nightingale was sorrowful and pale because
(a) she had been practising in the rain.
(b) she had been performing all night.
(c) she was losing confidence in herself.
(d) she was falling ill.

Ans. (b) she had been performing all night.

II. The audience was tired of her song because
(a) they had heard it many times.
(b) it had become mechanical.
(c) she looked tired.
(d) she had added trills to her song.

Ans. (b) it had become mechanical.

III. She no longer enjoyed singing alone as
(a) she wanted to sing only for a titled crowd.
(b) she was now used to the appreciation she got.
(c) the frog was no longer with her.
(d) she had become proud of herself.

Ans. (b) she was now used to the appreciation she got.

ON PAGE 94-95

Q.10 Answer the following questions briefly.

(a) How did the creatures of Bingle Bog react to the nightingale's singing?

Ans. All the creatures of Bingle Bog appreciated the nightingale's singing. They cheered and clapped at her songs. Creatures from far off places gathered to enjoy the melodious song. They listened to her with undivided attention and were totally enchanted.

(b) Which are the different ways in which the frog asserts his importance?

Ans. To assert his importance, the frog tells the nightingale that he is a great singer and the owner of the sumac tree. He declares that he is an expert singer and that he writes songs columns for the magazine 'Bog Trumpet'. He also informs her that he can give her training to sing better.

(c) Why is the frog's joy both sweet and bitter?

Ans. The frog's joy is sweet because he is earning money as he charges fees for hearing the nightingale. His joy is bitter because the nightingale has broken his self-proclaimed singing supremacy in the bog. He felt jealous of the popularity of the nightingale.

(d) Why was the frog angry?

Ans. The frog was angry because the nightingale's voice was no longer sweet and inspired. His long practice and over-rehearsal had made her voice sound mechanical and tired. As a result, he was not earning enough money.

(e) How did the frog become the unrivalled king of the bog again ?

Ans. The frog exploited the nightingale to the extent of causing her death. He made her sing day and night and in pouring rain. She was so exhausted that one of her veins burst and she died. In this way, the frog became the unrivalled king of the bog again.

ON PAGE 95

Q.11 Discuss the following questions and write the answers in your notebooks.

(a) Bring out the irony in the frog's statement – 'Your song must be your own'.

Ans. The statement made by the frog is ironical as he was the one who drove the nightingale away from her originality.

Initially, the nightingale's song was melodious as well as original. She had even defended herself against the frog's criticism, saying that her songs were her own. It was here that the harsh and jealous frog had cunningly convinced her that originality did not make much of a difference. During the training sessions, the frog made every possible effort to obstruct the original talent of the nightingale. He insisted that she should copy his style, as that was the fashion of the times. Thus, the frog's remark on maintaining the originality of art is quite ironic as he himself had manipulated the nightingale into following or imitating him.

(b) Do you think that the end of the poem is justified?

Ans. I think that the end of the poem is justified. The poet had purposely ended the poem to display the loss/death of innocence at the hands of evil. The nightingale symbolises innocence which is destroyed by the evil frog. The nightingale's end, then, shows how innocent people become victims to the upper-class, powerful and evil people in our real world.

(c) Do you think the nightingale is 'brainless'? Give reasons for your answer.

Ans. Yes, I find the nightingale to be truly 'brainless'. First, she couldn't see through the initial talk of the frog, when he impressed her with his knowledge and talent in singing.

Second, she couldn't make out why the frog had been making her sing non-stop. Furthermore, she couldn't understand that the frog was exploiting her and earning money when he talked of 'sixty shillings' that she owed him. In a way, she did not realise that the frog was slowly destroying her.

(d) In spite of having a melodious voice and being a crowd puller, the nightingale turns out to be a loser and dies. How far is she responsible for her own downfall?

Or **After reading the poem 'The Frog and the Nightingale', you are filled with compassion and sympathy for the nightingale. With reference to the poem, discuss how it was her timid and gullible nature that led to her downfall.**

Ans. One cannot deny that the evil and sly frog is very much responsible for the innocent nightingale's miserable death. However, one also has to agree that the nightingale is also to be blamed for her tragic end. The nightingale is too gullible, meaning that she is easily persuaded by the frog to believe what he says. That's why she is easily deceived by the sinister and cunning frog. She gets 'training' from the frog to give more pleasure to her audience.

She has no confidence in her own abilities. So, she easily gives in and follows the frog's commands in the name of training.

However, the greatest weakness of her personality is that she is unable to understand the intentions of the cruel frog who can't bear to see her talent.

(e) Do you agree with the frog's inference of the nightingale's character? Give reasons for your answer.

Ans. The frog's inference of the nightingale's character is absolutely right. He calls her timid and foolish.

He also says that she was far too prone to influence. The sly and cunning frog easily manipulated her, which finally led to her demise. The nightingale had no confidence. She easily believed whatever the frog told her.

Being flattered and submissive and timid, she invited her own death upon herself. She should have been able to see through the frog's plot and responded accordingly. However, her innocence didn't allow her to see through the cunning frog's tricks. Hence, his inference was correct.

DISCUSSION ON PAGE 95

Q.12 (a) How does a person try to put down another person when the latter is succeeding in his or her life?

Ans. There are many strategies used by people to put down another person who is succeeding in his/her life. These include

- Constantly complaining
- Finding faults
- Comparisons

(b) Our self-image is often based on what others make us believe. A poor self-image can do irreparable damage to us. Do you agree with this statement? Elaborate with suitable reasons and examples.

***Or* Our self-image is often based on what others make us believe we are. With reference to the poem 'The Frog and the Nightingale', write an article on "Poor Self-Image can be Self-Destructive".**

Ans. Poor Self-Image can be Self-Destructive
by Akansha

Our self-image is often based on what others make us believe we are. A poor self-image can do irreparable damage to us. This is evident from the poem 'The Frog and the Nightingale'.

The nightingale is melodious, simple-hearted and innocent but she lacks self-confidence. As a result, she easily allows herself to be exploited by the shrewd, crafty, and deceptive frog. The frog felt that the nightingale had threatened his sovereignty in Bingle Bog. So, he devised a plan to finish the nightingale.

The timid and under confident nightingale fell for the clever frog's word to ultimately lose her life.Just like the nightingale, who has a poor self-image, there are many people around us who are under confident. Such people do not believe in their capabilities and talents. As a result, they are suppressed and fearful. Their lack of confidence becomes an agency for the cruel, crafty and scheming people who exploit them. In the end, such people are at loss. They do not succeed and end up depressed as well as anxious.

WRITING TASK

Q.13 The nightingale has scaled the heights of success. But now the audience is dwindling, the frog is unhappy and reprimands her all the time. She is mentally and physically exhausted and fears failure. As the nightingale, write a diary entry highlighting her fears and analysing the reasons for her failure.

Ans. Wednesday, 19th November, 20XX 7:00 p.m.

Dear Diary

I am feeling very exhausted but I have to continue singing tonight due to my teacher's insistence that the show must go on.

I feel exhausted both physically and mentally and its impact is showing in my dwindling performance. My audience is getting bored with my monotonous singing. This is probably due to the non-stop singing I have been indulging in at the insistence of my teacher, the Frog. He keeps on pushing me to sing, although very often I do not feel I can go on any longer. The audience also does not cheer me, as they now rarely applaud my singing.

I am getting fearful that I will soon collapse from exhaustion. Tonight, I will muster up enough courage to tell the Frog that I need rest. If he does not agree, I may even fly away from Bingle Bog and settle on another tree somewhere else where I can get rest.

Wish me luck.

The Nightingale

Q.14 Write an obituary for the nightingale. You may begin like this:

May the kind soul .... (or you may make use of your own beginning).

Ans. May God give the kind departed soul peace and bless her!

The Nightingale was a simple, unsuspecting and talented bird. She personified ideal human qualities and had no ill-will against anybody. She did not suspect anyone of evil intentions, leave alone the frog, who she thought was her teacher. She believed that everybody was like her due to which she was deceived by the clever frog. She did not understand that he intended her to die with overexertion so that his singing could rule over Bingle Bog again.

She died a martyr to the cause of melodious singing. May she rest in peace!

REVIEW EXERCISE

Including Previous Years' and Practice Questions

Extract Based Questions

Read the following extracts carefully and answer the questions that follow.

1. Once upon a time a frog
Croaked away in Bingle Bog
Every night from dusk to dawn
He croaked awn and awn and awn.
Other creatures loathed his voice,
But, alas, they had no choice.

(a) What does 'Bingle Bog' refer to?

Ans. 'Bingle Bog' refers to a marshy land where the frog and the other creatures live.

(b) What does the phrase 'dusk to dawn' mean?

Ans. The phrase means that the frog croaked from evening to morning, i.e. throughout the night.

(c) What made the frog sing from dusk to dawn?

Ans. The frog thought that his voice was melodious. He sang from dusk to dawn to express his heart's elation.

(d) Why did other creatures loathe his voice?

Ans. The frog's cacophonous voice irritated others instead of pleasing them. So, they loathed his voice.

2. And the crass cacophony
Blared out from the sumac tree
At whose foot the frog each night
Minstrelled on till morning night.

(a) Why did the poet use the word 'minstrelled' for the frog?

Ans. 'Minstrels' were medieval singers. The poet used the word 'minstrelled' for the frog because the frog considered himself as one of them and sang till morning.

(b) The other creatures hate the frog's song. Why?

Ans. The other creatures hated his song because he had a very unpleasant and jarring voice.

(c) What does the word 'alas' signify here?

Ans. The word 'alas' here signifies the sorrow of other creatures.

(d) Why does the poet use the phrase 'blared out' here?

Ans. The phrase 'blared out' means to make an appalling noise like a sound causing irritation. The poet uses the phrase here to emphasise that the frog's cacophonous singing caused all the creatures much irritation.

3. Neither stones nor prayers nor sticks,
Insults or complaints or bricks
Stilled the frog's determination
To display his heart's elation.

(a) Give the rhyme scheme of the given stanza.

Ans. The rhyme scheme of the given stanza is *aabb*.

(b) What idea about the frog do you get from the above lines?

Ans. These lines show that the frog was stubborn.

(c) What is the synonym of 'elation'?

Ans. The synonym of 'elation' is 'joy'.

(d) Why did the frog continue singing despite complaints from the other creatures?

Ans. The frog continued singing despite complaints because he was a determined creature who wanted to express his joy of life, no matter what.

4. But one night a nightingale
In the moonlight cold and pale
Perched upon the sumac tree
Casting forth her melody.

(a) What change took place in the bog?

Ans. The change that took place in the bog was that a nightingale came and began to sing in a melodious voice.

(b) Where did the nightingale perch?

Ans. The nightingale perched upon the sumac tree.

(c) Select the phrase from the extract which signifies singing.

Ans. Casting forth her melody.

(d) Why was the moonlight 'cold and pale'?

Ans. The moonlight was cold and pale because it was the winter season.

5. Dumbstruck sat the gaping frog.
And the whole admiring bog
Stared towards the sumac, rapt,
And, when she had ended, clapped,
Ducks had swum and herons waded
To her as she serenaded.

(a) What was the frog feeling?

Ans. The frog was dumbstruck with amazement.

(b) The phrase, 'whole admiring bog' means ....

Ans. all the creatures of the bog admired the nightingale's singing

(c) Name the poetic device used in the last line.

Ans. Personification is used in the last line.

(d) What does the word 'rapt' mean here?

Ans. The word 'rapt' here means 'fascinated'.

6. I'm the frog who owns this tree.
In this bog I've long been known
For my splendid baritone
And, of course, I wield my pen for
Bog Trumpet now and then.

(a) Why is the frog famous in the bog?

Ans. The frog claims that he was famous in the bog for his singing skills. He was actually famous for his bad singing skills.

(b) Which characteristic trait of the frog is revealed from the above lines?

Ans. The given extract shows that the frog was jealous and manipulative. He tells the nightingale incorrect things to manipulate her views about him.

(c) Explain the term 'baritone'.

Ans. The term 'baritone' refers to a heavy male voice. Herein, it refers to the croaking noise created by the frog.

(d) How does the frog introduce himself?

Ans. The frog introduces himself as the owner of the tree on which the nightingale is perched. He adds that he is a great critic of music.

7. "Did you... did you like my song?"
"Not too bad - but far too long.
The technique was fine of course,
But it lacked a certain force."

(a) The word..........in the stanza is a synonym of 'devoid of.'

Ans. lacked

(b) The opinion expressed about the song ....

Ans. is to discourage the nightingale

(c) What does the first line reveal about the speaker?

Ans. The first line reveals that the speaker is feeling nervous and unsure.

(d) 'The technique was fine, of course'. What technique is being talked about?

Ans. The technique of the art of singing is being talked about here.

8. Now the nightingale inspired,
Flushed with confidence, and fired
With both art and adoration,
Sang – and was a huge sensation.
Animals for miles around
Flocked towards the magic sound,
And the frog with great precision
Counted heads and charged admission.

(a) What made the nightingale a huge sensation?

Ans. The nightingale's sweet and melodious singing made her a huge sensation.

(b) Why is the nightingale 'flushed with confidence'?

Ans. The nightingale was feeling 'flushed with confidence' because her singing had been appreciated.

(c) Which quality of the frog is evident?

Ans. The frog is money-minded and greedy.

(d) What does 'with great precision' mean?

Ans. 'With great precision' means 'to do something meticulously.'

9. "But I can't sing in this weather".
"Come my dear–we'll sing together.
Just put on your scarf and sash,
Koo-oh-ah! ko-ash! ko-ash!"

(a) Which quality of the frog is revealed here?

Ans. The frog's cunning and heartless quality is revealed here.

(b) Why can't the nightingale sing?

Ans. The nightingale couldn't sing as it was raining and her throat would go bad.

(c) The word .... in the extract means the same as 'a badge of honour.'

Ans. sash

(d) What weather is the speaker referring to in the first line ?

Ans. The nightingale is referring to the rainy weather in the first line.

10. Day by day the nightingale
Grew more sorrowful and pale.
Night on night her tired song
Zipped and trilled and bounced along.
Till the birds and beasts grew tired
At a voice so uninspired

(a) What made the nightingale sorrowful and pale?

Ans. Too much singing and humiliation by the frog made the nightingale sorrowful and pale.

(b) What does the word 'trilled' mean?

Ans. The word 'trilled' means shook and vibrated.

(c) Why did the birds and beasts grow tired?

Ans. The birds and beasts grew tired of the nightingale's uninspired songs.

(d) Why had the nightingale's singing become uninspired?

Ans. The nightingale's singing became uninspired because she had been demoralised by the continuous criticism of her singing by her teacher, the frog.

11. Now the frog puffed up with rage.
"Brainless bird - you're on the stage -
Use your wits and follow fashion.
Puff your lungs out with your passion."

(a) Why was the frog puffed up with rage ?

Ans. The frog was puffed up with rage because the nightingale's singing did not attract a huge audience anymore, resulting in less collections for the frog.

(b) Give the antonym of 'brainless'.

Ans. The antonym of 'brainless' is 'intelligent'.

(c) What happened when the nightingale puffed up her lungs?

Ans. When the nightingale puffed up her lungs, one of her veins burst because of the pressure and she died.

(d) Why did the frog call the nightingale 'brainless bird' ?

Ans. The nightingale's voice became uninspired which resulted in less income for the frog. Angry and concerned about his income, he called the nightingale a 'brainless bird'.

12. Well, poor bird – she should have known
That your song must be your own.
That's why I sing with panache:
"Koo-oh-ah! ko-ash! ko-ash!"
And the foghorn of the frog
Blared unrivalled through the bog.

(a) Why is the nightingale referred to as a poor bird?

Ans. The nightingale is being referred to as a poor bird because she was unable to understand the frog's cunningness, fell into his trap and ultimately died.

(b) What do you mean by the word 'foghorn' as used in the extract?

Ans. The word 'foghorn' means a loud and unpleasant sound.

(c) Which trait of the frog's character is reflected in these lines?

Ans. The frog's traits of jealousy and cunningness are reflected in these lines.

(d) Explain–'your song must be your own'?

Ans. This means that imitations lead us nowhere. One's own art and wit carries one forward in life.

Or

(a) How did the frog become 'unrivalled?

Ans. The frog became unrivalled by torturing the nightingale till her death. No other creature could compete with him in singing after the nightingale's death.

(b) Which poetic device has been used here?

Ans. Metaphor has been used in 'the foghorn of the frog.'

(c) What does the word, 'unrivalled' mean?

Ans. The word 'unrivalled' means to have none to match.

(d) What had happened just before this extract?

Ans. Just before this extract, the nightingale had died by bursting a vein due to overexertion.

Short Answer Type Questions

Answer the following questions in 30-40 words.

1. "To display his heart's elation." What do you understand by these words?

Ans. The frog considered himself a great singer but he had an unpleasant voice. The creatures of the bog did not wish to listen to his harsh and stupid singing. However, the frog's croaking couldn't be silenced as he was determined to express himself. The frog kept on singing as it filled his heart with joy.

2. What happened when a nightingale came and sang while sitting on the sumac tree?

Ans. One night, a nightingale came and sat on the sumac tree. She began to sing melodiously. Everybody was pleasantly surprised to hear such a melodious voice. They all admired her song. They were so charmed that they even asked her to sing once more.

3. The frog proudly countered the nightingale. Comment on this statement.

Ans. It is true that the frog proudly countered the nightingale on meeting her for the first time. He not only introduced himself as the owner of the sumac tree but also praised his own singing and said that he was famous for his fine sound. He boasted that in the capacity of a music critic, he wrote songs for the 'Bog Trumpet'.

4. In what ways had the nightingale's life changed after her arrival in the Bingle Bog? CBSE 2019

Ans. After arriving in the Bingle Bog, the nightingale's life changed dramatically. She rose to fame as a brilliant singer who had brought relief to the Bingle Bog's animals by taking on the sumac tree and outshining the frog's harsh voice. Furthermore, she also started giving great concerts under the guidance of the cunning frog. In addition, she had become used to her performances and applauses.

5. The frog judged the nightingale's song critically. Do you think he was fair in his judgment? Justify your answer.

Ans. The frog was not fair in his judgment. He was jealous of the nightingale's talent of singing and wanted to demoralise her. He intentionally criticised the nightingale's song by calling it "too long and lacking a certain force".

6. Explain the line, "But-oh, well-at least it's mine" in your own words.

Ans. The above line means that the composition, lyrics and tone of the nightingale's song were original. They were neither borrowed nor copied from anyone else. She was proud of singing her song without any training or instruction from anybody else.

7. Why do you think the nightingale lost her appeal for the masses?

Ans. The nightingale lost her appeal for the masses because her songs lacked originality. Moreover, her songs became stale, old and mechanical. Listening to her songs now gave no joy to the creatures of the bog and thus, gradually, the audience reduced in numbers.

8. What made the nightingale sad and sorrowful?

Ans. Excessive singing and harsh behaviour of the frog made the nightingale sad and sorrowful. She had to sing for long hours which made her throat harsh and rough. She lost the charm of her singing. All this drove her into an unpleasant situation.

9. Whose influence did the nightingale come under? What was its effect?

Ans. Gullible and foolish, the nightingale was easily influenced by the self-important frog. He ill-treated and exploited her for days together and she grew pale and sorrowful. After much humiliation and exploitation, the nightingale burst a vein and died.

10. How was the frog benefited by the nightingale's concerts?

Ans. The frog was benefited greatly by the nightingale's concerts. First, he made a lot of money from the nightingale's concerts. Then, he got rid of his rival by putting her through physical and mental torture and again established his supremacy.

11. Lack of confidence and her gullible nature led the nightingale to her unfortunate end. Elucidate.

Ans. The nightingale met an unfortunate end but to some extent she herself was responsible for her miserable fate. She had no confidence in her own abilities and was easily influenced and tricked by the frog. She was too gullible to understand that the frog was actually exploiting her.

12. Comment on the frog's character from the poem 'The Frog and the Nightingale'.

Ans. The frog is a manipulative and sinister personality. He is very cunning and shrewd. He tricks the nightingale into believing that he is a well wisher but exploits her to the extent of causing her death.

13. 'The Nightingale was a misfit in the world of the cunning.' Comment. CBSE 2020

Ans. Yes, we agree that the Nightingale was a misfit in the world of the cunning. The world is competitive and selfish and only those people who are cunning can survive in it. Gullible and innocent people like the Nightingale, who are trusting by nature, cannot survive in it and thus are considered a misfit.

14. The frog claims to be the best trainer in the field of music. Do you agree? Justify your answer.

Ans. It is absolutely wrong to say that the frog was a good trainer of music. Six hours of rigorous training in the rain, his constant rebuking of the nightingale and exploiting her mentally and financially, prove that he was a bad trainer who slowly but surely drove an innocent bird to a sudden death.

15. What was the frog's ulterior motive in making the nightingale add frills and trills to her songs?

Ans. The frog made the nightingale sing repeatedly with the aim of earning more money. He added more frills and trills to her voice so that, with time, her voice would be ruined and he would remain the sole superior singer of the bog.

16. Can you suggest an alternative ending for the poem?

Ans. The story could have ended with someone telling the nightingale about the frog's nature and jealousy. The nightingale would initially have been doubtful but with observation, she would have realised the frog's true intentions and would have left the bog for good.

Long Answer Type Questions

Answer the following questions in 150 words.

1. Contradict the fact that the nightingale did not deserve the frog's wrath.

Ans. The frog had been the sole singer of the Bingle Bog. Although the animals hated his voice, he had the freedom to sing unrivalled. However, when the nightingale came and sang her song, everything changed. Everyone, who hated the frog's voice, applauded the nightingale for her singing skills.

This hurt the frog and he took out his wrath of the nightingale. Even though, the nightingale nowhere deserved the frog's anger, he could only take it out on her as she seemed innocent enough to fall into his trap. If the nightingale had been confident in her abilities, she would not have accepted the frog's opinion or guidance. She may have even realised the frog's true intentions.

2. "Well, poor bird-she should have known that your song must be your own. That's why I sing with panache."

Though the nightingale is an excellent and naturally talented singer, she is called a poor singer and stupid animal by the frog. Explain how the nightingale lacked worldly wisdom which led to her miserable demise.

Ans. In today's world, it is required of a person to have worldly wisdom, otherwise she/ he has to face a similar fate as that of the nightingale. The nightingale sang beautifully but she was easily influenced by the cunning frog. Due to lack of worldly wisdom and being highly gullible, she believed whatever the frog told her and thus, was easily fooled by him.

Besides this, the nightingale believed the frog to be a great authority on music. Hence, she readily agreed to be coached by him. This was also due to her lack of confidence in her ability to sing wonderfully well. She did not use her intelligence and worked only according to the instructions of the frog, who earned money from her talent. He started torturing her and the nightingale became sorrowful and pale. Had she shown better self-confidence, she would not have been exploited by the dominating frog and her life could have been saved.

3. The nightingale placed her blind trust in the frog but he exploited her. With reference to the poem, elaborate on the statement 'Betrayal always comes from those whom you trust'.

Ans. The saying 'betrayal always comes from those whom you trust' has been depicted very well in this poem. Whenever we trust a person, we believe that everything he or she says or does is true and is done for our well-being. We trust such people completely and follow them blindly due to lack of confidence in ourselves. The people whom we trust completely often take advantage of the situation and betray us for their own selfish benefit. They do not bother what happens to us.

This is what happened with the nightingale. She placed her blind trust in the crafty frog who pretended to be her friend and well-wisher. He assumed the role of her trainer and subjected her to long and rigorous training. The nightingale felt that it would make her a better singer, whereas the frog actually intended to rob her of her natural talent and her original sweet voice. This helped the frog in successfully carrying out his evil intentions, ultimately resulting in her death due to overexertion.

4. "In today's manipulative world, it is not enough to have talent only, you also need to understand how to utilise it properly." Comment.

Ans. It is true in the modern world that, besides having talent, you must also know how to utilise it to your benefit. You cannot leave it to other people who are not known to be trustworthy as they may manipulate you for only their own benefit at your expense. In this poem, the frog manipulated the nightingale when he realised that she was gullible and unsure of her talent in singing. He made her feel that he was very knowledgeable about music and singing, whereas he was nowhere near her in talent.

Thus, it is necessary for talented people to have or develop commercial skills to utilise their talent properly and effectively for their own benefit. The nightingale did not have such skills and thus, was exploited by the cunning frog for his own benefit. The nightingale believed whatever the frog told her because she was easily persuaded. Ultimately, she died due to overexploitation by the frog.

5. 'The Frog and the Nightingale' is actually a fable, conveying a moral lesson. Discuss.

Ans. A fable is a fictional story, in prose or verse, featuring animals as characters and giving them human qualities. A fable usually conveys a moral lesson.

In the poem, 'The Frog and the Nightingale', animals have been used as characters and they have been personified.

The poem also leads us to a moral lesson. The frog is the evil villain while the nightingale is his innocent victim because she lacks experience, wisdom and self-confidence. The frog is full of hatred and jealousy for the nightingale and is determined to destroy his rival. He first befriends the nightingale, pretends to train her and then exhausts her original talent, leading to her ruin and ultimate death. He thus, succeeds in his evil intentions.

The moral conveyed here is that, in order to survive in today's manipulative world, it is important to have worldly wisdom and self confidence.

6. The poem 'The Frog and the Nightingale' exposes the role of critics towards fresh talent. After reading the poem you were quite disturbed. Write a letter to a friend mentioning how negative criticism can hamper the growth of genuine talent.

Ans. H. No. 243/A, Civil Lines
Delhi-110007

7th July, 20XX

Dear Nikhil

How are you keeping? I've not heard from you for some time.

I have been disturbed a lot after reading the poem 'The Frog and the Nightingale' in my literature course. It exposes the role of cunning critics towards fresh talent as they try to suppress budding artists for their own selfish purposes. In everyday life we do get negative criticism. However, sometimes it can hamper the growth of genuine talent. Negative criticism can discourage a budding artist, who may lose all his/her confidence. He/She may feel humiliated and lose his/her spontaneity and originality. As a result, he/she would not try anything new. Instead, he/she will try to follow his/her contemporaries. This would in turn result into monotony and lack of freshness, leading ultimately to failure. The critics should, thus, welcome fresh talent and inspire talented artists to achieve more. Their positive remarks and constructive criticism can motivate such budding artistes to reach the pinnacle of greatness.

Do reply soon.

With regards

Sameer

7. "Trembling, terrified to fail,
Blind with tears, the nightingale
Heard him out in silence, tried,
Puffed up, burst a vein and died."

Keeping the poem in view, write an article considering how selfish people try to exploit the innocent and what we must do to avoid being exploited like the nightingale.

Competency Based

Ans. **Don't Let Yourself be Exploited**
by Vicky

It is sad but true that there are people around us who try to take advantage of us and try to exploit us. Innocent and gullible people who are unsure of their own abilities trust others easily and are more prone to falling into traps set by cunning people. These selfish people always come up with ideas to benefit themselves at the expense of others. They exploit the innocence of the gullible people for their own benefit, making them suffer. As we cannot run away from them, we must try to counter every evil action that is targeted at us. We must be able to see through their mask to understand their real intentions. Unlike the nightingale, we must have faith in our own capabilities and strengths. We must not trust others blindly. People will try to manipulate us but we should not let others influence our thoughts. If we want to live a happy life, we cannot let ourselves be fooled.

ASSESSMENT EXERCISE

Extract Based Questions

Read the following extracts carefully and answer the questions that follow.

1. "Other creatures loathed his voice
   But, alas, they had no other choice".
   (a) Whose voice is being talked about in the above lines?
   (b) What was the reason the other creatures loathed his voice?
   (c) The word 'loathed' means ....
   (d) Who were the other creatures?
2. "Bravo!" "Too divine!" "Encore!"
   (a) Who uttered the above words?
   (b) The meaning of 'Encore' is ....
   (c) Why were these words spoken?
   (d) How did this contrast with what had been going on earlier?
3. "............This is a fairy tale-
   And you are Mozart in disguise ...."
   (a) Who was Mozart?
   (b) Why is the character addressed as Mozart?
   (c) Write two qualities of the character of the speaker of the above lines.
   (d) What sentiments are prevalent in the lines?

Short Answer Type Questions

Answer the following questions in 30-40 words.

1. What was the initial outcome of the nightingale's singing?
2. Explain the lines: "And the sumac tree was bowed, With a breathless titled crowd:"
3. "And the ticket office gross
   Crashed, and she grew more morose -"
   Why did the ticket office gross crash?'
4. What is the irony in the frog's statement, 'Your song must be your own'?
5. How did the frog bring an end to the nightingale?
6. Do you agree with the frog's view that he tried to teach the nightingale but she was a stupid creature? Give two reasons.

Long Answer Type Questions

Answer the following questions in 150 words.

1. 'The Frog and the Nightingale' is a satire on modern society in which success is determined by influence and not by talent. Discuss.
2. Cunning people have their own methods to exploit innocent people. How should we be careful of such cunning people? Write with reference to the poem, 'The Frog and the Nightingale'.
3. What was the philosophy of the frog? Do you agree with it? Why or why not?

Not Marble, Nor the Gilded Monuments

CHAPTER 2

by William Shakespeare

Introduction The sonnet 'Not Marble, Nor the Gilded Monuments' brings out the futility (uselessness) of statues and decorated monuments erected in the memory of the rich and the powerful kings and rulers to immortalise themselves. With passage of time, they stand lost and forgotten. However, the poet's work that is literary art will outlive the transient monuments and will be remembered in the times to come.

Stanzawise Explanation

Stanza 1

Not marble, nor the gilded monuments
Of princes, shall outlive this powerful rhyme;
But you shall shine more bright in these contents
Than unswept stone, besmear'd with sluttish time.

Explanation The poem begins with the poet, stating that the powerful princes, kings and rich men get their statues erected so that people remember them even after their death.

He clearly explains that neither of these marble statues nor the gold plated monuments will survive longer than this beautiful poem. According to the poet, the name of the listener or the person, whom the poem is dedicated to, will shine more brightly in the contents of this poem than the monuments. This is so because, with the passage of time, the monuments will decay. As the monuments will be left uncared for, they will go into utter ruin.

The poet has compared time to a slut in these lines because time is never faithful to anyone. It moves on without any care and everyone is equal before its eyes.

It is important to note here that the poet had established the superiority and permanence of poetry. The impact of poetry is such that the lives of great people will be preserved forever in them.

Stanza 2

When wasteful war shall statues overturn,
And broils root out the work of masonry,
Nor Mars his sword nor war's quick fire shall burn
The living record of your memory.

Explanation The poet further states that the marbled and gilded monuments are incapable of facing the wasteful wars, battles, Mars' sword (reference to the Roman God of war) and war's quick fire. The stone statues build by masons would be ruined and destroyed in wars that cause widespread death and destruction.

However, neither the war-like powers of Mars nor the fast moving fire of war will be able to destroy this written memory of the poet's loved one. The poem will continue to exist even after the loved one's death.

Stanza 3

'Gainst death and all oblivious enmity
Shall you pace forth; your praise shall still find room,
Even in the eyes of all posterity
That wear this world out to the ending doom.
So, till the judgement that yourself arise,
You live in this, and dwell in lovers' eyes.

Explanation Neither death nor the prejudice displayed by enemies can destroy or diminish the memory of the poet's loved one. It will remain alive in the lines of this poem. The praise of the poet's loved one will remain alive in the eyes of the coming generations as they would read the poem and remember it. This poem will last till doomsday or the day on which the last judgement will be given by God.

Through the poem and its words, the poet's loved one will find a permanent place in the eyes of lovers. Thus, the poem will not be destroyed with the passage of time and will be remembered for many years to come.

Poetic Devices Used in the Poem

Personification A figure of speech which is used for an inanimate object or animals/birds that look or feel human qualities.

- Time has been personified in the poem and is called heartless and cruel.

Alliteration Repetition of initial consonant sounds in the same line.

- Not marble, nor the gilded monuments
- you shall shine
- When wasteful war

Epithet A transferred epithet is a figure of speech in which an epithet (or adjective) grammatically qualifies a noun other than the person or thing.

- sluttish time
- unswept stone, besmear'd
- wasteful war
- ending doom

Allusion A reference to a statement, person, place, etc. from history, religion, literature or any other field.

- Mars, the Roman God of war
- Day of Judgement

Word Meaning

Word	Meaning
Stanza 1	
gilded	covered thinly with gold leaf or gold paint
monuments	buildings, statues built in the memory of persons
outlive	survive or last beyond
unswept stone	a stone monument which is not kept clean
besmear'd	damaged
sluttish	evil or immoral
Stanza 2	
broils	battles
masonry	stone work
Mars	the Roman God of war
quick	fast moving
living record	permanent written record
Stanza 3	
gainst	against
oblivious enmity	forgetful hostility which seeks to destroy everything
pace forth	move ahead
find room	be acceptable to
posterity	future generations, descendants
doom	doomsday, the last day of the world's existence
judgement	the day of the last judgement, when God will judge the moral worth of the whole human race

Textbook FOLDER

Here, we have covered questions given in the CBSE Textbook along with their answer

ON PAGE 99-100

Q.6 On the basis of your understanding of Shakespeare's sonnet, answer the following questions by ticking the correct options.

(a) The rich and powerful got ornate monuments made in order to

(i) show off their wealth
(ii) display their power
(iii) show their artistic talent
(iv) be remembered till posterity

Ans. (iv) be remembered till posterity

(b) The poet addresses his sonnet to

(i) time
(ii) war
(iii) the person he loves
(iv) powerful rulers

Ans. (iii) the person he loves

(c) In the line 'The living record of your memory', living record refers to

(i) the sonnet the poet has written for his friend
(ii) an existing statue of his friend
(iii) his friend who lives in the poet's memory
(iv) the autobiography of the poet's friend

Ans. (i) the sonnet the poet has written for his friend

(d) The poet's tone in the poem is ....

(i) despairing (ii) optimistic
(iii) loving (iv) admiring

Ans. (ii) optimistic

(e) The poem is set in ....

(i) the place where the poet meets his friend
(ii) a battlefield where Mars is fighting a battle
(iii) a city ravaged by war
(iv) the poet's study where he is writing

Ans. (iv) the poet's study where he is writing

ON PAGE 100

Q.7 Answer the following questions briefly.

(a) Why do you think the rich and powerful people get monuments and statues erected in their memory?

Or **Why do the rich and powerful erect monuments?**

Ans. The rich and powerful people get monuments and statues erected in their memory so that they may be remembered by generations to come and their name be noted in history. It reflects their desire to be immortalised.

(b) Describe how the monuments and statues brave the ravages of time.

Ans. Monuments and statues are made of strong materials like stone or metal. These stones and metals get disfigured, worn out and damaged by weathering. Even the metal plating that is used to stop them from getting worn out, wears out with time, thus indicating that monuments and statues are destroyed with time.

(c) Why does the poet refer to Time, as being sluttish?

Ans. In the poem, time has been referred to as 'sluttish' because time waits for none. Time passes by without any care or sense of responsibility for anyone. Further, it affects everyone equally. No one is free from its impact.

(d) The poet says that neither the forces of nature nor wars can destroy his poetry. In fact, even the godly powers of Mars will not have a devastating effect on his rhyme. What quality of the poet is revealed through these lines?

Ans. The qualities of the poet revealed through these lines are dedication, love and faith in the immortality of his poetry. It also reveals the confidence of the poet that he has the power to keep his loved one's memory alive forever.

Q.8 Shakespeare's sonnet has been divided into three quatrains of 4 lines each followed by a rhyming couplet. Each quatrain is a unit of meaning. Read the poem carefully and complete the following table on the structure of the poem.

	Rhyme Scheme	Theme
Quatrain 1		Comparison between poetry and monuments.
Quatrain 2		Ravages of time on monuments contrasted with ......
Quatrain 3		The recorded memory of ...... posterity
Couplet		Poetry immortalises friend.

Ans.

	Rhyme Scheme (Based on the entire poem)	Theme
Quatrain 1	a-b-a-b; the first line rhymes with the third and second line rhymes with the fourth line.	Comparison between poetry and monuments.
Quatrain 2	c-d-c-d; the first line rhymes with the third and second line rhymes with the fourth line.	Ravages of time on monuments contrasted with the indelible record of the sonnet.
Quatrain 3	e-f-e-f; the first line rhymes with the third and second line rhymes with the fourth line.	Immortality of poetry
Couplet	g-g; it is a rhyming couplet of two lines.	Poetry immortalises friend.

Q.9 **(a) The poet uses alliteration to heighten the musical quality of the sonnet. Working in pairs, underline the examples of alliteration in the poem.**

(b) Identify Shakespeare's use of personification in the poem.

Ans. Refer to poetic devices used in the poem.

REVIEW EXERCISE

Including Previous Years' and Practice Questions

Read the following extracts carefully and answer the questions that follow.

1. Not marble, nor the gilded monuments
Of princes, shall outlive this powerful rhyme;
But you shall shine more bright in these contents
Than unswept stone, besmear'd with sluttish time.

(a) What does the word 'marble' refer to?

Ans. The word 'marble' refers to statues made of marble.

(b) What does the phrase 'in these contents' mean?

Ans. The phrase 'in these contents' refers to this sonnet itself.

(c) Explain the phrase 'Than unswept stone'.

Ans. The phrase 'Than unswept stone' means the stone monuments that are often not cared for.

(d) The expression 'powerful rhyme' in line 2 means ....

Ans. this sonnet, which will outlive the monuments

2. When wasteful war shall statues overturn,
And broils root out the work of masonry,
Nor Mars his sword nor war's quick fire shall burn
The living record of your memory.

(a) Why are wars wasteful?

Ans. Wars are wasteful as they bring upon death and destruction.

(b) What does the phrase 'the work of masonry' refer to?

Ans. The phrase 'the work of masonry' refers to the statues and monuments built by masons for kings and rulers.

(c) Why can't war have any ill-effects on the poet's writings?

Ans. Unlike monuments and statues, the poet's writings are ideas, thoughts and emotions; they are not physical things. Hence, war can't have any ill-effects on them.

(d) What does the word, 'broils' mean?

Ans. The word 'broils' means tumult, fighting, disturbances, especially as a result of war.

3. 'Gainst death and all oblivious enmity
Shall you pace forth; your praise shall still find room,
Even in the eyes of all posterity
That wear this world out to the ending doom.

(a) What is meant by the word 'gainst'?

Ans. The word 'gainst' means 'against'.

(b) Explain "your praise shall still find room."

Ans. Through the phrase, the poet wants to say that his loved one would receive praise from future generations due to the poet's sonnet.

(c) What does the word 'doom' refer to?

Ans. The word 'doom' refers to the last day of judgement.

(d) How will the poet's loved one pace forth against death and oblivious enmity?

Ans. The memory of the poet's loved one will pace forth against death and oblivious enmity because the person will remain alive in the lines of his poem.

4. So, till the judgement that yourself arise,
You live in this and dwell in lover's eyes.

(a) 'You live in this'. What does 'this' refer to?

Ans. The word 'this' refers to this poem or verse.

(b) When does the poet expect that his beloved shall arise?

Ans. The poet's loved one shall arise on the day of the last judgement.

(c) What is meant by the word 'dwell'?

Ans. The word 'dwell' means to remain or reside.

(d) What did 'till the judgement' refer to?

Ans. The phrase 'till the judgement' refers to doomsday or the day on which the last judgement will occur.

Short Answer Type Questions

Answer the following questions in 30-40 words.

1. Explain "Of princes, shall outlive this powerful rhyme."

Or **In what way is the poet stronger than powerful rulers?**

Ans. The poet says that his poetry has great power. He says that all the marble structures or gold-plated monuments which are erected in the memories of powerful people like the princes cannot stand against the ravages of time. He believes that his loved one shall outlive these monuments as his poetry has the power to withstand time's destruction and to confer immortality.

2. How would wars prove ineffective in tarnishing the living record of 'your' memory?

Or **How will the 'living record' of the poet's beloved and his memory be more powerful than wasteful wars?**

Ans. War always brings destruction and death. It is a wasteful evil that destroys everthing except the name and fame of those personalities whose images exist in people's hearts. The poet knows that war cannot destroy the written memory of his loved one's life.

3. The poet says that neither forces of nature, nor war can destroy his poetry. What do you learn about the poet's character through these lines?

Ans. The given lines show that the poet is proud of creating art and literature. These are immortal whereas the material achievements of man are temporary. The poet is self-confident and contemptuous of arrogant rulers.

4. The poem 'Not Marble, Nor the Gilded Monuments' talls about the unmortality of poety. Elaborate. CBSE 2024 C, CBSE SQP 2024

Or **How does the poet glorify the power of poetry?**

Ans. The poet glorifies the power of poetry in an attractive manner. He shows faith in his poetry and says that even time and his own death cannot destroy it. The beauty of his poetry is more than that of the statues and gilded monuments of princes.

5. Explain "Gainst death and all oblivious enmity".

Ans. The poet says that no enemy will get success over his loved one. Neither death nor enmity that wipes out everything from people's memory can destroy the memory of his loved one. Noble souls such as of his loved one will continue to stride forward despite enemies and even after death.

6. What will the poet's friend learn when he arises on the 'Judgement Day' in the poem 'Not Marble, nor the Gilded Monuments'?

Or **What will Shakespeare's friend realise when he rises on the Day of Judgement?**

Ans. On the 'Judgement Day', the poet's friend will learn that due to the poem, he/she is still alive in the hearts and memories of the people.

7. How long does the poet feel can the lover live in the rhyme written by him?

Ans. The poet feels that by writing about his loved one, he has immortalised the person. As a result, even the coming generations will remember the person. He/She will continue to dwell (live) till the day of the last judgement.

8. Why does the poet believe that he has immortalised his friend? CBSE 2019

Ans. The poet believes that he has immortalised his friend by writing the sonnet as the poem will survive the test of time. It will not be destroyed by anything and will remain the memory of people till eternity.

9. Why and how, according to Shakespeare, is the pen mightier than the monuments or even the mighty kings? CBSE 2025

Ans. In Shakespeare's Sonnet 55, he says the pen is mightier than marble or kings because written words last longer than physical monuments. While statues or buildings fade with time, poetry and writing can live on for centuries, keeping a person's memory alive long after they are gone. Shakespeare believes his writing will make the person immortal, outlasting even the greatest kings and monuments.

10. Bring out the sum and substance of Shakespeare's sonnet, 'Not Marble, nor the Gilded Monuments'.

Or **What is the theme of the poem 'Not Marble nor the Gilded Monuments'?**

Ans. In this poem, the poet pays tribute to the quality of his verses and to the intensity of his love for his loved one. The poet is confident that his verses will continue to be read for ever. His loved one will outlive all other things of the world as he/she is described in the poet's verses.

11. Discuss how Shakespeare's sonnet Not Marble, Nor the Gilded Monuments conveys the theme of immortality through poetry.

Ans. Shakespeare's, 'Not Marble, Nor the Gilded Monuments', explores the theme of immortality through poetry by asserting the enduring power of written words to preserve a person's legacy. In the poem, Shakespeare contrasts impermanent physical structures with the eternal nature of poetry.

The very first line of them poem states that marble statues or gold-plated monuments are destined to decay. Even grand, wealthy tributes to rulers and kings cannot withstand the passage of time. In contrast, his poetry will endure forever, preserving the subject s memory. The poet emphasises that as long as the poem exists, so too will the memory of the person to whom it is dedicated.

The poem further explores the concept of immortality by mentioning how time, even as it destroys physical structures, will not be able to erase the memory of the subject through poetry. Even catastrophic events, such as wars, which might demolish buildings and monuments, cannot harm the lasting power of the poet's words. The theme of immortality is thus powerfully conveyed by Shakespeare as he links the endurance of poetry to the survival of a person's memory long after they are gone.

Long Answer Type Questions

Answer the following questions in 150 words.

1. "Not marble, Nor the Gilded Monuments, Of princes, shall outlive this powerful rhyme." How does Shakespeare emphasise the fact that immaterial things are imperishable whereas material things perish over a period of time. Explain with reference to the poem.

Ans. Shakespeare's sonnet, 'Not Marble, Nor the Gilded Monuments' portrays time as a mighty destroyer. According to the poet, all material things, worldly power, glory and prosperity, fade away with the passage of time. The princes, rulers and the rich try to perpetuate their memory through gold plated monuments, memorials and statues. However, all their attempts are in vain as over a period of time, such monuments and memorials lose their glory and fall to utter neglect, decay and deterioration. The ravages of 'sluttish' time destroy them.

However, immaterial things like great poetry and art are imperishable. They withstand the forces of decay over time and outlive all such monuments erected by princes and rulers. The words of this 'powerful rhyme' will be a living record of the memory of the poet's loved one. The poet asserts that his loved one will be remembered longer because of the poet having written about him/her.

2. "When wasteful war shall statues overturn, And broils root out the work of masonry." War is destructive in nature. It does not see anything or anybody when it comes; and leaves villages, towns, cities and kingdoms empty and without people. Now write an article on the topic 'War is Wasteful.'

Ans.

War is Wasteful

by XYZ

War is always wasteful, as it causes widespread death and destruction. It is never productive or creative for society. It is fruitless in the sense that it only kills happiness and hope for humanity. In earlier days, greedy kings followed the way of war to extend their kingdoms and to amass (collect) wealth. Man's ego, lust for power and false concepts of religion, caste, colour, creed or language gave birth to the evil of war.

Nobody wins in war as it does not give real happiness to anybody. Thousands of wars have been fought in human history and hundreds of kings have gained power, but to no use? They too had to bend before death and depart from this world. Were they really the winners? Actually, they were not. They were unable to achieve the happiness that they could get only in peace.

3. Materialistic things don't really last. What matters most are the people we care about and the values we live with. Explain this with reference to the poem 'Not Marble, Nor the Gilded Monuments.'

Ans. It is a well-known truth that materialistic things don't really last. All signs of worldly power, glory and prosperity fade away with the passage of time. Kings and princes get their monuments erected so as to be remembered by the future generations. However, all gold plated monuments, memorials and statues fall to utter neglect, decay and deterioration. They all meet the fate of destruction as they fail to outlive the ravages of time. In stark contrast stand our relationships. They are immortal and don't get destroyed by time. Rather, they get strengthened with the passage of time.

The poet is also of the opinion that riches don't matter much in this world. What is more valuable is his love for his loved one. Their love would live longer than any man-made monuments. Neither death nor war will be able to destroy her memory. Hence, it is our love and relationships which matter more in this world. All other things come to an end one day.

ASSESSMENT EXERCISE

Extract Based Questions

Read the following extracts carefully and answer the questions that follow.

1. But you shall shine more bright in these contents
Than unswept stone, besmear'd with sluttish time.
When wasteful war shall statues overturn,
And broils root out the work of masonry,
Nor Mars his sword nor war's quick fire shall burn
The living record of your memory.

(a) Name the two destructive forces mentioned in the extract.
(b) Why is the reference to Mars given here?
(c) What is the tone of the poet?
(d) What is the meaning of 'sluttish' here?

2. 'Gainst death and all oblivious enmity
Shall you pace forth; your praise shall find room,
Even in the eyes of all posterity
That wear this world out to the ending doom.
So, till the judgement that yourself arise,
You live in this and dwell in lover's eyes.

(a) Explain 'the ending doom' and the 'judgement'.
(b) The word 'oblivious' in the extract means........
(c) State the example of personification in the given lines.
(d) What is the rhyme scheme adopted in this paragraph?

Short Answer Type Questions

Answer the following questions in 30-40 words each.

1. Bring out the irony in the sentence "Nor Mars his sword nor war's quick fire shall burn the living record of your memory."

2. The poet himself desires the immortality he promises his beloved. Comment.

3. What does Shakespeare praise more in his poem 'Not Marble, nor the Gilded Monuments', poetry or beauty?

4. What mythological references does Shakespeare make in the poem?

5. Why does Shakespeare repeatedly use the word 'you' in the poem. What does he want to emphasise?

Long Answer Type Questions

Answer the following questions in 150 words each.

1. Since time immemorial, the human race has longed for immortality. What makes people desire immortality? Is it possible to achieve it? Discuss.

2. Ancient rulers spent a great deal of money and resources on building magnificent statues, huge forts and palaces, whereas they should have used the same money in the welfare of their subjects. It is not the display of wealth but the deeds and actions that make a ruler great. Comment on the short-sightedness of these ancient rulers.

Ozymandias

CHAPTER 3

by Percy Bysshe Shelley

Introduction The poem revolves around the foolish pride of an arrogant King Ozymandias, whose statue has been destroyed with time. Through the destroyed statue, the poet brings out the temporary nature of life fame and fortune. This poem reveals the truth that the power of arrogant people fails to permanently continue their name and fame.

Stanzawise Explanation

Stanza 1 (Lines 1-8)

I met a traveller from an antique land
Who said: Two vast and trunkless legs of stone
Stand in the desert. Near them, on the sand,
Half sunk, a shattered visage lies, whose frown.
And wrinkled lip, and sneer of cold command,
Tell that its sculptor well those passions read
Which yet survive, stamped on these lifeless things,
The hand that mocked them, and the heart that fed;

Explanation The poet narrates his meeting and conversation with a traveller who had come from an ancient land. The traveller described an unusual sight that he saw there to the poet. He told the poet about an old, fragmented statue that stood in the middle of the desert.

It was a broken statue with only two huge stone legs that stood on a very huge and high pedestal. The upper body of the statue was missing. The face of the statue was lying away from it. It was half buried in the sand.

The traveller further told the poet that the face had the expressions of frown and sneer (angry and unhappy expression). Looking at those facial expressions, one could easily guess that the sculptor was perfect in his art.

The traveller praised the sculptor saying that he had read/understood the emotions of the king very well. That's why he could carve them on the statue's face.

The sculptor had made fun of the passion that had flourished in the heart of the king, by carving those expressions on the statue's face.

Stanza 2 (Lines 9-14)

And on the pedestal these words appear:
"My name is Ozymandias, king of kings:
Look upon my works, ye Mighty and despair!"
Nothing beside remains. Round the decay
Of that colossal wreck, boundless and bare
The lone and level sands stretch far away.

Explanation The traveller informed the poet about the inscription that was engraved on the pedestal of the statue. The inscription gave the impression that Ozymandias considered himself to be the most powerful king. It showed Ozymandias' arrogant claim of being the mightiest of the mighty.

The king showed off that his achievements and his exploits were incomparable in the world. The king was proud of them and felt that all would despair in the face of his achievements. Ironically, none of Ozymandias' works can be seen in the vicinity (area) of the statue now.

The neglected and shattered statue highlighted the irony of his claims. Due to weathering over time, nothing else was left behind of Ozymandias' glory except the boundless sand which spread all around the broken statue. Time had wiped out all the power and position of this self-proclaimed mighty king and he had been forgotten.

Poetic Devices Used in the Poem

Alliteration Repetition of initial consonant sounds in the same line.

- boundless and bare
- cold command
- sands stretch
- lone level

Synecdoche It uses part for the whole or the whole for a part.

- the hand that mocked them

Anastrophe In which the normal word order of the subject, the verb and and the object is changed.

- well those passions read

Metaphor A device which compares two things or qualities which are unlike.

- Ozymandias is used as a metaphor for the ephemeral (temporary) nature of power as well as pride

Irony A contrast between reality and expectation, between what is said and what is meant, between what appears to be true and the real truth.

- There is use of irony in the lines, 'My name is Ozymandias, king of kings'. The irony is that the once great king is no more.

Symbolism Where an object, person or situation has another meaning other than its literal meaning.

- The statue is symbolic of Ozymandias' status, political tyranny and pride.
- The huge size of the statue is symbolic of the king's pride and ego.

Hyberbole Exaggeration of something.

- My name is Ozymandias, king of kings

Word Meaning

Word	Meaning
Stanza 1	
trunkless	without the upper body
shattered	broken
visage	face
frown	angry and unhappy expression of moving the eyebrows together
sneer	facial expression of scorn or hostility in which the upper lip may be raised
cold	indifferent herein
read	interpreted
stamped	engraved
mocked	made fun of
Stanza 2	
pedestal	a column where a statue stands
ye	you
mighty	powerful
despair	be disappointed
beside	else
colossal	enormous, huge
wreck	destruction
bare	without buildings, trees, people, etc.
level sand	plain desert
stretch	spreading

Textbook FOLDER

Here, we have covered questions given in the CBSE Textbook along with their answer

ON PAGE 102-103

Q.4 Answer the following questions by selecting the correct options.

(a) The poem is set in ....

(i) the wilderness (ii) an ancient land
(iii) a palace (iv) a desert

Ans. (iv) a desert

(b) The expression on the face of the statue is one of ....

(i) admiration (ii) anger
(iii) despair (iv) contempt

Ans. (ii) anger

(c) This poem throws light on the .... nature of Ozymandias.

(i) cruel (ii) arrogant
(iii) boastful (iv) aggressive

Ans. (iii) boastful

(d) The sculptor was able to understand Ozymandias' ....

(i) words (ii) expression
(iii) feelings (iv) ambition

Ans. (iii) feelings

(e) The tone of the poem is ....

(i) mocking (ii) nostalgic
(iii) gloomy (iv) gloating

Ans. (i) mocking

ON PAGE 103-104

Q.5 Answer the following questions briefy.

(a) "The hand that mocked them, and the heart that fed." Whose hand and heart has the poet referred to in this line?

Ans. The hand is that of the sculptor who made the statue and captured the king's feelings very well. The heart is that of the king who fed on the passion of his subjects.

(b) "My name is Ozymandias, king of kings:" Why does Ozymandias refer to himself as King of Kings? What quality of the king is revealed through this statement?

Ans. Ozymandias refers to himself as "King of Kings" to emphasise his power and superiority over other rulers. This statement reveals the king's qualities of arrogance, boastfulness and conceit. Ozymandias considers himself the most powerful king and no one is more powerful than him. He is proud of his achievements, strength, and power.

(c) "Look on my works, ye Mighty, and despair!" Who is Ozymandias referring to when he speaks of 'ye Mighty'? Why should they despair?

Ans. Ozymandias is referring to any warrior or king who thinks he is stronger than him when he speaks of 'ye Mighty'. He thinks that they would become afraid of him when they see his might and his works because they cannot match him.

(d) Bring out the irony in the poem.

Ans. The irony in the poem lies in the statement which is engraved on the pedestal, "Look upon my works, ye Mighty, and despair!" At the same place now, there is nothing around except for vast stretches of sand and desert. Through these words, the king was trying to show his grandeur in the form of his statue but now it stands broken in a place where time had destroyed everything.

(e) 'Nothing beside remains'. What does the narrator mean when he says these words?

Ans. When alive, Ozymandias hoped that his mighty works would be admired by the world. However, now, there is nothing left to see except his shattered statue. The poet means that Ozymandias' existence has passed into oblivion and no trace of his glory can be seen anywhere.

(f) What impression do you form of Ozymandias as a king?

Ans. Ozymandias appears to be a very arrogant king when he calls himself the king of kings. Through the lines on the pedestal, he wanted to show that he was the greatest king who ever lived.
This statement shows how conceited, powerful, arrogant and blind with power he was.

(g) What message is conveyed through this poem?

Ans. This poem conveys the important message that time is all powerful. No king or his power can defeat time. Nothing lives forever and all achievements are lost due to passage of time.
So, having pride in your achievements and showcasing them are meaningless.

ON PAGE 104

Q.6 Identify and rewrite the lines from the poem spoken by the narrator, the traveller and Ozymandias. What impact do you think these three voices have on the reader?

The Narrator

The Traveller

Ozymandias

Ans. **The Narrator**

I met a traveller from an antique land
Who said

The narrator's lines tell us that whatever he is going to tell is a narrative he had heard.

The Traveller

Two vast and trunkless legs of stone
Stand in the desert.
Near them, on the sand,
Half sunk, a shattered visage lies, whose frown,
And wrinkled lip, and sneer of cold command,
Tell that its sculptor well those passions read
Which yet survive, stamped on these lifeless things,
The hand that mocked them, and the heart that fed;
And on the pedestal these words appear :

The lines of the traveller seems to show a factual description of the destroyed statue and a sense of admiration for the sculptor.

Ozymandias

My name is Ozymandias, king of kings:
Look upon my works, ye Mighty, and despair!"

The lines on the pedestal seem to be spoken by Ozymandias. These lines show that Ozymandias was a proud, arrogant and a conceited king.

ON PAGE 104-105

Q.7 Shelley's sonnet follows the traditional structure of the fourteen-line Italian sonnet, featuring an opening octave, or a set of eight lines, that presents a conflict or dilemma, followed by a sestet, or a set of six lines, that offers some resolution or commentary upon the proposition introduced in the octave. Read the poem carefully and complete the following table on the structure of the poem.

	Rhyme Scheme	Theme
Octave		
Sestet		

Ans.

	Rhyme Scheme	Theme
Octave	abacaded	Description of the statue
Sestet	abacac	Power of time, Mortality of everything

ON PAGE 105

Q.9 Imagine that Ozymandias comes back to life and as he sees the condition of his statue, realisation dawns on him and he pens his thoughts in a diary. As Ozymandias, make a diary entry in about 150 words. You could begin like this: I thought I was the mightiest of all but.....

Ans. Wednesday, 10th July, 20XX 10:00 p.m.

Dear Diary

I thought I was the mightiest of all. However, today I was completely shaken to see my own statue shattered with my head rolling in the sand and the trunk missing. There was a time when ten men used to run to wipe even a speck of dust on my shoes. However, today my statue lay shattered with the head on the ground. No one was even bothered about it. It took me a while to understand that my world had disappeared and all that was left was barren land with sand everywhere.

My own words inscribed on the pedestal seemed to make fun of me. I had challenged the mighty to match my exploits and here my own words and works were ruined with time. Now, I know it is 'time' which is the mightiest. All else decays with time. Nothing is immortal.

Ozymandias

Q.10 'Ozymandias' and 'Not Marble, nor the Gilded Monuments' are on Time. Compare the two sonnets in terms of the way in which Time is treated by the poets. Write your answer in about 150 words.

Or **In the poems 'Ozymandias' by Percy Bysshe Shelley and 'Not Marble, Nor the Gilded Monument's by William Shakespeare, the concept of time is explored, but each poet treats it in a distinct manner. Elucidate.** **CBSE 2024**

Ans. The poems 'Ozymandias' by Shelley and 'Not Marble, nor the Gilded Monuments' by Shakespeare are related to each other through some similarities and differences. The main similarity between the poems is that both the poems are on the subject of 'time'.

In both these poems, the poets convey the message that riches and wealth are not lasting and they perish with time. In both the poems, the poets have treated 'Time' as a destructive agent. They describe the ravages of time taking their toll on all materialistic things.

The main difference between the two poems is that in 'Not Marble, nor the Gilded Monuments', Shakespeare treats love and poetry to be everlasting.

In 'Ozymandias', Shelley does not talk about poetry or love. He shows that even the mightiest decays with time. He stresses that nothing is immortal.

REVIEW EXERCISE

Including Previous Years' and Practice Questions

Extract Based Questions

Read the following extracts carefully and answer the questions that follow.

1. I met a traveller from an antique land
Who said: Two vast and trunkless legs of stone
Stand in the desert. Near them, on the sand,
Half sunk, a shattered visage lies, whose frown,

(a) Who does 'I' represent?

Ans. 'I' represents the poet.

(b) Where was the traveller coming from?

Ans. The traveller was coming from an ancient land.

(c) What effect does the fact the author met a traveller from an antique land create?

Ans. The fact that the author met a traveller from an antique land creates an atmosphere mystery and thrill.

(d) What had happened to the statue?

Ans. The statue got damaged with the passage of time. It lay in ruins.

2. Near them, on the sand,
Half sunk, a shattered visage lies, whose frown,
And wrinkled lip, and sneer of cold command,

(a) What lay near the trunkless legs of stone?

Ans. Near the trunkless legs of stone lay the partially buried broken face of the statue.

(b) Describe the expression on the face of the visage.

Ans. On the face of the visage, the traveller could see the expression of a frown, wrinkled lip and a sneer of cold command.

(c) What does 'sneer of cold command' mean?

Ans. The phrase 'sneer of cold command' refers to the facial expression of scorn or contempt in which the upper lip may be raised.

(d) What do you mean by 'shattered'?

Ans. The word 'shattered' means 'to be broken into pieces'.

3. And wrinkled lip, and sneer of cold command,
Tell that its sculptor well those passions read
Which yet survive, stamped on these lifeless things,
The hand that mocked them, and the heart that fed;

CBSE 2024 C

(a) Describe the setting of the poem.

Ans. The poem is majorly set in a desert amidst the ruins of the statue. It is a mysterious and thrilling setting as we know more about the dilapidated statue.

(b) Identify the poetic device used in the first line.

Ans. Imagery is used in the first line.

(c) What image of the sculptor can be formed after reading the above lines?

Ans. The colossal statue of Ozymandias gives a clear indication that the sculptor was a master artist. He had very beautifully carved every detail of the king's face. Even when the statue was lying in ruins, one could easily make out the arrogant expression on it.

(d) Explain the phrase 'The hand that mocked them, and the heart that fed'.

Ans. The given lines indicate that the hands of the sculptor mocked Ozymandias by etching the expressions of sneering, frowning and wrinkled lips. His face displayed the heart of king Ozymandias, which was the source of the feelings displayed on the statue's head.

Or

(a) What do 'lifeless things' mean?

Ans. The expression 'lifeless things' refers to the scattered fragments of the broken statue of Ozymandias, especially the shattered face.

(b) What does the expression 'well those passions read' mean?

Ans. The expression means that the sculptor skilfully interpreted the king's feelings.

(c) How did the heart feed the passions?

Ans. The passions which were depicted on the statue's face were those of vanity and self-importance. These were the emotions born and produced in the king's heart.

(d) Explain– "The hand that mocked them and the heart that fed".

Ans. The given line means that the sculptor tried his level best to understand the emotions of the king and mocked him by skilfully carving it out.

4. And on the pedestal these words appear:
"My name is Ozymandias, king of kings:
Look upon my works, ye Mighty, and despair!"

(a) **What do the lines on the pedestal suggest about Ozymandias?**

Ans. The lines on the pedestal suggest that Ozymandias was an arrogant king.

(b) **Bring out the irony of the poem.**

Ans. The irony of the poem is that time has claimed the great statue and the kingdom of Ozymandias. Everything lies in ruins.

(c) **Give the synonym of the word 'despair'.**

Ans. The synonym of word 'despair' is 'submit'.

(d) **What does 'my works' stand for?**

Ans. The phrase 'my works' stands for the many victories that Ozymandias achieved in his lifetime.

5. Nothing beside remains. Round the decay
Of that colossal wreck, boundless and bare
The lone and level sands stretch far away.

(a) **What does 'colossal wreck' refer to?**

Ans. The phrase 'colossal wreck' refers to the huge statue of King Ozymandias which lies in ruins.

(b) **What does the last line suggest?**

Ans. The last line suggests that time is a leveller and destroyer. It broke the king's arrogance by destroying his status. Now, only sand remains all around.

(c) **What does the expression 'Round the decay' mean?**

Ans. The expression 'Round the decay' means the destruction caused with the passage of time due to natural causes.

(d) **Why did nothing remain?**

Ans. Nothing remains as time has destroyed everything in the region.

Short Answer Type Questions

Answer the following questions in 30-40 words.

1. **What did the traveller see in the desert?**

Ans. The traveller from the ancient land saw a broken statue in the desert. There he saw two large legs of stone standing in the desert.

Near them, he saw the face of the statue that lay half buried in the sand. The trunk and hands of the statue were missing.

2. **What remained of the 'shattered' statue? What does it indicate?**

Ans. Time had claimed the statue. Its trunk and hands were somewhere lost in the vast desert. Only the two legs and the fragmented face of the statue remained. It indicates that time is a destroyer. It can consume even the most colossal statues and the glories of great kings.

3. **Describe Ozymandias' statue in your own words.**

Ans. Ozymandias' statue must have been a colossal statue in his days of glory. Now, only its ruins remain. The trunk of the statue is lost in the sand. Only two vast legs and a shattered face remain. His arrogant expression is still visible on the lifeless face.

4. **What does the dilapidated state of the statue suggest?**

Ans. The broken statue of Ozymandias was surrounded by vast stretches of sand and the loneliness of the desert. These ruins prove that the king's work and civilisation has crumbled to dust. Nothing lasts forever and even the biggest statue can't stand the test of time.

5. **What expressions of Ozymandias have been captured by the sculptor?**

Or **Describe the passions that were stamped on the lifeless stone of the broken statue of Ozymandias.**

Or **Describe the facial expressions of the broken statue of Ozymandias.**

Or **What do the expressions on Ozymandias' face reveal about him?**

Ans. The sculptor has carved Ozymandias' arrogance on the face of the statue. The statue had the expressions of a sneer and a frown. The grim, arrogant expression on his face reveals the excessive pride possessed by the king.

6. **What is ironic about the inscription on the pedestal of Ozymandias' statue?**

Or **The inscriptions on the pedestal of ozymandias was ironical. Justify.** CBSE 2024 C

Ans. The inscription on the pedestal of Ozymandias' statue is ironic because the once great king is no more. Moreover, his empire, his rule and his people are all gone and have disappeared with the passage of time. Even his statue is wrecked and lost in the sands of a far away desert.

7. **How does the poet present the overpowering nature of posterity upon glory?**

Ans. Posterity or the transition of time from one generation to another has an amazing influence over power and glory. Ozymandias was once a powerful king and was very certain that his glory will not fade.

However after many generations, his empire, his name, fame and even his statue were all forgotten with the passage of time.

8. What did Ozymandias expect from future generations? Was his hope fulfilled?

Ans. Ozymandias expected that the future generation would remember him till eternity. He was, in fact, very much confident that posterity would recall his achievements with amazement and admiration. His hopes have not been fulfilled as he has been forgotten and his statue lies broken and in complete neglect.

9. What quality of King Ozymandias does the poem reflect?

Ans. King Ozymandias appears to be an arrogant and a very conceited ruler. He seems to have no concern for his fellow beings. He is proud of his power, position and glory, and boasts of being the greatest of all kings. He looked down upon the other kings. His irrational approach to immortalise himself by getting a colossal statue carved of himself shows his arrogance.

10. How does the poem convey the briefness of human life?

Ans. The poem conveys the briefness of human life. Rich or poor, mighty or weak everyone has to leave this world. Time does not spare even the 'king of kings'.

The statues carved in stone, marble, etc. remind the world about them but with the passage of time, these statues also get shattered and the world gradually forgets them.

11. 'The vanity of human glory power is transient', Elucidate with reference to the poem 'Ozymandias'. **CBSE 2025**

Ans. In 'Ozymandias', the poem shows how human glory and power are short-lived. The statue of Ozymandias, once a symbol of his greatness, is now broken and buried in the desert. The inscription on the statue says, 'Look on my works, ye Mighty, and despair!' but all that remains is ruin. This shows that no matter how powerful someone is, time eventually fades all achievements, leaving nothing behind. The poem highlights the temporary nature of fame and power.

12. What moral is Shelley teaching through Ozymandias?

Ans. Shelley, through the example of a vain king, tries to teach us that nothing is permanent in this world. Ozymandias tried to make a failed attempt at eternal glory and lost. However, the sculptor's talent still survives, which means that only art and beauty, and not pride, is eternal.

13. How effective is the use of the phrase 'Nothing beside remains,' in conveying the theme of the transience and impermanence of power and human achievement, in Ozymandias by P.B. Shelley? **CBSE SQP 2023**

Ans. The use of the phrase is highly effective as it emphasises the idea that even the greatest accomplishments of human beings will eventually crumble and disappear, leaving behind only the inevitable march of time. By emphasising this theme, Ozymandias serves as a powerful reminder of the fleeting nature of human existence and the futility of pursuing power and glory at the expense of more meaningful pursuits.

14. The poem re-emphasises the idea that political power is transient but art is eternal and it survives. Do you agree? Why/ Why not?

Ans. No, I do not think that the poet re-emphasises the idea that political power is transient but art is eternal. According to the poet, nothing can escape time. Even art forms such as the sculpture made by Ozymandias fails the test of time.

Long Answer Type Questions

Answer the following questions in 150 words.

1. People with might and power are not always respected. What should be the qualities in a person that will gain him respect amongst his people?

Ans. It is true to say that people with might and power are not always respected. One such example is king Ozymandias, an arrogant and highly conceited ruler. He believed that no one will ever be able to equal his achievements. He regarded his subjects as inferior to him. However, now his shattered statue, half buried in sand with the waste and ruins around, prove that time has levelled his fame and achievements.

The ruins around the statue bear witness to the fact that nothing lasts forever. This is the true destiny of man. He is insignificant before the power of time.

The poem illustrates the vanity of human greatness.

It depicts that one must command respect and not demand it. As Ozymandias demanded respect, he never got it.

The mason who made his statue and even the poet mock Ozymandias for his arrogance.

To gain respect, one must never misuse power and might. Glorious deeds should be committed to get respect from future generations. Real power lies in winning the hearts and not in ruling the weak and needy.

2. The poem, 'Ozymandias' highlights the vanity of human glory and power. Elaborate.

Ans. The poem, 'Ozymandias' highlights the vanity of human glory and power. It conveys that no human emotions of haughtiness, sneer, pride and arrogance assure immortality and durability against the all powerful effect of time.

Everything in the world degenerates with the passage of time and under the powerful influence of the elements of nature. Even the mightiest of the mighty becomes dust. No trace of them is left on the sands of time. Ozymandias, a powerful king of Egypt, was proud of his glory and achievements. He desired to immortalise his name and constructed a statue of himself. But nothing could stand against time and the powerful elements of nature. The broken statue symbolises the destruction caused by time. The sand of the desert, boundless and bare, symbolises the power of the elements.

3. Overarching ambition can lead to great leaders and their downfall. Substantiate your position in favour or in opposition to this statement, with two points each. Competency Based

Ans. It is true to say that overarching ambition can lead to great leaders and their downfall. Ambition drives a man towards a goal. A man with an ambition would work hard with sincerity, dedication and perseverance to reach the goal and sustain it. It was Ozymandias' ambition that made him such a powerful king that he could boast of something.

However, over ambition often also leads to downfall. Ozymandias is an example of such overarching ambition. He felt that he as well as his fame would live through time such that he would be immortalised. But nothing of the sort happens. The statue he gets made is ruined and destroyed.

4. Time humbles even the greatest of the great. One should cultivate the quality of humility. Describe how time has reduced the mighty Ozymandias to nothing. CBSE 2018

Ans. It is true to say that time humbles even the greatest of the great and that one should cultivate the quality of humility. The truth of the statement is evident in the poem 'Ozymandias' in which a traveller from an ancient land saw the statue of the king Ozymandias. The statue was broken and lying in the desert with its trunk missing and sand surrounding it. The shattered face of the statue was lying some distance away from the legs, which were on a pedestal. The statue in ruins bears witness to the fact that nothing lasts forever. This is the true destiny of man, however powerful or famous he may be when he is alive. Thus, the passage of time had reduced the memory of a mighty king to only a broken statue. The king's power, pride and everything else had faded away with the passage of time. Time spares nobody and proves to be a great leveller. Man is insignificant before the power of time and everything is reduced to nothing with its passage.

5. 'None are so empty as those who are full of themselves.' Compare and contrast the characters of Mrs. Packletide and Ozymandias in light of this statement.

Ans. It is true to say that 'None are so empty as those who are full of themselves.' We have two people in our curriculum that evidently prove this fact. The first one is Mrs. Packletide who wants to always be on the top of everything. She is so jealous of the fame her rival is receiving that she plans to do something (hunt a tiger) to outdo her. She even plans to throw a lunch to show off and give a tiger claw brooch to her rival. However, in the end, she suffers monetary loss as to maintain the fame she has to hide the reality of the hunt.

Much like Mrs. Packletide, there is Ozymandias. Ozymandias is so sure of his power and fame that he gets a statue made to present it. He even goes on to say that he is the king of kings. However, in the end even his arrogance is broken as the statue, that he believed would display his power, was completely destroyed and ruined.

6. Imagine the traveller of the poem writes a diary entry, narrating his personal impressions about the trunkless statue and feelings about being in the antique land. You may begin like this...
The moment I saw the vast stretches of sand I couldn't contain my excitement. In the midst of this sandy desert, I saw...

Ans. The moment I saw the vast stretches of sand I couldn't contain my excitement. In the midst of this sandy desert, I saw two poles erected on a pedestal. I was shook. Why construct two poles on a pedestal? To seek my answer I decided to go near the poles. As I drew near, I realised that the poles were actually legs. It was a broken statue whose upper body was missing. Even the remaining part was on the verge of collapsing. I thought that if I look around I might find some other part of the statue.

And lo and Behold! I found the weird looking head. One look at it and you would know that the sculptor was skilled. The expression on the statue was precise. It showed pride, anger and coldness. After inspecting the face of the statue, I returned to the pedestal. There was an inscription there. It said that it was the statue of Ozymandias, the king of kings. He asked the looker to look at his fame and glory but I could see none. What an arrogant man must he be to think that he would survive the test of time. As I had been reading the inscription, I realised that I had to return to continue my journey.

The Traveller

7. In the poems 'The Frog and the Nightingale' and 'Ozymandias', discuss how the characters' attitudes towards power and influence contribute to their respective outcomes. **CBSE SQP 2024**

Ans. In 'The Frog and the Nightingale,' the frog's domineering and exploitative attitude towards power leads to the suppression and eventual demise of the nightingale. His desire for control and superiority blinds him to the nightingale's true talent and potential, resulting in her exploitation for his own gain. This attitude ultimately leads to the nightingale's tragic downfall. Similarly, in 'Ozymandias', the monarch's attitude towards power is depicted through his arrogance and pride. These, coupled with belief in his own invincibility lead to the construction of a grand monument which boasts of his power and greatness. However, his arrogant attitude towards power ultimately contributes to his downfall, as the ruins of his statue stand as a testament to the fleeting nature of human achievements and the inevitability of decline. In both poems, the characters' attitudes towards power and influence play a significant role in shaping their respective outcomes, highlighting the destructive consequences of unchecked power.

ASSESSMENT EXERCISE

Extract Based Questions

Read the following extracts carefully and answer the questions that follow.

1. I met a traveller from an antique land
Who said: Two vast and trunkless legs of stone
Stand in the desert.

(a) What did the traveller chance upon?
(b) What was his reaction?
(c) The word 'trunkless' in the extract means ....
(d) Where is the rest of the statue?

2. Which yet survive, stamped on these lifeless things,
The hand that mocked them, and the heart that fed;

(a) Whose hand is being referred to here?
(b) What is the reference to 'Which yet survive'?
(c) Give a synonym of 'mocked'.
(d) Why have the other parts of the statue not survived?

Short Answer Type Questions

Answer the following questions in 30-40 words.

1. Apart from the trunkless legs, what else did the traveller see there?

2. What idea do you get about the person whose statue lay in a dilapidated state in the desert?

3. Describe the expression of Ozymandias as captured by the sculptor.

4. Why did Ozymandias get such pompous words inscribed on the pedestal?

5. What idea do you form about the traveller from the poem?

6. Why do you think Ozymandias got such a colossal statue carved out?

7. Elaborate on Ozymandias' short-sightedness.

Long Answer Type Questions

Answer the following questions in 150 words.

1. The sculptor reads the passions of Ozymandias and transports it into his work of art. What do you understand about the character of King Ozymandias? What traits of the sculptor can be imbibed for developing one's craftsmanship skills?

2. The poem 'Ozymandias' highlights the hollow concept of man that objects such as statues, monuments and memorials can immortalise him. How far do you agree with this perception? Explain with reference to 'Ozymandias'. What, in your opinion, can make a man immortal?

3. "There is a great man who makes every man feel small. But the real great man is the one who makes every man feel great." In which category of great men would you place Ozymandias? Why? What qualities should a person have, according to you, to be really great? Give an example of one such person from real life.

The Rime of the Ancient Mariner

by Samuel Taylor Coleridge

CHAPTER 4

Introduction 'The Rime of the Ancient Mariner' is a ballad that demonstrates the importance of God's creations and the appreciation we should have for them, no matter how small or great. Through the poem, the poet brings out the suffering and the feelings of guilt faced by the Ancient Mariner, who, in a moment of cruelty, killed an innocent Albatross (a huge sea-bird).

Stanzawise Explanation

Stanza 1 (Lines 1-20)

It is an ancient Mariner,
And he stoppeth one of three.
'By thy long grey beard and glittering eye,
Now wherefore stopp'st thou me?
The bridegroom's doors are opened wide,
And I am next of kin;
The guests are met, the feast is set:
May'st hear the merry din.'
He holds him with his skinny hand,
"There was a ship," quoth he.
'Hold off! unhand me, grey-beard loon!'
Eftsoons his hand dropt he.
He holds him with his glittering eye-
The wedding guest stood still,
And listens like a three years' child:
The Mariner hath his will.
The wedding guest sat on a stone:
He cannot choose but hear;
And thus spake on that ancient man,
The bright-eyed Mariner.

Explanation The poem starts by introducing the central character of the poem-the old Mariner (sailor) who stops one of the three wedding guests going to attend a wedding feast. The old mariner has a long grey beard and eyes that are shining brightly. When the Mariner stops the wedding guest, the latter is surprised. The guest asks him how he has dared to stop him.

The annoyed wedding guest asks the Mariner if he cannot see that he is going to the wedding feast. The wedding guest mentions that he is a close relative of the bridegroom's family. So, his presence is essential. All the guests have arrived and the feast is laid on the table. He asks the Mariner if he cannot hear the noise of the festivities. He further tells the Mariner that he should let him enjoy the merry-making.

The Mariner holds the guest with his thin hand. He starts narrating his story by saying that there was a ship. The guest gets irritated and angrily calls the Mariner a crazy man while asking him to stay away from him. As soon as the Mariner hears this, he drops his hand but still holds him with his glittering eyes. Under its influence, the wedding guest gives all his attention to the Mariner and willingly listens to him. So, the wedding guest sits on a stone and the Mariner continues his story. The guest has no option but to listen to his story.

Stanza 2 (Lines 21-40)

"The ship was cheered, the harbour cleared,
Merrily did we drop
Below the kirk, below the hill,
Below the lighthouse top.

The sun came up upon the left,
Out of the sea came he!
And he shone bright, and on the right
Went down into the sea.
Higher and higher every day,
Till over the mast at noon-
The wedding guest here beat his breast,
For he heard the loud bassoon.
The bride hath paced into the hall,
Red as a rose is she;
Nodding their heads before her goes
The merry minstrelsy.
The wedding guest he beat his breast,
Yet he cannot choose but hear;
And thus spake on that ancient man,
The bright-eyed Mariner.

Explanation The Mariner begins his story by describing how his ship left the harbour and began its journey on a happy note. The Mariner and his shipmates cheerfully started the ship and it crossed the harbour and entered the open sea very quickly. As the ship sailed away from the coast, the church, the hill and the light house on top of the hill disappeared from the sailor's view.

The Mariner now describes nature and its very important element – the Sun. As they travelled, the Sun rose on the left hand side of the ship. It seemed as if it had came out of the sea. The Sun shone brightly during the day and then, set on the right side.

With the passing of each day, the Sun seemed to rise to greater heights. This indicates that the ship was moving towards the Equator. When the ship reached the Equator, the Sun was directly over the mast of the ship.

Although the wedding guest is patiently listening to the Mariner's tale, at this moment he started beating his breast because the sudden sound of the bassoon (a musical instrument) makes him impatient. He wanted to go and attend the wedding.

By this time, the bride had entered the hall. She was very pretty and looked like a beautiful red rose. She was entering the hall after the singers and musicians who were nodding their heads to the music.

The wedding guest could only beat his breast in disappointment and sorrow. Despite his protests, the wedding guest is made to hear the Mariner's story as he had no choice but to hear it. So, the old sailor continues with his story.

Stanza 3 (Lines 41-58)

"And now the storm-blast came, and he
Was tyrannous and strong:
He struck with his o'ertaking wings,
And chased us south along.
With sloping masts and dipping prow,
As who pursued with yell and blow.
Still treads the shadow of his foe,
And forward bends his head,
The ship drove fast, loud roared the blast,
And southward aye we fled.
And now there came both mist and snow,
And it grew wondrous cold:
And ice, mast-high, came floating by,
As green as emerald.
And through the drifts the snowy clifts
Did send a dismal sheen:
Now shapes of men nor beasts we ken-
The ice was all between.

Explanation Furthering his story, the Mariner tells the wedding guest that a strong storm arose in the sea. It was a very severe and powerful storm. The ship was forcibly thrown off its path and driven towards the South Pole. Here, the storm has been compared to a bird of prey or a winged monster which chases and pounces on the ship just like the bird does on its prey.

As the ship was caught in the storm, its front part had bent forward by the force of the wind. The poet compares the ship to a man being chased by an enemy, the storm here. As the enemy bent his head forward, the ship drove fast towards the South amidst the roaring sound of the storm. In other words, with the force of the storm, the ship was carried by the waves towards the South.

Now, the ship reached a place where there was a lot of mist and snow. The weather of this place was very cold. Icebergs as high as the mast of the ship were floating here and there. The poet says that the colour of the sea water was as green as an emerald and it was being reflected through the icebergs.

While the ship was moving through the floating ice and the steep sides of icebergs, there was no human being or animal to be seen around. The snow and the mist ensured that the light was dim.

Stanza 4 (Lines 59-82)

The ice was here, the ice was there,
The ice was all around:
It cracked and growled, and roared and howled,
Like noises in a swound!
At length did cross an Albatross,
Through the fog it came;
As it had been a Christian soul,
We hailed it in God's name.
It ate the food it ne'er had eat,
And round and round it flew.
The ice did split with a thunder-fit;
The helmsman steered us through!
And a good south wind sprung up behind;
The Albatross did follow,
And every day, for food or play,
Came to the mariner's hollo!
In mist or cloud, on mast or shroud,
It perched for vespers nine,
Whiles all the night, through fog-smoke white,
Glimmered the white moonshine."
'God save thee, ancient Mariner,
From the fiends that plague thee thus!-
Why look'st thou so?-"With my crossbow.
I shot the Albatross."

Explanation There was ice all around the ship and when it cracked, it made a growling or angry sound. The sounds produced by the splitting of the icebergs, their sliding and falling into the sea is described to be animalistic. They resemble the sound of the distance thundering and rumbling heard by a person in a fainting fit.

For many days, the ship sailed all alone in the icy ocean. After some time, an Albatross, a long-winged and large bird, flew over the ship. The bird came through the fog and mist. Believing in Christian theology, the sailors thought that just like them, the bird was also a creation of God. So, they welcomed it. Its arrival lifted their ship and brought some hope as well as excitement into their dull and boring journey.

The sailors gave the Albatross food items like meat, biscuits etc. They were sure that the bird had not eaten such food. It flew above the ship in anticipation of more food. Suddenly, the weather became favourable. The icebergs started splitting into pieces with thunderous noise. The helmsman found the way to steer the ship out of the land of mist and snow.

Then, the pleasant South wind started blowing. This was a good sign because now they could set sail and move. The sailors believed that it was the Albatross which brought the favourable weather and caused the wind to blow. The bird began to follow the ship. Every day the bird came to take food or play with the Mariners.

Whether it was a misty or a cloudy day, the Albatross sat on the mast or ropes tying the sails for nine days continuously. He sat on the mast at a fixed time everyday which was the hour of the church service. All this while, the pale light of the moon would shine dimly through the fog.

Then suddenly, the wedding guest noticed that the expression of the Mariner's face changed. It seems that something wrong and something bad had happened. He asked the Mariner why he was looking so terrified and tormented. The old mariner replied that he committed the cruel crime of killing the Albatross with an arrow from his crossbow.

Stanza 5 (Lines 83-102)

"The sun now rose upon the right:
Out of the sea came he,
Still hid in mist, and on the left
Went down into the sea.
And the good south wind still blew behind,
But no sweet bird did follow,
Nor any day for food or play
Came to the mariners' hollo!
And I had done a hellish thing,
And it would work' em woe:
For all averred, I had killed the bird
That made the breeze to blow.
Ah wretch! said they, the bird to slay,
That made the breeze to blow!
Nor dim nor red, like God's own head,
The glorious sun uprist:
Then all averred, I had killed the bird
That brought the fog and mist.
'Twas right, said they, such birds to slay,
That bring the fog and mist.

Explanation The Mariner continues his story. The sun now rose out of the sea on the right side of the ship but it was still hidden in the mist. In the evening, it sank into the sea on their left. The favourable South wind continued to blow. Everything remained the same but the only difference was that no bird followed them, responded to the Mariners' calls or ever came for food. Here, it is to be noted that the mariner calls the bird 'sweet'. So, there is a touch of regret and repentance in the Mariner's voice.

The ancient Mariner admitted that he had done an evil thing which would bring sorrow and grief to all of them. Everyone felt that it was bad on his part to kill the bird which had made the good South wind to blow. They declared the Mariner to be a wretched person for killing the Albatross-the good omen which had brought a ray of hope and relieved them of their physical and mental agony.

Soon, the weather changed and the mist and snow were wiped away. The Mariner continued his story by saying that the sun rose and looked like the radiant halo (a circle of light) behind God's head. Seeing this, the sailors changed their view. They, now felt that the Albatross had brought mist and snow, and that the Mariner had done the right thing to kill the albatross. This change of attitude in sailors shows that they are opportunistic and fickle-minded.

Stanza 6 (Lines 103-119)

The fair breeze blew, the white foam flew,
The furrow followed free;
We were the first that ever burst
Into that silent sea.
Down dropped the breeze, the sails dropped down,
'Twas sad as sad could be;
And we did speak only to break
The silence of the sea!
All in a hot and copper sky,
The bloody sun, at noon,
Right up above the mast did stand,
No bigger than the moon.
Day after day, day after day,
We stuck, nor breath nor motion;
As idle as a painted ship
Upon a painted ocean.

Explanation The favourable South wind continued blowing and the ship moved in the right direction. White bubbles formed by the ship's movement were scattered in all directions and the ship continued to move ahead, without a break. As a result, the sailors thought that they must be the first ones to come to such a silent sea where there were no storms or interruptions in their journey.

The wind stopped blowing suddenly and the sails of the ship dropped down. The ship was unable to move due to lack of wind and there was a sinister silence all around. This silence was broken only by the Mariners' voices.

The punishment of the sailors continued. The Sun burning at noon looked red like the colour of blood. The sky had become hot and copper-coloured. It was right above the mast and looked bigger than the size of the Moon.

The ship was stuck in this place as there was no wind or tide to allow its movement. In other words, the Ancient Mariner and his fellow sailors were stuck in the middle of the silent sea for a very long time. Their ship looked like painted ship on a painted ocean. It didn't give the appearance of a real ship.

Stanza 7 (Lines 120-143)

Water, water, every where,
And all the boards did shrink;
Water, water, every where,
Nor any drop to drink.
The very deep did rot: O Christ!
That ever this should be!
Yea, slimy things did crawl with legs
Upon the slimy sea.
About, about, in reel and rout
The death-fires danced at night;
The water, like a witch's oils,
Burnt green, and blue, and white.
And some in dreams assured were
Of the Spirit that plagued us so;
Nine fathom deep he had followed us
From the land of mist and snow.
And every tongue, through utter drought,
Was withered at the root;
We could not speak, no more than if
We had been choked with soot.
Ah! well-a-day! what evil looks
Had I from old and young!
Instead of the cross, the Albatross
About my neck was hung."

Explanation The suffering of the Mariner and his crew was increasing day-by-day. They were thirsty and had no potable water. There was water all around but they didn't have a single drop of water which they could drink. The sea water was saline and not fit for drinking. The weather was also getting so hot that even the wooden planks of the ship seemed to be shrinking.

The deepest part of the ocean started rotting. They had never thought that such a situation would arise. The mariners could see ugly sea creatures crawling with their ugly legs on the sticky glue like water of the sea. Death-fires, which are a kind of moth, were seen moving about in circular movements. The sea water took the colour of witch's oil, i.e. green, blue and white in colour. All this signifies evil and points towards the grave sin that the Mariner had committed by killing the Albatross.

Some of the sailors were convinced at this time that they were being followed by a vengeful spirit which they had seen in their dreams. The spirit was the guardian spirit of the Albatross and it was behind all that was happening with them. The spirit had followed them by remaining under the water from the land of mist and snow.

Due to immense heat and thirst, the sailors' mouths were parched and dry. They could not even speak! It seemed as if their mouths were filled with dust. The fellow sailors of the Ancient Mariner looked at him with eyes full of hatred, disgust and accusation. They blamed him for their sufferings in the silent sea. In anger, they took off the holy cross around the Mariner's neck and hung the dead Albatross around his neck as a reminder of his heinous sin and guilt.

It is interesting to note here that the 'very deep' sea which is stagnant and full of stench is symbolic of the Mariner's sinful soul which was rotting.

Poetic Devices Used in the Poem

Alliteration Repetition of initial consonant sounds in the same line.

- By thy long grey beard and glittering eye
- The merry minstrelsy
- The fair breeze blew
- The furrow followed free

Repetition Repetition of a word, a phrase or a full sentence.

- Higher and higher every day,
- Water, water, every where
- Day after day, day after day

Onomatopoeia Using a word which suggests the meaning by its sound.

It cracked and growled, and roared and howled,

Simile A device which compares two different things by using the words 'as' or 'like'.

- The bride hath paced into the hall, Red as a rose is she
- And ice, mast-high, came floating by, As green as emerald

Metaphor A device which compares two things or qualities which are unlike.

- Upon a painted ocean
- We could not speak, no more than if, we had been choked with soot

Personification It is used for an inanimate object or animals/birds that look or feel human.

- And now the storm blast came, and he was tyrannous and strong

Word Meaning

Word	Meaning
Stanza 1	
Mariner	sailor
stoppeth	stopped
glittering	shining brightly, with flashing points of light
wherefore	why
thou	you
kin	members of family
merry din	sound of festivities
loon	a mad person
eftsoons	at once
hath	had
spake	spoke
Stanza 2	
kirk	church
mast	pole
bassoon	a musical instrument
minstrelsy	singers and musicians
Stanza 3	
tyrannous	cruel, severe, harsh
prow	the front part of the ship
pursued	chased
treads	follows behind
foe	enemy
emerald	a precious stone, which is clear and bright green
drifts	floating ice
clifts	steep sides of icebergs
dismal	gloomy
sheen	a smooth and gentle brightness on the surface of something
ken	see

Word	Meaning
Stanza 4	
growled	rumbled
swound	a fainting fit
Albatross	a very large sea bird
helmsman	the person steering the ship
hollo	shout, call
shroud	sail
perched	sat on the edge of something
vespers nine	a fixed time everyday (the evening church service)
thee	you
plague	to bother, trouble
crossbow	a very powerful bow and arrow with a trigger
Stanza 5	
hellish	very bad, infernal
em	them
woe	great unhappiness and sorrow
averred	said firmly
wretch	someone you feel sorry for
uprist	rose up
slay	kill
Stanza 6	
furrow	the white foam created by the ship's movement
Twas	It was
Stanza 7	
deep	ocean
rot	decay
reel and rout	types of dance
fathom	a measurement of depth equal to six feet
withered	shrunken
soot	dirt

Textbook FOLDER

Here, we have covered questions given in the CBSE Textbook along with their answer

ON PAGE 110

Q.4 Here are some of the archaic words used in the poem; can you match them with the words used in modern English language that mean the same? The first one has been done for you as an example.

Stoppeth	Why
thy	Entered
Wherefore	Stopped
Stopp'st	You
Thou	Lunatic
May'st	At once
Quoth	Fainting fit
loon	Has
Eftsoons	Can't you
Dropt	Stopping
Hath	Church
spake	Enemy
kirk	Yes
Paced	See
foe	Call
Aye	Trouble
Ken	Looking
Swound	Your
Hollo	Said
Plague	Dropped
Look'st	Spoke

Ans.

Stoppeth	stopped
thy	Your
Wherefore	Why
Stopp'st	Stopping
Thou	You
May'st	Can't you
Quoth	Said
loon	Lunatic
Eftsoons	At once
Dropt	Dropped
Hath	Has
spake	Spoke
kirk	Church
Paced	Entered
foe	Enemy
Aye	Yes
Ken	See
Swound	Fainting fit
Hollo	Call
Plague	Trouble
Look'st	Looking

ON PAGE 111

Q.5 Using the words given above rewrite PART I of the poem in your own words. The first stanza has been done as an example:

It is an ancient Mariner,
And he stoppeth one of three.
'By thy long grey beard and glittering eye,
Now wherefore stopp'st thou me?

An old sailor stopped one of the three people passing by, who asked: "Old man, with your long grey beard and glittering eye, why are you stopping me?"

Ans. Refer to stanza wise explanation.

ON PAGE 111-113

Q.6 Answer the following by choosing the right option from those given below.

(i) The Ancient Mariner stopped one of the three wedding guests because......... .

(a) he wanted to attend the wedding with him
(b) he wanted him to sit with him
(c) he wanted him to listen to his story
(d) he wanted to stop him from going to the wedding

Ans. (c) he wanted him to listen to his story

(ii) The wedding guest remarked that he was 'next of kin' it meant that ....

(a) he was a close relation of the bridegroom
(b) he was a close relation of the bride
(c) he was next in line to get married
(d) he had to stand next to the bridegroom during the wedding

Ans. (a) he was a close relation of the bridegroom

(iii) 'He cannot choose but hear' means.........

(a) 'the mariner was forced to hear the story of the wedding guest.'

(b) 'the wedding guest was forced to hear the story of the mariner.'

(c) 'the mariner had the choice of not listening to the story of the wedding guest.'

(d) 'the wedding guest had the choice of not listening to the story of the mariner.'

Ans. (b) 'the wedding guest was forced to hear the story of the mariner.'

(iv) 'The sun came up upon the left, /Out of the sea came he;' This line tells us that the ship...... .

(a) was moving in the Northern direction

(b) was moving eastwards

(c) was moving in the Western direction

(d) was moving towards the South

Ans. (d) was moving towards the South

(v) The wedding guest beat his breast because......... .

(a) he could hear the sound of the bassoon

(b) he was forced to listen to the Mariner's tale when he wanted to attend the wedding

(c) the sound of the bassoon meant that the bride had arrived and the wedding ceremony was about to begin and he could not attend it.

(d) the sound of the bassoon announced the arrival of the bride and the start of the wedding ceremony

Ans. (c) the sound of the bassoon meant that the bride had arrived and the wedding ceremony was about to begin and he could not attend it.

(vi) The storm blast had been described as being tyrannous because.......... .

(a) it was so fierce that it frightened the sailors

(b) it took complete control of the ship

(c) the storm was very powerful

(d) the sailors were at its mercy

Ans. (b) it took complete control of the ship

(vii) The sailors felt depressed on reaching the land of mist and snow because...... .

(a) there was no sign of any living creature

(b) they felt they would die in that cold weather

(c) they were surrounded by icebergs and there seemed to be no sign of life

(d) everything was grey in colour and they felt very cold

Ans. (c) they were surrounded by icebergs and there seemed to be no sign of life

(viii) The sailors were happy to see the albatross because........ .

(a) it was the first sign of life and therefore gave them hope that they might survive

(b) it split the icebergs around the ship and helped the ship move forward

(c) it was a messenger from God and it lifted the fog and mist

(d) it gave them hope of survival by splitting the icebergs

Ans. (a) it was the first sign of life and therefore gave them hope that they might survive

(ix) The two things that happened after the arrival of the albatross were ....

(a) the icebergs split and the albatross became friendly with the sailors

(b) the icebergs split and a strong breeze started blowing

(c) the ship was pushed out of the land of mist and the ice melted

(d) the albatross started playing with the mariners and ate the food they offered

Ans. (b) the icebergs split and a strong breeze started blowing

(x) 'It perched for vespers nine' means......... .

(a) the ship stopped sailing at nine o'clock every day

(b) the albatross would appear at a fixed time everyday

(c) the albatross would sit on the sail or the mast everyday

(d) the albatross was a holy creature

Ans. (b) the albatross would appear at a fixed time everyday

(xi) 'God save thee, ancient Mariner, /From the fiends that plague thee thus! Why look'st thou so?' means.......... .

(a) the mariner wanted to know why the wedding guest was looking so happy

(b) the wedding guest wanted to know why the mariner was looking so tormented

(c) the wedding guest wanted to know whether some creatures were troubling the ancient mariner

(d) the ancient mariner wanted to know whether something was troubling the wedding guest

Ans. (b) the wedding guest wanted to know why the mariner was looking so tormented

ON PAGE 113

Q.7 Answer the following questions briefly. (Part I)

(a) How did the ancient mariner stop the wedding guest?

Ans. The ancient mariner stopped the wedding guest by holding him with his skinny hand and looking at him with glittering eyes. The wedding guest wanted to leave but was totally mesmerised by the glittering eyes of the Ancient Mariner.

(b) Was the wedding guest happy to be stopped? Give reasons for your answer.

Ans. No, the wedding guest was certainly not happy at being stopped. He was eager to go to the wedding. He grew restless as he was the next of kin of the bridegroom and needed to be present at the wedding.

(c) Describe the ancient mariner.

Ans. The ancient mariner was very old and thin. He had a grey beard which highlighted his old age. He also had glittering eyes which could spellbind others.

(d) How does the mariner describe the movement of the ship as it sails away from the land?

Ans. The ship was given a warm send-off from the harbour. It went easily and smoothly by the side of the church, the hill and the lighthouse.

(e) What kind of weather did the sailors enjoy at the beginning of their journey? How has it been expressed in the poem?

Ans. The sailors enjoyed fair weather at the beginning of the journey. This is indirectly expressed, starting from line 22 and going on till line 30. It has been expressed in a happy manner, as in line 22 it says, 'Merrily did we drop...'. This shows that they were happy with the progress of the journey.

(f) How did the sailors reach the land of mist and snow? Or Explain how the ship reached the land of mist and snow.

Ans. The sailors left the harbour in good weather and sailed South for many days. Then, the weather changed and they were driven further South by a storm. There they were surrounded by mist, snow and ice as high as the mast of their ship.

(g) How does the mariner express the fact that the ship was completely surrounded by icebergs?

Ans. The mariner describes how emerald coloured blocks of ice as high as the mast of the ship floated around the ship, blocking all view. There was no passage visible through which the ship could be steered. He gives a vivid and graphic description of the icebergs all around the ship.

(h) How do we know that the Albatross was not afraid of the humans? Why did the sailors hail it in God's name?

Ans. When an Albatross came on the ship, it ate food indicating that it was not afraid of the humans. The sailors hailed it in God's name because it was the only living creature they had seen since they reached the sea full of ice. The albatross seemed to be a representative of God there.

(i) What was the terrible deed done by the Mariner? Why do you think he did it?

Ans. The Mariner had killed the Albatross with his crossbow. He killed it due to some reason which he did not know himself. May be he did it out of monotony, as there was nothing to be done on the ship. It was a terrible deed because he had no reason to kill the Albatross. Killing a living being without reason is unjustified.

ON PAGE 113-114

Q.8 There are a number of literary devices used in the poem. Some of them have been listed below. Choose the right ones and write them down in the table as shown in the example. In each of the cases, explain what they mean. **(Part II)**

Simile, metaphor, alliteration personification, hyperbole, repetition,

1	The wedding guest stood still, and listens like a three years' child :	Simile; the wedding guest was completely under the control of the Mariner
2	Below the kirk, below the hill, below the lighthouse top	
3	The Sun came up upon the left, out of the sea came he	
4	The bride hath paced into the hall, red as a rose is she	
5	And now the storm-blast came, and he was tyrannous and strong :	
6	With sloping masts and dipping prow, As who pursued with yell and blow still treads the shadow of his foe	
7	The ice was here, the ice was there. The ice was all around	

Ans.

1	The wedding guest stood still, and listens like a three years' child :	Simile; the wedding guest was completely under the control of the Mariner
2	Below the kirk, below the hill, below the lighthouse top	Repetition; the word below repeats for emphasis.
3	The sun came up upon the left, out of the sea came he	Personification; the sun has been given the human quality as it is referred to as 'he'
4	The bride hath paced into the hall, red as a rose is she	Simile and Alliteration in 'red as a rose'; simile as the bride is compared to a rose using 'as'; Alliteration as the sound 'r' is repeated in nearly words.
5	And now the storm-blast came, and he was tyrannous and strong :	Personification and Metaphor; storm has been given the human quality using 'he', storm is compared to tyrannical ruler without use of any comparison word.
6	With sloping masts and dipping prow, As who pursued with yell and blow still treads the shadow of his foe	Personification; ship has been personified
7	The ice was here, the ice was there. The ice was all around	Repetition; the word ice is repeated

ON PAGE 116-117

Q.11 Answer the following questions briefly. (Part II)

(a) In which direction did the ship start moving? How can you say?

Ans. The ship was now sailing North. This is evident from the lines which state that the sun rose on the right (East) and went down in the sea on the left (West).

(b) Why does the mariner say that 'no sweet bird did follow'?

Ans. The Albatross was shot by the old Mariner and so no 'sweet bird' was following them. This line also shows that the old Mariner was feeling guilty after killing the poor bird.

(c) How did the other mariners behave towards the Ancient Mariner at first? How many times did they change their mind about the Ancient Mariner? What does this tell us about their character?

Ans. At first, the Mariners condemned the terrible act of killing the innocent and auspicious albatross. They believed that killing of such a lucky bird that caused the breeze to blow was a sin. It would bring woe and despair to them. They changed their stand when the ship got a favourable breeze. Now, they started justifying the killing of the bird that brought mist and snow.

Later on, they again changed their stand and condemned the killing of the Albatross when their ship was stranded in mid-ocean without any wind to drive it forward. This only shows their fickle-mindedness.

(d) How did the sailing conditions change after the ship had moved out of the land of mist and snow? What or who did the mariners blame for this change?

***Or* How did the killing of the Albatross prove to be a bad omen for the sailors?**

Ans. As soon as the ship moved out of the land of mist and snow, the sailing conditions changed. The breeze stopped blowing and the sails of the ship dropped down.

The sailors blamed this on the shooting of the albatross. They held the Ancient Mariner responsible for this change. Thus, they felt that the killing of the albatross had proved to be a bad omen for them.

(e) What is indicated by the lines 'The bloody sun, at noon,/Right up above the mast did stand,/No bigger than the moon'?

Ans. These lines clearly indicate that something ominous will happen soon. The weather had become unbearably hot. It threatened the lives of the sailors, and the ship was at a standstill due to no breeze.

(f) How does the Mariner describe the fact that they were completely motionless in the middle of the sea?

Ans. This is described in lines 117-118 as a 'painted ship upon a painted ocean' meaning that their ship was stationary, just like a painting.

(g) What is the irony in the ninth stanza (lines 119-122)? Explain it in your own words.

Ans. The ninth stanza presents an irony in stating that there was water everywhere but there was no drop of water which they could drink. Their supply of fresh water was exhausted and the water around them was saline and not fit for drinking.

(h) What is the narrator trying to convey through the description of the situation in the tenth and eleventh stanza (lines 123-130)?

Ans. The narrator is trying to convey that the ocean itself begins to decay and the sailors see many disturbing sights. By this, he probably means that due to dehydration, the sailors were having hallucinations and would die soon if they did not get fresh water.

(i) What or who did the mariners feel was responsible for their suffering?

Ans. The fellow mariners felt that the Ancient Mariner's shooting of the albatross was responsible for their sufferings. Hence, they hung the dead albatross around his neck to punish him.

(j) Describe the condition of the mariners as expressed in the thirteenth stanza (lines 135-138).

Ans. The condition of the Mariners as described in this stanza was miserable. Their tongues were withered by the lack of water. They could not speak anymore and felt as if their throats were choked with soot.

(k) Why did the Mariners hang the albatross around the neck of the Ancient Mariner?
***Or* Why was the albatross hung around the neck of the Ancient Mariner?**
***Or* How did the sailors react to the killing of the albatross by the Ancient Mariner?**

Ans. Since the sailors felt that the Ancient Mariner was responsible for their problems, they hung the dead albatross around his neck as a sign of his guilt. They wanted to punish him for the sin that he had committed by killing the albatross.

ON PAGE 117

Q.12 Like part one, the second part also has a number of literary devices. List them out in the same way as you had done in question number seven and explain them.

Ans.

The Sun now rose upon the right Out of the sea came the still hid in mist	Personification; The sun has been given the human quality of movement
And it would work'em woe That made the breeze to blow The fair breeze blew, the white foam flew The furrow followed free About, about in reel and rout	Alliteration; The sound of 'be' repeats in 'breeze', 'blow', 'blew'. The sound of 'f' repeats in 'form', 'flew', 'furrouwed', 'follow' and 'free'. The sound of 'r' repeats in 'reel' and 'rout'.
Nor dim, nor re, like gods own head, the glorious sun purist	Simile; the Albatross is compared to a God using 'like'.
Down dropped the breeze, the sails dropped down Day after day, day after day Water, water, everywhere	Repetition; The words 'dropped', 'day after day' and 'water' repeats.
As idle as a painted ship upon a painted ocean	Simile; the ship in the sea is compared to a painting using 'as'.
Water, water everywhere and not a drop to drink	Irony; The sailors are surrounded by water that they connot drink.
The bloody Sun	Metaphor; The Sun's colour is compared to the colour of the blood.
And every tongue, through utter drought, was withered at the root	Metaphor; The dry condition of the sailors' mouth is like that of a land suffering from drought.
Nine fathom deep he had followed us from the land of mist and snow	Hyperbole; The depth of sea is exaggerted to nine levels.
The water, like a witch's oils	Simile; The colour of the water of the sea is blue, white and black like the colour of the witch's oil.

Q.13 What is the rhyme scheme of the poem?

Ans. The poem follows the rhyme scheme of *abcb* except in the lines 45-50 where it follows the rhyme scheme of *aaabcb* and lines 91-96 and 97-102 where it follows the rhyme scheme of *abcbdb*.

Q.14 Find examples of the use of interesting sounds (Onomatopoeia) from the poem and explain their effect on the reader.

1.	The ice 'cracked and growled, and roared and howled'	Coleridge uses onomatopoeic words which use harsh 'ck' sounds to make the ice sound brutal. He also gives the ice animal sounds to give the impression that it has come alive and is attacking the ship.

Ans.

1.	The ice cracked and growled, and roared and howled'	Coleridge uses onomatopoeic words which use 'ck' sounds to make the ice sound brutal.
2.	The ship drove fast, loud roared the blast	Roared is connected here to the sound of wild animals like lion. The sound is used to depict the roaring storm coming alive and loudly towards the ship.
3.	He struck with his O'rtaking wings	'Struck' gives the impression of the storm hitting the ship.
4.	The fair breeze blew, the white foam flew	The two words blew and flew explain the movement of the wind and the foam in a mild way
5.	The ice did split with a thunder fit	The word split brought the sound of the ice during crack
6.	Came to the Mariner's hollo!	The word 'hollo' is the sound of the call of the Mariners to the Albatross.

ON PAGE 123

Q.15 The poem is full of strange, uncanny or supernatural elements. Discuss how these elements appear in the poem. You should consider

- the strange weather,
- the albatross as a bird of 'good omen'
- the spirit from 'the land of mist and snow'
- the strange slimy creatures seen in the sea
- the ocean appearing to rot
- the death fires and sea water being referred to as witch's oil

Now write a paragraph about the supernatural elements in the poem and how they add to the events that take place in the poem.

Ans. There are a number of supernatural elements in this poem. These elements were common superstitions that most people of his time believed in.

In the beginning, the sailors believed that the albatross brought them the South wind, as the bird was supposed to be a good omen. So, they were angry with the Ancient Mariner when he killed the albatross. They thought that his action brought them bad luck as the breeze stopped totally and the drinking water was finished. Other supernatural elements that the poet mentions include

(a) The strange weather, as there was a huge storm first and then there was no wind at all.

(b) The spirit from 'the land of mist and snow', meaning the ghost which had pursued them ever since the Ancient Mariner had killed the albatross.

(c) The strange slimy creatures seen in the sea, the ocean appearing to rot and the fires and sea water being referred to as witch's oil, which are all hallucinations of the sailors due to the excessive heat and their thirst.

ON PAGE 118

Q.19 In your groups discuss the following.

(a) Why did the Ancient Mariner stop the particular wedding guest to listen to his tale?

Ans. The Ancient Mariner stopped the particular wedding guest to listen to his story as he was able to get the man's attention.

(b) Why did he have to tell his tale to someone?

Ans. He had to tell his tale to someone because he was compelled to do so. The more the mariner tells his story to others, the more he reflects on his sins and guilt. This causes him to feel even more remorseful for his mistreatment of the albatross.

(c) What is the poet trying to convey through this poem?

Ans. The poet is trying to convey the importance of God's creations and the appreciation we should have for them, no matter how small or great they may be.

REVIEW EXERCISE

Including Previous Years' and Practice Questions

Extract Based Questions

Read the following extracts carefully and answer the questions that follow.

1. It is an ancient Mariner,
And he stoppeth one of three.
'By thy long grey beard and glittering eye,
Now wherefore stopp'st thou me?

(a) Who does 'one of three' refer to?

Ans. 'One of three' refers to one of the three wedding guests.

(b) Why did the Mariner stop one of them?

Ans. The Mariner stopped one of them because he wanted to tell him his story.

(c) Which word in the extract means the same as 'shining brightly'?

Ans. The word 'glittering' means the same as 'shining brightly'.

(d) What is the rhyme scheme adopted in these lines?

Ans. The rhyme scheme adopted in these lines is *abcb*.

2. He holds him with his glittering eye.
The wedding guest stood still,
And listens like a three years' child:
The Mariner hath his will.

(a) Was the wedding guest a willing participant to the Ancient Mariner's act?

Ans. No, the wedding guest was not a willing participant to the Ancient Mariner's act.

(b) Why did the wedding guest stand still?

Ans. The wedding guest stood still because the Mariner's eyes fascinated him and took all his attention.

(c) What was the Mariner's will?

Ans. The Mariner wanted to make the wedding guest listen to his woeful story.

(d) Explain 'The Mariner hath his will.'

Ans. This means that the Mariner at last was successful in persuading the wedding guest to hear his story.

3. The bridegroom's doors are opened wide,
And I am next of kin;
The guests are met, the feast is set:
May'st hear the merry din.'

(a) Who is 'I' in the above lines? Who is he talking to?

Ans. 'I' here refers to the wedding guest who was stopped by the Mariner. He is talking to the Ancient Mariner.

(b) What do you mean by 'The bridegroom's doors are opened wide'?

Ans. The expression means that the guests are being eagerly awaited for by the bridegroom's family.

(c) What do the last two lines suggest about the speaker?

Ans. The lines suggest that the wedding guest is eager and impatient to attend the wedding.

(d) What do you understand by the word 'feast' here?

Ans. The word 'feast' means a large and special meal meant for many people to celebrate the wedding.

4. Higher and higher every day,
Till over the mast at noon–
The wedding guest here beat his breast,
For he heard the loud bassoon.

(a) What went on higher and higher every day?

Ans. The Sun went higher and higher every day.

(b) How was the wedding guest frustrated in his attempt to attend the wedding?

Ans. The wedding guest was frustrated because his attempt to attend the wedding was stopped by the Mariner who wanted to tell him his story.

(c) A bassoon is ....

Ans. a musical instrument

(d) Write the meaning of 'mast.'

Ans. The word 'mast' is a tall pole on a boat or ship that supports the sail.

5.

The wedding guest he beat his breast,
Yet he cannot choose but hear;
And thus spake on that ancient man,
The bright-eyed Mariner.

(a) Why did the wedding guest 'beat his breast'?

Ans. The wedding guest could hear the sound of the bassoon and he realised that the wedding ceremonies had started. However, he could not go and was compelled to listen to the Mariner's story. So, he 'beat his breast' in frustration.

(b) Why was the wedding guest forced to hear the Mariner?

Ans. The wedding guest was perhaps hypnotised by the Mariner which made him spellbound. As a result, he was forced to hear the Mariner.

(c) What does 'ancient' mean?

Ans. The word 'ancient' here means 'old.'

(d) What rhyme scheme has been adopted in these lines?

Ans. The rhyme scheme adopted in these lines is *abcb*.

6.

"And now the storm-blast came, and he
Was tyrannous and strong:
He struck with his o'ertaking wings,
And chased us south along.

(a) Who was being chased and by whom?

Ans. The storm was chasing the Mariner's ship, meaning that it was blowing the ship southwards.

(b) What was the effect of the storm-blast?

Ans. The effect was that it blew the ship southwards.

(c) Which Literary device is used in the given lines?

Ans. Metaphor.

(d) What is signified by 'o'ertaking wings'?

Ans. The phrase 'o'ertaking wings' means that the storm was like a bird of prey and was pouncing upon the ship to devour it.

7.

At length did cross an Albatross,
Through the fog it came;
As it had been a Christian soul,
We hailed it in God's name.

(a) What was the atmosphere around the ship when the albatross came?

Ans. The atmosphere around the ship was cold and silent. The ship was surrounded by ice. There were no beasts or other men around.

(b) Why has it been called a 'Christian soul'?

Ans. The sailors thought it to be an angel sent by God to help them, as the conditions became favourable after its arrival.

(c) Which word in the extract is a synonym of 'greeted' or 'welcomed'?

Ans. The word 'hailed' is a synonym of 'greeted' or 'welcomed'.

(d) Explain 'We hailed it in God's name.'

Ans. This means that all the crew members welcomed the arrival of the albatross.

8.

It ate the food it ne'er had eat,
And round and round it flew.
The ice did split with a thunder-fit;
The helmsman steered us through!

(a) What do you mean by 'helmsman'?

Ans. The word 'helmsman' refers to the person steering the ship.

(b) What difficulty did the mariners face before 'it' arrived?

Ans. The difficulty faced by the mariners was that they were stuck in the ice. There was mist and snow all around.

(c) What happened after 'its' appearance?

Ans. After 'its' appearance, the ice split and the helmsman was able to steer the ship out of the ice.

(d) Explain 'round and round it flew'.

Ans. The phrase 'round and round it flew' means the albatross hovered around the ship.

9.

And I had done a hellish thing,
And it would work' em woe:
For all averred, I had killed the bird
That made the breeze to blow.

(a) Who is 'I' in the above lines?

Ans. 'I' in the above lines is the Ancient Mariner.

(b) What had he done?

Ans. He had killed the albatross which had proved lucky for them, as they thought that it had made the favourable wind to blow.

(c) Why is the act called a hellish thing?

Ans. It is called a 'hellish thing' because he had sinned by killing the albatross which had brought them luck.

(d) What would happen due to the 'hellish thing'?

Ans. Due to the Ancient Mariner killing the Albatross, the South wind would stop blowing and they would be stranded in the middle of the ocean.

10. Nor dim nor red, like God's own head,
The glorious sun uprist:
Then all averred, I had killed the bird
That brought the fog and mist.

(a) Why has the sun been described as 'glorious'?

Ans. The sun has been described as 'glorious' as it appears after many days of fog and mist.

(b) What does the word 'uprist' mean?

Ans. The word 'uprist' means 'rose up'.

(c) These lines indicate a change in the sailor's attitude. What is that change ?

Ans. The sailors are fickle-minded. To start with, they cursed the Ancient Mariner because they thought that the bird had brought them luck, but later praised him for killing the albatross as they were able to see the Sun after the bird was killed.

(d) Which figure of speech is found in the first line?

Ans. The figure of speech in the first line is a simile.

11. Down dropped the breeze, the sails dropped, down,
'Twas sad as sad could be;
And we did speak only to break
The silence of the sea!

(a) What is an antonym of 'silence' in the above lines?

Ans. 'Storminess' or 'turbulence' is an antonym of 'silence' in the above lines.

(b) Why were they sad?

Ans. They were sad as they had entered the silent sea. There was no movement there and the blazing sun was very hot.

(c) What did they believe was the reason for their misery?

Ans. They believed that they were suffering because the Ancient Mariner had killed the albatross.

(d) How was this different from what happened earlier?

Ans. This was different from what had happened earlier because then the South wind was blowing and their ship was sailing smoothly.

12. Water, water, everywhere,
And all the boards did shrink;
Water, water, everywhere,
Nor any drop to drink.

(a) Why did the boards shrink?

Ans. The heat of the sun dried the boards and shrank them.

(b) What caused the sailors to suffer?

Ans. The Sun was shining overhead and it was very hot. The sailors had no water to drink and were stuck in the middle of the ocean. All these caused the sailors to suffer.

(c) The given lines express ....

Ans. desperation.

(d) Which poetic device is there in these lines?

Ans. The poetic device employed here is repetition of the word 'water'.

13. And every tongue, through utter drought,
Was withered at the root;
We could not speak, no more than if
We had been choked with soot.

(a) Why were their tongues dry?

Ans. Their tongues were dry as they had no water to drink and the sun was very hot.

(b) Who was held responsible for their condition?

Ans. The Ancient Mariner was held responsible for their condition.

(c) What do you mean by 'withered'?

Ans. The word withered means 'shrunk'.

(d) Why had all this happened?

Ans. All this had happened because there was no wind blowing, their ship was at a standstill in the middle of the ocean and their drinking water had been exhausted.

14. Ah! Well-a-day! What evil looks
Had I from old and young!
Instead of the cross, the Albatross
About my neck was hung.

(a) Why did the speaker have evil looks from the mariners?

Ans. The speaker had evil looks from the mariners because he had killed the bird which had brought them luck. After the killing, the mariners had suffered many hardships.

(b) Why did they hang the albatross around the speaker's neck?

Ans. They hung the dead albatross around the speaker's neck as a punishment for his wicked deed of killing the albatross.

(c) What does the word 'evil' mean?

Ans. The word 'evil' here means 'bad'.

(d) The idiom 'Albatross around the neck' has been derived from this poem. What does the idiom mean?

Ans. The idiom 'Albatross around the neck' means 'a heavy burden of guilt that becomes an obstacle to success'.

Short Answer Type Questions

Answer the following questions in 30-40 words.

1. Whom did the Ancient Mariner stop and why?

Ans. The Ancient Mariner stopped one of the three wedding guests. He stopped him because he wanted to tell him about the sin that he had committed and the consequences he had suffered.

2. How did the wedding guest react when he was stopped by the Ancient Mariner?

Ans. When the wedding guest was stopped by the Ancient Mariner, he grew angry and irritated. He felt irritated as a crazy man had stopped him from attending the wedding of a close relative.

3. Why is the wedding guest restless?

Ans. The wedding guest is restless because he has been forcibly detained by the Ancient Mariner. Moreover, he is a close relative of the bridegroom and he does not want to miss the wedding celebrations.

4. Who is called 'a grey-beard loon'? Why?

Ans. The wedding guest calls the Ancient Mariner 'a grey-beard loon' because the Mariner is old and has a grey beard. He is thought as a madman (i.e. a loon) by the wedding guest as he stops the guest from attending the wedding.

5. Why has the wedding guest been called a 'three year' child?

Ans. The wedding guest wanted to go but he got mesmerised by the Mariner's glittering eyes. He had no intention to hear his story but somehow kept listening in rapt attention like a three-year-old child listens to a story.

6. Why does the wedding guest sit on the stone?

Ans. The wedding guest sits on the stone to listen to the Mariner's story. He feels helpless and immobile due to the Mariner's spell on him and no longer resists the Mariner. He surrenders to the Mariner's will and sits on the stone.

7. Why did the sailors hail the bird as a 'Christian soul'?

Or **Why did the mariners hail the arrival of the albatross?**

Ans. The ship had been trapped in ice and the sailors were losing hope. However, just then the Albatross arrived like an angel and everything changed. The weather changed and they got free from the ice. So, they hailed the albatross as a Christian soul because its coming ended their misery.

8. Why did the Albatross follow the ship and how did the sailors treat it?

Ans. The Albatross followed the ship due to the warm hospitality offered by the sailors. The sailors offered food and company to the albatross. It enjoyed food as well as playing with the sailors. The sailors treated the albatross very well and welcomed it like a Christian soul.

9. How did the mariners escape from the ice ?

Ans. The mariners escaped from the ice due to the arrival of the albatross. The arrival of the bird brought favourable weather conditions for the mariners. The icebergs started splitting and made a passage for the ship to steer clear of them.

10. Why was the Ancient Mariner deeply troubled ?

Ans. The Ancient Mariner was deeply troubled because he felt the guilt of killing the Albatross. His guilt compelled him to narrate his experience to the wedding guest as he believed that confession of a sin would lead to its redemption.

11. What was the crime committed by the Mariner? Why was it thought to be a crime?

Ans. The Mariner had wantonly (cruelly) killed the innocent albatross which had brought new hope to the sailors.

It was thought to be a crime as he killed a harmless creature which had brought a turning point for the better in their lives.

12. What is the significance of the lines 'Water, water every where'?

Ans. The lines 'Water, water every where' signifies the peculiar fate the sailors had to face. Although they were surrounded by water on all sides, they had not a drop to drink as it was salty sea water. Moreover, their own stock of fresh water was exhausted.

13. What was the experience of the mariners in the silent sea?

Ans. The mariners had a terrible experience in the silent sea. The breeze that carried the sails stopped blowing and the ship became motionless. It became extremely hot and there was no water to drink. Besides, slimy creatures began to emerge from the rotting sea.

14. What happened after the innocent bird was killed?

Ans. The Mariner had killed the innocent bird which had brought new hope and the blowing of the South wind. After the bird was killed, the ship was stuck in the middle of the hot sea as the wind had stopped blowing. With no water to drink and no ray of hope to brighten them up, the sailors underwent a lot of physical and mental agony.

15. The other mariners kept changing their opinion about the killing of the albatross. What does this reveal about their character?

Or **Human nature is very unpredictable. Justify this in the context of the poem, 'The Rime of the Ancient Mariner'.**

Or **"The sailors are fickle-minded". Justify this statement with reference to the poem 'The Rime of the Ancient Mariner'.**

Or **In the poem 'The Rime of the Ancient Mariner', what opinion do you form of the other crew members on the ship with the Ancient Mariner?**

Ans. The sailors on the ship are fickle-minded and utterly superstitious. They condemn the Ancient Mariner for killing the bird at first but later say that it was a wise decision. When they face difficulties again they again blame the mariner for their misery.

16. The poem invokes the concept of sin and repentance. How?

Ans. The Ancient Mariner kills the poor albatross for no reason. The other sailors considered it a sin, as he had no right to take away a creature's life. As a punishment for his sin, they hung the dead albatross round his neck.

17. Consider you are an animal rights' activist. Briefly mention how you could cite this poem to propose your points in defence of animal rights.

Ans. As an animal rights' activist, I will cite this poem to point out how the ancient Mariner had killed the innocent albatross for no reason whatsoever. Albatross, just like humans, is a creation of God. Hence, it has as much right to live as us humans. Thus, such senseless killing as done by the Mariner will be punished.

18. Interpret imagery and symbolism in 'The Rime of the Ancient Mariner', as elements that contribute to the poem's overarching themes of retribution and redemption. **CBSE SQP 2024**

Ans. In the poem 'The Rime of the Ancient Mariner', the albatross, which is initially a symbol of nature's grace, becomes a burden when the Mariner kills it. This represents his guilt. The ship's desolate imagery and the ghostly events reflect retribution for his actions. Furthermore, the eventual removal of the albatross and the Mariner's compulsion to share his tale symbolise redemption, showing his transformation through suffering and penance.

Long Answer Type Questions

Answer the following questions in 150 words.

1. 'One should respect and appreciate all of God's creations, no matter how great or small.' Elaborate this statement with reference to the poem 'The Rime of the Ancient Mariner'.

Ans. The given statement is true as a man who loves God and all of God's creations will have a better life than a man who doesn't. The poem 'The Rime of the Ancient Mariner' displays it. The Albatross was known as a symbol of good luck to sailors and brings favourable weather conditions. The Ancient Mariner kills the albatross for no reason at all which brings bad luck to the ship. The killing of the albatross results in the crew being cursed. The mariner gets bad luck and suffering because he disrespected God's creation and killed the bird for no good reason. Although the albatross appeared to be only a bird, its importance is emphasised as the ship has misfortunes from then onwards. This shows that the albatross was a blessing to have around. Later on, the Ancient Mariner regrets his decision to kill the bird. He seeks forgiveness for his wrongdoing.

The Ancient Mariner carries the guilt he feels from killing the Albatross and wishes that he had more respect for nature in the past. The mariner thus tries to convey the message that one should cherish God and his creations.

2. "As you sow, so shall you reap," is a well- known proverb which means that one has to face the consequences of one's actions. Comment on this statement with reference to 'The Rime of the Ancient Mariner'. What do you learn from the poem? **Competency Based**

Ans. It is rightly said that "as you sow, so shall you reap". The saying holds true in the light of the circumstances in the poem. The arrival of the albatross proved auspicious for the sailors. The South wind started blowing. The ice split and cleared the path for the ship. Then one day, without any motive or reason, the Ancient Mariner killed the Albatross. Soon, the troubles started.

The wind stopped. The ship couldn't move further. The stock of fresh water was exhausted. The sea water turned slimy. The sailors were convinced of some spirit haunting them. All of them condemned the Ancient Mariner and hung the dead body of the albatross around his neck. The Ancient Mariner, thus, faced the consequences of his evil deed.

We learn that no one can escape punishment for sin. One has to face the consequences for the crime one has committed.

3. Gilbert Parker said, "There is no refuge from memory and remorse in this world. The spirits of our foolish deeds haunt us, with or without repentance".

ST Coleridge highlights the concept of sin and repentance in his poem. What qualities do you infer from this poem?

***Or* The poem, 'The Rime of the Ancient Mariner' is based on the concept of sin and redemption / punishment. Justify.**

Ans. The poem 'The Rime of the Ancient Mariner' truly highlights the concept of sin and repentance. The Ancient Mariner killed the poor albatross without any valid reason even when the elements had turned in the sailors' favour after the bird's arrival. His sin was unpardonable.

The sailors believed that the killing of the bird was the right thing to do in the beginning because they thought that the bird had brought them bad luck. Later on, when the wind stopped and they were marooned in the middle of the ocean, they felt that killing the bird was wrong. So, their behaviour is questionable. The fickleness of their minds is at its extreme when they seek revenge and punish the Ancient Mariner for killing the albatross. The Ancient Mariner repents his deed and he wants to tell whoever is willing to listen to him about it, so that the burden of guilt on him is reduced.

4. As the wedding guest, write and describe your feelings in the form of a diary entry after listening to the Ancient Mariner's tale of sin and suffering. Also, write about what you learnt from his story.

Ans. Sunday, 17th January, 20XX 10 : 30 p.m.

Dear Diary

Today was a shocking day indeed. I was about to enter the hall for the wedding when an old, bearded man with strange eyes stopped me. He started telling me a story of his journey through the ocean. He and his sailors had ups and downs in the journey when an albatross visited them.

But one day, without any reason, the Mariner killed the Albatross. What followed next was very shocking. Their ship was marooned (stuck) in the middle of the sea and their stock of drinking water ran out. They started suffering from hallucinations. His story taught me the great lesson of *karma* that what goes around comes around. Those who harm and torture others can never experience peace of mind. The sinner is sooner or later punished by God. We should thus do good things and never hurt anyone. Even those who support sin are equally guilty.

The wedding guest

5. Respect for all forms of life is an essential value. Unmindful destruction of nature and its creatures deserves just punishment. Write in 150 words about this essential value as brought out in the poem 'The Rime of the Ancient Mariner.'

Ans. Life is a gift from God and nobody has the right to take away another's life, more so when there is no just or valid reason. Thus, respect for all forms of life becomes an essential value to be cherished by all. Coleridge's 'The Rime of the Ancient Mariner' too upholds this essential value besides the other things that the poem talks of.

The Ancient Mariner killed the albatross when he apparently had no reason to do so. He and his shipmates were punished for this sin when their ship reached a silent sea where there was no breeze to move the ship. The weather was extremely hot and there was no water to drink. Ultimately, the sailors started having hallucinations due to their deprivation in the middle of the ocean. Thus, the Ancient Mariner, along with the other sailors, is justly punished for his unmindful killing of the albatross.

6. From the poems 'The Rime of the Ancient Mariner' and 'The Snake', discuss how the characters, the albatross and the snake view human attitude and perspective towards creatures. **CBSE 2025**

Ans. In 'The Rime of the Ancient Mariner' by Coleridge and 'The Snake' by D.H. Lawrence, the albatross and the snake highlight human arrogance towards nature.

The **albatross**, a harmless guide for sailors, is killed by the Mariner without reason, showing reckless disregard for life. This act brings suffering upon him, as nature punishes his cruelty. Similarly, in 'The Snake', the poet admires the snake's beauty but, influenced by fear and societal beliefs, throws a log at it-an action he immediately regrets.

Both creatures symbolise nature's innocence, while human actions reflect thoughtless harm. The poems reveal how humans exploit or fear animals instead of respecting them.

ASSESSMENT EXERCISE

Extract Based Questions

Read the following extracts carefully and answer the questions that follow.

1. The ship was cheered, the harbour cleared,
Merrily did we drop
Below the kirk, below the hill,
Below the lighthouse top
(a) How was the ship cheered?
(b) Explain 'Merrily did we drop'.
(c) What does the extract describe?
(d) Explain 'below the lighthouse top.'

2. With sloping masts and dipping prow,
As who pursued with yell and blow
Still treads the shadow of his foe,
And forward bends his head,
The ship drove fast, loud roared the blast,
And southward aye we fled.
(a) What is the storm described as?
(b) In which direction did the storm push them?
(c) Describe the comparison made in the lines.
(d) What does 'blast' mean here?

3. The ice was here, the ice was there,
The ice was all around:
It cracked and growled, and roared and howled,
Like noises in a swound!
(a) What happened to the Mariner's ship?
(b) Name the figure of speech used in the third line.
(c) The word 'swound' means ....
(d) Why is the ice making such sounds?

4. "The sun now rose upon the right:
Out of the sea came he,
Still hid in mist, and on the left
Went down into the sea.
(a) What can you say about the tone of the given lines?
(b) Describe the weather in the above lines.
(c) What is 'mist'?
(d) Explain 'Still hid in mist.'

5. About, about in reel and rout
The death-fires danced at night;
The water, like a witch's oils,
Burnt green, and blue, and white.
(a) What do you understand by 'reel and rout'?
(b) Where did the death-fires dance?
(c) What happened to the water of the ocean?
(d) What do you understand by 'a witch's oils'?

Short Answer Type Questions

Answer the following questions in 30-40 words.

1. Whom does the Ancient Mariner stop and why?

2. How do his looks affect the person addressed?

3. What is a bassoon? How does it affect the wedding guest?

4. As the story progresses the wedding guest suddenly beats his breast. Why?

5. What happened to the ship soon after it was given a warm send off?

6. What happened when the Ancient Mariner's ship reached the Equator?

7. How was the arrival of the Albatross a good omen?

8. What do you understand by 'the furrow followed free'?

9. What painful experience did the Ancient Mariner undergo in 'the silent sea'?

10. In what way did the sailors react to the killing of the albatross?

Long Answer Type Questions

Answer the following questions in 150 words.

1. 'Punishment does catch up with the sinner although it may be delayed sometimes'. Comment on this statement with reference to the poem.

2. What were the mariners' reactions to the killing of the albatross ? Do you think that the sailors were justified in the punishment they meted out to the Ancient Mariner?

3. What is the lesson that the Ancient Mariner has learned from the terrible act of killing the bird ?

CHAPTER 5

Snake

by DH Lawrence

Introduction The poem 'Snake' revolves around the principle of peaceful co-existence. It tells the story of a snake that comes to drink water at the poet's water-trough. On one hand, the poet is in great admiration for the snake, on the other, he wants to kill him. The snake, rather than evoking a sense of mortal fear in the poet's mind, arises his curiosity.

Stanzawise Explanation

Stanza 1 (Lines 1-6)

A snake came to my water-trough
On a hot, hot day, and I in pyjamas for the heat,
To drink there.
In the deep, strange-scented shade of the great
dark carob-tree
I came down the steps with my pitcher
And must wait, must stand and wait, for there he
was at the trough before me.

Explanation The poet speaks about his encounter with a snake. It was a hot day and he was feeling thirsty. So, he, in his pyjamas, came to his water-trough to get some drinking water in his pitcher. He saw a snake in the shade of the distinctly scented carob-tree. The snake had come to his water-trough to drink water. The poet, further, describes that he came down the steps and had to wait because the snake came before him to drink water.

Stanza 2 (Lines 7-14)

He reached down from a fissure in the earth-wall
in the gloom
And trailed his yellow-brown slackness
soft-bellied down,
over the edge of the stone trough
And rested his throat upon the stone bottom,
And where the water had dripped
from the tap, in a small clearness,
He sipped with his straight mouth,
Softly drank through his straight
gums, into his slack long body,
Silently.
Someone was before me at my water-trough,
And I, like a second comer, waiting.

Explanation The poet says that the snake had come down from a crack in the earth-wall and moved its loose yellow-brown coloured belly on the edge of the stony water-trough. He rested his throat upon the stone and sipped the water that had dripped from the tap with his straight mouth. He softly and silently drank the water which went to his long boneless body. The poet felt an obligation 'to stand and wait' for the snake because it was there before him.

Stanza 3 (Lines 15-20)

He lifted his head from his drinking,
as cattle do, And looked at me vaguely, as
drinking
cattle do, And flickered his two-forked tongue
from his lips, and mused a moment,
And stooped and drank a little more,
Being earth-brown, earth-golden
from the burning bowels of the earth
On the day of Sicilian July, with Etna smoking.

Explanation The poet now describes the manner in which the snake drank water. The snake lifted its head from the water much like cows and buffaloes typically lift their head every now and then while drinking water. The snake looked vaguely (confusedly) at the poet. It moved its forked tongue around its lips, thought for a moment and bent down again to drink a little more water. The earth-brown or golden-brown snake had come out from under the hot ground. It was a hot day in July and the poet is reminded of Mount Etna in Sicily. When the poet says 'Etna smoking', he refers to the volcanic eruption that killed a large number of people.

Stanza 4 (Lines 21-25)

The voice of my education said to me
He must be killed,
For in Sicily the black, black snakes are innocent, the gold are venomous.
And voices in me said, If you were a man
You would take a stick and break him now, and finish him off.

Explanation These lines introduce the poet's inner conflict arising from the voice of his education which tells him to kill the snake. The poet says that according to what he has read or heard, black snakes are harmless but golden coloured snakes in Sicily are poisonous. The voice of his education tempted the poet to kill the snake by saying that if he were really a man he would kill the snake.

Stanza 5 (Lines 26-29)

But must I confess how I liked him,
How glad I was he had come like a guest in quiet, to drink at my water-trough
And depart peaceful, pacified, and thankless,
Into the burning bowels of this earth?

Explanation The poet here states that he liked the snake very much. He was happy and honoured that the snake had come as a guest to drink water at his water-trough and would return to its burrow peacefully after drinking water. He feels the snake is quite harmless and all it wants to do is to quench its thirst and depart peacefully.

Stanza 6 (Lines 30-36)

Was it cowardice, that I dared not kill him?
Was it perversity, that I longed to talk to him?
Was it humility, to feel so honoured?
I felt so honoured.
And yet those voices:
If you were not afraid, you would kill him!
And truly I was afraid, I was most afraid,
But even so, honoured still more
That he should seek my hospitality
From out the dark door of the secret earth.

Explanation The poet is now in a dilemma. He questions himself regarding his decisions and desires. He questions if his decision to not kill the snake makes him a coward. He further asks if his desire to talk to the snake was illogical and unreasonable or if him feeling honoured displays his kindness. The poet states that he felt honoured that the snake had come to his place and had given him a chance to be hospitable.

However still, in his subconscious mind, he feels that he should kill the snake. The poet thinks a lot about this conflicting situation. The poet feels that he was no doubt scared of the snake. However, he feels more honoured to think that the snake had come out from the secret part of the earth and sought his hospitality.

Stanza 7 (Lines 37-45)

He drank enough
And lifted his head, dreamily, as one who has drunken,
And flickered his tongue like a forked night on the air, so black,
Seeming to lick his lips,
And looked around like a god, unseeing, into the air,
And slowly turned his head,
And slowly, very slowly, as if thrice a dream,
Proceeded to draw his slow length curving round
And climb again the broken bank of my wall-face.

Explanation The poet comes back to describing the snake and states that it drank the water unaware of the poet and felt satisfied after drinking. After that, it raised its head slowly and moved its forked tongue as if it was licking its lips in satisfaction. Then, it looked around like a God and turned its head. Later, the snake very slowly started curving its long body and began to move back into the crack of the wall from which it had come.

Stanza 8 (Lines 46-50)

And as he put his head into that dreadful hole,
And as he slowly drew up, snake-easing his shoulders, and entered farther,
A sort of horror, a sort of protest against his withdrawing into that horrid black hole,
Deliberately going into the blackness, and slowly drawing himself after,
Overcame me now his back was turned.

Explanation The snake begins to withdraw very slowly and makes its way back to its home in the Earth. It puts its head first and then, slowly moves its shoulders and other body parts. At this point, a fear and protest overcomes the poet against its going back. He does not want the snake to withdraw into its world of darkness.

Stanza 9 (Lines 51-58)

I looked round, I put down my pitcher,
I picked up a clumsy log
And threw it at the water-trough with a clatter.
I think it did not hit him,
But suddenly that part of him that was left behind convulsed in undignified haste.
Writhed like lightning, and was gone
Into the black hole, the earth-lipped fissure in the wall-front,
At which, in the intense still noon, I stared with fascination.

Explanation The poet states that he protested against the leaving of the snake. So, quite instinctively, he put down his pitcher, picked up a log and threw it at the snake. He threw it near the water tap. The poet thinks that the stick did not hit the snake but the part of the snake that was still out of the hole moved violently and hurriedly.

It twisted and moved like a flash of lightning and speedily went inside the black hole in the crack in the wall from where it had come. The poet kept looking at that hole with deep interest.

Stanza 10 (Lines 59-63)

And immediately I regretted it.
I thought how paltry, how vulgar, what a mean act!
I despised myself and the voices of my accursed human education.
And I thought of the albatross
And I wished he would come back, my snake.

Explanation For a moment, regret engulfed the poet. He immediately felt sorry and repented his action. He felt that his action was cheap, worthless, rude and hasty. He hated himself and cursed the voices of education within him which had told him to kill the snake. The poet felt like the Ancient Mariner who had killed an Albatross without any reason. He felt the same guilt and wished that the snake would come back so that he could apologise to him.

Stanza 11 (Lines 64-70)

For he seemed to me again like a king,
Like a king in exile, uncrowned in the underworld,
Now due to be crowned again.
And so, I missed my chance with one of the lords
Of life.
And I have something to expiate A pettiness.

Explanation The poet here visualises the snake to be a royal king who had been banished from its kingdom or like an uncrowned ruler who was now ready to regain recognition and waiting to be crowned again. The poet feels that because of his mean action, he had lost the opportunity to be in the good books of the ruler of life, i.e. God. The poet thought he should make amends for his meanness. So, he utters regret and asks for pardon. He says that he missed the chance to welcome a lord of life into his home and must apologise for his petty behaviour.

Poetic Devices Used in the Poem

Personification A figure of speech which is used for an inanimate object or animals/birds that look or feel human qualities

- In the poem, the snake is personified and attributed human qualities.

Alliteration Repetition of initial consonant sounds in the same line.

- strange-scented shade
- slackness soft-bellied down
- And depart peaceful, pacified and thankless
- mused a moment

Repetition Repetition of words/phrases in the same line.

- On a hot, hot day
- And must wait, must stand and wait
- For in Sicily the black, black snakes
- I was afraid, I was most afraid

Simile A device which compares two different things by using the words 'as' or 'like'.

- And I, like a second comer, waiting
- He lifted his head from his drinking, as cattle do
- And looked at me vaguely, as drinking cattle do
- he had come like a guest

Onomatopoeia Using a word which suggests the meanings by its sound.

- The poet uses the word 'clatter' to describe a sound.

Allusion A reference to a statement, person, place, etc. from history, religion, literature or any other field.

- Sicilian July
- Etna smoking

Word Meaning

Word	Meaning
Stanza 1	
water-trough	a large container for storing water
carob-tree	a red flowered tree originally in the Mediterranean area
pitcher	tall, round container with an open top and large handle
Stanza 2	
fissure	crack
trailed	carried behind it
slackness	looseness
dripped	fallen in small drops
Stanza 3	
vaguely	confusedly, without concern
flickered	moved quickly
mused	thought
stooped	bent down, leaned over
bowels	bottom of earth
Etna	an active volcano in Italy
Stanza 4	
venomous	poisonous
Stanza 5	
confess	admit
pacified	satisfied
Stanza 6	
cowardice	fearfulness, weakness
perversity	quality of being unreasonable, illogical
humility	meekness, the quality of being humble
hospitality	friendliness, warm reception

Word	Meaning
Stanza 7	
dreamily	absent mindedly
forked	looking like a fork
unseeing	without noticing or seeing anything
thrice adream	extremely lazily
Stanza 8	
dreadful	horrible
horrid	unpleasant
deliberately	intentionally
Stanza 9	
clumsy	heavy
clatter	loud noise
convulsed	violent movement
haste	swiftness
writhed	twisted and turned
fissure	crack
Stanza 10	
regretted	felt sorry
paltry	worthless
vulgar	offensive
despised	detested
accursed	hateful
albatross	an allusion to the bird killed in the poem 'The Rime of the Ancient Mariner' for no reason
Stanza 11	
exile	banishment
expiate	make amends for
pettiness	meanness

Textbook FOLDER

Here, we have covered questions given in the CBSE Textbook along with their answers

ON PAGE 122-123

Q.4 Given below is the summary of the poem 'Snake' in short paragraphs. However they are jumbled. Work in pairs and put the summary into a logical sequence.

(a) After drinking water to his satisfaction, the snake raised his head dreamily and flickered his forked tongue and licked his lips. The snake looked around like a God and then slowly proceeded to curve round and move away from the water trough.

(b) The poet felt much like the ancient mariner who had killed the albatross for no reason. He wished that the snake would come back. He thought of the snake as a king in exile who had to be crowned again. He also regretted having missed his opportunity of knowing and understanding one of the lords of life.

(c) As the snake put his head into the hole to retreat into the earth, the poet was filled with a protest against the idea of the snake withdrawing into his hole. The poet put down his pitcher, picked up a log and hurled it at the snake. The snake twisted violently and with great alacrity vanished into the hole in the wall.

(d) A snake visited the poet's water trough on a hot afternoon to quench his thirst. The poet who had also gone to the trough to fill water in a pitcher waited for the snake to depart since he had come at the trough prior to the poet.

(e) The voice of education inside the poet which tells him that it was the fear for the snake that made him refrain from killing him. However, the poet felt that though he was quite afraid of the snake, he did actually feel honoured that a snake had come to seek his hospitality from the deep recesses of the earth.

(f) He is guilt-ridden and feels that he has to atone for the meanness of his action of throwing a log at the snake.

(g) The snake rested his throat upon the stone bottom and sipped the water into his slack long body. After drinking water, he raised his head just like cattle do and flashed his forked tongue, thought for a moment and then bent down to drink some more water.

(h) Education and social conventions make the poet think that the golden brown poisonous snake must be killed and that as a brave man he must undertake the task of killing the snake.

(i) The poet instantly felt sorry for his unrefined and contemptible act and cursed the voices of education and civilisation that had shaped his thought process and urged him to kill the snake.

(j) However, the poet instinctively likes the snake, treats him like a guest and feels honoured that it has come to drink at his water trough. The poet questions himself and wonders whether his not daring to kill the snake proves that he is a coward and whether his desire to talk to the snake reflects his perversity.

Ans. The logical sequence is (d) (g) (e) (h) (j) (a) (c) (i) (b) (f)

ON PAGE 123-124

Q.5 Based on your reading of the poem, answer the following questions by selecting the correct options.

(i) 'he lifted his head from his drinking as cattle do'-The poet wants to convey that the snake ....

(a) is domesticated

(b) is innocent

(c) is as harmless as cattle

(d) drinks water just like cattle

Ans. (d) drinks water just like cattle

(ii) *'Sicilian July'*, *'Etna smoking'* and *'burning bowels of the earth'* are images that convey that ....

(a) there are snakes in volcanic areas

(b) the poet lives in a hot area

(c) it is a really hot day when the snake comes

(d) Sicilian snakes are dangerous

Ans. (c) it is a really hot day when the snake comes

(iii) *'A sort of horror, a sort of protest overcame me'*- The poet is filled with protest because ....

(a) he doesn't want to let the snake remain alive

(b) he fears the snake

(c) he doesn't want the snake to recede into darkness

(d) he wants to kill it so that it doesn't return

Ans. (c) he doesn't want the snake to recede into darkness

(iv) In the line '*And as he slowly drew up, snake-easing his shoulders, and entered farther*', the phrase snake easing his shoulders means ....

(a) loosening its shoulders
(b) slipping in with majestic grace
(c) moving slowly
(d) moving fast

Ans. (b) slipping in with majestic grace

(v) '*He seemed to me like a king in exile...*' The poet refers to the snake as such to emphasise that the snake ....

(a) is like a king enduring banishment
(b) is like a king due to be crowned
(c) is a majestic king who came for a while on earth
(d) is a majestic creature forced to go into exile by man

Ans. (a) is like a king enduring banishment

(vi) '*I thought how paltry, how vulgar, what a mean act*'-The poet is referring to ....

(a) the snake going into the dreadful hole
(b) the accursed modern education
(c) the act of throwing a log of wood at the snake
(d) the act of killing the snake

Ans. (c) the act of throwing a log of wood at the snake

ON PAGE 125

Q.6 Answer the following questions briefly.

(a) Why does the poet decide to stand and wait till the snake has finished drinking? What does this tell you about the poet? (Notice that he uses 'someone' instead of 'something' for the snake.)

Or **Why did the poet wait for the snake to drink first from the trough?** **CBSE 2020**

Ans. The poet decides to stand and wait till the snake has finished drinking because he feels the snake was the first one to reach the water-trough and he himself had come second, so he must wait for his turn. This shows that the poet is civilised and well-mannered. He is treating the snake as his guest.

(b) In stanza 2 and 3, the poet gives a vivid description of the snake by using suggestive expressions. What picture of the snake do you form on the basis of this description?

Ans. On the basis of the poet's description, we get a vivid and beautiful picture of the snake. The snake is yellow-brown or golden-brown in colour. It weakly trails its soft belly over the edge of the stone trough. It appears to be tired and thirsty and drinks water slowly. Just like cattle, it raises its head and then drinks some more water. It sips water while keeping its mouth straight. It has a 'slack long body' and a two-forked tongue which it flickers while drinking.

(c) How does the poet describe the day and the atmosphere when he saw the snake?

Ans. The poet describes it as a very hot day. Humans and animals, all were turning to water to quench their thirst. The poet further uses words like 'Sicilian July', 'Etna smoking' and 'burning bowels' which highlight the hot atmosphere of the day.

(d) What does the poet want to convey by saying that the snake emerges from the 'burning bowels of the Earth'?

Ans. By saying that the snake emerges from the 'burning bowels of the Earth,' the poet wishes to convey that the snake lived inside the Earth which was heated up on that hot summer day. The insides of the Earth were so hot that they appeared to be burning.

(e) Do you think the snake was conscious of the poet's presence? How do you know?

Ans. The snake was not conscious of the poet's presence. It was very relaxed and moved leisurely and dreamily. If the snake had seen the poet, it would not be so relaxed. The poet uses the expression 'dreamily, as one who is drunk' to highlight this.

(f) How do we know that the snake's thirst was satiated? Pick out the expressions that convey this.

Ans. We know the snake's thirst was satiated as the snake lifted its head and smacked its tongue as if licking its lips in satisfaction.

The following expressions give us the information that the snake's thirst was satiated

- He drank enough
- And lifted his head, dreamily, as one who is drunk,
- And flickered his tongue like a forked night on the air, so black,
- Seeming to lick his lips.

(g) The poet has a dual attitude towards the snake. Why does he experience conflicting emotions on seeing the snake?

Or **What is the dilemma that the poet faces when he sees the snake?**

Or **Why does the poet experience conflicting emotions on seeing the snake?**

Or **Describe the poet's (DH. Lawrence) dual attitude towards the snake.** **CBSE 2024**

Ans. The poet experiences conflicting emotions on seeing the snake because his education tells him that Sicilian snakes of earth-brown or golden-brown colour are poisonous and must be killed.

He feared the snake but at the same time thought of the snake as his guest. His humanity and thinking of the snake as a guest conflicted with his education and inner voice. This led to his dual attitude towards the snake.

(h) The poet is filled with horror and protest when the snake prepares to retreat and bury itself in the 'horrid black', 'dreadful' hole. In the light of this statement, bring out the irony of his act of throwing a log at the snake.

Ans. The thought of the snake returning to the place it had just come out of filled the poet with protest and fear. He hated the idea of the snake going away and throws a log at the snake. He, thus, scares it, forcing it to escape and hide in its hole. The irony of the situation is that he forces the snake into the same hole to which he did not wish the snake to return earlier.

(i) The poet seems to be full of admiration and respect for the snake. He almost regards him like a majestic God. Pick out at least four expressions from the poem that reflect these emotions.

Ans. The following expressions show the poet's admiration for the snake

(i) But must I confess how I liked him

(ii) How glad I was he had come like a guest in

(iii) And looked around like a God

(iv) For he seemed to me like a king

(j) What is the difference between the snake's movement at the beginning of the poem and later when the poet strikes it with a log of wood? You may use relevant vocabulary from the poem to highlight the difference.

Ans. The snake's movement at the beginning is very leisurely and relaxed. It takes a lot of time to drink water, and sips and enjoys it. After drinking water, it moves very slowly and dreamily, and goes back to the crack in the wall. Later, when the poet throws a log at it, it vanishes very quickly with the speed of lightning and in an undignified manner.

(k) The poet experiences feelings of self-derision, guilt and regret after hitting the snake. Pick out expressions that suggest this. Why does he feel like this?

Ans. The expressions such as 'I thought how paltry', 'how vulgar', 'what a mean act!', 'I despised myself', 'to expiate', 'A pettiness' suggest that the poet experiences feelings of self-derision, guilt and regret after throwing a log at the snake.

He feels so because he had no reason to kill the snake. He regrets his action and realises that he shouldn't have thrown a log to hit the snake. He despises himself and accuses his human education for hitting the snake.

(l) You have already read Coleridge's poem 'The Ancient Mariner' in which an albatross is killed by the Mariner. Why does the poet make an allusion to the Albatross?

Ans. The Ancient Mariner's act of killing the albatross was similar to the poet's attempt to kill the snake. Just as killing of the harmless bird was a cruel and inhuman act of the mariner, the poet feels that his own act was also equally despicable as the snake was as harmless as the albatross. Hence, he makes an allusion to the albatross.

(m) "I have something to expiate"—Explain.

or **In the poem 'Snake', why does the poet say "I have something to expatiate"?**

Ans. The poet regrets his petty act of throwing a log at the snake and feels that this was something he had done which needed to be atoned for or made amends for. He wishes that the snake would return so that he could apologise to it.

Q.7 The encounter with the snake and the dual response of the poet to his presence at the water-trough reflect a conflict between civilised social education and natural human instincts. The poet writes a diary entry highlighting how he was torn between the two voices. Write his diary.

Ans. Wednesday, 15th July, 20XX 10:30 PM

Dear Diary

Today, I experienced something which made me realise that man is not always good or bad. His actions are guided by his civilised social education and natural instincts.

It was a very hot day today and I was feeling thirsty. I picked up the pitcher and went to fetch water from the trough. As I approached the trough, I saw a long earth-brown and golden snake drinking the water which had collected near the trough. My civilised education had taught me that in Sicily such snakes are poisonous and should be killed.

However, I felt the snake was not there to harm me; it was simply drinking water to quench its thirst. I was torn between my education and sentiments. It was a difficult situation and I struggled to argue with myself but my education won and I threw a log at the snake, although it slithered away immediately without being hurt.

David

REVIEW EXERCISE

Including Previous Years' and Practice Questions

Extract Based Questions

Read the following extracts carefully and answer the questions that follow.

1. I came down the steps with my pitcher
And must wait, must stand and wait, for
there he was at the trough before me.

(a) Who came down the steps and why?

Ans. The poet came down the steps because he wanted to quench his thirst.

(b) Which word in the extract means 'a large container for storing water'?

Ans. The word 'pitcher' means 'a large container for storing water'.

(c) Who was there at the trough before him?

Ans. The snake was there at the trough before him.

(d) Why was he carrying the pitcher?

Ans. The poet was carrying the pitcher to fill it with water which could then be drunk.

2. Someone was before me at my water-trough,
And I, like a second comer, waiting.

(a) Who was at the water-trough before the poet?

Ans. A snake came to the water-trough before the poet.

(b) Where had it come from? How has 'he' been described?

Ans. It came from the burning bowels of the Earth. 'He' has been described as yellow-brown in colour and having a soft-bellied and slack body.

(c) Why did the poet wait?

Ans. The poet was a civilised person and so, he waited for his turn because the snake had reached the water-trough before him.

(d) Which figure of speech has been employed in the second line?

Ans. The figure of speech used is simile.

3. He lifted his head from his drinking, as cattle do,
And looked at me vaguely, as drinking cattle do,
And flickered his two-forked tongue
from his lips, and mused a moment,
And stooped and drank a little more,

(a) What does the comparison indicate?

Ans. The comparison indicates that the snake was as harmless as cattle are.

(b) Explain– 'as drinking cattle do'.

Ans. The given lines indicate that the snake was drinking water like cattles. In other words, it was as harmless as cattle.

(c) Why did 'he' muse?

Ans. The poet thought that 'he' must be musing because it paused for some time while drinking the water.

(d) Which poetic device has been used in the above lines?

Ans. Simile has been used here.

4. But must I confess how I liked him,
How glad I was he had come like a guest in quiet, to
drink at my water-trough
And depart peaceful, pacified, and thankless Into the
burning bowels of this earth. **CBSE SQP 2023**

(a) What can be inferred about the speaker's attitude towards nature based on the excerpt?

Ans. On the basis of the given excerpt we can say that the speaker shares a complex relationship with nature, experiencing both admiration and fear towards its power.

(b) List the meaning of the phrase 'burning bowels of this earth.'

Ans. The phrase 'burning bowels of this earth' refers to the depths of the earth where it is hot and dark.

(c) How is the snake's arrival and departure symbolic?

Ans. The snake's arrival and departure is symbolic of a fleeting moment of connection with nature.

(d) The speaker compares the snake to the guest. Which word in the extract displays the snake's non-guest like behaviour?

Ans. The word 'thankless' displays the snake's non-guest like behaviour.

5. Was it cowardice, that I dared not kill him?
Was it perversity, that I longed to talk to him? Was it
humility, to feel so honoured?

(a) Who is the poet referring to as 'him'?

Ans. The poet is referring to the snake as 'him'.

(b) What can you say about the poet's feelings here?

Ans. The poet is experiencing mixed feelings about the snake's presence. He feels honoured but also feels like a coward.

(c) Give the antonym of 'perversity'.

Ans. The antonym of 'perversity' is logical.

(d) Why was the poet feeling honoured?

Ans. The poet was feeling honoured because he thought of the snake as a royal guest which had come to drink water from the poet's water-trough.

6. And truly I was afraid, I was most afraid,
But even so, honoured still more
That he should seek my hospitality
From out the dark door of the secret earth.

(a) Why was the poet afraid?

Ans. The poet was afraid because he had been taught that golden-brown snakes are poisonous and could be a threat to him.

(b) Why did the poet feel honoured?

Ans. The poet felt honoured because such a fascinating creature as a snake, whom humans were afraid of, had sought his hospitality.

(c) What do you mean by 'hospitality'?

Ans. Hospitality means a friendly and generous reception and entertainment of guests, visitors or strangers.

(d) Explain– 'the dark door of the secret earth'.

Ans. The phrase signifies the dwelling place of snakes, a hole below the ground which is usually dark.

7. I looked round, I put down my pitcher,
I picked up a clumsy log
And threw it at the water-trough with a clatter.

(a) The log was thrown at whom?

Ans. The log of wood was thrown at the snake.

(b) Why did the poet throw a log?

Ans. The poet was overpowered by the voice of education that taught him that the snake was poisonous and must be killed.

Hence, the poet threw a log at the snake to kill it.

(c) Was the poet right in throwing the log at the snake?

Ans. No, the poet was not right in throwing the log at the snake, as it was going away quietly without having any intentions of harming the poet.

(d) What do you understand by 'clumsy'?

Ans. The word 'clumsy' here means heavy.

8. But suddenly that part of him that was left behind
convulsed in undignified haste.
Writhed like lightning, and was gone
Into the black hole, the earth-lipped fissure in the
wall-front, At which, in the intense still noon, I stared
with fascination. And immediately I regretted it.

(a) Why did the poet stare with fascination?

Ans. The poet stared with fascination because the snake had its own beauty and grace while moving.

(b) Why did the poet immediately regret his action?

Ans. The poet immediately regretted his action as his act of throwing the log at the snake while it was retreating was mean and cruel.

(c) What has been described here?

Ans. The snake going away after drinking water at the poet's water-trough has been described here.

(d) Which figure of speech is used in the last line?

Ans. The figure of speech used is simile.

9. I thought how paltry, how vulgar, what a mean act!
I despised myself and the voices of my accursed
human education.

(a) Who is 'I' in the above lines?

Ans. 'I' refers to the poet.

(b) Which 'mean act' had he committed?

Ans. The poet had committed the mean act of throwing a log at his guest, the snake.

(c) Give the synonym of 'paltry'.

Ans. The synonym of 'paltry' is 'worthless'.

(d) Explain 'accursed human education'.

Ans. Human education teaches us to kill the snake as and when it is seen as it may be venomous. That is why the poet calls human education to be 'accursed'.

10. For he seemed to me again like a king,
Like a king in exile, uncrowned in the underworld,
Now due to be crowned again.
And so, I missed my chance with one of the lords
Of Life.
And I have something to expiate
A pettiness.

(a) Why is the snake described as 'a king in exile'?

Ans. The snake is described as one of the lords of life who has lost his crown under the ground, waiting to be crowned again.

(b) What does 'pettiness' refer to in the given lines?

Ans. The word 'pettiness' refers to the poet's mean act of throwing a log at the snake while it was going away.

(c) **What chance has been missed by the poet?**

Ans. The poet has missed the chance to honour such a fascinating creature as a snake.

(d) **What is the feeling of the poet at this time?**

Ans. The feeling of the poet at this time is one of repentance for his mean act of throwing a log at the snake without any provocation.

Short Answer Type Questions

Answer the following questions in 30-40 words.

1. How does the poet call the snake? What does this imply about the poet?

Or The poet refers to the snake as 'someone' not 'it'. Why does he do so?

Ans. He calls the snake 'someone' rather than 'something' and considers it as a 'guest' rather than an 'intruder'. He regards it as an individual. It shows that the poet has respect in his heart for nature's all creations.

2. What was the poet's reaction when he saw the snake at the water-trough?

Ans. When the poet saw the snake at the water-trough, he stopped immediately but was not afraid of it. Rather, he was curious. He observed its movements closely and was fascinated by the snake.

3. Why did the poet have to wait near the water-trough?

Ans. The poet had to wait near the water-trough because a snake was drinking water at the trough. Out of respect for the snake, whom the poet considered his guest, the poet decided to wait as he considered the snake as an equal co-owner of the earth's resources.

4. What is very special about the poet that makes him think that he was a second comer? What was his world view?

Ans. The poet was different from most men. He believed that he had reached the water-trough after the snake; thus he was second. He believed that snakes are God's beautiful creations and should be respected and treated equally with humans. The poet's views reflect his attitude.

5. What does the poet compare the snake's drinking habits to? Why?

Ans. The poet compares the snake's drinking habits to that of cattle. Cattle, while drinking water, are not aware of their surroundings nor are they worried about any possible threats.

They drink peacefully and do not cause any harm to anyone. Just like them, the snake in the poem drinks peacefully and lifts his head like a cattle.

6. What picture of the snake do you form on the basis of the poem?

Ans. From the poet's description, we can gather that the snake had a straight mouth, slack long body, a two-forked tongue, and it was earth-brown and golden in colour.

7. What did the voice of education say to the poet?

Or Why do the voices in the poet's mind advise him to kill the snake?

Ans. The voice of education refers to the knowledge that the poet had learned through books or by learning things. The voices in the poet's mind are due to his education, which taught him that snakes with yellow brown skin colour are poisonous. These voices advise him to kill the snake, as otherwise the snake may harm the poet if it feels threatened.

8. What is the poet's dual attitude towards the snake?

Ans. On one hand, the poet feels an instinctive fascination for the snake and thinks of it as a guest who has come to his place to quench his thirst. On the other hand, his voice of education tells him that it is a poisonous snake and he should throw a log at it to kill it. This shows the poet's dual attitude towards the snake.

9. Why was the poet glad to have the snake in his garden?

Ans. The poet was an educated man. He was of the opinion that a snake is a beautiful creation of God and should be respected. To have a snake in his garden was an honour to him. The snake was his guest and he felt honoured to extend his hospitality to it.

10. Why did the narrator want to hit the snake?

or Why did the poet throw the log at the snake?

Ans. The narrator wanted to kill the snake because the voices of education in his head told him that it was a poisonous snake that could harm him. He was so overpowered by the voice of his education that when the snake was going back to his home in the Earth, he threw a log at the snake to try to kill it.

11. What does the poet do which he calls as 'paltry, vulgar and mean'? Why?

Ans. The poet attacked the snake by throwing a log at it, when it was going away. The poet initially considered it a 'guest' and yet committed this vulgar and mean act. The snake had done nothing to deserve such a treatment. Hence, the act was paltry, vulgar and mean.

12. Why does the poet call his human education 'accursed'?

Ans. The poet calls his human education 'accursed' as it takes him away from the generosity of man, from the bond between human beings and other species.

His education teaches him to hurt a harmless, innocent animal. It builds barriers between him and the other creatures. Therefore, he calls it 'accursed'.

13. "I despised myself and the voices of my accursed human education". What made the poet despise these voices?

Ans. The poet despised himself and the voices of his education because they made him stoop so low as trying to kill a 'guest', the snake. The snake had done nothing to harm him, still the poet committed this inhuman act.

14. Why is the snake said to be one of the lords of life?

Ans. The snake is said to be one of the lords of life by the poet because he considers it as a majestic creature and as a beautiful creation of God, and thus calls it one of the lords of life.

15. How does Lawrence explore the internal conflict in Snake? **CBSE SQP 2024**

Ans. In the poem 'Snake', the poet explores internal conflict by portraying the narrator's struggle between his natural admiration for the snake and the real world conditioning to view it as a threat. The narrator's conflicting instincts lead to an impulsive act of violence, which is followed by regret, highlighting the tension between human instincts and society's expectations towards nature.

Long Answer Type Questions

Answer the following questions in 150 words.

1. Why does the poet experience feelings of self-derision, guilt and regret after throwing a log at the snake?

Ans. The poet experiences guilt and regret because he felt he had tried to hurt a creature which had caused him no harm. In fact, the snake was not even aware of his presence. Yet, the poet acted small and petty by attacking it when it had turned its back. The snake was just drinking water to quench its thirst on a hot day and the poet had been mean to attack it. He even compared the snake to cattle which are harmless. Thus, he regrets getting overpowered by the 'voice of education' which told him that the snake was poisonous and must be killed. Later, when the snake escapes and the poet reflects on his action, he condemns his act. He is filled with guilt and regrets his action.

2. The poem, 'Snake' by DH Lawrence reminds us of the fact that animals too have a right to life and we have no right to deny them their life. Elaborate.

Ans. The poem, 'Snake' reminds us of the fact that animals too have a right to life and we have no right to deny them their life. One should always listen to the voice of one's conscience that does not allow us to play with these innocent creatures. Man cannot afford to tamper with ecology as it has been carefully planned and laid out by nature. It may result in the extinction of wild animals and in the depletion of forests and their wealth.

Further, man will have to face dire consequences like landslides, floods, droughts and famines. Nature has supplied living creatures with abundant resources and man in particular has been able to co-exist with the least discomfort. So, it is our moral duty to have mutual respect for these creatures and believe in the principle of peaceful co-existence.

3. Earth has many species living on it. Every single species has the right to enjoy their existence. We humans call some species dangerous as they either have poison or claws or kill for a living. Still, we have no right to threaten their existence. Elaborate with reference to the poem 'Snake'.

Ans. It is important that man needs to learn to peacefully co-exist with nature and all living creatures. All the creatures of God have an equal right to a safe existence. As per our convenience, we have catalogued different animals as domestic and wild. We consider wild animals dangerous even when they pose no threat to us.

In the poem 'Snake', the snake came to the water-trough to quench its thirst.

Even though the snake was a poisonous one, it never tried to harm the poet or even display any intention of doing so. Thus, the poet had no right to threaten the existence of the snake. We must remember that even if the snake was a poisonous one, it was so because nature had made it like that. We have no right to interfere in nature's work or try to change it.

4. The poet talks to us indirectly about his inner voice and the need for man to forget age old prejudices and love nature's creations like the snake. Discuss this with reference to DH Lawrence's poem, 'Snake'.

Ans. We are often advised to stay away from animals like snakes. This is so because we have notions about other living species and consider some of them to be dangerous. In the poem, Lawrence talks about the inner voice that appeals to us to drop the age old prejudices that categorise some animals as dangerous.

Lawrence treats the snake as an equal. This shows that he doesn't consider other species to be inferior to him.

The snake never threatens or tries to harm the poet. It just quenches its thirst and retreats to his hole. However, the poet's education has taught him that snakes are dangerous and so, he attacks it. However, soon, the poet regrets his act. He feels guilty for his petty act and for not accepting his conscience. The poet's regret is important as it teaches us to show respect to the beautiful creations of God. We should learn to peacefully co-exist with the other species and protect their right to existence.

5. Whenever we act against the voice of our conscience, the result is suffering. Explain with reference to the poet's action against the snake and its consequences. **CBSE 2017**

Ans. Before the poet's 'voice of education' advised him to try to kill the snake, the poet's voice of conscience told him that the snake was his guest and was quenching its thirst at his water-trough. He felt that the snake was an honoured guest and should be satisfied by its visit. However, when the poet's 'voice of education' took over his thinking, he felt that the snake should be killed as it may be dangerous. So, the poet acted against the voice of his conscience by throwing a stick at the snake. The result was that the snake suffered by having to slither away very fast away from the place. However, the poet suffered more. This was so because he felt that his action had been arbitrary in nature and he had no reason to throw the stick at the snake as it was already going away after drinking water. The snake did not threaten the poet at all. So, the poet suffered remorse that he had listened to his 'voice of education' instead of listening to the voice of his conscience.

6. Animals too deserve respect and should not be harmed. Describe in about 150 words how the action of the ancient mariner in 'The Rime of the Ancient Mariner' and the poet in the poem 'Snake' highlight the regret of harming the animals.

Ans. Animals, like humans, are sentient beings deserving of respect and compassion. They play crucial roles in our ecosystems and contribute to the rich tapestry of life on Earth. The harm inflicted upon them not only disrupts natural balance but also causes deep moral and emotional consequences.

In Samuel Taylor Coleridge's The Rime of the Ancient Mariner. The mariner's fateful decision to kill the albatross symbolises a grave disrespect towards nature. This act leads to dire consequences-drought, despair, and the death of his sailors. This ultimately lead to the Ancient Mariner's profound regret. The mariner's suffering serves as a reminder of the moral responsibility humans hold toward animals.

Similarly, D.H. Lawrence's poem Snake illustrates the internal conflict of a poet faced with the urge to harm a beautiful serpent. The speaker grapples with societal expectations overshadowing his respect for the creature. Ultimately, the regret for contemplating violence against the snake evokes a powerful message: harming animals disrupts both nature and our own humanity. Both works point out the need to recognise and uphold the dignity of all living beings.

ASSESSMENT EXERCISE

Extract Based Questions

Read the following extracts carefully and answer the questions that follow.

1. Being earth-brown, earth-golden
from the burning bowels of the earth
On the day of Sicilian July, with Etna smoking.
   (a) What do you learn about the appearance of the item described in the above lines?
   (b) Why does the poet make a reference to 'Etna smoking'?
   (c) What do you mean by 'burning bowels'?
   (d) What is the item described here?
2. And voices in me said, If you were a man
You would take a stick and break him now, and finish him off.
   (a) Which voices does the poet refer to?
   (b) What do the voices tell the poet to do?
   (c) What do you mean by the phrase 'finish him off'?
   (d) Explain 'if you were a man'.

Short Answer Type Questions

Answer the following questions in 30-40 words.

1. What made the poet feel honoured to have a snake at his water-trough?
2. Do you think the poet was really afraid of the snake? Give reasons for your answer.
3. Will you say it was cowardice which prevented the poet from hitting the snake? Give reasons.
4. Why does the poet feel that the snake must be killed ?
5. What 'chance' did the poet miss by throwing the log at the snake?

Long Answer Type Questions

Answer the following questions in 150 words.

1. I thought how paltry, how vulgar, what a mean act!
I despised myself and the voices of my accursed human education.
The poet repents throwing a stick at the snake. He finds fault with the education he had for his deplorable behaviour and dual attitude. Write a letter to your friend justifying the above statements in the light of the general behaviour of people.
2. How does the poet satirise human education in the poem 'Snake'?
3. DH Lawrence's poem 'Snake' presents a conflict of human values—the natural ones and the acquired ones. Do you agree?
4. Imagine you are DH Lawrence. Write a diary entry describing how you were in two minds—whether to kill the snake out of fear or to feel honoured to have him as a guest. Mention your sense of regret and guilt for your act of hurling a log of wood at it.

Section D : Literature
Textbook : Interact in English (Drama)

CHAPTER 1

The Dear Departed

by Stanley Houghton

About the DRAMA 'The Dear Departed' is an extremely humorous play written by Stanley Houghton. The play exposes the materialistic mentality of modern day people. Here Houghton satirises the degradation of moral values in the British Middle-class. Mutual relations, love and compassion have no meaning for them. Blinded by greed, they ignore their responsibilities towards the elder generation.

Important Characters

- **Mrs. Amelia Slater** A greedy and materialistic (money-minded) woman who can stoop down to any level to satisfy her greed. She is a dominating wife and has no regard for her father.
- **Mrs. Elizabeth Jordan** A very clever woman. Like her sister, she too is very greedy and petty.
- **Mr. Henry Slater** A good husband who supports his wife and does nothing against his wife's wishes.
- **Mr. Ben Jordan** A jolly man who cracks jokes here and there. Like the two sisters, he too is interested in the old man's inheritance.
- **Victoria Slater** (Vicky) A ten year old girl. She is a smart and witty child who loves her grandfather very much.
- **Abel Merryweather** He is the grandfather. He believes in eating, drinking and being merry.

Scene of the Drama

The room where the whole drama is enacted is the drawing-cum-dining room of a small house in a poor area of a small town. On the left, there is a window with curtains. It has a sofa in front of it. On the right, there is a fireplace, with an armchair (comfortable chair) nearby. At the back of the stage, there is the door into the passage.

To the left of the door, there is a worn out chest of drawers. In the middle of the room, there is the dining table with chairs. Ornaments and a cheap American clock are placed on the mantelpiece above the fireplace, and in the hearth a kettle. A pair of new carpet slippers is kept nearby. The table is laid for tea as the time is late afternoon. Copies of an evening paper and of the magazines TIT-BITS and PEARSON'S WEEKLY are lying on the table. The front door of the house is on the left side of the passage and there is a staircase going up on the right side. In the passage, a hat stand is visible. When the curtain rises, Mrs. Amelia Slater is seen setting the table for tea. She is a strong, plump, red-faced, tough-looking woman, prepared to talk straight to make others agree with her views. She is wearing a black attire that represents that someone had died. However, she does not seem to be in complete mourning dress. She listens for a moment and then, goes to the window and opens it.

Summary of the Drama

Victoria is Told to Wear a Black Dress

Amelia Slater calls her daughter Victoria and scolds her for playing outside when her grandfather is lying dead upstairs. Amelia tells her to change her dress as her aunt Elizabeth and uncle Ben are about to come. Victoria is surprised to learn about their coming. Then, Henry Slater enters with a little paper parcel and sits on the armchair near the fire. Amelia is looking to outdo her sister by wearing a mourning dress. However, Henry is doubtful about Elizabeth's coming as she had once said after a fight with Amelia that she would never set foot in their house. However, Amelia is confident that Elizabeth would come for her share of what their father (Abel Merryweather) has left for them.

Grandfather's Bureau

Amelia advises her husband to start using the new slippers of the grandfather even though Henry believes that they will be very small for him. She also wants to shift grandfather's bureau (writing desk with drawers) to her room before Elizabeth's arrival. She believes that if her sister gets to know that the bureau belonged to their father then, she would surely try to take it.

Henry is surprised at such a suggestion. He thinks that it is not the right thing to do but constant persuasion (urging) from his wife gets him to agree. When Victoria learns that they are moving the bureau, she feels that they are stealing it. Henry is shocked to hear her views and makes up a false story to convince her about the correctness of the act. Meanwhile, Amelia enters with grandfather's clock. She tells Victoria not to mention anything about the clock and the bureau in front of her aunt Elizabeth.

Arrival of the Jordans

Victoria still feels that they have stolen the bureau and the clock. After a short while, when Henry and Amelia are moving the bureau, there is a knock at the front door. Amelia warns Victoria not to open the door if it is her aunt and uncle. Victoria peeps through the window and reports that her aunt and uncle have arrived. There is repeated knocking and it keeps on getting louder. After clearing up the mess and cleaning up the room, Mrs. Slater tells Victoria to open the door.

The Families Ridicule the 'Departed' Soul

Mrs. Amelia Slater discusses with her sister, Mrs. Elizabeth Jordan, their father's death and also tells her that their father became seventy-two years old just a fortnight (2 weeks) ago. The Jordans ask the Slaters whether they had called the doctor when his condition got serious. Amelia answers that Henry went immediately to call the family doctor but he was not at home. Ben Jordan reacts and says that then he should have looked for another doctor. Mrs. Jordan treats it as a big mistake on the part of the Slaters. Mrs. Slater tells them that the grandfather was quite happy that morning. He took his breakfast and went out to pay his insurance. They further discuss the last day of the father in a ridiculing manner.

Shrewd Nature of the Slaters and the Jordans

Mrs. Amelia Slater asks if they wish to go upstairs and look at grandfather now or would they have tea first.

Mrs. Jordan decides to have tea first. Henry suggests that the announcement of the death should be made in the newspapers by publishing an obituary. Then, the two sisters quarrel about grandfather's gold watch.

The topic shifts to grandfather's insurance money when Ben enquires about it, Victoria informs them that grandfather didn't go to pay his insurance. Instead, he met his friends and went to the Ring-o'-Bells public-house. They conclude that he had not paid the insurance money and it was overdue. At this point, Ben calls him a drunken old beggar. Mrs. Jordan says that her father did it on purpose just to annoy them. Amelia Slater sends Victoria into the grandfather's room to fetch the keys of the bureau so that they could find the receipt for the insurance premium paid by grandfather.

Elizabeth is shocked to see a new bureau and asks Amelia about it. Amelia tells her sister that Henry had bought it at an auction and that it is second hand.

The 'Departed' Wakes Up

Victoria reluctantly to her grandfather's room. She returns very scared and says that grandfather was getting up. Mrs. Jordan reacts with surprise and says that the child is crazy. Then, they look at the door.

The door opens, revealing an old man dressed in a faded but cheerful dressing-gown. Victoria wonders whether he is her Grandpa or his ghost. Grandfather (Abel) is surprised to see the Jordans. When Amelia asks if that is really him, he strongly replies by telling her to stop behaving in a foolish and silly manner. He also notices that Elizabeth is not very happy to see him. He, then, asks Amelia about his slippers which Henry Slater was wearing. She promptly tells him that she had given them to Henry as they were new and needed some stretching. Victoria moves towards Abel and tells him that she is happy to see him alive. Amelia Slater tells her in a whisper to keep quiet.

Silly Behaviour of Jordans and Slaters Continue

Abel is astonished to see everybody wearing black mourning clothes. So, Mrs. Slater makes an excuse and states that they are mourning for Ben's brother. However in reality, Ben did not have a brother. After hearing about it, Abel enquires about the brother and then, sits down to have tea with the family.

As they are drinking the tea, Ben starts asking about Abel's health and if he was sleeping. Abel replies that he was not sleeping but he was in a daze wherein he wouldn't move. However, he could hear and see everything.

Then, Mrs. Jordan asks Abel whether he had seen Henry or Amelia coming into his bedroom when he was lying down. Abel starts thinking and Amelia says that they should not force him to remember the details.

Truth Dawns Upon Abel

Suddenly, Abel remembers that the Slaters had been shifting his bureau. Then, he also notices his clock. He is puzzled and is not able to understand what was happening. Amelia and Henry try to calm the situation down. However, Mrs. Jordan reveals that Amelia and Henry had stolen the bureau and the clock. She also revealed that Amelia had believed him to be dead. This leads to a quarrel between the sisters. Soon, Abel realises that they were in mourning as they thought he was dead. He chuckles and takes his seat again. He tells Amelia and Elizabeth that he had a will which was kept in the bureau. However, now, he wishes to change his will.

Three Things to Do on Monday

Mrs. Amelia Slater requests Abel not to be so harsh on them and starts crying. Abel says that he does not want to be hard on anyone because he is going to make a new will, leaving all his things to whomsoever he is living with when he dies. Hearing this, the sisters begin convincing Abel to stay with them so they can get his property. In their fight, Amelia Slater reveals that the quarrel between them had happened because none of them wanted to keep Abel in their home. Hearing this, Abel realises their true feelings and states that he will live with someone else.

Mrs. Amelia Slater and Mrs. Jordan request their father not to do so. Ben also requests Abel that he has got to live with one of his daughters. However, Abel says that on next Monday, he has got to do three things. First, he will go to his lawyer and change his will. Second, he will go to the insurance office and pay his premium and third, he will go to St. Philip's Church and get married.

Abel Merryweather's Wedding

Ben and Henry are surprised to hear about the upcoming marriage. Mrs. Jordan is also surprised while Mrs. Slater says that he is out of his senses. She asks the name of the lady to whom he is going to be married. Abel replies that he is going to be married to Mrs. John Shorrocks, the widow who runs the 'Ring-o'-Bells' pub. He goes out saying that he is too much of a burden to them and adds that he wishes to see them at the ceremony. He further tells Amelia Slater that it was good she brought the bureau downstairs, as now it would be easy to shift it to the 'Ring-o'-Bells' after his marriage.

Word Meaning

Word	Meaning
TIT-BITS, PEARSON WEEKLY	British weekly magazines
sharply	strongly, angrily
blind	screen, shutter
precocious	a child whose mental abilities are developed beyond his/ her age
gallivanting	playing
in colours	wearing a colourful or gay dress
good gracious	a term expressing surprise
stooping	bending
drooping	hanging down
tailcoat	a man's formal coat, with a long skirt divided at the back into tails and cut away in front
sash	waistband
till our new black's ready	till our new mourning dress is ready
prying	excessively interested in a person's private affairs
bear up	manage
trifles	things of little value or importance
bureau	a writing desk with drawers
drive a hard bargain	argue in an aggressive manner
grubbing	searching
daft	foolish
bumping	crashing, loud
flushed	excited
ostentatiously	showily
complacent	self-satisfied
impassive	calm
air	manner

Word	Meaning
regrettable	mournful
chirpy	cheerful and lively
furtively	stealthily, secretly
piqued	irritated, annoyed
as merry as a sandboy	extremely happy and carefree
poetic license	the freedom poets/ artists enjoy to depart from facts or conventional rules of language
'Ring-o'-Bells'	the name of a public house
public-house	a place for sale of alcoholic beverages (also called a 'pub')
overdue	not having done by the expected time
swindling	cheating
disparagingly	in a derogatory manner
transfixed	motionless
chuckling	quiet, inward laughter
vigorous	energetic
malicious	intending to cause harm
tomfoolery	foolish behaviour
what the dickens	a term expressing annoyance or surprise
disconcerted	worried, confused
dazed	confused
begad	by God
drat me	shame on me
double-faced	deceitful
sneaked	entered stealthily
keen	eager, anxious
will	a legal document dealing with the transfer of a person's wealth/property after his death
fixed up	settled, arranged

Textbook FOLDER

Here, we have covered questions given in the CBSE Textbook along with their answers.

ON PAGE 150

Q.4 Given below are the main incidents in the play. They are in a jumbled order. Arrange them in the sequence in which they occur in the play.

1. Victoria is asked to fetch the bunch of keys to the bureau to look for the insurance receipt.
2. Mrs. Slater instructs Victoria to put her white frock on with a black sash.
3. Mrs. Slater discovers that grandfather is 'dead'.
4. The Slaters fetch the bureau and the clock from upstairs.
5. The family sits down to have tea.
6. Henry wears grandfather's new slippers.
7. Grandfather comes to know how his daughters were in a hurry to divide his things between them.
8. Grandfather announces his intention to change his will and to marry Mrs. Shorrocks.
9. Grandfather comes down and is surprised to find the Jordans.
10. They discuss the obituary announcement in the newspapers and the insurance premium payment.
11. The Jordans arrive and learn the details of grandfather's demise from the Slaters.

Ans.
3. Mrs. Slater discovers that grandfather is 'dead'.
2. Mrs. Slater instructs Victoria to put her white frock on with a black sash.
6. Henry wears grandfather's new slippers.
4. The Slaters fetch the bureau and the clock from upstairs.
11. The Jordans arrive and learn the details of grandfather's demise from the Slaters.
5. The family sits down to have tea.
10. They discuss the obituary announcement in the newspapers and the insurance premium payment.
1. Victoria is asked to fetch the bunch of keys to the bureau to look for the insurance receipt.
9. Grandfather comes down and is surprised to find the Jordans.
7. Grandfather comes to know how his daughters were in a hurry to divide his things between them.
8. Grandfather announces his intention to change his will and to marry Mrs. Shorrocks.

ON PAGE 151

Q.5 Answer the following questions briefly.

(a) How does Mrs. Slater plan to outshine the Jordans? What does it reveal about her character? CBSE 2016, 14

Ans. Mrs. Slater plans to outshine the Jordans by wearing new mourning dress and thinks that Ben and Elizabeth will never have thought about mourning yet. It shows her inhuman greedy and selfish character for she wants to outdo her sister even during a sad time.

(b) Why does Mrs. Slater decide to shift the bureau from grandfather's room before the arrival of the Jordans? How does Henry react to the suggestion?

Ans. Mrs. Slater decides to shift the bureau from grandfather's room before the arrival of the Jordans because she did not want her sister to claim it.

Henry was shocked at the suggestion because he felt that the sisters should amicably divide grandfather's things. He also felt that it was too heavy and moreover, he was worried about the arrival of the Jordans while they were shifting it.

(c) What is the reason for the Jordans taking a long time to get to the house of the Slaters? What does it show about the two sisters' attitude towards each other?

Ans. The Jordans take a long time to get to the house of the Slaters because they have to buy new mourning dresses as grandfather had died. This shows that the two sisters are very jealous and want to outdo each other even in the tragic hour of mourning.

(d) What does Mrs. Jordan describe as 'a fatal mistake'? What is the irony in the comment she makes on Mrs. Slater's defense?

Ans. Mrs. Jordan describes not calling another doctor when Dr. Pringle was out as a fatal mistake. The irony in the comment to Mrs. Slater's reply is that she mentions that there are many cases of people remaining alive even after they were thought to be dead and later on in the drama, grandfather is actually found to be alive.

(e) **Ben appreciates grandfather saying 'it's a good thing he did.' Later he calls him a 'drunken old beggar.' Why does he change his opinion about grandfather?**

Or **In the play 'Dear Departed', why did Ben Jordan refer to the grandfather as 'The drunken old beggar'?** **CBSE 2019**

Ans. Ben changes his opinion about grandfather when the family discusses that he may not have paid the premium and it might still be overdue. As a result, they may not get the insurance money now.

(f) **What change does grandfather make in his new will? What effect does it have on his daughters?**

or **What decision did Abel Merryweather take regarding his will? What were his future plans for himself?**

Ans. Grandfather decides to mention in his new will that all his things will belong to the person who he will be living with at the time of his death. Further, he is going to get married to the widow of John Shorrocks and will be living with her in future.

Both the daughters are shocked at this as now they will not get anything from their father.

(g) **What are the three things that grandfather plans to do on Monday next?**

Or **What were the programmes scheduled for Monday next by grandfather?**

Ans. The three things that grandfather plans to do on next Monday are

(i) to change his will

(ii) to pay the premium of his insurance.

(iii) to get married to Mrs. John Shorrocks at St Philip's Church.

Q.6 Answer the following in detail.

(a) **Bring out the irony in the title of the play.**

Or **Bring out the irony in the title of the play, 'The Dear Departed'.** **CBSE 2016, 14**

Ans. The title 'The Dear Departed' literally means that the person who is dead is much loved by the family members and hence the person is called 'the dear departed'. However, in the drama, no one has departed and no one is dear. The story presents how the grandfather is taken to be dead as he was lying down in a dazed condition. His daughter, Amelia Slater thinks that he has died. She doesn't even bother to call a doctor to confirm this. The only matter on her mind is stealing his possessions before her sister Elizabeth arrives and outshining her by wearing mourning clothes. When Elizabeth does arrive, instead of going to see her father, she prefers to have tea. The two sisters quarrel over his possessions. Finally, Abel realises that he is not at all 'dear' to them and, since he is not a departed soul, he decides to 'depart' from their lives.

(b) **How does the spat between his daughters lead to grandfather discovering the truth?**

Ans. In spite of being sisters, the two ladies, Amelia and Elizabeth, cannot stand each other. They are very jealous of each other and always make plans to outdo each other. Even at the time of their father's supposed death, they keep on fighting over his inheritance with the least concern for the mournful occasion. Both the ladies had their eyes on his possessions. When Abel comes down and observes that the Slaters have shifted his bureau, Elizabeth becomes furious. She calls the Slaters robbers and a heated quarrel begins. Amelia and Henry try to calm down the situation but an extremely angry, impatient and frustrated Elizabeth tells Abel everything.

Thereafter, Abel does not take too long to realise what has happened.

(c) **Compare and contrast Henry's character with that of his wife. Support your answer with evidence from the play.** **Competency Based**

Ans. Henry's wife, Amelia is a woman of a dominating nature. She is extremely jealous of her own sister and, at the time of tragedy of her father's assumed death, wants to outdo her. This shows her pretentious and selfish side. Henry's character does not show such strength. Amelia is also greedy and wants to remove the bureau before her sister arrives. Although Henry is startled to hear this, he helps her in shifting the bureau. He is even reluctant to take grandfather's slippers. This shows that Henry, though more sensitive than his wife, is a weak-natured person.

He is a subjugated (suppressed) husband who cannot raise his voice against his wife and follows her orders like a slave. Though Amelia seems to be the real culprit among the two, one cannot deny that Henry was her 'partner in crime'.

ON PAGE 151

Q.7 Bring out the traits in Mrs. Slater's personality, quoting evidence from the play.

Trait	Evidence from the Play
Greedy	(a).....................
Overpowering / dominating	(b).....................
Blunt / straight talking	(c).....................
Impolite	(d).....................
Insensitive	(e).....................

Ans.

	Evidence from the Play
(a)	I thought I would fetch this down as well. Our clock is nothing and this always appealed to me.
(b)	Don't look so daft. Why not?
(c)	After all I have done for him... It's nothing short of swindling.
(d)	No, If I am not to have him, you shan't either.
(e)	Well, will you go up and look at him now, or shall we have tea?

ON PAGE 151-152

Q.8 Answer the following with reference to the context.

(1) "Are we pinching it before Aunt Elizabeth comes?"

(a) What does 'it' refer to here?

Ans. 'It' refers to the bureau that was in grandfather's room.

(b) How does Victoria conclude that her parents are 'pinching it'?

Ans. When Victoria was told by her father that he and his mother were shifting the bureau downstairs, she concluded that her parents are 'pinching it' because everything that was in grandfather's room had to be equally divided amongst the two sisters.

(c) Mention the two reasons that Mrs. Slater gives for her action.

Ans. Mrs. Slater justifies her action of moving her father's bureau downstairs by saying that she had always liked it and wanted to have it. Further, she adds that if her sister got to know that she like it, her sister would not let her have it and would fight for it.

(d) What does it reveal about the difference between the attitude of the elders and that of Victoria?

Ans. The elders in the given extract come out as selfish and manipulative as they do things for their own benefit. Victoria, in contrast, seems to be an innocent child who loves her grandfather as lot.

(2) "I don't call that delicate stepping into a dead man's shoes in such haste."

(a) Who makes this comment?

Ans. Mrs. Jordan made this comment.

(b) What prompts the speaker to say this?

Ans. When grandfather sees Henry wearing it, Mrs. Slater quickly gives them back to him. This prompts Mrs. Jordan to make this comment.

(c) Bring out the significance of this statement.

Ans. Stepping into dead man's shoe is to take the position of the dead man although one might not be capable of it. Mrs. Jordan on seeing her brother-in law wearing grandfather's shoes feels that he was in too much of a hurry to step into the grandfather's shoes. He didn't even wait for his funeral.

WRITING

Q.9 Victoria Slater is truly attached to her Grandpa. As she sees the elders in her family quarrel over the inheritance, she is bewildered and upset by their attitude. As Victoria, write a diary entry outlining the incident and your feelings. (150 words)

Or **Victoria Slater is truly attached to her Grandfather. She is confused by the behaviour of the elders at home and their attitude towards the old man. As Victoria, write a diary entry in not more than 150 words outlining the incidents and the elders' feelings towards the misfortune.**

Ans. Friday, 4th March, 20XX 10 p.m.

Dear Diary

Today turned out to be a day of great emotional turmoil for me. My mother called me inside when I was playing outside my home and told me that Grandpa was dead. She ordered me to change my dress before Uncle Ben and Aunt Elizabeth came. Moreover, before their arrival, Mom and Dad started pinching grandfather's belongings.

I was very much upset at their greedy and insensitive behaviour. They were also quarrelling over the inheritance. I hated their selfish mentality.

When mother ordered me to go into Grandpa's room to bring a bunch of keys, I was terrified as I saw that Grandpa was getting up. He was not dead; he was just sleeping. I am very much happy that Grandpa is alive. But alas! He has decided to live away from us. All this happened because of the insensitive attitude of my parents. I will never forgive them for this.

Victoria

REVIEW EXERCISE

Including Previous Years' and Practice Questions

Extract Based Questions

Read the following extracts carefully and answer the questions that follow.

1. **Mrs. Slater:** (sharply) Victoria, Victoria! D'ye hear? Come in, will you? (Victoria comes in.)

   Mrs. Slater: I'm amazed at you, Victoria. I really am. Be off now, and change your dress before your Aunt Elizabeth and your Uncle Ben come. It would never do for them to find you in colours with grandfather lying dead, upstairs.

   Victoria: What are they coming for? They haven't been here for ages.

   (a) Who are 'They' in the above extract?

Ans. 'They' refers to Mr. Ben Jordan and Mrs. Elizabeth Jordan, Victoria's uncle and aunt.

   (b) What is the meaning of the word 'ages' in the extract?

Ans. The word 'ages' means 'a long period.'

   (c) What is the occasion that 'They' are coming for?

Ans. The occasion is to mourn the reported 'death' of grandfather.

   (d) What will 'They' do when they come?

Ans. 'They' will talk about sharing Grandpa's possessions and money with the Slaters after his reported 'death'.

2. **Mrs. Slater :** In the kitchen; but you want a new pair, those old ones are nearly worn out. You don't seem to realise what it's costing me to bear up like I am doing. My heart's fit to break when I see the little trifles that belonged to grandfather lying around, and think he'll never use them again. Here! You'd better wear these slippers of grandfather's now. It's lucky he'd just got a new pair. **CBSE 2024 C**

   (a) Whose slippers were completely worn out?

Ans. Henry Slater's slippers were completely worn out.

   (b) From the above extract, what can be inferred about the speaker's feelings for the grandfather.

Ans. We can infer that the speaker did really love the grandfather. She is finding it difficult to bear the little things, that the grandfather used, lying around.

   (c) Mrs. Slater was very disturbed. Justify.

Ans. Mrs. Slater was very disturbed because she had just lost her father. However, we know that she was disturbed at the thought of her sister laying claim on the things that she had wanted.

   (d) Find one word for the phrase 'a thing of little value or importance'.

Ans. Trinket

3. **Be quiet! It's ours now. Come, Henry, lift your end. Don't breathe a word to your aunt about the clock and bureau.**

   (a) The idiom 'not breathe a word' used here means ....

Ans. to not give any information

   (b) What is the item being referred to in the above extract when the speaker says "it's ours now"?

Ans. The item being referred to is grandfather's clock.

   (c) What is the intention of the speaker in asking the listener to 'be quiet'?

Ans. The intention of the speaker is to ensure that her sister does not come to know that she and her husband have taken away grandfather's bureau and clock.

   (d) Why does the speaker tell Henry to "lift your end"?

Ans. The speaker, Mrs. Slater, asks her husband, Henry, to lift one end of grandfather's bureau to shift it to her room before her sister comes so that Mrs. Slater can claim that the bureau is hers.

4. **That was a near thing. Open the door, Victoria. Now, Henry, get your coat on.**

   (a) In the extract, 'a near thing' means ....

Ans. that they have just managed to settle everything before Mr. and Mrs. Jordan enter.

   (b) Why was Henry asked to wear his coat?

Ans. Mrs. Slater wanted her husband, Henry, to wear his coat so that the visitors, Mr. and Mrs. Jordan, would think that he was ready and waiting for them.

(c) What was the reason for the visitors coming to their house for whom Victoria was asked to open the door?

Ans. The reason was that Mr. Slater had sent information to the Jordan family that Mrs. Jordan's father had 'died'.

(d) What had been happening just before the speaker said the words given in the extract?

Ans. Just before this, Mr. and Mrs. Slater had shifted grandfather's bureau to their room, so that they could pretend that the bureau was their own.

5. **Mrs. Slater :** Elizabeth's that sharp she'll see I'm after it, and we'll drive a hard bargain over it.

Henry : Perhaps she's got her eye on the bureau as well.

Mrs. Slater : She's got her eye on the bureau as well.

Mrs. Slater : She's never been here since father bought it. If it was only down here instead of in his room, she'd never guess it wasn't our own.

(a) What is 'it' in the present context?

Ans. The word 'it' here is grandfather's bureau, a piece of furniture he had bought recently.

(b) Who is 'she' in the present context?

Ans. The word 'she' in the present context is used to refer to Mrs. Jordan, the speaker's sister.

(c) Why does the speaker say these words?

Ans. The speaker, Mrs. Slater, says these words because she wanted her husband to help her shift the piece of furniture to their room before her sister arrived.

(d) Why does the speaker not want 'she' to guess that 'it' belonged to grandfather?

Ans. Mrs. Slater did not want Mrs. Jordan to guess that the bureau belonged to grandfather so that she could say that it belonged to her.

6. He always was thoughtful in that way. He was too honourable to have 'gone' without paying his premium.

(a) The word..........in the extract is a synonym of 'instalment.'

Ans. 'premium'

(b) Who is 'he' in the above extract?

Ans. The word 'he' refers to Abel Merryweather, also referred to as 'grandfather'.

(c) Where is 'he' supposed to have gone that morning?

Ans. 'He', that is Abel Merryweather, was supposed to have gone that morning to pay his insurance premium.

(d) Why is 'he' said to be thoughtful?

Ans. Abel Merryweather is said to be thoughtful because paying his insurance premium on time is a thoughtful action so as to prevent his insurance policy from lapsing.

7. **Henry:** I saw a verse in the Evening News yesterday. Proper poetry it was. It rhymed. (He gets the paper and reads) Despised and forgotten by some you may be, But the spot that contains you is sacred to we.'

Mrs. Jordan: That 'll never do . You don't say sacred to we.'

Henry: It's in the paper.

Mrs. Slater: You wouldn't say it if you were speaking properly, but it's different in poetry.

Henry: Poetic licence, you know.

(a) The speaker of these words is ....

Ans. Mrs. Slater

(b) What does the phrase 'it's different' refer to in the above extract?

Ans. The reference is to any expression, as in poetry we need not follow the rules of grammar.

(c) What were the reactions of the others seated there to what was said in the extract?

Ans. The response of Mrs. Slater's husband was that the phrase is allowed in poetry, whereas her sister's response was that for an obituary, a full poem should be there, not just one verse.

(d) What were the people discussing when the speaker said the words in the extract?

Ans. The people were discussing about what kind of obituary notice about grandfather's supposed death should be published in a newspaper.

8. **Mrs. Jordan:** No, that'll never do. We want a verse that says how much we loved him and refers to all his good qualities and says what a heavy loss we've had.

Mrs. Slater: You want a whole poem. That'll cost a good lot.

Mrs. Jordan: Well, we'll think about it after tea, and then we'll look through his bits of things and make a list of them. There's all the furniture in his room. (The Dear Departed) **CBSE 2024**

(a) What does Mrs. Jordan want?

Ans. Mrs. Jordan wants to publish a verse in honour of her father's death as his obituary.

(b) **Mrs. Slater does not want a whole poem to be published. Why?**

Ans. Mrs. Slater doesn't want the entire poem to be published because it would cost a lot of money to be printed in the newspaper.

(c) **"You want a whole poem. That'll cost a good lat." Mention one characteristic trait of Mrs. Slater through this line.**

Ans. This line indicates that Mrs. Slater was insensitive and stingy.

(d) **Which is more important for these speakers - mourning on their father's death or distributing his property between them?**

Ans. According to the given extract, the speakers are more interested in acquiring their father's wealth than mourning his 'supposed' death.

9. Abel What's the matter with little Vicky? (He sees Ben and Mrs. Jordan) Hello! What brings you here? How's yourself, Ben? (Abel thrusts his hand at Ben who skips back smartly and retreats with Mrs. Jordan to a safe distance below the sofa.)

Mrs. Slater (approaching Abel gingerly) Father, is that you? (She pokes him with her hand to see if he is solid.)

Abel Of course it's me. Don't do that, Amelia. What the devil do you mean by this tomfoolery?

(a) **The speaker in the extract is ....**

Ans. Abel Merryweather.

(b) **Who is Vicky?**

Ans. Vicky is Victoria Slater, the daughter of Mr. and Mrs. Slater and the speaker's granddaughter.

(c) **What makes the speaker say these words?**

Ans. Abel Merryweather says these words because Victoria was scared when she saw him alive thinking that she may have seen a ghost.

(d) **What is the outcome of these words?**

Ans. The outcome is that his daughters and their husbands cannot believe that he is alive as they thought that he was dead.

10. Abel I don't see them. (Observing Henry trying to remove the slippers.) Why, you've got' em on, Henry.

Mrs. Slater (promptly) I told him to put them on to stretch them; they were that new and hard. Now, Henry. (Mrs. Slater snatches the slippers from Henry and gives them to Abel, who puts them on and sits in armchair).

Mrs. Jordan (to Ben) Well, I don't call that delicate. Stepping into a dead man's shoes in such haste.

(a) **Why did Henry wear Abel's slippers?**

Ans. Henry wore Abel's slippers because his wife Amelia told him to wear them, as she thought that Abel was dead and would now not need the new slippers.

(b) **What does the phrase, 'got em, on' mean?**

Ans. The phrase means wearing them on his feet.

(c) **Infer the playwright's purpose of including some writing in brackets.**

Ans. The writing in brackets usually indicate the physical action, expression or the stage direction to be followed in the play.

(d) **State the word that classifies the genre of the drama from the given extract.**

Ans. Comedy

11. Aye, you both say that because of what I've told you about leaving my money. Well, since you don't want me, I'll go to someone that does.

(a) **Who is the speaker of these words?**

Ans. The speaker of these words is Abel Merryweather, also referred to as 'grandfather'.

(b) **Who are referred to as 'both' in the above extract?**

Ans. 'both' refers to the two daughters of Abel Merryweather, Amelia Slater and Elizabeth Jordan.

(c) **Why is the speaker insisting on going somewhere?**

Ans. Abel, the speaker, has realised that his selfish daughters don't care for him and he wants to live with someone who is willing to care for him.

(d) **What does the decision of the speaker say about him?**

Ans. The decision tells us that Abel is deeply hurt by his daughters' behaviour and doesn't want to remain a burden on his daughters.

Short Answer Type Questions

Answer the following questions in 30-40 words.

1. Explain, "I'm amazed at you, Victoria; I really am."

Ans. Mrs. Slater speaks these words to her daughter Victoria. She is somewhat disturbed at the behaviour of her daughter and says that her grandfather is lying dead and still she goes out and plays. She wants Victoria to change into a mourning dress.

2. Why were Aunt Elizabeth and her husband Uncle Ben coming to Mrs. Slater's house?

Ans. As Mr. Abel Merryweather had supposedly died, her daughter, Mrs. Slater, had asked her sister Elizabeth and her husband Ben Jordan to come to her house for mourning his death.

That is why they were coming to her house. They also wanted to participate in the last rites and discuss how to distribute the old man's property between themselves.

3. Why do you think Elizabeth would not make a claim for the bureau and the clock?

Ans. Elizabeth would not make a claim for the bureau and the clock because she was unaware that these had been purchased by the grandfather in her absence. Moreover, she had set her eyes on grandfather's gold watch which she desired for her son.

4. Explain "What have you got your coat off for, father"?

Ans. Victoria appears dressed as desired by her mother and asks her father why he had got his coat off. Her father replies that they are going to bring the bureau downstairs and that is why he is not wearing his coat.

5. What does the shifting of the bureau tell us about the character of Mrs. Slater?

Ans. The shifting of the bureau tells us that Mrs. Slater is very greedy and money-minded. Just after her father's death, when the lady is expected to be in mourning, she is more concerned about how to acquire her father's belongings and portray them as her own when her sister Elizabeth arrives at her house. She wants to keep the bureau for herself before Elizabeth can claim it.

6. What made Mrs. Slater believe that grandfather was 'dead'?

Ans. Before dinner, Mrs. Slater planned to serve some food on a tray to grandfather, as he did not want dinner. When she reached his room, the old man was lying on his bed. Mrs. Slater thought he was asleep. When she went to wake him up, she found him to be quite cold and believed he was dead.

7. Why was grandfather so keen on changing his will?

***Or* Why did the grandfather change his will?**

Ans. Grandfather was keen on changing his will because he realised that none of his daughters was to keep him and considered him a burden on them. Moreover, they wanted to take his belongings and had already proceeded with the division of his belongings between themselves. Grandfather, thus, decided to change his will and totally deprive his mean, selfish and greedy daughters of his inheritance.

8. What were the changes that the grandfather wanted to make in his will and why?

Ans. The grandfather wanted to change his will and make a new one. He wanted to leave all his belongings to the one with whom he would be living at the time of his death. He decided to do so as he came to know about his mean and selfish daughters who did not love him.

9. Do you think Abel Merryweather is justified in parting ways with his daughters?

Ans. It must have been really shocking and upsetting for Abel Merryweather to discover what his selfish and greedy daughters thought of him. When we think of Amelia and Elizabeth's insensitivity, indecent behaviour, greed and hypocrisy, then Abel's decision to part ways with them seems quite fair and just. However, his disowning the entire family is a little harsh and unjust towards little Victoria who truly loved her grandfather.

10. Describe your impression of both the sisters, Mrs. Slater and Mrs. Jordan.

Ans. Both the sisters were totally materialistic and inhuman, as they did not even pay respect to their supposedly dead father but were more worried about dividing his property among themselves. They were selfish and greedy and had no compassion or sympathy.

11. Do you agree that Mrs. and Mr. Slater loved Grandpa? Justify your answer.

Ans. After going through the play, I believe that Mrs. and Mr. Slater did not love Grandpa. They had consideration only for his assets. They found him a burden that was being carried unwillingly by them. They did not have a sense of responsibility or affection towards him.

12. In what way is the play 'The Dear Departed' satirical? Comment on the nature of its characters.

Ans. The play is a satire on the degrading values in modern society. Abel was not even buried when his daughters started fighting over his possessions. They felt that he was a burden on them. Children today don't care for their parents and are only concerned about their inheritance and other material gains.

13. Briefly describe the character of Victoria in the play 'The Dear Departed'.

Ans. Victoria is the precocious ten year old daughter of the Slater couple. She is compassionate and loves her grandfather. She is innocent but has some worldly wisdom which is clear from the fact that she understood that her parents had stolen grandfather's belongings.

14. What is Stanley Houghton's primary purpose in employing irony in the play 'The Dear Departed'?

Ans. Stanley Houghton's primary purpose in employing irony in 'The Dear Departed' is to satirise the societal values and behaviours of his time, particularly the greed and materialism of the middle class. The story also exposes the hypocrisy and moral bankruptcy of characters like the Slaters and the Jordans, who prioritise money and possessions over family and morality.

15. Bring out the significance of 'grandfather's bureau', in the play.

Ans. The 'grandfather's bureau' is an important tool used by the playwright to introduce the theme of selfishness in the play. It also brings out the rivalry between the two sisters. Mrs. Slater wants the bureau as she likes it. She knows that if her sister knows that she likes it, her sister will fight for it and will not let her have it. So, she decides to take the bureau herself and call it her own.

16. The character of Victoria is a stark contrast to that of her parents. Justify.

Ans. It is true to say that the character of Victoria is in stark contrast to that of her parents as she is an innocent 10 year old girl who loves her grandfather a lot. In comparison, her parents and uncle as well as aunt are selfish people who only care about material possessions.

Long Answer Type Questions

Answer the following questions in 150 words.

1. "Materialism makes way for shaky relationships." Do you agree with the statement? Explain with reference to the play 'The Dear Departed', highlighting the values required of the two sisters.

Or **For Mrs. Slater and Mrs. Jordan, greed for money is more important than their love for their father. Comment.**

Ans. Relationships that are guided by materialism are often not able to continue or be successful. The relationship between Abel Merryweather and his daughters Amelia and Elizabeth, particularly from the daughters' side, is based completely on monetary considerations. While the two sisters did not really do much for their father during his life, they are eager to derive maximum benefit from the old man's supposed death. Amelia Slater even tries to cheat her sister by appropriating some of her father's belongings and declaring them as her own.

Their relationship towards their father is devoid of feelings. When Abel Merryweather declares that he will leave all his belongings to the person with whom he will spend the last days of his life, both the daughters compete with each other to keep the old man with them, whereas earlier neither was interested in having the father at their home. The values required of them were to support and love their father in his old age without craving for his possessions, so that he remains happy with them.

2. Greed and deception govern the lives of the Slaters and the Jordans. Do you agree? Answer with reasons supporting your point of view.

Ans. The lives of the Slater and Jordan families are certainly governed by greed and deceit. On an occasion when we expect the characters to be sad, we are shocked by their greedy behaviour.

While Amelia Slater is keen to grab her 'dead' father's new pair of slippers for her husband, she also wants to appropriate his writing bureau and his clock.

Elizabeth Jordan too is no less insensitive. She chooses to have tea first rather than going upstairs to pay respect to her 'dead father'. She even suggests that they should look through their father's possessions and make a list of them. Though Henry Slater is not as money-minded as his wife, he hardly makes any attempt to stop her because he is a weak-willed character.

Thus, the entire family except Victoria seems to be governed by insensitivity, greed and hypocrisy.

3. Abel Merryweather, the grandfather, takes the decision of disowning his daughters and changing his will. Do you think the grandfather did the right thing? What message do you get after reading the play?

Ans. The grandfather's supposed death was an eye opener for him. It exposed the pettiness, greed, selfishness and hypocrisy of his ungrateful daughters, Amelia and Elizabeth, towards him. He realised this after he recovered from his temporary dazed feeling and came downstairs. He saw both his daughters together, which was a surprise for him. From the family's black clothing and conversation while having tea, he realised that all of them thought that he was dead and they had already taken possession of some of his belongings. So, he took no time to decide his course of action. He took the wise decision of disowning them and making his life more comfortable by remarrying.

The play, thus, conveys an important message that elderly people should be treated with great care and love and should not be regarded as a burden. Moreover, the old should make their will carefully without being affected by emotions and sentiments.

4. Victoria does not have the right role models to look up to. Discuss. What values are displayed by the members of the family?

Ans. Victoria is the only one in the family who loves her grandfather and is truly attached to him. The girl seems to have some respect for family values but unfortunately, she does not have the right role models to look up to. Both her parents are selfish and greedy for acquiring her grandfather's possessions. Not only that, they also want to show that they are better mourners of grandfather's death than Mr. and Mrs. Jordan. This demonstrates their hollowness of character, as even during a sad time, they want to outdo others. Victoria witnesses their manipulations and greedy behaviour.

Such hypocrisy is shocking for an innocent child of ten. As Victoria's elders, their duty is to create an ideal atmosphere for children to cultivate appropriate moral values.

5. 'The Dear Departed' highlights how we are treating our elders. Comment on the declining family values in modern society with reference to the play.

Ans. In this play, the parent-child relationship between the grandfather and his daughters has been shown as a farce (joke). The daughters are disrespectful to their father. They are only concerned with the money from his insurance policy and in acquiring his possessions. They have no feelings for their supposedly dead father who must have raised them up and got them married.

The daughters seem to have forgotten the hardships their father must have faced while fulfilling his filial duties. They feel that he is a burden to them in his old age. They only want to put up a show of mourning by dressing in mourning clothes. They also try to pull each other down by commenting on each other's actions.

All these events show that, due to materialistic pressures in modern society to look 'correct' and do better than others, the family values of unconditional love, respect for elders, etc. are rapidly declining. Not only this, greed for money and possessions dominates people's thinking.

6. Even though both, the frog from Vikram Seth's poem 'The Frog and the Nightingale' and Abel's children from the play 'The Dear Departed' display greed, there are differences. Elaborate, in about 150 words, how the greed of the frog and that of Abel's children differ in motivation, actions, relationship, and consequences. CBSE SQP 2023

Ans. It is true to say that even though both, the frog from Vikram Seth's poem, The Frog and the Nightingale and Abel's children from the play, The Dear Departed, display greed, there are differences between them. We can understand the differences in the following manner—

(i) **Motivation** The frog's greed is motivated by a desire for personal gain and success whereas Abel's children are motivated by a desire for material possessions and inheritance.

(ii) **Actions** The frog takes advantage of the nightingale's talent and exploits her while Abel's children scheme to acquire their father's belongings through deception.

(iii) **Relationship** The frog and the nightingale have a business relationship while Abel's children have a familial relationship with their father.

(iv) **Consequences** The consequences of the frog's greed result in the nightingale's demise while the consequences of Abel's children's greed result in a family dispute and moral dilemma.

7. Victoria is quite different compared to her mother and aunt. Her love for her grandfather is evident in the play. As Victoria, write a letter to a friend expressing her feelings highlighting the values depicted through her character.

Ans. 37G, Mathew Street
Birmingham

5th March, 20XX

Dear Celia

How are you? I want to tell you about an incident which occurred yesterday. Grandfather was lying down due to feeling dazed but my mother mistook him to be dead. She did not even call a doctor to confirm his supposed death. My father also sent a message to my Aunt Elizabeth about Grandpa's death. Then my mother, with the help from my father, quietly shifted some of Grandpa's belongings to her own room before Aunt Elizabeth came to mourn grandfather. She made Papa wear grandfather's new slippers, although they did not fit him. I was shocked to see my mother taking advantage of his assumed death by pinching his possessions. Actually, she should have been grieving over his 'death'.

Aunt Elizabeth also appears to be equally self-centred. My grandfather is a straightforward man with a decisive mind. I love him and share his pains. May God grant him a long life.

Convey my respects to your parents.

With regards

Victoria

ASSESSMENT EXERCISE

Extract Based Questions

Read the following extracts carefully and answer the questions that follow.

1. **Mrs. Jordan:** No! For myself it's such a relief to get into the black. And now perhaps you'll tell us all about it. What did the doctor say?

Mrs. Slater: Oh, he's not been near yet.

Mrs. Jordan: Not been near?

Ben: (in the same breath). Didn't you send for him at once?

Mrs. Slater: Of course I did. Do you take me for a fool? I sent Henry at once for Dr . Pringle, but he was out.

Ben: You should have gone for another. Eh, Eliza

Mrs. Jordan: Oh yes. It's a fatal mistake.

(a) What is 'another' referred to here?

(b) What is meant by 'fatal' here?

(c) What is the real intention of the two speakers in saying these words?

(d) Why was the mistake not really 'fatal'?

2. **Mrs. Jordan :** Well, we'll think about it after tea, and then we'll look through his bits of things and make a list of them. There's all the furniture in his room.

Henry : There's no jewellery or valuables of that sort.

Mrs. Jordan : Except his gold watch. He promised that to our Jimmy.

Mrs. Slater : Promised your Jimmy! I never heard of that.

Mrs. Jordan : Oh, but he did, Amelia, when he was living with us. He was very fond of Jimmy.

(a) Who is 'He' referred to in the present context?

(b) Synonym of 'promised' is ....

(c) Why does Mrs. Jordan make this claim?

(d) What did 'He' promise to Jimmy?

3. **Mrs. Jordan :** You know, father, it's quite time you came to live with us again. We'd make you very comfortable.

Mrs. Slater : No, he's not been with us as long as he was with you.

Mrs. Jordan : I may be wrong, but I don't think father will fancy living on with you after what's happened today.

Abel : It seems to me that neither of you has any cause to feel proud about the way you've treated me.

Mrs. Slater : If I've done anything wrong, I'm sure I'm sorry for it.

Mrs. Jordan : And I can't say more than that, too.

Abel : It's a bit late to say it, now. Neither of you cared to put up with me.

(a) What does 'it' refer to?

(b) Antonym of 'late' is ....

(c) What does the speaker imply when he says that neither of his listeners 'cared to put up with' him?

(d) What is the speaker complaining about?

Short Answer Type Questions

Answer the following questions in 30-40 words.

1. Why does Victoria think that her parents have pinched (stolen) the bureau?
2. Despite being very fond of her Grandpa, why was Victoria reluctant to go to his room to fetch his bunch of keys?
3. Why was the family surprised to see the grandfather alive?
4. "Drat me if that isn't my clock too. What the devil's been going on in this house?" Who says this and what exactly has been going on in the house?
5. How did Elizabeth treat Mr. Abel Merryweather?

Long Answer Type Questions

Answer the following questions in about 150 words.

1. "The old should make their will discreetly without being swayed by emotions and sentiments". Do you agree with the statement? Justify your answer with reference to Abel Merryweather's daughters.
2. The play conveys the message that old people deserve to be treated with great care and love. Write a paragraph on the topic "Old People Should be Loved."
3. Abel Merryweather is very upset at his daughters' behaviour. He expresses his feelings to a friend in a letter. As Abel, write the letter deploring the decline of values required in children when they become adults.

CHAPTER 2

Julius Caesar

by William Shakespeare

About the DRAMA Julius Caesar, an able general and a conqueror, returns to Rome amidst immense popularity after defeating the sons of Pompey. The people celebrate his victorious return and Mark Antony offers him the crown which he refuses. Jealous of Caesar's growing power and afraid that one day Julius may become a dictator, Cassius instigates a conspiracy to murder Caesar. He realises that to gain legitimacy in the eyes of the Romans, he must win over the noble Brutus to his side, as Brutus is the most trusted and respected in Rome. Brutus, joins the conspiracy feeling that everyone is driven by motives as honourable as his own. Ironically, Caesar is murdered at the foot of Pompey's statue.

Important Characters

- **Julius Caesar** He is the greatest and most powerful of the Romans. Being large-hearted, he thinks of common welfare. He is a courageous and brave general. He is assassinated by Brutus, Cassius and a band of conspirators who feel that Caesar is too ambitious and may aspire to apply for dictatorship over the Roman republic.
- **Calpurnia** She is Caesar's wife. Calpurnia is superstitious about her dreams. She takes her dream to be an evil omen which signifies murder of her husband. She is worried about her husband's well-being and warns Caesar against going to the senate that day.
- **Mark Antony** Mark Antony is a loyal friend and a devoted follower of Caesar. He is a very cunning man and is able to manipulate people. He is shattered by Caesar's death and wants revenge. He is a very effective speaker, who successfully dupes (misleads) Brutus to permit him to speak at Caesar's funeral and incites the crowd to rebel and take revenge for Caesar's assassination.
- **Marcus Brutus** Marcus Brutus is a true patriot, a judicial magistrate of Rome and a powerful public figure. He is a very dear friend of Caesar, but joins Cassius in the conspiracy to assassinate Caesar. He does so for his great love of Rome and for democracy.
- **Caius Cassius** Cassius is the mastermind and organiser behind the assassination of Caesar. He assembles all the conspirators and convinces Brutus to kill Caesar on the grounds of ambition and threat to the democracy of Rome.
- **Decius Brutus** Decius Brutus is the co-conspirator in Caesar's assassination. He is the one who persuades Caesar to attend the session at the Senate House by fabricating a positive interpretation of Calpurnia's dream.

Summary of the Drama

Stage Setting The play opens with Caesar at his home. The weather is bad with flashes of lighting and sounds of thunder.

Act II Scene II

Calpurnia's Interpretation of her Dream

Caesar comments that both the Earth and heaven are not at peace, as Calpurnia had thrice cried out in her sleep, "Help, ho! They murder Caesar!" He commands a servant to go to the priest and ask them to sacrifice an animal to find out the future events. Just then, Calpurnia enters and says that Caesar should not go out of his home today. However, Caesar is very arrogant and is adamant (firm) on going out. He dismisses her fears as something foolish.

Calpurnia is frightened as she dreamt of Caesar's bleeding statue and that many Romans dipped their hands in Caesar's blood with a smile. She depicts her dream to be an ill omen (bad sign) along with other horrifying things witnessed by the staff, watchman and others. These sights were a lioness giving birth on the streets, warriors fighting upon clouds, graves opening and the dead stepping out, etc. She becomes fearful that something unfortunate may happen to Caesar as these events are unusual and signified death and obstacles. Therefore, she requests Caesar to stay at home and not venture out.

Caesar gives in to Calpurnia's Plea and Agrees to Stay at Home

Caesar finds Calpurnia's fear and anxiety strange. He feels that if destiny has determined someone's death, it cannot be avoided. Besides, all the happenings were the same for the whole world and not only for him, so he would definitely go out. Just then, the servant comes back from his visit to the priest and states that the priests had advised him to stay at home because when they sacrificed an animal in Caesar's name, they found no heart within. This was an extremely bad omen. Hearing this, Calpurnia pleads with him to stay back. Caesar gives in to Calpurnia's request and agrees to stay at home.

Decius Brutus Comes to Fetch Caesar

Decius Brutus, one of the conspirators, arrives at Caesar's home to take him to the Senate House, where other conspirators are waiting to execute their plan and assassinate (kill) Caesar. Caesar informs Decius about his decision to stay at home and tells him to inform the senators about the same. Caesar also tells Decius about Calpurnia's dream and her interpretation of it.

Decius Brutus' Interpretation of Calpurnia's Dream

Decius Brutus is very clever in the art of flattery. To make Caesar come to the Senate House, he says that Calpurnia's dream has been interpreted wrongly. He tells Caesar that the smiling Romans who were dipping their hands in his blood signifies that Rome will revitalise itself due to him. Decius also tells him that his possessions will be fought for and preserved as immortal mementos of pride. He pampers Caesar's ego by telling him that if he refuses to go to the Senate House on the grounds of his wife's anxiety because of a dream, he will become a laughing stock. Further, Decius tells him that the senators have decided to offer him the crown and if he doesn't go, they may change their mind.

Caesar Agrees to go to the Senate House

Caesar falls into Decius' well-set trap, and decides to go to the Senate House. As per the conspiracy, all the conspirators, Brutus, Publius, Metellus, Ligarius, Casca, Trebonius and Cinna, arrive at Caesar's house. Caesar invites them to have wine with him before they leave for the Senate House together as friends. Brutus is disturbed and whispers aside that sometimes what is seen is not the truth. His heart grieves when he thinks that being 'like' a friend is not the same as 'being' a friend.

Act III Scene I

Caesar Arrives at the Senate House with the Conspirators

When everyone reaches the Senate House, the proceedings begin as planned. Trebonius takes Antony away to prevent him from interferring in their plan of assassinating Caesar. Suddenly, Metellus Cimber falls on his knees and humbly requests Caesar to revoke or cancel the order of his brother's banishment (exile). Caesar dismisses his request by saying that he is as stable as the Northern Star which is known for its fixed position and stability. Thus, such requests cannot move him. Caesar stays firm even when Brutus and Cassius join Metellus in his request.

Caesar's Assasination

Casca now grabs the opportunity to stab Caesar to death, followed by the other conspirators. Casca is the first one to stab Caesar and Brutus the last one. When Caesar sees Brutus as one of the conspirators, he is hurt at the betrayal from the one whom he confided in. Caesar thus cries "Et tu Brute!" (Even you, Brutus) before his last breath. Cinna and Cassius think that they must declare to the people of Rome that they are now free from the unseen tyranny of Caesar. After the death of Caesar, all the conspirators cry, "Liberty! Freedom! Tyranny is dead!"

Antony's Expression of Grief and Pleading for Death

Antony, who had been taken away by Trebonius, re–enters. He is devastated to see the noble Caesar reduced to a bleeding piece of flesh. He speaks to the dead body of Caesar in grief and love. He, then, turns to Brutus and begs to be killed if he is their target as well, for he preferred to be killed with the same dagger (knife/sword) and in the same hour as Caesar. Brutus feels sad for Antony and tells him not to request for his death. He tells Antony that they love him just as any other Roman and he is equally important as the others.

Antony's Pretentious Behaviour and Crafty Plans

Antony pretends a reconciliation with the conspirators and shakes hands with each one of them to gain their trust. He requests them to let him speak at Caesar's funeral as expected from a friend in the form of a farewell speech. Antony assures them that he is harmless and hopes that they would tell him the reasons that led them to put Caesar to death.

Brutus Allows Antony to Speak at Caesar's Funeral

Although Cassius is not in favour of allowing Antony to speak at Caesar's funeral, Brutus grants Antony the permission to do so. Brutus satisfies Cassius' objection by telling him that he had imposed two conditions on Antony. First, Antony will speak only after he (Brutus) will have addressed the mob (crowd) with the reasons of Caesar's assassination and second, Antony will speak only with their permission and definitely not against any of them.

Act III Scene II

Brutus Addresses the Romans and Expresses his Love for Liberty

At Caesar's funeral, Brutus steps up to the pulpit and addresses the crowd. He asks people to believe what he is about to tell them and to stay patient till the end. He expresses his love for his friend Caesar but he says that he loves Rome more than any other person. He justifies his role as a conspirator by saying that he pitied the wrong being done to the Romans. He tells them that Caesar had become very ambitious and his hunger for power may have reduced each one of them into slaves. He also tells the crowd that whenever needed, his countrymen could take his life.

The citizens of Rome accept his reasons and wish him to be crowned. Everyone is convinced that Caesar was a dictator and it is good that Rome has got rid of him. Brutus then directs the crowd to stay and listen to Mark Antony's funeral speech, which he is giving with their permission. Then, he departs from the place, where the crowd had gathered.

Antony's Speech

Antony is fully aware that the audience is against the noble Caesar. Therefore, he adopts a tactful manner to address the crowd. He proceeds to counter all the arguments given by Brutus one at a time. As he builds up his reasoning, the crowd seems to get influenced with his logic and sorrow. Antony tells the crowd that Brutus cannot be wrong because he is an honourable man and if he says Caesar was ambitious, he certainly must have been so.

Then, Antony reminds the public of how Caesar used to bring captives to his country and the ransom money he got from them went into the state treasury. He questions the audience whether an ambitious man would do such a thing. He also reminds the people how previously Caesar had refused the crown three times. If he had been ambitious, he would not have refused it. The citizens start analysing what Mark Antony tells them and they feel that Caesar had been wronged.

Antony Uses Caesar's Will to Influence the Crowd

Antony very cleverly tells the crowd that he has Caesar's will with him but he will not read it out. He says that if he reads it, everyone will become violent and he does not want to arouse a rebellion. The crowd gets excited on hearing this and wishes to know what is written in the will. Antony, as a brilliant orator, plays with words and makes everyone curious about Caesar's will.

He purposely emphasises on the most unkind wound i.e. the wound by Brutus, his dear friend, and how he hurt Caesar emotionally more than physically.

Then, the people are incited to anger by Antony. Antony reveals Caesar's love for Romans and why he deserved to be loved by them. He tells them that Caesar, in his will, has left his parks, orchards and all his land open for Romans for their common pleasures. He also tells them that they all are his heirs (inheritors) as he has left seventy five drachmas (silver coins) for each one of them out of his personal treasures.

The Crowd Turns Ferocious

After hearing Caesar's will, people are incited and filled with revenge. They want to burn down the conspirators' houses to ashes. Antony is pleased as his speech proves to serve the purpose he wanted to achieve. Now, the crowd is convinced that Caesar was not ambitious and Brutus was a liar and murderer.

After the Extract

After Antony instigates the mob to take revenge, he plans for the future threats with Julius Caesar's nephew—Octavius Caesar. Brutus and Cassius are defeated and they kill themselves.

Word Meaning

Word	Meaning
walk forth	venture out
stood on ceremonies	paid much attention to omens and forecasts
whelped	given birth
right form of war	correct battle order
hurtled	went through
beyond all use	most unnatural
blaze forth	announce
necessary	inevitable
augurers	persons who can tell the future
entrails	guts
thy	your
morrow	morning
in very happy time	at the right moment
graybeards	contemptuous term for the senators
lusty	strong; vigorous
portents	predictions
imminent	about to happen
blood	symbolises Caesar's spirit or influence
expounded	explained
great men ...... cognizance	great men shall gather around Caesar and stain their handkerchiefs in his blood which will serve as colours added to a coat of arms, an object of reverence, mementos and a badge of service
that every ...... think upon	My heart grieves when I think that being like a friend is not the same as being a friend
exeunt	exit
amiss	wrong
redress	correct
puissant	powerful
couchings and these lowly courtesies	bowing and bending
pre-ordinance	order that has existed from earlier times
first decree	law passed earlier
spurn thee like a cur	refuse you like a dog
enfranchisement	citizenship
pray to move	pray to others to change their minds
resting	permanent
fellow in the firmament	matching star in the sky
Et tu, Brute	even you, Brutus
tyranny	oppression

Word	Meaning
spoils	trophies of war
little measure	small piece of ground on which your body lies
beseech	ask
bear me hard	bear a grudge against me
reek	stench
master	powerful
in strength of malice	which may appear to be hostile
reverence	respect
dignities	honours
render	give
conceit	consider
grieve	cry
corse	corpse
modesty	understatement
compact	agreement
good regard	serious consideration
order	ceremony
will	will go
protest	announce
devise of	think of
woe	pity
prophesy	predict
light	fall
strife	war
cumber	burden
in use	common
Ate	Greek Goddess of revenge
carrion	dead
custom of fell deeds	terrible deeds shall become so familiar
carrion	dead
my cause	the cause that I represent
believe me for mine honour	believe me because you know I am respectable
censure	judge; criticise me harshly
senses	understanding
valour	bravery
bondman	slave
rude	uncivilised

Word	Meaning
do to Brutus	you may assassinate me if I become ambitious
question	reasons for
enrolled	recorded
extenuated	diminished
enforced	exaggerated; emphasised
the commonwealth	the free republic
slew	killed
lover	friend
parts	qualities
clamours	celebrations
blest	blessed
oft interred	often hidden
lupercal	the feast of the God Lupercus
disprove	contradict
stood against	overcome the opposition of
poor	humble
wrong the dead	be unjust to Caesar, who has been assassinated, by calling him ambitious
to wrong myself	by not speaking what I know
you	by allowing you to be deceived by Brutus

Word	Meaning
napkins	handkerchiefs
bequeathing	bestowing
issue	heirs
meet	fitting, proper
mantle	cloak
Nervii	the most war-like of the Gallic tribes
envious	malicious
ingratitude	the blow struck by Brutus' ingratitude
all the while ran blood	which was covered with Caesar's blood
flourish'd	triumphed
flood of mutiny	wave of violence
wit	intelligence
worth	authority
action	gestures
utterance	eloquence
right on	directly
wherein	in what way
drachmas	silver coins
royal	generous
afoot	started

Textbook FOLDER

Here, we have covered questions given in the CBSE Textbook along with their answers.

ON PAGE 174-175

Q.5 Answer the following questions by selecting the correct options.

(i) When Caesar says, "Nor heaven nor earth have been at peace tonight" he sounds

(a) worried (b) angry
(c) joyous (d) frightened

Ans. (a) worried

(ii) Caesar's reference to the senators as 'graybeards' shows his ....

(a) confidence
(b) cowardice
(c) arrogance
(d) ambition

Ans. (c) arrogance

(iii) Decius Brutus changes Caesar's mind about going to the Senate by appealing to his ....

(a) ambition (b) vanity (c) greed (d) generosity

Ans. (b) vanity

(iv) The offer that Cassius makes to Antony after Caesar's assassination is that

(a) the conspirators would like to be friends with him.
(b) he may take Caesar's body to the pulpit and speak to the crowd praising Caesar for his achievements.
(c) his recommendations will be as strong as that of the conspirators while distributing the powers and benefits to friends.
(d) he may join the conspiracy against Caesar.

Ans. (a) the conspirators would like to be friends with him.

(v) Cassius tries to stop Brutus from letting Antony speak at Caesar's funeral as he

(a) knows the Roman mob loves Caesar and Antony
(b) knows Brutus is not a good orator
(c) knows they should not have killed Caesar
(d) knows Antony is a good orator who can sway the mob

Ans. (d) knows Antony is a good orator who can sway the mob

(vi) What prophecy does Antony make over Caesar's dead body?

(a) Romans will see Caesar's ghost roaming on the streets
(b) Rome will experience fierce civil war in which many people will die
(c) Rome will be ruled by Ate
(d) Roman women will smile at the death of Caesar

Ans. (b) Rome will experience fierce civil war in which many people will die.

(vii) After listening to Brutus' speech, the Third Citizen says 'Let him be Caesar'. This clearly shows he ....

(a) has not understood Brutus' reason for killing Caesar
(b) loved Caesar more than he loves Brutus
(c) loves Brutus more than he loved Caesar
(d) thinks Brutus killed Caesar to assume power

Ans. (c) loves Brutus more than he loved Caesar.

(viii) When Antony's calls the conspirators, 'honourable men', his tone is ....

(a) admiring (b) flattering
(c) angry (d) mocking

Ans. (d) mocking

(ix) Antony's reference to Caesar's conquest of the Nervii is to ....

(a) remind the mob of Caesar's greatness as a warrior
(b) make the mob feel afraid of being attacked by the war-like race
(c) make the crowd weep for Caesar who died at war
(d) stop and collect his emotions as he is feeling very upset

Ans. (a) remind the mob of Caesar's greatness as a warrior.

(x) Antony remark : Mischief, thou art afoot, Take thou what course thou wilt!, shows him to be

(a) a ruthless manipulator
(b) an honourable man
(c) a loyal friend
(d) a tactful man

Ans. (d) a tactful man

ON PAGE 176-177

Q.6 Answer the following questions in about 30-40 words.

(a) How do the heavens 'blaze forth' the death of Julius Caesar?

Ans. Whenever a bright shooting star falls down from the sky and leaves a blazing light behind it, it signifies the death of a prince or king. Thus, when Caesar died, a star blazed forth in the sky.

(b) What does Calpurnia try to convince Caesar of?

Ans. Calpurnia tries to convince Caesar to not venture out on that day as she had dreamt of a bleeding statue of Caesar in which smiling Romans were dipping their hands. She considers it to be a bad omen and pleads with Caesar to stay indoors.

(c) Why does Calpurnia say "Caesar's wisdom is consumed in confidence"? What does she mean?

Ans. Calpurnia says this because Ceaser has refused to stay at home inspite of the ill-omens. When Calpurnia says this she means that Caesar's over confidence has overpowered his wisdom and analytical mind.
This is why he is willfully disregarding the overwhelming presence of ill-omens.

(d) What does Calpurnia dream about Caesar? How does Decius Brutus interpret the dream?

Ans. Calpurnia dreamt that Caesar spouted blood from a hundred places and many Romans came and washed their hands in it. Decius Brutus interprets Calpurnia's dream in a positive light to change Caesar's mind about not going to the Senate House that day. He tells Caesar that the bleeding statue which Calpurnia saw in her dream signifies that Rome depends on him to renew its vitality. He also says that the smiling Romans who bathe their hands in his blood will consider having his belongings as treasures.

(e) What are the arguments put forward by Decius Brutus to convince Caesar to go to the Capitol?

Ans. To convince Caesar to go to the capitol, Decius Brutus put forward many arguments. First, Decius Brutus convinces Caesar that Calpurnia's dream is a good omen. Second, he says the senators want to crown him. If he does not go to the Senate, the senators may change their minds.

(f) Why is Decius more successful than Calpurnia in persuading Caesar?

Ans. Decius is more successful than Calpurnia in convincing Caesar as he appeals to Caesar's vanity. He tells Caesar that the senators want to crown him, whereas Calpurnia only talks about her dream. He also interprets Calpurnia's dreams as positive indicating the importance Caesar has in the Roman Empire. As a result, Caesar is flattered and convinced to go the capital.

(g) What is the petition put before Caesar by the conspirators? How does Caesar respond to it?

Ans. The conspirators put a request before Caesar to repeal the banishment of Metellus Cimber's brother. Caesar responds to it by refusing the appeal. He says that he is as unchanging as the Northern Star, which is known for its fixed position. Hence, he will not revoke his order at any cost as this will undermine his authority and also render the laws made earlier meaningless.

(h) Who says 'Et tu Brute'? When are these words spoken? Why?

Or **'Et tu Brute' These were the last words of Julius Caesar's. Elucidate with reference to the drama 'Julius Caesar'. Why did Caesar say these words before his death?** **CBSE 2024**

Ans. The words 'Et tu Brute' are the last words spoken by Caesar just before dying. It means, 'You too, Brutus?' Caesar speaks these words as he had not expected such a treacherous and disloyal act from Brutus, his trusted friend.

(i) In the moments following Caesar's death, what do the conspirators proclaim to justify Caesar's death?

Ans. In the moments following Caesar's death, the conspirators proclaim that Caesar's oppression is over with his killing. They announce 'liberty, freedom and enfranchisement' (right of citizenship), at public places to justify Caesar's murder. This announcement is made to convince the Romans that with Caesar's murder, democratic rights will be restored to them.

(j) Seeing the body of Caesar, Antony is overcome by grief. What does he say about Caesar?

Ans. After seeing Ceaser's dead body, Antony praises Caesar in every way possible. He recollects his conquests, glories, triumphs and spoils. He calls him 'mighty' and wonders how 'low' he lies in his death. He pays him a warm tribute by calling him a 'bleeding piece of earth' and 'the ruins of the noblest man'.

(k) Whom does Antony call "the choice and master spirits of this age"? Why?

Ans. Antony calls Brutus and the other conspirators the choice and master spirits of this age because they had murdered Caesar and now Rome would be ruled by them. He uses such flattery to win them over.

(l) How do Brutus and Cassius respond to Antony's speech?

Ans. Brutus and Cassius had earlier refused Antony when he begged for his death. Now, they offered him a share of their power in reply to Antony's speech.

(m) Why does Cassius object to allowing Antony to speak at Caesar's funeral? How does Brutus overcome this objection?

Ans. Cassius does not want Brutus to allow Antony to speak at Caesar's funeral because he is fearful that something unfortunate might happen to them, in case his words move the crowd. However, Brutus overcomes Cassius' objection by assuring him that he himself will address the people before Antony with the reasons for Caesar's assassination and that Antony will not speak against them in any way.

(n) What are the conditions imposed by the conspirators before allowing Antony to speak at Caesar's funeral?

Or Antony was permitted to address the Romans on Caesar's funeral on a few conditions laid down by the conspirators. State the conditions. **CBSE 2024 C**

Ans. The conspirators laid down the following conditions on Antony's speaking at Caesar's funeral

(*i*) He will speak only after Brutus has finished speaking.

(*ii*) He will not blame the conspirators for killing Caesar.

(*iii*) He can speak whatever good he wants of Caesar, but must mention that he is speaking this with the permission of all of them.

(o) When he is left alone with the body of Caesar, what does Antony call Brutus and the others?

Ans. When Antony is left alone with the body of Caesar, he refers to the conspirators, Brutus and the others as butchers as they stabbed Caesar without any pity and hesitation. He also seeks forgiveness from Caesar for being polite with the conspirators.

(p) What prediction does Antony make regarding the future events in Rome?

Ans. Antony predicts that the country will witness a civil war which will be very destructive. Foul deeds will be so common that all feelings of compassion will vanish from the hearts of men. The ghost of Caesar shall roam about to take revenge and punish his enemies. The earth will be polluted by the evil smell of rotting bodies.

(q) What reasons does Brutus give for murdering Caesar?

***Or* Why does Brutus kill Caesar?** **CBSE 2016**

Ans. Brutus gives various reasons for assassinating Caesar. He says that Caesar had become ambitious and would have wronged the Romans if he had lived and became a dictator. He justifies Caesar's killing by stating that he loved Caesar as a friend but not more than Rome and so conspired against him for the sake of their country.

(r) Who says, 'Let him be Caesar'? What light does this throw on the speaker?

Ans. The third citizen, who signifies the common citizens of Rome, speaks these words after Brutus has finished his speech justifying the reasons for Caesar's death.

This shows that the citizens are fully satisfied with the reasons given by Brutus and they are all in praise for Brutus. They praise Brutus and show their sympathy for the act.

(s) Why is Antony's speech more effective?

Ans. Antony appeals to the basic sentiments of the common people. He very cleverly directs his speech towards Caesar's greatness as a human being. He arouses the citizens' feelings of revenge against the conspirators. So, his speech proves more effective than Brutus' speech, as it is more logical and appeals to the minds of the people.

(t) At the end of the scene, what is the fate of Brutus and Cassius?

Ans. At the end of the scene, Antony had finished his speech and succeeded in arousing the feelings of anger and revenge amongst the citizens of Rome. Following this, a vicious civil war broke out in Rome. Brutus and Cassius ultimately killed themselves after their armies were defeated.

ON PAGE 177-178

Q.7 Julius Caesar and Antony reveal something about their character in their words and actions. We also learn about them from what other people say. Can you pick out the words that describe them from the box given below? Also, pick out lines from the play to illustrate your choice.

superstitious arrogant loyal clever overconfident manipulative good orator ambitious brave great conqueror generous fearless loves flattery firm shrewd crafty

Person		Extract from play		What it tells us about the character
Julius Caeser	1.	The things that threaten'd me Ne'er look'd but on my back; when they shall see The face of Caesar, they are vanished.	1.	Arrogant
	2.			
	3.			
	4.			
	5.			
	6.			
Mark Antony	1.		1.	Loyal
	2.			
	3.			
	4.			
	5.			

Ans.

Person		Extract from play		What it tells us about the character
Julius Caeser	1.	The things that threaten'd me Ne'er look'd but on my back; when they shall see The face of Caesar, they are vanished.	1.	Arrogant
	2.	Cowards die many a times before their deaths: the valiant never taste of death but once	2.	Brave
	3.	What can be avoided whose end is purposed by the mighty gods?	3.	Fearless
	4.	Shall Caesar send a lie? Have I in conquest stretch'd mine arm so far, To be afraid to tell graybeards the truth?	4.	Great conqueror
	5.	From you great Rome shall suck reviving blood, and that great men shall press for tinctures, stains, frelics and cognizance.	5.	Loves flattery
	6.	Caesar doth not wrong, nor without cause will he be satisfied.	6.	Overconfident
Mark Antony	1.	shall it not grieve thee dearer than thy death, to see thy thy Anthony making his peace, shaking the bloody fingers of thy foes	1.	Loyal
	2.	I know not, gentlemen, what you intend, who else must be let blood, who else is rank: If I myself, there is no hour so fit	2.	Fearless
	3.	Good friends, sweet friends, let me not stir you up to such a sudden flood of mutiny	3.	Shrewd
	4.	My heart is in the coffin there with Caesar, And I must pause till it come back to me	4.	Manipulative
	5.	I will not do them wrong; I rather choose to wrong the dead, to wrong myself and you, than I will wrong suck honourable men.	5.	Crafty
	6.	For I have neither wit, nor words, nor worth, action, nor utterance, nor the power of speech, to stir men's blood	6.	Oratory

ON PAGE 179

Q.8 In the play 'Julius Caesar', we meet the Roman mob. We find that as Brutus and Antony speak, the mob displays certain qualities and characteristics.

Given below are some characteristics of the mob. Complete the table by quoting the lines wherein these are revealed.

Words/ actions of the mob		Characteristics
1.		Foolish
2.		Does not understand the ideals of democracy
3.		Emotional
4.		Greedy
5.		Fickle
6.		Violent

Ans.

	Words/ actions of the mob	Characteristics
1.	'bring him with triumph home unto his house'. 'methinks there is much reason in his sayings'. 'I fear there will a worse come in his place'.	Foolish
2.	'let him be Caesar'. 'Caesar's better parts shall be crown'd in Brutus	Does not understand the ideals of democracy
3.	'revenge! About! Seek! Burn! Fire! Kill! Slay! Let not a traitor live!'	Emotional
4.	'they were villains, murderers: the will! Read the will'. 'the will! Let's stay and hear the will'. Most noble Caesar! We'll revenge his death'. 'o royal Caesar!'	Greedy
5.	'this Caesar was a tyrant'. 'if thou consider rightly of the matter, Caesar has had great wrong'. 'Away, then! Come, seek the conspirators'.	Fickle
6.	we'll mutiny'. 'we'll burn the house of Brutus'.	Violent

Q.9 Antony employs a number of devices to produce the desired effect on the mob. These devices maybe described as rhetorical devices. He first speaks in such a manner that it seems to the mob that he is in full agreement with Brutus about Caesar. Then step by step he moves away from Brutus' position, depicting Brutus as a villain and Caesar as a wronged man. Copy and complete the following table by showing how Antony builds the argument in Caesar's favour.

	Antony's words	Arguments
1.	I come to bury Caesar, not to praise him.	Does not eulogise Caeser
2.	The noble Brutus Hath told you Caesar was ambitious: If it were so, it was a grievous fault, And grievously hath Caesar answer'd it.	Seemingly agrees with Brutus
3.		
4.		
5.		

Ans.

	Antony's words	Arguments
1.	I come to bury Caesar, not to praise him.	Does not eulogise Caeser
2.	The noble Brutus Hath told you Caesar was ambitious: If it were so, it was a grievous fault, And grievously hath Caesar answer'd it.	Seemingly agrees with Brutus
3.	He hath brought many captives home to Rome Whose ransoms did the general coffers fill: Did this in Caesar seem ambitious? When that the poor have cried, Caesar hath wept: Ambition should be made of sterner stuff.	Counters the charge of ambition put by Brutus
4.	You all did see that on the lupercal I thrice presented him a kingly crown, Which he did thrice refuse: was this ambition?	Reminds people of familiar incident
5.	I speak not to disprove what brutus spoke, But here I am to speak what I do know	Cautious: does not want to annoy the mob

ON PAGE 180

Q.10 Read the extracts given below and answer the questions that follow.

I. CAESAR Cowards die many a times before their deaths;
The valiant never taste of death but once.
Of all the wonders that I yet have heard.
It seems to me most strange that men should fear;
Seeing that death, a necessary end,
Will come when it will come.

(i) Whom is Ceasar speaking to? Why does he say these words?

Ans. Caesar is speaking these words to his wife Calpurnia. Caesar's wife sees a horrible dream and bad omens signalling death and disaster. She requests him not go to the Capitol. As a reply, Caesar states these words, highlighting that he is not a coward who is always afraid of his death.

(ii) What fears has the listener expressed?

Ans. The listener expresses the fear that all those ill-omens and horrid sights signal the death of some prince and naturally he will be Caesar.

(iii) What is the basis for the fears expressed?

Ans. Calpurnia's fears find basis in the unearthly events reported in the past few days and the strange dream which she had the previous night.

II. But here's a parchment with the seal of Caesar;
I found it in his closet, 'tis his will:
Let but the commons hear this testament—
Which, pardon me, I do not mean to read—
And they would go and kiss dead Caesar's wounds

(i) Who speaks these words? Where is the speaker at this moment?

Ans. Antony is speaking these words to the Roman mob while standing on the pulpit in the market place.

(ii) What are the contents of Caeser's will he is referring to?

Ans. Caesar's will gives every Roman seventy-five drachmas. Moreover, he has left all his walks, new orchards to the common men. He had made them his 'heirs' and opened everything for common pleasures.

(iii) Why does the speaker read Caesar's will to the citizens?

Ans. Antony reads Caesar's will to the citizens to play on their sympathy, and to make Caesar look like a great and kind ruler.

(iv) What is the reaction of the listeners to the reading of the will?

Ans. The listeners are convinced that Caesar was not ambitious and he was brutally murdered by the conspirators for their own selfish ends. Now they are after the conspirators and ready to burn their houses.

ON PAGE 180-181

Q.11 Given below are some questions based on a reading of the play 'Julius Caesar.' These questions are not for testing in the exam. These are for deeper understanding of the play and characters.

(a) Why was the conspiracy to assassinate Julius Caesar hatched?

Ans. The conspiracy to assassinate Caesar was hatched to prevent Caesar from being crowned as the king of Rome. Cassius and Brutus didn't want Caesar to become the dictator of Rome and rule over Romans, though for different reasons.

(b) Was Caesar really ambitious? Find evidence from the play to support your answer.

Ans. Caesar was not ambitious at all. He was an able and patriotic leader who had brought many glories to Rome. He was sympathetic towards the poor. He refused to be crowned thrice and was selfless as he promised seventy five drachmas (silver coins) to every Roman out of his possessions. Thus, he cannot be called ambitious in any way.

(c) What was Cassius' motive for murdering Julius Caesar?

Ans. Cassius was jealous of Caesar's growing popularity. He was afraid that Caesar will become the dictator of Rome soon. So, he wished to murder Caesar.

(d) Why was it essential for the conspirators to include Brutus in the conspiracy?

Ans. It was essential for the conspirators to include Brutus so that their cause could be sustained in front of the Romans. They tricked Brutus to join them in the conspiracy to escape the blame for the unreasonable killing of Caesar.

(e) What were the mistakes made by Brutus that led to the failure of the conspiracy?

Ans. Brutus' ignorance towards Cassius' fear and objection to not let Antony speak at Caesar's funeral led to the failure of the conspiracy. It was because of Brutus' faith in Antony that gave the opportunity to Antony to turn the crowd against them and win over the Romans to Caesar's side.

(f) Comment on Caesar's friendship with Antony.

Ans. Antony was a dear friend of Caesar and vowed upon Caesar's dead body to take revenge for his death. Antony held a special place in Caesar's heart and life. This is evident as the conspirators take him away before assassinating Caesar. They knew that he would intervene and save Caesar. Thus, Caesar's and Antony's friendship was deep and true.

(g) Write a brief character sketch of Antony.

Ans. Antony is a noble and strong Roman. He is a devoted follower of Caesar. He has a reputation of being militarily accomplished, politically shrewd and a skilful orator. His attitude persuades the conspirators to allow him to give a speech and his impactful speech moves the crowd against the conspirators. In short, he is an able and wise leader.

(h) What is the role of Julius Caesar's ghost in the play, Julius Caesar?

Ans. The ghost of Julius Caesar appears twice in the play. Once, before Brutus when he is sleeping in a tent, it stood by his bedside and said nothing. The second time, it appears in the battle at Philippi, in front of Antonius and Octavius. The purpose of Caesar's ghost was to make Brutus realise his mistake and repent for it.

(i) Why does Antony call Brutus 'the noblest Roman of them all'?

Ans. Antony's comment that Brutus was 'the noblest Roman of them all' is laced with sarcasm. He do so because he was the only conspirator who stabbed Caesar for the love of Rome, and to gain the trust and sympathy of the Romans.

(j) How do Brutus and Cassius meet their end ?

Ans. Brutus states that their forces should move to Philippi and attack the enemy. Cassius does not agree and leaves. On the plains of Philippi, Brutus and Cassius reach with their forces.

With Octavius' interference, their wrongdoing comes to an end. Then the forces of Cassius and Antony fight, in which Antony emerges victorious. Cassius could not accept this defeat and commits suicide. Brutus too is disheartened and kills himself with his own sword.

ON PAGE 181

Q.12 A reporter covers the event of the assassination of Julius Caesar in the Senate giving graphic details and a catchy headline. Write the newspaper report in about 150 words.

Ans.

Julius Caesar Murdered

by a Press Reporter

Today was a dark day in Rome's history. A great commander and general was assassinated in broad daylight by a group of conspirators.

Julius Caesar came to the Senate House expecting to be crowned as the king of Rome. When Metellus Cimber requested Caesar to repeal his brother's exile from Rome, Caesar refused it despite the request being seconded by Brutus and Cassius. On Caesar's refusal, the conspirators stabbed him one by one. Brutus, a good friend of Caesar, was the last one to stab him.

Caesar was shocked to see that his good friend had also stabbed him. He cried, "You too, Brutus!" before he fell down and died. Then, the conspirators shouted slogans of liberty, freedom and independence over his dead body. When Mark Antony, another good friend of Julius Caesar, saw this, he was shocked and asked the conspirators to kill him too but Brutus refused his request.

It is believed that Calpurnia, Caesar's wife, had a premonition about Caesar's death. She requested him to not step out from his home that day. However, Caesar did not listen to her and paid for it with his life. Thus, a great general's life has been extinguished due to the dark deeds of some conspirators.

The fact that this act of inhuman violence happened inside the Senate where all weapons are banned makes sure that this day will be remembered in history as the black day when Romans forsook their vows.

REVIEW EXERCISE

Including Competency Based Questions

Extract Based Questions

Read the following extracts carefully and answer the questions that follow.

1. **Caesar shall forth** the things that threaten'd me
Ne'er look'd but on my back; when they shall see
The face of Caesar, they are vanished.

   (a) Where is Caesar planning to go to?

Ans. Caesar is planning to go to the Senate House.

   (b) What does the word 'vanished' mean in this context?

Ans. The word 'vanished' here means 'gone away'.

   (c) Caesar said these words in reply to what request?

Ans. Caesar said these words in reply to his wife Calpurnia's request to not go out of his home that day.

   (d) What omens were responsible for the other person making this request?

Ans. The bad omens responsible for Calpurnia making this request were a lioness giving birth on the streets, the dead coming out of their graves, blood of warriors falling on the Capitol and other ominous happenings.

2. **Do not go forth to-day** call it my fear
That keeps you in the house, and not your own.
We'll send Mark Antony to the senate-house:
And he shall say you are not well to-day:
Let me, upon my knee, prevail in this.

   (a) What was Calpurnia's fear? What made her feel so?

Ans. Calpurnia's fear was that something bad was going to happen to Caesar. Her dream and the bad omens made her feel so.

   (b) Which word or phrase in the extract means 'request'?

Ans. The phrase 'prevail in' means 'request'.

   (c) How did Caesar react to her fear?

Ans. Caesar did not seem to be affected by her fear but he did not want to increase her anxiety. So, he decided to stay at home.

   (d) Was Caesar's decision changed later on? Why?

Ans. Caesar' changed his decision to not go to the Capitol that day later on due to Decius Brutus appealing to his vanity.

3. Shall Caesar send a lie?
Have I in conquest stretch'd mine arm so far,
To be afraid to tell graybeards the truth?
Decius, go tell them Caesar will not come.

   (a) What place was Caesar supposed to go to?

Ans. Caesar was supposed to go to the Senate House that day.

   (b) Who are the 'graybeards' that Caesar is referring to?

Ans. The 'graybeards' that Caesar is referring to are the senators of Rome.

   (c) Why had Decius come to Caesar's place?

Ans. Decius had come to persuade Caesar to go to the Senate House.

   (d) What was Caesar's final decision? Was it wise?

Ans. On the persuasion of Decius, Caesar decided to go to the Senate House. But it was not a wise decision because Caesar was killed there.

4. **Decius Brutus** This dream is all amiss interpreted; It was a vision fair and fortunate: Your statue spouting blood in many pipes, In which so many smiling Romans bathed, Signifies that from you great Rome shall suck Reviving blood, and that great men shall press For tinctures, stains, relics and cognizance. This by Calpurnia's dream is signified.

   (a) Which 'vision' is referred to here?

Ans. The 'vision' referred to here is Calpurnia's dream in which she saw Roman people washing their hands in Caesar's blood.

   (b) The word .... in the extract means the same as 'incorrectly' or 'wrongly'.

Ans. 'amiss'

   (c) What is the speaker's interpretation of the vision?

Ans. Decius Brutus interprets the dream as a happy one. He feels it signifies that the Roman people depend on Caesar for their revitalisation and prosperity.

   (d) What was Caesar's reaction to what is said in this extract and its interpretation by the speaker?

Ans. Caesar's reaction to Decius Brutus' interpretation of Calpurnia's dream was to agree with Decius.
It prompted Caesar to go to the Senate House.

5. How foolish do your fears seem now, Calpurnia!
I am ashamed I did yield to them.
Give me my robe, for I will go.

(a) Where did Caesar decide to go?

Ans. Caesar decided to go to the Senate House.

(b) What does the word 'them' in the extract signify?

Ans. The word 'them' signifies Calpurnia's fear that the omens forecast Caesar's death.

(c) Why was Calpurnia afraid?

Ans. Calpurnia was afraid that the unnatural occurrences and her dream served as omens predicting Caesar's death as well as the end of peace in Rome.

(d) What prompted Caesar to go where he wanted to go?

Ans. Decius Brutus' positive interpretation of Calpurnia's dream and his mentioning that the senators wanted to crown Caesar that day prompted Caesar to go to the Senate House.

Or

(a) What were Calpurnia's fears? **CBSE 2020**

Ans. Calpurnia fears that her husband Caeser's life is in danger.

(b) Why did they seem foolish to Caeser?

Ans. They seemed foolish to Caeser because another Senator named Decius Brutus has manipulated Calpurnia's dreams as good omens.

(c) Where did Caeser want to go?

Ans. Caeser wants to go to the Senate House.

(d) What does the word 'yield' mean?

Ans. The word 'yield' means 'give way under force or pressure.'

6. I could be well moved, if I were as you:
If I could pray to move, prayers would move me:
But I am constant as the Northern Star,
Of whose true-fix'd and resting quality
There is no fellow in the firmament.

(a) By what and whose prayers is the speaker not moved?

Ans. Caesar is not moved by the prayers of Metellus Cimber to free his brother from banishment.

(b) Which word in the extract is an antonym of 'variable'?

Ans. The word 'constant' is an antonym of 'variable'.

(c) Where was the speaker when he said these words?

Ans. Caesar was in the Senate House when he said these words.

(d) What was the ultimate outcome of Caesar's refusal?

Ans. The ultimate outcome of Caesar's refusal was that he was stabbed and killed by the conspirators.

7. If thou dost bend and pray and fawn for him,
I spurn thee like a cut out of my way.

(a) Identify the speaker of the above extract.

Ans. The given lines are spoken by Julius Caeser.

(b) Who was bending, praying and fawning?

Ans. Metellius Cimber, along with Cassius and Brutus was bending, praying and fawning.

(c) In what context have the above words been spoken?

Ans. The given words are spoken by Caeser to refuse Metellius Cimber's request for freeing his brother from banishment.

(d) What do these words reveal about the character of the speaker?

Ans. The given lines indicate that the speaker is a strong-willed individual who does not tolerate traitors.

8. Antony O mighty Caesar! dost thou lie so low? Are all thy conquests, glories, triumphs, spoils, Shrunk to this little measure? Fare thee well. I know not, gentlemen, what you intend, Who else must be let blood, who else is rank: If I myself, there is no hour so fit As Caesar's death hour, nor no instrument Of half that worth as those your swords, made rich with the most noble blood of all this world.

(a) Why was Caesar lying so low?

Ans. Caesar was lying so low because he had fallen down after being murdered by the conspirators.

(b) What is meant by 'little measure' in the extract?

Ans. It means the small piece of ground on which Caesar's body was lying.

(c) Who were responsible for Caesar lying low?

Ans. Cassius, Brutus, Casca and a few other conspirators were responsible for Caesar's assassination.

(d) What did the speaker request the others immediately after this?

Ans. Immediately after saying this, Mark Antony, the speaker, requested the conspirators to kill him too.

9. I know not, gentlemen, what you intend,
Who else must be let blood, who else is rank:
If I myself, there is no hour so fit
As Caesar's death hour, nor no instrument
Of half that worth as those your swords, made rich
With the most noble blood of all this world.

(a) **Who does the 'gentlemen' refer to?**

Ans. The word 'gentlemen' refers to the conspirators who killed Caesar.

(b) **What does the speaker request the 'gentlemen'?**

Ans. The speaker, Mark Antony, requested the 'gentlemen' to kill him too.

(c) **Why did the speaker give this request?**

Ans. Mark Antony gave this request knowing very well that they would not kill him at present, as their enmity was only against Caesar and not him. The request was simply to know their attitude towards him.

(d) **What was the response by the 'gentlemen' to the request?**

Ans. The response by Brutus, a conspirator, was that they would not kill Antony because they had killed Caesar for his ambitions of tyranny.

10. O Antony, beg not your death of us.
Though now we must appear bloody and cruel, Yet
see you but our hands
And this the bleeding business they have done:

(a) **What reason had been given by Antony for begging his death and from whom?**

Ans. The reason given by Antony for begging his death from the conspirators who murdered Caesar was that he felt that it was the best hour to die along with Caesar as he was such a great man.

(b) **What does 'bleeding business' refer to?**

Ans. The phrase 'bleeding business' refers to the assassination of Caesar by the conspirators.

(c) **What had happened just before this conversation?**

Ans. Just before this conversation, Caesar had been stabbed to death by the conspirators.

(d) **What reason was given by the speaker for what had happened?**

Ans. The reason given by the speaker, Brutus, for what had happened was that Caesar was a turning into a tyrant who would have terrorised Romans.

11. You know not what you do: do no consent
That Antony speak at his funeral

(a) **Identify the speaker of the given lines.**

Ans. The given lines are spoken by Cassius, a senator and conspirator of Caeser's assassination.

(b) **Whose 'funeral' is being talked about?**

Ans. Caeser's funeral is being talked about in the given lines.

(c) **Why did the speaker raise this objection?**

Ans. The speaker, Cassius, raises this objection because he fears that Antony, a great friend of Caeser's, could sway the masses against them for murdering Caeser.

(d) **Give the antonym of the word 'consent'?**

Ans. The antonym of the word 'consent' is 'dissent'.

Or

(a) **To what does the speaker object?**

Ans. The speaker (Cassius) objects to Brutus consenting to let Antony speak at Caesar's funeral.

(b) **What does the word 'moved' mean in the extract?**

Ans. The word 'moved' here means 'affected emotionally'.

(c) **What does the speaker anticipate will happen if Antony is allowed to speak at the funeral?**

Ans. The speaker anticipates that the Romans will be so emotionally affected by Antony speaking at the funeral that they may turn against the conspirators.

(d) **Was the speaker's apprehension justified? Why?**

Ans. Yes, Cassius' apprehension was justified because Antony was a fiery speaker and he enabled the Roman people to revolt against the conspirators.

12. Brutus Mark Antony, here, take you Caesar's body.
You shall not in your funeral speech blame us,
But speak all good you can devise of Caesar,
And say you do't by our permission;
Else shall you not have any hand at all
About his funeral: and you shall speak
In the same pulpit whereto I am going,
After my speech is ended.

(a) **Identify the speaker.**

Ans. The speaker of these lines is Brutus.

(b) **Who is being granted permission ?**

Ans. Antony is being granted permission to speak at Caesar's funeral.

(c) **What is the speaker afraid of?**

Ans. The speaker, Brutus, is afraid that Antony may speak against Brutus and the other conspirators, so he warns Antony to speak only about Caesar and not about them at all.

(d) **What opinion do you form of the speaker ?**

Ans. From these lines, we understand that the speaker, Brutus, is a fair man because he allows Antony to speak at Caesar's funeral, despite knowing that Antony was very close to Caesar.

13. O, pardon me, thou bleeding piece of earth,
That I am meek and gentle with these butchers!

(a) What is the 'bleeding piece of earth' referred to here?

Ans. Caesar's dead body is referred to as 'bleeding piece of earth' here.

(b) Which expression in the extract means 'I seek your forgiveness'?

Ans. The expression 'pardon me' means 'I seek your forgiveness'.

(c) Why was the speaker 'meek and gentle'?

Ans. Antony was 'meek and gentle' with the conspirators because he wanted them to let him speak at Caesar's funeral so that he can expose them and avenge Caesar's death by inciting the Roman people to revolt against them.

(d) Did the speaker later on change his attitude of being meek and gentle? With what effect?

Ans. Antony later on changed his attitude when he gave a fiery speech at Caesar's funeral. The effect was that the Roman people revolted against the conspirators.

14. Had you rather Caesar were living and die all slaves, than that Caesar were dead, to live all free men?

(a) Who is speaking these lines to whom?

Ans. Brutus is speaking these lines to the citizens of Rome who have gathered for Caesar's funeral.

(b) What does 'rather' mean here?

Ans. The word 'rather' means 'prefer that' here.

(c) How did the speaker justify his action before this speech?

Ans. Brutus justified the killing of Caesar by telling the people that Caesar was highly ambitious and all the Romans would soon have become his slaves if he had not been stopped.

(d) Who gave his speech after this speaker had finished?

Ans. Mark Antony gave his speech after Brutus had finished.

15. He was my friend, faithful and just to me:
But Brutus says he was ambitious;
And Brutus is an honourable man.

(a) Who is the speaker and who is he referring to as his friend?

Ans. Mark Antony, Julius Caesar's loyal friend is the speaker here. He is referring to Caesar as his friend.

(b) What is the significance of the word 'but' in the context?

Ans. The word 'but' brings out the sarcasm or mockery behind Antony's words.

(c) What impact do these lines have on the listeners?

Ans. Antony succeeds in appealing to the emotions of the listeners who believe that a great wrong has been done to Caesar. They become enraged and decide to avenge Caesar's death.

(d) Besides speaking about his friend's faithfulness to him, what other good qualities of his friend does the speaker talk about?

Ans. Mark Antony talks of Julius Caesar's many good qualities which benefited ordinary Roman citizens like ransom money for prisoners filling the state's treasury, donating in his will all his property for use by Roman citizens, etc.

16. He hath brought many captives home to Rome
Whose ransoms did the general coffers fill:
Did this in Caesar seem ambitious?
When that the poor have cried, Caesar hath wept:
Ambition should be made of sterner stuff:
Yet Brutus says he was ambitious;

(a) What were the speaker's sentiments at this time?

Ans. Antony was filled with grief as well as anger at the brutal murder of Caesar.

(b) What is the meaning of 'ransoms' in the extract?

Ans. The word 'ransoms' here refers to the money paid into Rome's treasury for return of the prisoners captured by them in various battles.

(c) "Caesar hath wept" tells us what about him?

Ans. Caesar's weeping tells us that he had compassion for poor Romans.

(d) What was the intention of the speaker in recounting Caesar's good qualities?

Ans. Antony's intention in recounting Caesar's good qualities was to make the Romans feel that the conspirators were wrong in murdering Caesar.

17. Antony If you have tears, prepare to shed them now.
You all do know this mantle: I remember
The first time ever Caesar put it on;
'Twas on a summer's evening, in his tent,
That day he overcame the Nervii:
Look, in this place ran Cassius' dagger through:
See what a rent the envious Casca made:
Through this the well-beloved Brutus stabb'd;
And as he pluck'd his cursed steel away,

CBSE SQP 2023

(a) How does Antony use visual imagery to make his point about the assassination of Caesar?

Ans. Antony uses visual imagery to appeal to the imaginations of the citizens. By creating the illusion of the original scene, Antony succeeds in making the citizens feel as if they were present to witness those historical events of Caesar's greatness.

(b) What is the significance of the mantle that Antony refers to in his speech?

Ans. The mantle refers to the red cloak owned by Caesar that was presented to him by Mark Antony after he won the battle of Nervii. The mantle was a symbol of Caesar's military accomplishment and his good deeds for the citizens of Rome.

(c) Identify the tone of Antony's statement when he says, "If you have tears, prepare to shed them now".

Ans. The tone of Antony's statement when he says, "If you have tears, prepare to shed them now" is dramatic and tragic. He aims to appeal to the empathy of the citizens of Rome.

(d) What does Antony's reference to the Nervii suggest about Caesar's military prowess?

Ans. Antony's reference to the Nervii suggests that Caesar possessed unrivalled military prowess. The statement stands to prove that Caesar was a great and unparalleled military leader.

18. O judgment! thou art fled to brutish beasts,
And men have lost their reason. Bear with me;
My heart is in the coffin there with Caesar,
And I must pause till it come back to me.
First Citizen Me thinks there is much reason in his sayings.
Second Citizen If thou consider rightly of the matter.
Caesar has had great wrong. **CBSE SQP 2024**

(a) What does the phrase 'O judgment! thou art fled to brutish beasts' tell us about the speaker's thoughts?

Ans. The phrase tells us that the speaker was appalled at the lack of logic and fairness in the surrounding events.

(b) Select the line that indicates the speaker's deep grief and emotional connection with Caesar.

Ans. The line 'My heart is in the coffin there with Caesar' shows the speaker's deep grief and emotional connection with Caesar.

(c) What do the responses of the First and Second citizens reflect about the impact of the speaker's words?

Ans. The responses of the First and Second citizens show that they are beginning to question the justice of Caesar's assassination, suggesting that the speaker's emotional appeal is having an effect on the audience.

(d) What about the extract signifies shifting sentiments among the citizens?

Ans. The line -Caesar has had great wrong- indicates that the citizens had begun to view Caesar's assassination as an act of injustice.

19. Decius Brutus
And know it now : the senate have concluded
To give this day a crown to mighty Caesar.
If you shall send them word you will not come,
Their minds may change.
Caesar
How foolish do your fears seem now, Calpurnia!
I am ashamed I did yield to them.
Give me my robe, for I will go. **CBSE 2025**

(a) How does Decius Brutus persuade Caesar?

Ans. Decius Brutus persuades Caesar by cleverly reinterpreting Calpurnia's dream and appealing to Caesar's ego.

(b) What did Calpurnia's fears make her do?

Ans. Calpurnia's fears made her try to prevent Caesar from going to the Senate on the Ides of March. After having a troubling dream, she became deeply anxious about his safety and believed that something bad would happen to him if he went.

(c) What do the above lines tell you about Caesar's character?

Ans. The above lines reveal that Caesar is somewhat arrogant and easily swayed by flattery, particularly when it boosts his sense of pride and ambition.

(d) Why does Caesar say that he was ashamed of himself?

Ans. Caesar says that he is ashamed of himself because, after being persuaded by Decius Brutus, he realises that he was initially swayed by fear and hesitation, especially in response to Calpurnia's troubling dream.

Short Answer Type Questions

Answer the following questions in 30-40 words.

1. What did Caesar ask his servant to tell the priest? What was its result ?

Ans. Caesar asked his servant to bid the priest to perform a sacrifice in the name of the almighty for success and security. However, the augurers (fortune tellers) sent a message to Caesar not to step outside his home on that particular day as they could not find a heart in the sacrificed beast.

2. Why did Calpurnia try to stop Caesar from going to the Senate?

Or **Why did Calpurnia try to prevent Caesar from going to the Senate House? Did she succeed in her attempt?**

Ans. Calpurnia feared that something terrible would happen to Caesar. She felt this because in her dream she saw Caesar's statue with many spouts, out of which blood was oozing and that the Romans were washing their hands with his blood.

No, she did not succeed in her attempt because just when she was able to convince him, Decius Brutus very cunningly convinced Caesar to go to the Senate House.

3. How did nature foretell Caesar's death?

Or **What were the events which Calpurnia had heard about and what effect did they have on her?**

Ans. There were several unnatural occurrences that foretold Caesar's death. Calpurnia had heard that a lioness had given birth on the streets. The graves had opened, with the dead coming out. Fierce warriors were seen fighting in the clouds and blood was drizzling upon the Capitol. Neighing of horses was heard. Dying men were groaning and ghosts were heard shrieking about the streets.

All this resulted in Calpurnia feeling that something bad would happen to Caesar that day if he ventured outside his home.

4. What was Caesar's belief about death?

Ans. Caesar's belief about death was very practical. He believed that death is inevitable and that cowards fear death and experience it often before their actual death. In contrast, the brave taste death only once. He found it very strange that men fear death, knowing that it is a necessary end.

5. How does Decius Brutus interpret Calpurnia's dream?

Ans. Decius Brutus interprets Calpurnia's dream as a good omen. He explains that Caesar's statue spouting blood in many pipes in which many smiling Romans bathed signifies that due to his influence, Rome will revive. He adds that great men shall gather around Caesar and stain their handkerchiefs in his blood which will serve as colours added to their coat of arms.

6. Why does Decius Brutus interpret the dream to flatter Caesar?

Ans. Decius Brutus interprets Calpurnia's dream to change Caesar's mind about staying back at home. He flatters Caesar because he had taken the responsibility of bringing Caesar to the Senate House where the conspirators had planned to assassinate him. Their plan would have failed if Caesar would not have changed his decision.

7. The word 'Aside' has been frequently used in the play. What is meant by it? **Competency Based**

Ans. 'Aside' is a literary device which is frequently used in plays. It is used to depict the thoughts in the back of the mind of the character. These thoughts are conveyed to the people watching the play but are not known by the other actors in the play. As a play is being played on a stage, it adds an element of reality to the characters.

8. Was Julius Caesar proud and overconfident? Why ?

Ans. Julius Caesar was a great warrior and leader. He was proud of his achievements. He was overconfident and thus, paid a very heavy price. Because of his overconfidence and ignorance about his wife's intuition and potential of his conspirators, he lost his life.

9. Was the plea of Metellus Cimber the actual reason to stab Caesar to death?

Ans. No, the plea of Metellus Cimber for his brother Publius Cimber was not the actual reason to kill Caesar. In fact, this was used as an excuse to bring out Caesar's arrogance so as to stab him to death.

10. Bring out the irony in Caesar's decision to go to the Senate House in the light of the incidents that happen over there.

Ans. Caesar feels that Calpurnia's dream had been misinterpreted by her and Decius had justified its significance appropriately. As a result, he decides to go to the Senate House. However, when Caesar arrives at the Senate House and dismisses Metellus' plea, he is brutally assassinated by the conspirators. Hence, his decision proves to be ironical.

11. Why does Cinna says 'Run hence, proclaim, cry it about the streets'? What does he mean?

Ans. Cinna says this after assassinating Caesar. He means that they should now declare the freedom of Rome from the tyranny of Caesar in front of the public in the streets.

12. Was Brutus noble in his intention to assassinate Caesar?

Ans. Yes, Brutus was noble in his intention to assassinate Caesar. Brutus had no personal grudges to have been involved in the conspiracy. However, he was influenced to become a part of Caesar's assassination. Brutus did so as he was a patriotic leader and loved Rome more than anything else. His misjudgement of Caesar as ambitious and his fear that Caesar would become a tyrant convinced him to become a part of this conspiracy.

13. What were Cassius' reasons to kill Caesar?

Ans. Cassius was jealous, envious and insecure due to Caesar's growing popularity among the Romans. He was afraid that Caesar may become a dictator one day. These reasons sowed in him the seeds of conspiracy to assassinate Caesar.

14. How can you say that Brutus was a supporter of the republican and democratic spirit?

Ans. Brutus was a noble and patriotic leader. He was an avid supporter of free representative government. It is evident from his active part in Caesar's assassination because his sole reason of participation was protecting and safeguarding the freedom of Romans against the misjudged ambitious Caesar.

15. Who do you think is a manipulative leader out of Brutus and Cassius? **Competency Based**

Ans. Cassius is indeed a manipulative leader out of Brutus and him as he successfully draws Brutus into the conspiracy in the name of democratic Rome and Caesar's ill ambitions.

He asserts his strong will to assassinate Caesar to Brutus. Brutus, on the other hand, fails to question Cassius' intentions even once and misjudges Caesar.

16. How does Brutus convince the Romans that Caesar deserved death?

Or **How does Brutus win the heart of the Roman mob?**

Or **What argument did Brutus put forward in defence of Caesar's murder?**

Ans. Brutus satisfied the hearts of the Roman mob by giving several reasons which were the grounds for Caesar's assassination. He told the Romans that Caesar had become ambitious and wished to enslave them all. He masked Caesar's patriotism with selfish motives and misinterpreted them as his greed for the crown and power.

17. Bring out the irony in the lines, "Good countrymen Let me depart alone. And, for my sake, stay here with Antony"?

Ans. The irony in the above lines is that Brutus, unknowingly, sets the stage for Antony to inflame the crowd to avenge Caesar's death through his oration. By telling the crowd to stay and listen to Antony, he digs his own grave.

18. Why does Antony refer to 'Brutus' cut on 'Caesar's body as 'the most unkindest cut of all'?

Ans. Antony refers to Brutus' cut as 'the most unkindest cut of all' because Brutus was a very dear and trusted friend of Caesar. Caesar did not expect him to be a part of his assassination and thus, the cut by Brutus stabbing him not only hurt him physically, but also emotionally.

19. How did Caesar's will infuriate the Romans?

Ans. Caesar's will infuriated the Romans because it showcased Caesar's selflessness and love for them and the country. The fact that Caesar had left all his private walks and orchards for common pleasures and seventy five drachmas for each Roman out of his personal possessions enraged the public regarding his assassination and made them realise that Caesar had been wronged.

20. How did Mark Antony prove to be Caesar's true friend?

Ans. Mark Antony was very close to Julius Caesar and Caesar held a special place in his heart for Antony. Antony was very loyal and faithful towards Caesar. Caesar's death shook him deeply as he genuinely cared and wanted to see him crowned as the king of Rome. Antony proved to be a true friend as he avenged Caesar's death successfully.

21. Was Caesar really ambitious ? How can you say so ?

Ans. No, Caesar was not ambitious on personal grounds. In fact, he didn't crave any post, as he refused the crown thrice. Another fact that also proves his generous attitude towards the Romans was that, in his will, he opened his parks and gardens for the Romans and also gave seventy five drachmas to each one of them.

22. Analyse Brutus's reasoning for joining the conspiracy against Julius Caesar in the excerpt of Shakespeare's play Julius Caesar. **CBSE SQP 2024**

Ans. Brutus's reasoning for joining the conspiracy against Julius Caesar is rooted in his belief that Caesar's ambition could threaten the Roman Republic's democratic principles. Brutus fears that Caesar's rise to power might lead to tyranny. His decision is driven by a sense of duty to protect Rome from despotism, illustrating the complexity of his character as he balances loyalty to a friend with loyalty to the republic. However, this reasoning also reveals Brutu's vulnerability to manipulation by others in the conspiracy.

Long Answer Type Questions

Answer the following questions in 150 words.

1. **Both Adolf Hitler and Gandhiji were said to be great orators. While Gandhiji used his skills to spread non-violence, Hitler used his skills to push the world into a World War. What do you think good orators should be like? Using references from the chapter, answer in 150 words.**

Ans. Gandhiji used his oratorical skills to spread the message of non-violence so that the country could obtain its freedom from the British through peaceful means. He used this method because he realised that Indians could not match the British in terms of firepower. Thus, violent means like an armed rebellion would not be successful as had happened during the 1857 mutiny. In contrast, Hitler used his oratory skills in an evil way. Though his intentions were to uplift his nation, he plunged the world into a war.

Actually, a great orator should utilise his power of persuasion with utmost care. If one has this power, then one should choose one's words very wisely, as they make a deep impact. In the play 'Julius Caesar', Antony displays the qualities of a true orator. First, he convinces the conspirators to not kill him and let him speak to the crowd. Then, he instigates the crowd for the greater good. Thus, a good orator should always think of what he can bring about through his words which will be good for the majority of people.

2. **"Not that I loved Caesar less, but I loved Rome more." Brutus says this as he justifies to the Romans why Caesar was assassinated by them. Do you agree with Brutus? Justify your answer in 150 words by giving examples from the play. What values does Brutus display as he says this line to the Romans?**

Ans. Yes, I agree with Brutus' justification for killing Julius Caesar. Brutus was patriotic and felt that Rome would be ruined if Caesar was crowned as then Caesar would rule like a dictator. Although Brutus himself was a great friend of Caesar, he sacrificed his friendship for the betterment of his countrymen. This is proved when he says "Not that I loved Caesar less, but that I loved Rome more" and "As Caesar loved me, I weep for him; as he was fortunate, I rejoice at it; as he was valiant, I honour him: but, as he was ambitious, I slew him." By saying these lines, Brutus displays the values of idealism, patriotism and sacrifice. He was willing to go to any lengths, including his reputation as an honest and upright citizen, to protect his countrymen from what he thought would be a despotic rule by Julius Caesar.

3. **"O, pardon me, thou bleeding piece of earth that I am meek and gentle with these butchers!" Antony proves to be a true friend and an ideal citizen who plans revenge for a wrong deed done. Impressed by his true friendship and loyalty, write an article on the topic 'Friendship and Loyalty Makes Life Worth Living.'**

Ans.

**Friendship and Loyalty
Makes Life Worth Living**

Any person's life is a unique and interesting experience for that person. It takes one through myriad experiences of success, failure, betrayal and much more. What comes as a cool breeze in this desert of continuous struggles is friendship and loyalty of close friends and associates, just like Antony's loyalty to Julius Caesar did in ancient Rome.

Such friendships truly make life worth living as they perform a number of functions which make life truly enjoyable. They heal the wounds others, our 'enemies', have created. Loyalty enriches our life in a positive way so that we feel happy that we have loyal friends. Personal relations sometimes get clouded due to personal motives, greed and jealousy but friendship and loyalty always remain pure. Thus, we must strive hard to overcome personal shortcomings and be an ideal friend to those whom we consider as having similar values in life as us. In that way, we can make their life worth living.

4. **"This was the unkindest cut of all,
For, when the noble Caesar saw him stab,
Ingratitude more strong than traitor's arms,
Quite vanquished him."
According to Antony, when Brutus stabbed Caesar, a bloody deed was compounded with ingratitude. It wasn't the wound that killed Caesar, says Antony, but Brutus' ingratitude. Keeping the above views in mind, write about the importance of gratitude in one's life.** Competency Based

Ans. Gratitude is one of many positive emotions. It's about focusing on what's good in our lives and being thankful for the things we have. Gratitude is pausing to notice and appreciating the things that we often take for granted like having a place to live, food, clean water, friends, family and even access to computers. It's about taking a moment to reflect on how fortunate we are when something good happens, whether it's a small thing or a big thing.

Making a habit of gratitude can also be good for us. Like other positive emotions, feeling grateful on a regular basis can have a big effect on our lives.

Antony feels Brutus had been ungrateful to his friend Caesar and that, more than the wound, it was his act of ingratitude that killed Caesar. Brutus forgot his friendship due to his blind faith in the conspirators. Brutus was not fair to Caesar and, when Caesar realised this, he lost his will to live.

5. "Cowards die many times before their deaths;
The valiant never taste of death but once.
Of all the wonders that I yet have heard.
It seems to me most strange that men should fear.
Seeing that death, a necessary end
Will come when it will come."

It is true that a coward dies many times as he sacrifices himself, his respect and his wishes many times. But brave people live a life of dignity and die only once. Inspired by this discussion, write a letter to your cousin discussing the value of bravery in life. You are Kriti.

Ans. A-23/Central Street
Bangalore - 560023
19th November, 20XX

Dear Samrat

How are you doing? I am doing good here and hope the same for you. I have written this letter after reading Julius Caesar. The play reminded me of the conversation we had regarding cowardice and death. Julius Caesar had also said something about it which I feel echoes the thoughts of many great thinkers of this world. He said that cowards 'die' many times during their lives while valiant people die only once. Fear of losing someone or something, fear of pain, fear of suffering, etc. make us cowards. But, in order to get rid of these fears, we lose our respect, our willpower and our confidence.

On the other hand, brave people die only once. They live a life of principles on their own terms and for the values which they hold dear to their hearts. Thus, they explore infinite possibilities of life and die only once, and that too gracefully. Their death does not lower their esteem or their respect in other people's minds.

I have told you what I feel about it. Now, I hope you will write to me about your opinions. I will be eagerly waiting for your reply. Give my love to everyone.

Yours lovingly
Kriti

6. Now let it work. Mischief thou art afoot,
Take thou what course thou wilt!

Antony seeks justice by getting the crowd to kill the conspirators. But to correct a wrong, one cannot commit another wrong. Write a speech for the school assembly on 'The Ends do not Justify the Means'.

Ans. Respected Principal Sir, learned teachers and my dear friends. Today I, Vinita Singh of Class X-B, will speak on the topic, 'The Ends do not Justify the Means'.

In the historical play, 'Julius Caesar', it is shown that the conspirators murdered Caesar because they felt that he may become a dictator. However, they should not have taken law into their own hands. Any person cannot be punished for the crimes that they may commit. Although they achieved their goal, they did not employ proper means. They could have found other acceptable means to curb Caesar's ambition. Mark Antony found an acceptable method to avenge Caesar's murder by inciting Roman citizens against the conspirators. The hunting down of the conspirators due to a popular revolt by the citizens was an acceptable means of taking revenge for Caesar's murder.

Thank you!

7. Do you agree that the assassination of Julius Caesar was a deliberate move to satisfy the ambitions and aspirations of a few? Justify. **CBSE 2019**

Ans. I agree with the statement that the assassination of Julius Caesar was a deliberate move to satisfy the ambition and aspiration of a few. The play 'Julius Caesar' essentially shows how political ambitions can be dangerous.

Julius Ceasar, a just and practical general of Rome was assassinated by a few Senators who feared Caesar's power. They were jealous of Caesar's growing fame and popularity. Hence, they did not want him to become the king. They wanted to usurp the power and keep it for themselves.

We can see the evidence of their malicious motives in the way they react to the fact that Antony would be allowed to speak at the funeral. They knew that if Antony is allowed to speak at Caesar's funeral their true motive of personal vengeance would come forward. They also knew that they had no real reason to kill Caesar and thus, would not be able to justify their actions to the Roman masses.

ASSESSMENT EXERCISE

Extract Based Questions

Read the following extracts carefully and answer the questions that follow.

1. And you are come in very happy time, To bear my greeting to the senators And tell them that I will not come to-day: Cannot, is false, and that I dare not, falser: I will not come to-day: tell them so, Decius.

(a) About what did Caesar want Decius to inform the senators?

(b) What is meant by 'very happy time' in this extract?

(c) What decision had Caesar taken just prior to this?

(d) Why had Caesar taken this decision?

2. That every like is not the same, O Caesar, The heart of Brutus yearns to think upon

(a) Who is saying this to whom?

(b) What does the speaker mean by 'that every like is not the same'?

(c) What was the reason for the speaker speaking these lines?

(d) What happened after the speaker spoke these lines?

Short Answer Type Questions

Answer the following questions in 30–40 words.

1. What does Calpurnia's pleading show about her?

2. How can you say that Caesar loved his country?

3. What impression do you form about Caesar at his refusal to be crowned three times?

4. Antony was a skilled orator. Elaborate.

5. Were the conspirators right in what they did? Explain.

Long Answer Type Questions

Answer the following questions in 150 words.

1. Death did not hurt Caesar more than being stabbed by his dear friend. Friendship is a bond of trust between two people. Do you think Brutus was a true friend? What qualities do you think a true friend possesses?

2. "If thou dost bend and pray and fawn for him, I spurn thee like a cur out of my way."

Caesar was indeed an able general and a brave conqueror. Do you think this gave him the right to be arrogant and overconfident? Give reasons for your answer highlighting how this proves to be his undoing.

3. Caesar, I never stood on ceremonies, Yet now they fright me. There is one within, Besides the things that we have heard and seen, Recounts most horrid sights seen by the watch.

After reading the play and analysing Calpurnia's character, you realise that many people fall in the trap of superstitions. Write an article whether or not believing in such things is a trait of an intellectual person.

ASL

Assessment of Speaking and Listening Skills

CBSE has clearly outlined the significance of Speaking and Listening Skills as a part of co-scholastic areas of achievement by every learner and also stressed the clear integration of Assessment of Speaking and Listening Skills as a part of the curriculum.

As good communication skills raise the self-esteem of a student, CBSE essentially desires that the students acquire proficiency in it by the time they leave school. In the present day global markets, speaking and listening are considered to be the essential skills of real life. So, it has been felt for a long time that CBSE must focus on assessing speaking and listening skills for qualification in examination.

Considering this, CBSE has proposed to give 5% weightage to the Assessment of Speaking and Listening Skills from 2017-18 onwards. Therefore, the Assessment of Speaking and Listening Skills will be done formally at the term-end examination. Schools may conduct ASL themselves as per the guidelines provided by the CBSE.

The overall purpose of the test is to help improve and standardise students' communicative skills. Thus, in keeping with the international standards, the CBSE has put this assessment in place.

Listening Skills

The **Listening Comprehension** section tests the student's ability to listen for basic interpersonal, instructional and academic purposes. A number of sub-skills need to be developed in the everyday classroom transaction. Given below are some of the sub-skills of listening which need to be assessed.

(i) Listening for specific information
(ii) Listening for general understanding
(iii) Predictive listening
(iv) Inferential listening
(v) Listening for pleasure
(vi) Intensive listening
(vii) Evaluative listening

Role of Examiner

Here, the Examiner is assigned the job of assessing a candidate's performance in any of the skills that is to be assessed.

It is extremely important to keep in mind the factors listed below as they can significantly influence the expected outcome of the Listening Test.

- Size of the room
- Seating arrangement
- Acoustics of the room
- Equipment used
- Quality of the recording of the listening input
- Quality of the oral rendering of the listening input (in case it is to be read aloud by the Examiner), in terms of volume, clarity, enunciation, intonation, pace, etc.

Test Administration For the Examiner (Teacher)

- Select the time and date of the assessment.
- Plan the seating arrangement in advance.
- Decide exactly as to how much time is to be reserved for instructions or any possible interaction regarding clarifications, etc and for the actual test.
- Make the announcement giving general instructions directed to the candidates before the recording is played or before the reading of the text.
- Adhere strictly to the time specified for each of the three phases of the Test (Pre-listening, While listening and Post-listening)
- The general instructions given below should be followed while conducting the test.

The Listening Assessment

The Listening Assessment comprises of a variety of tasks. These tasks are graded according to the length of the task and the difficulty level. Schools may download the sample tasks and reorganise them into two parts - transcripts and the marking scheme for the examiner and the worksheets for the students on which students will write answers.

General Instructions for Students

- You are not allowed to ask questions or interrupt the Examiner at any point.
- You are being tested on your Listening Skills.
- You will hear a set of recordings of the Listening Input or listen to a reading of the Listening Input.
- Each of the recordings will be played twice. In case there is an oral rendering of the Listening Input, it shall take place twice.
- You are required to answer a set of questions based on each of the Listening Inputs.
- The assessment consists of 4 sections.
- You are required to attempt all 4 sections of the assessment.
- Familiarise yourself with the questions on the worksheet. It will help you to answer them later on.
- After you have listened to the input, you will be given specified minutes to answer the questions on your worksheet.
- You may answer the questions on your worksheet while listening.
- Do not interact/comment until you have moved out of the examination room.

PRACTICE ASSIGNMENT

Instructions

There are ten questions in this test.

Answer the questions as you listen to the transcripts.

You will listen to four short extracts. As you listen to each one, answer the questions.

TASK 1

Through the given QR code or link you will hear to the news reports about some incidents happening worldwide. Read the sentences below then listen to the news and write the correct answer for the given questions. You will hear to the recording twice.

TO LISTEN THIS TRANSCRIPT

Link https://goo.gl/fLXnyk OR **Scan the Code**

Transcript

1. **Kathmandu, May 14** Thirteen Indians were among the 15 people killed when their 20-seater aircraft slammed into a cliff in Western Nepal, less than seven months after 10 Indian tourists were killed in an air accident. Six people miraculously survived the crash.
2. E-mailing has enabled us to communicate messages to one another at a very fast pace. However, there are times when we have to post important letters and documents by surface or air mail. The postal department is very slow.
3. City dwellers often depend on cars, buses or metros to travel from one place to another. Bicycles used to be a popular mode of travel once. I think we need to popularise them once again if we need to tackle the pollution problem.
4. 'The Mars Rover, Curiosity, landed on the Martian surface to begin a two-year mission, seeking evidence that the Red Planet once hosted ingredients for life'. NASA said.

   Mission controllers at the Jet Propulsion Laboratory near Los Angeles burst into applause and cheered as they received signals relayed by a Mars orbiter confirming that the Rover had survived a make-or-break descent and touched down within its landing zone.
5. A V-chip has been developed. In addition to spelling out the age-based ratings, letters will be displayed to warn parents if a show contains violence or other objectionable content. A group of major networks and producers have agreed to go along with the system, but NBC will not.

Questions

1 What is the news report about?

(a) There was an explosion before the crash.

(b) The crash was a consequence of collision with a cliff.

(c) There have been several air crashes in the recent past.

(d) Indians always die in the air crashes in and around Nepal.

Answer ____________________

2 After listening to the comment by an officer to his colleague, what option do you think the speaker would opt for?

(a) E-mail
(b) Air mail
(c) Postal department
(d) Surface mail

Answer

3 Now listen to an environment activist who is talking to one of his friends. The speaker advocates the use of ....

(a) cars
(b) buses
(c) bicycles
(d) metros

Answer

4 What is the news report about?

(a) Invention of Curiosity
(b) Landing of Curiosity
(c) Happiness at the Jet Propulsion Laboratory
(d) Possibility of life on Mars

Answer

5 What does the V-chip do?

(a) It allows the cable company to monitor what TV programmes you watch.
(b) It turns your TV into a "virtual reality" computer.
(c) It allows parents to block out certain programmes, so their children cannot watch them.
(d) It reduces the use of the remote control device.

Answer

TASK 2

Through the given QR code or link you will hear a talk about the tigers and wildlife tourism. Read the statements below, then listen to the text (talk) and answer the questions given below. You will hear the talk twice.

TO LISTEN THIS TRANSCRIPT

Link https://goo.gl/KAWXWj OR **Scan the Code**

Transcript

Tigers are being loved to death. Tourists desperate for a glimpse of a tiger are damaging the habitat and harassing tigers. This by no means decides that tiger tourism or wildlife tourism is a bad thing. Wildlife tourism has a lot of advantages. Wildlife tourism helps people of the area who get employment in tourism. In this way, wildlife is valued, rather than poached or encroached upon.

Wildlife also inspires the people who see it. For many, a dramatic view of one of the world's great beasts—a tiger, a leopard, a whale—is a life-changing experience. Such a sighting makes people aware of the fragility of the planet and the folly of our short-term thinking. Above all, it prompts people to step back from our traditional chauvinism. Wildlife tourism is similarly equivocal. When carried out with wisdom and responsibility, it is the best possible news for the creatures and the people of the area and for the people doing the touring. Wildlife tourism can sometimes, with the best of intentions, be stupid, greedy and destructive.

An adjustment of practice in India's wildlife tourism is a good thing. It is not tourists that are killing off tigers : it is, above all, the world's ever-increasing human population, and its incontinent need for room to live in.

Questions

1 State whether the following statements are True or False.

(a) People's fascination with the tigers is causing them harm.

(b) Wildlife tourism should be banned.

(c) Tiger tourists are destroying their living places.

2 Fill in the blanks with a word or phrase.

(a) Wildlife tourism helps in ....

(b) .... and .... behaviour is expected from tourists who go for wildlife sightings.

☑ TASK 3

Through the given QR code or link you will hear a lecture about libraries. Read the questions below, then listen to the extracts and choose the correct option from a, b or c to complete the statements in each questions. You will hear the recording twice.

TO LISTEN THIS TRANSCRIPT

Link https://goo.gl/LGrbVH OR **Scan the Code**

Transcript

Libraries It has been a great pleasure to be here this evening and to hear all the things that have been said about libraries in general, and the librarians, without whom the libraries would be of little use. What libraries mean is fairly obvious to all of us, especially to those who are here this evening. We know that without libraries, we cannot have educated people who will carry out their jobs successfully. But as I sat here I was worried about the fact that there are so many places in the world that have no libraries and that have no way of getting books. A lack of money for the books and the librarians is a problem in some places, but I wonder if the biggest problem is really that no one is interested in reading anymore?

Young students often go straight to the internet for readymade notes on a subject. They no longer want to go to libraries to do their own research. Although many students will use the library when they have an examination to study for; once the exams are over, they never return. Even reading books for fun and relaxation is no longer popular amongst the young. A young man, I interviewed recently admitted that he could not name a single book by an Indian author that he had read recently. Demand for non-fiction increases every year, particularly career-oriented books. Students want just to pass an examination and get a job; they no longer have time to read stories.

The more I have thought about the problem, the more I have felt that we do not use all our opportunities to develop an interest in books. Today everything in which people are interested, the radio, the movies - all of these - should, if properly used, stimulate reading. For instance, if there is a remarkably good film 'The Life of Pasteur', I think it should be used by teachers to create an interest in the life of that person. So, in studying Pasteur's achievements and the people around him, students can then use their libraries to read more about the lives of great and famous people. I am sure that if we put our minds to it, there are a great many ways in which we can use the electronic media, films and the internet to stimulate an interest in books and reading. Maybe then our young people will visit libraries more often.

Questions

1 The speaker thinks that librarians ....

(a) are very important for libraries

(b) fulfill, many functions in a library

(c) are more useful today than previously

2 **The speaker says that libraries have an obvious effect on ....**

(a) schools (b) cities (c) business

3 **According to the speaker, there are not enough libraries in the world because ....**

(a) it is hard to build libraries in some areas (b) libraries are very expensive
(c) there is a lack of interest in books

4 **According to the speaker, students are using libraries less because the internet ....**

(a) makes research easier for them (b) has more up-to-date information
(c) give them answers to exam questions

5 **Today, students do not read books because they have no ....**

(a) interest (b) money to buy books (c) motivation

6 **The speaker says that the demand for fiction books is ....**

(a) decreasing with young audiences (b) being replaced by exam books
(c) focused on non-Indian authors

7 **The speaker believes that film and radio can ....**

(a) be a good alternative to reading (b) encourage people to read more
(c) teach us about famous people

8 **What example does the speaker give of a way to increase interest in reading?**

(a) Good books (b) Famous people (c) Historical films

9 **The speaker feels that it is possible to encourage interest in reading if ....**

(a) we spend more time on the internet (b) we think about how to use electronic media
(c) we visit the library more often

10 **Young people can use the library more if they ....**

(a) stop buying books (b) take interest in electronic media, films and internet
(c) have an access to it

☑ TASK 4

Through the given QR code or link you will hear 5 short extracts of friends talking about the significance of sports and games in their life. Read the statements below, then listen to the extracts and match each statement A–G to each Friend 1–5. There are two statements you do not need. You will hear the recording twice.

TO LISTEN THIS TRANSCRIPT

Link https://goo.gl/1LJw1E OR **Scan the Code**

Transcript

Friend 1 Friends, we should play sports and games regularly, because I believe that they are the most important source of entertainment. We enjoy and please ourselves when we play sports and games.

Friend 2 For me the best use of sports is earning a livelihood. These days the people who play games and sports not only earn a lot of money but also are given a great deal of money as prizes. Therefore, I strongly believe that playing games and sports is a very good way of earning a comfortable income.

Friend 3 Sports and games are very good way of keeping good health. All those who play games regularly remain healthy for a longer time. So, if we really wanted to be healthy, we must regularly play outdoor games of our choice.

Friend 4 Dear friends, I believe that we should play games to keep ourselves occupied. If we regularly play sports and games we keep ourselves busy in constructive work.

Friend 5 Sports and games make us both mentally and physically strong to face the challenges of life. The discipline and practice of games and sports give us enough strength to bear the harsh realities of life.

Questions

Which of the following statements are true?

A. Sports and games keep you in good health.
B. Playing sports gives you a feeling of entertainment.
C. Sports and games make you intelligent.
D. Sports are a good source of earning money.
E. Sports make you strong to face challenges.
F. Sports make you grow tall and attractive.
G. Playing sports is a good way to avoid bad company.

TASK 5

Through the given QR code or link you will hear an interview with veterinarian Dr Mohit Sharma on the importance of keeping pets. Read the sentences below, then listen to the conversation and choose A, B or C for each sentence. You will hear the recording twice.

TO LISTEN THIS TRANSCRIPT

Link https://goo.gl/97WvUC OR **Scan the Code**

Transcript

Interviewer You are a great advocate of keeping pets. Would you like to tell our listeners something about them?

Dr. Sharma Pets make great friends for everyone in the family because they are a great source of love and friendship. Pets are playful beings in the house as they keep everyone, young and old, happy.

Interviewer That's really true, but do you think that pets also help people make friends.

Dr. Sharma Having a pet at home, you often need to go out for walks every day. Initially you may not like it, but over a few days you'll begin to love the routine.

Interviewer What is the impact of the pets on people's moods?

Dr. Sharma Oh yes! Pets really boost your mood. Playing with the pet, can increase the brain activity and enhance pleasure and tranquility.

Interviewer Do pets help in inculcating educational values?

Dr. Sharma Yes, they do and that's true! With pets, children also learn basic lessons on building a strong character like loyalty and trust.

Interviewer What is the impact of pets on their owner's fitness levels?

Dr. Sharma Having a pet at home you are on your toes at all times. Pets make you more agile in the house, they expect you to play with them, be concerned for them.

Interviewer Don't you think that it is very stressful having to care for a pet?

Dr. Sharma No. not at all. In fact people with pets have lower blood pressure and stress levels as compared to the people without pets.

Questions

1 Pets make great friends because they are

A. very attractive B. great achievers C. good companions

2 Pets help you make new friends as they make you

A. appear more beautiful B. go out for a walk C. change your attitude

3 Pets boost your mood because

A. playing with pets makes you feel fresh. B. they help you pass time

C. they love you so much

4 Pets inculcate educational values because

A. they are very valuable and precious B. they make you study more and more

C. they enable you develop habits of daily care

5 Pets help you remain fit because

A. they make you to eat less food B. they make you go to the gym

C. they make you more active

6 Pets help you in being in good health because

A. your blood pressure is maintained B. you don't have to visit your doctor

C. you care about your pet a lot

Answers

Task 1

1. (b) The crash was a consequence of collision with a cliff **2.** (a) E-mail

3. (c) bicycles **4.** (b) Landing of Curiosity

5. (c) It allows parents to block out certain programmes, so their children cannot watch them.

Task 2

1. (a) True (b) False (c) True

2. (a) employing people/generating employment (b) Wise; responsible

Task 3

1. (a) are very important for libraries **2.** (c) business

3. (c) there is a lack of interest in books **4.** (a) makes research easier for them

5. (a) interest **6.** (a) decreasing with young audiences

7. (b) encourage people to read more **8.** (c) Historical films

9. (b) we think about how to use electronic media **10.** (b) take interest in electronic media, films and internet

Task 4

Friend	Statement
1	B
2	D
3	A
4	G
5	E

Task 5

1. C **2.** B **3.** A **4.** C **5.** C **6.** A

Speaking Skills

Speaking skill has acquired a very important place as a communication skill. Like listening skill, a number of sub-skills of speaking need to be consciously developed among students. Some of the sub-skills which can be assessed are as follow

- Speaking intelligibly using appropriate word stress, sentence stress and intonation patterns.
- Narrating incidents and events, real or imaginary in a logical sequence.
- Presenting oral reports or summaries; making announcements clearly and confidently.
- Expressing and arguing a point of view clearly and effectively.
- Taking active part in group discussions, showing ability to express agreement or disagreement, summarising ideas, eliciting the views of others and presenting own ideas.
- Expressing and responding to personal feelings, opinions and attitudes.
- Participating in spontaneous spoken discourse in familiar social situations.

General Instructions

1. The total administration time for the speaking assessment is approximately 10-12 min.
2. The speaking assessment will be conducted for two students at a time.
3. There will be a single teacher to function as the examiner.
4. The examiner should be a qualified English teacher.

Role of Examiner

- The examiner should ensure that the room is quiet and has good acoustics.
- The tone, manner and body language of the examiner should be relaxed, encouraging and pleasant. Care should be taken to make the candidates feel at ease.
- Students must not be discouraged from making a fresh start in case they are unable to do so at the first attempt.
- The examiner needs to be flexible, sympathetic and reassuring in her/his demeanour.
- The examiner should also be a proficient user of the language in order to conduct the speaking assessment successfully. For example, the examiner should be skilled in elicitation techniques, so that questions such as... "Explain how"/"Why"..."Tell me what you think of" .... may be asked. Yes/ No questions should generally be avoided.
- Ideally, the examiner should award marks after the candidates have left the examination room. If necessary, notes can be made discreetly to be used later in the scoring, so that it does not make the candidates unduly tense and self-conscious.

The Speaking Assessment is divided into three stages

Stage 1 General Introduction

The aim of this introductory task is to put the candidate at ease through some general, open-ended questions, thereby creating a space for the candidate to respond with personal feelings and opinions. Simple warm up questions based on the candidate's name, place of residence, leisure preferences, etc are asked.

Stage 2 Topic Presentation

This can take the form of PowerPoint/ OHP presentations, book reviews, debates, speech, etc. The focus of this task is to assess a candidate's ability to sustain a straightforward, subjectwise description, mapped out in a fluent and cohesive style.

In this section, the examiner gives each candidate the choice to pick up a Role Card or a Cue Card with a topic written on it. The candidates are given 1 minute to prepare. The examiner should be ready with sheets of paper and a pencil. Candidates may organise their thoughts and ideas. Prior to the day of the speaking assessment, as an assistance to students to prepare for the presentations, the teacher can give a choice of 20 to 30 topics in class to students so that they can prepare presentations based on the topics and organise their ideas. Similar topics can be given in the actual; assessment.

Students are not allowed to write full length answers. They may jot down points only in the sheets given by the examiner. Therefore, a pencil and sheet of paper should be provided on the table. Students are not allowed to carry pen, paper or mobile phone to the examination room. After a minute for making notes, each student will be given 2 minutes each to present his/ her ideas. In case a student is unable to speak during/ for the allotted time, the Examiner may ask some rounding off questions.

Stage 3 Problem Solving (Pair Interaction)

The third section of the test is for 3 minutes. Both students are given a verbal or visual stimulus and asked to respond to it. Both the students are given a total of 3 minutes to interact. Both of them will talk together. After 2 minutes the examiner can ask questions based on their discussion.

Closing

The closing is for 1 minute duration only. In case a student has not been able to speak or has been unable to speak owing to nervousness, the dominance of the second candidate or any other factor, then the examiner may use the 1 minute to give a fresh opportunity to that student.

CBSE Assessment of Speaking and Listening (ASL) Descriptors for Assessment of Speaking

Interactive Competence	5	4	3	2	1
Task Management	Contributions are highly effective and fulfill the task. Can fulfill the communicative functions of the level with spontaneity.	Contributions are effective and fulfill the task. Can fulfill the communicative functions of the level.	Contributions are adequate and fulfill the task. Can fulfill functions of the level but may not do so consistently.	Contributions are limited and there is some attempt at the task which is not fulfilled and/or may be repetitive.	There is almost no contribution and/or contributions may not be related to the task.
Initiation and Turn-taking	Is prompt to initiate discussions on the themes/ functions at the given level appropriately. Contributes spontaneously to keep the interaction going; takes turns appropriately.	Is easily able to initiate discussions on the themes/ functions at the given level appropriately. Contributes effectively to keep the interaction going and takes turns appropriately.	Is able to initiate discussions on the themes/ functions at the given level. Makes an effort to keep the interaction going; takes turns.	Struggles to initiate discussions on the themes/functions at the given level. Makes little effort to keep the interaction going;	Does not initiate discussions. Makes no effort to keep the interaction going.
Appropriacy and Relevance	Speaks with a clear sense of purpose and audience in both formal and informal situations. Contributions are always appropriate to the context/ situation.	Speaks with a fair sense of purpose and audience in both formal and informal situations. May be less confident in normal situations.	Speaks with an awareness of purpose and audience may not adapt register effectively. Contributions are appropriate to the context/ situation.	Has unclear sense of purpose and may be unable to adapt register. Contributions may be unconnected to the context/ situation.	Has hardly any sense of purpose and cannot adapt to register.

Fluency	5	4	3	2	1
Cohesion and Coherence Speed of Delivery	Presents information in a logical sequence of linked utterances with a clear connection between ideas, arguments and statements. Uses a range of cohesive devices. Speak fluently with minimal hesitation. Intelligible speed of delivery.	Presents information in a logical sequence of linked utterances with a connection between ideas, arguments and statements. Uses with ease some cohesive devices. Speaks fluently with some hesitation. Intelligible speed of delivery.	Presents information generally in a logical order but overall progression may not always be clear. Uses a range of cohesive devices but some over/under use. Coherence may be affected by hesitancy or rephrasing. Intelligible speed of delivery.	Presents information but without clear progression. Uses limited cohesive devices repetitively. Severe hesitation may impede communication. Speed of delivery impedes understanding.	Presents information with no progression and/ or little control of organisational features. May use only isolated words and phrases.
Pronunciation	**5**	**4**	**3**	**2**	**1**
Pronunciation, Stress and Intonation	Has clear, natural pronunciation that can be easily understood by the listener. Varies stress and intonation in keeping with the task, content and meaning.	Has pronunciation that can be easily understood by the listener. Varies stress and intonation in keeping with the task, content and meaning.	Is intelligible though there are examples of some mispronunciation. Tries to speak, varying stress and intonation according to task, content and meaning.	Is not always intelligible and the listener may have to ask for repetition from time to time. Flat intonation and/or inappropriate stress for the task, content or meaning.	Is not intelligible.
Language	**5**	**4**	**3**	**2**	**1**
Accuracy	Uses a range of grammatical patterns with accuracy, including some complex forms. Makes only negligible errors.	Uses a range of grammatical patterns with accuracy, including few complex forms and makes only noticeable errors.	There may be some mistakes which affect meaning but there is an attempt to correct most of these mistakes.	There are mistakes which affect meaning but there is hardly an attempt to correct these mistakes.	Communicates with fragments of words and structures but does not manage to bridge the gaps or correct his/her mistakes.
Range	Uses an expressive and appropriate range of structures, words and phrases on topics appropriate to the level and to deliver an effective message.	Uses an expressive and appropriate range of words and phrases on topics appropriate to the level. These may be repetitive.	Can use the language of the level but is repetitive. May search for words with the risk of the message becoming weaker.	Uses basic, simple words and phrases for the level. There may be an effort to find suitable words, which may hamper the message.	Uses simple, isolated words for the level. There is little effort to find words.

AN OVERVIEW OF SPEAKING TEST

STAGE 1

1 INTRODUCTION (1 min)

Section Time	Procedure
10 secs	Examiner Hello, please sit down. My name is X. What's your name? *(to Candidate A)* And what's your name? *(to Candidate B)* So, your names are *(name and serial number A)* and *(name and serial number B)*.
25 secs	*(Candidate A)*, tell me something about *(e.g. where you live)*. Candidate A responds.
25 secs	*(Candidate B)*, tell me something about *(e.g. your school)*. Candidate B responds.

STAGE 2

2 TOPIC PRESENTATION (4 min)

Section Time	Procedure
5 secs	Examiner Now *(Candidate A)*, you are going to tell us about your topic. When you have finished, *(Candidate B)* will ask you a question and then I will ask you some more questions. Would you like to begin please?
1 minute	Candidate A speaks.
15 secs	Examiner Thank you. *(Candidate B)* can you ask *(Candidate A)* a question please? Candidate B asks question; Candidate A responds.
40 secs	Examiner asks 2 or 3 follow-up questions as appropriate from the topic prompt list Stage 2 example follow-up questions How often do you .... ? Why? When you .... do you .... ? Why do think .... is important?
5 secs	Examiner Thank you. Now *(Candidate B)*, you are going to tell us about your topic. When you have finished, *(Candidate A)* will ask you a question and then I will ask you some more questions. Would you like to begin please?
1 minute	Candidate B speaks.
15 secs	Examiner Thank you. *(Candidate B)* can you ask (Candidate A) a question please? Candidate A asks question; Candidate B responds.
40 secs	Examiner asks 2 or 3 follow-up questions as appropriate from the topic prompt list.

STAGE 3

3 PROBLEM SOLVING (3 min)

Section time	Procedure
25 secs	Examiner Thank you. Now let's go to the next task. I'm going to give you a card which has information about a problem. I'd like you to read the information and then discuss together how you are going to solve the problem. You have 2 minutes to do this. Here is your problem. Stage 3 sample problem solving card *Your classmates have not been keeping the school tidy. After lessons there is litter in the classrooms and in the halls.* *With your partner, discuss this problem and decide what you can do to make the school a nicer, cleaner place for everyone.* Candidates read card (20 secs) then asked to start speaking.
2 mins	Candidates discuss the problem and a solution.
35 secs	Examiner OK, can you stop now please. Option A (for candidates who have reached a solution). Thank you. (Move straight on to a question) Option B (for candidates who have not reached a solution). Can you agree on a solution? What is it? Candidates explain. Then examiner asks 1 or 2 follow-up questions as appropriate from the list of problem solving prompts. Stage 3 example follow-up questions • Do you think your (solution) will be effective enough? Why?/Why not? • What role do you think .... plays in this problem? Why? • .... sounds interesting. Could you tell me more about that/this? Please stop here. That's the end of the test. Thank you and goodbye.

PRACTICE ASSIGNMENT

Instructions

1. The speaking test will be conducted for two students at a time.
2. Students should not have pen, paper, mobile, etc.
3. The teacher will act as the Examiner (who is involved in a conversation) as well as an assessor who will also give marks to the candidates.

STAGE 1

1 GENERAL INTRODUCTION (1 min)

The Examiner makes the students feel comfortable.

Examiner	Hello! Good morning, I am .... May I know your name please?
Student A	My name is ..../ I am ....
Examiner	And yours? *(Looking at student B)*
Student B	....
Examiner	Where do you live? *(To student B)*
Student B	....
Examiner	How about you? *(To student A)*
Student A	....
Examiner	What do you do in your leisure? *(To student A)*
Student A	....
Examiner	And what do you do in your free time? *(To student B)*
Student B	....
Examiner	What hobby would you like to cultivate? *(To student A)*
Student A	....
Examiner	How about you? *(To student B)*
Student B	....

STAGE 2

2 PRESENTATION (5 min) In this part of the test, teacher will give 1 min to prepare and 2 min each to both students to present

The oral examiner can frame any input; the following two frames are suggested

1. **To student B** Describe something that you own and you value tremendously. You have 1 min to prepare and 2 min to present.
   - Where did you get it from?
   - What do you use it for?
   - How long have you had it?
   - Why is it so important for you?

   If the student is not able to speak at length, the teacher could ask rounding off questions.
   - Did you buy it/ was it a gift?
   - Is it valuable in term of money?
   - Would it be easy to replace it?

2. **To student A** You will be given 1 minute to prepare based on your most memorable journey and you will have 2 minutes to describe your journey. (Each student is given 2 minutes to present.)

For Student A

- Where did you travel to?
- What was the highlight of your visit? (monument/ temple/park/relatives)
- Which place would you like to visit next?
- Why are such journeys relaxing?

If the student is not able to speak at length the teacher could ask rounding off questions

- Was it a trip organised by the school?
- Did you go with the family?
- Was it a place you had never seen before?
- What fascinated you?

Ask student B to ask a question.

To student A (Repeat)

Qualities that I Value in a Friend

For Student B

- Qualities I like in a friend
- Why do I consider these qualities important?
- How many of these qualities do I have?
- What is that one quality that I would like to inculcate?

If the student is not able to speak at length, the teacher could ask rounding off questions

- Do you have a lot of friends?
- Why did you pick on them?
- Why do your friends care for you?

Ask student A to ask a question.

Changing Role of Women

- Varied jobs
- Working mothers
- Financial security
- Economic/social independence

If the student is not able to speak at length, the teacher could ask rounding off questions.

- Do women in your family work outside the house?
- Do you appreciate women working? Why?
- Do you think the advantages outweigh the disadvantages?

STAGE 3

3 PROBLEM SOLVING (3 min)

(a) **Teacher to both students A and B**

Look at the visual carefully. Talk together for 2 mins.

Students are given 1 min to think and prepare. And then they respond to the visual/ verbal stimulus.

1. Child Marriage

2. Growing Obesity

Verbal Stimulus

3. **How do you imagine life in cities in the future?**

The examiner can give the following hints

- Work
- Leisure/Entertainment
- Travel

4. **What responsibilities do you think individuals have towards the environment?**

The examiner can give the following hints

- Lifestyle
- Shopping
- Finance

CLOSING (1 min)

Thank you very much. That was the end of your test. The examiner retrieves the pencil and paper.

Suggested Topics for Presentation

1 Violent Computer Games Should be Banned
2 My Choice of a Career
3 E-learning
4 Demonetisation
5 Gender Discrimination
6 Peer Pressure—*Harmful or Beneficial*
7 Beauty Pageants Just a Way of Objectifying Women
8 Bullying
9 Problem of Child Abuse
10 Honour Killings in India
11 Importance of good health
12 Drug Abuse
13 Extreme Sports—*The Risks and the Thrill*
14 Uniforms are Better
15 Animal Dissection Should be Banned
16 Should Juveniles be Tried as Adults?
17 Are Social Networking Sites doing us Any Good? or Are They Just a Sophisticated Way of Stalking People?
18 Are Security Cameras an Invasion of Privacy?
19 News Channels have Turned into Entertainment Channels
20 Caste System has Completely Ruined Us

Suggested Questions for Problem Solving Task

1 Some of your classmates persuade you to watch a movie after school hours. However, your parents have instructed you to come straight home after school hours. Now you are worried that the other students will laugh at you if you tell them the truth. With your partner, discuss what you should do in the situation.

2 The drinking water taps on the ground floor of your school building are not working properly. Water is always found to be leaking from one tap or the other. With your partner, discuss this problem and decide what you can do to reduce the wastage of water.

3 Some of the senior boys are often seen bullying their juniors. It has caused fear among the students and they perform the tasks given to them out of terror. With your partner, discuss what could be done to help them.

Sample Question Paper 1 (Solved)

A Highly Simulated Sample Question Paper for CBSE Class X

English Communicative

Time : 3 hrs	M.M. : 80

General Instructions

1 This question paper has 12 questions. All questions are compulsory.

2 This question paper contains four sections Section A : Reading Skills, Section B : Writing Skills Section C : Grammar Section D : Literature Textbook

3 Attempt all questions based on specific instructions for each part. Write the correct question number and part there of in your answer sheet.

4 Separate instructions are given with each question/part, wherever necessary.

5 Adhere to the prescribed word limit while answering the questions.

Section–A (Reading Skills)

[22 Marks]

1. Read the following passage. **(12 M)**

1. Very often, we do not take the first step towards a good cause because we say to ourselves, "The task is so big. What can I do alone?" So nothing gets done. There is much talk about environmental protection, air pollution and saving our forests. Do we really care? If we do, here are a few things we can do to make our surroundings more pleasant.
2. It is good to adopt a two-uses-attitude! By putting an article to a second use, we are giving it a longer lease of life and using up less raw material from nature. One of the worst things we do is the abuse of paper. The clean sides of envelopes can be used to write small notes, lists and reminders around the house. The more paper we use, the more trees will have to be cut down. For the same reason, we should avoid the use of paper napkins or paper plates. Cloth napkins are just as good, for they can be washed and used over and over again.
3. Another area which needs the most urgent attention is effective garbage disposal. People who are conscious about it follow rules and laws strictly. As a result, their neighbourhoods are clean and beautiful. Similarly, each one of us can contribute to a cleaner environment. All kitchen waste should be collected separately. Those of you who have green fingers can turn this into valuable manure. Dig a pit and put the kitchen waste into it. When the pit is a little over half full, cover it up with mud. Let nature do the rest. Within three or six months, we will have a good garden manure. It can also be done as a community project by digging a large pit in the colony). Do take help of all the members, for nothing succeeds like co-operation.
4. A lot of people don't care about the environment because they don't understand the adverse effect that society has on it. It is important to convince people to care about the environment. The first step would be to convince people to change by providing simple alternative solutions and ways' of doing things. The internet is a powerful tool and a group on social media of like-minded people can be formed. People can share environmental stories and issues, as well as pool in solutions and alternatives to educate one another. With the current state that our planet is in, it is imperative that people actively care about the environment and most importantly to act now.

Answer the following questions based on the passage above.

(i) According to the author, why does nothing get done? **(1)**

(a) We do not want to do any task

(b) We do not take the first step towards the task

(c) We feel that our actions are small

(d) We do not have time for many things

(ii) The writer would agree with the following statements, except **(1)**

(a) Awareness is the key towards change

(b) We need to follow the 3R's- Reuse, Reduce and Recycle

(c) Paper use needs to be significantly reduced

(d) Individual actions triumphs community actions

(iii) Complete the given sentence appropriately. **(1)**
An effective garbage disposal ensures ....

(iv) Rectify the given False statement. **(1)**
The internet cannot be used towards the cause of the environment.

(v) List any one thing that we can do to avoid the abuse of paper? **(1)**

(vi) How can people of an area convert making garden manure to a community project? **(1)**

(vii) Comment on the writer's statement that 'we do not take the first step towards a good cause'. **(2)**

(viii) What procedure can one adopt for kitchen waste? How long does it take to make good garden manure? **(2)**

(ix) Explain the purpose of the given passage. **(2)**

2. Read the following passage carefully and answer the questions that follow. **(10 M)**

(1) Ratan, a global brand in Dairy products, works on a business model popularly known as, 'The Ratan Model'. This model aims to provide value for money to the customers and protect the interests of farmers simultaneously.

(2) The Ratan Model is a three-tiered structure that is implemented in its Dairy production : Firstly, Ratan acts as a direct link between milk producers and consumers that removes the middlemen. Secondly, farmers (milk producers) control procurement, processing and marketing. Thirdly, it is a professionally managed organisation.

(3) One can understand the Ratan Model better by taking cognizance of 'Ratan's Target Audience', where it has targeted the mass market of India with no premium offerings and works on providing the best quality products at affordable prices.

(4) So, Ratan formulates its pricing policy on the low cost price strategy which has attracted a lot of customers in the past and it continues to do so.

(5) Another stance used by Ratan's Target Audience is based on customer-wise targeting and industry wise targeting. This strategy divides the target audience on the following two bases.

(6)

Segment wise break down of Customer-Based target Audience	
Customers	Ratan products
Kids	Chocolate, Ratan cool, Ratan milk
Youth	Ratan Pizza Cheese, Cheese spread

The above table showcases how Ratan has a diversified customer base.

(7) Industry Based Target Audience: Ratan has segmented milk for various industries such as ice-cream manufacturers, restaurants, coffee shops, and many similar- industries. Further, it has segmented butter, ghee and cheese for bakeries, snack retailers, confectioneries and many more.

(8) The target audience study tells us that Ratan has a strong presence in both Business to Business and Business-to-Customers.

(9) Ratan's marketing campaigns and strategies are implemented in a very attractive way. For example, the story of the 'Ratan Girl' is a popular 'ad' icon. It is a hand drawn cartoon of a young girl.

Answer the following questions based on the passage above.

(i) Complete the sentence appropriately. **(1)**
The most loved ad icon of Ratan is ....

(ii) Fill in the blank with one word/phrase. **(1)**
The Ratan Model is a .... that is implemented in its Dairy production.

(iii) Which of the following products can be targeted for health conscious people ? **(1)**
(a) Coconut milk (b) Cold coffee (c) White butter (d) Flavoured curd

(iv) Select the option that states the purpose of the table given along with the passage. **(1)**
1. To show how Ratan diversified customer base
2. To show the Ratan model's focus
3. To point out how Ratan's model is customer oriented
4. To show how Ratan dairy became popular

(a) 1 and 2 (b) Only 1 (c) 3 and 4 (d) Only 4

(v) What does 'The Ratan Model' aim at? **(2)**

(vi) Name the two basis on which Ratan divides the target audience. **(2)**

(vii) 'Ratan acts as a direct link .... '. Explain. **(1)**

(viii) 'Ratan Target Audience' is described as a diversified market. Explain with reference to the given table. **(1)**

Section–B (Writing Skills) [22 Marks]

3. Write an e-mail to your Principal to make arrangement for extra coaching in Mathematics as the teacher was on long leave and the course could not be completed. **(3)**

You may copy the given template to write your e-mail.

From	
To	
Cc	
Date	
Subject	

4. Write a factual description of a person you once lived with, in not more than 100 words. **(4)**

5. (A) You are Shubha/Krushna Mohanty, residing in Subhadra Apartments, Bhubaneswar, Orissa. You have observed, with increasing concern, that garbage collection continues to be done without segregation in your neighbourhood. Write a letter to the Editor of The Real Times, Bhubaneswar, explaining your concern along with the rationale behind the importance of garbage segregation. Suggest ways in which the RWAs can participate in this program with reference to Unit Environment. **(7)**

Or

(B) Mountview Public School, Kalka is run by an NGO to give quality education to the children of the deprived sections of society. The Principal of the school feels that blackboards in the classrooms need to be replaced. She decides to ask the chairperson of the NGO named 'Education for All' for funds. Write her letter with reference to the MCB Unit Education.

Clues

- Initiation of funds for new boards
- Replace the blackboards with whiteboards
- Whiteboards are more durable and necessary
- Release funds at the earliest
- Contact local supplier

6. (A) While reading about new places and searching for them online has its merits, the advantages of actually travelling to various destinations far exceed them. Write an article in 150 words for the magazine 'Travel Times', evaluating both these options. You may use the clues given below along with your own ideas referring to the Unit Travel and Tourism. You are Amrit/Amrita. **(8)**

Clues

- Builds confidence
- Make friends and memories
- Experience new cultures
- Expands knowledge

Or

(B) We cannot imagine life without our mobile phones, TV sets and other modern gadgets. Write an article on 'Role of Modern Gadgets'. You are Rashi/Rishi. You can take help from the given clues and also refer to the Unit Science of your MCB.

- What are Gadgets?
- Importance of gadgets in everyday life
- Disadvantages of using gadgets
- Step to ensure proper usage of gadgets

Section–C (Grammar)

[10 Marks]

7. Complete the tasks A-C, as directed.

(A) Fill in the blanks (i)-(iii) with the appropriate option from those in the brackets. **(3)**

Three tourists **(i)** .... (by/from/for) Delhi decided to visit Goa last year. While standing on Calangute beach, two of them decided to have a dip in **(ii)** .... (a/an/the) sea. While playing in the water, they were swept away by the current. The lifeguard at the beach **(iii)** .... (try/tried/trying) to save them but did not succeed. The bodies were later washed up the coast two kilometres away.

(B) In the following passage, one word has been omitted in each line. Write the missing word, along with the word that comes before and the word that comes after it, in any four lines of the given paragraph in the space provided. **(4)**

	Word before	Omission	Word After
(a) Corvus is the Latin name the crow family.	....	....	....
(b) I have started calling my pupil this name.	....	....	....
(c) At first, he would turn stare at me;	....	....	....
(d) but now he has begun respond verbally.	....	....	....

(C) Do as directed.

(i) Rearrange the following word clusters to make a meaningful sentences. **(1)**

One night Charley worked late at the office.

He was in a hurry to get to his apartment.

the subway/so he/Grand Central/take/from/decided/to

(ii) Report the dialogues to complete the paragraphs that follow. **(1 + 1)**

Mother: You seem so tired. Take some rest.

Suraj: I can't even think of relaxing. I have lots of homework to do.

Mother: You should not take so much of stress.

Suraj: Don't worry. Please give me a hot cup of tea.

Mother said to Suraj that .... (a) .... Suraj replied that .... (b) .... The mother advised him not to take so much of stress. Suraj told his mother not to worry and requested her to give him a hot cup of tea.

Section–D (Literature Textbook)

[26 Marks]

8. Read the given excerpts and answer the questions briefly, for any two excepts, of the three given. **(4 + 4 = 8)**

(A)

But one night a nightingale
In the moonlight cold and pale
Perched upon the sumac tree
Casting forth her melody.

(The Frog and the Nightingale)

(a) How has the atmosphere being described before the nightingale perched on the tree? **(1)**

(b) How did the nightingale's song affect the audience and the atmosphere of the bog? **(1)**

(c) What does 'casting forth her melody' mean? **(1)**

(d) What does the use of the word 'but' indicate in the lines? **(1)**

(B) "You're to exert your influence. Get all your friends and acquaintances to stop using the Ouija board, and then we'll start helping you to write."
"But ..."
There was a footstep outside my door.
"John! Oh, John!" called the voice of my wife.
I waved my arms at the ghost with something of the motion of a beginner when learning to swim.

(A Shady Plot)

(a) Who said these words to whom? **(1)**

(b) What did the speakes want the listener to do? **(1)**

(c) Select the line that indicates that I did not want his wife to meet the speaker. **(1)**

(d) Why did the speaker say these words? **(1)**

(C) **Victoria** What are they coming for? They haven't been here for ages.

Mrs. Slater They're coming to talk over poor grandpa's affairs. Your father sent them a telegram as soon as we found he was dead. (A noise is heard.)

Good gracious, that's never them. (**Mrs. Slater** hurries to the door and opens it.) No, thank goodness! It's only your father.

(Henry Slater, a stooping, heavy man with a drooping moustache, enters. He is wearing a black tailcoat, grey trousers, a black lie and a bowler hat. He carriers a little paper parcel.) *(The Dear Departed)*

(a) Who are 'They' in the above extract? **(1)**

(b) What is the meaning of the word 'ages' in the extract? **(1)**

(c) What is the occasion that 'They' are coming for? **(1)**

(d) What will 'They' do when they come? **(1)**

9. Answer any five of the following six questions in about 30-40 words each. **(5 × 2 = 10)**

(a) Why was there a change in the sailors' attitude when the sun rose? **(2)**

(b) How does the poet assess the power of his poetry in 'Not Marble, Nor the Gilded Monuments'? **(2)**

(c) Who was Patol Babu's mentor? How did his words help Patol Babu in enacting his role? **(2)**

(d) Mrs Slater plans to outshine the Jordans. How? What does it tell about her character? **(2)**

(e) What message is conveyed through the story 'Mrs Packletide's Tiger'? **(2)**

(f) State one aspect that might have led the narrator to think that the boys must be saving to emigrate to America. **(2)**

10. Answer any one of the following two questions in about 150 words. **(8)**

A. There is an old Latin proverb - 'A jealous woman will set a whole house on fire'. Discuss the evils of jealousy that can be learnt from Saki's story 'Mrs Packletide's Tiger' and Stanley Houghton's drama 'The Dear Departed' in about 150 words.

Or

B. In 'The Rime of the Ancient Mariner' and 'Snake', how do the narrators' expressions of guilt and subsequent reflections on their actions reveal their evolving perceptions of innocence and the natural world, and what does this suggest about their journeys towards redemption and self-awareness?

Answers

1. (i) (b) We do not take the first step towards the task
(ii) (d) Individual actions triumphs community actions
(iii) a cleaner neighbourhood and a cleaner environment
(iv) The internet is a powerful tool that can be used towards the cause of the environment.
(v) To avoid the use of paper, we can use the blank sides of any used paper like the clean sides of an envelope to write small notes, lists and reminders around the house.
(vi) People of an area can convert making garden manure to a community project by digging and making large pit in the colony and then throwing kitchen waste into it.
(vii) The given statement by the writer indicates that the writer blames each one of us as individuals for the lack of change in anything. The writer believes that our lack to take initiatives because we feel that the task is too big and we cannot do anything alone had resulted in our condition as far as the environment is concerned.
(viii) All the kitchen waste can be collected separately and turned into manure. People can dig a pit and put kitchen waste into it. When the pit is half full, put some mud over it. After some time, we will have good manure to be used. It takes 3-6 months to make good garden manure.
(ix) The purpose of the given passage is to suggest to us that if we want something to changes, we should bring the change ourselves. We should not wait for others and be the first one to do something. The author uses the example of our roles in reducing waste and promoting a positive as well as healthy environment to do so.

2. (i) the tale of the 'Ratan Girl.' It features a young girl in a hand-drawn cartoon
(ii) three-tiered structure
(iii) (a) Coconut milk
(iv) (b) Only 1
(v) The Ratan Model aims to provide value for money to the customers and protect the interests of farmers simultaneously.
(vi) The basis on which Ratan divides the target audience are
- Customer-wise targeting
- Industry-wise targeting

(vii) The given phrase indicates that Ratan closely connects milk producers and customers through the three-tiered structure of the Ratan Model, which is used in its dairy operations. As a result, farmers (milk producers) have control over purchasing, processing and marketing.
The farmers receive the entire benefit as a result, and intermediaries cannot earn from a commission.
(viii) The 'Ratan Target audience' is said to as a diverse market because every sort of client is taken into consideration while releasing the items. For example, chocolate, Ratan cool, and Ratan milk are marketed to children; pizza cheese and cheese spread are marketed to young people; and Ratan Shakti and RatanLite butter are marketed to consumers who are health conscious.

3. From: students@gmail.com
To: principalxyz@gmail.com
Cc: abc@gmail.com
Date: 10th April, 20XX

Subject Extra coaching for Mathematics

Respected Sir/Ma'am

On behalf of all the students of Class X, I XYZ, would like to request you to make an arrangement for extra coaching in Mathematics after school timings. Our honourable teacher is making a sincere effort to complete the syllabus. However, since, he was on long leave, our course will not be completed with the regular classes only. Further, you know that Mathematics is a subject that requires a lot of practice after learning once.

Therefore, we all are ready to attend extra classes in the evenings. We shall be highly obliged to you for your kind consideration.

Thanking you

Yours obediently

XYZ

4. I lived with my parents and siblings for most of my life. However, when I shifted to the school boarding I started living with a friend named Sienna. She was a Class XII student who became my roommate.

I was nervous of living with someone I did not know first. However, we became best friends and we were lucky to have each other as roommates and friends. She was very supportive, compassionate, talented, helpful and humble. Our friendship became so strong that when we could have had a single room for each of us and live separately, we did not do that. We preferred to live together. Sienna was the sister I never had! Since both of us had took the same stream, we studied together. Sienna helped me in completing our assignments and also prepared me to ace my exams. We also planned for our extracurricular activities together. Today, our bond is so strong that we talk everyday.

5. (A) Subhadra Apartments
Bhubaneswar, Orissa

16th May, 20XX

The Editor
The Real Times
Bhubaneswar
Odisha

Subject Non-segregation of Garbage by Residents

Sir/Ma'am

Through the columns of your esteemed daily, I would like to bring to your notice the issue of non-segregation of garbage by the residents of my area JP Nagar, Bhubaneswar. Despite promotion by the municipal body and the media on the benefits of garbage segregation, the residents in our area continue to resort to the old practice of garbage dumping.

Most of the residents in the area do not segregate their waste. For the ones who are practicing this religiously, their efforts go in vain as the garbage collector puts all the waste in one bag. The Resident Welfare Association (RWA) in the area should promote the benefits of garbage segregation by pasting posters, playing audio message on the collection vans, etc. The people who practice segregation should be awarded a certificate. The RWAs should also watch the CCTV footage to penalise the residents who are not doing this.

I sincerely hope that all this would help in making this initiative a success.

Thanking you

Yours sincerely

Shubha/Krushna Mohanty

Or

(B) Mountview Public School
Kalka, New Delhi

16th March, 20XX

The Chairperson
Education for All
New Delhi

Subject Funds Required for Replacement of Blackboards

Respected Sir/Ma'am

Your NGO is taking good care of the children of deprived sections of society by providing them education. Your efforts towards education can be seen in the innumerable schools that you have opened across the country, just like mine. I have written this letter to inform you that now the school is completing almost ten years of its existence. As a result, some of the fixtures need to be replaced. The most urgent need at present is of replacement of the blackboards in the classrooms, as they are either damaged, worn out or totally unusable.

I suggest that we should replace them with permanent whiteboards, as these are more durable and can be also used to project slides as well as for using audio-visual teaching equipment, necessary in today's education scenario.

Therefore, I request you to release funds for this purpose at the earliest.

Thanking you

Yours sincerely

Shweta Pandit

6. (A) **Travelling in 2020**

by Amrita

Travelling is a great thing. It refreshes our minds and makes us aware of other places and cultures. Some people do screen travelling these days. By 'screen travelling', I mean that they discover the new places on their personal computers, laptops, tabs, mobiles, etc. By doing this, they get to know a lot of about the places. It educates them about new places and their cultures, histories, etc.

They also get to know about the experience of other travellers. However, travelling to a place physically is a unique experience. It builds our confidence by exposing us to new experiences. We get an opportunity to meet new people and make friends. We also get to make memories in this process by clicking pictures, creating blogs, videos, etc. Travelling widens our horizons by exposing us to different languages, cultures, festivals, etc. We get to know about the demography of a country through travelling.

So, all in all travelling physically to a place is much more exciting than screen travelling. We must try to travel new places whenever we get the opportunity.

Or

(B) **Role of Modern Gadgets in Our Life**

by Rishi

It is difficult to imagine a life without modern gadgets. Gadgets are electronically simplified applications that have been designed to make our life simple and convenient. Over the years, gadgets like mobiles, laptops, tvs, etc. have gained so much popularity and wide use that today they have become an integral part of our lives.

Each and every aspect of living today is associated with gadgets. We can perform all tasks with a simple click on our mobiles. Be it business, studying, looking for recipes or even switching off the lights, gadgets have come to our rescue.

While these gadgets are a great addition to our lives, they bring many cons too. Overuse of gadgets has led to an addiction wherein we are constantly glued to them. As a result, our lifestyles have deteriorated.

This does not mean that we abolish new scientific advancement. It good to use gadgets in our lives, but to a certain limit only, and everyone must spend some qualilty time with family members instead of being engrossed in mobiles of watching TV.

7. (A) (i) from (ii) the (iii) tried

(B)

	Before word	Omission	After word
(a)	name	of	the
(b)	pupil	by	this
(c)	turn	and	stare
(d)	begun	to	respond

(C) (i) So, he decided to take the subway from Grand Central.

(ii) (a) he seemed so tired and advised him to take a rest.

(b) he could not even think of relaxing as he had lots of homework to do.

8. (A) (a) Before the nightingale perched on the tree, the atmosphere was cold and gloomy. There was no joy in the bog.

(b) The nightingale's song effects the audience and the atmosphere of the bog positively. Her presence and song brings joy to the bog making it lively.

(c) The phrase means, 'spreading sweetness all around with her melodious singing.'

(d) The use of the word 'but' indicates a contrasting change that came in the bog with the presence of the nightingale.

(B) (a) The ghost of Helen said these words to John Hallock.

(b) Helen wanted John to persuade people around him to not use the Ouija Boards.

(c) The line would be "I waved my arms at the ghost with something ...." This line indicates that 'I' wants the speaker to go away.

(d) The ghost of Helen said these words because she and the other ghosts were getting tired in answering the questions of the persons using Ouija Boards.

(C) (a) 'They' refers to Mr. Ben Jordan and Mrs. Elizabeth Jordan, Victoria's uncle and aunt.

(b) The word 'ages' means 'a long period'.

(c) The occasion is to mourn the reported 'death' of grandfather.

(d) 'They' will talk about the Slaters after his reported 'death'.

9. (a) Before the sun rose, the ship was surrounded by snow and ice and the sailors felt very cold. The sailors felt that the killing of the albatross by the Ancient Mariner was its cause. However, when the Sun rose and the ship cleared the ice, they felt that the albatross had brought mist and snow. They changed their attitude and felt that the old Mariner had done the right thing by killing the bird.

(b) The poet in 'Not Marble, Nor the Gilded Monuments' glorifies the power of poetry in an attractive manner. He shows faith in his poetry and says that even time and death cannot destroy it. The beauty of his poetry is more than that of the statues and gilded monuments of princes.

(c) Mr. Pakrashi was Patol Babu's mentor and guru. His words proved to be a source of inspiration to Patol Babu is enacting his role to perfection. After remembering his words, he was able to fight with his initial apprehensions and go ahead with enacting his role.

(d) Mrs. Slater plans to outshine the Jordans by wearing a mourning dress and thinks that Ben and Elizabeth will never have thought about mourning yet. It shows her inhuman character, wanting to outshine her sister even at a sad time.

(e) The story 'Mrs. Packletide's Tiger, conveys the message that those who consider themselves smart enough to outshine other often get outsmarted themselves. The actions of such people can backfire on them. Thus, before targeting anyone, they must not forget that even a biter can be bitten.

(f) The narrator thought that the boys must be saving to emigrate to America because the boys worked day and night doing odd jobs to earn money and yet did not each much. They only ate black bread and some figs.

10. (A) In Saki's 'Mrs. Packletide's Tiger', jealousy drives Mrs. Packletide to orchestrate a tiger hunt solely to outshine her rival, Loona Bimberton. This jealousy leads to a contrived and farcical event, exposing her vanity and pettiness. Similarly, in Stanley Houghton's 'The Dear Departed', jealousy and greed between sisters Mrs. Jordan and Mrs. Slater over their father Abel Merryweather's possessions reveal their moral decay. Their competitive desire for inheritance results in deceit and conflict, further eroding familial bonds. Both stories illustrate how jealousy incites destructive behaviour, undermining relationships and integrity. The proverb, 'A jealous woman will set a whole house on fire,' aptly encapsulates the chaos and moral disintegration caused by envy, as portrayed in these narratives. Through satire and drama, Saki and Houghton expose the evils of jealousy, urging readers to recognise and combat this vice to preserve personal and familial harmony. across as harbingers of the values of altruism, diligence, grace and self-respect.

Or

(B) In 'The Rime of the Ancient Mariner', the Mariner's overwhelming guilt for killing the albatross manifests as physical and spiritual suffering, symbolising a profound moral transgression against nature. His journey towards redemption begins with his recognition of the natural world's beauty and interconnectedness, culminating in his spontaneous blessing of the sea creatures. Similarly, in 'Snake', the narrator's guilt for throwing a log at the snake stems from his realisation of having acted against his initial instinct to admire the creature. This act of violence against an innocent being reveals his internal conflict between societal conditioning and innate reverence for nature. Both narrators' guilt and reflections indicate a deepening understanding of innocence and the intrinsic value of the natural world. Their paths to self-awareness and redemption are marked by this newfound respect for nature, emphasising the moral imperative to harmonise with rather than dominate the natural order.

Sample Question Paper 2 (Solved)

A Highly Simulated Sample Question Paper for CBSE Class X

English Communicative

Time : 3 hrs	M.M. : 80

General Instructions

1 This question paper has 12 questions. All questions are compulsory.

2 This question paper contains four sections Section A : Reading Skills, Section B : Writing Skills Section C : Grammar Section D : Literature Textbook

3 Attempt all questions based on specific instructions for each part. Write the correct question number and part there of in your answer sheet.

4 Separate instructions are given with each question/part, wherever necessary.

5 Adhere to the prescribed word limit while answering the questions.

Section–A (Reading Skills) [22 Marks]

1. Read the following passage. **(12 M)**

1. Twenty-six-year-old V Khanna is not your garden variety green crusader. He's on a mission to cure 'tree blindness'- the habit of not looking at trees. "People just walk past them", he complains. Khanna, as part of the New Delhi Nature Society (NDNS), is educating Delhiites about trees in a unique way- by teaching them how to climb them.
2. A generation ago, the practice was commonplace, but with today's increasingly indoor living, learning to scale the neem next door sounds like a spot of daredevilry. "Spending time with nature and climbing trees has become a spiritual exercise for me. Once you're in a tree, you become part of its ecosystem, which includes birds, insects, fruits and flowers", says Wadhwa, who can spend 40-45 minutes hanging out on tree branches, sometimes with a cup of green tea in hand.
3. But it's all about barking up the tree right. "It depends on how and where you sit", Khanna points out. "You have to find a cosy nook, maybe a Y-or a V-shaped branch. Find a hook to rest your arm. Or, you can lie down. It can get so comfortable that I have to warn people from falling off to sleep." A trained commercial pilot, Khanna organises periodic campouts around Delhi where he not only teaches members how to climb trees but also to make a fire, count GPS satellites and count stars.
4. While Khanna provides tents and other equipment on these free tutorials, participants have to bring their own food. The tree-lover funds his woody ambitions with his day job as business developer, and as a light painting artist at OLE India – a collaborative of professionals and free thinkers. He has also uploaded tree-climbing tutorials on YouTube. When climbing a straight trunk (coconut or palm), ascend using both arms in tandem (like in a hug) instead of alternating them. But banyan trees, with thick, low-lying branches and vines, offer a relatively easy climb.
5. Anyone can join NDNS and it's free. The year-old society has been attracting members through word of mouth and sight - the image of men and women sitting atop trees in various city parks. Khanna has organised six outdoor camps in the past year and has taught around 30 people to climb trees. Once up, he briefs participants about the tree and its ecosystem. Details like what kind of fruits and flowers it bears, their benefits, the shape and size of leaves, kinds of insects, birds and squirrels living on it, and any folk tales associated with it are discussed and shared.

6. If you want to do your climbing yourself, look for a sturdy tree which doesn't have red ants on its branches and is clear of broken glass or injury-causing material at its base. Its branches should be thicker than your arm. When you climb, never go right to the edge of the branch. The aim is not to climb high but to find a comfortable resting place with a good back rest. Climb slowly and keep close to the tree; it will support you. Neem, mango and banyan trees are easy to climb. Newbies should have a friend on the ground to watch out for them.

Answer the following questions based on the passage above.

(i) What is the aim of climbing a tree if you want to do it yourself? **(1)**

(a) Go as high as possible to get a good view.
(b) Climb only neem, mango and banyan trees.
(c) Find a comfortable resting place with a good back rest.
(d) None of the above

(ii) Pick the option that is not the final feelings of V Khanna with reference to the climbing experience. **(1)**

(a) Satisfying (b) Sustainable (c) Spiritual (d) Emotional

(iii) Complete the given sentence appropriately. **(1)**
Khanna's way of teaching about the trees is unique because ....

(iv) Rectify the given False statement. **(1)**
The most suitable title for the above passage will be Teaching Tree Blindness.

(v) Comment on the writer's statement that climbing trees is a spot of daredevilry now. **(1)**

(vi) Why does the writer call disregard for trees as 'tree blindness'? **(1)**

(vii) List the activities that the members of the NDNS club participate in. **(2)**

(viii) The NDNS initiative does not only teach people how to climb trees but also teaches them about the trees and its ecosystem. Do you agree? Give reason for your answer. **(2)**

(ix) Do you think that there is a specific reason for not planting oak trees? Explain your answer. **(2)**

2. Read the following passage. **(10 M)**

The given dialogue fast forward's to some years after Ivan and Natalya get married Natalya and Ivan are expecting a child and are arguing about the name of the baby

Ivan Honoured Natalya. I think that we can name our child Nastasya Mihailovna after dea cyoung aunt who ....

Natalya Excuse my interrupting you. But are you suggesting we name our child after your aunt who ran away with an architect. Not while I am alive.

Ivan What are you talking about?

Natalya I'm speaking of your younger aunt Nastasya Mihailovna who ran away with an architect.

Ivan No, you're mistaken, honoured Nataiya Stepanovna

Natalya Yes, yes, My father told me all about it. Just think. Ivan Vassilevitch! Do you remember spending time with your aunt?

Ivan Do I? For as long as I can remember.

Natalya Really, you won't get me to believe that!

Ivan But you can see from the Photographs. Its true, that she liked an architect but now everyone knows that they were respectively married. There is nothing to argue about it. It was in fact your aunt who ran away with a priest.

Natalya No, it isn't at all like that! Both father and grandfather told me that she died because of fever I really don't sea what is there to argue about it is simply silly that you believe my aunt ran away.

Ivan I'll simple show you the photos of my aunt and then you" believe.

Natalya No, you're simply joking or making fun of me What a surprise! I have always been told that your aunt ran away and mine died and now suddenly you say it is the appasite Ivan Vassilevitch, I can hardly believe my own ears. Now, generally it would not concern me but I would not let you name our child after your runaway aunt.

Ivan	Hear me out, or just see the photos.
Natalya	I can't mke head or tail of all this aunts and uncles. I know that you aunt ran away and mine died.
Ivan	Not true

Answer the following questions based on the passage above.

(i) Complete the given sentence with the appropriate reason. **(1)**

Natalya does not believe that her aunt ran away because ....

(ii) Select the correct option to fill in the blank and complete the analogy. **(1)**

.... : Argumentative :: Ivan : Logical

(iii) Natalya says that she can't make 'heads or tails' of the subject. This means that she is **(1)**

(a) confused (b) angry (c) disgusted (d) sad

(iv) What does the given lines tell us about Natalya? **(1)**

Natalya is

1. short tempered 2. submissive 3. stubborn 4. Homely 5. Humble

Select the correct option.

(a) 1 and 3 (b) 2 and 5 (c) 1 and 4 (d) Only 3

(v) Why does Natalya want to name her child after Ivan's aunt? **(1)**

(vi) What gets Natalya agitated? **(1)**

(vii) What proof does Ivan give to disagree with his wife? **(2)**

(viii) Identify the person who is likely to believe in everything others say and support your choices with one reason. **(2)**

Section–B (Writing Skills) [22 Marks]

3. Write an email to the Principal of your school requesting him to grant you leave for week as you are suffering from typhoid. **(3)**

You may copy the given template to write your e-mail.

From	
To	
Cc	
Date	
Subject	

4. Describe something special you brought home from a holiday. **(4)**

5. (A) You are Kavish/Kavita, a resident of Amar Colony, New Delhi. You have noticed all kinds of people throwing discarded packaging materials, used cigarette stubs and other garbage at every crossing and on the roads and pavements. They do not throw these in the garbage bins provided by the Municipal Corporation. Write a letter to the Editor of 'The Times of India', New Delhi, emphasising the importance of cleanliness amongst people for a healthy life. (120 words) **(7)**

- Cleanliness is important for healthy environment
- Need to learn hygiene and sanitation
- Dirty places breed diseases
- Important to adopt good and healthy practices
- Keep surroundings clean and not litter at public places
- Cleanliness is next to godliness

Or

(B) You are Abhinav, a sports lover. Write a letter to the Editor of a Local Daily expressing your views on improving facilities for sportsmen. You can use the following clues and refer to Unit I- Health and Medicine.

- Facilities provided are pathetic
- No facility of international standards
- Poor performance in overseas tournaments
- Need of action for improvement

6. (A) Some colleges conduct entrance test for admission to their professional courses. Do you think that the entrance test is the right method for selecting students? Write an article for your school magazine on this issue. You are Kavita/Himanshu Manchanda, a student of Class XII-A. You can use the following clues. (8)

- Necessity of written entrance test
- Aptitude developed
- Rote learning at school level
- Tests will bring out true capabilities

Or

(B) Compulsory value-based education is the only remedy for inculcating values among the future citizens of the country. This will also help in the prevention of crime in the country. Write an article on the need of compulsory value-based education in about 150 words. Use the ideas that you may have gathered from MCB Unit 2 : Education and Unit 6 : National Integration.

Section–C (Grammar) **[10 Marks]**

7. Complete the tasks A-C, as directed. (3)

(A) Fill the blanks (i)-(iii) with the appropriate option from those in the brackets.

Hello, this is Arjun. I am (i) ...... (speak/speaks/speaking) from Oxford, where the finals of the World Quiz Championship will be held tomorrow. The favourite is Arvind Ghoshal (ii) ...... (for/from/to) India, the man who (iii) ...... (know/knows/knowing) everything. A few months ago, no one had heard of Arvind, but today he is famous. He is likely to win the Championship if he does not commit a blunder.

(B) The following passage has not been edited. There is one error in each line. Write the incorrect word and the correction in your answer sheet in any four of the given blanks against the correct blank number. (4)

		Incorrect	Correct
(a)	Often these days we hear and speak of the conquered	....	....
(b)	in nature, 'the taming of a river', 'the war against insects'	....	....
(c)	and so on. Often these phrases being used without consciously	....	....
(d)	attaching any value to them, but those have an underlying attitude of hostility towards nature and nature's creatures.	....	....

(C) Do as directed.

(i) Rearrange the following jumbled words/ phrases in the given information to create a meaningful sentence. (1)

for many/on/relied/dogs/people have/generations

They have been used for hunting and companionship.

A dog's nose and ears are very sensitive.

(ii) Report the dialogue to complete the paragraph that follows. (1 + 1)

Anil : Why is there such a big crowd on that street?

Ravi : A new shop selling sports goods is opening today.

Anil : Is a filmstar doing the opening ceremony?

Ravi : I heard that Sachin Tendulkar is inaugurating it.

Anil : Is shop offering any discount on the first day?

Anil asked Ravi (a) .... Ravi replied that a new shop (b) .... Anil enquired whether a filmstar was doing the opening ceremony Ravi replied that he had heard that Sachin Tendulkar was inaugurating that

Section–D (Literature Textbook)

[26 Marks]

8. Read the given excerpts and answer the questions briefly, for any two excepts, of the three given. **(4 + 4 = 8)**

(A) And so, I missed my chance with one of the lords
Of Life.
And I have something to expiate
A pettiness. *(Snake)*

(a) **What chance has been missed by the poet?** **(1)**

(b) **What does 'pettiness' refer to in the given lines?** **(1)**

(c) **What does the word 'expiate' mean?** **(1)**

(d) **What is the feeling of the poet at this time?** **(1)**

(B) At the top was a picture of the second Sheriff. This time though, he was wearing jeans and a sweatshirt. Printed over the bottom was a message. I'M STUCK, PLEASE HELP TO RETREIVE ME. *(Virtually True)*

(a) **Who was the message from?** **(1)**

(b) **What suggestion did the message-writer give?** **(1)**

(c) **The word 'retreive' in the extract means ....** **(1)**

(d) **Which game had the narrator just finished playing?** **(1)**

(C) These couchings and these lowly courtesies
Might fire the blood of ordinary men,
And turn pre-ordinance and first decree
Into the law of children.
Thy brother by decree is banished:
If thou dost bend and pray, and fawn, for him,
I spurn thee, like a cur, out of my way. *(Julius Caesar)*

(a) **Who is the speaker of these lines?** **(1)**

(b) **Who is being addressed and why?** **(1)**

(c) **What fails to influence Caesar?** **(1)**

(d) **What does he warn him of?** **(1)**

9. Answer any five of the following six questions in about 30-40 words each. **(5 × 2 = 10)**

(a) Describe the place near the post office. (The Letter) (2)

(b) What moral does the poem 'Ozymandias' teach? (2)

(c) Why does Caesar say 'Et tu Brute'? (2)

(d) Explain the line, 'Gainst death and all oblivious enmity' in the poem Not Marble, Nor the Gilded, Monument. (2)

(e) Why do the voices in the poet's mind advise him to kill the snake? (2)

(f) John's apprehension about his wife's reaction to the encounter with the ghost is unfounded. Justify. (2)

10. Answer any one of the following two questions in about 150 words. **(8)**

(A) Imagine you are Mrs. Packletide. After being betrayed by Louisa Mebbin, you learnt a lesson for life. Now, you are completely changed. You are purged of all ill-will and dislike that you nursed for Loona Bimberton. Write a letter of apology to Loona Bimberton telling her how you were blackmailed because of your craze for fame.

Or

(B) Discuss how the theme of art and legacy is explored in Shakespeare's 'Not Marble, Nor the Gilded Monuments' and Shelley's Ozymandias'. How do the poets use the contrast between physical structures and artistic expressions to convey the enduring power of art?

Answers

1. (i) (c) Find a comfortable resting place with a good back rest.

(ii) (b) Sustainable

(iii) he makes people aware of the trees and their ecosystem by teaching them how to climb trees and not just give factual information or organise excursion to parks and gardens.

(iv) The most suitable title for the pasage will be Curing Tree Blindness.

(v) According to the writer, climbing trees is a spot of daredevilry now because people today spend their time indoors and do not come out of the houses to enjoy nature.

(vi) The writers call the disregard for trees as 'tree blindness' because people know that there are trees around them but they just ignore them and move a ahead without paying attention to them.

(vii) The two activities in which the members of the NDNS participate in are
- teaching how to climb trees but also to make a fire, count GPS satellites and count stars
- Guerilla gardening.

(viii) Yes, I agree, with the statement that the NDNS initiative does not only teach people how to climb trees but also teaches them about the trees and its ecosystem. This is so because Khanna after making people climb the tress give them information about the tree and its ecosystem. He tells them about the kind of fruits and flowers it bears, their benefits, the shape and size of leaves, kinds of insects, birds and squirrels living on it, and any folk tales associated with it.

(ix) Yes, there may be a specific reason for not planting oak trees. According to the passage, we look for trees whose branches are thicker than one's arm. This ensure arms that one can climb the tree easily. Hence, oak trees may not have thick arms, making the people climbing it vulnerable to injury.

2. (i) her father and grandfather had told her that she had died.

(ii) Natalya

(iii) (a) confused

(iv) (a) 1 and 3

(v) Natalya does not want to name her daughter after her husband's aunt because his aunt had run away with an architect.

(vi) Ivan's statement that it was Natalya's aunt that has run away with a priest and that she is not dead gets Natalya agitated.

(vii) Ivan, to prove that her aunt had not in fact run away, had photographs in the form of a proof to disagree with his wife.

(viii) Natalya is the person who is more likely to believe in everything others say as she believes in her father regarding her husband's aunt even though her husband has proof to prove her incorrect.

3. From: students@gmail.com

To: principalxyz@gmail.com

Cc: abc@gmail.com

Date: 10th April, 20XX

Subject Leave application for four days due to sickness

Respected Sir/Ma'am

This is to inform you that I, XYZ, am a student of your school. I have written this email to inform you that I have been suffering from typhoid since yesterday. The doctor has advised me to take complete bed rest for four days. So, I request you to grant me leave for four days from 8th March, 20XX to 11th March, 20XX.

Medical certificate is attached herewith. I shall be highly obliged to you for the same.

Thanking you

Yours obediently

XYZ

Attachment : Med

4. Call me 'frugal' or 'not-interested-in-random-things', I seldom buy anything, when I am on a holiday trip, unless of course, they are exceptionally beautiful. However, when I went on a holiday trip last winter, I bought something special without worrying about its price at all. It was an extraordinarily-beautiful looking quilt blanket that was quilted with the utmost care and love from start to finish. It was a homemade quilt which used some traditional cotton fabrics in many different colors joined together in abstract pattern both at its top and bottom. Not sure, how many layers are used in this quilt or what kind of materials are used to make it soft and smooth from the inside, but those materials surely made this quilt very comfortable and light. The quilt was something special, primarily because of the way it was made. After all, it was quilted with some extraordinary designs and artworks.

5. (A) H. No. 86

Amar Colony

New Delhi-110024

24th March, 20XX

The Editor

The Times of India

New Delhi

Subject Importance of Cleanliness for Healthy Living

Sir/Ma'am

Through the columns of your esteemed newspaper, I would like to voice my concern on the issue of the dirty and unhygienic state of the roads and pavements we use regularly.

Cleanliness is one of the most important practices for a clean and healthy environment. It is essential for everyone to follow the practices necessary for maintaining cleanliness, hygiene and sanitation. Many public places in our city are left messy by our own citizens throwing packaging material, used cigarette stubs and other rubbish on our roads and nearby areas. These places look unsightly and breed fast spreading diseases like dengue, malaria, swine flu etc. Thus, it is important to follow practices like keeping our surroundings clean, avoiding littering of public places, disposing garbage at designated places, etc.

It is rightly said that cleanliness is next to godliness, as it is an all-embracing ethic of sound living.

Thanking you

Yours sincerely

Kavita

Or

(B) 32/4, Sector-4

Rohini, New Delhi-110088

6th December, 20XX

The Editor

Local Daily

Delhi

Subject The State of Sports Facilities in India

Respected Sir/Ma'am

Through the columns of your esteemed newspaper, I would like to draw the attention of the concerned authorities towards the pathetic condition of sport facilities in India.

If we look at the condition of the sports facilities, we will get to look at the shocking condition of the location as well as the equipment of all the sports except cricket. Given that most of our sports person practice in these facilities and then, go on to represent our nation on the international platform, the facility do not even stand close to the international standards. There are no artificial grass surfaces, the shooting range is not maintained and there is a lack of equipment.

All this results, the poor overall performance of the athlete in oversees games. It is time for the government and all the concerned authorities to take actions to improve this condition.

Thanking you

Yours truly

Abhinav

6. (A) **Admission Tests for Undergraduate Courses**

by Himanshu Manchanda

A new trend has developed in the process of admission for professional courses in some colleges. This is the written entrance test which is necessary to be cleared before any candidate is called for counselling. Some candidates and their parents feel that it is totally unnecessary because admission to other courses does not need any entrance test. They think that it would result in being too strict for students opting for such a course. However, such tests are required for many reasons. It is said that the aptitude of students for a subject or profession is never tested in schools. Clearing the Board exams does not reveal the true potential of the child as they can be passed by rote learning in most cases.

Instead, entrance tests try to bring out the student's true capabilities. Only those students who are serious about the course will prepare and take the tests. So, these entrance tests for professional courses are necessary and should be introduced by all colleges offering professional courses.

Or

(B) **Need for Value-Based Education**

by XYZ

Value-based education is an educational philosophy, an approach to teaching and learning that underpins away a school organise itself relationships and promotes positive human values. Schools that adopt such an approach report that there is a qualitative improvement in pupils' attitude and behaviour. The purpose of value-based education is to help the school community think about and reflect upon positive universal values and practical implications of expressing them in relation to themselves and the community as a whole.

Value-based education also supports schools in promoting an inclusive school ethos and the methods of working raise achievements and help pupils to raise their self-esteem and take responsibility for their own behaviour and learning. It also enables students to examine the kind of life that is worth living and to consider what kind of life they want for themselves. At the core of value-based education lies an agreed set of principles, deeply held convictions that underpin all aspects of school life and work. The process is holistic and developmental, demanding a greater deal from the school's community. Value-based education is, thus, a philosophy for developing and supporting schools of excellence.

7. (A) (i) speaking (ii) from (iii) knows

(B)

	Incorrect	**Correct**
(a)	conquered	conquest
(b)	in	of
(c)	being	are
(d)	those	they

(C) (i) For many generations, people have relied on dogs.

(a) why was there such a big crowd on that street

(b) selling sports goods was opening that day

8. (A) (a) The poet has missed the chance to honour such a fascinating creature as a snake.

(b) 'Pettiness' refers to the poet's mean act of throwing a log at the snake while it was going away.

(c) The word 'expiate' means 'to make amends'.

(d) The feeling of the poet at this time is one of repentance for his mean act of throwing a log at the snake without any provocation.

(B) (a) The message was from Sebastian Shultz.

(b) The message writer asked for help and asked the reader to try the game 'Dragonquest'.

(c) 'to get or bring something or someone back from somewhere'

(d) The narrator, Michael, had just finished playing the game called Wildwest.

(C) (a) Julius Caesar is the speaker.

(b) Metellus Cimber is being addressed as he is asking for a repeal for his brother's banishment.

(c) The couching and lowly courtesies fail to influence Caesar.

(d) He warns Cimber to stop his low courtesies or he will spurn him away like a dog.

9. (a) The author describes the place near the post office in an impressive way. Trees stood in a line on one side of the road and on the other side was the public garden of that town. At the end of the garden, there was a building in the newest style. It was the post office.

(b) Shelly, through the example of a vain king, Ozymandias, teaches us that nothing is permanent in this world. Ozymandias tried to make a failed attempt at eternal glory, but time is a great leveler. However, the sculptor's talent still survives, which means that only art and beauty, and not pride are eternal.

(c) The given words are supposedly the last words of Caesar after he was stabbed by the conspirators. These words mean 'Even you, Brutus' and express the shock that Caesar got when Brutus stabbed him. He never expected such a treacherous act from a 'friend'.

(d) The poet in 'Not Marble, Nor the Gilded Monuments' says that no enemy can wipe out the memory of his beloved. Neither death nor enmity that wipes out everything from people's memory can obliterate her memory. Noble souls such as of his beloved continue to be remembered even after death.

(e) The voices in the poet's mind are due to his education, which taught him that snakes with yellow brown skin colour are poisonous. These voices advise him to kill the snake, as otherwise the snake may harm the poet by biting him if it feels threatened.

(f) John was of the view that Lavinia would faint on seeing a ghost. Whenever Helen came to John, he tried to prevent Lavinia from seeing her. When Helen came last time, Lavinia managed to see Helen but she didn't faint. She began to smile and later, talked to Helen. So she was quite normal. Hence, the apprehension of John was indeed unfounded.

10. (A) #15, Curzon
Street London
24th June, 20XX

Dear Loona,

You will be shocked to receive my letter as we were never the best of friends. It's been almost five years now since we last met. As I look back on the events that went by, I feel very pity and ashamed for having conducted myself in such a poor manner. I realise that I have been vain and insensitive.

All the pomp and glory that accompanied the tiger shooting incident has revealed unconditionally my ridiculously vainglorious nature. I hate myself for having been in continuous competition with you. How lovely it would have been if we were congenial with each other!

I have a confession to make to you. The entire incident surrounding the tiger shoot was only partially true. I had not killed the tiger. It had succumbed to a natural cause. I did not disclose the truth, neither did my associates, the villagers and my paid companion, as I had paid them handsomely to buy their silence. However, I paid a heavy price for my falsehood. Louisa blackmailed me into buying her a weekend cottage to guard my secret. This shattered my self-confidence.

Realisation has dawned and I have decided to turn over a new leaf. Time has been a great teacher. It taught me that fame and money are transient, whereas human relationship is not. Loona, I earnestly wish to seek your pardon for my deplorable behaviour towards you. I extend to you my hand of friendship.

Hope you would keep in touch.
Your friend
Ruby Packletide

Or

(B) In 'Not Marble, Nor the Gilded Monuments', Shakespeare asserts that poetry transcends the physical decay of monuments. The sonnet argues that while grand structures crumble, the words of a poet can immortalise an individual's essence, preserving their legacy beyond temporal confines. Conversely, Shelley's 'Ozymandias' illustrates a ruined statue as a testament to the fleeting nature of earthly power and grandeur. The sculptor's skill, however, endures through the lifelike depiction of the king's visage and the inscribed words, which convey a timeless message about human hubris. Both poets contrast the impermanence of physical monuments with the enduring nature of artistic expression, suggesting that art captures the true essence of human achievements and legacies. Shakespeare and Shelley highlight the supremacy of art in preserving and conveying powerful messages across generations, outlasting the inevitable decay of material constructs.

Sample Question Paper 3 (Unsolved)

A Highly Simulated Sample Question Paper for CBSE Class X

English Communicative

Time : 3 hrs	M.M. : 80

General Instructions

1 The question paper is divided into four sections–*A, B, C and D*.
 Section A : Reading Skills
 Section B : Writing Skills
 Section C : Grammar
 Section D : Literature Textbook

2 There are 10 questions in the question paper. All questions are compulsory.

3 Answers should be brief and to the point.

4 You may attempt any section at a time.

5 All questions of that particular section must be attempted in the correct order.

6 Instructions are given with each section and question, wherever necessary.

Section–A (Reading Skills) [22 Marks]

1. Read the following passage. **(12 M)**

1. While there is no denying that the world loves a winner, it is important that you recognise the signs of stress in your behaviour and be healthy enough to enjoy your success. Stress can strike anytime, in a fashion that may leave you unaware of its presence in your life. While a certain amount of pressure is necessary for performance, it is important to be able to recognise your individual limit.
2. Stress is a body reaction to any demands or changes in its internal and external environment. Whenever there is a change in the external environment such as temperature, pollutants, humidity and working conditions, it leads to stress. In these days of competition, when a person makes up his mind to surpass what has been achieved by others, there is an imbalance between demands and resources, which causes psycho-social stress.
3. Stress reduces productivity and pressure to the management of organisations. Today companies prefer women to men as employees because of the hope that they bring additional qualities such as innovation, patience and dedication in the workplace. But due to increased pressure for women both at the workplace and at home, they face stress. Thus, any employee will make the maximum effort and give the maximum contribution when kept happy and without any stress. Hence, to increase productivity, it is the responsibility of the employer to keep the employees free from stress. Hence, it is essential to take steps to minimise the effects of determinants of stress and help individuals and organisations evolve newer and more effective coping strategies.
4. Stress takes a different meaning, depending on the stage of life you are in. The loss of a toy or a reprimand from the parents might create a stress shock in a child. An adolescent who fails in examination may feel as if everything has been lost and life has no further meaning. In an adult, the loss of his or her companion, job or professional failure may appear as if there is nothing more to be achieved.
5. Such signs appear, in the attitude and behaviour of the individual, as muscle tension in various parts of the body, palpitation and high blood pressure, indigestion and hyperacidity. Ultimately the result is self-destructive behaviour such as eating and drinking too much, smoking excessively or relying on tranquilisers. There are other signs of stress such as trembling, shaking, nervous blinking, dryness of throat and mouth and difficulty in swallowing. The professional under stress behaves as if he is a perfectionist.

6. A person under stress reacts in different ways and the common ones are flight, fight or flee depending upon the nature of the stress and capabilities of the person. The three responses can be elegantly chosen to cope with stress so that stress does not damage the system and become distress.
7. When a stress crosses the limit peculiar to an individual, it lowers his performance capacity. Frequent crossings of the limit may result in chronic fatigue, in which a person feels lethargic, disinterested and is not easily motivated to achieve anything. This may make the person mentally undecided, confused and accident prone as well. Diet, massage, food supplements, herbal medicines, hobbies, relaxation techniques and dance movements are excellent stress busters.

Answer the following questions based on the passage above.

(i) Complete the sentence by choosing an appropriate option. **(1)**

A certain amount of pressure is ....

(a) not necessary for performance
(b) necessary for under performance
(c) necessary for performance
(d) necessary for failure

(ii) The writer would not agree with the given statements based on paragraph three, EXCEPT **(1)**

(a) stress increases productivity.
(b) women face stress only due to increased pressure at home.
(c) an employee will give an average contribution when kept happy and without stress.
(d) to increases productivity the employer should keep his/her employees free from stress.

(iii) Complete the given sentence with an inference with respect to the following. **(1)**

The writer quotes the example of a child, an adolescent and an adult in Paragraph 5 in order to highlight that ....

(iv) Rectify the statement if it is False. **(1)**

Chronic fatigue' occurs when stress frequently crosses a limit that a person can handle effectively.

(v) List the symptoms of stress in individuals. **(1)**

(vi) What are the causes of stress? **(1)**

(vii) List the ways in which a person under stress behaves. **(2)**

(viii) List the symptoms of stress in individuals. **(2)**

(ix) How can the solutions suggested in the last paragraph best be described? **(2)**

2. Read the following passage. **(10 M)**

1. Forest fire is a major cause of injury and loss to forests. With the population increase, the frequency and subsequent damage due to forest fire is increasing day by day. The impact of the fire is diverse on the forest ecosystem. Besides directly damaging the forest trees, the fire also adversely affects forest regeneration, microclimate, soil erosion and wildlife, etc.
2. Very Heavy fire, frequent forest fire and occasional fire damage is noticed only over 0.84 per cent, 0.14 per cent, 5.16 per cent and 43.06 per cent of the forest areas, respectively. Only 6.17 per cent of the Indian forests are subjected to severe fire damage annually. In absolute terms, out of around 63 million hectares of forests, an area of around 3.73 million hectares can be presumed to be affected by fires annually.
3. In most of the cases, the forest fire causes retrogression of forest vegetation. Forest fire is one of the major degenerating factors, which extensively damages the growing stock and its generations and making area vulnerable to erosion. It has wide-ranging adverse ecological, economic and social implications.

   Forest fires in India are generally ground fires. About 35 million hectares of forest area is affected by fires annually. About 95 per cent of the forest fires are caused by human beings, especially to promote new flush of grasses, collection of minor forest produce or to prepare land for shifting cultivation. While statistical data on fire loss in India are very weak, it is estimated that the proportion of the forest areas prone to forest fire annually ranges from 33% to over 90% in different states.

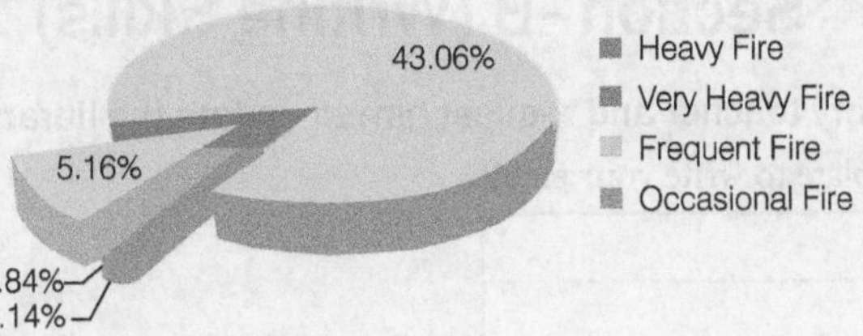

Answer the following questions based on the passage above.

(i) Complete the sentence suitably.

Some forest fires are deliberately created to .... **(1)**

(ii) Select the appropriate option to fill in the blank.

From Paragraph 1, we can infer that the increase in population has resulted in the .... of forest fires. (increase/stabilisation) **(1)**

(iii) Which of the following is not True as per the passage? **(1)**

(a) Most deforestation occurs due to forest fires.
(b) The frequency of forest fires has increased rapidly.
(c) The ecosystem is heavily damaged due to forest fires.
(d) None of the above

(iv) Select the chart that appropriately represents the cause of forest fires. **(1)**

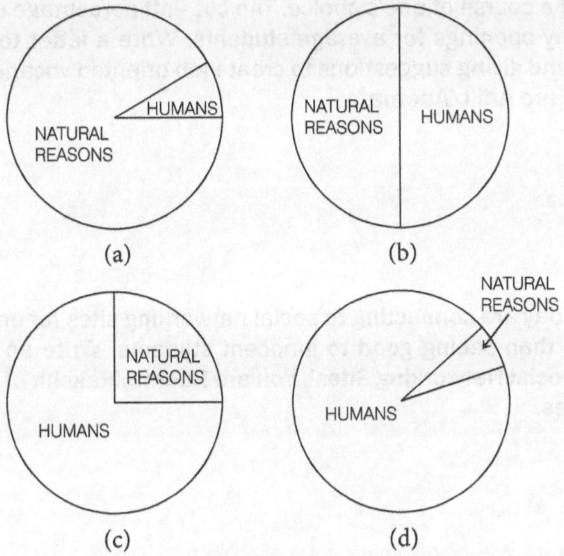

(v) List 2 things that a forest fire affects in an unfavourable way? **(1)**

(vi) According to the passage, what results in forest fires and what do forest fires result in? **(1)**

(vii) Justify the following forest fire is not a major concern in India. **(2)**

(viii) How much is the estimated forest cover in India? **(2)**

Section–B (Writing Skills)

[22 Marks]

3. Write an email to your library teacher and request him to update the library with some new books. **(3)**

You may copy the given template to write your email.

From	
To	
Cc	
Date	
Subject	

4. Write a factual description of handmade gift you have treasured in not more than 100 words. **(4)**

5. (A) You are Sridhar/Smita, the Head Boy/Head Girl of Gemini Public School, Jayanagar, Bengaluru. An excursion has been planned for the Class X students from your school to Mysuru. Write a letter to the Secretary, Deeka Youth Hostel, Mysuru, requesting him to provide accommodation for 15 girls and 20 boys for three days. (120 words) **(7)**

Or

(B) A student's anxieties never end. After clearing the Class XII Board Examination, there is the uncertainty of getting admission in a college and a course of one's choice. The cut –off percentage in good colleges rises every year. There are hardly any openings for average students. Write a letter to the Editor of a National Daily stating the problems and giving suggestions to create job-oriented vocational courses for students after passing Class XII. You are Arijit/Aperna.

Clues

- Cut off percentage rising
- Students are inable to get admission
- Increasing demotivation in students
- Create job-oriented courses

6. (A) You notice that a lot of youngsters today are connecting to social networking sites for one reason or the other. At times, it brings more evils than seeing good to innocent students. Write an article for your school magazine on 'Bad effects of Social Networking Sites'. You are Reema/Rakshit of Class XII-C. You can take help from the following clues. **(8)**

- Mania of sites
- Keeps one distracted
- Information that is fake or distorted
- Necessity of counselling

Or

(B) Places of pilgrimage have turned into tourist spots. As a result of this, they are losing their importance and grace, thereby disturbing nature too. You are Swati/Sandeep, a columnist for an e-zine. Draft an article on the theme of maintaining the grace of places of pilgrimage. Explore possible reasons for the prevailing situation and include suggestions for addressing it. You may use the clues given below.

- Flooded with tourists
- construction of roads, hotels, etc
- Litter and pollute pilgrimages
- Realise the real essence
- Located on high mountains
- Excess footfall

Section–C (Grammar)

[10 Marks]

7. Complete the tasks A-C, as directed.

(A) In the passage given below, fill in any four of the blanks with the most appropriate tenses of the verbs given in brackets after each blank. Write the answers in your answer sheet against the correct blank numbers. **(3)**

Yesterday, Savita **(i)** .... (come) to my house to give me the happy news of her standing first in the Board Examination. I **(ii)** .... (be) overjoyed to know this. We **(iii)** .... (share) our views regarding the latest trend in paper setting. She also told me that she attended all the classes regularly.

(B) In the passage given below, one word has been omitted in each line. Write any four of the missing words along with the word that comes before and the word that comes after it in your answer sheet. **(4)**

	Before	Missing	After
(a) Egyptian pyramids served tombs for kings	....	....	....
(b) and queens, but they also places of ongoing	....	....	....
(c) religious activity. After a ruler died, his her	....	....	....
(d) body carefully treated and wrapped to	....	....	....
(e) preserve it a mummy.	....	....	....

(C) Do as directed.

(i) Rearrange the following jumbled words/phrases in the given story to create a meaningful sentence. **(1)**

a/time/upon/there/a/was/merchant/once/rich

He was coming back from a fair. He had a large sum of money with him. The merchant as well as his money got wet. He had to hurry up home to dry his money.

(ii) Report the dialogue to complete the paragraph given below **(1 + 1)**

Mom	Tomorrow is Diwali, so I am going to the market. Do you want anything?
Shreya	Shall I come along, mom?
Mom	No Shreya, I want you to do some cleaning.
Shreya	Fine mom, I will stay at home and do the cleaning.

Mom told her daughter Shreya that *(a)* .... she also asked Shreya *(b)* .... The daughter asked if she could come along with her, to this Mom replied in negative and added that she wanted her to do the cleaning. The daughter agreed to it and stayed back.

Section–D (Literature Textbook)

[26 Marks]

8. Read the given excerpts and answer the questions briefly, for any two excepts, of the three given. **(4 + 4 = 8)**

(A) Not that the lust to kill had suddenly descended on her, or that she felt that she would leave India safer and more wholesome than she had found it, with one fraction less of wild beast per million of inhabitants.

(a) Identify 'she' in the extract given above and list two of her characteristics? **(1)**

(b) Why did she want to shoot a tiger? How does it display her vanity? **(1)**

(c) Examine the use of the word 'lust' in the extract'. **(1)**

(d) What is the tone of the author? **(1)**

(B) 'And some in dreams assured were
of the spirit that plagued us so;
Nine fathom deep he had followed us
From the Land of mist and snow.'

(a) Who are 'us' in the above lines? (1)

(b) What does the word 'plague' indicate? (1)

(c) How are the speakers feeling in the extract? (1)

(d) Whose spirit plagued 'us' and why? (1)

(C) Mrs. Slater : She's never been here since grandfather bought it. If it was only down here instead of in his room, she'd never guess it wasn't our own.
Henry : (startled) Amelia! (He rises.)
Mrs. Slater : Henry, why shouldn't we bring that bureau down here now? We could do it before they come.
Henry (stupefied) : I wouldn't care to.
Mrs. Slater : Don't look so daft. Why not?

(a) What is 'it' in the present context? (1)

(b) Who is 'she' in the present context? (1)

(c) Why does the speaker say these words? (1)

(d) Why does the speaker not want ' she' to guess that 'it' belonged to grandfather? (1)

9. Answer any five of the following six questions in about 30-40 words each. (5 × 2 = 10)

(a) What reason did Mrs. Slater give when grandfather found Henry wearing his slippers in the play 'The Dear Departed'? **(2)**

(b) In what ways does the Frog assert his importance in the poem 'The Frog and the Nightingale? **(2)**

(c) "The heavens themselves blaze forth the death of princes." Elaborate as per the drama Julius Caesar. **(2)**

(d) Why did Nishikanto Babu give Patol Babu's address to his youngest brother-in-law? **(2)**

(e) Explain why Ozymandias' boast could never be justified. **(2)**

(f) What problems did Helen, the ghost cause in John Hallock's life in 'Shady Plot'?

10. Answer any one of the following questions in about 150 words. (8)

(A) "Punishment does catch up with the sinner although it may be delayed sometimes." Comment on this statement with reference to poem 'The Rine of the Ancient Mariner' and the drama 'Julius Caeser'.

Or

(B) Do you think computer games like the ones Shultz and Michael played can be used to teach or inculcate positive values among children? Give reasons in support of your answer.

Sample Question Paper 4 (Unsolved)

A Highly Simulated Sample Question Paper for CBSE Class X

English Communicative

Time : 3 hrs	M.M. : 80

General Instructions

1 The question paper is divided into four sections–*A, B, C and D.*

Section A : Reading Skills
Section B : Writing Skills
Section C : Grammar
Section D : Literature Textbook

2 There are 10 questions in the question paper. All questions are compulsory.

3 Answers should be brief and to the point.

4 You may attempt any section at a time.

5 All questions of that particular section must be attempted in the correct order.

6 Instructions are given with each section and question, wherever necessary.

Section–A (Reading Skills) [22 Marks]

1. Read the following passage. **(12 M)**

1. An urgent problem is now threatening libraries throughout the world. Their collections, which are crucial for diverse purposes as economic development, educational research and recreational pursuits are in danger of disintegration.
2. The problem is mainly due to one cause–the type of paper on which books have been printed for the past one and a half centuries. Until the 1850s, paper was produced from linen or cotton rags and proved to be relatively long-lasting. In the mid-19th century, however, the popular demand for paper and the commercial need for an economic method of production led to the use of mechanically ground wood pulp. Paper manufactured from wood pulp is highly acidic and therefore, inherently unstable. It contains lignin which causes paper to discolour and disintegrate.
3. Programmes are now being developed with two main aims in mind: on one hand, to improve the physical condition of library collections, especially by the process called 'mass deacidification' (to eliminate acid from the paper of published books and insert a buffer compound that will provide protection against future) and on the other, to transfer the contents of existing books to another medium.
4. Libraries will only be able to carry out these special tasks with the assistance of experts such as book conservators and high technology specialists. But, there is another group whose cooperation will be crucial, if the problem of decaying collections is to be arrested: the printing and publishing industries. The existing problem that of book collections already assembled in libraries is of vast proportions. It is intensified by the continuing use of acid-based paper in book publishing. The key issue is, how to preserve the books of the future, not simply those of the past.
5. If the future dimensions of the conservation problem are to be curbed, there will be a necessity of widespread adoption of paper which is of archival quality.
6. This change does not relate to a narrowly perceived need because the long-term preservation of library collections is important both for the overall social benefits they bring as well as for the special advantages they bestow on the printing and publishing industries.

7. In the first place, libraries are of critical importance to the well-being of citizens, since they provide the knowledge base of society. They contain the record of humanity, the accumulation of ideas and insights and discoveries on which social effort and progress are possible. The destruction of libraries would represent an immense cultural loss, a form of amnesia, which would affect every member of society.

Answer the following questions based on the passage above.

(i) Libraries can save their collections by .... **(1)**

(a) storing them in air-conditioned rooms
(b) laminating the pages
(c) creating a dust-free atmosphere in their premises
(d) widespread adoption of paper of archival quality

(ii) The writer would agree with the given statements based on Paragraph 2, Except. **(1)**

(a) The paper produced from wood pulp is not everlasting.
(b) The paper produced from wood pulp is acidic in nature.
(c) The paper produced from wood pulp is still being produced.
(d) The paper produced from wood pulp is prone to discoloring.

(iii) Complete the sentence appropriately. **(1)**

The need to produce mechanically ground wood pulp arise during the mid-nineteenth century because ....

(iv) Rectify the given False statement. **(1)**

Libraries are gaining back their significance in the 21st century.

(v) Comment on the importance of libraries referred to in the paragraph one. **(1)**

(vi) Why are the printing and publishing industries crucial to cause of protecting libraries? **(1)**

(vii) List the two ways in which a book by Robert Frost could be saved from deterioration and loss. **(2)**

(viii) According to the passage, linen or cotton rags were used as paper until the 1850's. Based on your understanding of the passage, state whether you promote going to back to using them as paper. Give reason for your answer. **(2)**

(ix) How can the tone of the passage be best described? Give reason for your answer. **(2)**

2. Read the following passage. **(10 M)**

1. The North-East of India is a melting pot of variegated cultural mosaic of people and races, an ethnic tapestry of many hues and shades. Yet, these states are lesser explored as compared to the rest of the country. The new generations of travellers who are 'money rich and time poor ' are increasingly looking for unique experiences —a phenomenon being called the emergence of the 'Experience Economy'. For this new and growing breed of tourists, the North-East with its variety and uniqueness holds immense attraction.

2. A study conducted in 2020 by Dr. Sherap Bhutia, revealed that the foreign tourist arrival in the North-East increased from 37,380 persons in 2005 to 118,552 in 2014. The overall growth rate of tourist (both domestic and foreign) in the North-East was as high as 26.44% during 2005-06. A high and positive growth of 12.53% was registered in foreign tourist visits to North-East States of India during 2012 from 2011, which further rose to register a growth of 27.93% during 2013 from 2012. Foreign tourist arrivals in the North-East witnessed a growth of 39.77% during 2014 from 2013, according to data provided from the Ministry of Tourism, Government of India.

3. The study recommendations for tourism planners included the need to concentrate on some key areas like enhancement of tourist facilities, tourism financing, focus on community involvement and others for the formulation of a sustainable tourism strategy in the North-East States of India.

Answer the following questions based on the passage above.

(i) Complete the sentence appropriately.

Travellers advocating the 'experience economy' seek a holiday package with .... (1)

(ii) Complete the following analogy correctly with a word/phrase from Paragraph 1. (1)

Aroma : Cooking :: .... : Painting

(iii) Fill in the blank by selecting the correct option. (1)

The study of tourist travel statistics in the North-East, from 2005 to 2014 showed .... results.

(a) expected (b) encouraging (c) inconsistent (d) questionable

(iv) Select the appropriate option to fill in the blanks. (1)

From Paragraph 1, we can infer that the .... and .... of the North-Eastern states aid attracting the 'money rich and time poor' tourists.

1. distinctiveness 2. conventionality 3. diversity 4. uniformity

5. modernity

Codes

(a) 1 and 3 (b) 2 and 4 (c) 2 and 5 (d) 1 and 4

(v) Infer one reason for the following based on information in paragraph 1. (1)

The rate of tourism in the North-East of India puzzles tourism officials.

(vi) List one reason why the researchers recommend that the formulation of a tourism strategy in the North-Eastern States of India be sustainable. (1)

(vii) List any 2 examples of 'tourist facilities' as referred to, in Paragraph 3. (2)

(viii) Describe the trend of foreign tourist travels in the North-East, from 2011-2014 as per Paragraph 2. (2)

Section–B (Writing Skills)

[22 Marks]

3. Write an email to the Principal of your school requesting him to arrange extra classes for computers. (3)

You may copy the given template to write your email.

From	
To	
Cc	
Date	
Subject	

4. Write a factual description of your favourite teacher in not more than 100 words. (4)

5. (A) You are Sunidhi Prakash, the Vice Captain of Brilliant Vidyalaya, Barra, Kanpur. You have recently noticed several posters around your school premises conveying a hazardous message. (7)

Lose weight in just a month!

"A WONDER DIET comes to your rescue...

A privilege available for only a few!"

Write a letter to the Editor of The DWA, in not more than 120 words, drawing attention towards harm caused by such advertising. Propose the implementation of 'Wholesome LunchMonth' in schools as an idea to address such practices, mention the advantages and share suggestions to foster healthy eating routines and develop positive body image among youngsters you can use the ideas that you have gathered from to MCB Health and Medicine.

Or

(B) You are Samina Zaveri, Class X, Vadodara, Gujarat. You come across the following information on a local library's notice board.

Create Your Own Board Game Competition!

Create Your Own Board Game Competition! Create an educational board game, and send it to us at Teen-Toggle Games Pvt. Ltd, 307, Satija building, Colaba,Mumbai by July 2022. The top 10 winning board games will be featured on our international portal. Attractive scholarships for the winners!

You wish to participate but require more information. Write a letter to Teen-Toggle Games Pvt.Ltd in about 120 words, enquiring about rules, scholarship details and deadlines. Also enquire about specifications for solo or group entries.

6. (A) You are Rahul of Class XII B. Information technology has brought about a global revolution in all fields. Computer aided education is fast becoming the order of the day. The market is flooded with educational CDs and online learning is a new phenomenon. Write an article on 'Computers Replace Classroom Teaching' for your school magazine. Use the given clues along with your own ideas and those that you have gathered from Unit 2: Education (150 words) **(8)**

- Advent of technology
- Anywhere and at anytime
- Lecture recorded
- Audio-visual method
- Combined theory and practical

Or

(B) The sports field is said to be a minifield of life. Whatever we experience or learn here serves as an invaluable experience to us for life. Write an article on 'More Lessons are Learnt on the Sports Field than in the Classroom' in 150 words. You are Sarika/Sandeep. You can use the following clues.

Clues

- Cooperation, teamwork, leadership
- Tolerance and understanding
- No caste and religious prejudice
- Healthy life

Section–C (Grammar) [10 Marks]

7. Complete the tasks A-C, as directed.

(A) Fill the blanks (i)-(iii) with the appropriate option from those in the brackets. **(3)**

Gavri was only eight years old, but **(i)** .... (a/an/the)mountain of family responsibilities had already **(ii)**......... (descends/ descended/descending) **(iii)** ....(on/over/to) her head.

(B) The following passage has not been edited. There is one error in each line. Write the incorrect word and the correction in your answer sheet in any four of the given blanks against the correct blank number. The first one has been done as an example. **(4)**

	Incorrect	**Correct**
The passenger were waiting at the	passenger	passengers
(a) station when five policemen rushing	....	....
(b) into difference compartments of a	....	....
(c) train. After some times one of them	....	....
(d) comes out with two young men	....	....
and soon the other policemen joined her.		

(C) Do as directed.

(i) Rearrange the following word clusters in the given information to make meaningful sentence. (1)

Moths are insects like butterflies. They also go through metamorphosis and are nocturnal.

lay/which/turn/they/into/eggs/caterpillars

(ii) Report the dialogues to complete the paragraph that follows. (1 + 1)

Charlie: Dear Santa, here is a list if what I want.

Patty: How do you suppose Santa Claus can afford to give away all those toys?

Charlie: Promotion! Don't kid yourself ...... Everything these days is promotion! I will bet if the truth were brought about, you will find that he's being financed by some big eastern chain!

While making the list of what Charlie wanted from Santa Claus, he asked Patty how ....(i)............ all those toys. She said that ....(ii)............ and that it was possible as Santa was being financed by some big eastern chain big eastern chain.

Section-D (Literature Textbook) [26 Marks]

8. Read the given excerpts and answer the questions briefly, for any two excepts, of the three given. (4 + 4 = 8)

(A) And immediately I regretted it.
I thought how paltry, how vulgar, what a mean act!
I despised myself and the voices of my accursed human education.

(a) What is the poet regretting? (1)

(b) Why does he call his education 'accursed'? (1)

(c) Give the synonym of the word 'paltry'. (1)

(d) What was the result of the poet's action? (1)

(B) "My hero! she squealed. 'Take me away from all this'. "Behind me I could hear the dragon roaring".

'Never mind her,' came a voice and a second knight appeared from the wardrobe. 'It's me who needs rescuing!'

Sebastian? I said.

(a) Who is the speaker? (1)

(b) Why did 'she' squeal? (1)

(c) Who is the hero? Explain the context of the given lines. (1)

(d) Explain "Take me away from all this". (1)

(C) "Elizabeth's that sharp she'll see I'm after it, and she'll drive a hard bargain over it.
Eh, what it is to have a low money grubbing spirit!"

(a) What is the relation of the speaker with Elizabeth? (1)

(b) What does 'it' in this extract stand for? (1)

(c) What bargaining is being discussed here? (1)

(d) Explain the meaning of the expression 'a low money grubbing spirit'? (1)

9. Answer any five of the following six questions in about 30-40 words each. **(5 × 2 = 10)**

(a) 'Ali displays qualities of love and patience'. Elaborate as per the story 'The Letter'. **(2)**

(b) What made Lavinia buy an Ouija board in 'Shady Plot' ? How did the narrator react to her doing this? **(2)**

(c) Why does the narrator address the two boys as gentlemen in the story 'Two Gentleman of Verona'? **(2)**

(d) How does the poem 'Ozymandias' convey the briefness of human life ? **(2)**

(e) Mark Antony is a skilled orator. Justify with reference to play Julius Caesar. **(2)**

(f) What was the intitial outcome of the nightingale's singing ? **(2)**

10. Answer any one of the following questions in about 150 words. **(8)**

(A) A person who is vain is full of self-importance and can only think of himself/ herself. He/ She can go to great lengths to prove his/her superiority. Do you think Mrs. Packletide is vain? Give reasons in support of your answer.

Or

(B) In your opinion, is the Ancient Mariner's punishment for killing the albatross fair? Whose fate is worse, the Ancient Mariner's or the sailors'? Why?

Sample Question Paper 5 (Unsolved)

A Highly Simulated Sample Question Paper for CBSE Class X

English Communicative

Time : 3 hrs	M.M. : 80

General Instructions

1 The question paper is divided into four sections–*A, B, C and D.*

Section A : Reading Skills

Section B : Writing Skills

Section C : Grammar

Section D : Literature Textbook

2 There are 10 questions in the question paper. All questions are compulsory.

3 Answers should be brief and to the point.

4 You may attempt any section at a time.

5 All questions of that particular section must be attempted in the correct order.

6 Instructions are given with each section and question, wherever necessary.

Section–A (Reading Skills) [22 Marks]

1. Read the following passage. (12 M)

1. World Conservation Day is celebrated internationally to increase awareness about the best practices needed to protect our natural resources. The Earth is supplied with a limited amount of resources that we all rely upon, like water, air, soil and trees. The World Nature Conservation Movement is a great opportunity to celebrate the progress we've made and determine to take action, wherever needed. It is time to remind ourselves that we need to give back to nature instead of just using resources without thinking about conservation. There is a need to replenish and recycle the resources we consume from nature.
2. Our forests, rivers, oceans and soils provide us with the food we eat, the air we breathe, the water we irrigate our crops with. We also rely on them for numerous other goods and services. We depend on them for our health, happiness and prosperity. We have a cycle of biodiversity which needs proper conservation.
3. The population explosion remains one of the major reasons why natural resources are getting depleted at a very fast rate. Technological advancement and luxurious lifestyles have led to several environmental problems like global warming, ozone layer depletion, river water pollution and deforestation which threaten the planet's future.
4. Humans, animals, marine creatures and the environment, all need to be protected and conserved for the planet's future well-being. There are many examples of conservation. One is a programme to try to preserve wetlands, or a programme to try and save old buildings. Another example is of an attempt to minimise the amount of electricity used by turning off lights when leaving a room, or an attempt to turn off the running tap to avoid wastage of water. There are lots of examples like these which need implementation.
5. Following these small steps in our daily lives we can help to maintain the balance of nature, thereby saving humankind from the kinds of natural disasters we may face in the near future.
6. Nature also has a profound impact on our minds and our behaviour, helping reduce anxiety, brooding, and stress and increase our attention, capacity, creativity and ability to connect with other people. So there is a need to save nature if we want to save life as the two are interconnected and need each other. If we hurt or destroy the environment, surely we will be ruined. We must create awareness among family members, and try and practise a sustainable lifestyle to protect and conserve nature.

Answer the following questions based on the passage above.

(i) Why is there is an urgent need to conserve our natural resources? (1)

(a) We are aimlessly using the natural resources and not replenishing them.

(b) They will be replaced by manmade resources.

(c) Serious efforts are needed to cut down the consumption of these resources.

(d) We must become alert before it is too late.

(ii) How can the solutions suggested in Paragraph 4 be best described? (1)

(a) Unrealistic (b) Short term (c) Practical (d) Challenging

(iii) Complete the sentence appropriately. (1)

It is fair to say that population explosion remains one of the major reasons why natural resources are getting depleted rapidly because ....

(iv) Rectify the sentence if it is False. (1)

The suitable title for the given passage is Save Nature Save Life.

(v) In Paragraph 1, the writer talks about 'celebrating the progress'. Explain in context. (1)

(vi) In the context of the given passage, what is the synonym of 'replenish' Paragraph 1? (1)

(vii) In the opinion of the writer, which are the primary natural resources without which our life is not possible? (2)

(viii) List two ways in which forests and rivers help mankind. (2)

(ix) Why does writer quote the example of family awareness? (2)

2. Read the following passage and answer the questions that follow. (10 M)

1. Access to primary education is a basic right of every child. An effective primary education can build a solid foundation and open avenues for future success. With its profound implications on both the individual and society, primary education plays a crucial role in reducing extreme poverty and promoting social changes. The Sustainable Development Agenda acknowledges the importance of primary education in Goal 4 which stipulates that by 2030, the world should ensure inclusive and equitable quality education and promote lifelong learning opportunities for all, including a target on universal access to primary education. Though there are varying standards, primary education is typically designed for children 6 to 11 years of age.
2. Significant progress has been made toward achieving universal primary education. Globally, the adjusted net attendance rate reached 87 per cent in 2019 and about four out of five children attending primary education completed it. Additionally, over the past two decades, the number of out-of-school children was reduced by over 40 per cent. However, there is still a long way to go: 58 million children of primary school age remain out of school, with the majority of them coming from marginalised groups. In addition, recent Multiple Indicator Cluster Surveys (MICS) results show that many children do not have foundational reading and numeracy skills, highlighting the massive challenge to achieving inclusive and equitable quality education for all.
3. Globally, a lower proportion of children from the poorest families attend primary education compared with their wealthier peers. While almost all children from the top wealth quintile attend primary education, only 75 per cent of children from the bottom wealth quintile do.
4. Across different regions, household wealth impacts primary school completion rates differently. West and Central Africa has the largest gap of 58 percentage points in primary school completion rates between the richest and poorest quintiles. In contrast, in East Asia and the Pacific and Latin America and the Caribbean, children from the top and bottom wealth quintiles complete primary school at more similar rates, with a gap of just 13 percentage points.
5. In the past 20 years, the number of out-of-school children of primary education age fell by more than 40 per cent, from 99 million in 2000 to 58 million in 2019. However, 54 per cent of these out-of-school children were girls. Despite this tremendous progress, the world must accelerate the pace at which the number of out-of-school children is reduced, as the total has remained stagnant since 2007.

Answer the following questions based on the passage above.

(i) Complete the following sentence. (1)

.... and .... have the highest rates of primary education completion in the rich quintile.

(ii) Complete the following analogy correctly with a word/phrase from the passage. (1)

Usual: Strange :: .... : Miniscule

(iii) "In 2019, about four out of five children attending primary education completed it suggests that (1)

(a) less than 80% children completed primary education
(b) almost 100% children completed primary education
(c) more than 80% children completed primary education
(d) about 80% children completed the primary education

(iv) What do you think could be the reasons for not completing primary education? (1)

1. Poverty 2. Inaccessibility 3. Feasibility 4. Discrimination
5. Child labour and trafficking 6. Displacement

Codes

(a) 1, 2 and 3 (b) 3, 4, 5 and 6 (c) 1, 4, 5 and 6 (d) All of these

(v) State one target related to primary education. (1)

(vi) How much decline in the number of out-of-school children of primary education age is seen in the past two decades? (1)

(vii) How is primary education critical to both an individual and a society? (2)

(viii) How does the sustainable development goals give importance to primary education? (2)

Section–B (Writing Skills) [22 Marks]

3. Write an email to your Principal asking him to start skill development programmes in the school. (3)

You may copy the given template to write your email.

From	
To	
Cc	
Date	
Subject	

4. Write a factual description of the most important technological advancement in not more than 100 words. (4)

5. (A) Write a letter to a training institute enquiring about the various courses available there for building a scientific temperament among students. You are Rishi/Rashi of Patel Nagar, Delhi. (120 words) (7)

Or

(B) Read the following advertisement for products using solar energy.

- Solar Power Systems For A Greener India
- Excellent Offers
- Solar Cookers
- Solar Lanterns
- Solar Heating/Cooking Systems
- Solar Water Heater
- Raj Solar Sales and Service 45-Panchkuian Road New Delhi

Write a letter to the editor of an English daily, making a plea to the common people to switch over to solar energy to conserve electricity and limit electricity bills.

6. **(A) You are Shruti of Class XII-D. You are a member of the Environment Society of your school. Write an article on 'Reduce Environmental Pollution Through Education and Legislation'. You can take help from the following clues.** **(8)**

- Environment getting destroyed due to pollutants and exploitation of natural resources
- Contamination of environment causes many diseases
- People need to be educated about using environment friendly items

Or

(B) Every activity that man indulges in creates pollution and waste of some kind. In fact, the need of the hour is to reduce pollution in all possible ways. Write an article on the topic 'Reducing Pollution—Need of the Hour'. You are Brinda, an environmentalist. You can take help from the given clues.

- What is pollution?
- Reasons behind increase in pollution
- Harmful effects of pollution
- Steps to reduce the pollution
- Government role

SECTION–C (Grammar)

[10 Marks]

7. **Complete the tasks A-C, as directed.**

(A) In the passage given below, fill in any four of the blanks with the correct forms of verbs given in brackets immediately after each blank. Write the answers in your answer sheet against the correct blank numbers. **(3)**

There (i) .... (live) many rabbits in their burrows in the lake area. When the herds of elephants (ii) .... (walk) around they (iii) .... (stamp) the burrows with their heavy feet.

(B) In the passage given below, one word has been omitted in each line. Write any four of the missing words along with the word that comes before and the word that comes after it in your answer sheet. The first one has been done as an example. **(4)**

	Before	Missing	After
When in evening Hari Ram's son did not come, he	in	the	evening
(a) and his wife very much sad and worried. The son	....	....	....
(b) arrived three days. When Hari Ram asked him where	....	....	....
(c) he was for three days, he replied that he had to Goa	....	....	....
(d) and not return due to the late running of the train.	....	....	....
(e) Hari Ram asked him to inform him he went out again.	....	....	....

(C) Do as directed.

(i) Rearrange the following word clusters in the given information to make meaningful sentences. **(1)**

The earthworm is the worm we know best.
An earthworm wriggles like most worms do.
Some worms have no legs but they can swim.
Earthworms live in the ground.
rainy/season/come/during/in/large/numbers/they/out

(ii) Report the dialogues to complete the paragraphs given below **(1 + 1)**

Yashvi How did you spend your holidays?
Saksham I went for cricket coaching. What did you do?
Yashvi I went for the NTSC coaching classes.
Saksham At least during the holidays you could have enjoyed yourself.

Yashvi asked Saksham ....*(a)*.........his holidays. Saksham said that ....*(b)*......... for Cricket coaching and wanted to know she had enjoyed going for during holidays. When Yashvi told him that she has gone for the NTSC coaching classes, Saksham told her that she could have enjoyed herself during the holidays.

SECTION–D (Literature Textbook) [26 Marks]

8. Read the given extracts below and answer the questions briefly for any two extracts of the three given. **(4 + 4 = 8)**

A. He holds him with his skinny hand,
"There was a ship", quoth he.
'Hold off! unhand me, grey-beard loon'
Eftsoons his hand dropt he.
(The Rime of the Ancient Mariner)

(a) Synonym of 'skinny' is .... (1)

(b) Why does 'He' hold 'him' with his skinny hand? (1)

(c) Who is the 'grey-beard loon' here? (1)

(d) Whose hand was held by 'He'? (1)

B. I waited outside until the boys rejoined me, then drone them back to the city. They sat beside me, not speaking. for my part, I did not say a word ... . I knew they would prefer to feel that they had safely kept their secret. Yet their devotion had touched me deeply. War had not broken their spirit. Their selfless action brought a new nobility to human life, gave promise of a greater hope for human society. *(Two Gentlemen of Verona)*

(a) Whose devotion is the narrator talking about? (1)

(b) What does the narrator mean by 'their devotion'? (1)

(c) What proves that they are true gentlemen? (1)

(d) What can be synonym of the word 'nobility'? (1)

C. "Well, I don't call that delicate, stepping into a dead man's shoes in such haste." *(The Dear Departed)*

(a) Who makes this comment? (1)

(b) What prompts the speaker to say this? (1)

(c) What does the speaker mean by 'delicate'? (1)

(d) What was done in haste? (1)

9. Answer any five of the following six questions in about 30-40 words each. **(5 × 2 = 10)**

(a) Was the nightingale really stupid? Comment. **(2)**

(b) Who was Helen ? Why had to come to John Hallock? **(2)**

(c) What is the 'Ring-o' Bells' and how is it important in the play 'The Dear Departed'? **(2)**

(d) Describe the snake in the poem by DH Lawrence. **(2)**

(e) How does Shakespeare put his poetry on a pedestal in the poem, 'Not Marble, nor Gilded Monuments'? **(2)**

(f) Why had Michael and his father gone to the computer fair in the story 'Virtually True'? **(2)**

10. Answer any one of the following questions in about 150 words. **(8)**

(A) Human relationships often cause a lot of pain and anguish to the people concerned. Do you agree? Write with reference to the story 'The Letter'. What values do you think can minimise such sufferings?

Or

(B) The human race longs for immortality. To what extent do people go to achieve it? Is it possible to achieve it? Is it even necessary? Discuss, with reference to Ozymandias.

CBSE
Examination Paper 2025

ENGLISH COMMUNICATIVE

Time : 3 Hours **Max. Marks : 80**

General Instructions

Read the following instructions very carefully and strictly follow them :

(i) The question paper is divided into **four** sections—A, B, C and D.

Section A — Reading Skills	**22 Marks**
Section B — Writing Skills	**22 Marks**
Section C — Grammar	**10 Marks**
Section D — Literature Textbook	**26 Marks**

(ii) There are **10** questions in the question paper. **All** questions are **compulsory**.

(iii) Answers should be brief and to the point.

(iv) You may attempt any section at a time.

(v) All questions of that particular section must be attempted in the correct order.

(vi) Instructions are given with each section and question, wherever necessary.

Section–A (Reading Skills)

[22 Marks]

1. Read the following passage carefully. **(12)**

(1) India, often celebrated as a land of diversity, is a unique blend of various cultures, languages, religions, and traditions. Known for its rich historical heritage, India stands as a testament to the coexistence of a multitude of identities harmoniously under one nation.

(2) The Indian subcontinent is home to a multitude of languages. The Constitution of India recognises 22 official languages, with Hindi being the most widely spoken. Besides, there are over a thousand dialects spoken across the country. This linguistic diversity is reflective of India's cultural richness and its people's adaptability and acceptance of varied means of expression.

(3) Religion plays a central role in the lives of many Indians, contributing significantly to the country's cultural diversity. India is the birthplace of major religions such as Hinduism, Buddhism, Jainism, and Sikhism, and also harbours significant populations of Muslims, Christians, Sikhs, Buddhists, and other communities. Religious festivals like Diwali, Eid, Christmas, and Vesak are celebrated with great enthusiasm, showcasing this unity in diversity.

(4) The Indian cuisine is another example of regional diversity turning into a national treasure. From the fiery dishes of the South to the rich curries of the North, and from the sweets of Gujarat to the street food of Mumbai, each region contributes to the subcontinent's eclectic palate. This culinary variety not only highlights India's diverse geography but also brings people together through a shared love for food.

(5) Cultural practices vary widely across regions. (Traditional dance forms like Bharatanatyam from Tamil Nadu, Kathak from North India, and Odissi from Odisha, along with classical music forms like Carnatic and Hindustani, illustrate the rich tapestry of regional art forms that together represent India's cultural unity.

(6) The principle of unity in diversity is perhaps best reflected in the Indian democratic system, where people from diverse backgrounds come together to participate in the world's largest democracy. The Indian Constitution guarantees Fundamental Rights and freedoms to all its citizens, ensuring equality and justice by transcending regional and cultural barriers.

(7) Challenges to this unity arise, such as regional conflicts and cultural misunderstandings, but the overarching narrative of mutual coexistence persists. India's ability to embrace diversity as a strength rather than a hindrance sets it apart globally as a symbol of unity.

Answer the following questions based on the above passage.

(i) The celebration of various festivals in India demonstrates. **(1)**

(a) Expertise (b) Skills (c) Regionalism (d) Diversity

(ii) What role does language play in Indian diversity? **(1)**

(a) It is a unique blend of various religions. (b) It stands as a testament to South-East Asia.

(c) It reflects India's cultural richness. (d) It ensures justice for all.

(iii) Complete the following suitably. **(1)**

India stands as a testament to the coexistence of a multitude of identities harmoniously because ....

(iv) Rectify the given false statement. **(1)**

The linguistic diversity is reflective of the people's intolerance of varied means of expression.

(v) List any one classical music form mentioned in the passage. **(1)**

(vi) What does the Indian Constitution guarantee to all its citizens? **(1)**

(vii) How is Indian cuisine an example of regional diversity? **(2)**

(viii) Explain in about 30-40 words, how the various Indian art forms represent cultural unity. **(2)**

(ix) What is the overarching narrative of India's existence as per the passage? **(2)**

2. Read the following passage carefully. **(10)**

Why do people travel?

(1) There are many reasons for travel. Most tourist trips can be placed under the following categories.

(2) Leisure tourism trips make up 42% of travel. The main purpose is relaxation, rest and enjoyment. Most holidays are taken in family groups, couples or with groups of friends. Sometimes, people may choose to go on holiday by themselves to be on their own, or perhaps to meet new friends. Short breaks of less than one week are also becoming increasingly popular as second holidays. People choose to spend 2 or 3 nights away from home on a short break over a weekend or mid-week to relax and de-stress. These holiday choices are driven by what memorable experiences we hope to create and what we class as our definition of spending quality time together.

(3) Health and fitness tourism, such as a cycling tour, trekking, or a walking holiday (5%), is growing in popularity amongst the youth today. Also, sports tourism (3%) wherein sports tours are taken as a spectator, such as a visit to a major sporting event like the Olympics or a World Cup in another city or country.

(4) Health tourism (10%) implies going to a different country to have an operation or medical treatment not available or too expensive in the country where the person usually lives. This is making India a popular destination because of the excellent medical facilities it has to offer.

(5) Educational tourism (3%) covers school and college visits and foreign language exchanges linked directly to study experiences and are short visits made by high school students as they prepare for further studies.

(6) Spiritual tourism (2%) is where people travel both inbound and outbound to places of worship according to their beliefs.

(7) Business tourism (35%) many people have to travel in the course of their business life apart from making a regular journey to and from where they normally work. It may involve driving to a meeting or flying to another country for conferences or corporate events. Business tourism is very important to the travel and tourism industry as it takes place all through the year and some travel and tourism businesses, such as budget hotel chains, rely heavily on income from business travellers.

Answer the following questions based on the above passage.

(i) Complete with a suitable reason. **(1)**

People go on holidays together to ....

(ii) Fill in the blank with an appropriate word/phrase. **(1)**

The phrase driven by in paragraph (2) suggests that the choice of holiday destination .... people's experiences.

(iii) Short holidays of 2-3 days are becoming popular **(1)**

(a) because people have limited holidays.
(b) because people have increased their holiday budgets.
(c) to take a break from the stress of daily life.
(d) to visit historical places.

(iv) Why do tourists travel abroad for sports tourism? **(1)**

I. It is more economical.
II. To watch family members play.
III. To be spectators at world events.
IV. It doubles up for both sports and leisure.
V. To train for sporting events.

Select the correct option.

(a) Only I (b) II and V (c) II, III and IV (d) Only III

(v) Why is India a popular destination for health tourism? **(1)**

(vi) Which is the most popular form of tourism and why? **(2)**

(vii) Explain why business tourism is important for the travel industry. **(2)**

(viii) According to the above statistics, which form of tourism is the least popular at the present moment? **(1)**

Section–B (Writing Skills)

[22 Marks]

3. You are Rishabh/Rishita, Class Prefect of Class IX A. Write an e-mail, in 50 words, to the Principal of your school, requesting him/her to provide an interactive board in your classroom. **(3)**

Include valid reasons for your request.

You may copy the given template to write your e-mail.

From	
To	
Cc	abc@xyzschool.com
Date	16th April, 20XX, 03:45 p.m.
Subject	

4. Write a factual description, in not more than 100 words, of a working model of 'Save Your Earth' that you have prepared for your school's Earth Day Exhibition. **(4)**

5. (a) The National Bravery Awards are given to honour those children who have demonstrated selfless courage in the face of all odds. These awards serve as inspiration to other children and motivate them to follow in their footsteps. Similarly, the government should institute National Environment Crusader Awards for children who dedicate themselves to spreading awareness about saving the environment. Write a letter to the editor of a national daily, in 120 words, expressing your views on the above. Use your own ideas along with ideas from the unit Environment, to write the letter. **(7)**

Or

(b) 'Atithi Devo Bhava' has been India's stand since times immemorial. However, you feel, to attract tourists, only tourism promotional drives do not suffice. It is important to sensitise those in the tourism industry to conduct themselves with propriety as hosts, and they must treat the tourists with respect, ensure their safety and support them during their visit. As Herbu R., write a letter to the Tourism Department expressing your concerns. Use your own ideas along with the ideas from the unit: Travel and Tourism, to write the letter in not more than 120 words.

6. (a) 'Laugh out loud and feel happy and fit inside out' for laughter is the best medicine. With stress mushrooming all around and among all ages, Laughter Yoga seems a great alternative way to physical and mental health. Use cues given below along with your own ideas and those you may have gathered from the unit: Health and Medicine, to write an article for your school magazine in about 150 words describing benefits of Laughter Yoga. **(8)**

- Improves Cardiovascular health
- Boosts Immune System → production of antibodies → activation of immune cells
- Reduces stress
- No special equipment required
- Cost effective

Or

(b) To meet the employment needs, the youth today are venturing into startups. As Veena/Veer of Class X A, write an article in about 150 words, for your school magazine discussing the merits of startups as a boon to self-reliance.

Use the cues given below along with your ideas and those you may have gathered from the unit: Education, to write the article.

- From job seeker to job creator
- Self-reliance
- Flexible working conditions
- Economic growth
- Decision-making freedom

Section–C (Grammar)

[10 Marks]

7. Complete the tasks from (a)-(c), as directed.

(a) Fill in the blanks (i)-(iii) with the appropriate option from those in the brackets. **(3)**

Prerna and Sushil (a)......... (has/have/had) spent years together. On growing up they (b) .... (had got/have got/got) separated and went their own ways. Sushil (c) .... (becomes/became/had become) a well-known sports personality while Prerna pursued her artistic passion.

(b) In the following paragraph, one word has been omitted in each line. In your answer sheet, remember to write the missing word along with the word that comes before and after it as shown below. The first one has been done as an example. **(4)**

No.	Text	Word before	Omission	Word after
e.g.	A particular mineral that will formed from a certain combination of elements.	will	be	formed
i.	This depends the physical			
ii.	and chemical conditions under the material forms.			
iii.	This results a wide range of colours,			
iv.	hardness, crystal forms, lustre density that a particular mineral possesses.			

(c) Do as directed.

(i) Rearrange the following jumbled words/phrases in the given dialogue to create a meaningful sentence. **(1)**

The King summoned his ministers who were Whispering to each other and said to them:

The King What are you whispering about?

Minister 1 Your highness, we were talking about the new education policy in the country.

Minister 2 education experience/a morg dynamic/for a holistic/the NEP is/and wholesome/pave the way/approach/which will

(ii) Report the dialogues to complete the paragraph that follows. **(1 + 1)**

The King summoned his ministers who were whispering to each other and said to them

The King How will the new policy benefit college students?

Minister 2 The policy will provide for an interdisciplinary education that has flexible study plans.

The King asked Minister 2 how would the new education policy benefit college students?

Minister 2 told the king that the new education policy .... interdisciplinary education .... flexible study plans.

Section–D (Literature Textbook) **[26 Marks]**

8. Read the following excerpts and answer the questions briefly, for any *two* excerpts, of the given three, (a), (b), (c). **(4 + 4 = 8)**

(a) I am important to her. She comes and goes. *
Each morning it is her face that replaces the darkness.
In me she has drowned a young girl, and in me an old woman
Rises toward her day after day, like a terrible fish. *(Mirror)*

(i) Why is the mirror important for her? **(1)**
(ii) With what hope does the woman keep coming back to the mirror every day? **(1)**
(iii) Which young girl has been drowned? Where and how? **(1)**
(iv) Name the literary device in 'like a terrible fish'. **(1)**

(b) '...... that now, forgetting his sport, he would become lost in the admiration of the green cornfield. He reflected deeply, and came to the conclusion that the whole universe was built up through love and that the grief of separation was inescapable.' *(The Letter)*

(i) Why has Ali forgotten his sport? **(1)**
(ii) What do the above lines tell you about Ali's attitude towards nature? **(1)**
(iii) What did his deep reflection of life make him realise? **(1)**
(iv) What does the writer mean by 'grief of separation'? **(1)**

(c) **Decius Brutus**

And know it now : the senate have concluded
To give this day a crown to mighty Caesar.
If you shall send them word you will not come,
Their minds may change.

Caesar

How foolish do your fears seem now, Calpurnia!
I am ashamed I did yield to them.
Give me my robe, for I will go.

(i) How does Decius Brutus persuade Caesar? **(1)**
(ii) What did Calpurnia's fears make her do? **(1)**
(iii) What do the above lines tell you about Caesar's character? **(1)**
(iv) Why does Caesar say that he was ashamed of himself? **(1)**

9. Answer any *five* of the following six questions in 30-40 words each. **(5 × 2 = 10)**

(i) Despite such a tender age, what made the two boys– Nicola and Jacopo work so hard? **(2)**
(Two Gentlemen of Verona)

(ii) 'The vanity of human glory power is transient'. Elucidate with reference to the poem 'Ozymandias'. **(2)**

(iii) What does Ouija board in 'A Shady Plot' ? **(2)**

(iv) How, according to you, did Sebastian's normal life get revived? Give an argument in support of your answer. **(2)**
(Virtually True)

* *8(a) This chapter is not in the syllabus and in CBSE Textbook.*

(v) Why and how, according to Shakespeare, is the pen mightier than the monuments or even the mighty kings? *(Not Marble, Nor the Gilded Monuments)* **(2)**

(vi) Why, according to you, did Patol Babu long to act? Cite reasons from the story. *(Patol Babu, Film Star)* **(2)**

10. Answer any *one* of the following two questions in about 150 words. (8)

(a) From the poems 'The Rime of the Ancient Mariner' and 'The Snake', discuss how the characters, the albatross and view human attitude and perspective towards creatures.

Or

(b) Both, the poem 'The Frog and the Nightingale' and the story 'Mrs. Packletide's Tiger', reflect themes of exploitation of others in pursuit of personal benefit. How, according to you, do each of these literary works manipulate situations to attain their personal desires and with what consequences?

Answers

1. (i) (d) Diversity

(ii) (c) It reflects India's cultural richness

(iii) Indian citizens embrace diversity as a strength rather than an hindrance.

(iv) The linguistic diversity is reflective of the people's adaptability and acceptance of varied means of expressions.

(v) Carnatic Music form

(vi) Indian Constitution guarantees fundamental rights and freedoms to all its citizens.

(vii) Indian cuisine is an example of regional diversity as the palate of the whole country is flavorful and eclectic. We usually see fiery dishes in South, rich curries in the North, sweets in Gujarat and street food of Mumbai. The culinary variety brings together people through a shared love for food.

(viii) India has a wide cultural variety with multiple art forms across various regions. From traditional dance forms like Bharatanatyam, Kathak, Odissi, etc, to music forms like Carnatic and Hindustani. These diverse forms represent the feeling of unity in India's cultural tapestry.

(ix) The overarching narrative of India's existence is Unity in Diversity. India does not count diversity as a hindrance, it is a strength for the country. Despite various challenges and diverse cultural background across states, there is a feeling of unity that fosters in the heart of people. India also safeguards its citizens by giving Constitutional rights and duties.

2. (i) relax, rest and enjoy

(ii) influenced

(iii) (c) to take a break from the stress of daily life.

(iv) (c) II, III and IV

(v) India is a popular destination for health tourism because it has excellent medical facilities available at a reasonable cost.

(vi) The most popular form of tourism is Leisure tourism. This makes up for around 42% of travel. It is the most popular form because people love taking holidays for relaxation and recreation.

(vii) Business tourism is important for travel industry because it takes places throughout the year. Some travel businesses such as budget hotel chains rely heavily on income from business travellers.

(viii) According to the given statistics, spiritual tourism is the least popular form at the present moment.

3. **From** rishitamishra66@gmail.com
To principal@xyzschoolsnoida
Cc abc@xyzschool.com
Date 16th April, 20XX, 03:45 p.m.

Subject Request for an Interactive Board in Class IX A

Respected Principal
I request you to kindly provide an interactive board in our classroom. It will enhance learning through visual explanations, make lessons more engaging, and improve understanding. Digital tools will also help teachers explain complex topics effectively. We believe this will greatly benefit our studies.

Thanking you
Yours sincerely

Rishita Mishra
Class Prefect, IX A

4. Our working model, 'Save Your Earth', is designed to spread awareness about simple yet effective ways to protect the environment. At the centre, a rotating globe represents our planet, surrounded by displays on afforestation, waste management, and renewable energy. A small solar panel powers an eco-friendly house, showing the benefits of clean energy. There's also a water filtration system and a composting unit to highlight conservation and recycling. Interactive buttons provide useful tips on reducing pollution and saving resources. Through this model, we hope to inspire others to take small but meaningful steps towards a greener future.

5. (a) A4, 1202
Supertech Ecovillage 1
Noida- 201306

18th February, 20XX

The Editor
Times of India
Noida- 201301

Subject Request to Institute National Environment Crusader Awards for Children

Respected Sir/Ma'am
Through the columns of your esteemed newspaper, I want to express my concern regarding environmental degradation and to propose an initiative that can inspire young mind to take action. The National Bravery Awards honour children who show extraordinary courage, inspiring others to do the same. Similarly, I strongly believe that the government should introduce National Environment Crusader Awards to recognise young environmentalists who actively promote eco-friendly practices.
Many children today are taking significant steps to protect nature-organising cleanliness drives, spreading awareness about pollution, and encouraging tree plantation. Recognising their efforts will not only reward their dedication but also inspire more young minds to take responsibility for our planet. At a time when environmental issues are a global concern, such an initiative will encourage future generations to work towards a sustainable future.
I hope my suggestion is considered.
Yours sincerely
Neha Vats

Or

(b) 1911, Maharani Bagh
New Delhi -110034

18th February, 2025

The Director
Tourism Department
Delhi

Subject Promoting Responsible Conduct in the Tourism Industry

Respected Sir/Ma'am
I am writing this letter to express my concern regarding the need for greater senitisation among those working in tourism industry. India has always believed in Atithi Devo Bhava, but to truly make tourists feel welcome, promotional campaigns alone are not enough. It is equally important to ensure that those in the tourism industry-guides, drivers, and hospitality staff-treat visitors with respect, offer help when needed, and prioritise their safety.
Unfortunately, incidents of overcharging, misguidance, and security concerns can leave tourists with a negative impression. Proper training and awareness programmes on responsible and ethical hospitality would make a huge difference.
A positive experience encourages more travellers to visit, benefiting both tourism and the country's reputation. I sincerely hope the department takes steps to address this concern.
Yours sincerely
Herbu R.

6. (a) **Benefits of Laughter Yoga**

by XYZ

They say laughter is the best medicine and Laughter Yoga proves it! In today's stressful world, where people of all ages struggle with pressure, this simple and enjoyable practice offers many health benefits. Laughter Yoga combines deep breathing with playful laughter exercises, improving heart health by boosting oxygen flow and blood circulation. It also strengthens the immune system, helping the body fight diseases. Most importantly, it reduces stress, lifts mood, and promotes a positive mindset. The best part? It needs no special equipment and is completely free, making it easy for anyone to practise.
Whether young or old, anyone can enjoy Laughter Yoga and feel its benefits. It not only improves physical and mental health but also strengthens social bonds, making people feel happier and more connected. A few minutes of laughter everyday can make a big difference in our lives. So let's laugh more, stay healthy and live stress free!

Or

(b) In today's world, where employment opportunities are limited, many young people are choosing to become job creators instead of job seekers. Startups have become a powerful way to achieve self-reliance, allowing individuals to turn their ideas into successful businesses.

One major benefit of startups is their role in economic growth. By creating jobs, they reduce unemployment and contribute to the nation's progress. Entrepreneurs also enjoy decision-making freedom, where they can shape their businesses according to their vision and creativity. Unlike traditional jobs, startups offer flexible working conditions, giving individuals the freedom to manage their time and work on their own terms. Most importantly, startups empower young minds to think innovatively and take charge of their own success. Instead of depending on others for employment, they build opportunities for themselves and others. With passion, hard work, and the right mindset, startups are truly paving the way for a self-reliant future.

7. (a) have, got, became

(b)

	Word Before	Omission	Word After
(i)	depends	on	the
(ii)	and	the	chemical
(iii)	results	in	a
(iv)	forms	and	lustre

(c) (i) The NEP is a more dynamic and wholesome approach which will pave the way for a holistic education experience.

(ii) would provide, that has

8. (a) *

Or

(b) (i) Ali has forgotten his sport because he has become deeply absorbed in the beauty of the green cornfield. As he observes the field, he is moved by its peacefulness and harmony, which seem to stir a profound reflection within him.

(ii) The lines suggest that Ali has a deep and contemplative attitude towards nature. His reaction to the green cornfield shows that he is not just appreciating its beauty on the surface but is also moved by it in a way that triggers profound thoughts.

(iii) This deep reflection on life made Ali realise that the entire universe is built on the foundation of love, and that the grief of separation is an inevitable part of life.

(iv) By 'grief of separation', the writer refers to the inevitable pain and sorrow that comes when people, or even aspects of life, are parted from each other.

(c) (i) Decius Brutus persuades Caesar by cleverly reinterpreting Calpurnia's dream and appealing to Caesar's ego.

(ii) Calpurnia's fears made her try to prevent Caesar from going to the Senate on the Ides of March. After having a troubling dream, she became deeply anxious about his safety and believed that something bad would happen to him if he went.

(iii) The above lines reveal that Caesar is somewhat arrogant and easily swayed by flattery, particularly when it boosts his sense of pride and ambition.

(iv) Caesar says that he is ashamed of himself because, after being persuaded by Decius Brutus, he realises that he was initially swayed by fear and hesitation, especially in response to Calpurnia's troubling dream.

9. (i) Despite being so young, Nicola and Jacopo worked hard because they loved their sick sister, Lucia. They took on tough jobs to earn money for her treatment. Their goal was to help her get better, so they were willing to work tirelessly, even though they were just kids. Their love for their sister and their sense of responsibility made them work so hard.

(ii) In 'Ozymandias,' the poem shows how human glory and power are short-lived. The statue of Ozymandias, once a symbol of his greatness, is now broken and buried in the desert. The inscription on the statue says, 'Look on my works, ye Mighty, and despair!' but all that remains is ruin. This shows that no matter how powerful someone is, time eventually fades all achievements, leaving nothing behind. The poem highlights the temporary nature of fame and power.

(iii) In 'A Shady Plot', the Ouija board symbolises the characters' curiosity about the supernatural and their desire to communicate with spirits. It represents both their fascination with the unknown and the potential dangers of trying to control or connect with forces beyond their understanding.

(iv) Sebastian's normal life was revived when Michael successfully rescued him from the virtual world by completing Warzone. This is confirmed by a newspaper article stating Sebastian had recovered from his coma. The story suggests a mysterious connection between virtual reality and real life, where Michael's actions influenced Sebastian's survival.

(v) In Shakespeare's Sonnet 55, he says the pen is mightier than marble or kings because written words last longer than physical monuments. While statues

* 8 (a) *This chapter is not in the syllabus and in CBSE Textbook.*

or buildings fade with time, poetry and writing can live on for centuries, keeping a person's memory alive long after they are gone. Shakespeare believes his writing will make the person immortal, outlasting even the greatest kings and monuments.

(vi) Patol Babu longed to act because it was his lifelong passion. Once a talented stage actor, he missed the joy of performing. The film role rekindled his excitement, and despite its small size, he embraced it with dedication, proving his love for acting was driven by fulfillment, not fame.

10. (a) In 'The Rime of the Ancient Mariner' by Coleridge and 'The Snake' by D.H. Lawrence, the albatross and the snake highlight human arrogance towards nature.

The albatross, a harmless guide for sailors, is killed by the Mariner without reason, showing reckless disregard for life. This act brings suffering upon him, as nature punishes his cruelty. Similarly, in 'The Snake', the poet admires the snake's beauty but, influenced by fear and societal beliefs, throws a log at it-an action he immediately regrets.

Both creatures symbolise nature's innocence, while human actions reflect thoughtless harm. The poems reveal how humans exploit or fear animals instead of respecting them.

(b) Both 'The Frog and the Nightingale' by Vikram Seth and 'Mrs. Packletide's Tiger' by Saki explore exploitation, where individuals manipulate situations for personal gain, leading to ironic or tragic consequences. In 'The Frog and the Nightingale', the frog, an arrogant singer, exploits the nightingale's innocence. He convinces her she needs his training, imposes harsh demands, and charges fees, ultimately breaking her spirit. His relentless pressure leads to her untimely death, ensuring he remains the sole singer of the bog. This highlights how power and manipulation can crush true talent.

Similarly, in 'Mrs. Packletide's Tiger', Mrs. Packletide, driven by jealousy, arranges a staged tiger hunt for social prestige. She bribes villagers to present her with a weak, old tiger, hoping to claim false glory. However, her deception backfires when Miss Mebbin, her companion, blackmails her, forcing her to pay a heavy price to maintain her reputation. Though she achieves her goal momentarily, she ultimately suffers financial loss and humiliation, proving that manipulation often leads to downfall.

Both works caution against exploiting others for selfish gains. While the frog's greed leads to the tragic loss of talent, Mrs. Packletide's vanity results in embarrassment. In the end, deception and selfishness bring irony and regret rather than success.